CONVERSATIONS

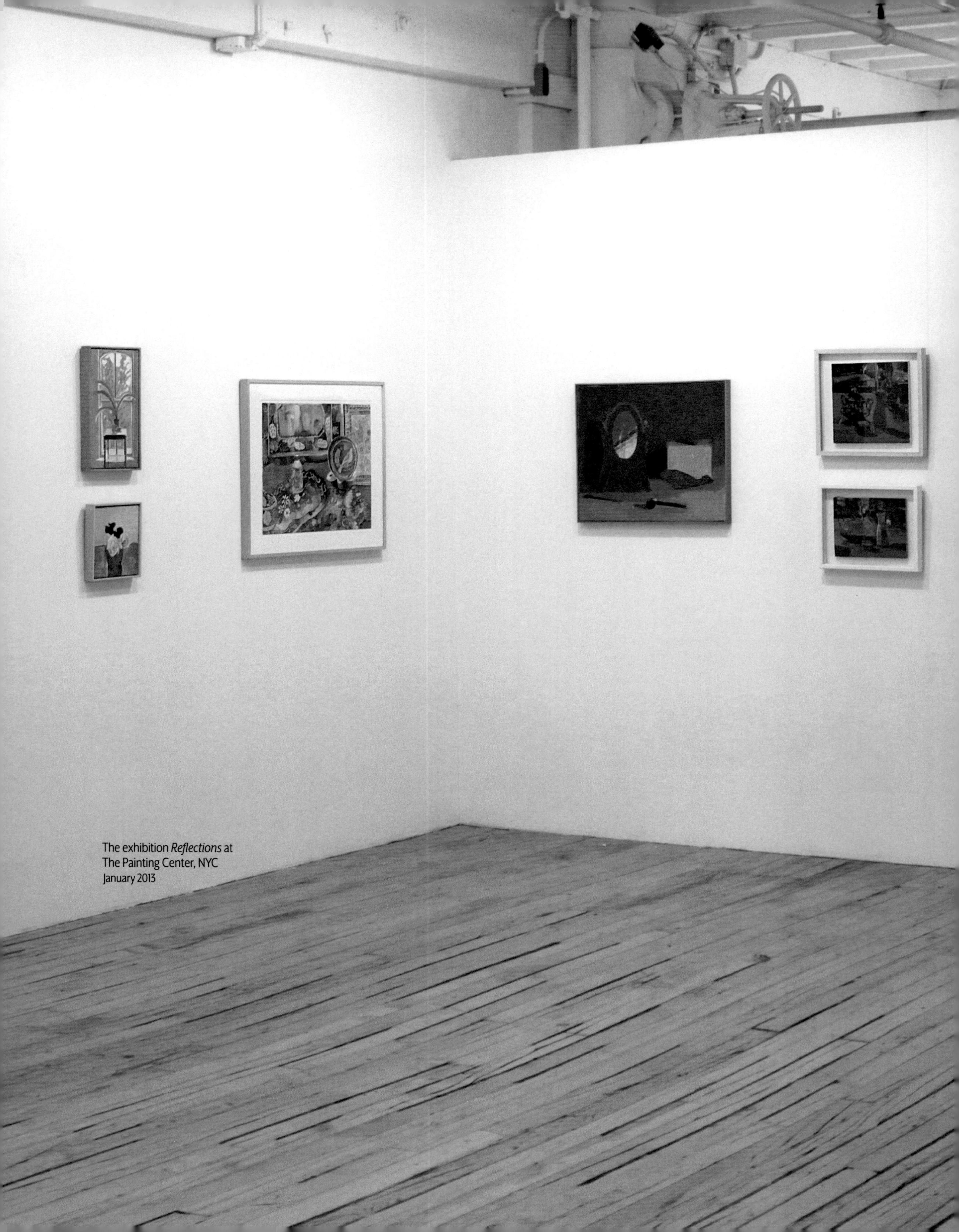

The exhibition *Reflections* at
The Painting Center, NYC
January 2013

CONVERSATIONS

23 Interviews with Still Life Artists

Organized and created by Zeuxis

Zeuxis
New York, NY

Published by Zeuxis in 2024
135 West 26th Street #9B
New York, New York 10001

Conversations: 23 Interviews with Still Life Artists
represents the culmination of a collaborative effort, conducted 2020-2023, to capture the views and achievements of more than 60 still life painters from across the United States.
Conversations was organized by Zeuxis, the association of still life painters based in New York City.
These interviews and images were originally published 2020-2023 on www.zeuxis.us.

Editors: Seth Schonberg and Phyllis Floyd
Proofreaders: Kathleen Craig and Nancy Granda
Designers: John Goodrich, Kayla Edmonston and Cheryl Conrad
Black and white gallery photographers: John Goodrich and Ying Li
Printer and binder: The Studley Press, Dalton, MA
Images accompanying interviews were supplied by participants

ISBN 979-8-218-35977-5

Printed in the USA

Contents

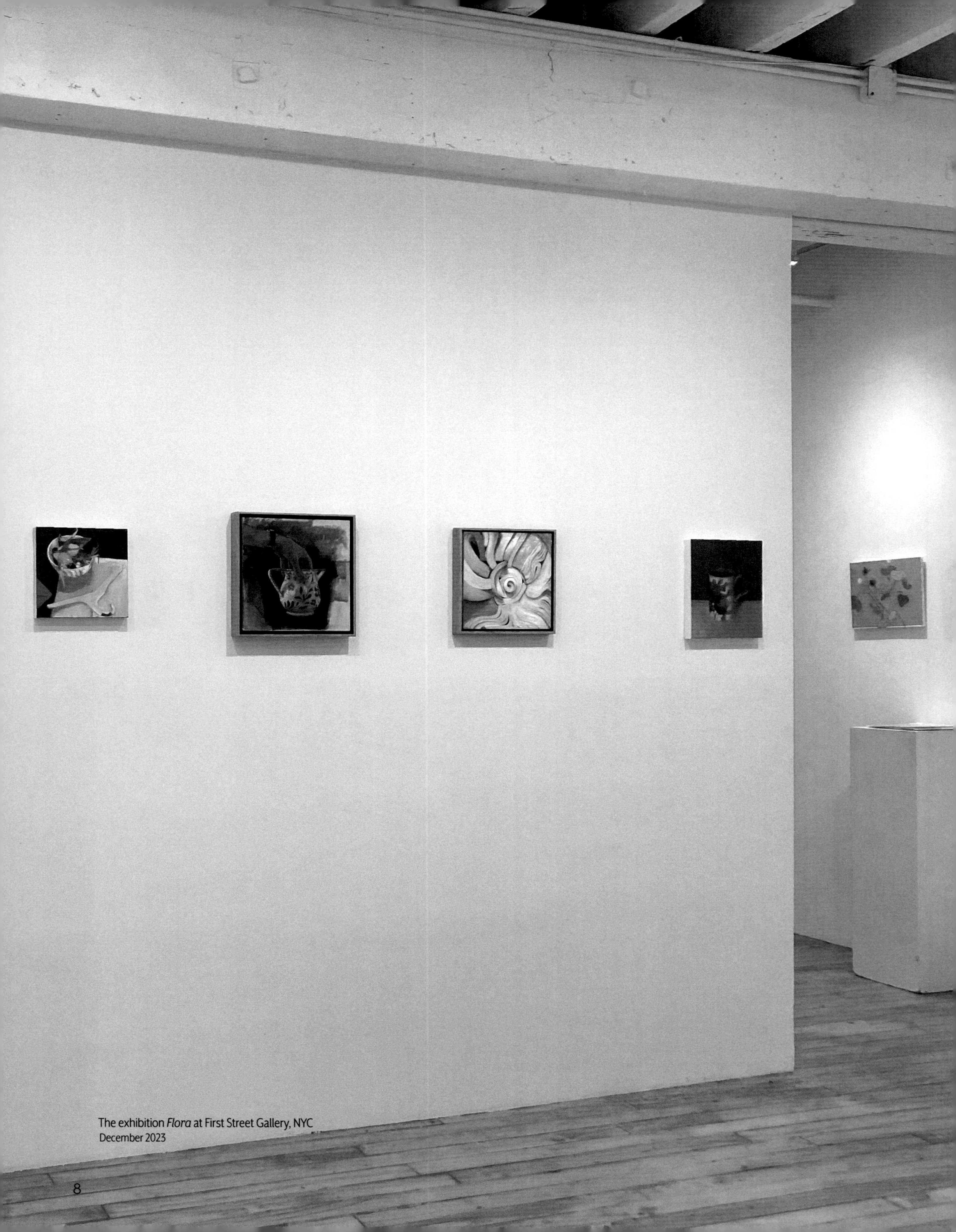

The exhibition *Flora* at First Street Gallery, NYC
December 2023

Foreword

Seth Schonberg

December 2023

The story of *Conversations* starts in May 2018 with the creation of the THERE art space. Phyllis Floyd, director of Zeuxis, an Association of Still Life Painters, decided to offer a section of her loft for the purpose of showing artwork by Zeuxis artists and guests. I, as the association's administrator, helped bring the plan to fruition and over the subsequent three years we organized six exhibitions with a myriad of themes.

"GEMS: Small Still Lifes" in Spring 2020 brought together members of the Midwest Paint Group with Zeuxis in an ambitious exhibition featuring the work of thirty-two artists and a full color catalog. Lynette Lombard was a member of the M.P.G., and she became liaison between the two associations. For the closing of the exhibition it was proposed that Lombard and Matt Klos of Zeuxis join in a talk to be moderated by artist and critic Xico Greenwald. The topic was to be "From Still Life to Abstraction." No one in New York could have guessed how truly abstracted our world would soon become. GEMS was slated to close on April 4th but mere days after the March 12th opening COVID-19 closed down the city, shuttering the art world, and the talk was cancelled.

We at THERE were immediately impatient with the inaction and began looking for something substantial to offer our painters. All opportunities to show their work had evaporated. Inspired by the sudden pivot to the internet that the entire social world underwent, we proposed hosting the artist talk on our website. The five of us—Greenwald, Klos, Lombard, Floyd, and I—settled on the simple medium of a written dialog to be held via email. We encouraged Greenwald to lead and edit the interview. "The Act of Seeing: In Conversation with Matt Klos and Lynette Lombard" was published on April 30, 2020. While I was responsible for the design and appearance of the interviews for two more years, the structure and style that Greenwald introduced to the interview shaped the entire series. Z

"The world about us would be desolate
except for the world within us. There is the
same interchange between these two worlds
that there is between one art and another,
migratory passings to and fro, quickenings—
Promethean liberations and discoveries."

— *Wallace Stevens*

Conversation Piece: A Writer Looks at Still Life

Imogen Sara Smith

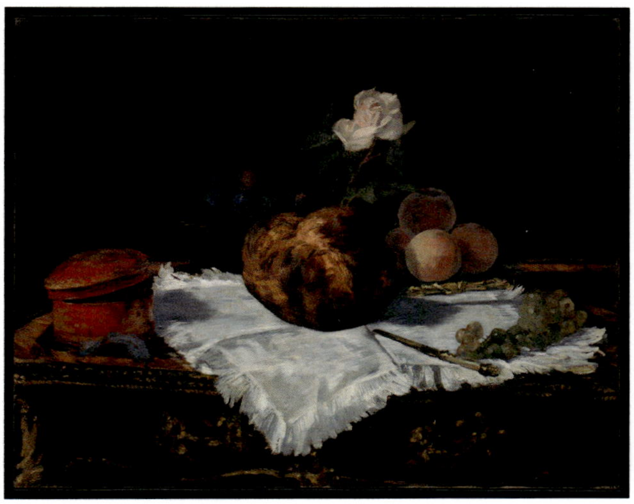

Edouard Manet *The Brioche*
1870, oil on canvas, 25 5/8 x 31 7/8 in., The Met

"They talk to each other, these folks," Cézanne said affectionately of the pieces of fruit he painted. Still life might be thought of as a quiet art, hushed by the muteness of inanimate objects, but its practice—one might even say its purpose—is to put things in conversation with each other. What does this mean, besides a rather clichéd figure of speech? A good conversation is an exchange that is balanced but unpredictable, that has both flow and tension, energy and freedom. It is not competitive like a debate or an argument, but in any good conversation the participants are changed in some way, just as forms and colors are changed by their proximity to others. Pictures hanging together also influence, question, challenge, amuse, disturb or flatter each other, and the group shows of still life organized by Zeuxis are conversations in which diverse voices speak about the same subject. They all talk at the same time, yet every voice is clear.

Still life usually omits the human figure, yet two people are present in every painting: the artist and the viewer. This is true of any picture, but perhaps you feel it more with a still life because faces and figures don't get in the way; because the painter's role in staging and presenting the subject is so undisguised; or even because the communication between artist and viewer often happens, like so many conversations, across a table. Still life is an art of nearness, of being, in Walter Benjamin's words, “tête-à-tête with things.” One more link between still life and conversation is suggested by an older meaning of the word: “close familiarity, intimate acquaintance, as from constant use or study.”

It was a happy accident of proximity that connected me to Zeuxis. I got to know the group’s co-founder Phyllis Floyd through my friendship with her daughter, Zoe Waldron, whom I first met when she and I shared adjacent cubicles at the New York Public Library for the Performing Arts. In 2009, Phyllis asked me to write a catalogue essay for “The Common Object,” an exhibition for which each artist was asked to submit a painting that incorporated an identical dishtowel—white with a grid of blue lines—an item they shared in common and that was chosen partly for its humble, everyday associations. Phyllis sent me a quote from John Updike about “giving the mundane its beautiful due,” which became a touchstone for the essay, and for me. I was also invited to moderate a panel discussion for the show’s opening at the Lancaster Museum of Art. On a snowy January evening, I joined four artists to talk about such topics as whether still life can have a narrative component; the spectrum of approaches to the genre from formal “pure painting” to sensual evocations of the physical world; and still life’s association with theater and elements of illusion and drama.

Before this, I had always felt rather lonely in my enthusiasm for still life. I am a writer not a painter, and among my art-loving friends and family, I found that the majority thought of still life as boring, something you walk past in a museum on your way to look at a portrait or a landscape. But in my teenage and college years I was increasingly drawn to the genre, and keen to understand what it was that I found so deeply beguiling and moving about Chardin’s copper pots and earthenware mugs and broken hunks of bread; the velvety fuzz on Manet’s peaches and the frail, luminous flowers he painted during his last illness; the glistening facets of cut lemons and spiraling curls of peel and fragile flutes of glass in Dutch breakfast pieces; or Cézanne’s justly famous apples.

Several things fed my fascination. Virginia Woolf, for years my idol, had a lot to do with it: in her short story “Solid Objects,” her memoir “Moments of Being,” and throughout her work, she infuses ordinary things with luminous, palpitating intensity and unsettling power. This enchantment of the everyday, the sudden flush and concentration of beauty in a glass of water or a colored pillow case or an onion or an egg, was part of what drew me to still life paintings. Woolf was surrounded by painters, including her sister Vanessa Bell, and she wrote a biography of the art historian Roger Fry, another member of her circle. She made no secret of the way she envied visual artists for their ability to deal directly in color, shape, and abstraction, while she had to evoke these things with words. But she also embraced the challenge. “I see why I like pictures,” she wrote plainly; “It’s as things that stir me to describe them.” The same was true of me.

Still life has also attracted many writers and critics as a vehicle for ideas. About material culture and our relationship to the physical world, whether through celebrations or critiques of luxury and excess; austere reminders of mortality and decay; or tender attention to the quotidian. About the paradox of motion within stillness: static images of inanimate objects that prove nothing is ever completely still, unchanging, or dead. (As a writer, my primary subject is film—itself a form of stillness in motion.)

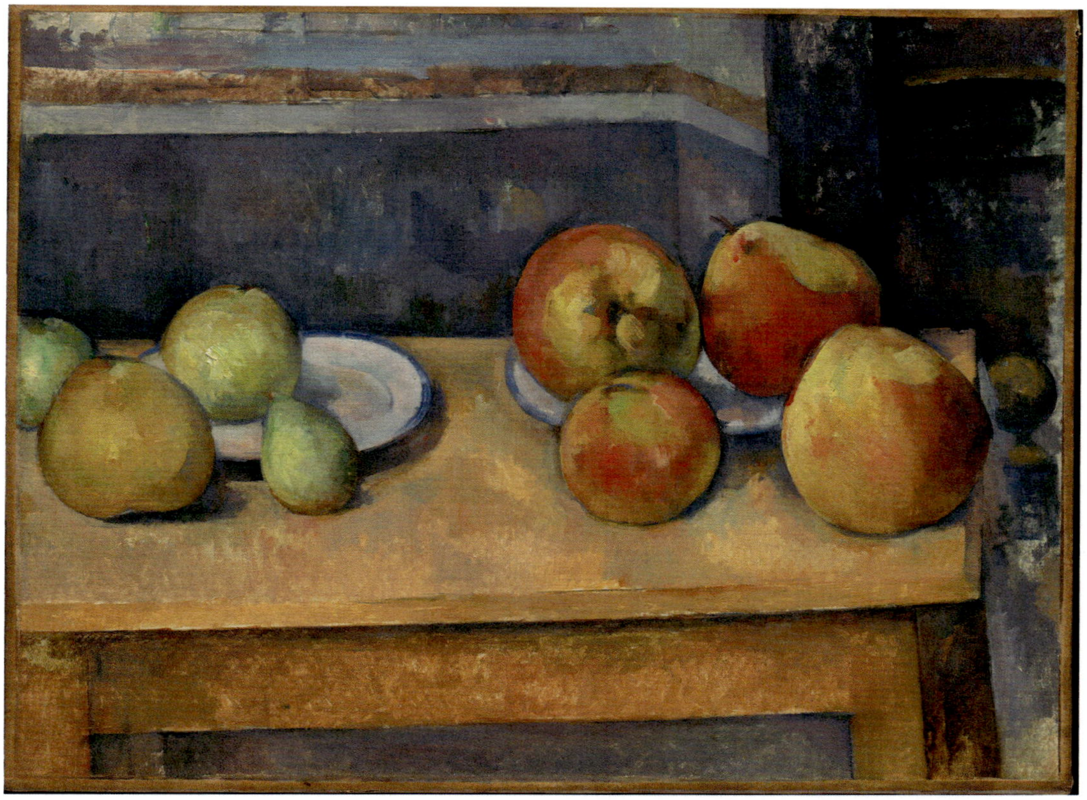

Paul Cézanne *Still Life with Apples and Pears*
c. 1891–92, oil on canvas, 17 ⅝ x 23 ⅛ in., The Met

Zeuxis engages with ideas through the themes of its shows—for which artists create work in response to a prompt, which could be anything from a dishtowel to the influence of Chardin—as well as through panels, talks, published essays, and now the series of "Conversations" gathered here. This is one of the things that has made it exciting for me to collaborate with the group: for instance, I not only contributed an essay for the exhibition "Still, Blue" in 2013, but got involved with an event—another of Phyllis's brain-children—that brought jazz into the gallery, connecting the color that unified the show with the notion of blue as a musical tone or mood.

My third essay was for "My Studio," exploring how artists represent their own working spaces. With Giorgio Morandi as its presiding spirit, this essay from 2019 eerily prefigured the hermetic mood that would engulf us all during the Covid lockdown, and offered encouragement that the whole world could be found in a single room, through engaging afresh with objects that are furred with the dust of familiarity. I dug deeper into these themes in the one "Conversation" that I moderated. Still life has always been quietly radical, and today it offers a much-needed antidote to the haste and waste of our "attention economy," a model of sustained engagement with the overlooked stuff of life.

While researching my essay for "The Common Object," I learned that one of the earliest forms of what we would now call still life painting was the Greek *xenia*, images of delicacies that represented the gifts of food presented to visiting guests. The word *xenos* can mean guest or host. Is the viewer of a painting the guest of the artist, or is the artist the guest of the viewer? The answer, obviously, is both. I am grateful to the artists of Zeuxis for welcoming me into their works, their community, and their conversations.

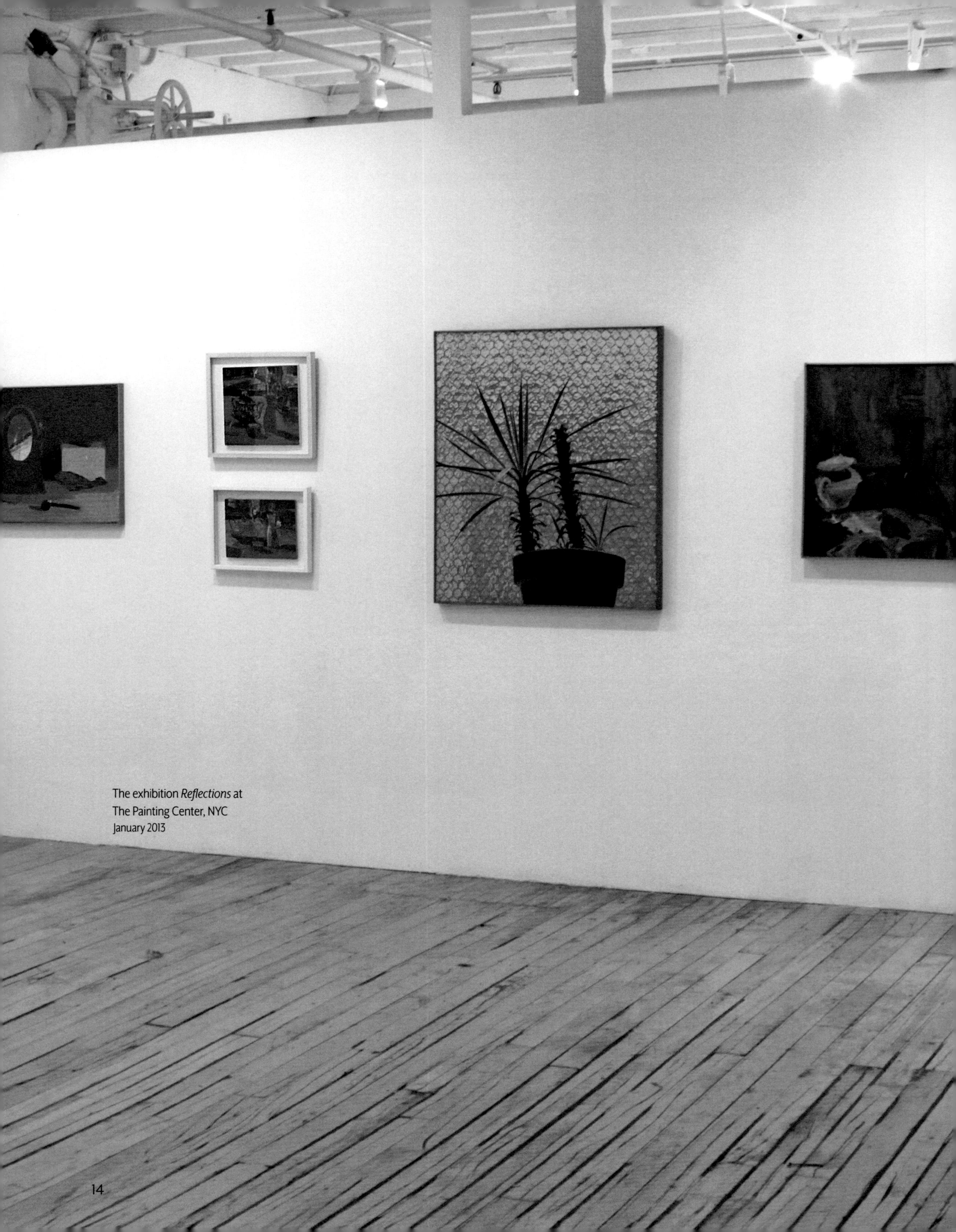

The exhibition *Reflections* at
The Painting Center, NYC
January 2013

The Act of Seeing

Xico Greenwald interviews

Matt Klos and Lynette Lombard

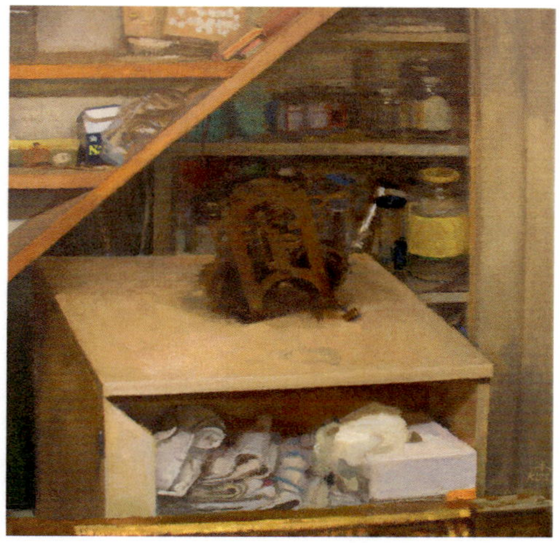

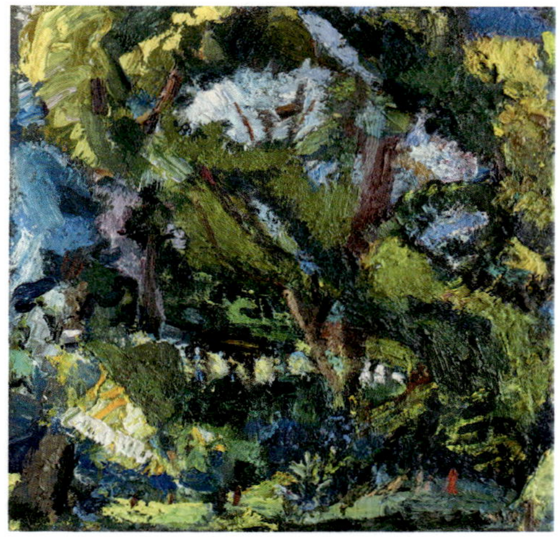

Matt Klos *Keeping Time*, 2018, oil on linen, 12 x 11 in.
Lynette Lombard *Spring Rising* (detail), 2001, oil on canvas, 24 x 18 in.

Xico Greenwald: *Two artist collectives, one in New York, one in the Midwest, joined forces this spring to mount an exhibition of diminutive still life paintings.*

New York–based Zeuxis bills itself as an association of still life painters. Zeuxis artist and founding member Phyllis Floyd describes the collective as a grassroots project she started in 1994 "to take the measure of contemporary still life painting."

Midwest Paint Group comprises artist-members working in America's breadbasket. Its website says members create "Post-Abstract Figuration," a revival of representational art that emerged out of Abstract Expressionism.

"Gems: Small Still Lifes," a group show at THERE, an art space in Manhattan, is presenting works by 21 Zeuxis artists and 12 Midwest Paint Group members.

I was slated to moderate a conversation between Midwest painter Lynette Lombard and Zeuxis member Matt Klos at the Chelsea exhibition space this month. That event, like all in-person public

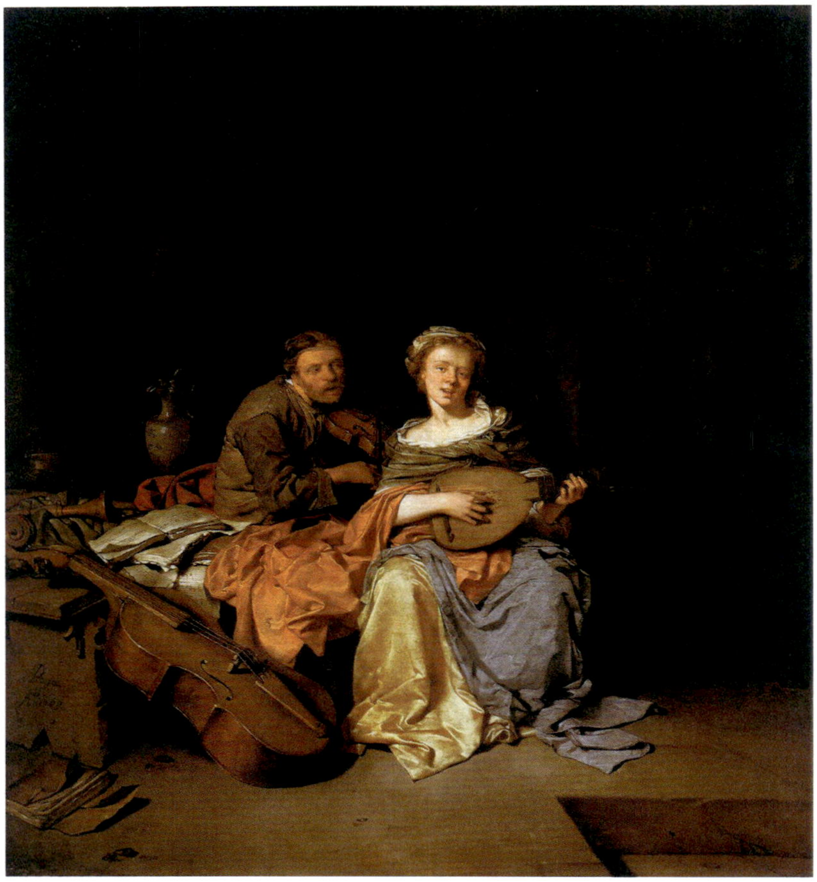

Cornelis Bega *The Duet*
1663, oil on canvas, 17 ¾ x 16 ¼ in.

gatherings, has been called off as New York City combats the corona virus.

Rather than fold up our tents, we moved the conversation online. Lombard and Klos were kind enough to answer my questions about the exhibit over email. What follows is an edited version of that exchange.

XG: *The paintings you are showing in "Gems" are small works. In general, how do you think about scale? Does the size of your canvas change drastically from painting to painting? Do you prefer to work a certain size?*

Matt Klos: I paint both large and small pictures. For the last twenty years or so I've always had both large and small paintings going in my studio at the same time. When painting small, my field of vision encapsulates the entire picture plane. Also, I can be quite indecisive about color and I tend to nudge the paint to adjust temperatures and tonalities. Working in a diminutive scale is less physically laborious for me. Working large is a core part of my practice, but it isn't my default setting.

A couple years ago, at "Vermeer and the Masters of Genre Painting" at the National Gallery, Cornelis Bega's painting, "The Duet" blew me away. The painting is a wonderful example of the power a small picture can possess. In this tiny interior scene, Bega creates an overwhelming sense of space. Scrutiny and close observation can be a vehicle for creating a sense of visual poetry.

The passage along the bottom of that painting, from book to stone step, shows a leak of light revealing and concealing color in violet-grays and green-browns. This acuity of visual phenomena is one of the things I like best about painting. That subtle negotiation of lightness, darkness, and saturation that describes something unnameable and purely visual. I feel that most days in the studio, I'm simply setting the stage for those few moments when a work is nearing completion and very particular negotiations can finally be made. After seeing that painting, I resolved to make some small paintings again. I went home and made a handful of them. My work for "Gems" was all done around that time.

Lynette Lombard: I find the size on which I work varies. It's personal. There are certain times when I need to work big. For example, a landscape I'm painting might evoke such a sense of expansiveness that I feel the need to capture that sensation on a large scale, say around five by seven feet, so that I feel as though I am engulfed inside a place.

Most of the time, though, I work best on a medium scale, around 30 by 45 inches. This easel-size scale is larger than my head; it's torso-sized, yet small enough so I can see the whole image at once. Working back and forth from the whole to the parts, and back to the whole, has a more fluid dynamic on a medium scale for me.

Yes, my paintings in this show are small. Traditionally, my small-scale paintings are studies for larger paintings. However, my paintings in this show are memorial paintings of an object my late father used—his hairbrush. A hairbrush is an intimate, personal thing. The scale of the paintings is

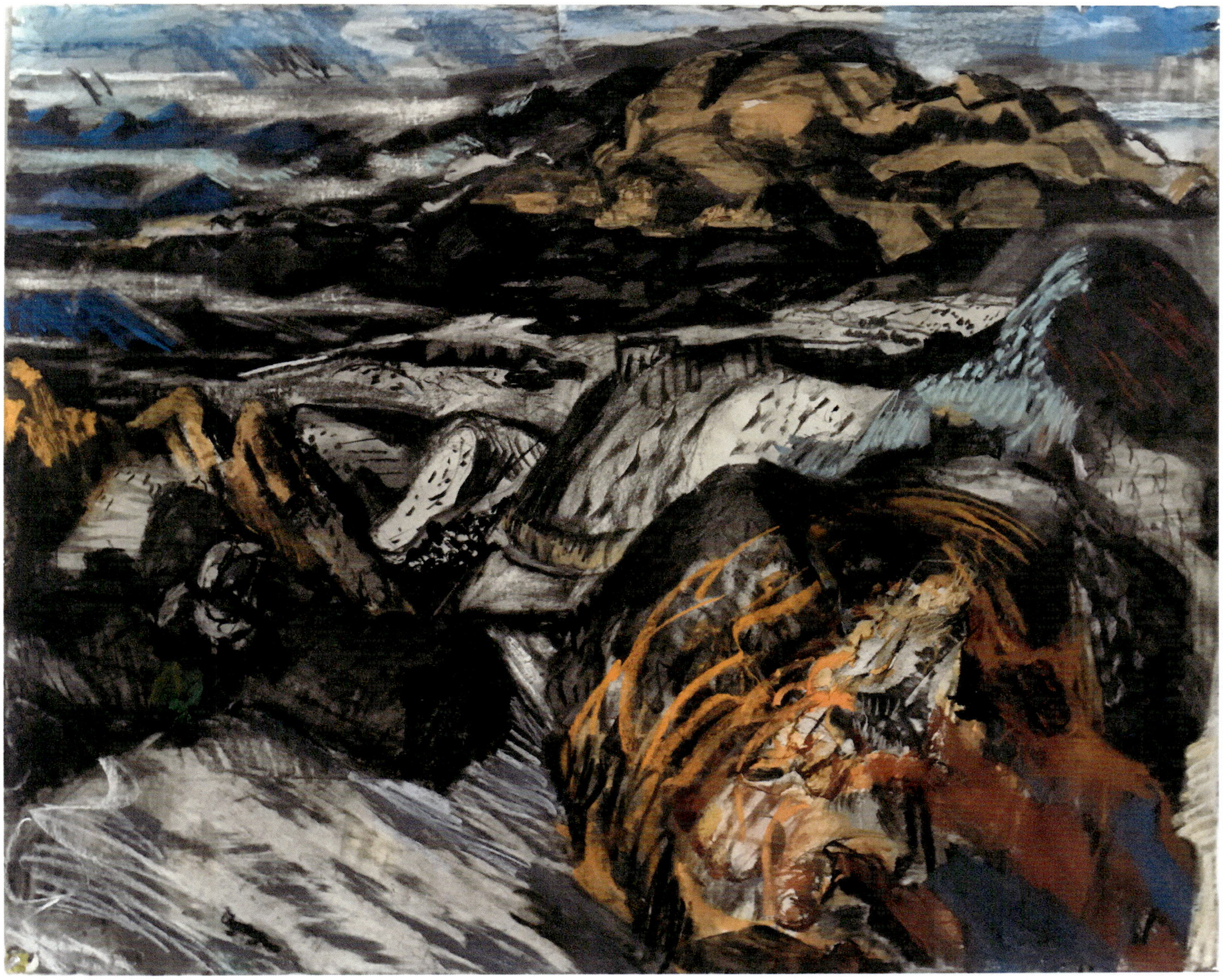

Lynette Lombard *Valley of Turre from Cabrera*
charcoal, chalk pastel on paper, 38 x 46 in.

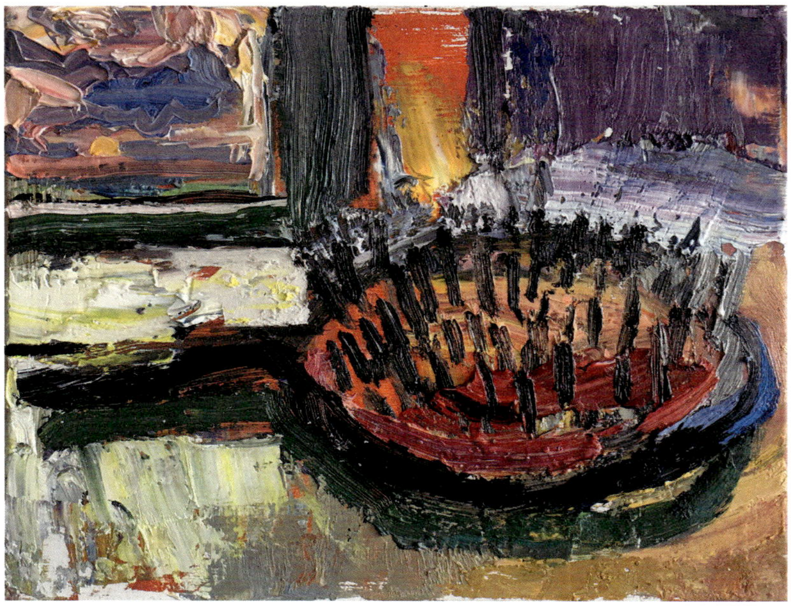

Lynette Lombard *Hairbrush #6*, 2020, oil on canvas, 11 x 14 in.

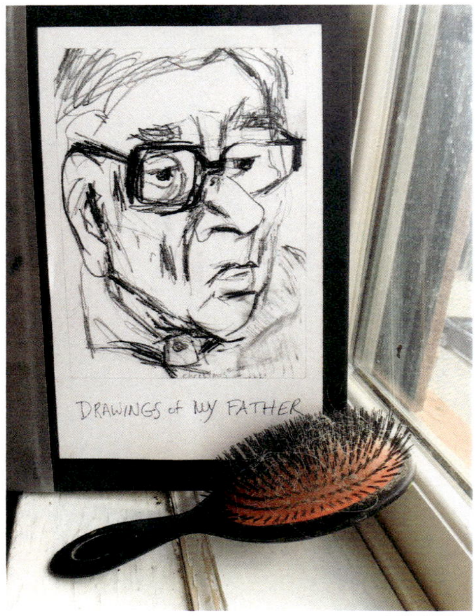

The hairbrush of Lynette Lombard's father

reflective of the intimacy I felt when painting the hairbrush. For me, the challenge of working small-scale is to express a sense of monumentality.

XG: *Do you both work from direct observation? Can you describe the process you went through making your paintings in this show?*

LL: Yes, I mainly work from observation. Working from life is unpredictable and challenging and it keeps me honest. I need what I call "the third thing," a triangular dialogue among the painting, the subject matter and me. Painting becomes a dance or a struggle really, culminating, hopefully, in a convincing, plastic, whole reality. Inevitably, when working from perception looking at the work and analyzing the painting as a painting is part of my practice, too.

The process I went through to make the paintings in this show demanded a different kind of focus for me. As usual, I painted, built, sanded, rebuilt, scraped and worked the image into existence, but they are memorial paintings about the absence of my father, and I would sometimes hold the hairbrush and paint from it to imagine him holding it and to feel his presence. And the hairbrush had a few last wisps of his amazing hair, so there's a tenderness I felt when painting. I had to use a smaller brush, which is not part of my practice usually.

Part of my process is finding the specific focus and particularity within the relationships of each new painting. In Hairbrush #1, I painted over an older painting and I left some of the underlying geometry showing through to locate the hairbrush in a slightly disjointed space. In Hairbrush #6, I placed the hairbrush in my studio space with a view out my window as the sun was setting, an apt metaphor. I've always thought painting is an act of holding time. I also like the idea that liquid paint turns to stone over time. This makes painting a sort of temporal contradiction: it preserves, memorializes even, several moments of time in one image set in stone; yet, it also conveys movement, tensions and energies, among other things, to connect to life as a life force.

MK: I, too, primarily work from direct observation. The three paintings in "Gems" were completed in my basement studio. My studio was filled with mid-century, middle-class artifacts when I moved in fifteen years ago—teapots, knick-knacks, tchotchkes. I've slowly, reluctantly, gotten rid of many things and kept those things that are most interesting.

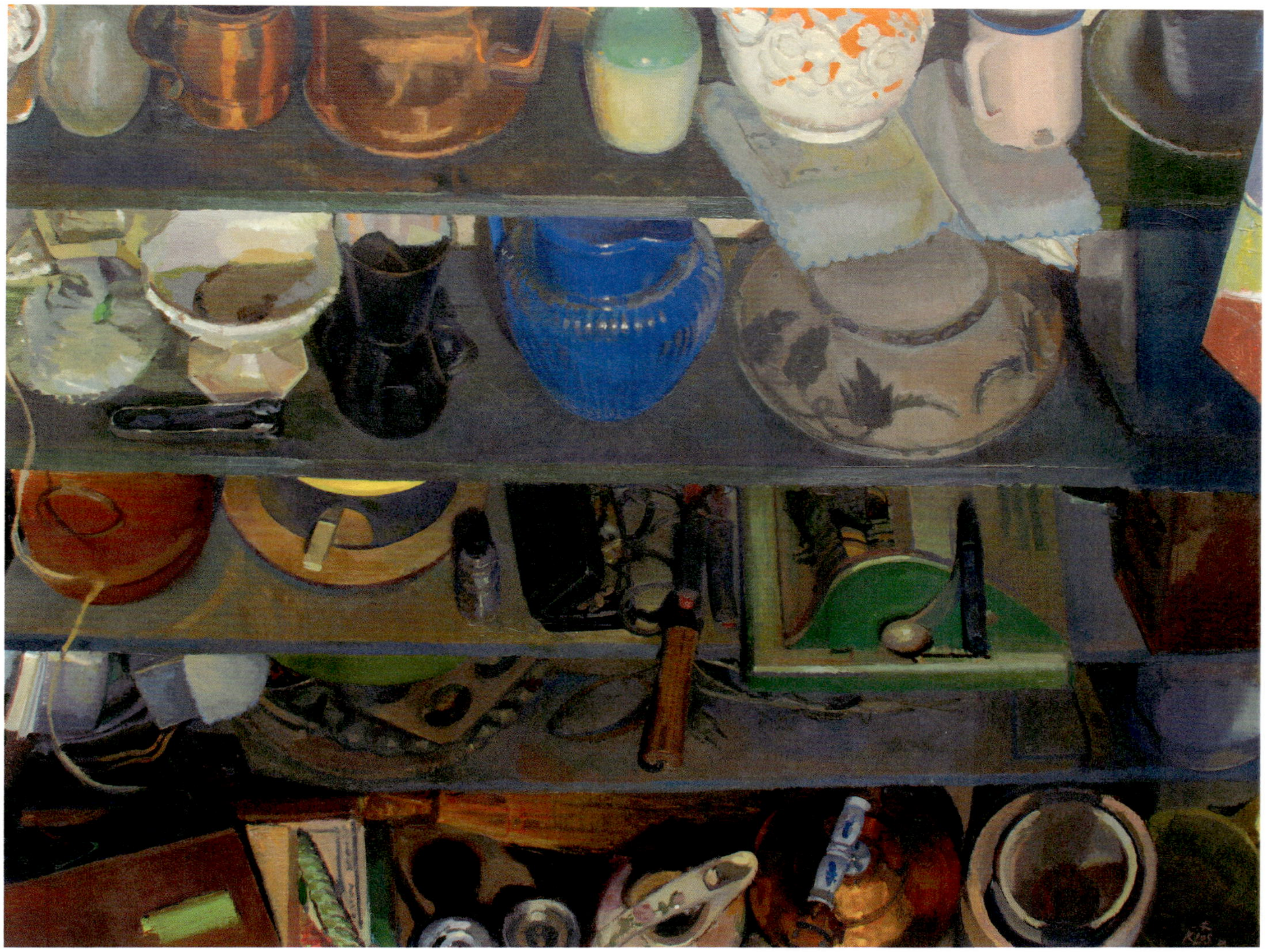

Matt Klos *Shelves*
2020, oil on canvas, 30 x 40 in.

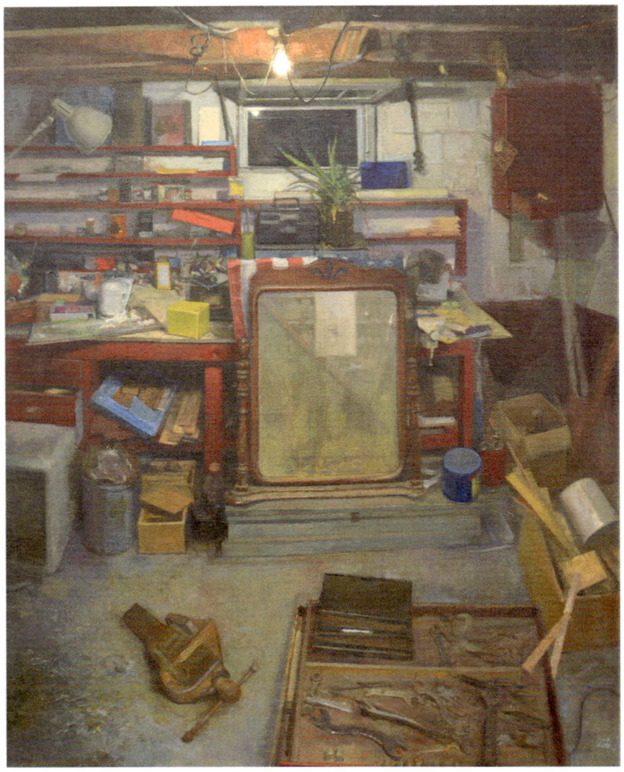

Matt Klos *Looking Back*
2009-2012, oil on linen, 46 x 36 in.

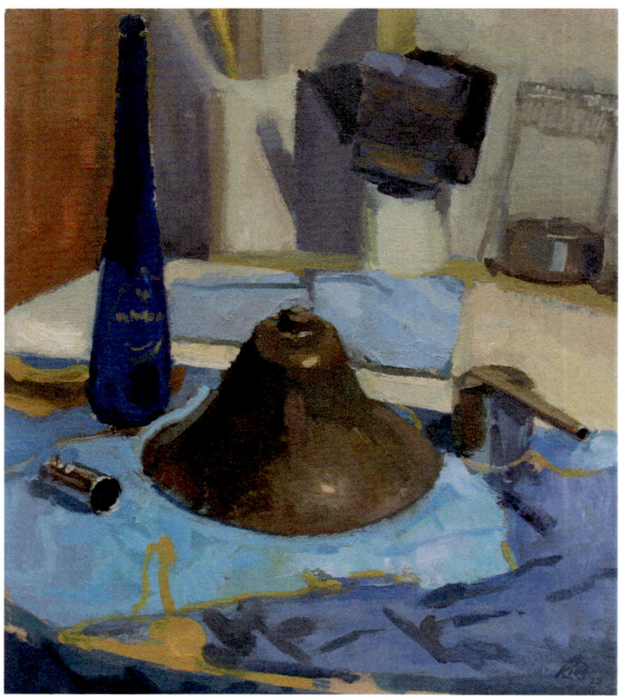

Matt Klos *Brass Bell*
2022, oil on panel, 10 x 8 in.

There is an object on the surface in "Keeping Time." It is the heart of an old clock. All the metal gears and springs converge coiled together ready to spring back to life. It's a beautiful thing. I wanted the gears to be in front on the tabletop but wanted the vibrant colors of the jar lids in the background cabinet to make you see beyond the machine to the shallow space. The gears become strangely ephemeral and almost solid when looking beyond them. Finding truth in observation is most challenging. I want my paintings to look like the act of seeing; if I bring everything up into a highly-focused description, the painting loses its relationship to natural vision. Perhaps my greatest struggle is knowing which elements of the scene before me ought to be carried further or pulled back.

XG: *What's it like to be in an art collective? How long have you been in your group and what role has it played in your artistic development?*

MK: Participating in an art collective is a great thing. I've been a member of Zeuxis for seven years and, initially, my main reason for joining was to have the opportunity to contribute work to annual traveling exhibitions, most of which have a stop in New York City. I realize now that the exhibitions are just one of the many benefits of the collective. Zeuxis members are artists but they are also curators, writers, professors, and the list goes on. Joining a collective has been a way for me to build connections with other serious painters that I might not have come to know otherwise. Several collaborations have grown out of it. I've hosted a Zeuxis show in Annapolis, MD, shown the work of a couple Zeuxis members in my Baltimore gallery, Exeter, and been invited for some terrific studio visits. Most importantly, I've been challenged to make new work for certain exhibitions that I certainly would not have made on my own.

LL: I agree. It's been beneficial. Thanks to my participation in Midwest Paint Group, my artwork is exhibited in a number of shows throughout the year. It's also beneficial to belong to a group of painters who, although quite diverse in our approaches to painting, nevertheless share a belief in being part of an informed, visual pictorial plastic tradition. I can't quite remember when I became a member of Midwest Paint Group, perhaps around 2007.

Besides Midwest Paint Group, I'm also a member of The Confluence Collective and 7 on Site. Thanks to my participation in collectives, I've exhibited my work nationally and internationally. Tim King, director of Midwest Paint Group, has been generous in designing and producing catalogues for our numerous shows. I think my participation in these collectives stretches my usual repertoire of subject matter and expands the venues that exhibit my work, such as being with Zeuxis in the "Gems" show. What a dynamic show. My work is in such good company and at a great venue in Manhattan.

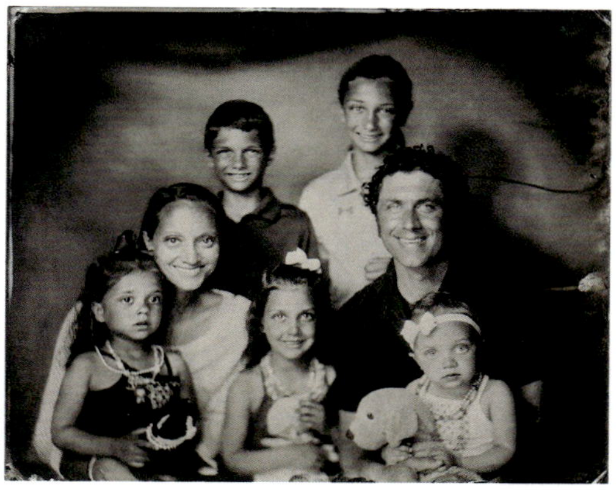

Photograph: Jay Gould

Klos Family portrait
Tintype photograph

***XG:** I hope you are both staying safe during this pandemic. How are you dealing with the quarantine? Has it affected you or your artwork?*

LL: As a professor, I've had to learn new strategies and platforms for teaching two studio art courses online. It has been challenging and nerve-racking to say the least, especially since the whole practice of painting and drawing is physical, experiential and direct. Critiquing images online is an acquired art, but we're all doing the best we can, I think. It's weird. In terms of my friends and family, I miss the physical camaraderie of being with them and seeing them in an actual space. My pets are happy though.

I'm at home more and it's been great to have more time to paint. Not being able to go outside and paint is a real drawback, but I feel as if there's more time to contemplate work in my studio. The impact on my painting has been not only an increased urgency to paint this strange time, but I am even more physical with paint now. The absence of engaging physically with the world has made me realize how much I miss the visceral and so that somatic desire is pushed into using even more, thicker paint than usual. What I paint out my window now is an urban landscape depleted of people, with only a few cars and a vacancy more akin to a ghost town.

MK: It has been a difficult time for me too. I miss my students and have concerns about online teaching. It was discouraging to cancel the opening of "Gems," where I was looking forward to seeing friends again and meeting members of the Midwest Paint Group.

Also, this spring I was set to open a two-part exhibit I curated with my colleague, Teddy Johnson, at Anne Arundel Community College in Maryland. We now plan to stage the exhibition in late summer or fall. But we are reeling from the news that one of the seven artists included in this group exhibit passed away from Covid-19. It's a surreal time for everyone and I know many people who have stories like these.

The greatest challenge of this quarantine has been what feels like a lobotomizing of the future from the present. I didn't realize how much my feelings about today were affected by the plans I have in place for tomorrow. I felt that my work has always been about being present and documenting my firsthand experiences. It seemed like it was always about measuring one decision against another and certainly my memories of the past played a role. Thousands of decisions to make one bedrock of truth. I feel now that my paintings must be made, in part, by dreaming up possible solutions, too. As I have continued to work in the studio, I'm more aware of a future tense and how it plays a crucial role in my creative process. It's been important to dream about the future in a positive light to keep things moving forward in the present. Z

Lynette Lombard in Andalusia

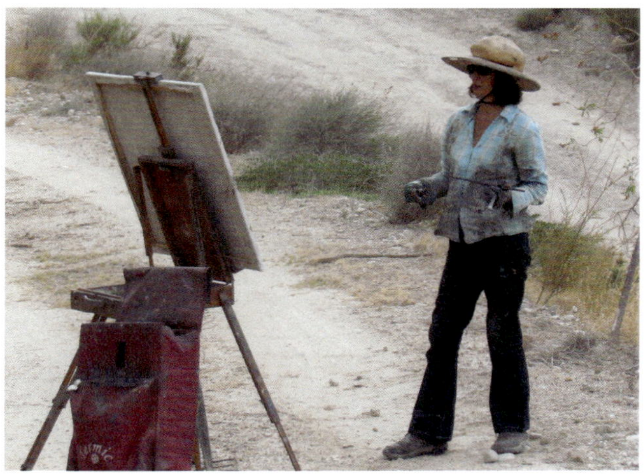

Postscript

Xico Greenwald, December 2023

I first met Lynette when we taught together at Mount Gretna in 2014. She brought a seriousness of purpose with her that I saw rub off on her painting students that summer. Reading over this interview today, a month after her passing, reminds me of her devotion to her artwork, her energy and her ambition. I send my sincerest condolences for this great loss to her family, her many friends and the many students whose lives she touched.

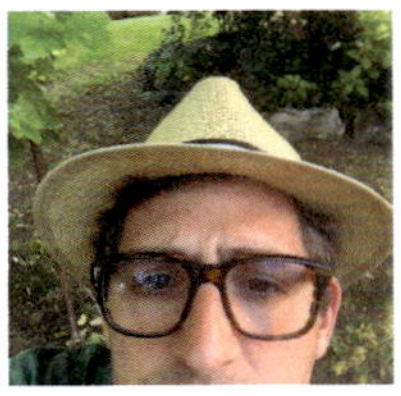

Xico Greenwald is a New York City-based artist. He teaches art at Borough of Manhattan Community College. In addition to painting and teaching, Xico writes and edits art criticism. His essays, reviews and interviews have been published in The New York Sun, Delicious Line, The Epoch Times, artcritical.com, Painting Perceptions and Painters' Table.

www.xicogreenwald.com

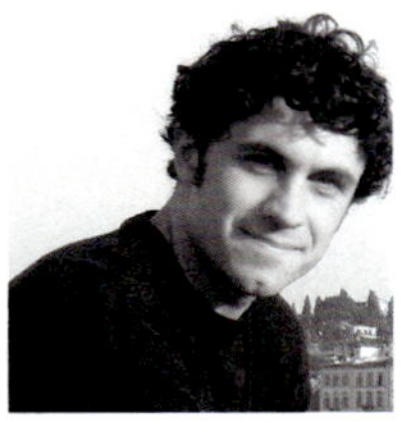

Matt Klos is a recipient of three Individual Artist Awards from the Maryland State Arts Council (2016, 2012 and 2008). His work has been featured in numerous group and solo exhibitions including the Prince Street Gallery in Chelsea, NY in 2011. He was awarded first place in the Bethesda Painting Awards in 2007 and received an Elizabeth Greenshields Foundation Grant in 2001. Klos currently teaches drawing and painting full-time at Anne Arundel Community College in Arnold, MD and has served as a guest lecturer/critic at various institutions including the New York Academy of Art, Towson University, and the University of Missouri. He is a member of the collective Perceptual Painters, www.perceptualpainters.com and Zeuxis, www.zeuxis.us. He lives in Baltimore, MD with his wife and children.

www.mattklos.com

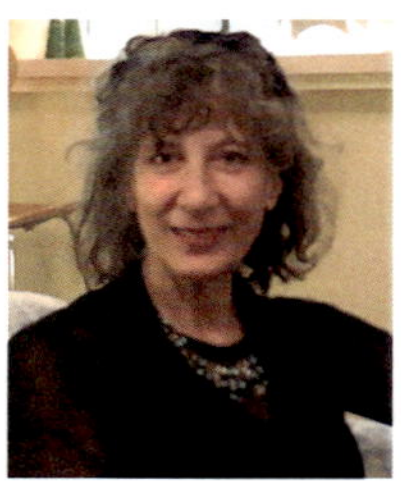

Lynette Lombard was a Professor of Art at Knox College, Galesburg, Illinois and a member of the Bowery Gallery, NY. She exhibited nationally and internationally, especially in Spain. She received her MFA from Yale University, BA Honors from Goldsmiths' College of Art, University of London and attended the New York Studio School for two years.

www.lynettelombard.com

The Art of Seeing

Jane A. Black interviews

Jean Koeller and John Benton

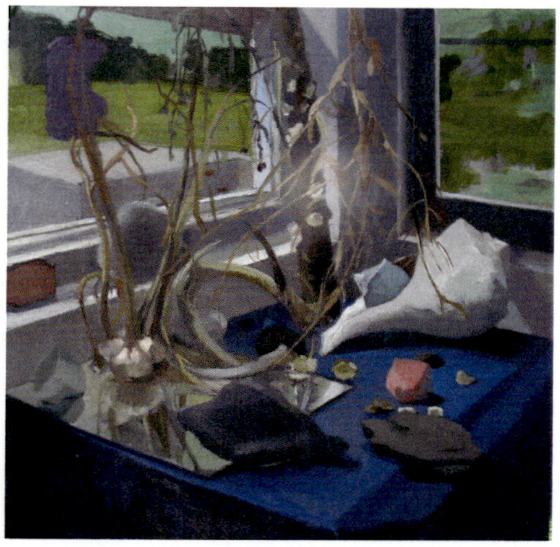

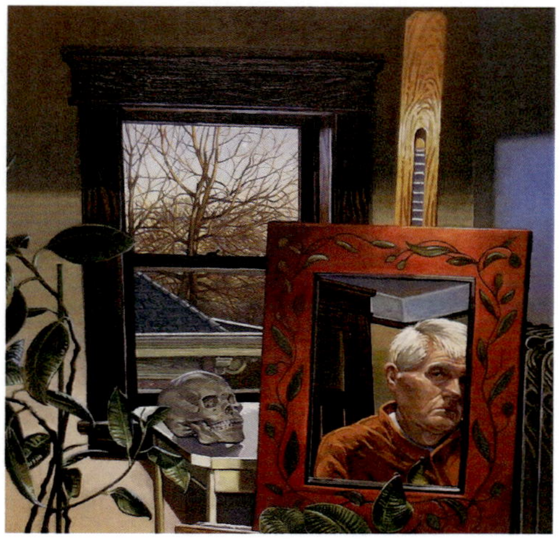

Jean Koeller *Landscape Parts II*, 2018, oil on panel, 24 x 24 in.
John Benton *Point of View* (detail), 2021, oil on canvas, 20 x 24 in.

Jane A. Black: *Jean Koeller, of New Carlisle, Ohio, chose John Benton, of Chicago, Illinois, with whom to have a conversation. By video conference, I asked them what they have in common, in addition to painting the landscape. These conversations were lightly edited for length and clarity.*

Jean Koeller: John is the most humble person I've met—his work is extraordinary. We come from similar educational backgrounds with common teachers, so we share a language. But we have very different voices. We both love the landscape and how it gets recorded formally. We have conversations about in-between color—how you see it. Also, we talk about how to sustain a painting by working on it over time. Things can happen in the studio—neither of us is afraid to go back to older work to see if we can figure it out. And, we both pretty much paint for ourselves.

John Benton: Jean and I met through mutual friends at Wright State University, where we both did our undergraduate work, and there were a couple of alumni shows we both were in. I admired her work a lot, so I sought her out. There's a similar way we both explore the landscape, but not stylistically. The way she journeys through a painting seems very familiar to me, and so I'm drawn to that. I am a tonal painter—I understand light and dark very well, but I don't feel like I always understand color. I see the world in a series of tones getting from one point of color to another point of color with darker to lighter

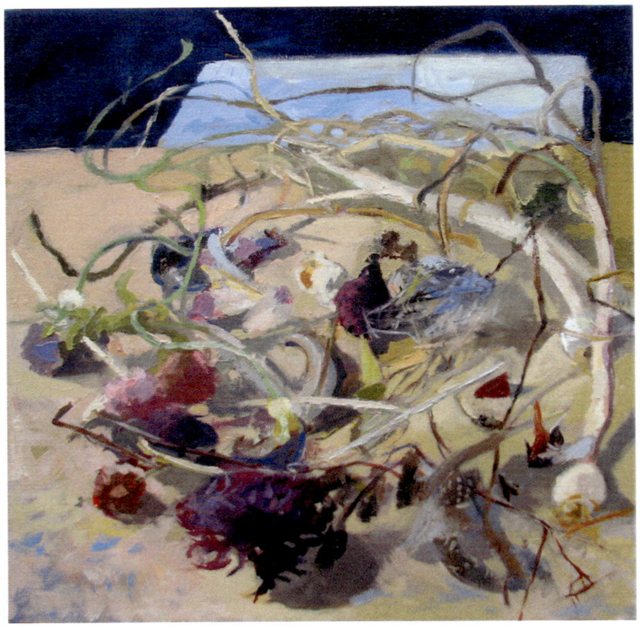

Jean Koeller *Landscape Parts IX*
2012, oil on canvas, 17 x 17 in.

tones. I can mold an object from light to shadow with progressions of tone (white, gray, black) believably. Those middle colors can throw me. One of the things Jean and I have talked about is getting from one color to another color in unexpected ways.

JAB: *I am interested in your thoughts about line—about the way you demarcate space by division—or leave that moment open to proximity.*

JK: I use ballpoint pen to draw, because it doesn't smear, but I don't really think about line anymore. I think about how to move across a surface or create something on the surface to express space, color, form. Line in my work is more implied. Of course, it becomes a descriptive thing with the branches; they are literally linear, although there is still a left or right, a top or bottom. They're never a singular line. I think I use line in a more abstract way—compositionally. I am looking for how things line up spatially and how to create juxtapositions. I am thinking in terms of parts, big to the little areas, and how much detail is needed. I am thinking about how to get the air and space and color. It's not about mark-making. I'm thinking how much I need to say, how to divide shapes, how one thing meets another.

JB: I use line a lot more than Jean does. She paints more with gesture and blocks, whereas I am more aware of edges, and edges meeting edges. I often use liner brushes or smaller brushes and draw with the paint, almost as if I'm using a pencil. Then I will move the colors into each other. I am a stronger draftsman than colorist, which is why this discussion of middle colors is much on my mind. They are key to the transition from edge to edge.

JAB: *What are some of the important lessons you have learned—in art or life —from experience or education? How are they part of your art practice?*

JK: I know now that I was harder on myself than anyone else could be, and I didn't balance that with the good parts, hearing the positives along with the negatives. Growing up when I did, female voices were not heard. Women had to be more articulate in order to make points in a critique or be taken at all seriously. Teaching young, less affluent students, listening to how those kids would beat themselves up, I thought, "I did that, too," and I saw how destructive that was. And, when I could talk them out of it, they did the most amazing things. It was eye-opening; I was ready to see it. Make your work, and make it as you see fit. Build context as you go; don't forget, but don't put a value judgment on it. See the world a different way—your way—and then see it another way. It's okay to be vulnerable, to be wrong. Another super important lesson was to leave your comfort zone, where you reside; I learned that from teaching abroad. When you go to another place and make work, you

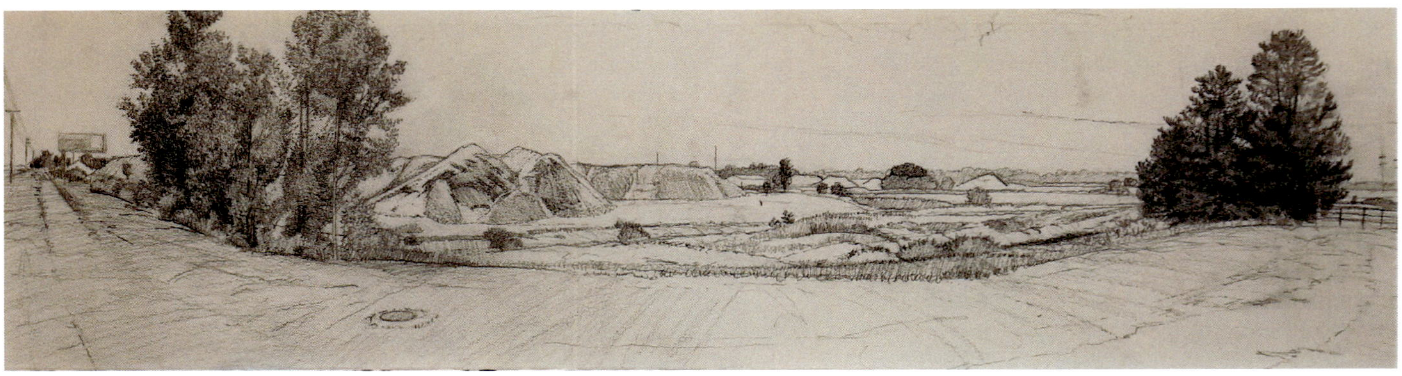

John Benton *Study for Early Sunday Morning*
2019, pencil on paper, 29 x 7 in.

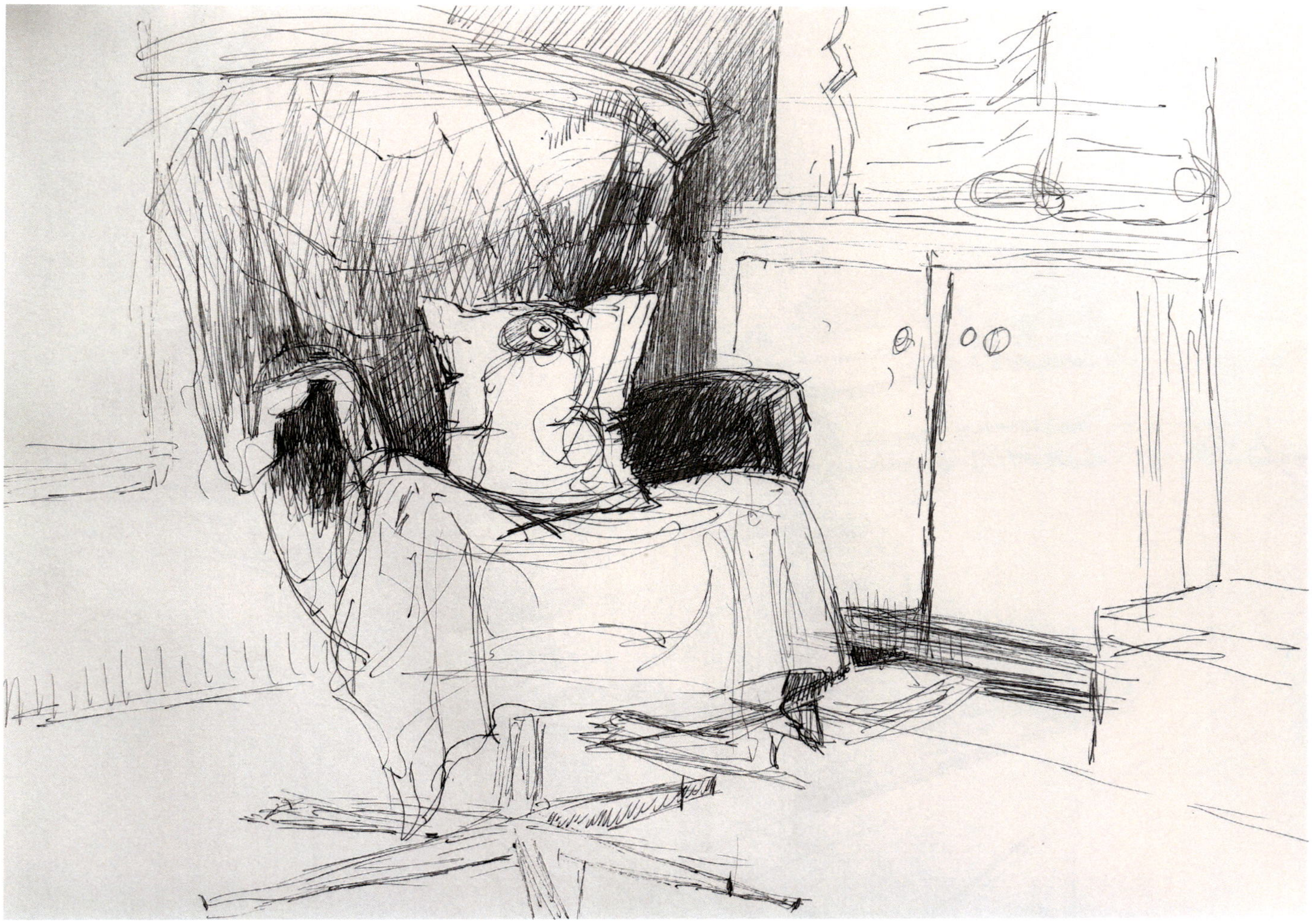

Jean Koeller *Untitled*
2015, black ball point pen, 8 ½ x 12 in.

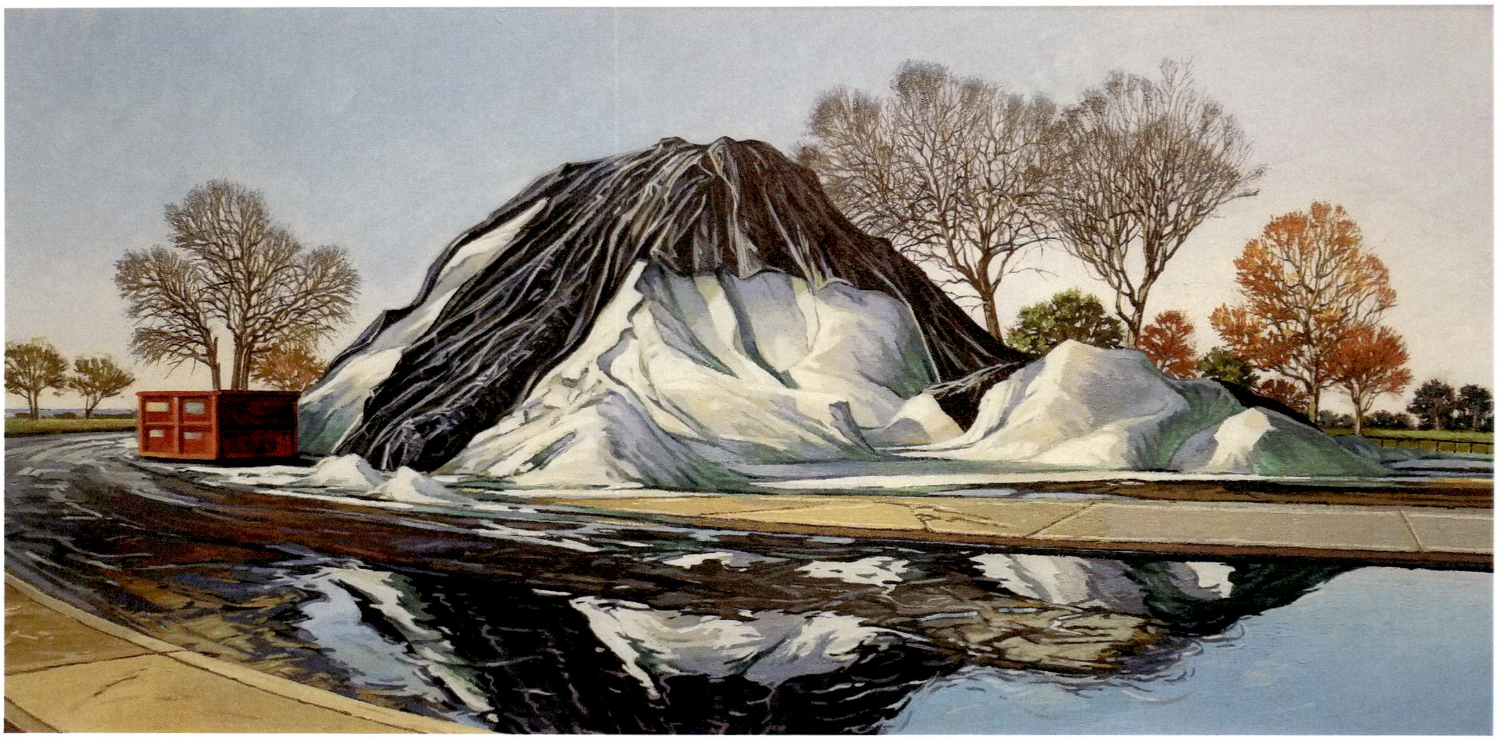

John Benton *Chicago Canal*
2023, oil on canvas, 12 x 24 in.

bring something back. It helps you to see what you know with fresh eyes. I knew it was important to go look at great artwork and experience it in relationship to your own body and mind. Same as the adventure of living in any other kind of culture—it's important to keep providing that for yourself. It's up to you to choose it. Painting has taught me self-care—emotionally, mentally, intellectually and physically.

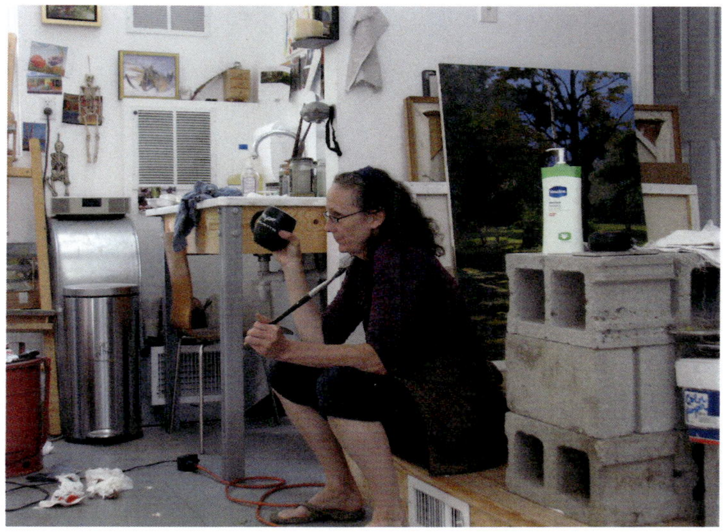

Jean Koeller in her studio

JB: Well, I feel as if the older I get and the more I figure out, the less I know. There is something that painting gives me that nothing else does—it's become something I just have to do, for my own health and wellbeing. It's a way of possessing the world, understanding and seeing it. One of my teachers, Neil Welliver, once said his wife refused to ride with him, because she said, "You paint while you drive." I do that, too! I am constantly painting even when I'm not painting. I ask myself, "How is that color laying against that color? Why is that line so distinct and that one is not?" There's so much to see.

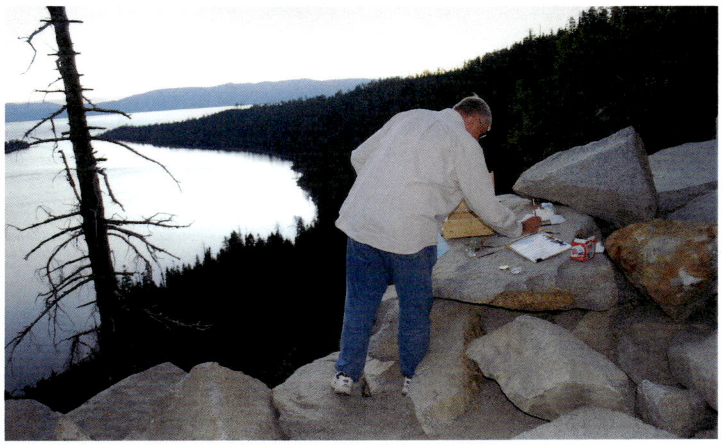

John Benton painting by Lake Tahoe

JAB: *What is something in your work that has changed over time but, looking back over many years, you can identify as an ongoing presence? Do you see it as a pathway through or an arc over your work—or something else?*

JK: I would choose color; it's been one thing I've loved, no matter what. My work has always been tonal, but it has become more about color interaction than ever. It is an arc in that way, I think you can see my color choices becoming more sophisticated. I still take a lot of pleasure in trying different palettes, colors that I've combined in the past. No matter what genre I'm painting, color has always been central. The landscape is contemplative. When I turn up the color, it's based on an idea, something I want to express, something I am feeling. I'm happy with the paintings I am making. Painting can capture and hold time in place. Time is expanded; the painting suspends disbelief—it's not a reality, but you believe it. I also love that I can walk up to a painting and identify what colors were used to make it.

JB: I started out mostly making still life paintings that were very symbolic. They were autobiographical, and after a while I found myself not engaging with them. It was almost as if I had the painting done before I started it. Landscape was a way of breaking myself of knowing where the painting was going to go. I see a lot of correlation between landscape and still life, but I wanted to allow the landscape to present itself... to find my way into the landscape. At some point, I realized I wanted to walk around and move through the space. I started doing horizontal paintings to allow that. So my progression was to start allowing others to experience the painting the way I do. I try not to make an obvious focal point, so you have to look harder and are rewarded. It's another reason I am attracted to Jean's paintings—they also allow you in to walk around. So, perhaps the overarching presence in my work is a lack of focal point. I still do still life paintings, but they are as much about the space between the objects as the objects themselves. I have gotten away from a central focal point.

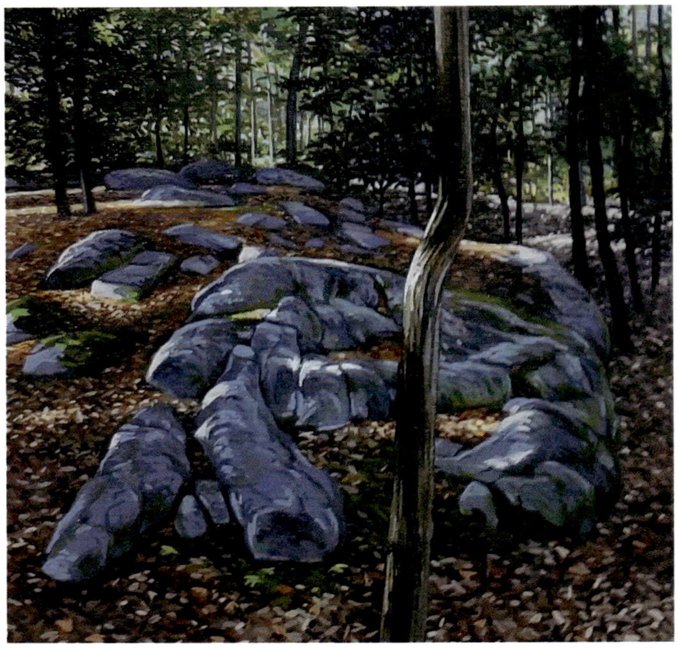

John Benton *Bouldered Ledge*
2020, oil on canvas, 10 x 10 in.

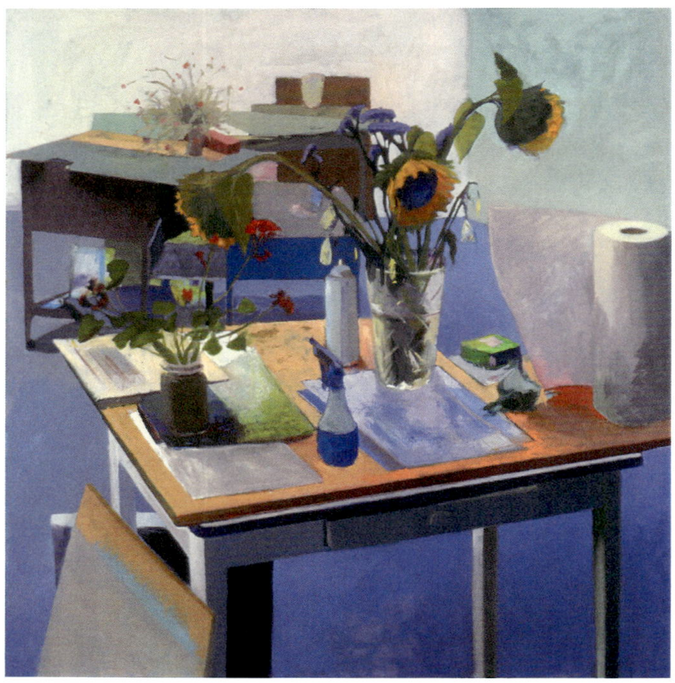

Jean Koeller *French Still Life II*
2000, oil on canvas, 48 x 46 in.

JAB: *At this strange moment in time, are your paintings suffused with a different set of concerns, changed vision, more emotionally charged? Or is the act of painting a refuge from the present, a way to reach a familiar balance?*

JK: Painting is a balance, and during this pandemic it has been a way to ground myself. I returned a bit to what I know. I have needed something really solid that I could hang on to that seemed okay. Being out here, on the land, I know I haven't felt the pandemic like friends in New York whose world has totally changed. It is not lost on me how lucky I am to have so much room to move around. It was hard to paint in the beginning—it seemed frivolous. I spent a lot of time cleaning house. But, I got past that. I honestly can't tell you if the pandemic is affecting my work, because I am in it now and can't see it yet.

JB: While the current situation isn't reflected in my paintings, it is very much a part of my being. I have health issues that make me high-risk for the virus, so I have been seriously quarantining since the beginning of March. And while painting has always been a place where I lose myself, it is not a means to avoid dealing with the realities of the world. I'm very much aware of my environment, but I'm not sure if that is something that will come out in the final work. When I am painting, I become so focused that I am unaware of time, the world, problems, even breathing. I think it is something a lot of creative people experience, and it has especially been a place to relieve the stress from all of the chaos of this new world order. When I'm working on a landscape, I enter another state. It is meditative—a state of mind that releases you from your concerns. The paintings are helping me get through these times. I am so grateful to have this practice. Z

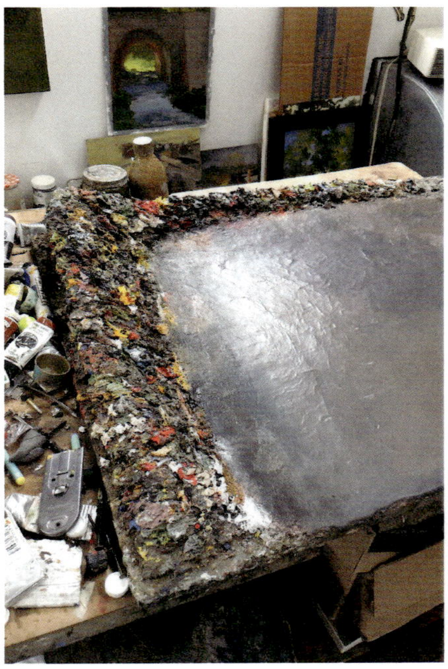

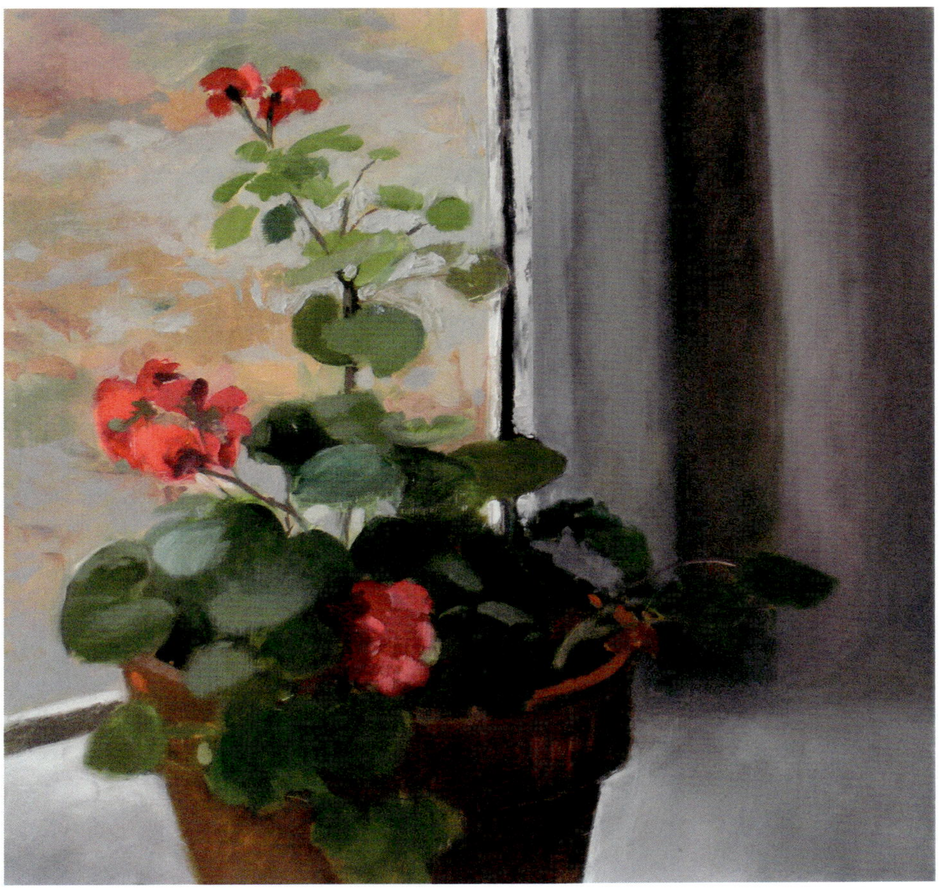

LEFT TO RIGHT:
Jean's palette
Jean Koeller *Geranium Day*
2010, oil on canvas, 15 x 15 ½ in.

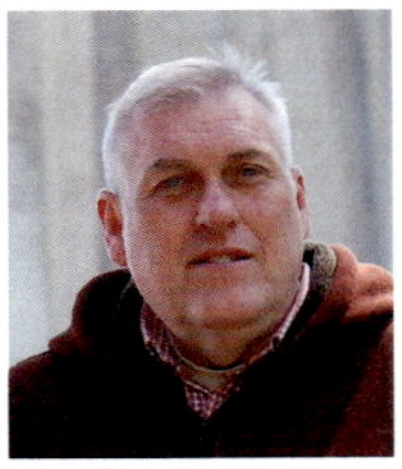

John Benton grew up in Ohio but currently lives in Chicago with his husband Dennis. He studied painting at Wright State University and received his MFA from the University of Pennsylvania. He has exhibited work at several museums, including the Butler Institute of Art, the Swope Art Museum and the Taubman Museum of Art, as well as galleries in the Midwest, New York City and elsewhere on the East coast.

www.johnbentonpainter.com

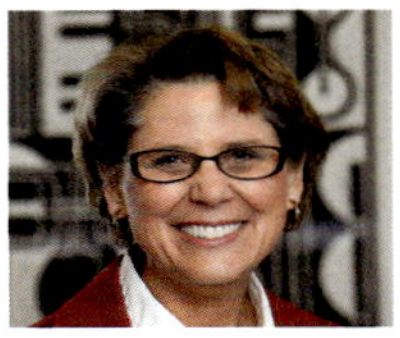

Jane A. Black has had a long and varied career as a writer, artist, juror, panelist, curator, nonprofit executive leader and business owner. A native of Ohio, she now lives in Portland, Oregon, where she is a specialist in grant writing and development for TriMet, the region's multimodal public transit agency.

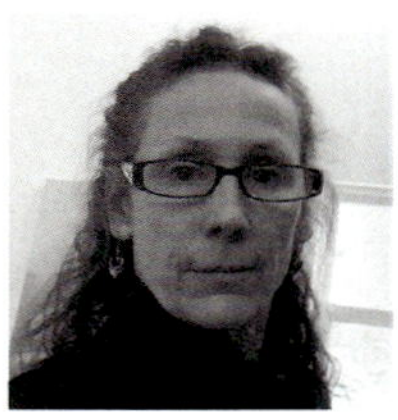

Jean Koeller lives and works in Ohio where she paints primarily still life and landscape. Her work explores these genres while employing observation, memory and invention. Art and nature draw her equally into their respective worlds. "I find that my painting is seamlessly about both, since long ago I lost any ability or desire to separate the two. Paintings always start with an inclination, a visual stimulus and then lead me through the process of what needs to happen. If I learn something new, then it's a success. The process constantly presents new possibilities, both from and away from nature. I just need to be present at all times." Jean shows with the Dana Wiley Gallery.

www.jeankoeller.com

The Quiet Work of Looking

Gael Mooney interviews

Richard La Presti and Deborah Rosenthal

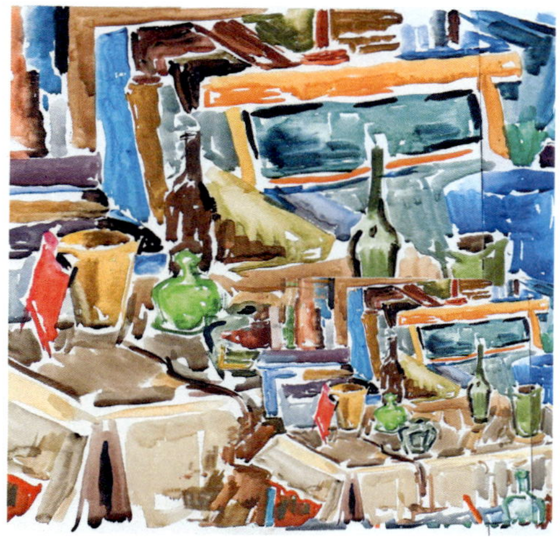

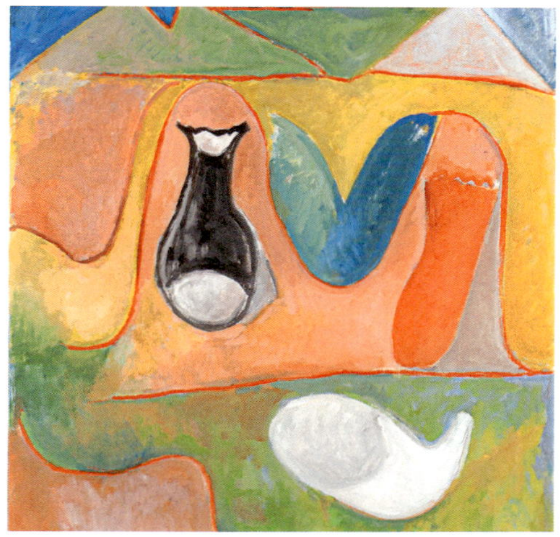

Richard La Presti *Horizontal* (detail), 2023, Watercolor, 18 x 36 in.
Deborah Rosentthal *Animate* (detail), 2020, Oil on linen, 30 x 24 in.

Gael Mooney: *At the invitation of Zeuxis, I spoke with Deborah Rosenthal and Richard La Presti. I've had an opportunity to get to know them and to follow their work thanks to our association with the Bowery Gallery—an artist collective in New York to which La Presti and Rosenthal have belonged since the mid-80s.*

Rosenthal's painterly abstractions explore the myths, metaphors and symbolism hidden beneath everyday appearances, whereas La Presti is a figurative painter who works primarily from life. I was curious to learn what, if any, common ground might exist between these two artists who approach painting from such different standpoints.

In my conversation with them what stood out is the degree to which even now, in the midst of a pandemic, they are each thinking about the art that they have seen in the museums and galleries and during their travels prior to the lockdown or even in years past.

I see in the work of Rosenthal and La Presti the influence of the long hours they have spent looking at and studying the art of the traditions in which they have immersed themselves. Richard's paintings of his studio and of his natural surroundings reflect the purity and chromatically rich colors of modernist masters such as Matisse and Dufy, their intricate scaffolding, and his belief (derived from Giacometti and others) that drawing and color are inextricably intertwined. The shapes, colors and patterns of Rosenthal's paintings similarly reflect the rich and diverse range of sources—both medieval and modern—that she's been looking at and studying her whole life.

As I think about the extent to which the vital role of the tradition informs the work of each, their apparent stylistic differences seem to be of secondary importance. Instead, what impresses me the most, to use a phrase of Rosenthal's, is the extent to which they are each engaged in the quiet work of looking.

GM: *The closure of museums, galleries and other cultural institutions during the pandemic is keenly felt by artists who rely on them for inspiration and source material for their work. How are you coping with the resulting cultural void and where are you finding inspiration these days for your work?*

Richard La Presti: Over the last few years I've been going to shows at the National Gallery in Washington DC—Corot and Tintoretto, for example. Now during these difficult times I look to nature and my work in the studio. I've been doing mostly small, spontaneous works of my studio and the outdoor environment. When you live in a rural area you are aware of the landscape at all times.

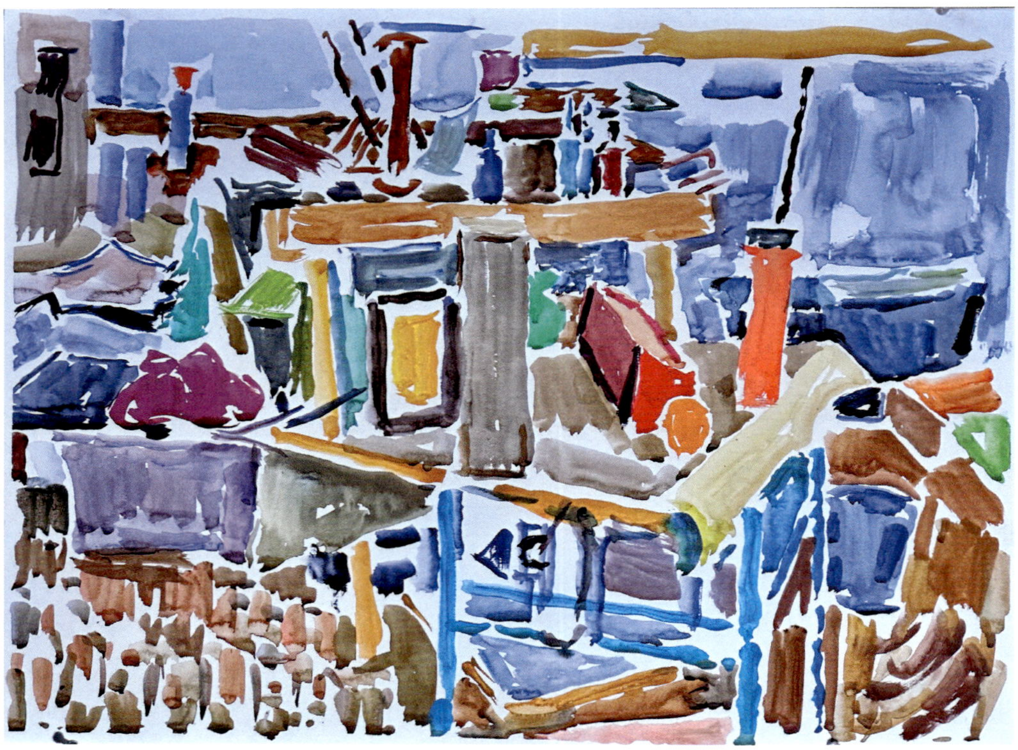

Richard La Presti *Yellow*
2023, Watercolor, 18 x 24 in.

Deborah Rosenthal: In this terrible moment of disease and death, murder and racism, chaos and social/political collapse, the dark and viewer-less galleries of the museums seem emblematic of it all. And the fact that this is occurring worldwide is terrible—one can't even escape in one's mind to a foreign country to see the great things there without thinking, "How and when will I ever see these things again?" There's no end in sight...

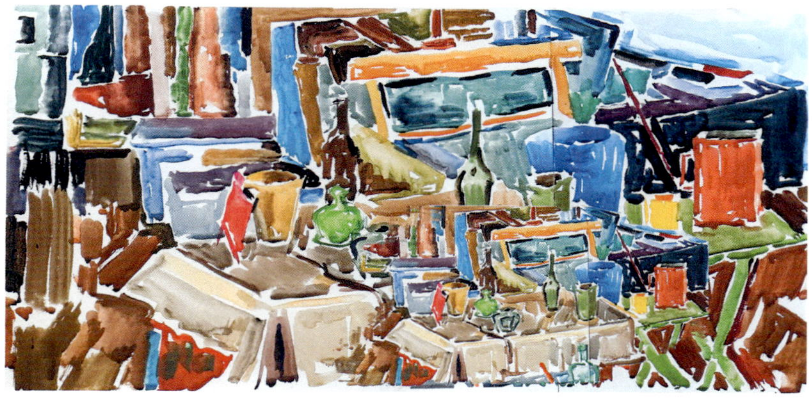

Richard La Presti *Horizontal*
2023, watercolor on paper, 18 x 36 in.

But I grew up in New York and have been lucky to live here my whole life and to look and draw in its museums. This past fall I traveled as I often have to look at paintings abroad. So I carry a large freight of painting, sculpture and architecture in my head and in my sketchbooks which, along with my art books and postcards, are always important references for me. I'm worried about the younger painters, such as my former students, who need to be discovering themselves but are losing this time and missing out on these experiences.

But I also feel that the chaotic and dark character of the world right now seems to be catching up to the craziness and decadence of the art world of recent years. I don't recognize in most mainstream galleries and publications the world I live in—where people are carrying on a discourse with the past and struggling to embody a vision in paint or with clay. In many ways it seems we're revisiting the issues of the 1930s—"paint me a painting with social significance" and with extra-aesthetic considerations and commercial concerns outweighing what art really does. And that puts up a lot of barriers to the quiet work of looking.

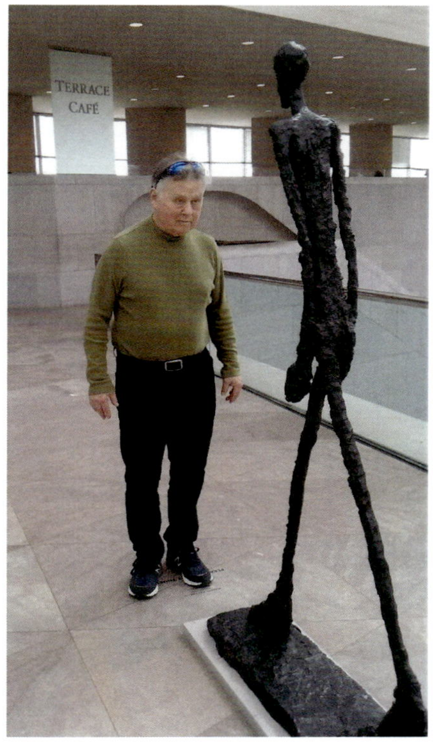

Richard La Presti

***GM:** The work of each of you draws on the traditions of both figuration and abstraction. Richard, your work appears to be primarily inspired by direct observation of still lifes, interiors and landscapes. Deborah, your paintings explore the language of metaphor, mythology and symbolism. How would you describe your process of making art and has this changed over time?*

RL: Before moving to the Catskills, I spent most of my adult life in New York City. When I lived in the city, I often painted at night. But since moving to the country I almost always paint during the day, working directly from the motif. Here in the Catskills with the beaches now "closed for the season" I work instead from the landscape surrounding my home and studio. In my still life paintings I generally work spontaneously, accepting the environment that my studio presents. I don't arrange things. With my landscape and still life paintings I like to add or to take out parts to make a clearer composition. I often incorporate elements of collage to achieve this.

DR: My painting reflects my belief that for an artist the past is open. Growing up in New York, I was enthralled by the modernists at MOMA—the complicated space in Braque; the avid imagination of Picasso. But in my first year of grad school, I saw the Mondrian retrospective at the Guggenheim, and recognized that what I had to say in painting would be in an abstract language. During the next few years I began to study the abstractions of 20th century artists such as Paul Klee, Wassily Kandinsky, André Masson, S.W. Hayter and Jean Hélion; another important influence was the American Mondrianist, Ilya Bolotowsky, with whom I had a few critiques and many long talks. And I first

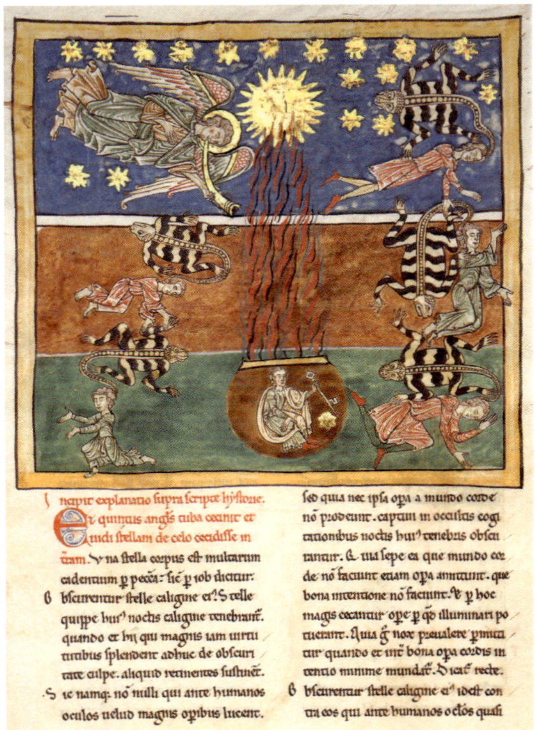

Beatus Manuscript, Clarion of the Fifth Angel's Trumpet (Book of Revelation)
c.1180, tempera, gold, and ink on parchment,
detail from 17 ½ x 11 ¾ in. sheet

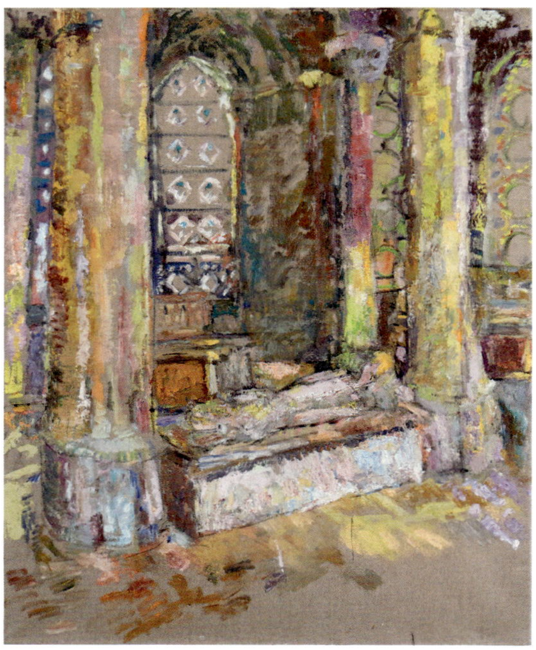

Gael Mooney *Gisant (Robert d'Artois) Basilique de Saint-Denis*
2019, oil on linen, 35 x 25 ½ in.

read The Thinking Eye, Klee's teaching and lecture notes on metaphoric abstraction, which I think of now as my graduate-school curriculum.

Over the next decade, I constructed my path through an artistic past, perhaps most significantly by returning to an earlier interest in medieval art when I first saw the Morgan Beatus, an important Spanish medieval manuscript, in an exhibition in New York. In that manuscript, as well as the Romanesque painting and sculpture that I saw on trips to Europe, I found a world that, as Klee put it, "I would like to see"—a world of characters and symbols located in the imagination. The path I laid out for myself years ago includes by now so many signposts—Odilon Redon, William Blake, El Greco, Islamic calligraphy, Coptic textiles, Borromini's architecture, Poussin and Claude Lorrain's poetic mythological landscapes. These artists describe a universe in which human experience—whether structured as a still life, landscape, or figure composition—traces the action of forces beyond and underneath the immediately perceptible world of things. How to construct such tensions in a modern painting? I find symbols or metaphors not only in the visionary artists of the past, but also in the expanded modern perception of the natural world that includes not only the animal, vegetal, and mineral, but also the cosmic, microscopic, and X-ray paradigms of vision. When drawing from sources such as geometrical, botanical, astronomical, or anatomical diagrams, I don't reduce from nature; I try to fuse new images to elaborate on my own experience of the world.

GM: *The work of each of you is characterized by luminosity created through your chromatically rich and vivid palettes. How do you think about the role of color and light in painting and which artists or art historical periods inform the way you think about this?*

RL: I frankly don't think about it much and would say that some of our best figurative artists—Kossoff and Giacometti for example—really were not as much involved with color as with drawing and structure. While I derive inspiration from all periods of art history in terms of color—I'm particularly fond of the modern masters such as Matisse, Dufy, Derain and Mondrian. The Peabody Museum in Salem, Massachusetts presented a retrospective of Hofmann last year that was also very interesting.

DR: Color and light are very mysterious, I think, and as hard to describe in words as the precise taste of something on your tongue. Light and dark, primary and secondary, warm and cool, having sunk pretty deeply into me after a lifetime of painting are by now matters that I feel rather than think about.

There are a few artists' truisms on color that always percolate around in my head—"find the perfect values;" "it's always easy to get the saturated colors;" "it's the intermediates—the grays—that are really hard to get." But best of all, I think, is Matisse's remark that each brushstroke on the canvas destroys or diminishes the previous ones. What I like about the comment is that it captures the dialectic of construction and destruction that putting a colored shape next to another colored shape entails—and the recognition that each new colored passage challenges whatever is already there. These challenges become enactments of tensions—the undercurrent of dynamism in a picture.

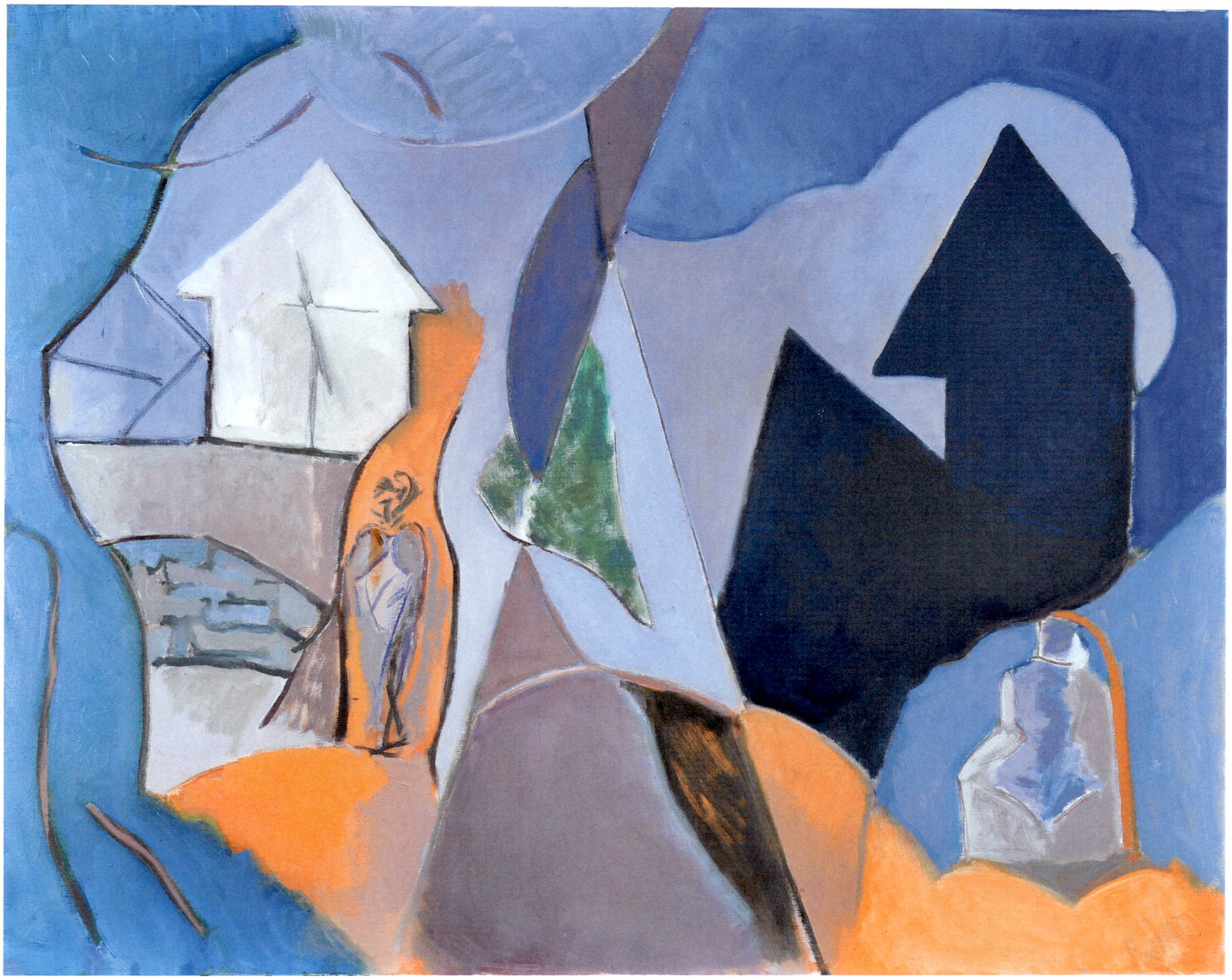

Deborah Rosenthal *Paired Scenes*
2011, oil on linen, 35 x 50 in.

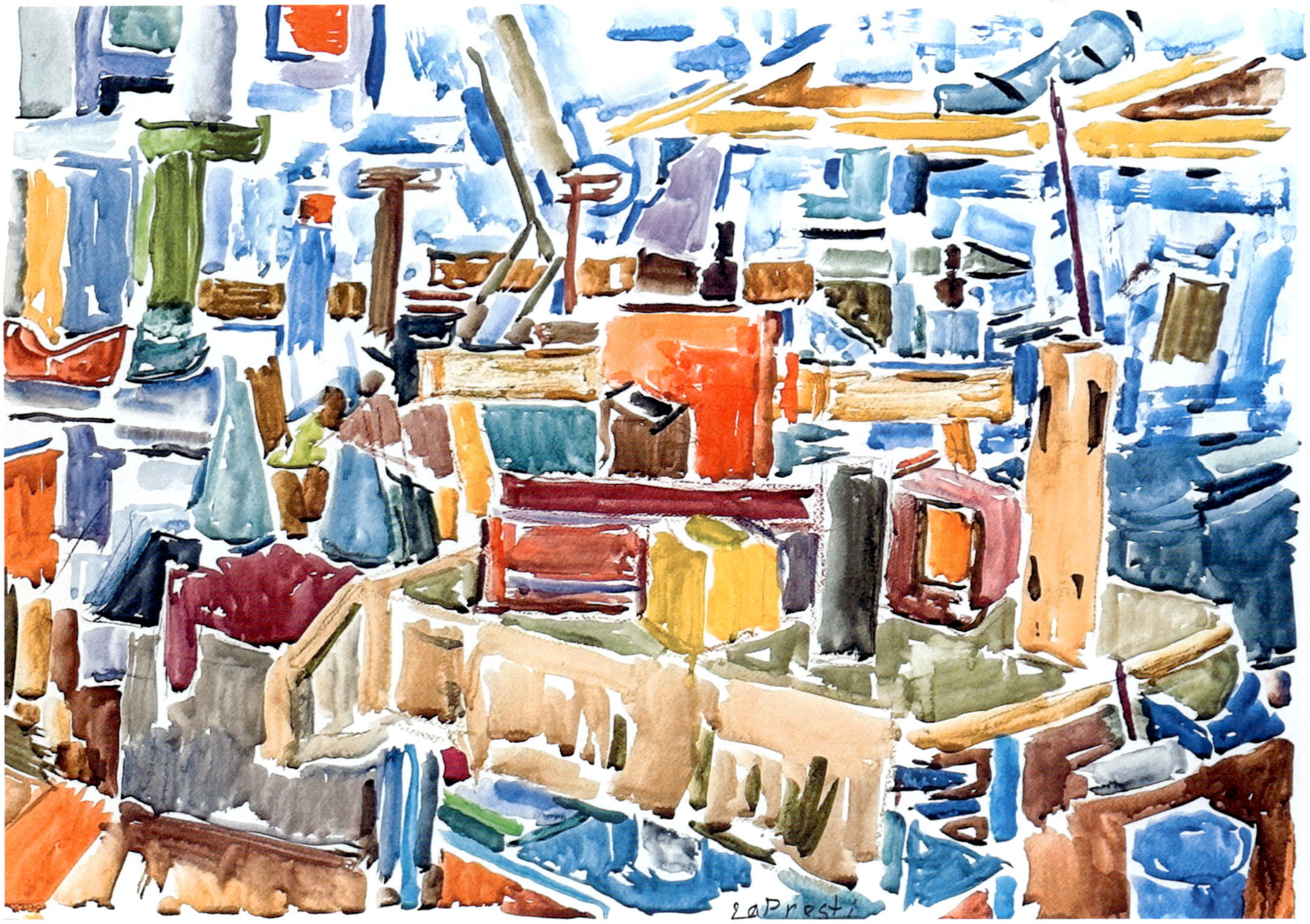

Richard La Presti *Pyramid*
2023, watercolor on paper, 18 x 24 in.

So that's the way I feel my way through color in each painting. And though I don't have a color theory, I do have an underlying principle about how color has to work in my painting, which doesn't start with reference to the local color of objects. For me, each metaphor from which I construct my pictures demands its own palette. I have no single, characteristic palette. In some, I may use tonal color; in others, I use schematic color—primaries or complementaries. The various palettes suggest different moods, lighting effects and so on. Paint handling—touch or attack—can't be separated from color. I sometimes lay in translucent layers of color, making for ambiguous space as planes overlap; in other pictures I apply color alla prima, impastoed or simply applied through thin opaque layers. Or in still others I may inundate almost the whole canvas in a single color, making a kind of slow or quiet movement, or through use of a schematic palette consisting of two complementaries a more emphatic one, like a brisk march or the striking of a gong. Through such variations—too numerous to describe now—I'm able to arrive at a different metaphor or at least a different take on the original one.

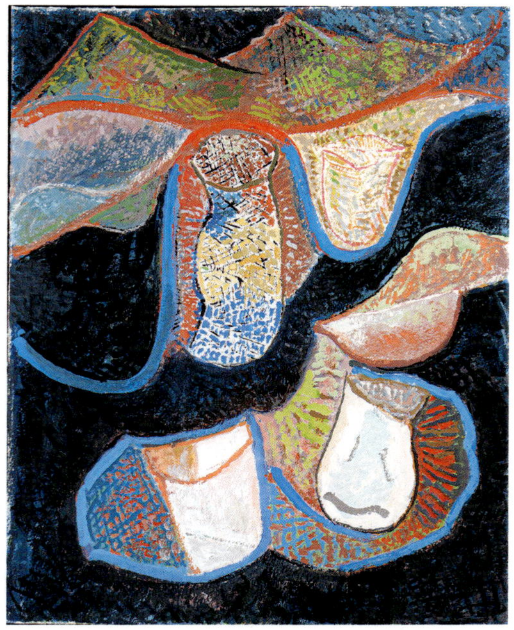

Deborah Rosenthal *Dark Still Life*
2021, gouache on paper, 16 x 12 in.

GM: *In addition to your longstanding membership in the Bowery Gallery you are connected to each other through your close ties to Barbara Goodstein—Richard's spouse and Deborah's close friend of many years—who sadly died in December, 2015. Your involvement with Barbara's art continues today through your work on behalf of the Barbara Goodstein Foundation which was founded to support and promote her legacy. How do you view the significance of Barbara Goodstein's art and example for you personally and for future generations?*

RL: Barbara Goodstein was a modern figurative artist with an interest in Byzantine, medieval and tribal art. She had an innate sense of structure and composition that made her work and opinions unique. She encouraged me to view my motifs (particularly the beach paintings) from different angles and to eliminate stereotypical figures that had no special meaning.

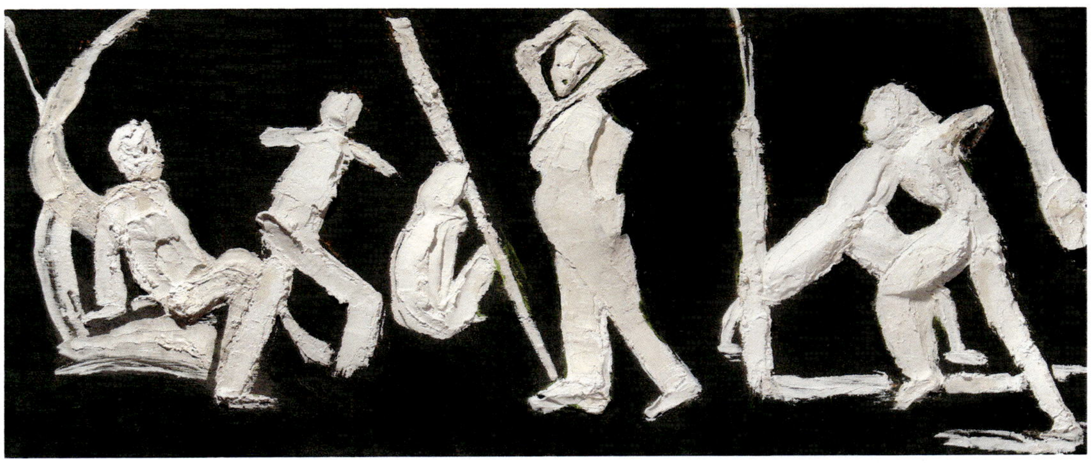

Barbara Goodstein
The Battle of the Sexes
1989, acrylic plaster, modeling paste and ground pumice on painted board, 15 x 36 in.

DR: Barbara Goodstein and I were close friends for forty-odd years. She was the artist I felt closest to. Our studio practices were different; she more often than not began by working from life, and I never do. But we shared similar sensibilities, including a love of medieval and Byzantine art, and of particular artists both past and present. Passages in some of my paintings show the influence of her plaster-drawing reliefs, and I recognize passages in her work that reflect the close attention she gave my paintings. She was an extraordinarily sophisticated artist who was even capable of humor in her sculpture —not an easy thing to do—with a great critical eye and straight-ahead personal vision. She was an original. Z

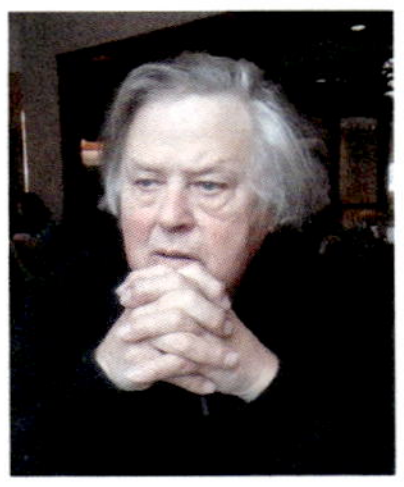

Richard La Presti was born in the Bronx and spent most of his adult life in Manhattan's East Village. In 2010 he moved to the Catskills where he now resides. La Presti's work focuses on landscapes, still lifes, portraits and bathers at the shore. Painter Gabriel Laderman wrote, "[La Presti] is a very passionate man. His paintings are, in fact very meditative, but they are also full of passion. Passion for people, the sky and the clouds, the land, the trees and foliage, [his work is] full of zest and verve." He holds a BFA from the Pratt Institute and is an associate member of the Bowery Gallery in New York and a member of Zeuxis, an association of still life painters. In 1993, La Presti was the recipient of the Ingram Merrill Award for Painting.

www.zeuxis.us/lapresti

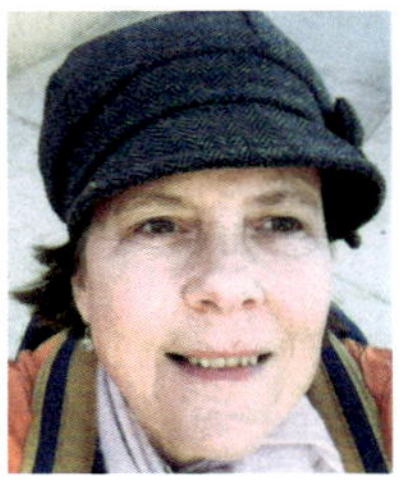

Gael Mooney a New York City based artist and an associate member of the Bowery Gallery. Her art criticism has appeared in www.artcritical.com. Among her publications exploring the intersection between art and spirituality are two essays exploring the symbolism of George Rouault's clowns.

www.gaelmooney.com

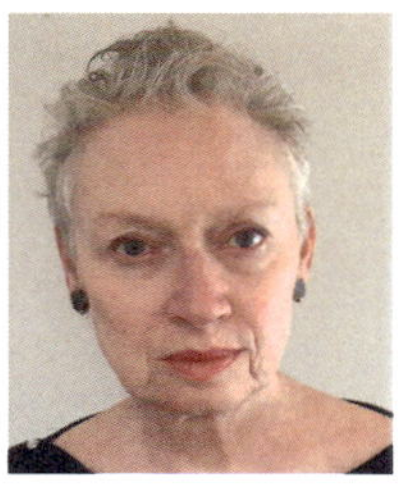

Deborah Rosenthal was born in New York and lives and works there and in the Catskills. She has a BA in English literature from Barnard College, and studied with Leonard Baskin at Smith College; her MFA in printmaking is from Pratt Institute. Rosenthal has had numerous solo shows of her paintings and prints since 1984 at the Bowery Gallery in New York, and had a 10-year retrospective at Hebrew Union College in NY; she's shown in many group shows nation-wide. For her writing on art that has appeared in publications including Arts, Modern Painters, The New Criterion, and Art in America, she received an NEA Critic's Grant. Rosenthal was the founding editor of Artists and Art, a series of books for Arcade Publishing. She taught painting and drawing at numerous institutions, and is a Professor Emerita of Fine Arts at Rider University.

www.deborahrosenthalstudio.com

Three Painters Unbound

John Parks interviews

Neil Callander and Catherine Kehoe and Tim Kennedy

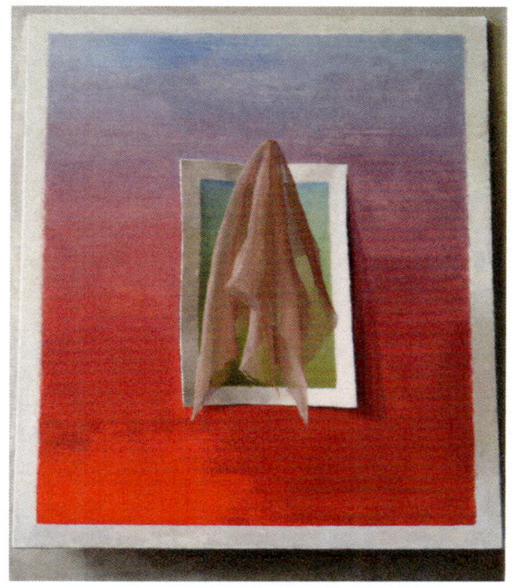

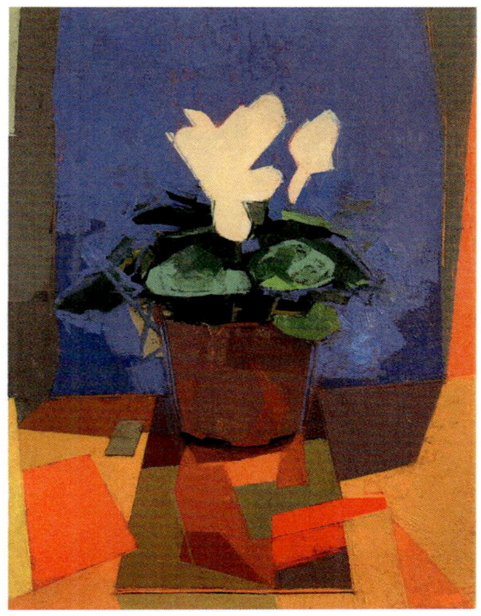

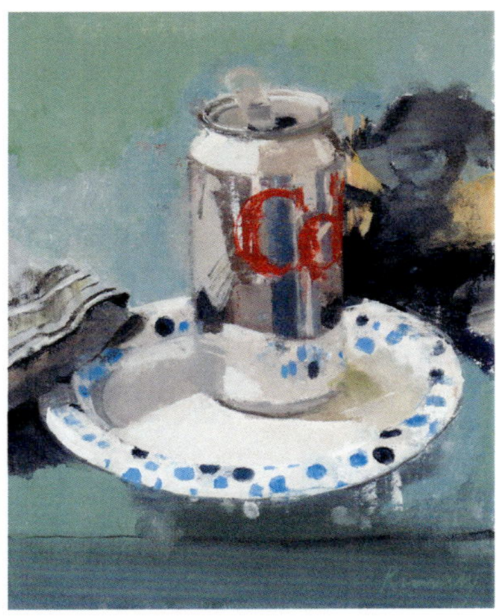

Neil Callander *Gradation #1*
2018, oil on linen on panel, 16 x 20 in.

Catherine Kehoe *Cyclamen*
2020, oil on linen on panel, 8 x 6 in.

Tim Kennedy *Holiday Can*
2013, oil on muslin on panel, 10 x 8 in.

John Parks: *At first glance Catherine Kehoe, Tim Kennedy and Neil Callander, are simply very different artists at different stages of their careers. I was intrigued that they wanted to be interviewed together, but quickly discovered that their work shares far more than at first appearance. All three are representational artists but none would fit in the "realist" category. Rather they each apply an open-ended painterly sensibility to the business of looking at the world around them and reconstructing it in paint. Their work involves considerable filtering of visual information, both in terms of subject matter and in the process of simplification and clarification that each engages in. Each of them is also highly selective in terms of color, creating color worlds rich in atmospheres, associations, feelings and aesthetic pleasures.*

Perhaps most remarkably each of these artists has covered an extraordinarily wide range of territory. Tim started as an abstract painter in college and has since explored still life, interiors, narrative figure paintings, landscape and portraiture. Catherine's work has ranged over portraiture, still life, figure painting, and painting from historical sources. Neil's paintings include still life, interiors, narrative scenarios, portraiture, landscapes, semi-abstract and wholly abstract paintings. It is this inclusive, spirited and adventurous quality that I found most attractive. These are not artists who are interested in carefully branding a product and engineering a career, rather they are creative spirits deeply involved in engaging and exploring the life around them. In doing so they are willing to take risks, make changes in approach and take on new challenges. The resulting artworks are fresh, insightful, often quite beautiful and always rewarding to contemplate.

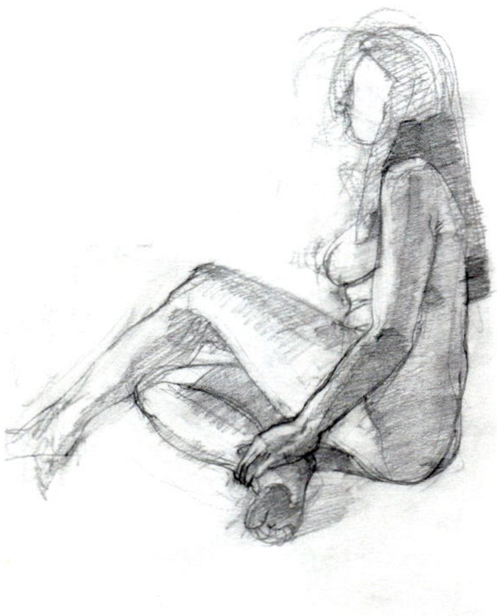

Tim Kennedy *Figure*
2012, graphite, 12 x 9 in.

JP: *Each of you has made a body of work that is surprisingly broad in range. What is it that drives you to venture into such a variety of approaches and such a diverse set of subject matter?*

Tim Kennedy: An answer off the top of my head is, "That's what artists do." I must have an image burned into my mind of artists like Matisse or Cézanne, who I grew up admiring, working in a variety of genres. I suppose that I wanted to do that too. During my undergraduate and graduate years I painted abstractly and after that things seemed to evolve naturally. When I finished graduate school and was still living in New York, I started painting very artificial, arranged still lifes of manufactured objects that reflected themes I had aimed for in abstraction. I relocated to the Midwest in 1996, which turned out to be liberating. It felt like I had taken a cork out of something. Space and air were not as constrained as they had been in the city. I started painting landscapes and interiors, and also started using models. Models were too expensive in New York, plus I couldn't imagine situations that I would put them in there. In the Midwest, models became stand-ins for my wife, Eve, and me and the places we lived. In New York my joke had been that I didn't have a life to paint. Now I had one.

Catherine Kehoe: Four genres have been central in my recent work: still lifes and self-portraits done from observation, paintings of my Polish ancestors derived from old photographs, and copies after paintings from art history.

Still life painting makes it possible to compose a world that remains constant, and under my control. Working from an unchanging subject, the process isolates and reveals the unstable nature of perception. Invention enters the process in the arrangement of objects and the selection of what goes into the rectangle.

With my self-portrait heads I can focus on a subject that is always there. Sometimes I develop these paintings over weeks of searching and scraping. Other times, at the end of a frustrating painting day, I put aside a still-life and make a quick study of my head with the remaining paint, energy, and light. I quickly forget I am looking at myself; when I see the resulting paintings, it is as if someone has captured my image without my knowledge.

When I work from art history, I look deeply at images and generate permutations through simplification and abstraction. This rigorous analysis of images from my painting ancestors

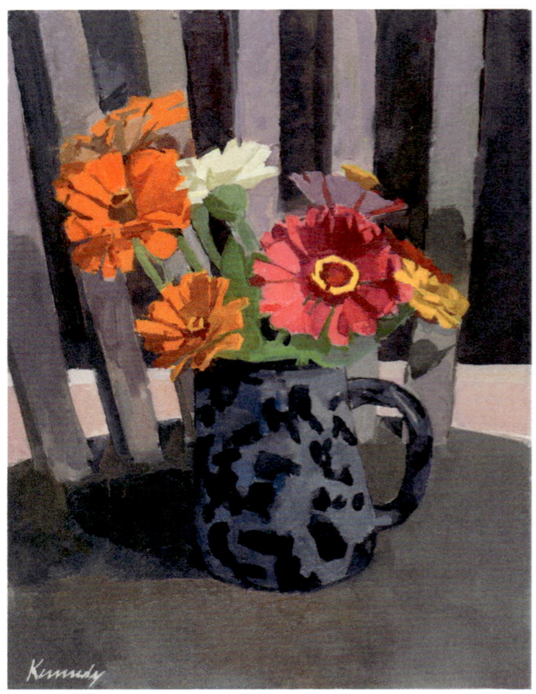

Tim Kennedy
Zinnias in Bennington Cup
2021, oil on muslin on panel, 12 x 9 in.

feeds my own work and imagination as I engage with images that speak to me across time. I wanted to imagine the people I could know only through faint photographs. I began with heads and later began relating people to each other and to space. I did not copy the photographs, but used them as a source to make paintings. In some cases I added images from different sources to give a context to the figures.

I circle around this handful of genres to keep myself interested. I would get bored repeating the same motif. As I move from one interest to the next, and back again, I realize that the subject is less important than the act of creating a design in a rectangle.

Neil Callander: I hope people don't consider me a fickle painter. My painterly ambition does retain a clear line of inquiry. I work entirely from perception and so, regardless of subject, the through-lines are perceptual color relationships and a corrective type of mark-making. Even the abstractions are sourced from perceptual phenomena. I paint my world; however, it would be very difficult to paint a car crash or howling dog from direct observation, so working this way places limitations on subject and I don't see a reason to limit it further.

I guess I'm a reactionary when considering the capitalist urge to brand oneself. There is hubris related to the idea of personal branding—it seems so declarative and tactical and increasingly passé. On the flip side, brands do represent the potential for a kind of immortality. I wonder without a clear brand if my identity as a painter will quickly dissolve after my death. When left to historians, archivists and collectors will my work be difficult to categorize and weave into the tidy narrative of art history?

JP: *Although each of you professes an interest in painting the world, none of you have pursued what we might call a relentlessly realist agenda. You don't engage in high finished rendering, photo finishes, or rigidly academic techniques of representation. Rather you each present a view of a world transformed in various ways. Please talk a little bit about how you feel your work varies from a realist approach and the kinds of expression this allows you to pursue.*

NC: A lot depends on what is meant by "realism." Most illusionistic realist painting has been shunted out of the critically informed art world and seems to be mainly interested in skill. I admire that branch of the painting world and am glad for the torch they bear. But, we're in a moment that encourages a subjective understanding of the world. That one's identity and unique experiences are paramount may be the closest we will come to a 21st century art movement. Realist paintings understood in this context should, by nature, look diverse.

My work reflects my relation to the world as a gardener—literally and figuratively—focusing in on and tending to a small plot of land, a house, a few beloved people, my community and

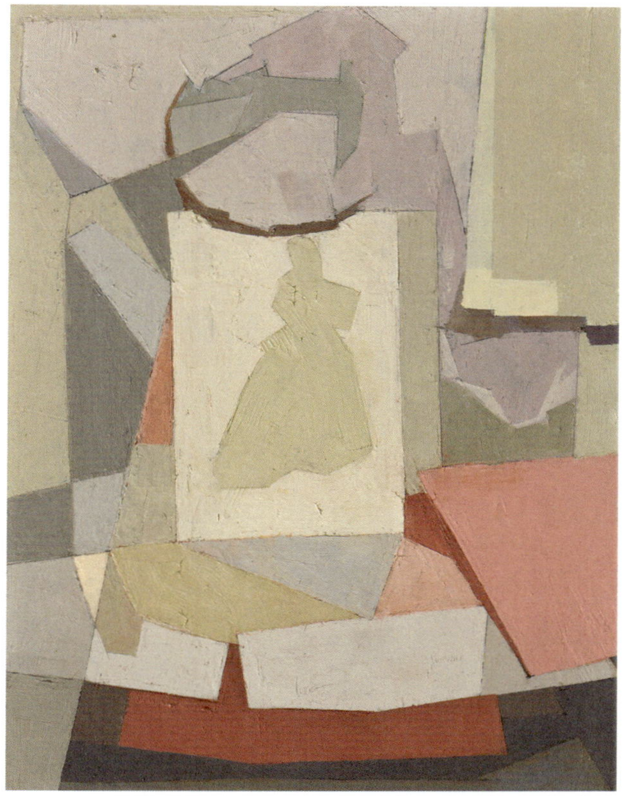

Catherine Kehoe *Delicate Situation*
oil on panel, 8 x 6 in.

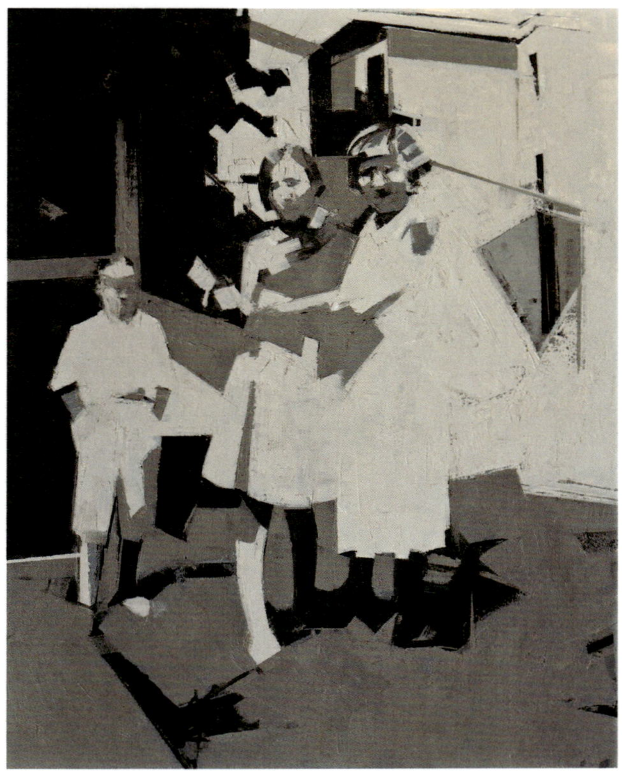

Catherine Kehoe *Stanley, Helen and Emilia*
2019, oil on panel, 8 x 10 in.

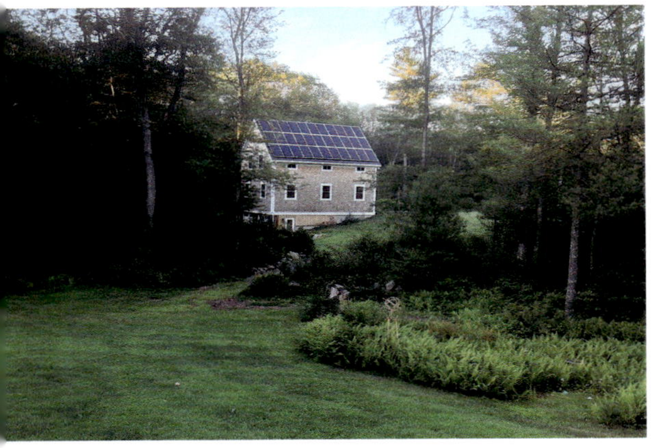

Catherine Kehoe's studio

the craft of painting. I sometimes daydream about the ideal venue to display my paintings and it is not a blue-chip gallery in a faraway cosmopolitan city. Imagining perfect lighting and walls, I dream of exhibiting in public libraries, farmers markets, lodges at state parks.

CK: I don't identify with the word realism. It is a label too confining for my painting interests. My paintings refer to the world as filtered through my eyes, my mind, and my nervous system. The relationships between the shapes in the rectangle have equal importance as the image itself. Anything can be expressed with a shape and a color made of paint next to another shape and color made of paint. A rectangle filled with these things in the right relationships to each other can add up to any number of illusions or truths.

TK: I like the list of things that you do not see in our work. I agree that there is no highly polished sense of finish that competes with photography in any of our paintings. I do not use academic techniques and I would be surprised to learn if either Catherine or Neil did. Realism does not interest me much as a term. The qualities that you allude to are not things I strive to achieve.

In Neil's previous answer he referred to perception. That is the arena I feel most comfortable situating myself in. I am very conscious of being a kind of perceiving machine. I constantly look at the world around me as a series of potential paintings. I notice how light collects, how reflection influences color, how I perceive distance and space, how or if my seeing "apparatus" (my eyes) gives me a true picture of the world. I try to record what I am seeing in "real," physical, tactile ways. Hopefully, as I paint, I am able to leave enough evidence of the process so that viewers will empathetically identify with the creation of the work.

JP: *One of the ways in which all of you filter the world concerns color. You might say that each of you offers a different "color universe," one that goes hand in hand with your overall vision. Catherine has explored the evocative power of limited color in her "Direct Descent" paintings, and often achieves highly emotive results in combining muted color pitched against combinations of very saturated color in her still life and figure paintings. Neil's representational paintings draw us into a world where the color is heightened and tends to be saturated in specific ranges, sometimes creating a curious sense of iridescence. His abstract paintings go further in exploring color gradients. Tim offers quite a wide-ranging palette, making paintings in which the color is often slightly over-saturated and simplified, generally conveying a sense (at least to my eyes) of general warmth and well-being.*

How far are your color choices the result of a perceptual process that you engage in as you look at your subject matter and how far are they creative acts, a deliberate strategy to present a particular "look" or "feel" in your paintings?

CK: The color in my paintings starts as a response to what I am looking at. The attempt to find relationships between colors in the motif is the starting point. As accurate as I try to be, the results are usually surprising and unexpected. When the painting extends over time, I sometimes find I want different relationships between parts. Sometimes I change the setup (I put a different color fabric behind my head, or I replace an object in a still life with another object). Sometimes, lately, when I am in the final stages of a painting, I invent relationships to serve a pictorial idea about space.

TK: You allude to each of us as having a filter to encounter the world with—I like that idea. I suppose that much of my choosing in relation to color takes place in response to a perceived subject that attracts me. I don't think it is mutually exclusive to use color in a deliberate, creative way and yet also seek perceived color as a goal. I sometimes think of finding the fullness of a color or colors in relationship as similar to slowly filling a glass of water until it bulges slightly above the brim.

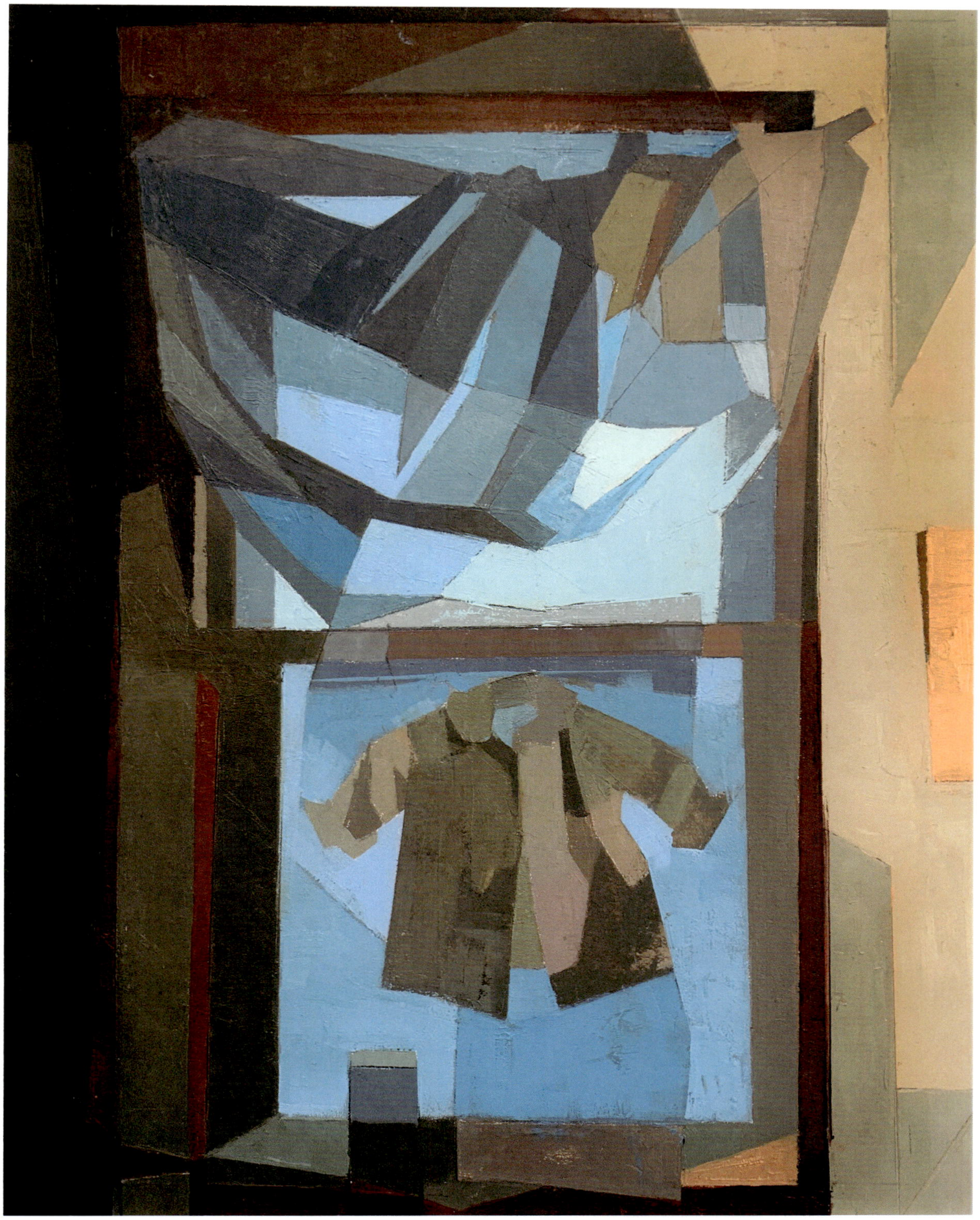

Catherine Kehoe *Little Jacket*
2016, oil on panel, 8 x 6 in.

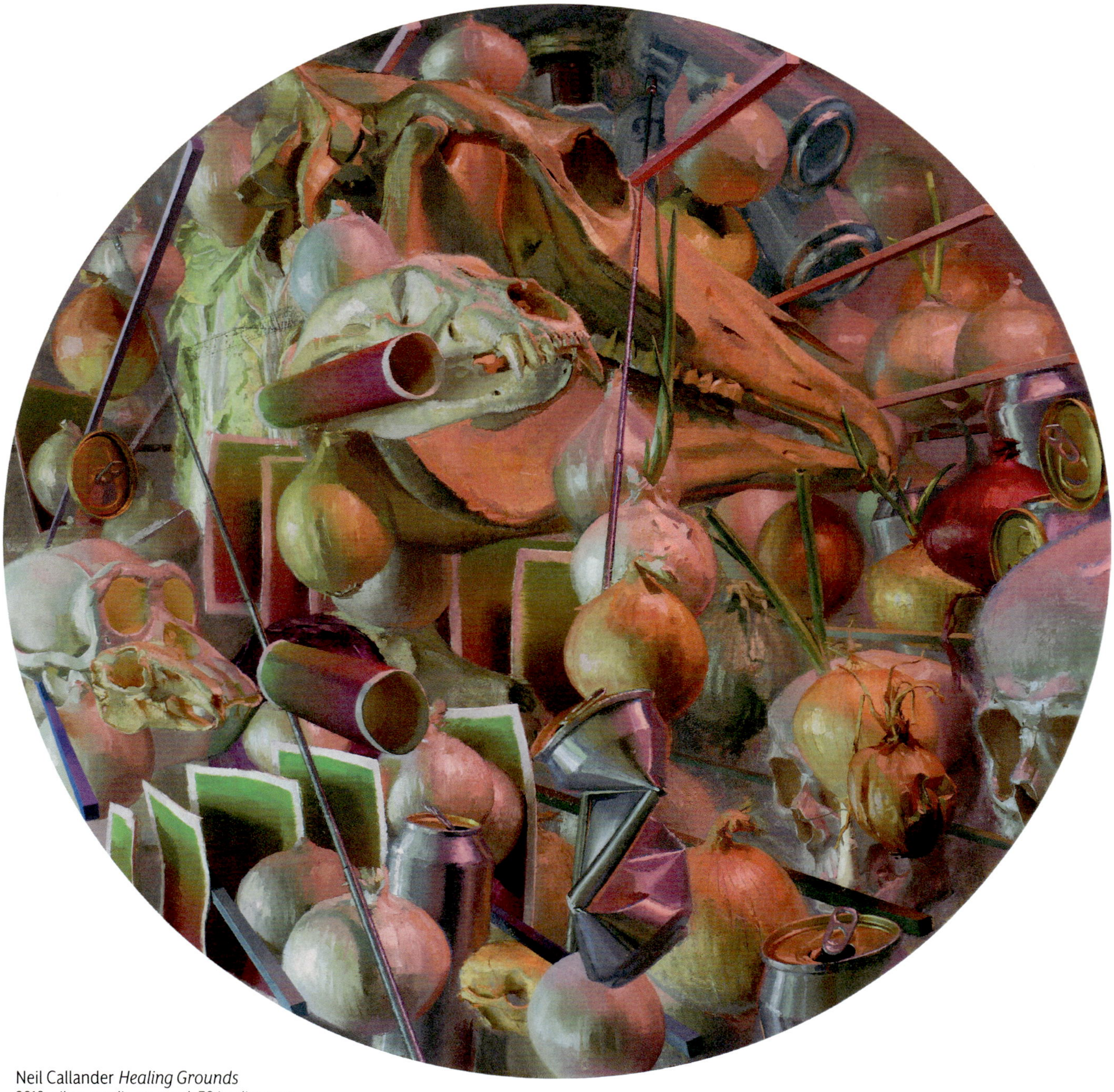

Neil Callander *Healing Grounds*
2010, oil on muslin on panel, 30 in. diameter

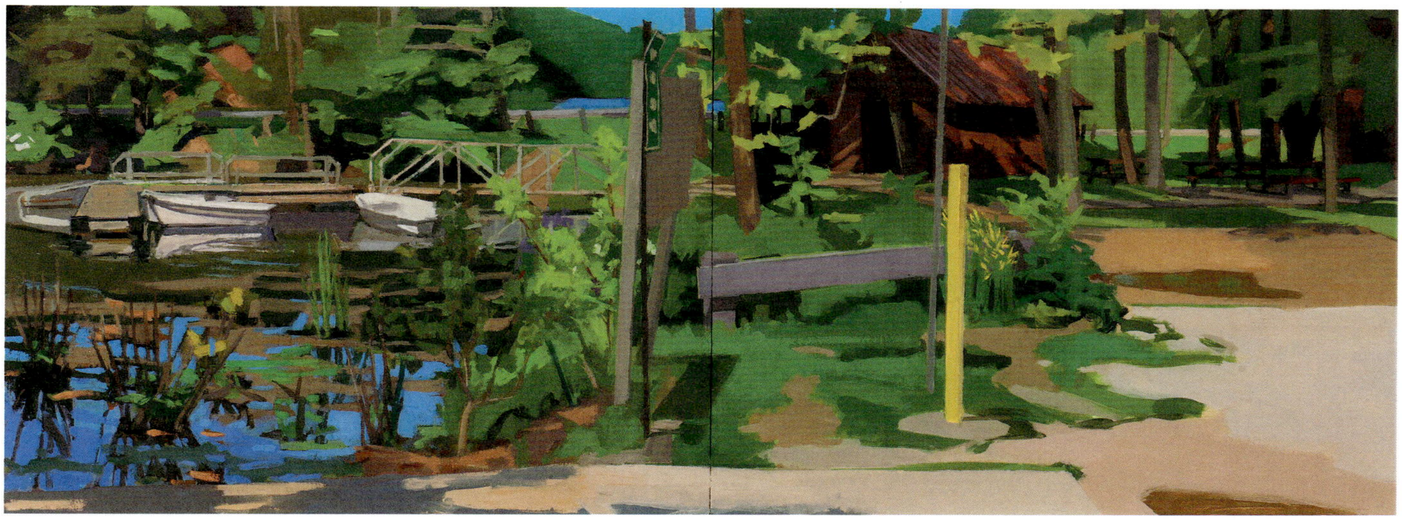

Tim Kennedy *Griffy*
2017, oil on muslin on panel, 14 x 36 in.

I can see dramatic color in a motif and respond to it but I am reluctant to impose something that feels arbitrary onto a subject. On the other hand, as I have gotten older, I probably give myself more latitude in relation to what I am seeing. I might see a possibility in a perceived color but it might slide into something quite different. There is a quote from Nietzsche that I am not quite remembering. The gist is that the artist seeks to capture nature but in reality the artist is intrinsically attracted to what he or she is able to paint.

NC: The effects of adjusting your palette can be like the difference between humming Bach or playing it on harpsichord. Every painter limits their palette whether for expression or by necessity. My color strategy begins with identifying the complementary color relationship that always exists between light and its accompanying shadow. I'll search around until I've found about seven colors that can recreate this relationship. Out of necessity Michelangelo advanced this notion of "cangiante"; Pontormo picked it up and did wonderful things. Now the notion has morphed and in modern painting parlance we talk about the cool/warm color relationship.

In Iceland I arrived at a limited palette through painting the shifts of green as the perpetual daylight reflected off the grasses (Indian Yellow Deep, Venetian Red, Mars Violet, Perylene Black, Scheveningen Blue, Cobalt Blue and Flemish White). Without a true red, my Icelandic palette leans towards a secondary triad of green, orange, and violet. I've continued to use this limited palette and its intrinsic moodiness has infused my recent paintings with some of the vivid peculiarity of an Icelandic summer.

JP: *Each of you deploys a process of simplification of form and shape. Catherine often reduces her drawing to much-clarified planes, resolving some areas to completely flat shapes. Tim maintains a more continuous three-dimensional space through his paintings but still simplifies areas considerably into clear and discrete shapes. Neil has been more variable in his approach to simplification, with paintings that range closer to an inclusive kind of realism, to severely simplified and even completely abstract paintings. Please talk a little bit about your strategies for simplification and what you feel it achieves for your painting.*

CK: I am not sure I have coherent or successful strategies for simplification. My main strategy is trial and error. The word that comes to mind is "enough." I have conflicting pictorial impulses. Often I start with the wish to describe something I see as well as I can, in detail (the dewdrop on the grape). Other times, I lean toward geometric abstraction, often in the same painting.

I sometimes start with a painting idea: Low contrast and muddy color, or the opposite. Sometimes the painting idea is to put two colors together, for example coral pink and yellow ochre. Sometimes the idea has to do with light: overhead, or from below. Or the idea is about scale. Often the painting idea does not translate from idea to painting. So I try a different approach.

Other times I start with a plan for a composition, and that plan seems boring when executed, so I eliminate parts and replace them with flat shapes that I hope will stand for the eliminated detail. Most often the catchphrase "Less is More" rings true for me. The more I leave out, the more I like the painting.

NC: Could one substitute the word "abstraction" for "simplification" in a painting context? I bet Tim, Catherine and I are trying to achieve some of the same things when attending to the inherent abstraction of a painting—light, space, and a compelling arrangement of shapes. Compositionally, I'll often conceive of a simple form that underlies and organizes the shapes; paintings that bulge in the middle are "bubble" compositions, and if they have an empty center they are "donuts."

Increasingly what's important to me is a visual language that is distinct to painting—not the even level of detail that photography offers, and not the construction of form through contour that comes naturally when drawing with line. Painting's vernacular is shape-based and deals with the expressive quality of variable edges. This is something I learned from Tim directly (as a student) and Catherine indirectly (through her paintings).

TK: Breaking objects visually into a series of discreet shapes is integral to how I see things. It is something that I stress when I teach too. Hopefully as I paint, I am able to keep the work evolving in this abstract fashion with shapes and colors pushing against each other without being distracted by my subject too much. I see these types of things in Catherine's and Neil's work too, which is what I respond to when I see their paintings.

Neil Callander *Skyblue Gradation Large*
2019, oil on linen on panel, 48 x 48 in.

But like any painter I can get lost in the particulars. On campus in our drawing studio we have a New Yorker cartoon pinned to the wall. In the cartoon Satan is receiving a new soul at the Gates of Hell, noting that in a figure drawing class from 1974 he had gone straight into doing details—I guess that's why he is there. Sometimes I'm that guy.

I like Neil's idea about bubbles and donuts. I do not have very many exalted ideas about composition. As a tendency I think I gravitate toward oblique motifs. I find that orientation to be more dynamic and it involves me on a visceral level more quickly.

JP: *I've often finished interviews by asking artists what they think their vision adds up to—what it is that they think their art brings to the world, and how they would like the viewer to respond to it. I've found that this is often a very difficult question to answer, almost as though the most important thing about a work of art is, in some way, hidden from its creator. It's simply very hard to see your own paintings. So this time, since I am*

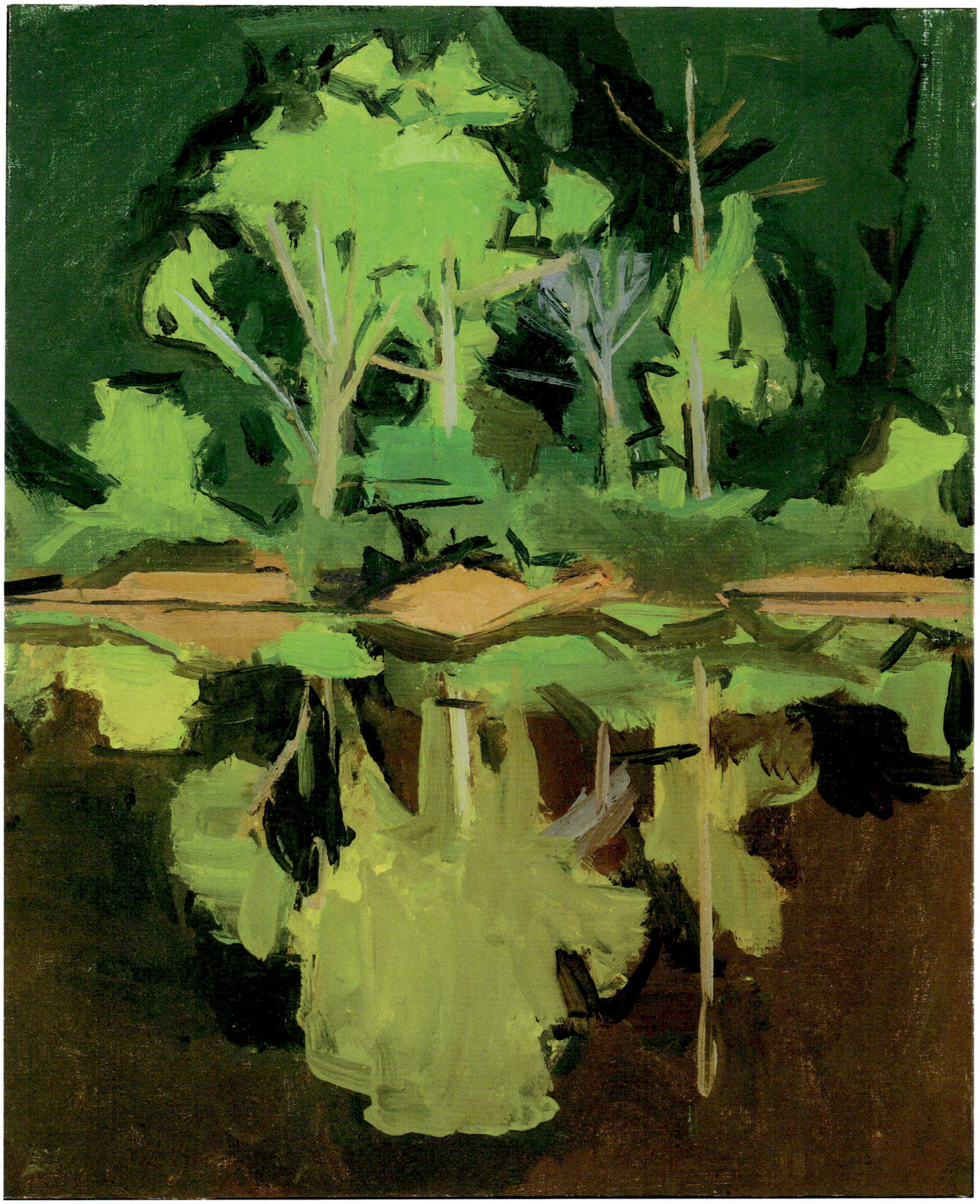

Tim Kennedy *Trees and Reflections*
2016, oil on muslin on panel, 8 x 10 in.

interviewing three artists at once, I'm going to ask you about how you respond to each other's work. "What is it about the work of your two fellow artists that is distinctive, compelling and beguiling? What is it that you think their work brings to the world?"

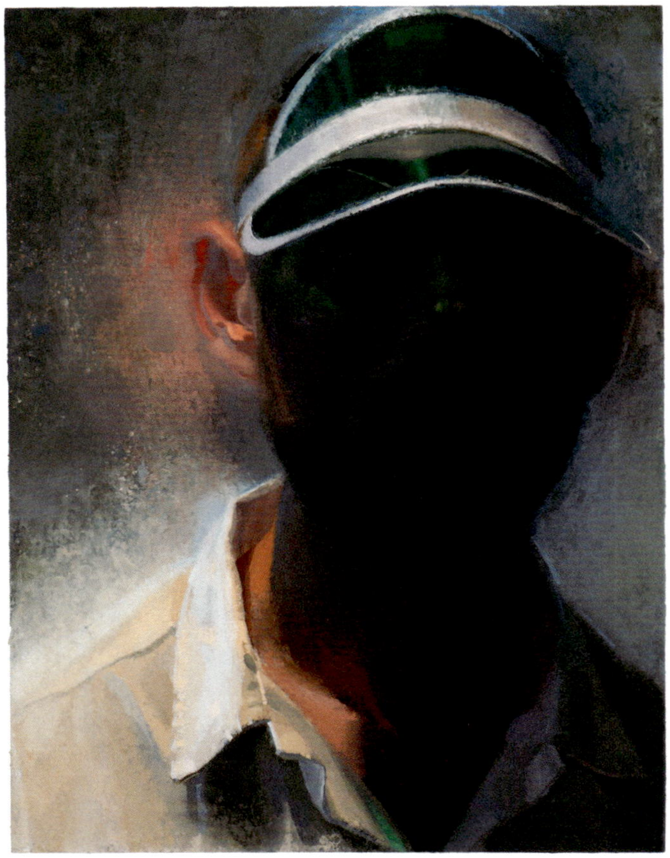

Neil Callander *Self-Portrait with Eyeshade*
2022, oil on panel, 24 x 18 in.

NC: On one level, both Tim's and Catherine's work is very instructive. I look at their paintings in the studio when I feel I'm making things more complicated than they need to be, and I regularly use them both in the classroom to illustrate the mechanics of painting. There isn't much mystery in how they apply paint—adjacent shapes of opaque color. In some of Catherine's paintings you can count the number of shapes on two hands. One can imagine oneself making those marks—it's very accessible and grounding.

Tim and Catherine are putting forth painterly versions of the world. By this I mean creating representational images that are distinctly not photographic. Instead of framing the world as frozen moments, their paintings take time to make and show evidence of a long sequence of decisions. Tim's genre paintings especially feel painterly and human to me. The motif is complex and he orchestrates the forms inside the rectangle with only gentle cropping. I particularly love Catherine's still life paintings when the space is intimate and inescapable and the objects feel monumental.

CK: For me, painting is a wordless activity, while Tim and Neil are both eloquent in paint and words. An even greater pleasure has been the chance to look more deeply into the paintings by Tim and Neil, in this case online.

I have seen Tim's paintings several times in person over the years and have always been struck by the clarity and sensitivity of touch in his work. The relationships in his paintings are delicate and surprising; the compositions, especially in the still life paintings, are inventive. I love this line from one of Tim's essays about painting: "It is explanation without speech. It reveals by allowing the pieces of a disjointed world to lock into place."

There is a thread that runs through Tim's work: he is convinced of the importance of appearances, and the personal meaning he finds in translating them to a painting.

It is easy for a painter to feel isolated, and that there is little appetite in the world for what we do. The greatest consolation might be knowing that our work, driven by personal necessity, feeds and enriches the work of other painters. Tim's work does this for me.

I have not had the pleasure of seeing Neil's work in person, but am dazzled by the breadth and range of his work, and the ability to take on complex scenes and make sense of them in brilliantly inventive compositions. His work is literally all over the place, a strength and a virtue, to my eye.

TK: What I admire about Catherine's and Neil's work is that they both have a cool, intelligent formal sense that is informed by a personal sensibility. In recent years Catherine's work has taken on an increasingly geometric character which acts as a filter that simultaneously constructs and deconstructs her image. Her color choices are fabulous both in the heads and the still lifes. The colors are frequently secondary and tertiary triads that pull subtly against one another. The personal and peculiar assert themselves. In her recent series of copies of paintings from history she may work with a small portion of an Uglow or even a Gilbert Stuart—a singular choice in itself.

Neil's paintings consistently flirt with the miraculous. His color is spectral and hints at other worlds. Not many artists would have the desire or inclination paint a giant ball of tin foil having the appearance of a forlorn and wayward planet, but it seems at home in Neil's body of work. I knew Neil when he was a student and even then, he had the ability to find things that touched him personally and that he managed to wring meaning from. The portraits, whether self-portraits or portraits of his son Finn, carry real feeling. Z

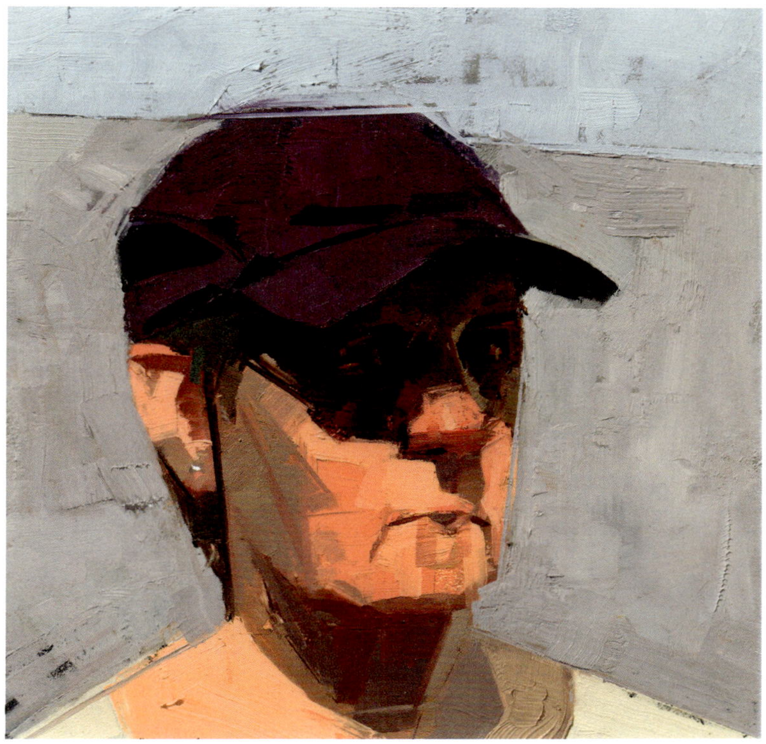

Catherine Kehoe *Purple Hat*
2018, oil on panel, 5 x 5 in.

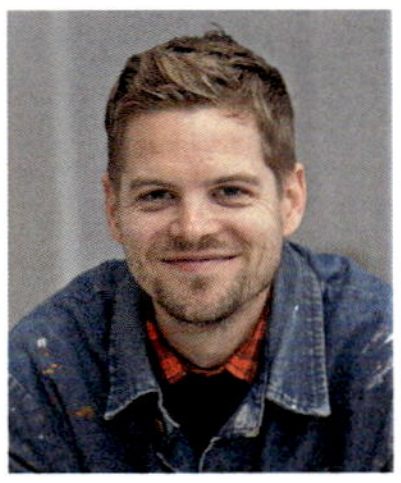

Neil Callander is an artist and educator. Born in Louisville Kentucky, Neil earned his BFA from Indiana University and an MFA from Rutgers University. In 2005 he received a full fellowship to attend the Skowhegan School of Painting and Sculpture. After graduate school he worked as a painter for the artist Jeff Koons in his New York studio. In 2007 Neil and family left New York City to pursue careers as artists and academics. Neil and his wife are currently Assistant Professors of Art at the University of Arkansas. Neil has exhibited widely and often presents publicly on his work and practice.

www.zeuxis.us/callander
www.neilcallander.com

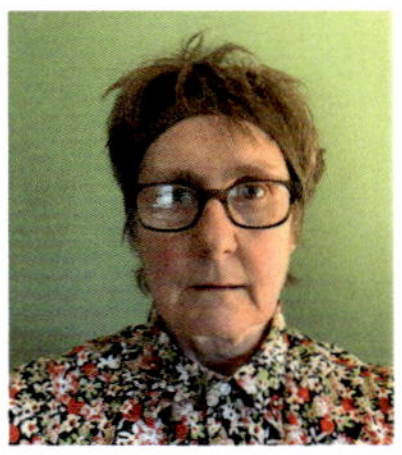

Catherine Kehoe earned her BFA in painting from Massachusetts College of Art and Design and her MFA in painting from the School of Visual Arts, Boston University. She has received numerous awards including the Massachusetts Cultural Council Fellowship in Painting, a Pollock-Krasner Foundation Grant and the Berkshire Taconic Artist's Resource Trust Grant. Her paintings are represented by Anderson Yezerski Gallery, Boston. Kehoe has taught painting and drawing at Massachusetts College of Art and Design and Brandeis University. She is a co-founder of Black Pond Studio in southeastern Massachusetts.

www.catherinekehoe.com

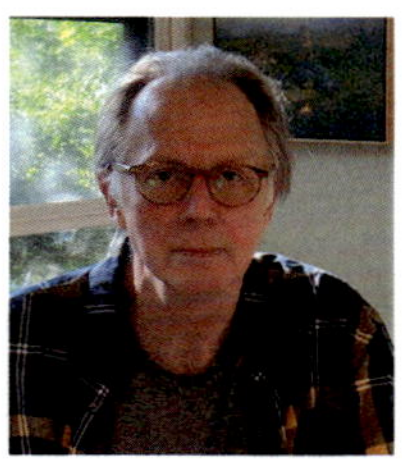

Tim Kennedy was born in Buffalo, New York. He received his BFA from Carnegie-Mellon University in 1977 and an MFA from Brooklyn College in 1984. He attended the Skowhegan School during the summers of 1979 and 1980. Kennedy has received individual artist grants from the Pollock-Krasner Foundation, the Indiana Arts Commission, the Arts Council of Indianapolis and the Clark Hulings Fund. He exhibits his work at First Street Gallery in New York where he has had eight solo exhibitions. Kennedy is a Senior Lecturer of Painting at Indiana University in Bloomington where he has taught since 2000.

www.zeuxis.us/kennedy
www.timkennedypaintings.com

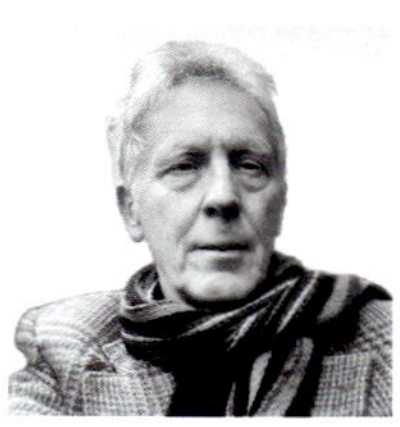

John A. Parks is a painter, writer and filmmaker. He studied at the Royal College of Art in London and has shown his paintings widely for the last thirty-five years. He is represented by Thomas Jaeckel Gallery in New York. Parks is a member of the faculty of the School of Visual Arts in New York where he teaches drawing, realist techniques and portrait painting. His writing credits include The New York Times, the Smithsonian Museum as well as many features for a variety of art magazines. Parks's paintings are represented in the collections of the Victoria and Albert Museum, the Royal College of Art Collection, the Museum of the Rhode Island School of Design, and many private collections.

www.johnaparks.com

On Observation, Memory, and Joy

Imogen Sara Smith interviews

Megan Williamson and Kathleen Craig and Richard Castellana

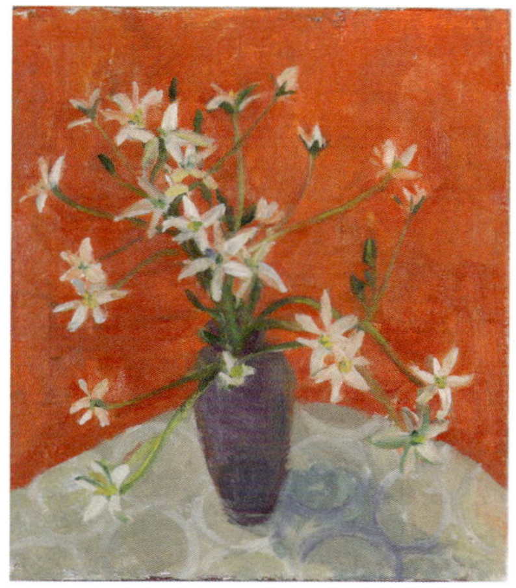

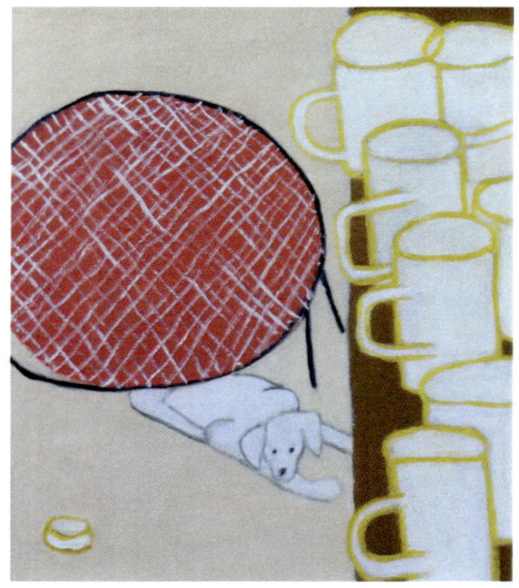

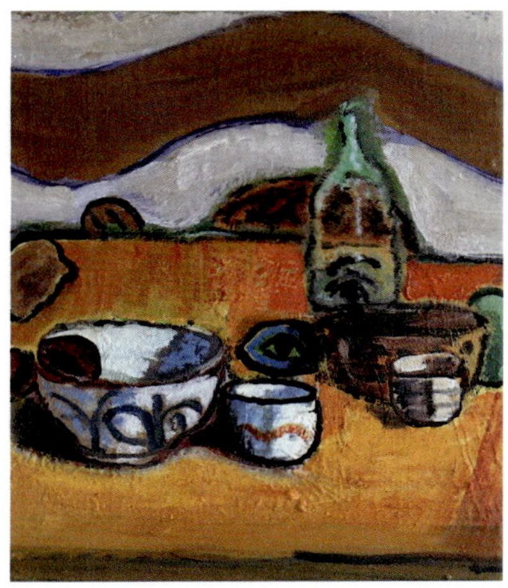

Megan Williamson *Flowers from Someone Else's Garden* 2019, oil on canvas, 13 x 11 in.

Kathleen Craig *Under the Table series I* (detail) 2020, oil on canvas, 17 x 17 in.

Richard Castellano *The Eyes Have It* (detail) 2020, oil on canvas, 18 x 24 in.

Imogen Sara Smith: *In 2019, I wrote an essay to accompany the Zeuxis exhibition "My Studio," in which I explored artists' relationships to the spaces in which they work. Revisiting the essay this past spring, I was struck by how some of its themes resonated during this time of quarantine and sheltering in place: the idea of still life as an art that allows us to see familiar, quotidian objects freshly; the way that artists were reflecting on their own processes and habits by looking at the studios where they worked. In particular, I found myself thinking again about Giorgio Morandi, who chose to spend his whole career working in a single room in his family's apartment, painting variations on a collection of familiar objects. Morandi said: "One can travel this world and see nothing. To achieve understanding it is necessary not to see many things, but to look hard at what you do see."*

Richard Castellana, Kathleen Craig, and Megan Williamson, the three artists I spoke with, have all cited Morandi as an influence, and I was intrigued by their statements about the interplay between observation, imagination, and memory in their practice. All of these artists paint still lifes, figures, landscapes, and abstractions, but I have chosen to largely focus on still life in honor of Zeuxis' mission. Our conversation ranged from Morandi to Matisse, and from working

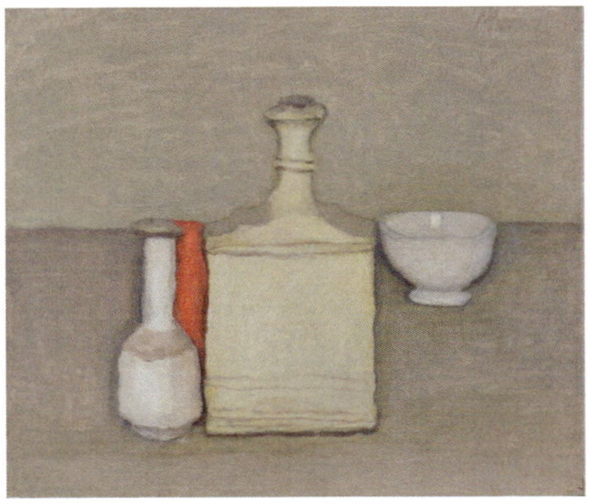

Giorgio Morandi *Still Life*
1957, oil on canvas, 14 x 16 in.

during the quarantine to the role of joy and comfort in art. I would like to thank these artists for generously sharing their time and thinking deeply about these questions.

IS: *How has Morandi been an influence on you? In light of the quote from him above, do you think still life has something to teach us in this moment, as we all experience a new reality largely confined to our homes?*

Megan Williamson: I was introduced to Morandi's work when I was an undergraduate. I couldn't understand why it appealed to me, but he still informed my own work. He was the first painter's painter I was drawn to.

I continue to look and find layers of meaning in his work. As with other Masters' work—the more I paint and the deeper I go in my own work—there is constantly more to see in what they did.

I went from reproductions to seeing his work in person. We all know what a revelation that can be! The subtleties of his tone and color, and how he applied the paint was so much more meaningful in person. It made me want to... be a better painter.

Another time I thought about him a lot was when I started going to Umbria. I recognized that the light I was seeing there was also the light I had seen in his work! He fused the light of the place with the light of his mind—inspiration from his environment that went beyond a tabletop or a landscape. And his connection to Piero [della Francesca] and Giotto was so clear when I saw all of their work in person—where it was originally painted. He came out of the long Italian tradition of Grand Painting and made his contribution to it.

In Italy I also learned that though he may have had a simple home and studio, he was a sophisticated painter who was known by many of his contemporaries. He had one foot in the past and one in the present.

As for his quote about seeing—it reminds me of the old Roman saying "everywhere is nowhere."

When I was a young painter I needed inspiring landscapes and interesting still life set ups to keep me at the easel. The longer I paint the less I need to get and keep me going. It's the landscapes (or still lifes) within...

Kathleen Craig: My first paintings were still lifes of faded milk cartons, sometimes with straws. This was because they were easy to draw; also the nondescript colors made it easier to focus on representing light. During this time several helpful friends informed me that I must be an admirer of Giorgio Morandi. Who? I had to look him up before I could see what they meant.

So to start with, I felt less influenced by Morandi than akin to him, as if "23 and Me" had put me face to face with a new family member. One who was a really big deal. My favorite way to draw was and is blind contour drawing—peering at the subject without looking at what my hand is up to. This can extend to memories of people, actions, feelings, and landscapes—in my head they will obligingly hold still for me. The simplified, gawky forms I wind up with do seem to belong somewhere in Morandi's extended family.

But kinship isn't influence. Morandi's influence on me started with kinship and with permission—what I was doing was okay because a great painter did it. It developed into respect, admiration, almost love. I came to believe that what set him apart was more than intent staring. Most artists stare intently. Morandi had a kind of internal serenity, a certainty about what he needed to paint that overcame whatever desire he had to go with the flow. It allowed him to dig in.

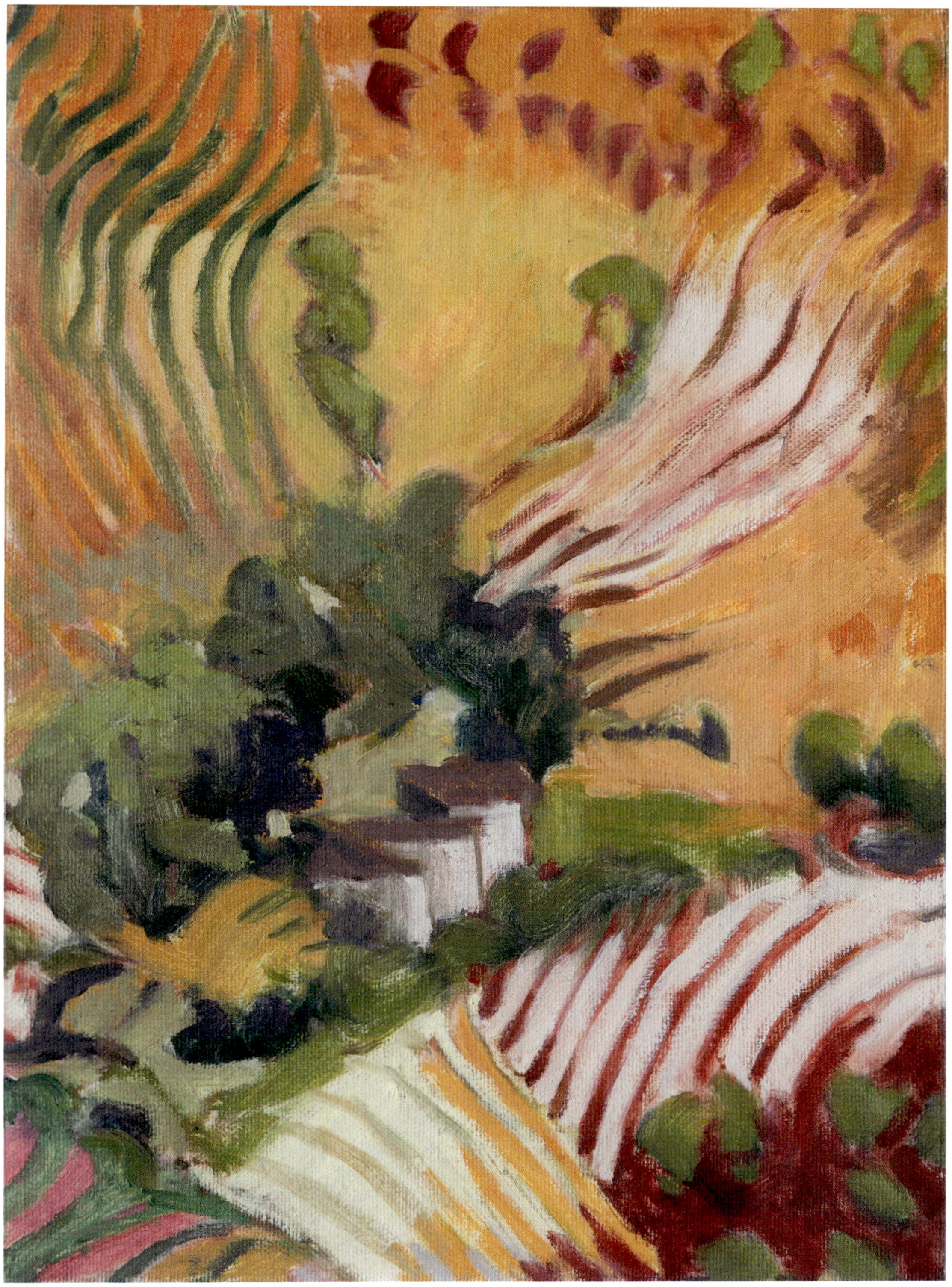

Megan Williamson *Italian Farmhouse & Fields, Umbria*
1991, oil on canvas, 14 x 10 in.

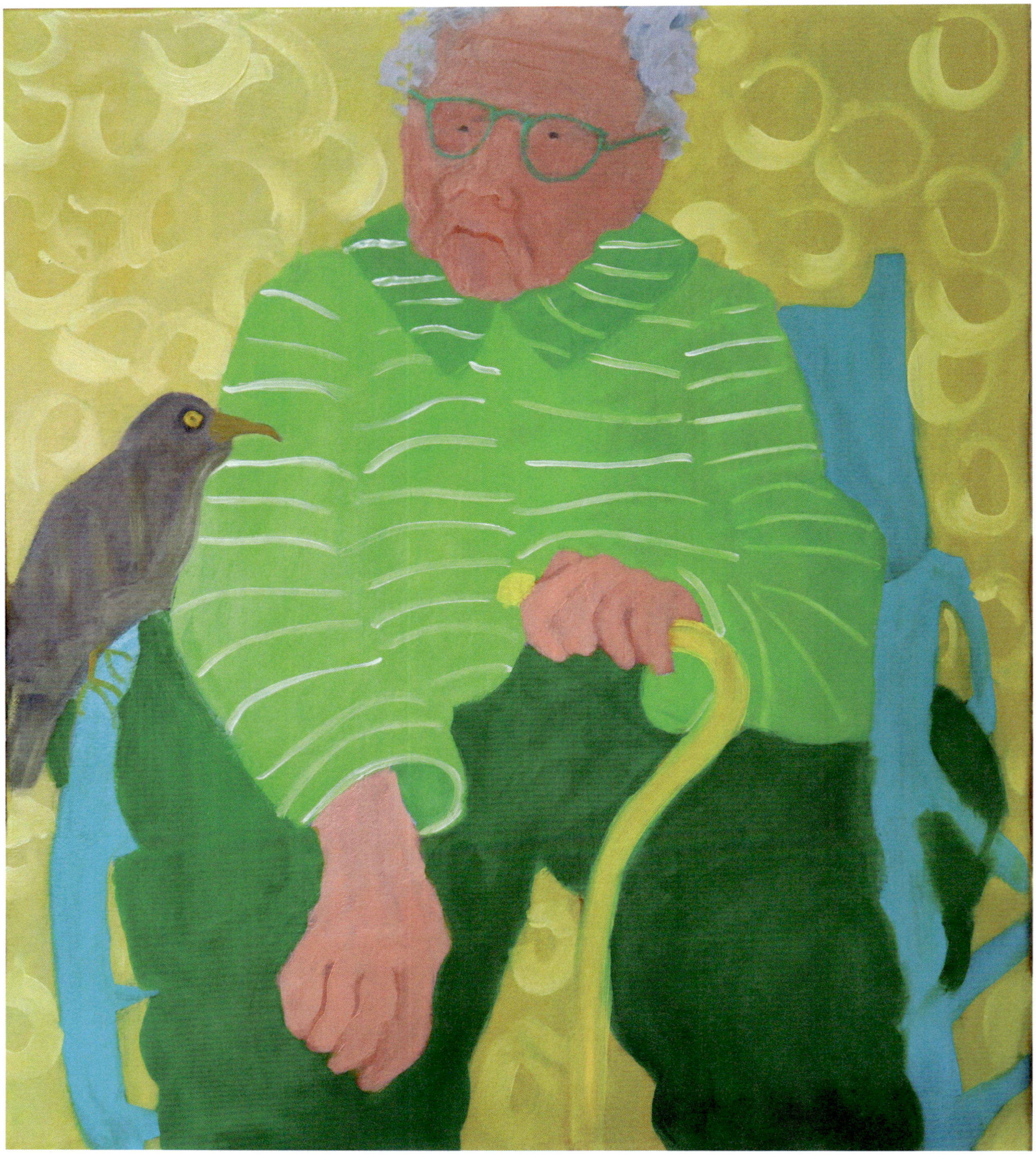

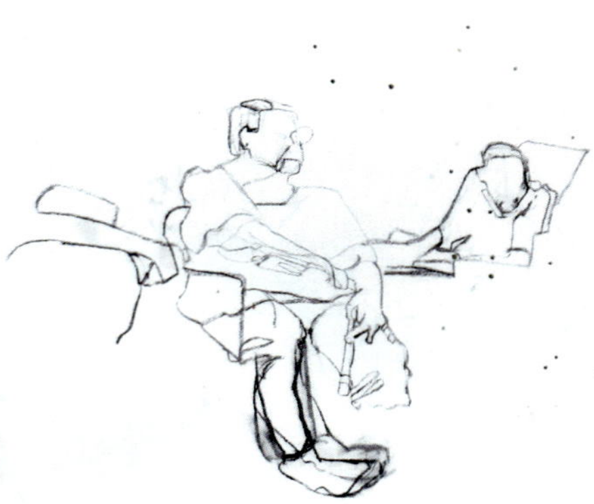

Above:

Kathleen Craig *Pet Crow*
2019, oil on canvas, 28 x 24 in.

Left:

Sketch for *Pet Crow*

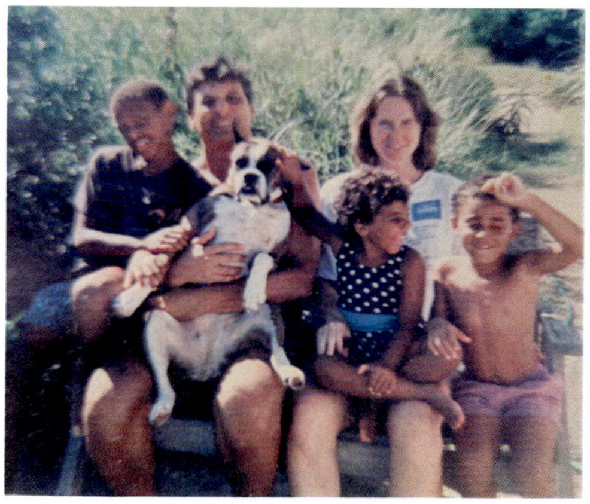

Kathleen Craig family photo

I met a person once who was the world's greatest expert on ants. He was legally blind, with the thickest glasses I have ever seen, and explained that his interest in ants came from this. As a child he could lie down on the ground and peer at his subjects at one-inch range—he couldn't really see anything farther away than that. My response to my own nearsightedness had been denial, pretending to see when I couldn't, hating my horrible thick glasses that distorted my face, and painful contact lenses. In other words, my nearsightedness connected us but my response to it had been superficial, skating over rather than digging in.

I understood pretty quickly that my "kinship" to Morandi didn't come close to approaching his intensity and self-confidence. His influence on me was, and is, that I keep trying to work toward a more independent spirit.

These days, as families Zoom and galleries shut down, as I fear that I'll never again sell a painting or hug my children, I try to use anxiety as a propeller to sharpen the intensity of my looking and the sincerity of my efforts. I don't know if the still life form has a lot to give but I think painting—if you are a painter—can help us cope with what can't be helped.

Richard Castellana: These quotes by Morandi resonate with me:

"I am essentially a painter of the kind of still life composition that communicates a sense of tranquility and privacy, moods which I have always valued above all."

"I am comforted by the knowledge that in all my endeavors, even in the moments of greatest uncertainty, my personality has always managed to come through."

"Everything is a mystery, ourselves, and all things both simple and humble."

"The feelings and images aroused by the visible world are very difficult to express or are perhaps inexpressible with words because they are determined by forms, colors, space and light."

I have always felt an affinity with the "sense of tranquility and privacy" and mystery that characterizes the work of Morandi and Piero della Francesca: a mysteriously calm stillness, expressed with subtle, yet glowing, light and color; a simple, yet strangely complex, architecture of forms and space; the way figure gives way to ground. When I first got my footing as a painter, I was surprised by what I saw, something that I hadn't consciously put in the paintings: myself, or at least a part of myself, the part of me that values mystery, tranquility and privacy. Painting is a process of self-discovery. There is another part of me, a more agitated part, that is expressed in my figure painting, not in still life.

On the "interplay of memory and observation": When I first began painting, I could only paint from observation. At the NY Studio School, Mercedes Matter set up elaborate, complex still lifes and

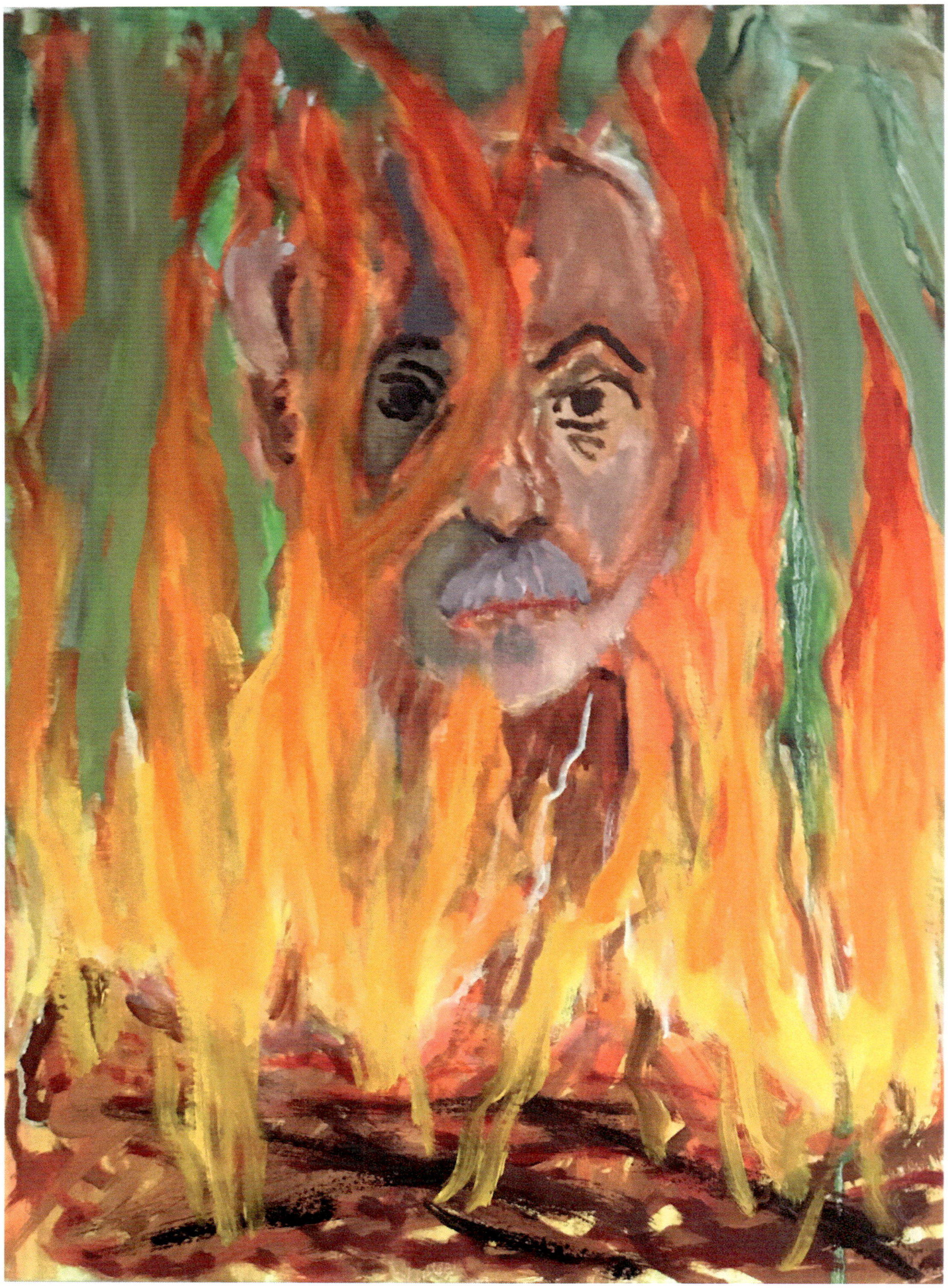

Richard Castellana *Self Portrait–Fire*
2020, oil on canvas, 24 x 18 in.

taught me to focus on the intervals and spatial tensions among objects; the objects themselves were less important, fractured as in cubism. When I encountered Morandi, the objects became more important to me—I even searched for objects similar to his. However, I had a problem with arranging them. Morandi is said to have spent days, even weeks, arranging his still lifes before beginning to paint; I never had the patience. I would arrange and when the composition didn't work, re-arrange, add, or omit and continue painting. Gradually I developed a technique: set up a still life, paint from observation until I hit a roadblock, look around the room for objects and ideas, then only on the canvas rearrange, add, and omit. Often I stop looking around the room and simply invent. I am less interested in the play of light than Morandi, more interested in color, largely invented; a sort of a combination of Morandi and Matisse.

As for memory, it is not something I consciously draw on for my still-lifes, but nothing can be done without implicit, subconscious memory. Memory is a product of experience, and experience (plus genetics and environment, of course) makes us who we are. If painting is an expression of personality, it can't be done without memory.

IS: *Richard mentioned Matisse in his response, and Kathy also brought him up in a separate email, so I'd like to turn to him next. What is it that draws you to Matisse, or in what way has he influenced you?*

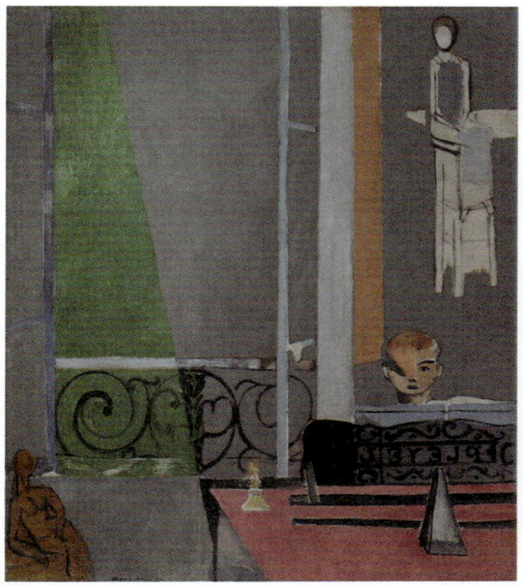

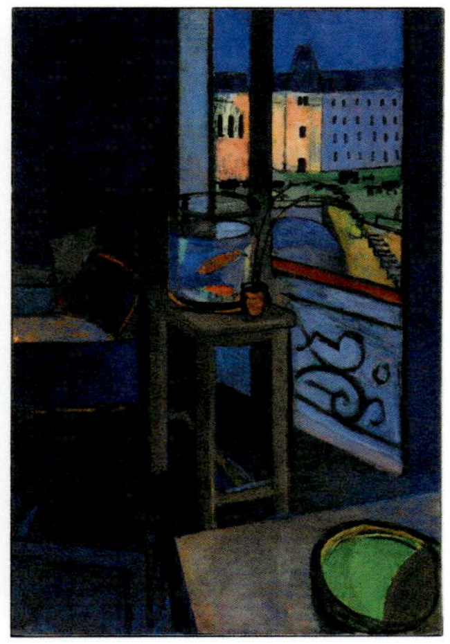

LEFT TO RIGHT:

Henri Matisse
The Piano Lesson
1916, oil on canvas,
96 ½ x 83 ¾ in.

Henri Matisse
Interior with Goldfish
1914, oil on canvas,
58 x 38 in.

I have two Matisse postcards hanging above my desk where I write: The Piano Lesson *(1916), and* Interior with Goldfish *(1914). They both embody for me a fusion of energy and calm, of stillness and joy.*

I remember a short story by the English author A.S. Byatt ("The Chinese Lobster," originally published in The New Yorker *and then in her collected* Matisse Stories*), in which she talks about this notorious quotation:*

"What I dream of is an art of balance, of purity and serenity, devoid of troubling or depressing subject matter, an art which could be for every mental worker, for the businessman as well as the man of letters, for example, a soothing, calming influence on the mind, something like a good armchair which provides relaxation from physical fatigue."

Byatt has one of her characters say, "Matisse knew the most shocking thing he could tell people about the purpose of his art was that it was designed to please and be comfortable."

Why is this so shocking? Has the idea of art bringing joy or solace become unfashionable, or even taboo in modern times?

KC: First, I love Matisse's circus of colors. I admire the way he uses them in patterns (like wall paper) to make very simple paintings that are simultaneously very complicated.

Second, like Morandi, he achieved a highly individual style that is all his own. I know—and how!—that trying to internalize its influence without merely imitating is very difficult. You have to follow him by finding the way to be only yourself and no one else. That's a long journey.

Finally—I think this may address the second part of your question—I like Matisse's paintings because they are fun. I like fun, whether it's serene or action-packed or delicious. How could anyone have a problem with that? The fictional character who suggests that Matisse wished to shock by

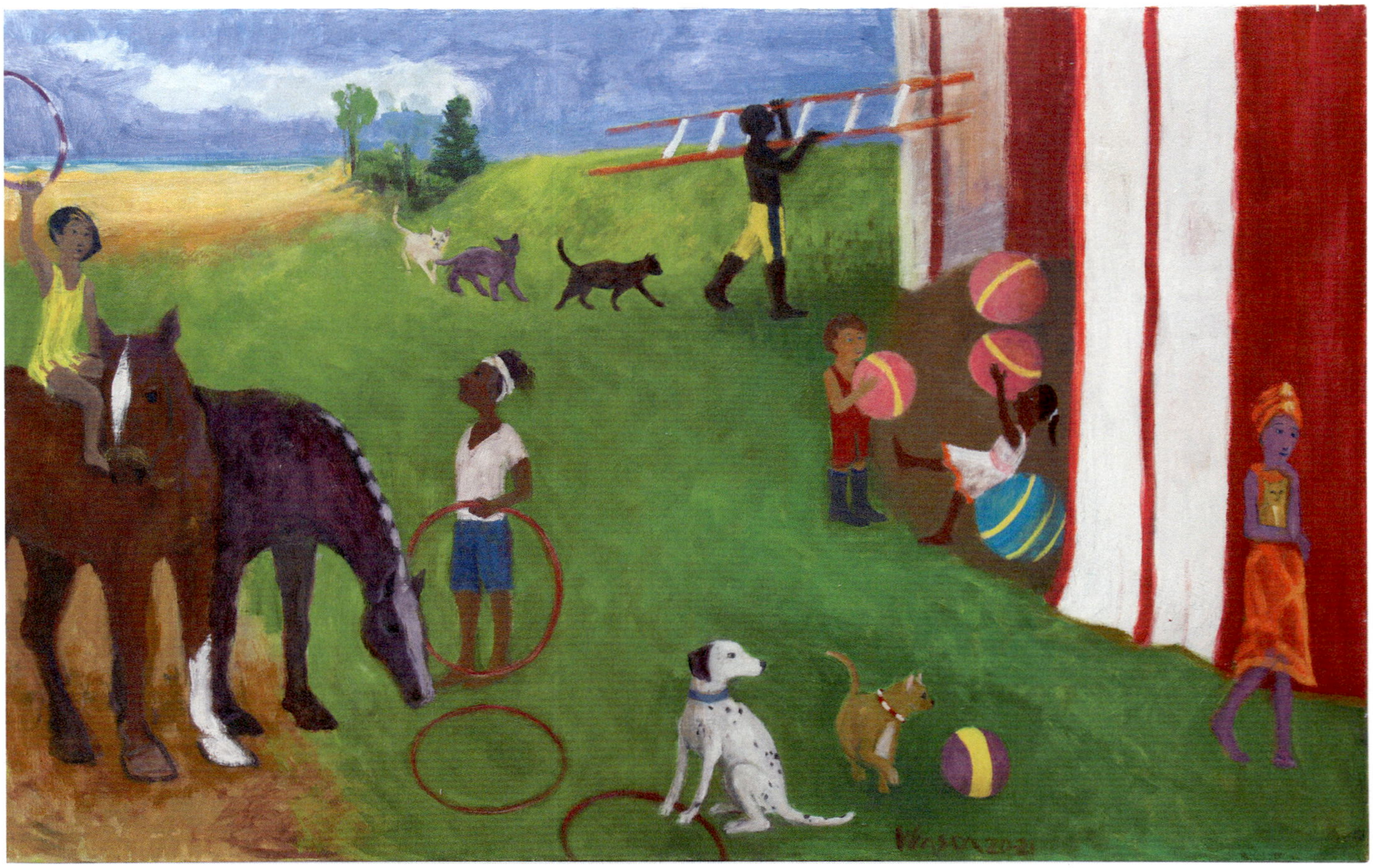

Megan Williamson
Circus II: commission for Rush Pediatric Oncology Infusion Waiting Room
2021, oil on canvas, 30 x 46 in.

recommending life on the La-Z-Boy is misreading the quotation. What his words actually say is that the goal of balance, purity and serenity is to give rest to the weary and relief to the strung-out. When "mental workers" have done their high intensity intervals they need to stop, catch their breath, and reset. It seems to me like a recipe for maintaining a healthy mind.

Indeed, I think Matisse probably had a better chance of achieving his goal than the artist who hopes their work will somehow inspire and energize people to go out and change the world. They can forget it—unless the people being influenced are also artists. In their case any good art will be stimulating.

Unlike Matisse, I don't paint with a goal in mind. I only get into trouble if I try to stick to a set purpose. I am happy if, when I stop work, the painting has some emotional effect—fun, sad, happy, stimulating. All good if the painting is good.

I don't know if political or meaningful or "impactful" are the fashion right now or not. I do know that fashion and taboos have no place in art, and very little to do with artists, except if the wheel of fashion happens to stop on what you happen to be making at the time.

MW: [Max]Beckmann said Art serves understanding, not entertainment. What I have always taken from the Matisse quote was the truth of the last part, about being a soothing, calming influence on the mind. He may have said the whole thing tongue-in-cheek, but we all know about the famously photographed figure painting he did over the course of more than a dozen sittings, and how he had the canvas stripped down at the end of the day so he could begin anew. The struggle and work that went into it wasn't something that he showed. He wasn't bringing the viewer on that trip. The final painting looks spontaneous and effortless. Matisse does often bring us to places of, as you said, stillness, energy, calm and joy.

The tension between the effort and the final painting interests me a lot. I want to put everything I can into my work, but I don't want the viewer to feel overwhelmed or assaulted by it (I do a lot of putting down and taking out myself). And however in or out of fashion joy, solace or beauty is right now, it is where I go. While I am not painting symmetrical mandalas, I do think a painting of mine is successful when it can (among other things) act as a visual meditation—where everything is connected to something else and can create all kinds of pathways and arabesques for the viewer to follow. This is especially true in my still lifes. I absolutely learned about this from Matisse. The joy being held in one of his paintings is like nothing else. There is something unexplainable about Matisse's fluidity and light and color and harmony that inspires me keeps me coming back. Of course everyone has their own reason, impulse and drive that keeps them painting. I think whatever it is, Luxe, Calme, et Volupté or Guernica, the joy or the tragedy (or both) has to come through the artist and the act of painting. It is the years and decades of painting that leads there. Political, satirical, deconstructed, ugly or beautiful—we don't get to choose as much as we might think. It bubbles up through us and if we can stay still, as Kafka urged in the quote from the last email, we can see what happens and maybe paint something good.

I just finished a commission for a painting where I really had to think about this. It hangs in a pediatric oncology infusion waiting room. Those are heavy places to be. My intention is that children and adults can find joy in it. And when they come back again and again they can find something new, or just enjoy the comfort of a summer day full of people and animals beside a circus tent. I still employed a layered, nuanced composition through color, light, shape and placement—but I was conscious as never before of wanting there to be joy.

RC: What draws me to Matisse is his color, or rather the color symphony he orchestrates on the canvas.

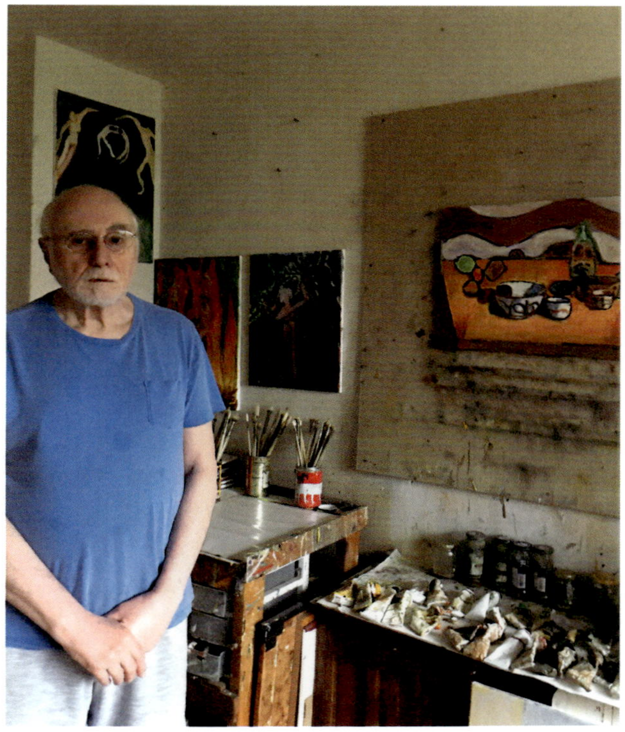
Richard Castellana in his studio

You wrote, "*The Piano Lesson* (1916), and *Interior with Goldfish* (1914)... embody for me a fusion of energy and calm, of stillness and joy." This statement confused me at first, how could he fuse energy with calm, stillness with joy? After puzzling over it, I concluded that it is true, although, for me the feeling of energy and joy are primary, calm and stillness, secondary. His distortions of form and color are unnatural; yet they harmonize and cohere in a way that seem natural, which is calming. In comparison, I associate Morandi's calm stillness with mystery. Both artists use horizontals and verticals to keep things quiet, but in different ways; Morandi's are explicit: objects are usually vertical, canvases usually horizontal. His subtle use of value, temperature, and color, and the simplicity of his compositions also contribute to the calm stillness and mystery. Matisse's use of horizontals and verticals is often, but not always, implicit. They tame the energetic color and the flowing arabesques that create the sense of joy and energy.

Matisse also influences the way I work. He wrote, "A distinction is made between artists who work directly from nature and those who work purely from imagination. Neither of these methods should be preferred to the exclusion of the other. Often both are used in turn by the same artist..." This and another quotation (which I could not find after a lengthy search on the internet) went something along these lines: to get away from the danger of unimaginatively copying what one sees (something I sometimes succumb to), it is best to have the model on the first floor and the easel, paints, and canvas on the third. This is more or less my method, although in my tiny studio the "model" (still life) is behind me. I paint large landscapes in the studio from sketches and when I'm stuck go back to the motif for ideas. My small landscapes are usually from direct observation.

You ask, "Has the idea of art bringing joy or solace become unfashionable, or even taboo in modern times?" It is certainly unfashionable in certain circles, unfortunately in the circles that dominate the current scene. It is certainly not taboo, not at least in the circles where I travel. Art can do

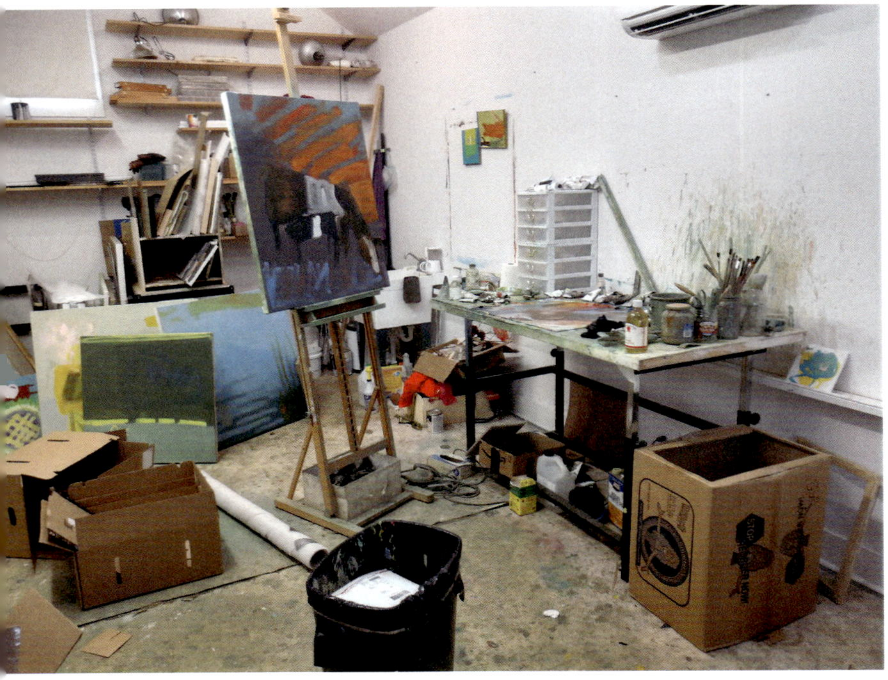

Kathleen Craig's studio

many things, it can be done for its own sake, be playful, psychological, social, political, conceptual, beautiful, and religious, bring joy, solace, or anguish. I do not believe any of these should be taboo; each goes in and out of fashion as time goes by.

IS: *All of you, in your responses to this last question, talked a bit about the working process: about the tension between the effort and the final result; about the balance between observation and imagination or memory; about to the journey to finding your own style. I'd like to dig into this a little more. I'm especially interested in hearing about how observation, imagination, and memory intersect—if they do—especially in your work with still life. And have you found that the quarantine has had any effect on your working process or the way you approach your work?*

RC: If I were to rate their importance to my still life paintings, I would give imagination and observation a tie for first place, memory a second (or is it third?). I start from observation and as I run into trouble, rearrange, move, add, subtract, and/or invent objects. "As for memory," as I said earlier, "it is not something I consciously draw on, but nothing can be done without implicit, subconscious memory. Memory is a product of experience, and experience (plus genetics and environment, of course) makes us who we are. If painting is an expression of personality, it can't be done without memory."

To expand on that, sometimes an accidental arrangement of objects on a table or shelf inspires me to start a painting, or I make what I know is only a provisional arrangement (I prefer to create the composition in the process of painting). Either way, I notice that objects might accidentally huddle, stand in the foreground or the background, lean on, obscure, bump into one another, stand alone, stand out, couple up, or cast shadows on each other. These remind me of human interactions, relationships, and the feelings associated with them. Usually, I exaggerate the human attributes as I re-arrange (in reality or solely on canvas) objects until I am satisfied with the composition. Is memory involved? If so, it is memory of a generic sort, not memory of specific events or relationships. I doubt I am alone in thinking a still life can stand as a metaphor for human life.

KC: Observation and memory go together for me. Once I have observed something it becomes a memory.

Often those two qualities—this is just me—are very left-brain. That is, words usually insist on standing in for them, even if the memory is something nonverbal, like the taste of ice cream.

I once wanted to write fiction but I lacked imagination—just couldn't make up anything by using words. Picture (!) my delight, long after I gave up writing, when I discovered that my imagination could go wild as long as I left words out of it.

First, learning to draw, I discovered the "drawing on the right side of the brain" phenomenon—blanking your verbal coding and focusing on visuals, or at least concentrating on geometric abstracts: angles, relative sizes and distances. Nose is a pyramid, eyeball is a sphere, etc. Then, when I went "abstract," I found it worked with color and shape, so well that I could live in the world of a painting with no more words than, perhaps, "Nope," or "Yes, got it, got it, got it!"

Now, still life. For some time I have been trying to find a place between "pure abstract" and "realism," partly because I empathize with people who need words for what they are looking at. Also, my strong left brain keeps intruding into my imaginary playground, reminding me that oh, that looks like a boat, or a person, or a flower. I have found that the best (that is, easiest) way to find a good balance is through direct observation. I don't know how it works. But in order to transform "real life" into an expressive, imaginative painting that I approve of, I need to look hard at the real thing (and avoid looking at the canvas until I have stopped moving my arm). Still life is convenient for this. Weather of one kind or another precludes outdoor painting much of the year (heat, wind, bugs, snow). Models are expensive. I do use photographs for people and cows, but the feeling I need is hard to access because I had to think "cow" before I google its image and now that stupid word is in my head.

As for Covid-19 and the shut-down, I think that the hiatus of connections to brick and mortar galleries and the lessening of pressure to produce inventory has had some effect on my work. I seem to be traveling on a continuum that moves slowly from floundering to resolution (maybe). I have been experimenting with mediums in a more organized way than usual, testing different combinations and writing down results, times, "stinkiness" levels. I have a roll of high quality oil-primed paper that I bought ages ago; finally I can work on finding the best way to use it. I have tried a few ways to turn my collages into multi-media affairs—this has been frustrating. I revise endlessly. In short—art-making is so self-centered—having a little more time on my hands has forced me to reacquaint myself generally with my own limitations, and their advantages.

IS: *Due to a loss in her family, Megan Williamson was unable to respond to the final question. Our thoughts and sympathy are with Megan in this difficult time.*

Before we started this Conversation, Megan and I spoke on the phone to get to know one another and discuss the topics we wanted to explore. We learned that we shared a love for Bologna, Italy, the lifelong home of Giorgio Morandi—its light, colors, and incredible food. In talking about the experience of sheltering at home during the pandemic, we discovered that we were both fascinated by the same quote from Franz Kafka, with which I will leave you:

"There is no need for you to leave the house. Stay at your table and listen. Don't even listen, just wait. Don't wait, be completely quiet and alone. The world will offer itself to you to be unmasked; it can't do otherwise. In ecstasy it will writhe before you." Z

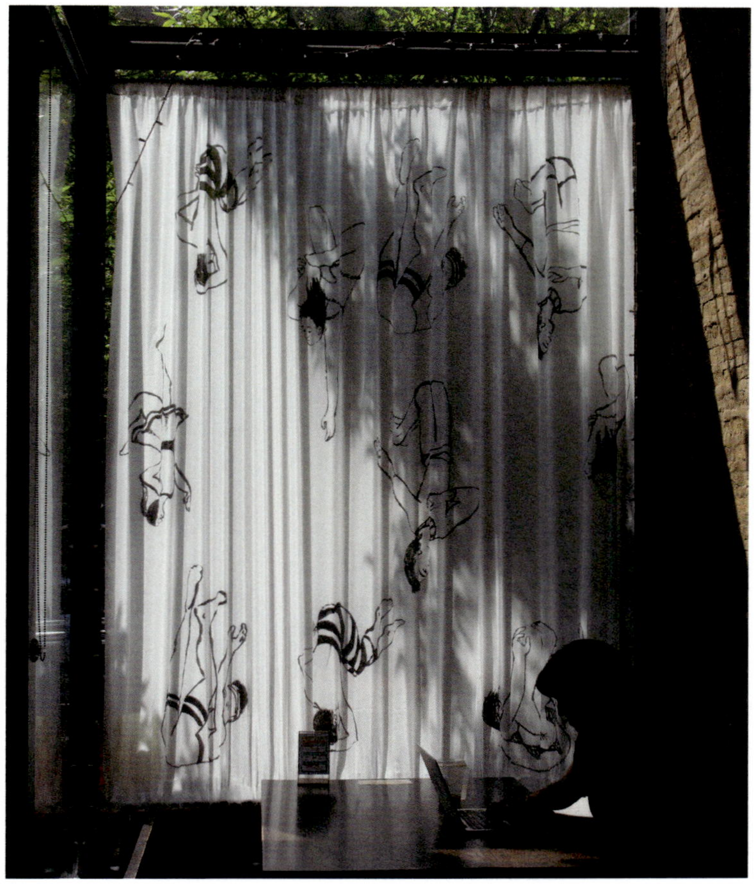

Megan Williamson *Falling (Ipsento)*
Installation view at a coffee shop in Chicago, Ipsento 606
2022, sumi ink on silk, 67 x 114 in.

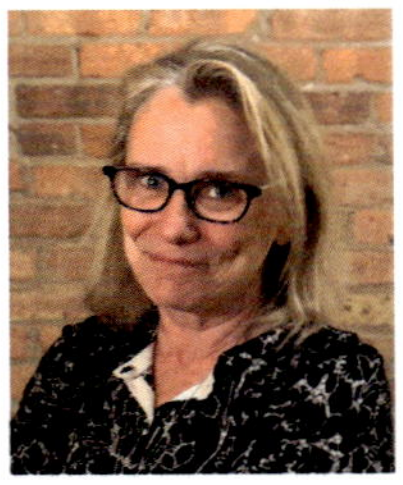

Megan Williamson is a still life and landscape painter who looks for a combination of beauty, complexity and simplicity in her subject matter. The artist's work emerges from of a modernist and cubist understanding of space, light and construction. Her influences include Matisse, Morandi, Pollock, Islamic tile patterns, Bonnard, Braque and her friend, mentor and teacher Nicolas Carone. Ms. Williamson lives in Chicago.

www.zeuxis.us/williamson
www.meganwilliamson.com

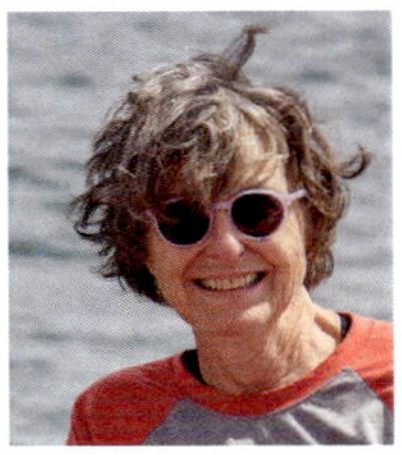

Kathleen Craig paints abstract still lifes, landscapes, and figures, working from observation and memory, with an emphasis on color, composition, and expression. Her work has been influenced by Giorgio Morandi, Nicolas de Stael, and Ken Kewley's essay on color. She currently exhibits with Nancy Margolis Gallery (NYC), Elder Gallery of Contemporary Art (Charlotte, NC), Cerulean Arts (Philadelphia) , and Bonvoey Gallery (Cleveland).

www.zeuxis.us/craig
www.kathleencraig.net

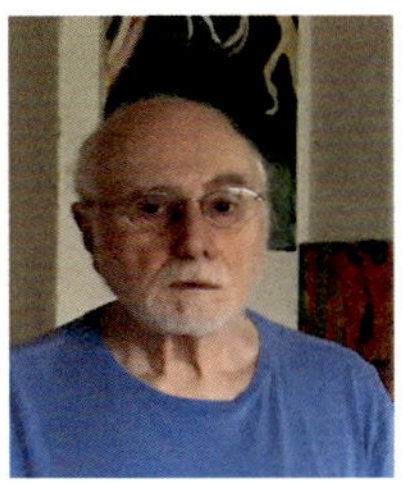

Richard Castellana paints still life, landscape, and figure compositions from a mix of observation, imagination, and memory. He is a member of the Blue Mountain Gallery and lives and works in New York City. Since the 1970's he has exhibited widely and received national and international recognition and awards for his work. Castellana studied at the Art Students League, New York Studio School, and Queens College. His teachers included Edwin Dickinson, Charles Cajori, Mercedes Matter, Esteban Vicente, John Ferren, and Louis Finkelstein. Castellana taught at Fairleigh Dickinson University for over 25 years, retired in 2013 as director of the B. A. in Interdisciplinary Studies program, and is now Professor Emeritus of Humanities and Fine Arts program, and is now Professor Emeritus of Humanities and Fine Arts.

www.richardcastellana.com

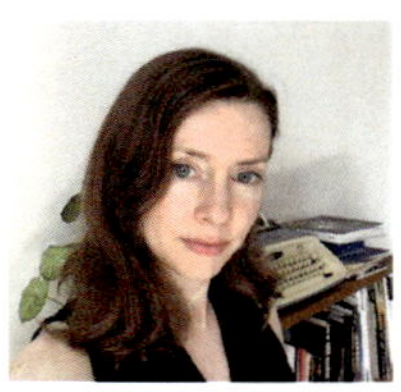

Imogen Sara Smith is a freelance writer and film critic based in New York City. She is the author of two books, *In Lonely Places: Film Noir Beyond the City*, and *Buster Keaton: The Persistence of Comedy*. Her writing has appeared in *Film Comment, Sight and Sound, The Criterion Collection, The Threepenny Review,* and many other publications. She is a frequent speaker on cinema, and she teaches film history at the School of Visual Arts. Imogen has written essays for several Zeuxis exhibitions and moderated events with Zeuxis artists in New York and Lancaster.

The Quiet Work of Looking

Gaela Erwin interviews

Sheldon Tapley
and
Emil Robinson

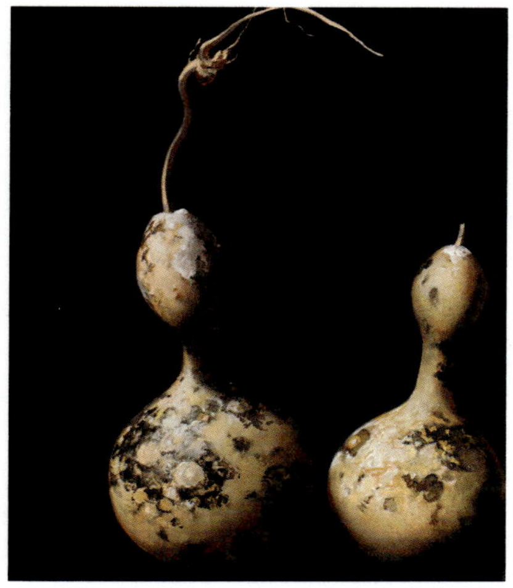

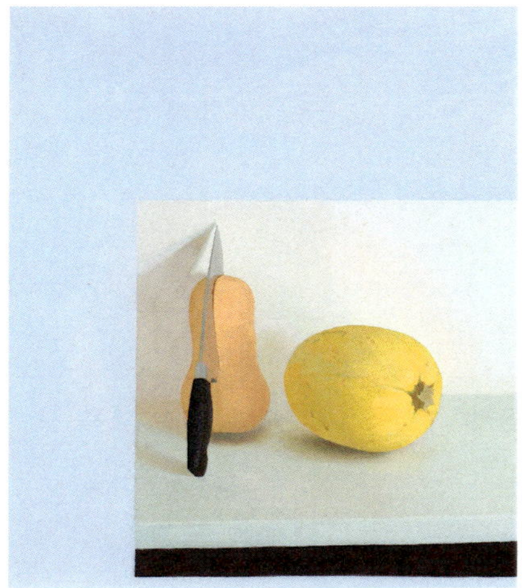

Sheldon Tapley *Two Gourds*
2016, pastel on paper, 23 x 17 in.

Emil Robinson *Arrangement with Knife and Gourds*
2015, oil on panel, 35 x 22 in.

Gaela Erwin: *When I was asked to do this interview, I was honored to have the opportunity to engage Sheldon and Emil in a dialogue about their work. I have had the privilege occasionally to spend time with them throughout many years thanks to summer gatherings at Centre College and participation in exhibitions together. Though their approaches to art differ, they have a shared integrity regarding the indispensability of perceptual painting in all its forms. Both Sheldon's and Emil's paintings, whose work I admire greatly, have always inspired my own studio efforts.*

Due to the Covid virus, it was necessary to communicate by e-mail, phone calls and Zoom. With this technology, we were able to have a series of dialogues about the conceptual genesis of their paintings, as well as influences, subject matter and personal histories.

GE: *How have your influences on one another shifted as former student Emil became fellow professor? What is that dialogue like now as colleagues, years later?*

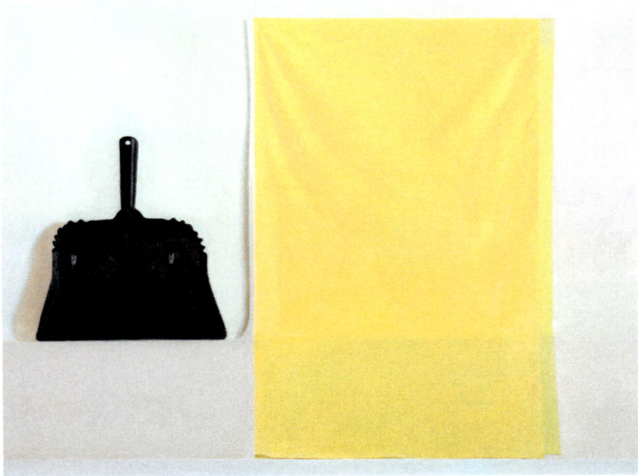

Emil Robinson
Dust Pan and Yellow Curtain
2020, oil on panel, 36 x 39 in.

Sheldon Tapley: Our works do not have an obvious stylistic link, but there are underlying commonalities, because we have many shared interests and respect each other's art. I admire his brilliant drawing, inventive and sensitive use of color, and his searching responses into so many different kinds of art. For me, Emil is a trusted critic. Conversations with him bring new insights; he has introduced me to artists and artworks I didn't know.

Emil Robinson: I remember first meeting Sheldon in 2001 when I was thinking about attending Centre College. There was an ease to his bearing that made me feel comfortable. He was complimentary about my work, but more than that I sensed that we were complementary as individuals. Sheldon modeled a kind of life that appealed greatly to me; a serious studio practice, a loving home life, and a passion for teaching. Sheldon and I are friends. He continues to be a mentor, but our relationship has deepened over the years. I am close with his family as well. I don't know anyone else who has the same open heart towards the stories and lives of those around him. I think this is an enduring quality of his art—an open heart. Sharing a beer with Sheldon while rambling through the history of art and its current manifestations is a cherished activity. He's a great talker—the good and the bad punctuated with rich guffaws and serious wisdom. I think it mystifies him that many of his art heroes were difficult people—he returns to that again and again in descriptions of the great artists from history. He's immensely serious about his work, the story he tells, and a warm loving person.

GE: *How do the objects you choose to represent in your paintings personify some aspect of spirituality and create the magical, transformative aspects I hear you both strive for?*

ER: Spirituality is an open experience for me. I grew up with the rituals of Catholicism, memorized prayers, standing at certain times, kneeling at certain times… I also grew up with parents who insisted that the spiritual was in all mundane things. My objects are never willfully symbolic or narrative driven. I choose them quickly in moments of insight. Some of them have personal meaning for me, and all of them were chosen in particular instances, but those stories are not important for the viewer. My spirituality does not reside in names or function. If anything, the painting begins as a series of meaningless declarative statements which might transform into something prayerful if I have enough faith. In this case "prayerful" means that the objects embody something other than themselves.

GE: *Emil, if I understand you correctly your studio experience is about your being present in a liminal space between perception and a metaphysical awareness that transcends the objective aspects of the still life. That said, the observation of every aspect of light and particularly color in the context of your studio is informed by the physical architecture of the room. What part does your work environment play in your paintings? Can you describe the function and selection of the objects you choose to paint?*

ER: My specific physical environment is very influential to my work. My current studio is a small room with a high ceiling, white walls and a gray floor. The room has the kind of subtle architectural details that reveal its domestic bones. There are large floor-to-ceiling, west facing windows on one wall. There is also a white mantel where I stage the objects for my still life paintings. The windows make a glowing colorful light and shadow, and the lightness of the whole room amplifies this effect. There is a pervasive atmosphere that is embodied by the quality of light, and this lightness is the common ground of my paintings.

The objects I choose are from different settings, but they share a personal language of form and color. The function of the objects is to manipulate and embody painted space. A knife collects light and color along its blade leaving its dark handle inert and certain in its dimensions. Everything I paint contains some paradox of the substantial and unsubstantial. The light and atmosphere, these are the real subjects, and the nameable objects in the painting are just a place for light and color to gain personality and voice.

GE: Sheldon, your still life paintings and drawings have an autobiographical feel to them. The choice of your subject matter has the appearance of being painted with a compassionate gaze. When I look at your still lifes, I see a portrait of objects that invite the viewer to intuit clues reflecting the dimensions and interests of the artist. How do you choose the objects you paint and how are they autobiographical? Do the physical aspects of your studio reflect in some way your painting process? The 1950's era enamel top table with the red trim, in particular, comes to mind.

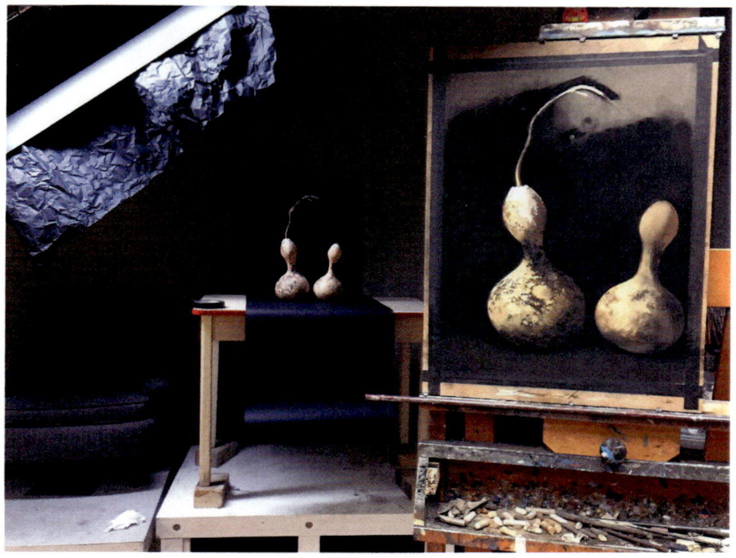

Sheldon Tapley's studio with *Two Gourds* in-progress

ST: That yellow enamel table caught my eye some years ago when I was helping my parents relocate to a smaller home, late in life (it is seen here in the photograph of my studio and in the painting Solitaire, below). They had acquired it in 1952, during their first year of marriage. Seeing it again, I experienced the visual hunger that often leads me to paint things. The color, the surface, and the family history attached to it have given it favored place in my studio.

Much of my painting is driven by visual appetite. Sometimes it is difficult to find a subject: nothing excites my eye. Other times, a thing presents itself and I sense its potential. It may be the way light falls on it rather than the object itself. It may be a change within me—I rarely question why it happens. Nevertheless, I have learned to seize that opportunity, to draw or paint it first and ask questions later.

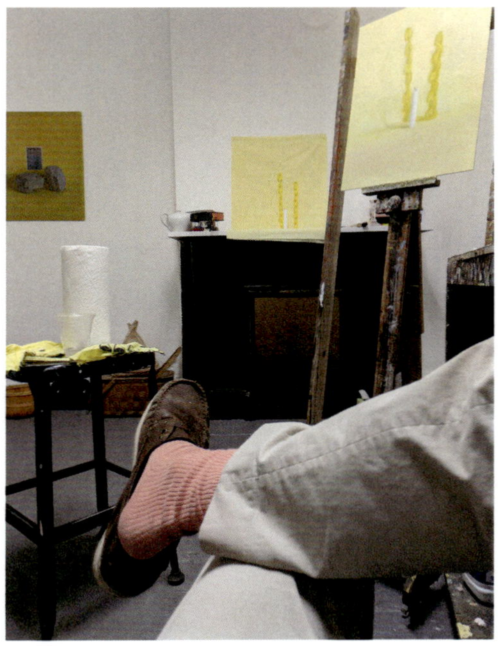

Emil Robinson in his studio

Some objects come into my studio to stay. If they did not have personal significance to begin with, they accrue it by appearing repeatedly in my images. A handblown glass pitcher brought home long ago from Mexico became an important motif in just that way. The body of the pitcher is nearly spherical, and that geometric form attracted me, as did its rich color. In the studio I found that it reflected images of the whole space, me included. That dark cobalt-blue surface made the reflections mysterious. The more I worked with it, the more it offered, so that it showed up in many drawings and paintings.

Autobiography is not really the goal of my still life paintings. I want the painting to be a gift to the viewer that will reward long looking. It needs to have a lot more in it than just little old me, and there is a whole world of things that are more interesting. Nevertheless, autobiography is sometimes impossible to avoid, simply because I am so often describing things, places and people in my life. And, the human desire to make stories out of everything is powerful, so maybe I am doing that without consciously aiming for it.

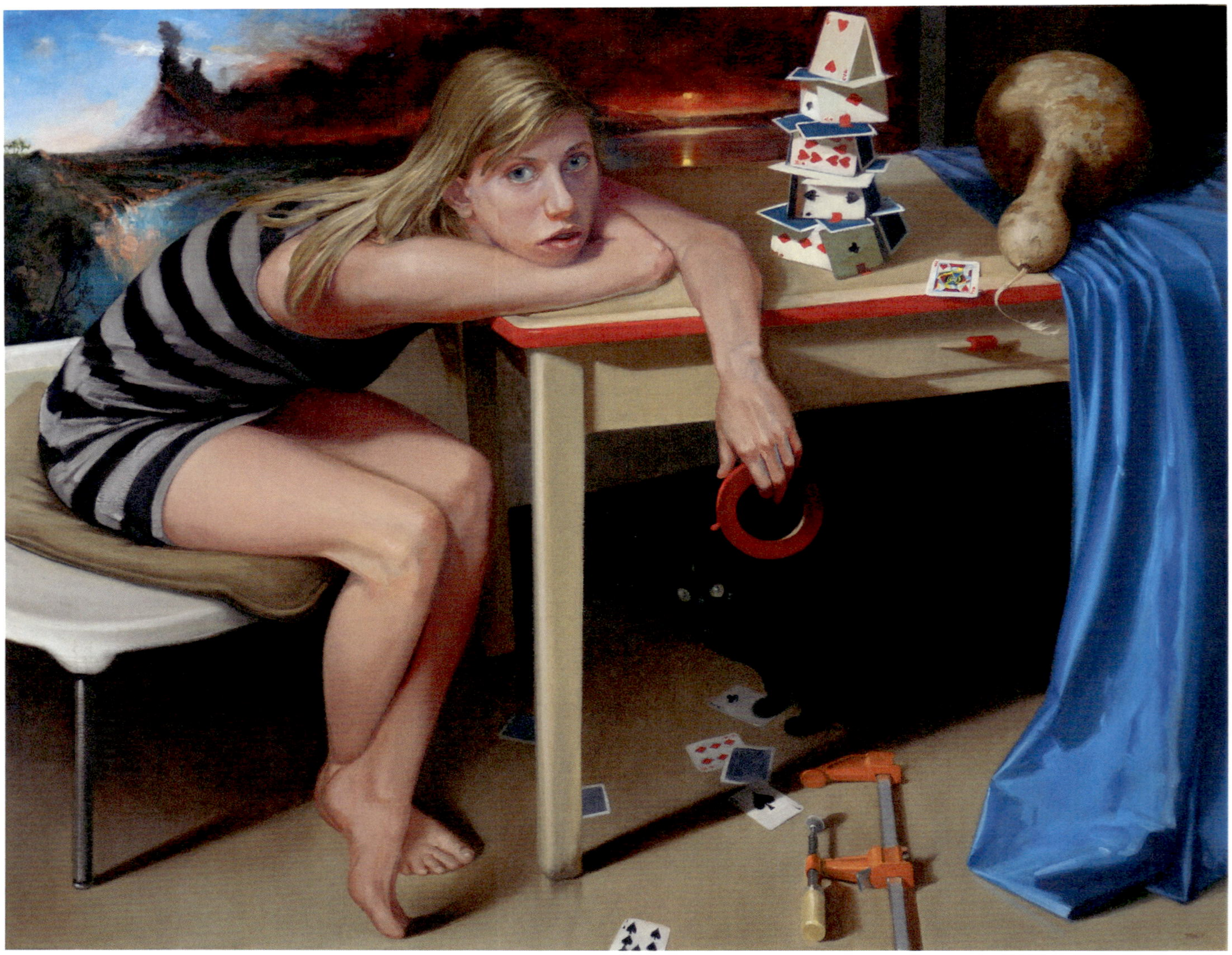

Sheldon Tapley *Solitaire*
2013, oil on linen, 36 x 35 in.

In still life, I am not drawn to any object that is obviously sentimental or precious. That would oversimplify the goal of painting, and undercut the imaginative purposes of art. But emotional and physical attachment are everywhere in the things we use. They are not hard to find, just difficult to translate into art. Many of the objects I paint have been in our family home, others came to me from friends. I have enjoyed many gifts of wonderful found objects, including tortoise shells, bird nests, gourds and flowers. Painting those things records that personal connection. That is important, but not more so than the visual qualities of the object, or the visual potential. It is my job to find the correct union of vision and feeling.

GE: *You have very different ways of approaching the painting of objects that transform their quotidian utility. You have both referred to two 17th century Spanish masters, Zurbarán and Cotán, as influences. Can you reflect on how these artists inspire you, even though your respective paintings appear very different in many aspects?*

ST: That's a wonderful idea—that objects are transformed by the artist. It's very appealing to think of oneself as a kind of magician. But I also think of the transformation of subjects as an ordinary responsibility of the artist: to paint something so that it is worth a second look; so that it might be affecting and memorable. Otherwise, we could just look at the object itself and not bother with the painting.

ER: I will double down on what both of you said here about how a painting transforms the identity of objects, that's beautifully said, and of course the whole point. The normal utility of objects is beside the point for how I paint. I am drawn to objects which mingle with an interior experience I am having. I trust my interior experience and have built it with respect and patience over my time as a painter. I notice elements of my surroundings and invite them to embody my intangible experience. Maybe that could be called "daydreaming." Painting is my bridge between an internal world and the external world of objects. This might be called vision. Whatever it's called, it's the place I put my effort hoping to become a better artist. I choose objects as a temporary home—a foil of sorts. Something seemingly sturdy, but only useful to me if it can open into a painted world. My studio is a place of non-utilitarian logic—I like the paradox of looking right at an object but painting something totally different.

ST: About Zurbarán and Cotán: I admire the dramatic power with which they present objects in their still-life paintings, and have learned much from studying their work, especially Cotán's, but I am wary of imitating any historical master too closely. My experiences and ways of thinking are so different from theirs that any honest attempt to represent the material world must necessarily be different.

Cotán's *Quince, Cabbage, Melon and Cucumber* is one of my favorite still-life paintings. I am particularly attracted to the painter's use of geometric proportion: the fruits and vegetables, shown in sunlight at the opening of a dark root cellar, are arranged in a beautiful arc. Their material existence is given an idealized conceptual order.

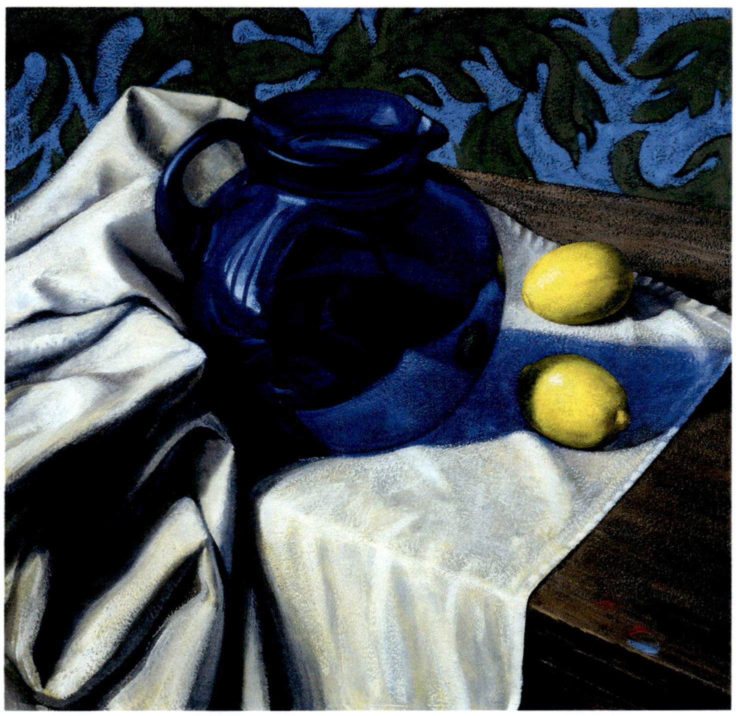

Sheldon Tapley *Water and Lemons*
2004, oil on aluminum panel, 18 x 18 in.

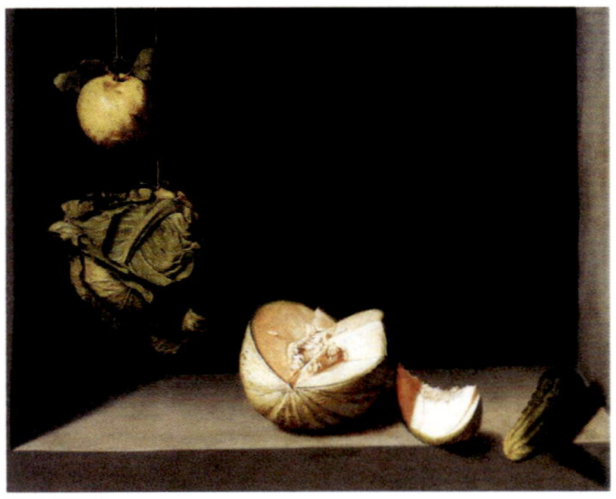

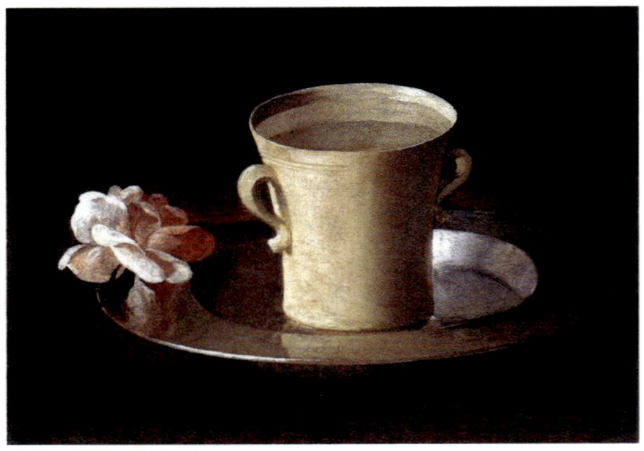

LEFT TO RIGHT:

Juan Sánchez Cotán
Quince, Cabbage, Melon and Cucumber
1602, oil on canvas

Francisco de Zurbarán
Cup of Water and Rose
1630, oil on canvas

It seems natural to me, when making preliminary drawings for a still life, to look for underlying geometric order. It is one of the ways that my experience of the material world can be infused with abstract thinking; it transforms what I see. That is particularly important when I am drawing, as opposed to painting. Line drawing is deceptively simple; a subtle and powerful abstraction of nature, and the foundation of most of my paintings.

ER: I appreciate the environment that Zurbarán presents in his work. It is the qualities of his paintings as whole images that make him powerful to me. The way his subjects feel elevated, ritualized and intense. The Cotán shown here is an amazing painting, but the Zurbarán strikes a poetic note which fits my particular needs. The explanatory manner in which Cotán presents his design, its iconic clarity, doesn't interest me as much. Cotán's objects have "lighting" on them whereas Zurbarán presents light as an embedded quality. Likewise, the clear factual drawing in the Cotán is impressive, but the Zurbarán is a tightly woven matrix of decisions and counter decisions. All objective ideas of perspective and traditional drawing are useless in describing what makes the Zurbarán hold together. The forms are balanced and counter balanced—each curve and surface given tender persistent attention in service of the painting's singularity. The difference between the two artists is a matter of theatre perhaps, and personality. I admire the Cotán and find it remarkable, I would gladly live with its friendly and intelligent wit, but the Zurbarán fills me with mystery.

ST: I love the way Emil is able to evoke feeling in his paintings. His response to the mystery in Zurbarán's paintings makes perfect sense; it helps me see it the way he does. And it makes me realize that I spend a lot of energy trying to make things clear and orderly. So, the way we have each responded to these paintings is quite revealing, even enlightening.

ER: It is interesting you say clear and orderly, part of my admiration for your work is in response to how open you are to a range of interesting subjects, like the Cotán, you generously give us diverse things to look at. Perhaps you perceive a certain quality in yourself that you identify as clear or orderly, but I feel my own sensibility is also too clear—I empty my paintings out! Of course, it's a choice I stand behind, but it has its own antiseptic implications!

GE: *Emil, I had a hard time "getting" the other inspirational sources that you mentioned in our preliminary conversation, including Josef Albers, Helen Lundeberg, and Holly Coulis. As a realist painter who works to create form by observation of light, I had some difficulty understanding the work of these artists that defied the norms of representational realism.*

After reviewing my notes from our discussion, I took my usual walk down the alley. I suddenly stopped short in front of a simple shed. I had seen it thousands of times before and yet had never really seen it until then. The building was completely unremarkable, painted humbly with two closely related house paint colors. Yet, the shed's utilitarian plainness, situated at the end of an alley, revealed in an instant all that we had discussed. The geometry, close range of values, and its oneness all seemed to encapsulate a new experience for me.

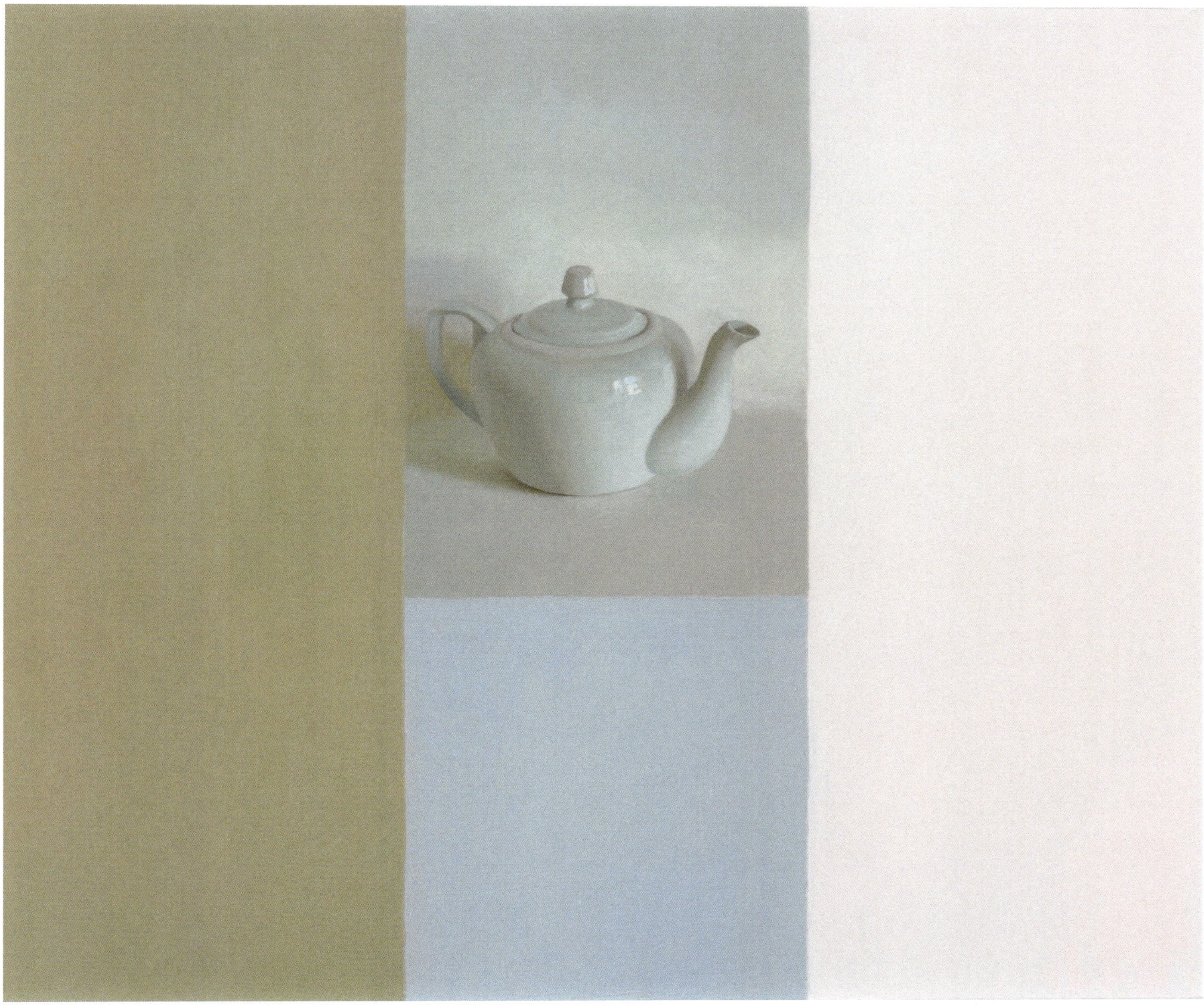

Emil Robinson *Arrangement with Teapot*
2020, oil on panel, 20 x 16 in.

Tell me how your work invokes that sense of consciousness through the conceptual choices you make in your paintings.

ER: My current still life paintings are built in response to particular needs. I paint illusionistic objects to respond to tangible space and the effects of light and atmosphere. I paint expanses of clear color to respond to the abstract interaction between feelings and fleeting environmental observations. The gap between formal elements in my paintings mirrors the gap between the physical world and the interior world of rumination, full of conflicting ideas which must be resolved or ignored.

I keep my compositional structures simple because I spent a number of years exploring other options without clarity. My current combination of carefully drawn objects and precisely calibrated colors is a poetry that feels both focused and free.

The shed is a nice metaphor, I'll use it to further answer your question. The painting and its internal logic are utilitarian like a shed, although the observations that are coming together in my paintings do not exist in one physical object or moment of space—they are built in my mind as disparate experiences which I allow to co-exist. Put another way, a single literal shed might not inspire me to paint, but if I perceive a oneness across a boundary of vision and internal experience, I try to paint a surprising unification.

I discover the colors I need in my environment. This space extends into different times of day and different physical locations. When I am working on a painting, I am working on it even when I am not in front of the painting. It's like leaving a door open to let the weather in.

I suppose that's part of what abstraction is about for me—building a painted experience that is logical yet undefined, just like the strangeness of our relationship to the physical world. Abstraction makes sense to me in this way, but realism does as well. I think realism is a type of visual potency that works productively in tandem (friction?) with the expanses of color in my paintings.

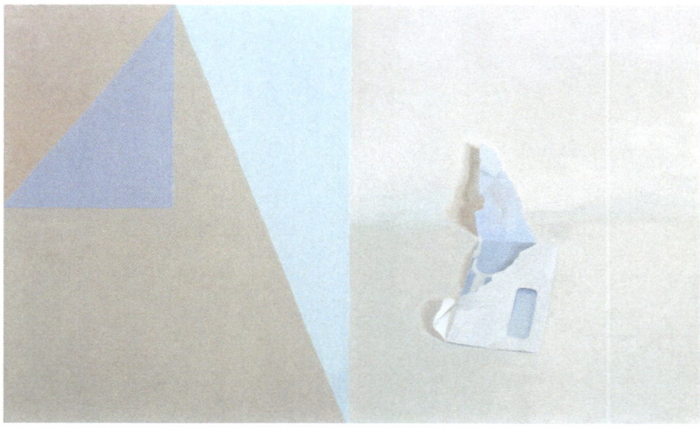

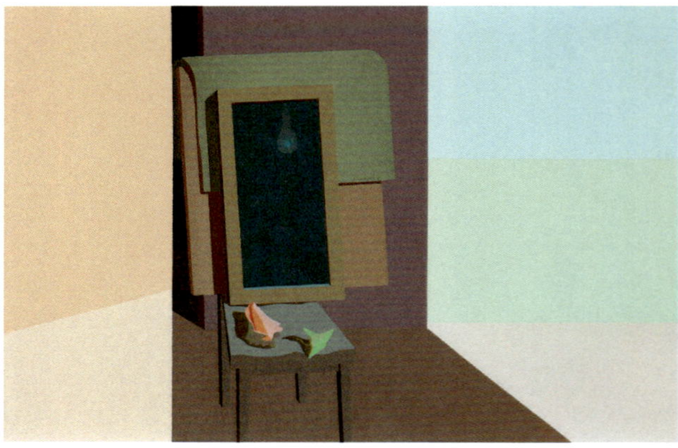

LEFT TO RIGHT:

Emil Robinson
Arrangement with Therapy Bill
2020, oil on panel, 16 x 20 in.

Helen Lundeberg *The Mirror*
1952/69, acrylic on canvas, 40 x 60 in.

The artists I listed as influences are more like partners than heroes. In their works I can read a shared set of goals. I can sense their curiosity, and I identify with their ambition. Albers is a father figure for me, his trust in the range of experience afforded by color broke new ground in my mind. Helen Lundberg is a newer acquaintance of mine, but her ambitions and association with the California light and space movement make her very relevant to my interests. I like how she operates between abstraction and realism in a focused cerebral way. Her mind is an inspiration. I've known Holly Coulis's work for quite some time, and her still life paintings of the last 3-5 years show an insight into a range of expression. Humor, joy and irony seem available in her paintings, which is a generous and exciting combination.

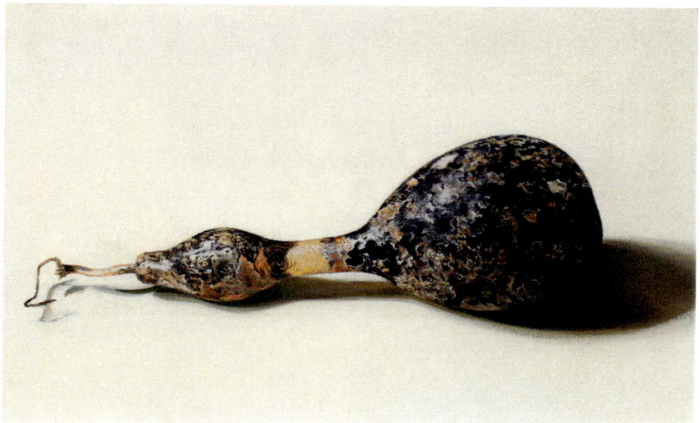

Sheldon Tapley *Black Gourd*
2016, oil on linen, 24 x 30 in.

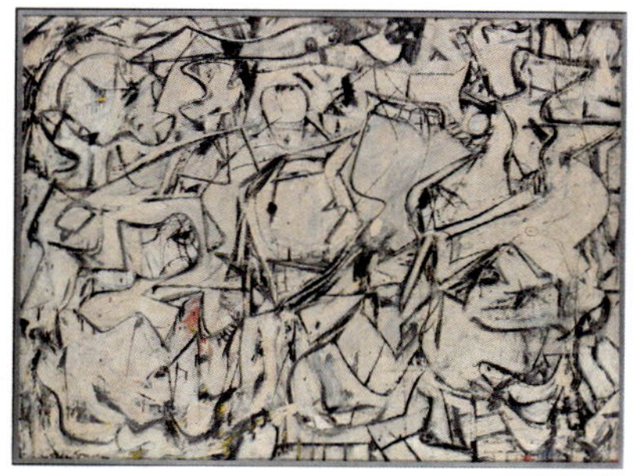

Willem De Kooning *Attic*
1949, oil, enamel, and newspaper transfer on canvas, 62 x 81 in.

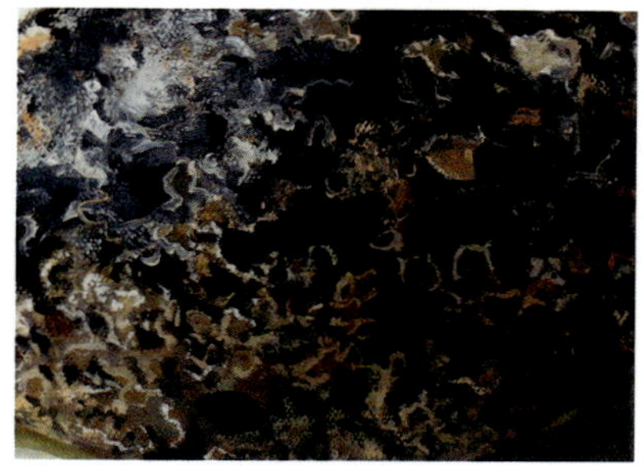

Black Gourd detail

GE: *After reading your response it appears that color works as an inspiration from an object observed within a particular environment. But more importantly, color acts as the springboard for the much more difficult investigation and immersion into the depths of the interior self. To return to the shed analogy, seeing the shed and the color created by the play of light may initiate interest in painting it but the perceived image functions only as the structural element for the conceptual process.*

ER: Yep, that seems right. I know it's a confusing paradox—maybe just shy of nonsensical, especially when written down. The painting is inspired by a moment shared with the shed but is not a painting of the shed. The moment of insight which is coincidental with seeing the shed is the real focus of the painting. So, the choices in the painting bend to fit the richness of feeling that was the sensation of seeing the shed and having something happen inside your mind.

GE: *Sheldon, I had a moment when, upon reviewing the examples of other artists you hold in high esteem, I came across your choice of de Kooning's* Attic. *My perception has been that you and I have always been closely aligned in a classical approach to representational painting. When I saw the de Kooning image with its abstract monochromatic shapes encrusted over the entire canvas, I could only scratch my head with incredulity. I could think of no greater contrast between two artist's paintings than yours and his. Your response to my inquiry on the subject was brilliant and another case of something that was right in front of my nose. Please share the story for your attraction to Attic.*

ST: I have loved de Kooning's paintings since I was first introduced to them as an undergraduate. They are such a familiar part of my own roster of favorites that I was a little surprised when you asked me about him. That is a healthy reminder that my own thoughts about my painting may seem clear to me while remaining opaque to others.

Patterns and textures are visually fascinating for me. Complex patterns, especially those that seem random, have a kind of hypnotic allure. That is part of my attraction to speckled gourds, which have become a regular subject in my work. Drying them in my garage over the winter allows them to become covered in unpredictable patterns caused by mold and weather, as if natural forces have created a kind of Action Painting. When I am imitating the black-and-ochre patterns on the skin of a gourd, I find that I am using a palette and making marks that remind me of some of de Kooning's paintings. It is like doing a miniature abstract painting, tucked into a larger recognizable image. A pictorial surprise. I have included here a detail of Black Gourd that I hope shows that. Z

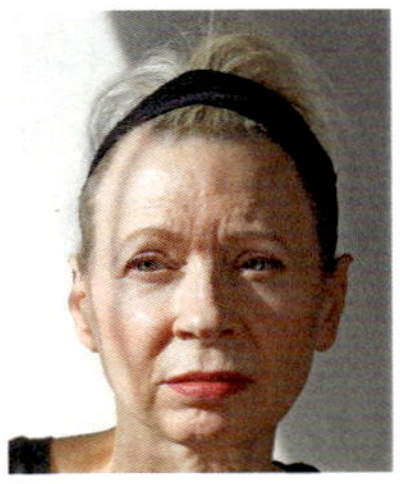

Gaela Erwin is a figurative painter whose portraits in pastel and oil have been exhibited nationally and internationally. The BP Portrait Award 2018 competition, sponsored by the National Portrait Gallery in London, England, selected Erwin's painting and named it second place in the People's Choice Award. Erwin's solo museum exhibitions and inclusion in permanent collections include the 21c Museum Hotel, Speed Art Museum, Indianapolis Museum of Art, Ogunquit Museum of Art, the Huntsville Museum of Art, to name a few.

www.gaelaerwin.com

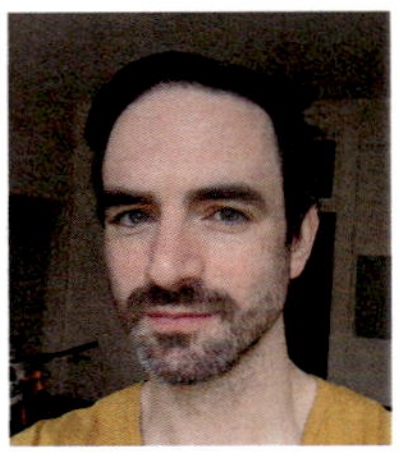

Emil Robinson is an artist known for paintings of light filled space and psychological precision. He is an Assistant Professor of Art and Design at the University of Cincinnati.

www.emilrobinson.com

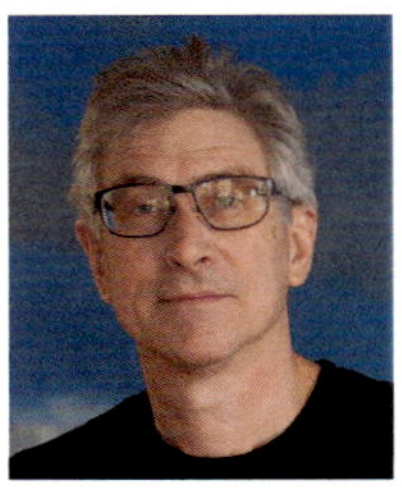

Sheldon Tapley's careful observation and playful invention are the roots of his art. He loves painting directly from life and hopes that it gives his images greater vitality. Still life is an important element of his work, and has also become the foundation for images that invoke memory and imagination. Tapley is the Stodghill Professor of Art at Centre College, where he has enjoyed working with his students for many years.

www.zeuxis.us/tapley
www.sheldontapley.com

Painting Choices

Matthew Lopas interviews

Eleanor Ray
and
Edmond Praybe
and
Joe Morzuch

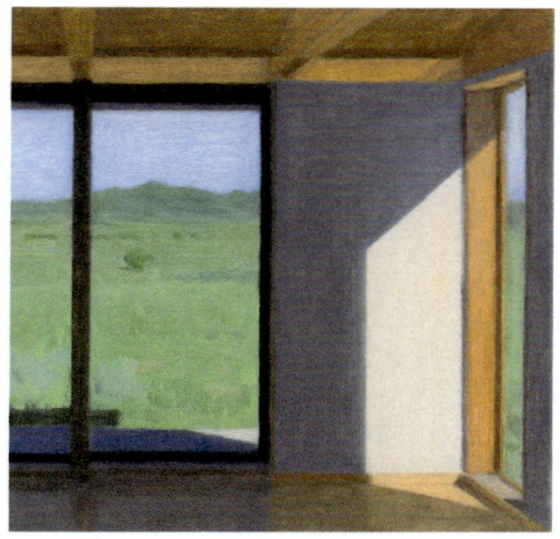

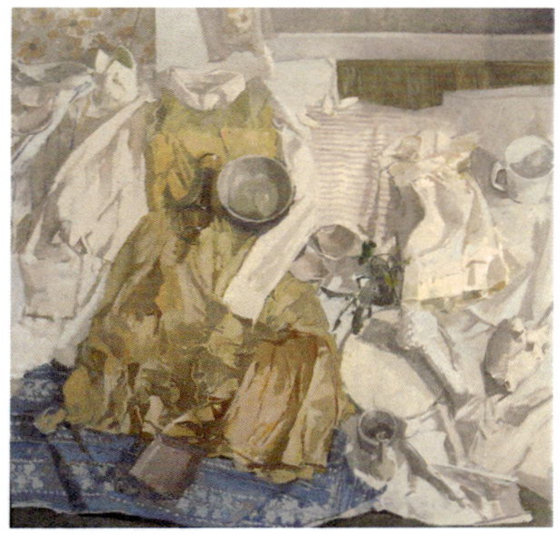

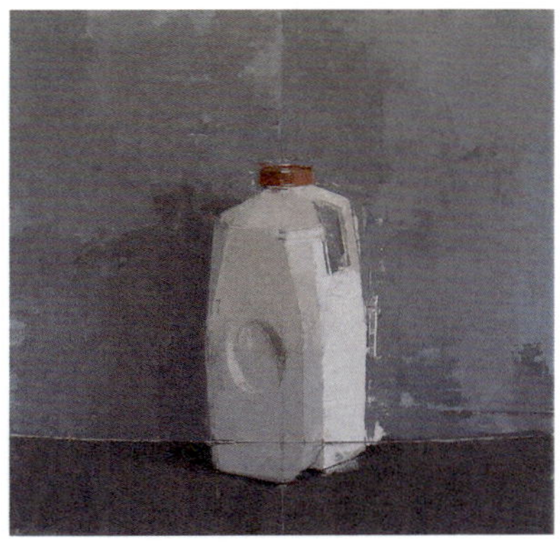

Eleanor Ray *Nevada Window, June*
2019, oil on panel, 6 ½ x 8 ½ in.

Edmond Praybe *Patterns and Folds*
2018, oil on panel, 36 x 36 in.

Joe Morzuch *Milk Carton*
2019, oil on canvas on panel, 17 x 17 in.

Matthew Lopas: *These three representational painters all share a deep engagement in their craft, light, and composition, yet are of course very different from the other. Eleanor Ray works from memory and photos, and is engaged with geometries that emphasize horizontals and verticals. She often directs the viewer to gently lit spaces out a window or through a door. The delicacy of her brush and quietness of her images brings the viewer to an almost prayerful state.*

Joe Morzuch works from observation and is interested in very rigorous measurement in the vein of Coldstream. His spare images and sometimes shifting elements show a love of humble objects and a zeal to the act of looking and representing. The unflinching intensity of his gaze imbues every subject with real significance.

Ed Praybe is interested in overall complexity and unpredictable geometries, a value I myself share. Rather than hit the viewer with an initial direct focus, Praybe invites the viewer to wander and discover. He often negates the customary desire to paint what is right in front of oneself, choosing instead to look directly down. His still lifes reinvigorate the genre, becoming swaths of landscape seen from above.

What follows is the record of an email conversation I was lucky enough to have with these three very engaging people. I asked some general questions about painting issues that have been on my own mind.

ML: *Question One—Subject Choice. So many representational painters become inarticulate when discussing the intent and effect of what they choose to paint. Many avoid the question all together. Because Modernism has taught us that illustration and specific stories are bad, it is easier to revert to conversations about the painting process that obsesses us. Yet the artist's motivation regarding the psychological or emotional impact, mood or even social context of what they paint often creeps out anyway. In that light why, really, do you paint what you paint? What is the full importance of your subject to you? Does your subject carry any meaning before it is painted, or is it just some random thing that gives you something to do? If it is random why should a viewer be interested in an empty room? A milk jug? Objects strewn on the floor? If it is not random, how do you communicate that meaning to the viewer?*

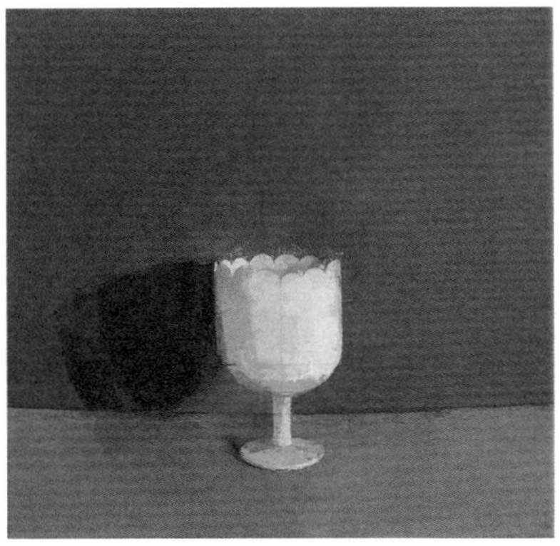

Joe Morzuch *Compot*
2020, oil on canvas on panel,
17 x 17 in.

Joe Morzuch: I grew up in a working-class suburb of Chicago. In my family, we took care of the things we used. We cherished objects that had passed through generations, not for their monetary value, but because of their age, utility, and connection to loved-ones. I was raised Catholic, and as a child was introduced to the idea that objects play essential roles in various rituals, profane and divine alike. Even now, I feel that objects ring with the residue of their use. I have always felt a connection to objects, which is why I use them in my paintings.

I like to think that my studio practice is open enough to allow me to work with any subject that I am interested in at any particular time. What unifies my work, from series to series, is how it's made (working observationally) and the challenge of translating my perceptions into a painting. This is always my first and foremost concern; how a subject will "work" as a painting.

However, I recognize that I am drawn to certain types of objects. My choice of subject matter starts with registering what I see on a daily basis. I always paint the things around me, the things that are familiar to me or objects I use every day. Looking back at older paintings and considering them against my most recent work, the types of objects I paint fall into two distinct categories.

Discarded, or broken objects: For a number of years now, I have been interested in using discarded, fragmented, or otherwise non-functioning objects as subjects for my paintings. There is a degree of abstraction present in this kind of motif. The forms are recognizable, but can be manipulated, altered, or all-out transformed to suit the needs of the painting. I might paint a tire tread that I found on the side of the road for its ability to snake through a composition, or a pile of cinder blocks in an effort to create a kind of architectural space. It is important that these objects no longer function as specific, nameable things, but rather as abstract, sculptural forms that can be arranged for the purpose making a painting.

Single, isolated objects: I recently completed a series of paintings of single, empty containers: a milk carton, paper bag, bowls, and boxes. These are things that connect with a viewer because of their familiarity and everyday use. The containers are painted at life-size and within reach of the viewer. They are empty, but nevertheless hold the space they occupy. Painting, for me, requires a high degree of focus and attention. I am interested in using objects that are so commonplace they often go unnoticed, and presenting them in paintings imbued with this level of focused attention. I am in love with the problem of trying to make arresting, engaging paintings of such unremarkable things.

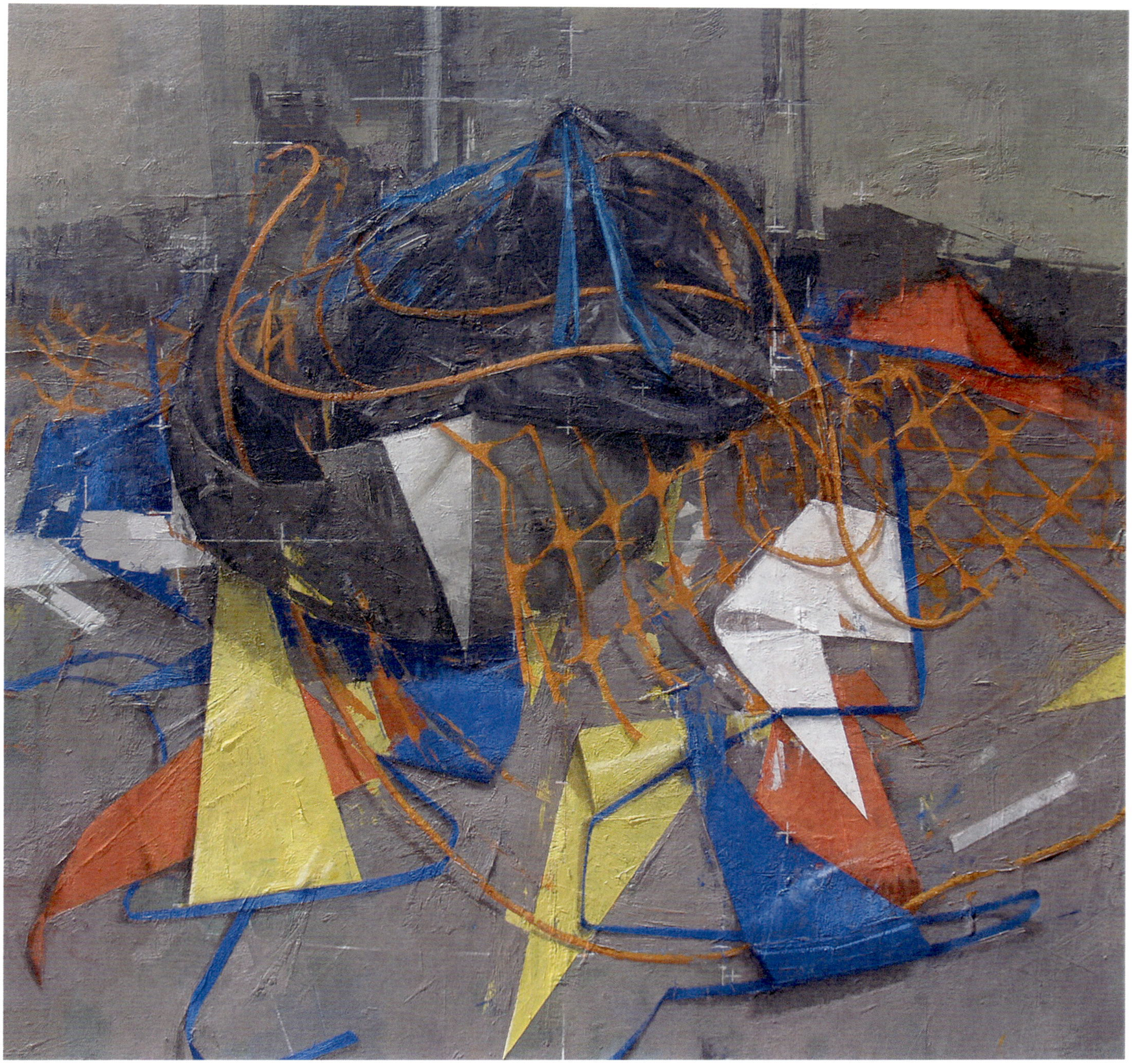

Joe Morzuch *Garbage Bag with Flags and Plastic Netting*
2015-19, oil on canvas on panel, 34 x 35 in.

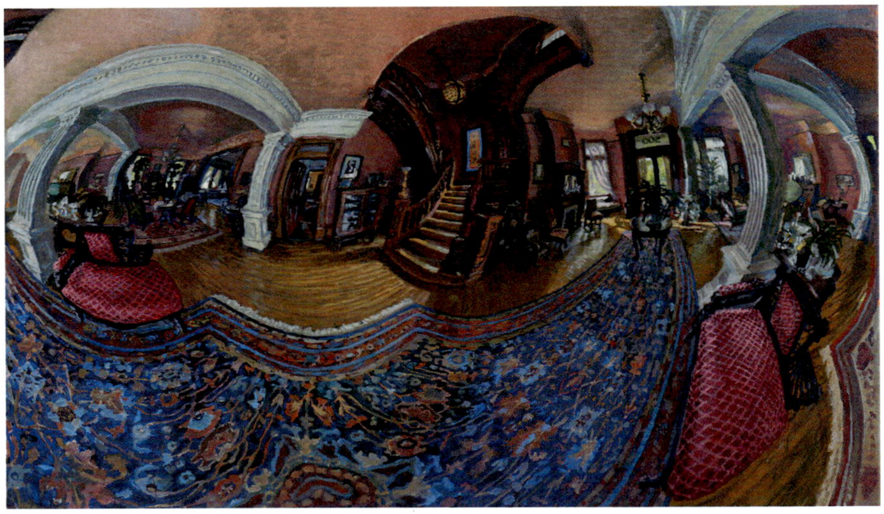

Matthew Lopas *Zoeller House*
2015, oil on canvas, 55 x 95 in.

ML: *Great answer. I felt struck to the core when you talked about your family tradition of cherishing objects. I am in the process of selling my mom's 20-year-old car that she gave to me a while back. Too many mixed feelings. I experience a huge nostalgia and sense of loss when I consider it. I spent a good deal of time in it with my now deceased dad and my presently infirm mom.*

In this context, I think I could invent a story about why you are attracted to "discarded" and "empty" objects beyond your ability to abstract them. What exactly is the "residue of their use"? There might be a sense of loss in something that has been discarded. It once meant something to someone, and now it doesn't. Perhaps the act of painting it gives it life again? Or perhaps the discarded object is something that feels the pain of its neglect and we are led to feel it too? Again, in the context of personal connection to objects through family or religious ritual, one might make of your attraction to empty quotidian objects an embodiment of the need to imbue such things with a soulful significance when, in fact, they are empty and thus have nothing really to offer beyond what we put in. A kind of atheist's relic? No? Yes?

JM: Thank you for this. Yes to everything you mentioned! The residue of use, for me, is very much about recognition and memory. I think we see an object, especially one that has been thrown away or set aside, and are triggered with memories of using it (or something similar). This then connects us to where we were, what we were doing, and who were with while using that object. Objects transport us. They take us out of the here and now. This tension is what I find most interesting about still life. The genre is ultimately about projection and transcendence, but lives so completely in the present moment.

There is a sense of loss in something isolated, empty, or discarded. To engage with an object like this is an affirmation of that thing's continued significance, despite its condition. This is where I feel the objects operate metaphorically, representing the body, a specific individual, or most often myself. Yes, I feel that the act of painting, in this context, is reanimation.

Eleanor Ray: My choice of subjects has become more specific and deliberate in recent years. It's not the painting process that obsesses me, but the experience of looking at art, specific places, nature, changing light. This is one reason I've always had trouble working on site; I'd rather walk around and see more, painting from memories and source images much later. It can be overwhelming how much there is to notice in our surroundings, an inexhaustible variety with elements always in flux. There's a freeing severity to the selectiveness of painting, and its self-containment.

My subjects do have meaning for me, and often for other people, before they're painted, as either well-known art-historical sites or specific landscapes. They're places I've fallen in love with, or where I've felt my perspective shift, places that have surprised me. Painting something also inevitably brings it into a conversation across a group of works, opening different possible routes to follow.

Places where artists worked, sometimes in the distant past, are compelling to me for what they can communicate and for what remains mysterious. I feel a visual and intellectual engagement with the art, its location, and its layers of historical and personal associations. I love the feeling of identification with distant people through encounters with their work, and making paintings is a way of looking at that experience, or answering in conversation. This is just one example; I don't want to make rules for myself about painting only certain things.

There's also a chance element, often out of my control, of what subjects might bring something interesting to the medium of paint, and to the way I paint in particular, which is something that shifts over time. I think there's a mysterious relationship between one's way of working and one's choice of subject, an uncertain cause and effect; this is different than "something random that gives you something to do." Why did Vermeer paint that particular street in Delft, of all the possible similar views he could have chosen? That subject lives on multiple levels—there's the specific place seen in a specific time and light, and also the life of the paint on a surface, the way it builds a space, and the way all the details, window frames and painted walls, vibrate with a tension specific to the medium, and specific to Vermeer. I love the pared-down, almost anonymous quality of Morandi's still lifes, where that life of paint, perception, and abstraction become primary, but that can happen in different ways across the subject-matter spectrum, from Vermeer's ordinary street to the religious scenes of early Renaissance paintings. I love that Philip Guston called the art of the Renaissance "a hidden art," pointing to this other current that's always running alongside the overt imagery. But imagery matters to me too—painting is a way of giving attention to certain moments, and I want to make that count.

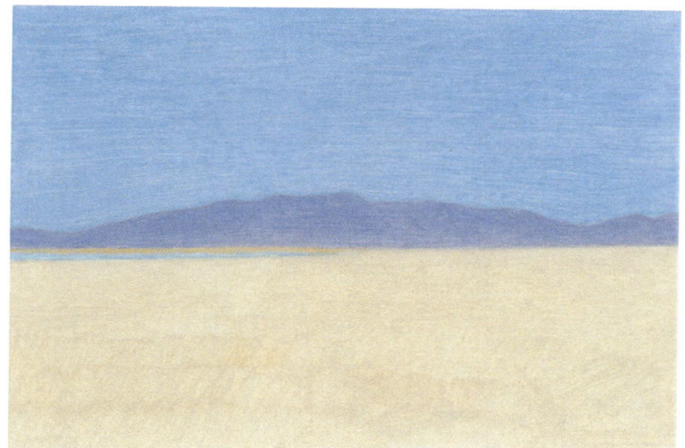

Eleanor Ray *Utah Field*
2019, oil on panel, 5 ½ x 7 ¾ in.

ML: *Eleanor, I saw a piece you did a few years ago of the Basilica di San Francesco in Arezzo where the Piero mural is.*

I instantly recognized it, and felt the presence of the greater, older conversation that you write about. I really enjoyed that you painted the place of the church itself, rather than just the fresco. I myself instantly thought it would be great to set up an easel right there. Here are a couple of shots I took instead. Seeing those frescos in person is such a different experience than seeing a typical reproduction.

With that in mind, there must be some places that immediately strike as something you want to make a painting of. Others you may have to consider for a while. Perhaps only then you reject or paint it. What is that period between experiencing the place and painting it like? What issues do you think about? How, specifically, do you decide?

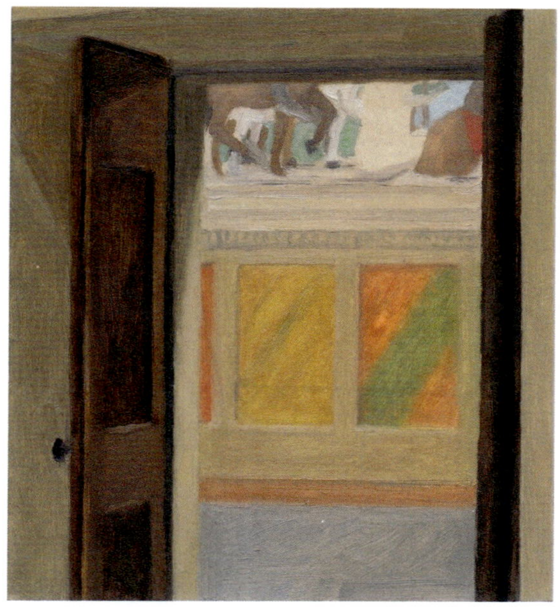

Eleanor Ray *Arezzo*
2018, oil on panel, 6 ¾ x 6 in.

ER: It's interesting that you chose this one to ask about because that space was particularly strange to me. When I first saw it, I'd just been to see the Fra Angelico frescoes at the San Marco monastery in Florence, and the Giotto frescoes in Padua, both of which feel so unified with their surroundings in an exciting way, and which offer amazing first glimpses, like Fra Angelico's large Annunciation rising above you as you come up the stairs. In contrast, the Piero frescoes here felt surprisingly compartmentalized in that back chapel, within this much larger church, with many more things competing for visual attention. The paintings felt like a slower read within the space, sneaking up on you a bit. The glimpses of detail through that doorway

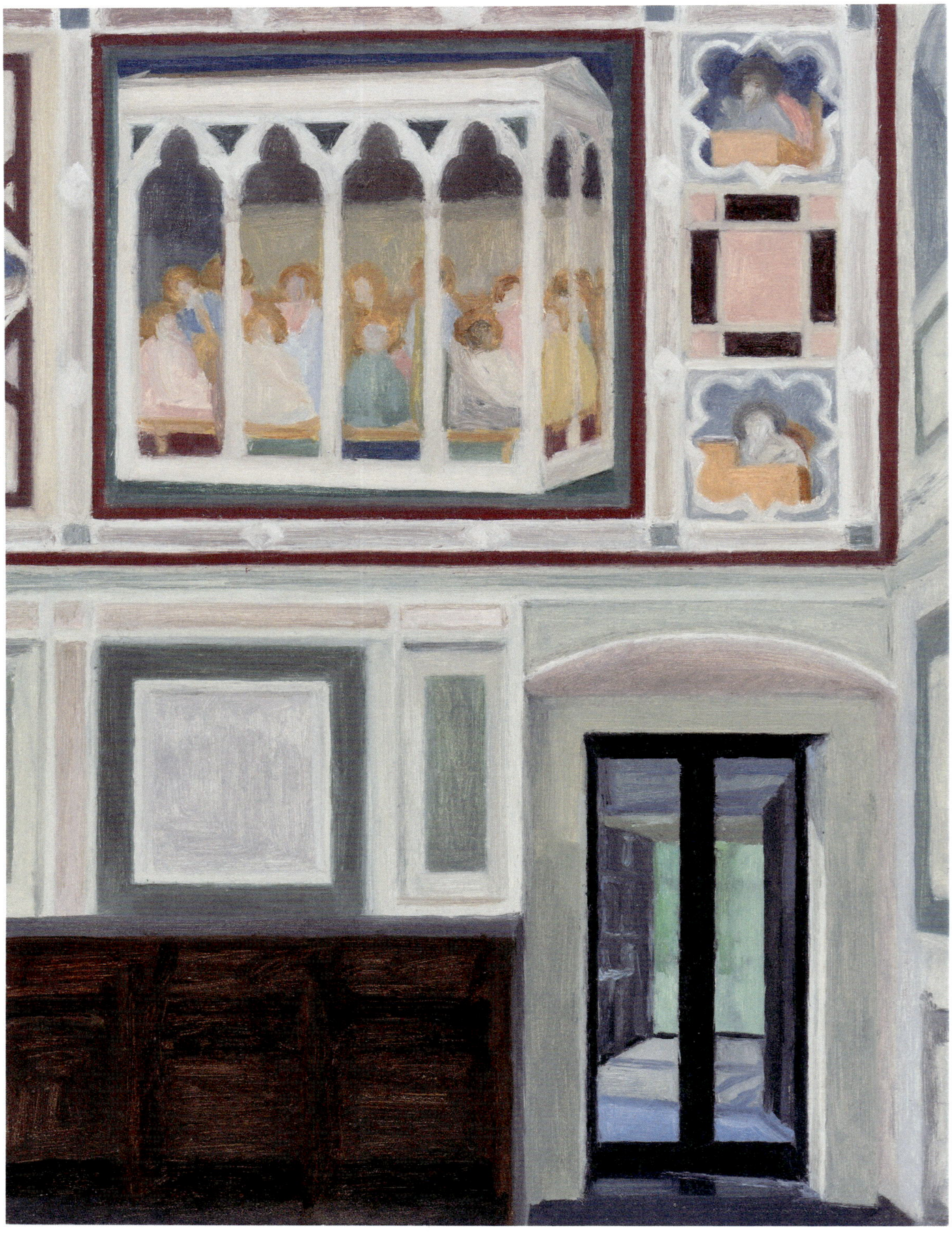

Eleanor Ray *Scrovegni Chapel, Padua*
2018, oil on panel, 8 ½ x 6 ½ in.

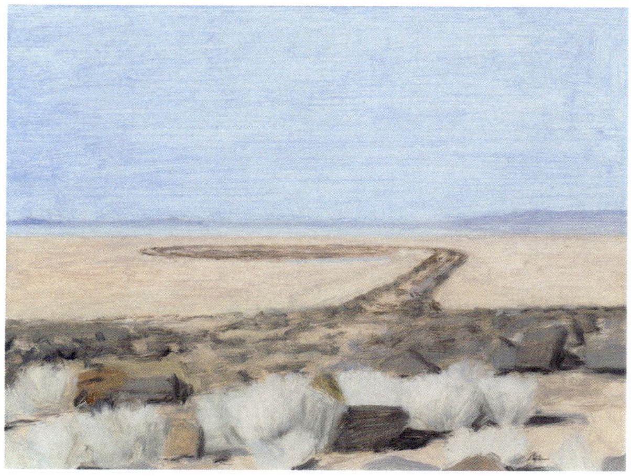

Eleanor Ray *Spiral Jetty*
2017, oil on panel, 6 ¼ x 8 in.

are so different than how you first see only the upper part of the fresco from across the cavernous space of the church, from the front entrance. Then once you're standing in the smaller chapel with the paintings, looking up at them, you're immersed, and the daylight feeling of Piero's color is such a contrast to the warm light bulbs of the contemporary church interior.

I love the experience of walking into a space and seeing a painting for the first time at its real scale, in its environment, whether that environment is disappointing or completely exceeds expectations. The painting is sort of brought down to earth, as something you're sharing space with. Having seen it in reproduction beforehand almost makes it more exciting. That perceptual moment, the surprise of it, is something I'm often wanting to paint. A moment when everyday things, like a doorway, are more charged or focused. I think about analogous moments in different contexts too. I like to wait and be intuitive about the decision of what exactly to paint, letting memory be its own editor. Some things take longer to show up as painting ideas, and I try not to worry about that too much. Certain visual moments retain a kind of clarity, sticking with you over time, or standing out more with distance. I feel really lucky to have been able to visit these sites, to have the memory of moving through those spaces and then stepping back out onto a blindingly sunny square.

ML: *"... letting memory be its own editor." Those are words to live by. That really sums up the creative mind for me.*

Edmond Praybe: I feel like there is a split between representational painters today. One camp is highly motivated by imagery and its impact on the viewer while the second is concerned more with process and formal concerns. The split, of course, is not always harshly pronounced and there are many painters operating in the porous border between the two approaches. I developed as a painter more closely aligned to the second camp, being brought up under the ethos of "it's not what you paint, but how you paint it." However, I do feel that subject matter is an important choice and greatly influences not only how the work looks, but what it ultimately says and how it is perceived by the viewer.

These days I mostly paint still lifes and a majority of them consist of arrangements of objects on the floor of my studio viewed from above. These objects I choose to paint have many origins, but were collected over the years by me and my wife. They've come from other family members or friends, from thrift stores or yard sales, from walks in the woods, pilfered from abandoned structures, or held onto from childhood. As far as I can think I have never bought or scavenged an object with the sole purpose of painting it. The objects that appear in my paintings usually sit dormant somewhere in the house for years before they come into rotation in my work. My still lifes are constructed from objects that I live with which seems important to me somehow. The act of painting them forces me to see beyond their overall impression and to focus on the specific characteristics. This could be a physical quality: color, texture, scale, shape, etc. or something more elusive: the sense of nostalgia, history

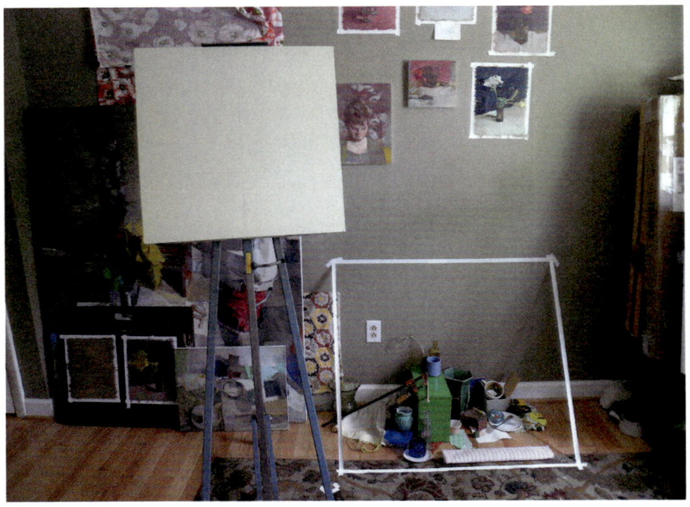

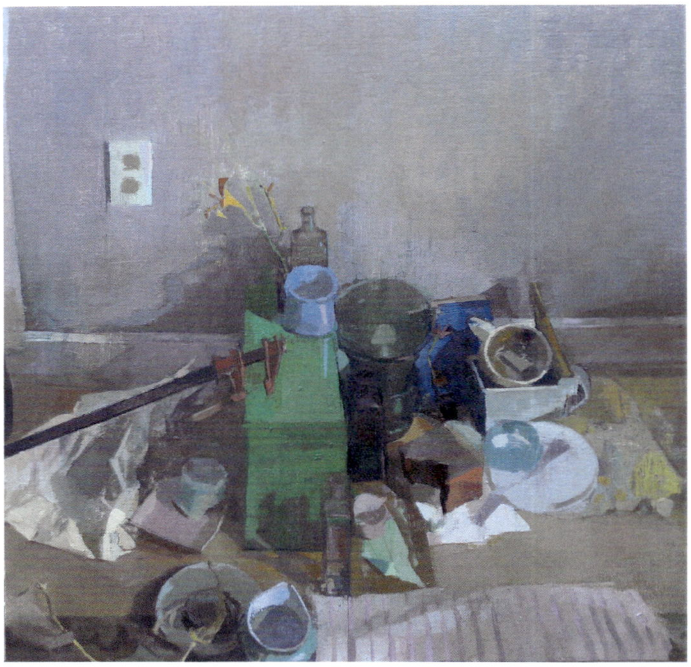

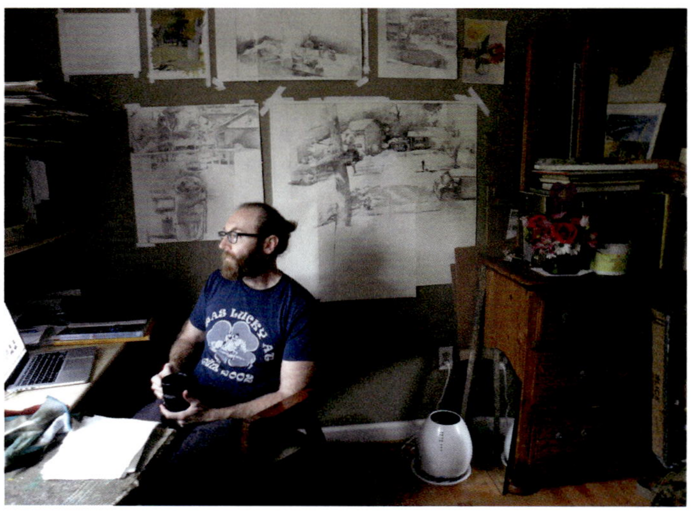

or psychology that a certain object brings to mind. The fact that these things have a life and history beyond me is of interest—where did this particular thing come from, who used it, why and what for? I think of them as people gathered on a city street at any given time, all coming with their own personal history and individual traits, but momentarily sharing the same space. From that point they disperse and regroup in different spaces and points in time. These objects existed beyond my life for a while, came together (in my possession), I painted them and some will probably go on to have a life in the possession of someone after me. There is an ordinariness to many of the individual items, but I'm looking for the unique expression that reveals itself in the relationships between these objects when grouped together.

I tend towards a mix of objects that directly relate to human use: cups, plates, tools, etc. and those that relate to the naturalist's world: bones, plants, shells and insects. I cannot claim that this was initially a purposeful decision. It is an organic reflection of my own life and what I (or simply my eye) is drawn to. As the paintings have developed I am more aware of the balance of man made and natural objects. I need both in the still lifes for them to feel complete, even if it is heavily skewed one way or the other. I enjoy being out in the quiet of the woods somewhere scooping up bits of plants or bones, but I'm also a homebody, surrounded by all the usual everyday domestic items. Both of these personality aspects converge and coexist in the paintings, so that hopefully a sense of tangible individual presence emerges out of these stand-ins for my experiences.

I'm also curious about the tension between a human presence and its absence. The human hand is present not only in the painting itself and the deliberate arrangements, but also in the function of many of the objects. However, figures themselves are mostly absent from the scene, or otherwise cropped and/or fully immersed in the tangle of the arrangement's clutter. The play between objects that could and obviously have been touched and placed by a human hand against the lack or diminishment of a visible figurative form raises questions concerning the value and meaning of the objects themselves. The only answer I have is that they make up a part of my life in small ways—this cup

Top to bottom:

Edmond Praybe studio with composition of *Remembering Remembering*, 2020, oil on linen on panel, 24 x 24 in.
Edmond Praybe in his studio

or plate is from a grandmother's house, these pine cones and buckeyes are from a trip to the Smoky Mountains, this dress of my wife's as a baby and so on.

Aside from my interest in the particular objects that I paint are my reasons for working with still life in terms of process: still life allows me complete control over arrangement, it is an immediately available source, it is a solitary pursuit and the objects are virtually unchanging in nature. I work best directly in front of my subject and begin with a loose direct approach. As the painting starts to develop I find it necessary to manipulate the actual objects in the set-up to achieve any number of outcomes—an exciting composition, better color relationships, more compelling negative spaces, generally keeping the painting open and alive and so on. Still life allows me to push these changes in ways that are harder or impossible in other observational genres like landscape or figure work. Another benefit, in the most practical sense, is that these objects are always available and remain constant—they do not have a schedule like a model or change with the seasons like a landscape. The only variables are light source, my physical relationship to the objects and any projected emotional, psychological or narrative meaning I find in them. Lastly, still life is a solitary genre. It is not dependent on a portrait model nor is there usually any interaction with passers by as with painting outdoors. As much as I enjoy and often work within the other observational motifs, I feel I work best in isolation, just me, the objects, and the painting.

ML: *Question Two—Difficulty and Progress*

The process of painting can be very difficult. When is that most true for you? Please describe the sensation of crisis, struggle, or trouble in a painting. How does it change the image? How do you overcome it? What do you do if you feel you cannot overcome it? When do you abandon an image? Do you carry that emotion over into other things?

Many young artists experience a sense of crisis as they learn to define themselves. But since you've become a mature artist, when do you question your process? Have you ever had a personal or artistic crisis that effected your whole creative self? How did it effect your work and your life? How did you immerse yourself in or find your way out of it? How do you move forward?

ER: I think about these things as they relate to the work on a longer time scale, more than within the making of any one individual painting. I think I'm an outlier in this group here, in not working on single paintings for so long. If a painting doesn't work out, I'll abandon it, and often try a few more approaches to a similar idea or image. But I'm not always deciding whether something worked right away. The painting process itself is more self-contained for me, and I don't want it to reflect a sense of struggle exactly.

As for broader, ongoing questions about process, I think there are two sides to it. On the one hand, there can be a gradual acceptance of the way you operate, the approaches that suit your individual interests, and an abandoning of concerns that feel less close or relevant to you. And, on the other hand, I think making art requires a certain degree of comfort with uncertainty, and with not knowing the path forward for your work all the time. That sort of difficulty never goes away, but my relationship to it fluctuates. I remind myself that this is a rich and interesting problem to have, more a privilege than a struggle. And, the longer you've been working on something, the more memories you have of times you believed you were really stuck but were later able to move forward, so it becomes possible to trust that that will happen again.

I definitely carry the emotions into other things, though! Many of the best things I've read about creative difficulty and a sense of defeat are in Agnes Martin's writings. She's so clear. I can identify with her emphasis on solitude as an opportunity to see your own responses and move forward. And her focus on responsiveness and openness to beauty, as priorities beyond one's individual art making, is inspiring.

ML: *Eleanor, thanks for the response. I actually hesitated to ask you this question because I get a feeling of peace, not struggle, from your paintings. The paint film is thin with a very light touch. There is no angst. The work seems to be about letting a certain space be in you, rather than asserting your presence in the space.*

ER: Thank you Matthew, that was nice to hear! That's how I'd hope the paintings feel; that focused, peaceful state is important to me.

EP: Eleanor, I really enjoyed your response. I particularly like the line about "a gradual acceptance of the way you operate." I remember studying with someone (can't remember who it was, may have even been at NYSS) and they were talking about how you develop the amount and type of facility that you need to say what it is that you need to say. I think that's true, but figuring out what you want to say and figuring out which approaches work best takes time and a lot of failure.

There's something uncomfortable about the level of self-awareness that you need in order to approach the work with a personal honesty, casting aside the irrelevant concerns that may pop up along the way.

JM: Concerning difficulty and progress: painting is hard. That's why I like doing it. I used to be an athlete, and continued half way through college until an injury forced me to quit. Today, I lift weights and run long distance. I think it's about reaching for goals I set for myself, each one a bit farther than the last. And coming to things consistently, with effort. I approach painting the same way. I feel defined by the goals I'm moving towards. They give me purpose. Even if, as with painting, those goals are sometimes abstract or less than concrete. I also just like being busy.

"Crisis" is a strong word for me. My paintings are about a kind of restraint, a subduing of extremes. I'm becoming more comfortable with my relationship to time and the role it plays in the studio. I trust it and know that as long as I keep working I will reach some kind of conclusion (I'm often surprised where a painting ends versus the intentions I had when starting). The conversation between myself and my paintings, the fact that they change so much during the process of their making, and the pure excitement to see "what happens if..?" keeps me going.

Certain difficulties do push back with the paintings. More often than not, they have to do with composition. My compositions are starting to empty out, or rather open up. Reducing a space to its most essential while painting forms that hold that space convincingly, and with resolve, is an interesting problem. I'm thinking a lot now about orchestration and air within the paintings; how the more I take out, the more important what remains becomes. A question I'm currently asking myself is how to pair forethought and planning in the beginning, with openness and improvisation later on, as they relate to space, scale, the panel's four edges, and composition.

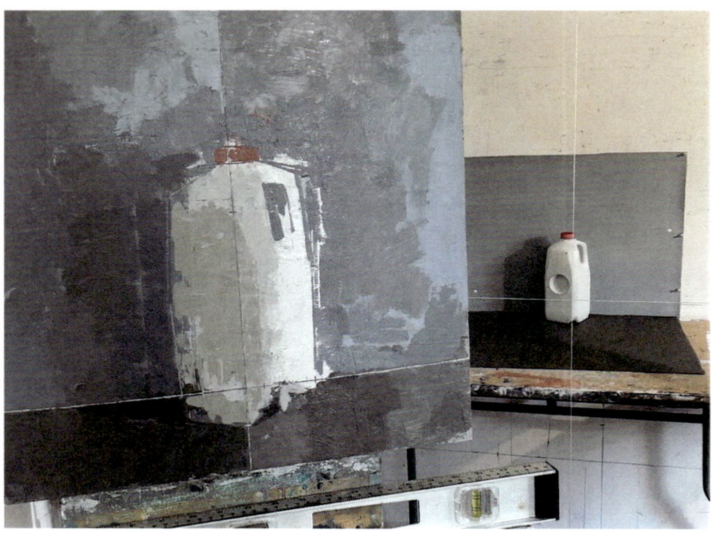

Joe Morzuch's studio with composition *Milk Carton*

I also know a painting isn't going well when I have lost sight of the whole of it. As an observational painter, I use a good deal of measuring. It helps to translate what's in front of me in the motif to the two-dimensional space of the painting. It is an incremental process, and so I often find myself wrapped up in minutiae. I aim to develop a specificity of placement, proportion, and spatial proximity, but to describe these relationships with an abbreviated, painterly touch. When the paintings become stiff or lifeless, or I can feel myself beginning to render, I know it's time to regroup and reassess my priorities. I hardly ever abandon an image, even if what was initially there gets painted over and completely changes. I believe these are all steps along the way in of the evolution of the work. Five years ago, I lost two loved ones within months of each other. It was a time of deep sadness and, despite my best efforts, left me unable to paint for about three years. During that time, I worked in my sketchbooks, journaling at first, and then eventually drawing, (mostly sketches of my dog and people I'd see at the coffee shop). The writing was a way to process thoughts and emotions, and the drawing kept my eye and hand engaged. When I can't paint, for one reason or another, I write and I draw.

ML: *Joe, Thanks for that. I identify with your process in relation to difficulty—setting hard-to-reach goals, strong work ethic, staying in a painting mode rather than rendering frame of mind, focusing on the composition, risking changes as you paint. But I especially relate to what you did when you could not paint. For different reasons, I went through a similar period when I could not paint. My teaching job changed and I lost my subject. The things I painted seemed empty. I spent several years sketching in ink and gouache till I could work in oil again. To the right is my last large painting and then what I did afterwards to start to rebuild myself.*

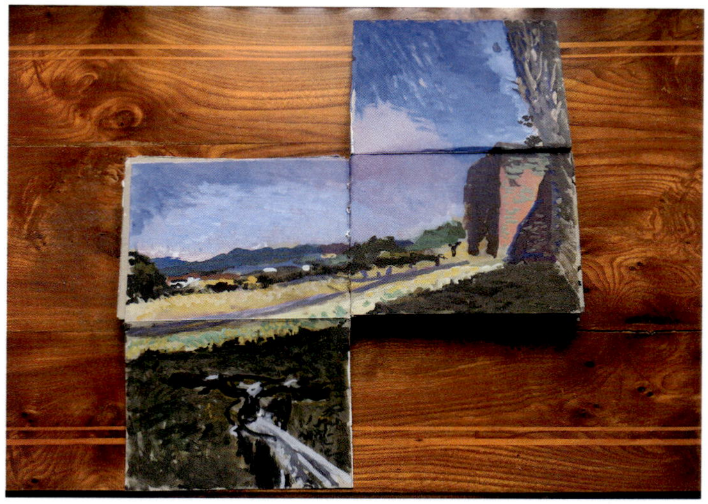

Matthew Lopas
Arezzo Wall
2017, goauche on Strathmore toned paper, 18 x 18 in.

EP: Joe, I found myself shaking my head in agreement with much of what you were saying here. Starting out with the simple statement "Painting is hard" is a great way to remind us that it's not supposed to just happen. I doubt any of us would be interested in continuing to do it if it wasn't difficult or challenging in some way. It would be like playing against an opponent that you beat every time—there's no growth.

I respond pretty strongly to the idea of trusting that you will reach some kind of conclusion if you just keep working. I think you need that sort of mindset to keep pushing through the awkward ugly stages. Taking some paintings to places where you do lose sight of the whole and fall into rendering in the end sometimes makes them stronger—if only because you have to work that much harder to find a way to bring it back to a unified image. The history of that negotiation becomes embedded in the final painting in unexpected ways. I see the beautiful evidence of that process in your paintings.

ER: I relate to what you said, Joe, about balancing planning and openness, too. Maybe a little anxiety in the planning or in between time helps the painting itself have more ease and clarity.

EP: When the image is beginning to take shape and things are falling into place, but the statement doesn't yet feel complete, that is when the painting becomes most difficult. The urge to finish rather than ride the momentum of the painting's true trajectory starts to sneak in and sabotage all the preceding work. The unity breaks and areas start to separate into pockets of rendering—"if I can just paint the glint on that cup or the pattern on that fabric THEN it will all make sense."

The more I paint the more I want out of my paintings. I sometimes think I want them to do or be too many things all at once. That is when it gets tough and I have to decide what is really important in that specific painting. I need to figure out how to best express or highlight that aspect—rather than trying to stuff the whole world of my experiences, training and painting interests into it. The two major concerns that I fall back on to pull a painting out of the mess are color and composition. Is the composition and space arranged in a way that feels purposeful, but not rigid and is the color operating on that line between descriptive and organizational? If I can get the painting to answer yes to both of these questions then most of my other hang-ups tend to resolve themselves or fall away as non-essential. This is a give and take process and happens over several stages. Even when a piece

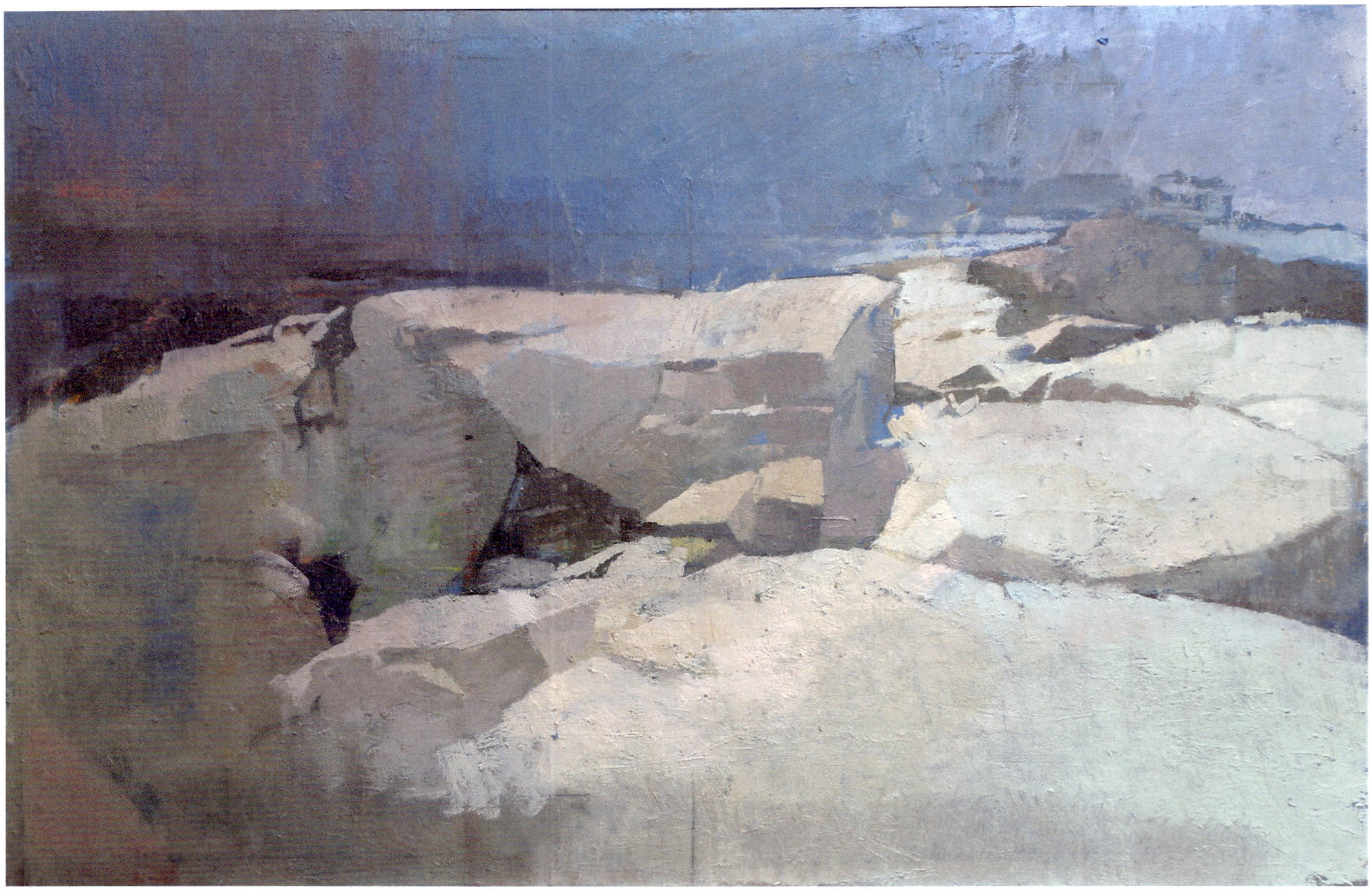

Edmond Praybe *Otter Point*
2019, oil on panel, 24 x 36 in.

is troublesome I rarely abandon a painting on purpose. I always have a couple pieces going at once and some end up getting less attention than others. Maybe eventually I lose interest or circumstances change to where I am not able to continue on it and it remains as-is in the studio or it gets painted over.

Every few years I have a crisis or freak out about my entire body of work. Is this what I should really be doing? Is this all a build up to something else? Am I really making the work that I want to make? Do I have a real vision or statement? These questions usually pop into my head after particularly long stretches of bad and/or uninteresting paintings, but not always. Sometimes I consider these thoughts when things in the studio seem to be going really well. These are hard, painful thoughts and are severely anxiety inducing when I'm in the thick of it. However, coming out of the other side I realize I need to keep questioning what I'm doing otherwise I could just as easily be mindlessly "getting up to make the donuts" everyday as one of my teachers once put it. Unfortunately when a painting is going poorly or when I'm feeling self-conscious about my work as a whole I definitely carry that over into other parts of my life. I'm not great at hiding my emotions when it comes to certain things and my work is one of those things. Taking breaks from painting and doing other activities like hiking, reading or even catching up on busy work helps me to get out of that mood and realize that a bad painting is just a bad painting and it doesn't mean all is lost.

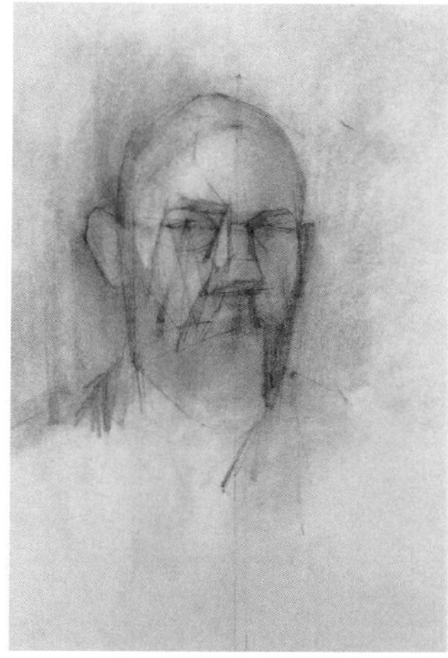

Joe Morzuch *Self Portrait*
2017, charcoal on paper, 24 x 16 in.

Time is the most important factor for figuring out how to overcome a difficult phase. Not looking at a painting for a while and then returning to it when I'm not so close to it is helpful. Doing something drastic like sanding the whole surface, painting out a section with a jarring color or shifting my viewpoint (the actual physical relationship of my head/eyes to what I am painting from) helps me move forward sometime as well. Working in other media helps me get through hard spots in painting. I take breaks from working in oil every so often to just draw or work in watercolor. I feel less anxiety about working in these materials. The self-imposed stress of trying to make the painting be the "ultimate thing" is not present and I can just look, work, respond, mess it up or throw it out. For a big part of a year after grad school I made large semi-abstract paintings on paper in oil or acrylic and house paint. I never showed them to anyone and never photographed them. I needed to follow this tangent in order to keep moving, not necessarily moving forward, but just to make something that I could engage with without knowing what I wanted or where it would end up. Not knowing exactly how a painting will turn out is important for me. Of course I have some idea, but when it goes exactly how I thought it would I feel let down somehow. It becomes execution rather than problem-solving and I think painting is about inventing your own way out of a problem.

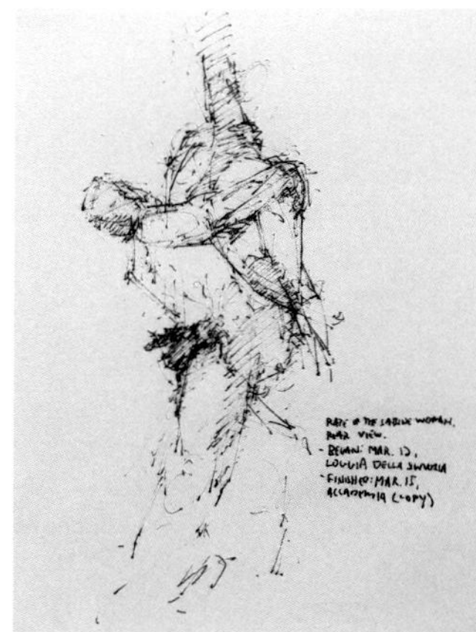

Joe Morzuch *Sketchbook Page, Florence*
2017, ballpoint on paper, 12 x 9 in.

ML: *I've been asking you all questions that I myself think about. So I can't help but take a stab at this one myself. My own relationship with difficulty in painting has changed a lot recently. I used to scrape and repaint often. I now see that as a function of my personal anxiety and lack of skill. I questioned what and why I painted. At one point, my painterly dissatisfaction led me to change my direction and lose a relationship with a very good gallery. There were also many paintings where I did not understand the tension between conventional and curvilinear perspective in a rectilinear format. This created huge difficulty as I turned my head and painted. These paintings were daunting adventures in unlearning preconceptions and discovering new truths. But this led to knowledge. I currently run into difficulty when my idea of what I want to paint will not conform with my imagined image. And given the strangeness of curvilinear space, one cannot just hold up a viewfinder and see how things might look in a rectangle. I threw out a painting two months ago because of that. I had such high hopes for it! But if the painting becomes a through line from intent*

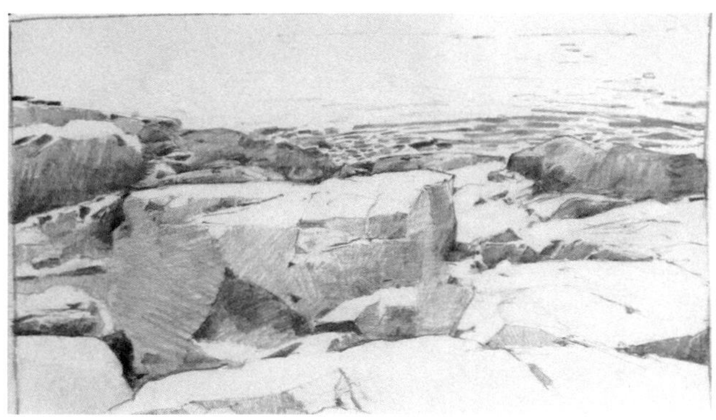

Edmond Praybe *Maine Drawing*
2019, pencil, 9 x 12 in.

to completion, when it only becomes more complex and expansive as I work, the process actually becomes easier and easier. I then experience an extended period of bliss. I walk around with butterflies of joy.

EP: Matthew, It's great to hear your response to this question. This idea of difficulty is such a complicated, troubling and very personal thing. I appreciate everyone sharing so openly their struggles and ideas on the topic.

The fact that you needed to change direction in your work to such a degree that you lost a relationship with a good gallery is very telling—not everyone would be able/willing to take that leap! But with the alternative being making work that is frustrating and dissatisfying only for the sake of production and exhibition, the choice to change clearly seems necessary for growth (and sanity!). What I appreciate about your work is how bizarre, but overwhelmingly felt and experienced the spaces appear. It's a true painting kind of space. I pick up on your overarching interest in curvilinear space and perspective from work to work, but each piece feels unique and arrived at without the appearance of a set system at play. Idea, perception and execution are all working together towards an image.

ML: *Thanks, Edmond! Question Three—Rejected Processes and Red Lines. Is there an approach or process that you dedicated yourself to earlier in your career that you either now completely reject or have just left behind? How and why did that happen? Are there any red lines in your current processes that might be easy to cross, but that you will not? Why?*

EP: There are not many things that I won't do if I think it could make a painting work or help it along. Although I mostly work directly from life, I still occasionally use photo, drawing and imaginary/memory sources. I'm not a purist about my approach. My preference for direct observation has mostly to do with my engagement level in the resulting work, not necessarily about a certain stance on process. I have difficulty making a painting feel whole when removed from observation. They become disjointed or flat (in feeling/conviction mostly as opposed to pictorially).

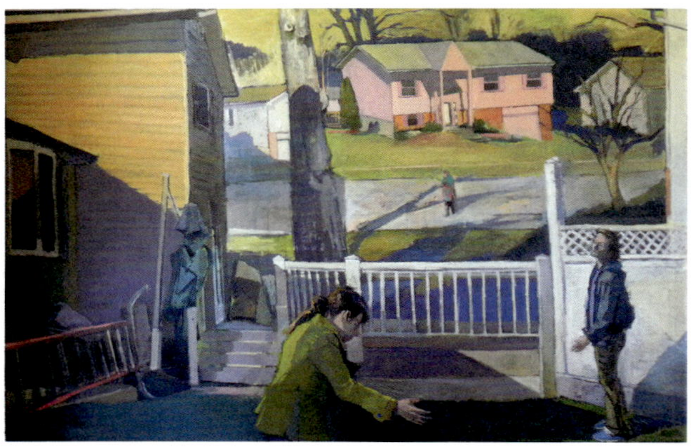

Edmond Praybe
Autumn Dream
2013, oil on canvas, 48 x 72 in.

I used to make larger paintings built from a combination of drawings and smaller painting studies. I was very interested in the classical approach to constructing a painting from separate sources. I liked that I could create a brand new scene from various parts and ideas in my studio, but one that somehow felt linked to reality. This way of working has more or less fallen off.

I have made paintings based on drawing sources as recently as earlier this year, but the goal was not the same. It was a landscape based on travel drawings from Maine. The coastline there has become such a rich and loaded motif for painters (Porter, Wyeth, Hartley, Hopper, Marin...). I knew that I would not be able to make the paintings I would like to while actually onsite. The time restrictions and access to certain views were prohibitive, so I made sketchbook drawings in the landscape. I didn't make them as sources for painting, but when looking back they seemed like perfect starting points. Having the drawing/structure worked out allowed me to focus on painting handling and color in a way internal to the picture, which was exciting for me. It was less about constructing an image and more about pushing the memory of a place and trying to develop it more fully from a distance—what falls away, what stays and what morphs through memory.

As for another wayward practice: For several years I painted almost exclusively with a palette knife, even on pretty large surfaces. I wanted the density and clarity of color that can only come from opaquely applied paint using the knife. The limitations of this method have a way of helping you edit out certain non-essential things as well. I worked this way for a good three years or so and figured out some valuable things about building planar form and color relationships. I gradually reintroduced brushes and now paint mostly with them and very little palette knife. I have a better appreciation of the versatility of the mark I can get with them.

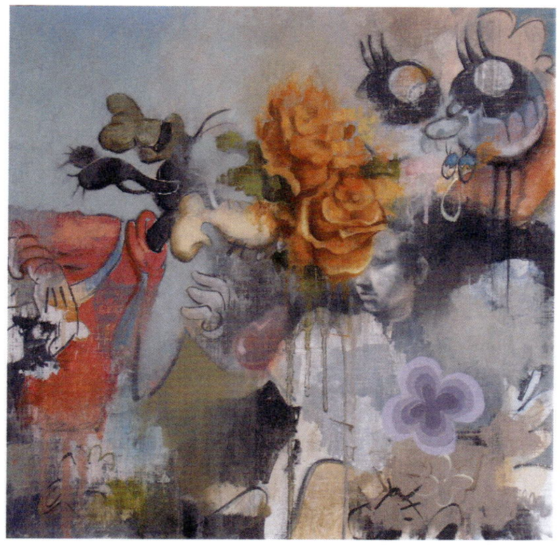

Joe Morzuch *Blossom*
2010, oil on canvas on panel, 20 x 20 in.

JM: For most of my time as a painter, I've worked observationally. It began in college, where I was introduced to the challenge of working from life and the potential to make really diverse work grounded in looking. That choice has never been about limiting my practice. It's really about seeing all the different possibilities within a bracketed, defined means of working.

I don't believe in artists limiting themselves. I have moved through bodies of work that for one reason or another failed to keep my interest. I love print-making, and that process-heavy, dirty kind of work still informs my painting and drawing. For a few years after graduate school I made strange pastiche paintings based on collages of various sources from comic book imagery to Baroque "old master" paintings. I've made paintings that were completely abstract and nonobjective. Even though I moved through and ultimately abandoned these series, they have all affected what I'm doing today. One example being the idea that multiple spaces can exist, or rather be pictured within the unified space of a single painting. I tend to lose interest in a body of work when I start making the same decisions over and over again. That's why I never tire of working from direct observation. One is always presented with new, unforeseen problems, and the process is malleable enough to keep me invested. I'm at a point now where each painting is basically a response to the one that preceded it. That's the thread that connects each individual work. To facilitate this, I need to be open to any kind of possibility creeping into the studio, while keeping some parts of my practice consistent. Often times it's only after making a group of paintings that I realize what I was painting about in the first place; their reason and meaning becoming clear after the fact. Working from life provides a constant that allows for variation elsewhere.

I admire artists who freely shift processes, media, and materials. Some of my favorites include Louise Bourgeois, Janine Antoni, and Kiki Smith. I see their work as an extraordinary marriage of form and content. The scope of their ideas, which are so perfectly tied to the materials they employ, require exploration across disciplines. On the other hand, I think of Morandi, working away in a small bedroom year after year, making paintings of the same handful of bottles and boxes. There is something about that slow evolution that is a bit more my speed. Plus, I problem-solve as a painter. I'm confident that if that were to change I would have no issue adopting alternative materials/ processes.

ER: I don't think I've strongly rejected earlier ways of working as much as slowly shifted. I also started out painting observationally, working from still life set-ups and models in college and at the beginning of grad school. That experience was really formative for me in learning about color, temperature, building a space, relationships across a painting, close looking... all things that are still with me.

In college I studied photography too, working with different kinds of cameras and printing. I'd always been interested in photography, and made pinhole cameras as a kid, printing little photos in an improvised darkroom at home. After painting mostly from observation for four or five years, I started to feel limited in terms of what I could paint working that way, and my own photographs were a natural resource for working more indirectly.

I suppose one informal rule I have is painting only places where I've been, using my own source material, rather than something found, since I'm working with particular memories and a sense of the surrounding context.

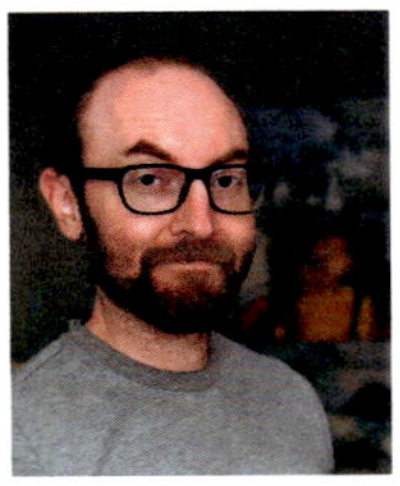

Edmond Praybe received his BFA from Maryland Institute, College of Art and MFA from the New York Studio School. His work has been shown in venues across the U.S. including Manifest Gallery in Cincinnati, OH, Stephen F. Austin State University in Nacogdoches, TX, The University of Mary Washington in Fredericksburg, VA, Prince Street and Bowery Galleries in New York City and The Mitchell Gallery at St. John's College in Annapolis, MD. Notable art critics Jed Pearl and David Cohen have included Praybe's work in juried exhibitions. He has been the recipient of the Hohenberg Travel Grant and the artist-in-residence at Catoctin Mountain Park. Edmond teaches classes and workshops, and lectures regularly at institutions including Anne Arundel Community College, New York Studio School and Maryland Hall for the Creative Arts. He is currently represented by Y Art in Baltimore and First Street Gallery in New York City. Edmond lives and paints just outside of Annapolis, Maryland with his wife and two cats.

www.zeuxis.us/praybe
www.edmondpraybe.com

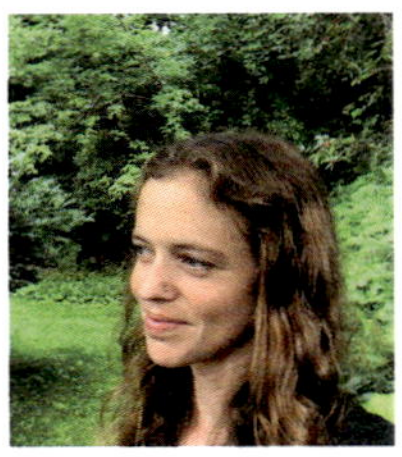

Eleanor Ray makes small-scale paintings of encounters with specific places, including well-known or art-historically significant sites, and others more anonymous. She received her BA in English and Art & the History of Art from Amherst College, and her MFA in Painting from the New York Studio School. Her work is represented by Nicelle Beauchene Gallery in New York, and has been supported by recent residencies at Steep Rock, The Montello Foundation, and Yaddo. Her critical writing has appeared in The Brooklyn Rail.

www.eleanorkray.com

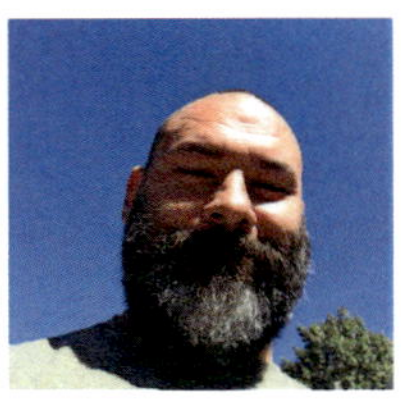

Joe Morzuch is an observational painter currently residing in Starkville, MS. In addition to his studio work, he is an Assistant Professor at Mississippi State University where he teaches courses in foundations, painting, and drawing. In 2006 he received his MFA from Southern Illinois University Carbondale. He has taught at the college level for the past 15 years and actively exhibits his work nationwide.

www.zeuxis.us/morzuch
www.joemorzuch.com

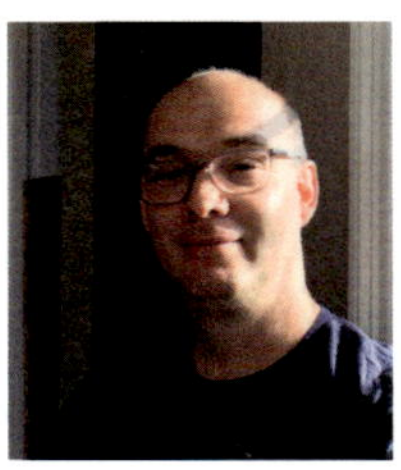

Matthew Lopas has been painting interiors lit by warm light for nearly 25 years. For him interiors suggest the lives that people them. He paints "global panoramas"—representing everything that can be seen from a single point in space. Lopas paints homes that have a sense of memory, loss, and rebirth. Lopas was born in 1965 in Chicago. He has shown in New York, California, Chicago, Connecticut, Atlanta, Cardiff, and Little Rock. He is represented in Little Rock by Boswell Mourot Fine Art. Lopas has a BA in Chinese Studies from the University of Michigan, a BFA from the School of the Art Institute in Chicago, and an MFA from Yale. Lopas resides in Conway, Arkansas, and is a Professor of Art at Hendrix College. He is married to Susan Clark and has three children.

www.instagram.com/matlopas/
www.facebook.com/Painting360

Two Painters and a City

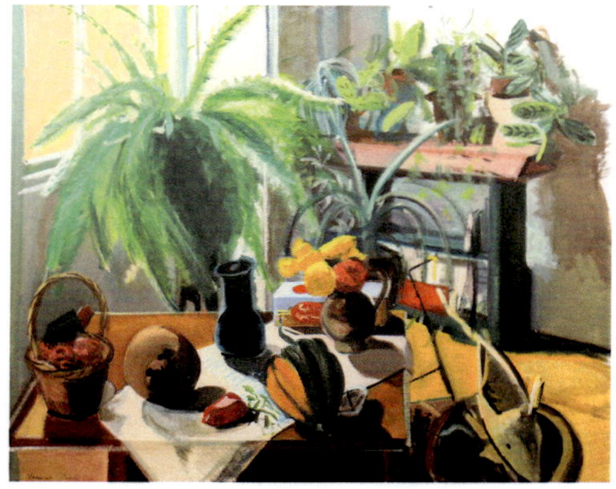

Meredith Fife Day interviews

Temma Bell and Phyllis Floyd

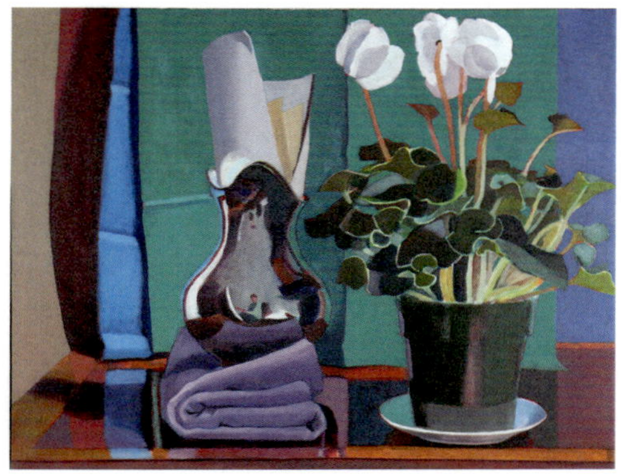

Temma Bell *Fern Basket and Strawfish*, c. 1970, oil on canvas, 33 x 48 in.
Phyllis FLoyd *Cyclaman and Pitcher*, 1999, oil on linen, 20 x 30 in.

Meredith Fife Day: *The two painters in this conversation are Zeuxis founder Phyllis Floyd and longtime member Temma Bell. The city is, of course, New York. Its place as destination and point of departure for artists is legend. As headquarters for the 26-year-old Zeuxis association of artists, the city figures prominently in the studio and exhibition lives of many of its members. When I approached Phyllis about including the City of New York as a part of our conversation, she answered with her natural candor, "I like thinking about New York."*

Having read Temma Bell's bio, along with being familiar with—and admiring—her parents' work, I suspected painting and her New York connections were at the center of a peripatetic life. Temma's long affiliation with Bowery Gallery was another clue. Like Phyllis, Temma was unaffected and open about her life and how New York figures into it.

The warm, personal stories of Phyllis and Temma were a refreshing antidote to wall text and resumes in laying the groundwork for my questions. They added genuine delight to the honor of learning about these two accomplished painters. What I thought would be an interview easily turned into conversation and anecdotal recall. Early on I had learned that neither artist was interested in talking about her paintings. Rather, they wanted to explain what led them to paint in the first place. When and where did it all begin? How did they become painters?

MD: *If you were to write a bio of your linear personal history as a painter in New York City, where would you begin? How would you describe your relationship with the city, and how did that fit with your expectations? What choices did you make to live, paint and exhibit here, and what challenges, if any, came with those choices?*

Phyllis Floyd: Meredith, I'm glad you asked about New York.

On a morning in August 1950, my mother drove me to the Pasadena train station where I boarded the El Capitan bound for Chicago. This was not going to be one of those prosaic trips that were habitual in our family—one that took us to visit my grandmother or an aunt no farther east than the Rocky Mountains. No, I was on my way to New York and to Paris.

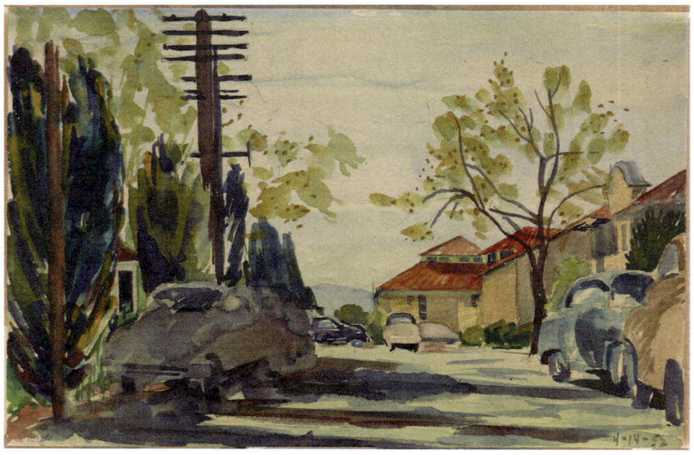

Phyllis Floyd *Stanford University*
1952, watercolor on paper, 14 x 21 in.

My memory of the three-day train ride has blurred except for the glorious morning we rolled along parallel to the Hudson River and entered Grand Central Station. My uncle met me, put me up, and did his best to "show me the town." Every meal took place in a different restaurant offering native cuisine from countries of the world. Thus we had a German lunch in Yorkville and a Chinese one in Chinatown, but the most exotic was at Katz Delicatessen—crowded and noisy. In the evenings I was treated to theatrical performances on Broadway. After a week, it was time to sail, and my uncle gave me a tour of New York Harbor as we headed for the dock of the Nieuw Amsterdam in Hoboken.

One note on the year in Paris: Back in California a friend kindly trying to save me pain advised, "If you think everything on your trip will be out of this world, you're going to be sadly disappointed." She was 180 degrees wrong.

A year later I returned to one of those hot New York summers and sadly to California and my last year of college. I had not many practical ideas for the future, but an offer of a job in New York brought me to a quick decision. In January 1953 I flew to the city leaving behind a suburban life—one that featured barbeques, discussions about sports, and two alcoholic parents. As I lay sleepless on my last night in California, I took stock of all that awaited me. I said to myself that I'd become a painter and that I'd marry a painter. No, I must choose a writer instead because two painters might unhappily compete with each other.

New York was Fred Astaire—glamorous and impressive. It offered anything I wanted all within walking distance. Purposeful people darted by, many well turned out. There were artists of all sorts, and even the longed-for writer turned up. From him I began to see how to manage a future as artist with single-minded focus. He was a mentor. In those years I was interested in my clothing and my social life, and not yet committed to painting. I told everyone I knew about my new life and urged them to move to this exciting city. I must have sounded like a representative from the Chamber of Commerce because one of them said, "You know not everyone likes what you like."

The many people I met had one thing in common—they all talked about housing. No sooner had I made a friend than he or she moved away because they couldn't afford a nice apartment. Somehow, I escaped housing woes. First I lived with two friends in a seedy apartment on the Lower East Side, then in a dreamy studio apartment in a brownstone on West 11th Street—rent was $85/month.

The writer and I moved to Long Island in 1960. There we had two daughters and a life again in the suburbs. After a few years, the writer left. I earned an MFA and had a stint at teaching in a college nearby. But I was a

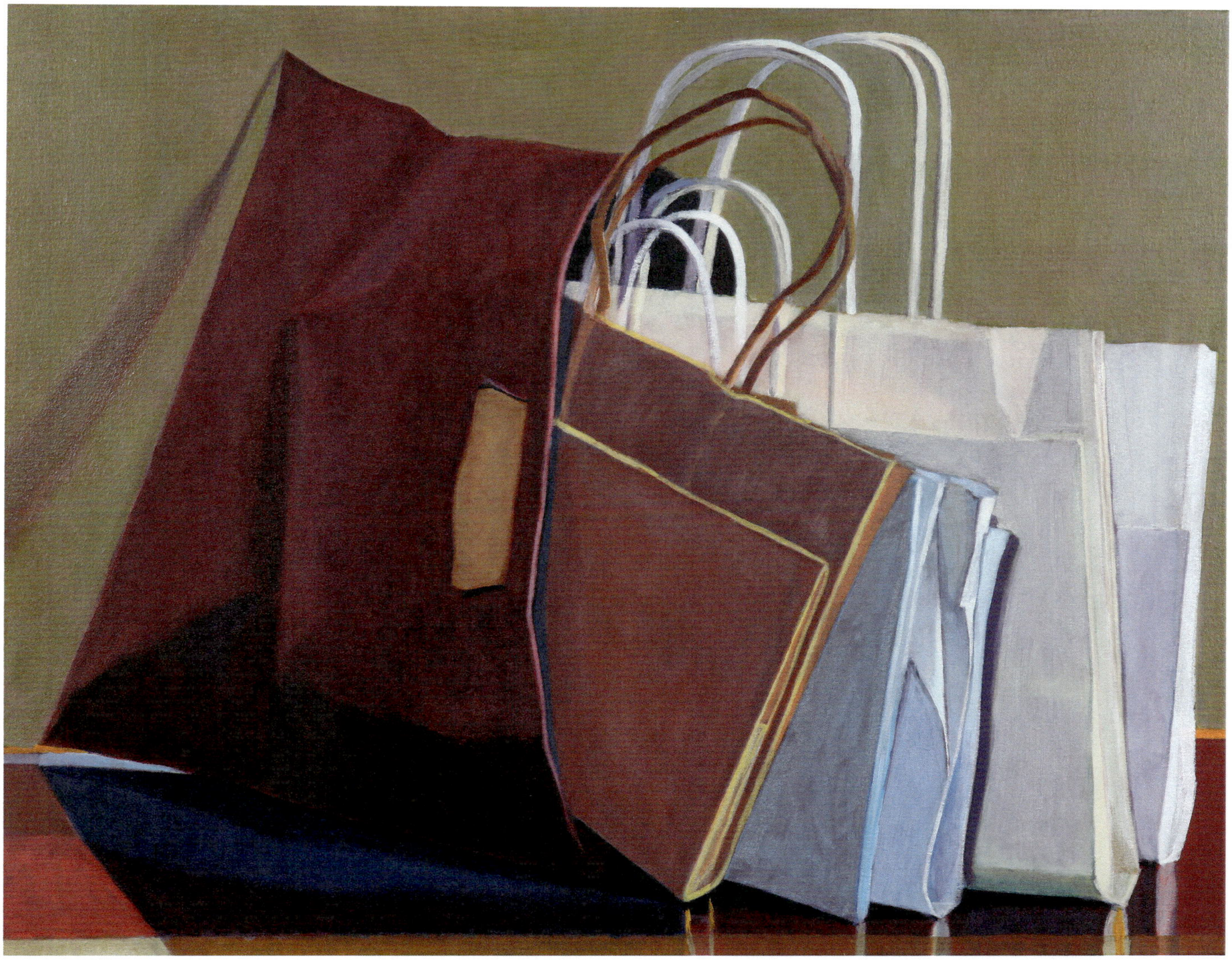

Phyllis Floyd *An Emanation*
2005, oil on linen, 24 x 28 in.

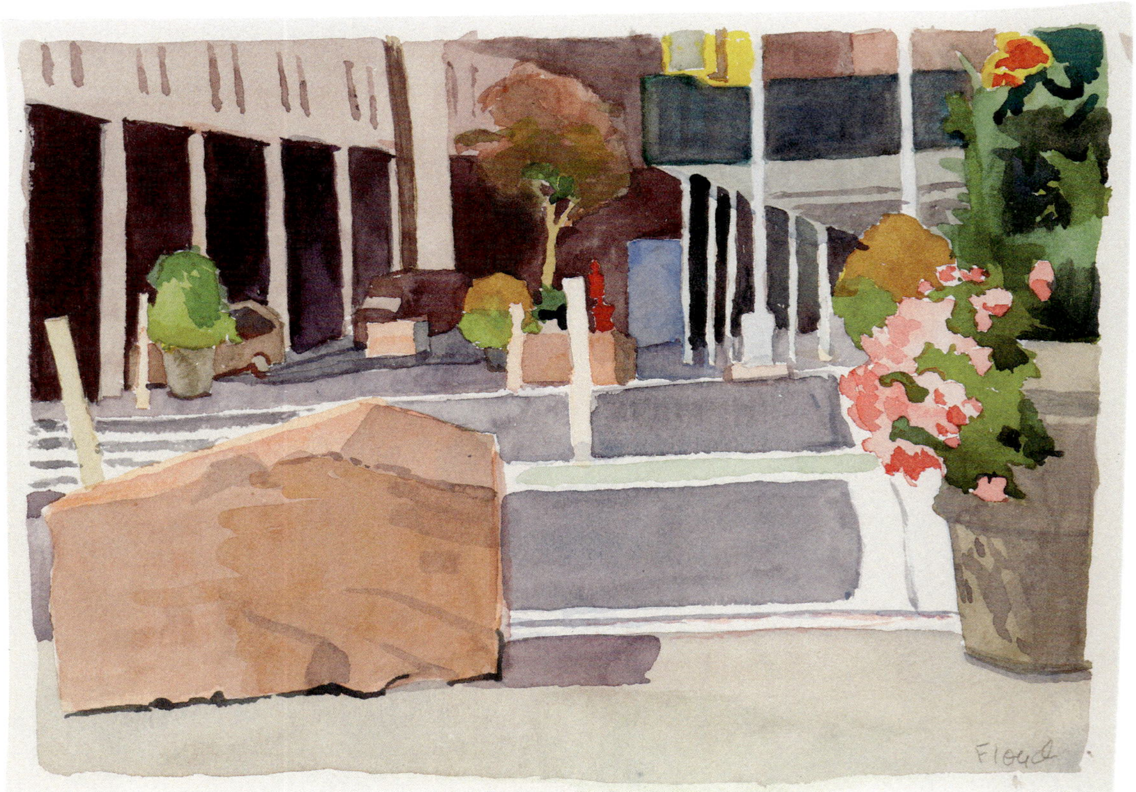

Phyllis Floyd *Flatiron #25*
2013, watercolor on paper, 10 x 14 in.

fish out of water, and in 1976 the three of us moved back to the city where I scrounged around for a way to make a living. Those were hard years.

They were lightened however by luck once again with housing. We moved into a rent-stabilized loft, and I have remained here all these years. I have ample space in which to paint, although often I go outdoors to do watercolors. In earlier years, my hangouts were Madison Square Park and Bryant Park. This summer I did a series of watercolors in the Flatiron district.

We here are all spoiled by the numerous galleries and museums offering first-rate exhibitions. Living in New York, I've been able to manage Zeuxis, an association of still life painters. Work for Zeuxis has occupied much of my time since 1995, and I'm proud of the many artists whose paintings we've been able to show both in New York and around the country.

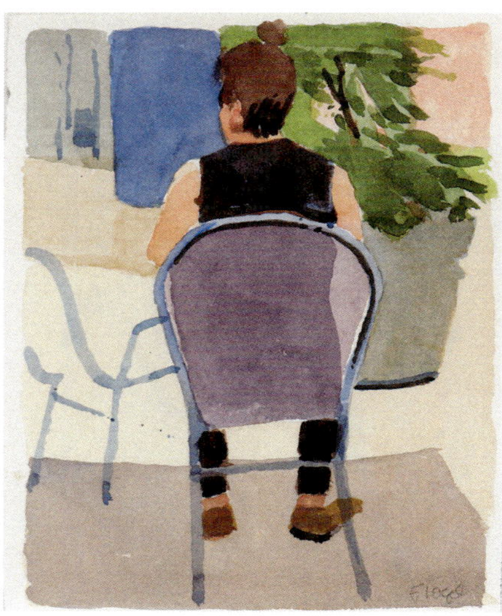

Phyllis Floyd *Flatiron #8*
2020, watercolor on paper, 9 x 12 in.

Temma Bell: I was made, I think, and born in New York City. My parents had met in New York. My mother, who had come from Iceland to study in New York City ended up studying with Hans Hoffman. My father, also a painter, met my mother at a party hosted by painter and fellow student Nell Blaine.

From 1945 on I was part of their world... painting, painting, painting. We first lived on Hudson Street in a building where the French painter Jean Hélion had a studio. My father had managed to get an apartment there in return for being a janitor so that he could visit Hélion's studio. Hélion was very impressed with how much New York janitors knew about painting. After that we went to visit my mother's family in Reykjavík.

We came back, I think in 1948 and moved to Bathgate Avenue in the Bronx. There my parents both painted, and they painted me as well. When I was four or five we went back to Iceland and then on to Paris, more specifically Montreuil. There I learned to read.

After that year we went back to my grandmother's in Reykjavik, where I briefly went to the school that my mother had attended. Then it was back to New York City.

My parents found accommodations at an NYU fraternity as house mother and father. In 1954, my father's father bought an old boarding house to house his son and daughter and their families, not very far from where I was born in the New York Infirmary for Women and Children on 15th Street. We lived in the bottom while my parents were fixing up the rest of the house.

I had a room with a tangerine floor. This was my first room—I had usually slept in my father's studio. From then on my parents had a studio they shared. My aunt and her family lived downstairs.

The house was definitely a work place. Both my parents were very private, and spent their days painting. I was a part of that. My mother would do housework when my father was teaching, so as not to disrupt their usual painting routine.

When I was in eighth grade I applied to the High School of Music and Art. My father helped me put my portfolio together. I was doing a self-portrait in charcoal and he came to give me a crit. He took the piece of charcoal and drew a straight line for the mouth. I was quite offended and rather angry that he drew on my work. He must have thought I was being too prissy or something. This is the only time I remember his giving me a crit without my asking for it. Otherwise my parents were supportive and left me alone unless I asked.

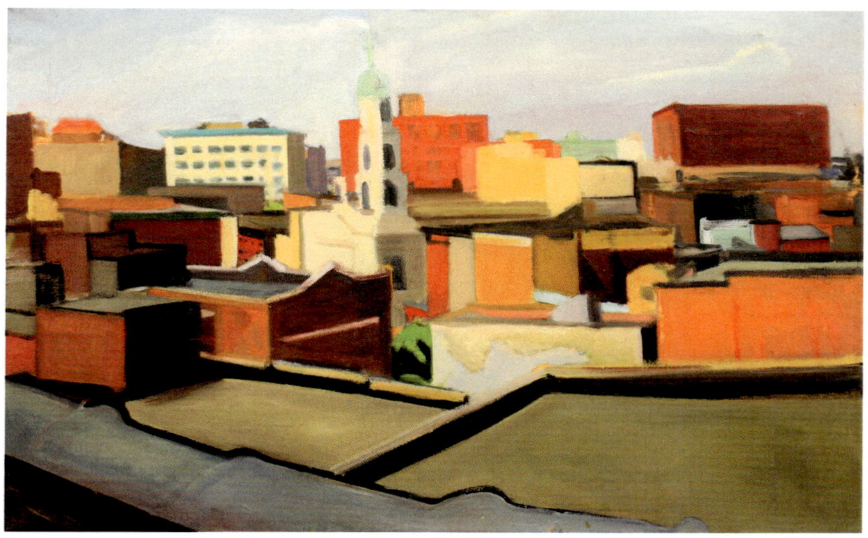

Temma Bell *Bleecker Street Rooftops*
c. 1972, oil on canvas, 23 x 36 in.

When I was a young child, my parents would take me with them to museums and galleries. To me they were all just paintings but I remember how impressed I was with my father—he knew all the different artists. I was constantly surrounded by art.

In 1962 I spent the summer in Aspen where my father was teaching and I painted the landscape. Then that fall we went to Paris, where I was a senior at the American School of Paris. The next summer I spent in Iceland, and then entered Boston University as a freshman, thinking I would study French Lit. However, the summer after that my father was teaching at the Yale Summer School and I painted there.

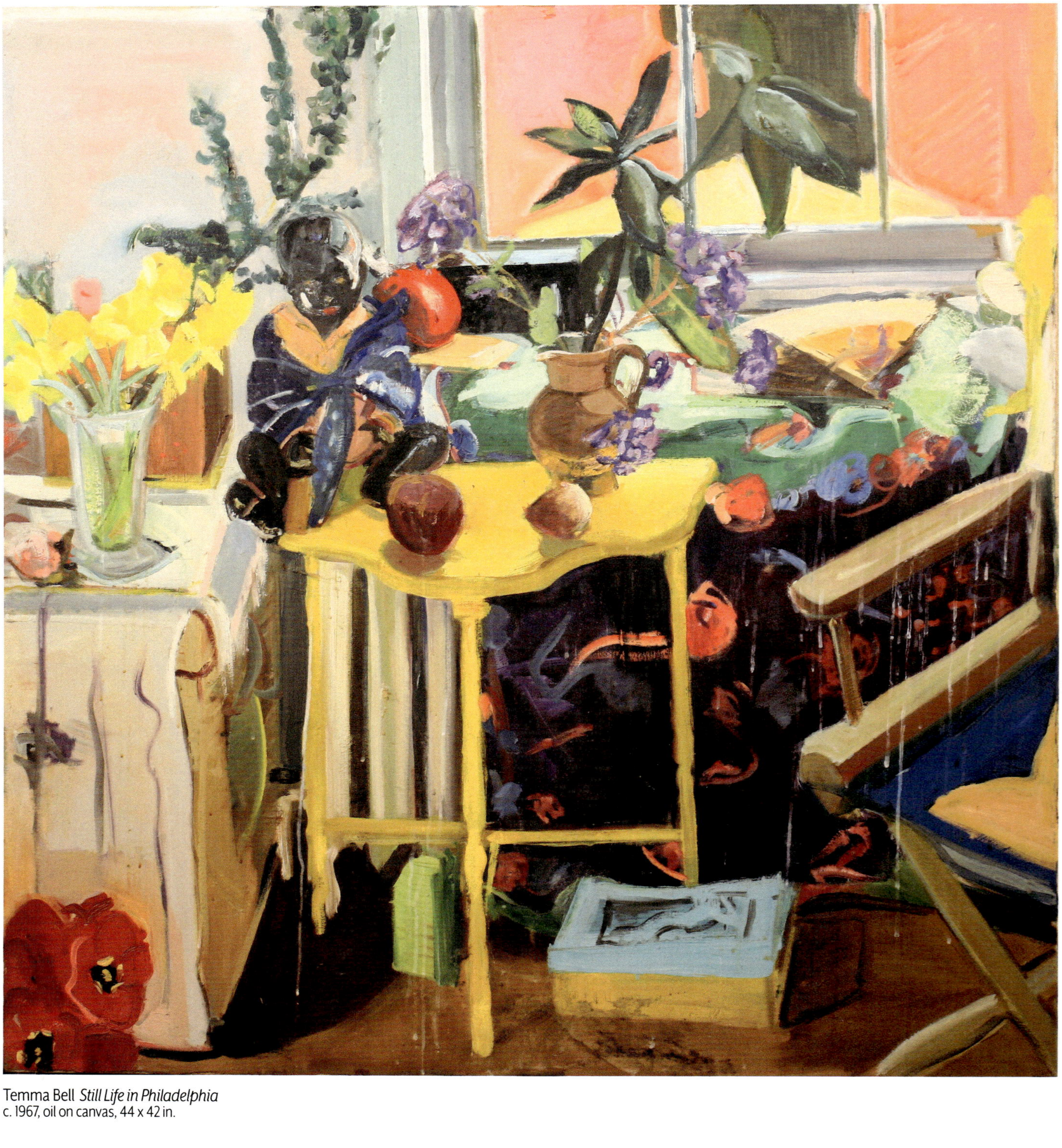

Temma Bell *Still Life in Philadelphia*
c. 1967, oil on canvas, 44 x 42 in.

Then I decided I did want to paint, and was able to follow my parents to Bloomington, Indiana, where my father was teaching. After that I transferred to Philadelphia College of Art. That summer I went to Iceland and then to Paris where I shared an apartment with two painters, Sue Daykin and Suzanne Gilliard. We all had a room to paint in and took trips to various museums in Europe. I did come back to Philly and got my degree. Then I went back home to New York City, where I was able to paint in the house where we all had a place to paint.

MD: *Temma, "I was a part of their world... Painting, painting, painting... I went back home to New York City, where I was able to paint in the house where we all had a place to paint." Because you are a native of NYC and were raised by two parents who painted there and everywhere they traveled, can you talk about how, along with your parents, the City of New York made it likely that you would "paint, paint, paint"—anywhere you went?*

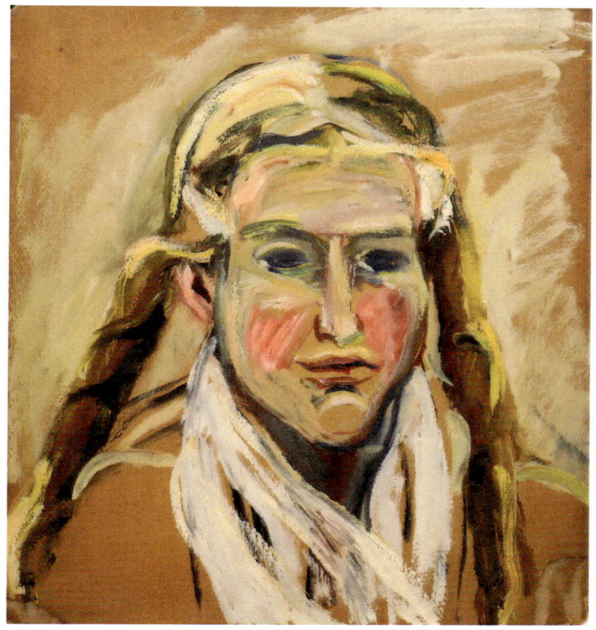

Louisa Mattiasdottir *Temma with Braids*
c. 1954, oil on paper, 17 x 16 in.

TB: My father taught at the New York Studio School and after I graduated from PCA in 1964, and returned to the city, I became friends with some of the students there and would sometimes go to lectures, however I must admit I preferred going to museums and galleries and painting to attending lectures. I have never felt compelled to articulate. I would rather paint.

In 1977, my husband and I married in Reykjavik, where we had met. I continued going back and forth to New York and had some shows at the Bowery Gallery. We moved back to the states after having lived in Reykjavik for five years and where two of our four daughters were born.

From 1982-96, we lived in Warwick, NY, about an hour-and-a-half from Chelsea. Now we live in Delhi, NY, quite a bit farther upstate, about a three-hour drive.

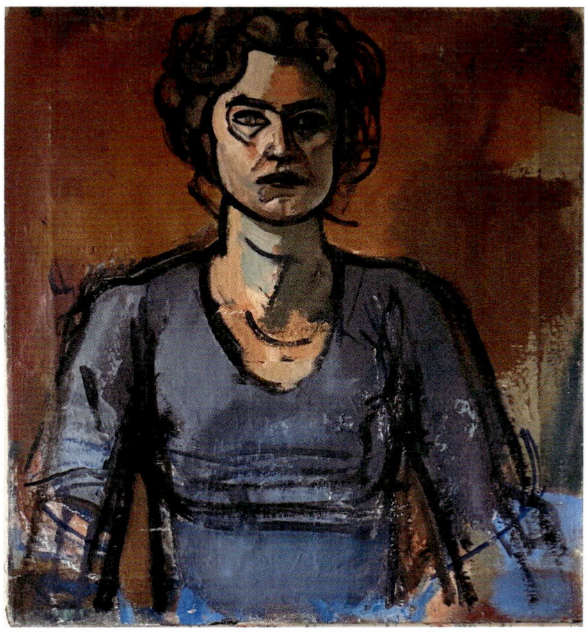

Leland Bell *Portrait of Temma*
c. 1975, oil on canvas, 22 x 20 in.

MD: *Phyllis, "I said to myself, I'd become a painter..." Can you elaborate on your education at Stanford as part of the life you left in California? Was it in, or related to, the visual arts? Was your uncle who introduced you to the city a New Yorker? Was your study at Academie Julian during your year in Paris? Part of your Stanford BA? Did becoming a painter seem possible or probable before you were in NYC?*

PF: Beginning in 1941, I had the good fortune to attend children's classes Saturdays and summers at the Otis Art Institute. These were taught by Donna Florine Schuster (born 1883) who is categorized as a California Impressionist. The first day of class has stayed with me because I was all keyed up. Miss Schuster's assignment was to draw a giant S as the basis for our compositions. After a year or two she asked my mother if she could paint my portrait. She had a magnificent home and studio overlooking Griffith Park with huge windows like those seen in photographs of Cézanne's studio in the south of France. She lived

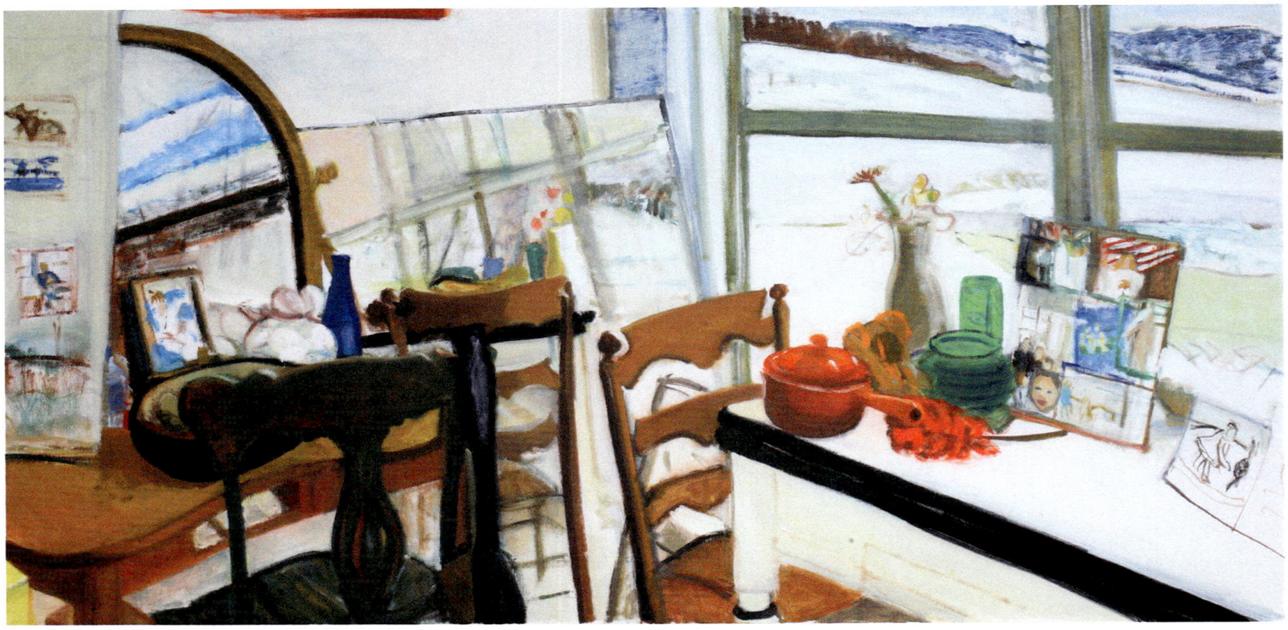

Temma Bell *In the Studio*
2019, oil on linen, 24 x 48 in.

there with her demented mother and a cat. In my high school years I took life-drawing classes with adults at Otis.

I entered Stanford in 1948 majoring in Art with a minor in French. It should be said that painting is not an academic subject, and Stanford was not known for its art department. However, several of the professors at Stanford were outstanding. I came to appreciate Victor Arnautoff just recently when I read in *The New York Times* that a mural he painted on the walls of a post office in San Francisco was about to be demolished because of a misunderstanding of its racist nature. Arnautoff became a Communist during the time he taught Stanford students a most conservative class, "Artists' Materials and Techniques." To pass the course, we were required to make one of the mediums from scratch as artists had done for centuries before the advent of art material stores. Daniel Mendelowitz (author of *A Guide to Drawing*) taught watercolor and several years before my time had persuaded Diebenkorn's parents to set him up with a studio. Mendelowitz seemed to like the watercolors I did on campus but it never occurred to me to stay in touch with him, and anyway I was much too shy. Another impediment to networking (a word that did not exist in 1952) was that the professors bonded more easily with the male students

Leland Bell *Family Group with Butterfly*
c. 1975, acrylic on paper on board, 9 ¾ x 19 ¼ in.

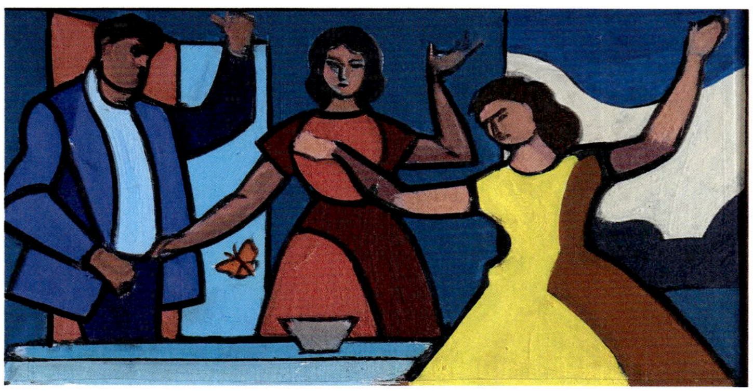

Temma and I have discovered that we were in Paris the same year—she as a child with her parents, and I as a student at the Sorbonne (mornings) and Academie Julian which I attended every afternoon, six days a week, from 2 to 6 o'clock. This was the original atelier on the Rue du Dragon which later was to become a renowned art school. I walked there from the apartment where I was living in the 7th arrondissement. There were always two nude models and three still lifes to work from. Once a week the arrival of the painter Chapelain-Midy elicited a cry of "Maitre." The monitor brought him a tray holding orange juice and two lumps of sugar, and most of the students followed him around from easel to easel while he did critiques. I have a clear memory of a hullabaloo surrounding a painting that one of the French students brought to class. It was Abstract Expressionist in style, and I said to myself, "Interesting, but this is not what I want to do." The year in Paris was laissez-faire—

Stanford had yet to institute "Junior Year Abroad"—all to my benefit because I stayed with a cultured French family, rather than with American students in a dormitory. In Paris I saw that the friends of the people where I lived visited art galleries regularly and talked with each other about these exhibitions—not a feature of life in southern California.

In New York I pursued the MFA at Pratt as a route to supporting my family. I was unhappy with the studio program there, except for Gabriel Laderman's class which introduced me to oil painting. Gabriel died in 2015, and I miss him. I believe he was a great painter, and it is sad that he is remembered by so few. George McNeil taught Art History, and when I went for an interview about my thesis paper, he complimented me on my graduate exhibition. Because he was an Abstract Expressionist, I was incredulous and blushed from the tip of my toes to the top of my head. Here is one of the paintings in the MFA (image right).

Many years later I enrolled for a time in the Art History department at New York's Hunter College. The legendary professor Howard Davis gave a course on Jan van Eyck that stopped me in my tracks. It was a joy to hear him hold forth on the International Style and the Dukes of Burgundy. I still have the pack of cards he passed out with images of the paintings he planned to speak about. I also retain the lecture notes from his classes, and there are former students from around the world who remember him as I do. According to the Columbia University Record, he and medical students were mutually attracted!

To some degree at least, we choose the courses we will take and the programs we will follow. We do not, of course, choose the family we are born into, and that family is perhaps the most important factor in determining the education we are to have and the life we are to lead and the person we are to become. Painters, writers, and composers of music have sometimes described the mental illness, alcoholism, chaos and pain they grew up with. Some might see their discordant childhoods as a spur to artistic achievement. I am among that group. After a long life I see that I have wished for serenity in my paintings. At the same time I have come to understand the struggle that my parents, too, experienced growing up with pioneering families in the western United States

MD: *For those of us who are not New Yorkers but are in love with painting, the city is a place where we can see "the numerous galleries and museums offering first-rate exhibitions" that Phyllis mentioned earlier. I will never forget driving to NYC on my own in 1981 to see Morandi's paintings at the Guggenheim. Two years before that I had feasted on Chardin at the Museum of Fine Arts in Boston shortly after moving there from Missouri.*

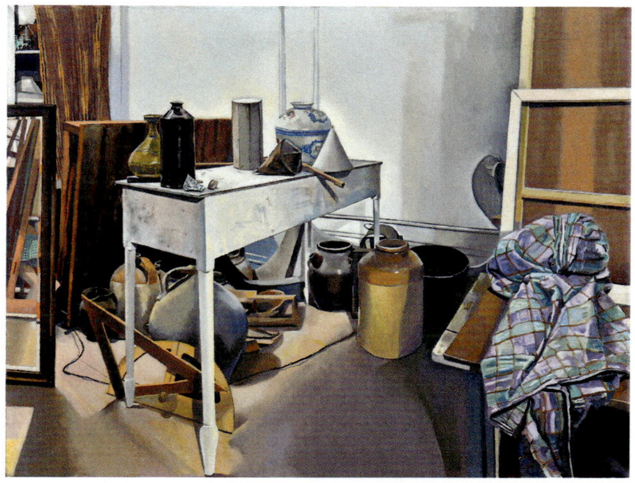

Gabriel Laderman *Still Life with Order and Chaos*
1983-1984, oil on canvas, 28 x 36 in.,
property of The Spurzem Family Collection

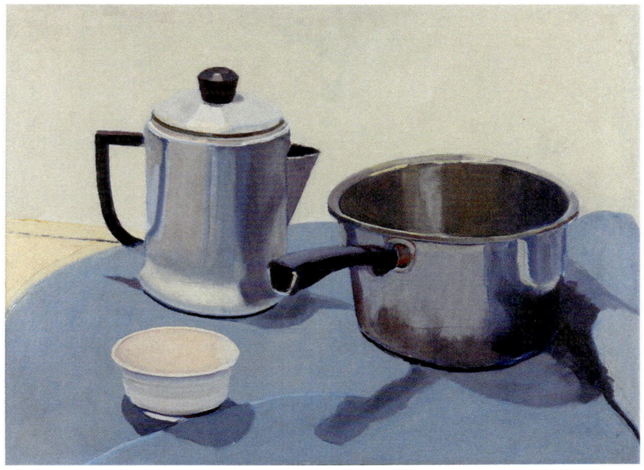

Phyllis Floyd *Pratt Still Life*
1966, oil on linen, 18 x 24 in.

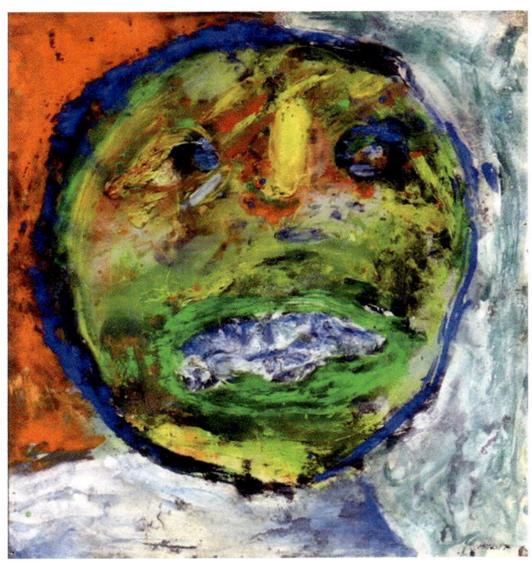

George McNeil *Blue Mouth*
1974, oil on paper, 22 x 20 in.

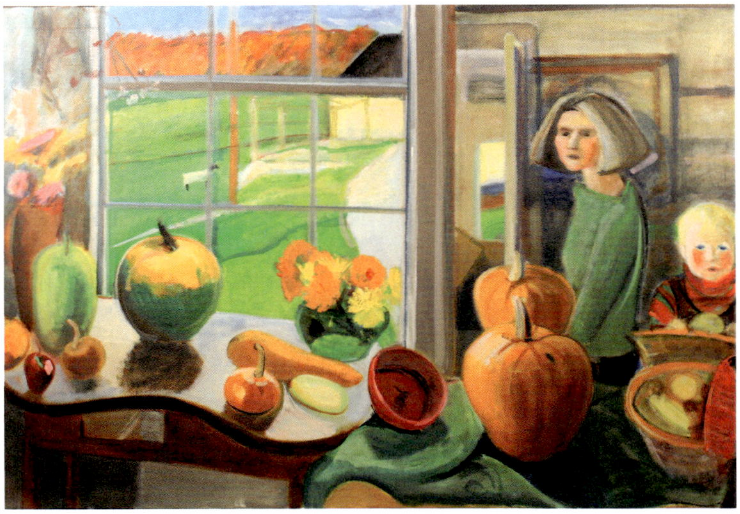

Temma Bell *Keith's Pumpkins*
c. 1988, oil on canvas, 37 x 53 in.

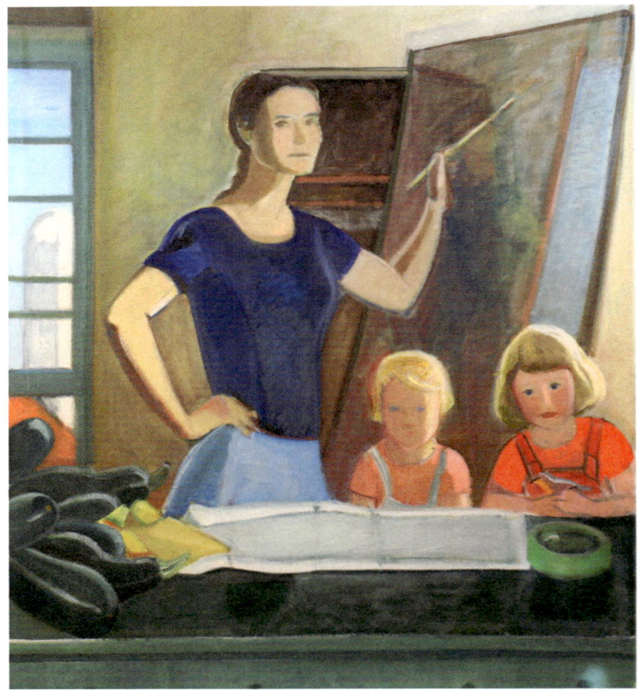

Temma Bell *Self with Ulla and Melkorka*
c. 1983, oil on canvas, 52 x 46 in.

Seeing exhibits like those give me something I feel I need as a painter. What are your peak experiences with looking at the art NYC has to offer? Which museums and galleries give something you need that you cannot get on a regular basis anywhere else?

TB: This is a hard one, I find it difficult to remember specific shows in the city. One visited the Met, the Frick Collection, the Museum of Modern Art and, way back in the '50s the Pierre Matisse Gallery and the Sidney Janis Gallery stand out. One was spoiled I guess, and there weren't crowds of people going from one work of art to the next, and having to negotiate as one moved through the exhibition.

There just was so much to see in the city and I had grown up going to galleries and museums all my life. It is almost as if I remember more going to places outside of the city like the Barnes Foundation. I do remember one amazing retrospective of Bonnard that I saw in Paris in the '60s that had a great effect on me, as did seeing the Frans Hals portraits in Haarlem—they were very moving—and then seeing the Prado that year. When I moved back from Iceland, I was concentrating on my family and painting, that was the important thing. I guess I never felt starved for art. The city was and is still always in me. I do regret not seeing the Chardin show that was in Boston though.

PF: My forays into museums and such began in Paris when I was 19. Sundays were reserved for those expeditions. It was also in Paris that I learned to appreciate city living. Back in New York, the writer took me around to some of his haunts. The semester with Howard Davis at New York's Hunter College provided inspiration for a trip to Paris, Bruges, Ghent, and London. I wanted to look up as many van Eycks as possible, and I managed to see a large portion of his output. I remember most vividly the self portrait in the National Gallery of London. I can never forget those two weeks. In the early sixties, there was an exhibition of van Gogh at the Guggenheim. I am next to positive that I crossed paths with his famous nephew who was tall and thin and wearing a beret. What a kick!

In 2017 The Morgan Library mounted an exhibition from Stockholm called "Treasures from the National Museum of Sweden: The Collections of Count Tessin." I had never heard of this connoisseur who traveled to Paris in 1740 to buy works for the King of Sweden. Included in the exhibition at the

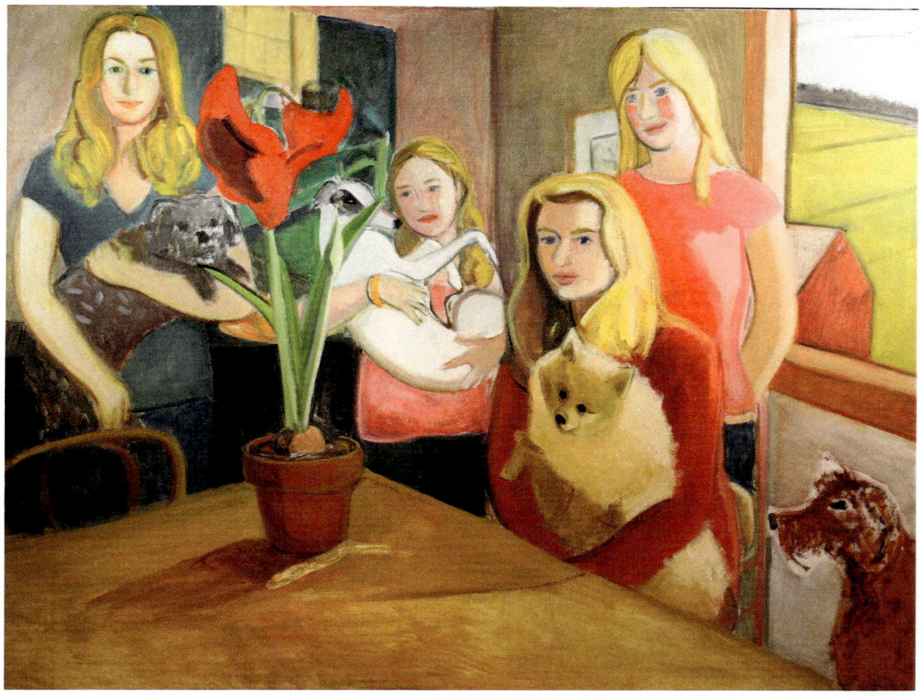

Temma Bell *Four Daughters*
2006, oil on canvas, 52 x 68 in.

Morgan was a large Chardin still life depicting a dead animal and some quite small genre scenes. These paintings were new to me. I love the Morgan Library. It is not overwhelming like the Metropolitan Museum. It is within easy walking distance, and I used to pop in there often. These days one has to plan ahead and make a date to see its exhibitions, and these restrictions conflict with my lifestyle. I went there recently with my daughter, and we saw the David Hockney portraits executed on paper over many decades. The atmosphere in the Morgan was dreary because hardly anyone was there—no tourists. My daughter says she feels relaxed after viewing an exhibition while I am likely to feel contemplative.

During the years I was teaching, I used to come in from Long Island to see as many shows as I could cram in. I continued in this vein when we returned to the city. Now I prefer one excursion; one show at a time. In talking with Trevor Winkfield now and then over the years, I remember a story he told about a one-day trip to the High Museum in Atlanta. I recently emailed him to learn the details, and here is his response:

> *I flew down for the day to see Cézanne's Mardi Gras, which formed part of a group of paintings on temporary loan from the Pushkin Museum in Moscow (undergoing renovation at the time, hence the loan exhibition). That must have been around fifteen years ago. I'd long loved the painting in reproduction, and knew I'd never visit Moscow, hence my flight. I spent about four hours looking at the painting (giving my eyes a rest every quarter hour, looking at other Pushkin loans, not one of which I recollect!). Then flying back to New York late afternoon. Well worth the effort and expense. I later wrote about the painting in Tether no. 1 (2015).*

Just yesterday, Dec. 12, 2020, I hiked over to the Chelsea art district. I saw exhibitions of work by Harriet Korman, Anne Truitt, Frank Auerbach, and Benny Andrews. This time one excursion, four shows. At the front desk, they asked for my name and email address because I had not made appointments. There looked to be no more than ten masked people in each gallery. Benny

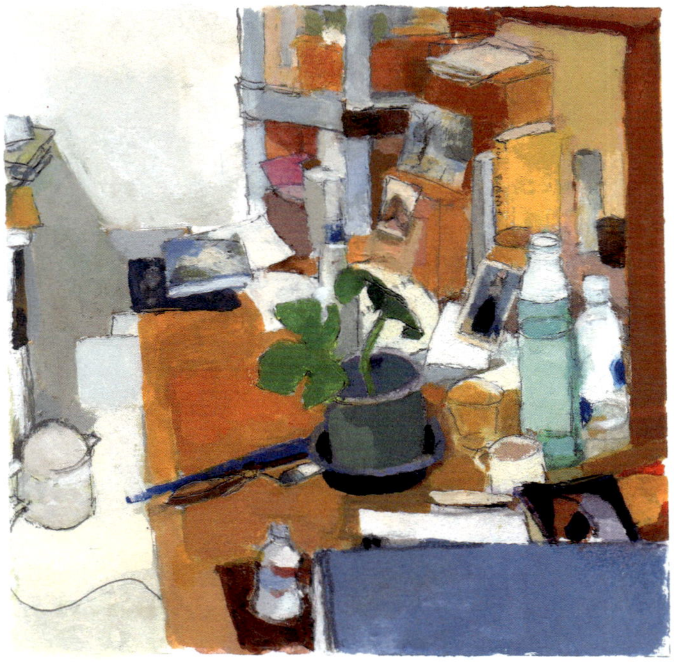

Meredith Fife Day *Broken Fig Leaves*
2018, gouche on paper, 13 x 13 in.

Andrews used to live directly across the street from me. I went to a party at his loft one time because my daughter was in school with his son. I saw none of the remarkable works that were on display yesterday.

MD: *As we are learning from the Covid-19 pandemic, our social connections are essential to our well-being. Involvement in community can counter the isolation and distancing as well as the solitude that is usually a part of making art. While Zeuxis is the obvious community in this conversation, I would like to hear of other communities that have helped to enrich and sustain your painting life in New York City.*

TB: In 1970, I joined the Bowery gallery which had been founded in 1969, There were four of us who got in that second year. I have had at least 15 solo exhibitions there. The first 11 years I was basically in the city. Then I spent five years in Reykjavik, where I met and married my husband, and where we had the first two of our four daughters. We moved back to the states in 1982 and lived on a farm in Warwick, NY. So I have been involved with the gallery for 50 years, and that has been my "artistic community."

Then I was invited to join Zeuxis in 2009, and have been showing with its artists ever since. Zeuxis is another artistic community for me. I haven't painted in the city for a number of years, but I did enjoy painting still lifes.

I have always loved painting indoor/outdoor motifs. I remember doing that first in Paris. I worked on still lifes in the city, but not with city views.

In New York City, I did paint on rooftops, and out in the land-scape near the East River, with Margaret Grace who had a car.

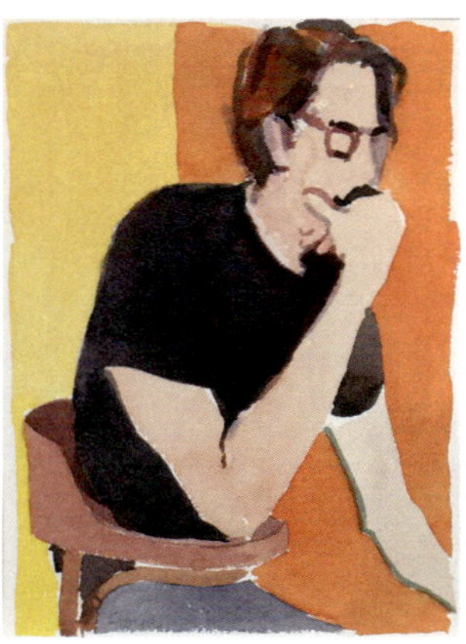

Phyllis Floyd *Seth #2*
2018, watercolor on paper, 10 x 14 in.

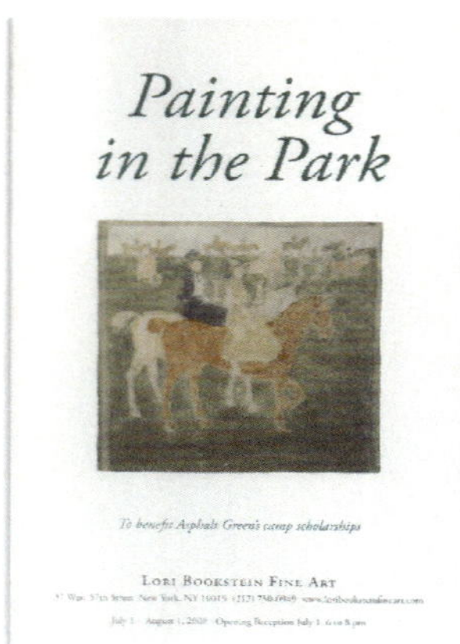

Publication for "Painting in the Park." 2008, Lori Bookstein Fine Art

PF: My community is composed of Zeuxis artists. Administratively, we have been through several permutations; I've managed to trudge on, with or without a committee. Begun in 1994 or 1995, Zeuxis has flourished because we have attracted artists who are excellent at painting still life and because through hard work we've organized admirable group shows. Ideas for themes come from our painters. It must be obvious that I chose the title for our upcoming show "Composing in the Key of S."

Seth Schonberg is an outstanding assistant. He is good on the computer while I am not. Though only in his 20s, he is wise in making crucial decisions. Because of him, too, Zeuxis has been successful. Like Temma, he is a native New Yorker, but one who has so far stayed put.

I enjoy getting to know the artists we promote. Sometimes I imagine that one or two of them might be struggling with a still life for our next show while I am doing the same. So I feel a kinship even though they are out of sight.

Our paintings are exhibited in New York galleries—Lori Bookstein has hosted several of our shows—and in nonprofit spaces. A New York-style incident occurred several years ago when one of the artists removed his painting from the wall and put another in its place almost causing us who knew about it to give up in despair. I trust that when our shows travel throughout the country, behavior is more orderly.

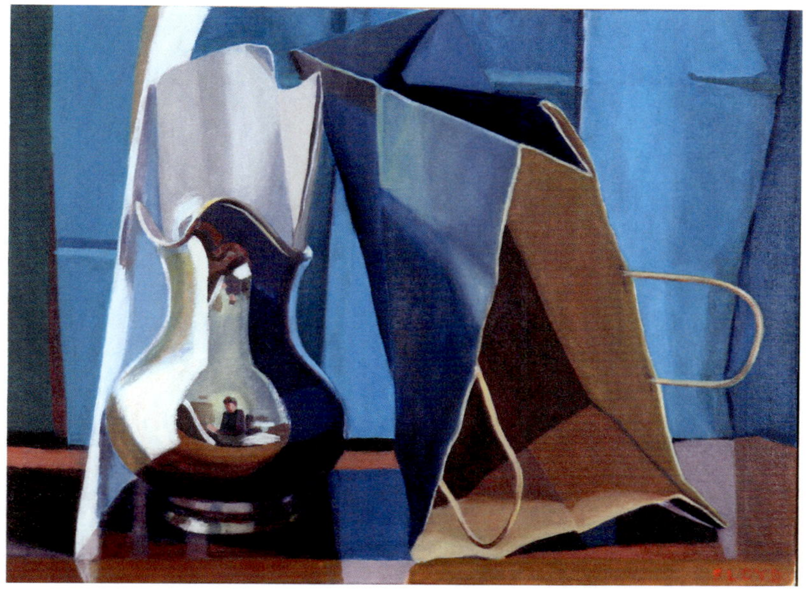

Phyllis Floyd *Blue*
2013, oil on canvas, 19 x 24 in.

Some of the Zeuxis people contribute by finding venues for our traveling shows, another one (John Goodrich) hangs our work in New York and writes much of our publicity, others tell us frankly how we can improve our operation.

It turns out that I have more room than I need for living and painting. Recently, Seth and I found a way to make about half of the loft function as a space to view work. The space is called THERE. We have had six exhibitions, and once enough people are vaccinated, we'll open up again.

We are left now with questions:

Will we be able to have a real reception when "Key of S" opens next year?

Will we be able to connect with some English still life painters?

If art departments around the country are shutting down, why are there so many painters?

What is the best education for a would-be painter?

What is our world going to look like in six months or a year?

What is to become of our New York? Z

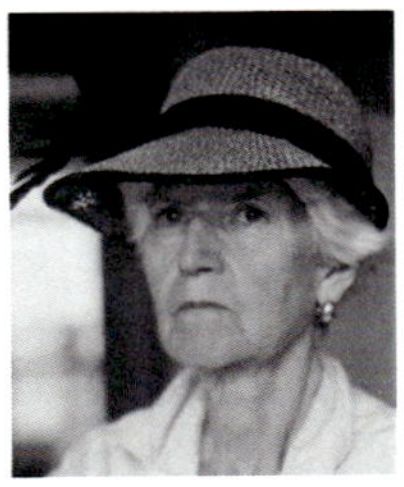

Temma Bell a painter born in New York City, currently lives on a farm in Delhi, New York, where she continues to paint landscapes (both interior and exterior), friends, family and surrounding animals. She frequently travels to Iceland, where she has been painting the landscape for more than 50 years. She shows at the Bowery Gallery in New York City.

www.zeuxis.us/bell
www.temmabell.com

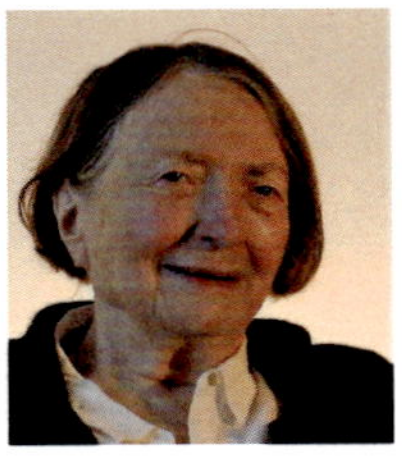

Phyllis Floyd lives and works in a loft in midtown Manhattan, a short walk from the Chelsea art scene. When not attending to Zeuxis matters, she gives her full attention to oil painting and to watercolor, a medium that forces one to "get it right" the first time.

www.zeuxis.us/floyd
www.phyllisfloyd.com

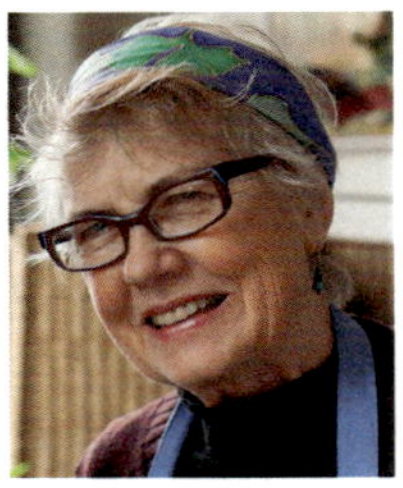

Meredith Fife Day is a painter, writer, teacher and lover of art. She is an advocate for equitable access to the arts and free education in the visual arts for children.

www.meredithfifeday.com

A Conversation with Painters

John Goodrich interviews

Ken Kewley and Mary Prince

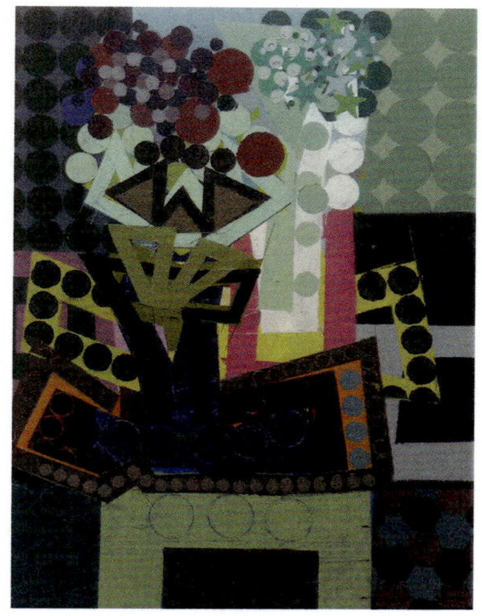

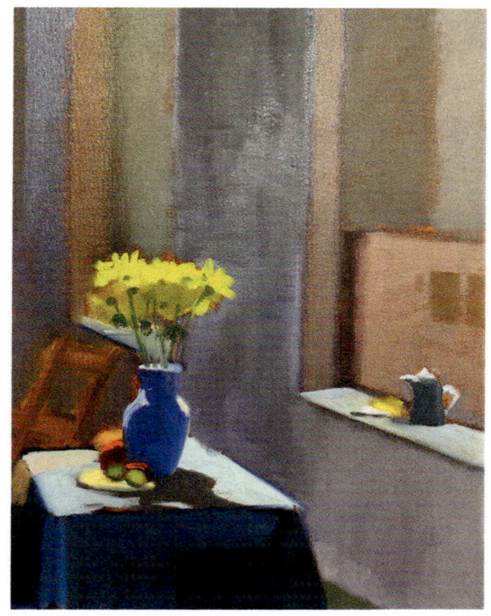

Ken Kewley *Bouquet I*
2015, acrylic on board, 24 x 18 in.

Mary Prince *Spring Flowers*
2020, oil on panel, 16 x 12 in.

John Goodrich: *This double interview took place over the course of two weeks in December, with Ken Kewley and Mary Prince taking turns responding to my questions and to each other in a single Google Doc. Many thanks to them both for their time and highly articulate thoughts.*

JG: *In what ways has the pandemic and social unrest this past year affected your work?*

Ken Kewley: Not the work itself. All I do is compose color shapes. The news, politics, thoughts, and feelings, are all separate from that. I listen to too much news. It's best if I'm moving shapes around at the same time.

The pandemic has stopped my workshops. Not teaching has surely taken something away. It has also kept me from taking the bus into New York, from going to the Met. But my work can do without that for awhile.

If not for the pandemic, I might have hired a model, I might have gone out painting, but I have not done either of those things for a few years.

Mary Prince: My interest lies in the dynamics of light in the physical world, how it intensifies color and creates shadows and shapes. The political turmoil and the pandemic have little influence on my motifs.

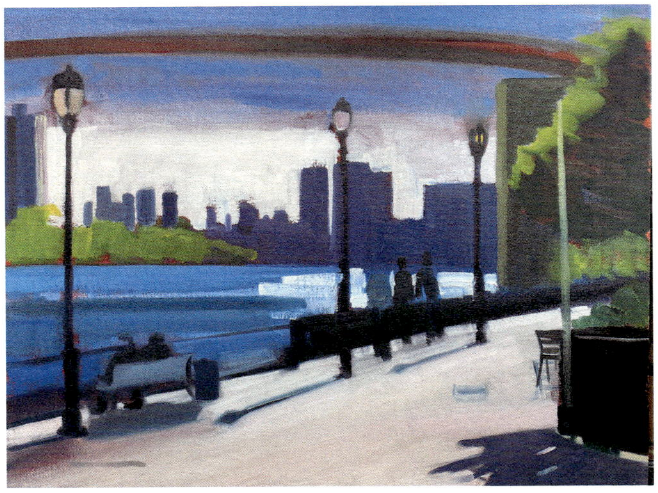

Mary Prince
Untitled (Green Plate)
2019, oil on panel, 14 x 18 in.

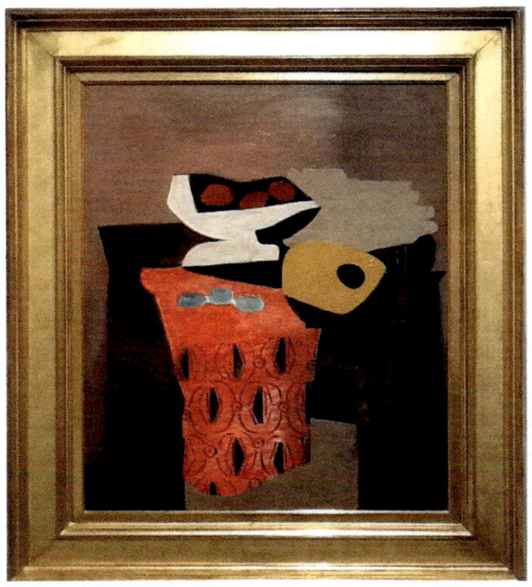

Pablo Picasso *The Red Foulard*
1924, oil on canvas, 39 ½ x 32 in.,
Norton Museum of Art

Initially, the pandemic robbed me of my summer painting time as I had to establish my teaching online. I sorely miss going to the Met and painting with my friends. On the flip side, the pandemic has recently given me more time to observe nature, reflect and experiment.

JG: *Have your hopes or expectations of paintings changed in this last year?*

KK: Every year, I'm trying to push the work. Trying to strengthen the work. Hopefully having the shapes lose less strength as they combine to make the subject. I am a realist. But I try to stay off the contours and surfaces of nature, while still getting the excitement of nature.

MP: I trust that if I keep my focus on the work, it continues to evolve as an inner dialogue that manifests on the pictorial plane. I am feeling more confident to focus in places I know need attention, and that focus likely brings fresh insights in my paintings. I'm working on new and challenging compositions and motifs. Sometimes I'm pleased and other times the challenge forces me to turn the painting to the wall for a while and have a look later.

KK: Yes, if I have a painting turned against the wall, when I turn it around, if it surprises me, I take that as a good sign.

I don't want to know my own work. I would never sit in a chair and study it. I give it a side glance as I leave my studio, that's enough.

MP: I like that you say you don't study your own work. I'm often advised to analyze my paintings, but I generally resist, as I move on to the next piece. Like you, Ken, I find myself eyeing it out of the corner of my eye often in surprising situations.

JG: *What shows or artworks had the greatest impact on you in recent years?*

MP: The Climax of Cubism at the Helly Nahmad Gallery was a show that recently inspired me with the simple shapes and bold colors of the paintings as well as the innovations of the work. It was a treat to see Braque, Gris, Léger and Picasso, my favorite modernists, displayed. These paintings remind me of Picasso's *The Red Foulard* that I saw with you, Ken, in Florida at the Norton Museum of Art. I remember we spent a long time reflecting on this simplified, bold and modernist painting. Another favorite show was Matisse: In Search of True Painting at the Met. Matisse's mastery at approaching the motif repeatedly with new inventions is brilliant. It's an invaluable concept for artists: we need to address a motif in different manners to realize the promising, multiple potentials. Ken, don't you do this when you print out an image and take it in a new direction?

KK: Yes Mary, it is just shapes, arranged, and rearranged. There are hundreds of Picasso still lifes with the same objects, where the shapes, the abstraction, have been rearranged. Once one realizes this, that it is the abstraction, the shapes, more than the objects, that one moves around, that one composes, it is endless.

Looking at the Helly Nahmad show online right now. Great things. Great shapes. I regret not seeing it.

MP: This concept of moving shapes around is a keeper. I've been thinking along the lines of the three knights of painting: hue, value and intensity combined with the presentation of a hierarchy that allows the painting to sing. It's a puzzle-like challenge that has to be solved. When I'm painting, I remind myself if I can get the color relationships working with the shapes and the appropriate values, I might be surprised by the results.

KK: Somewhere along the line I became focused on the work of Georges Braque. In 2014 I went to Paris to see the large retrospective of his work. I went every day for a week. During that week I also went to the Louvre a few times. Braque composed shapes as well as anyone in that great museum.

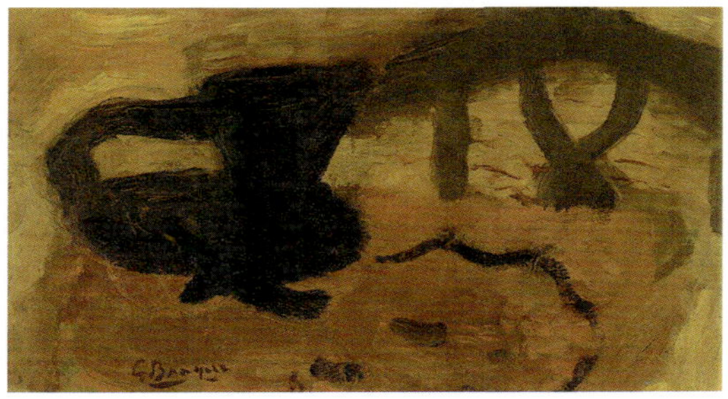

Georges Braque *Le Pichet Noir*
1943, oil on canvas, 7 ¾ x 13 ¼ in., Norton Museum of Art

James Castle is right up there also. As for those working right now, I look at Robin Sanford, Rotem Amizur, Ben Huberman, Clara Kewley. All great shape makers, and shape placers.

***JG:** James Castle for me is unique—the only painter I know of who, being deaf-mute, could attach no verbal meanings to things, only visual ones. And these meanings seem so private and intense. Do you think there is anything unique we can learn from him?*

James Castle *Untitled*
after 1945, soot on white found paper (commercially printed Amalgamated Fine Granulated Sugar wrapper), 4 ¼ x 10 ¼ in.

KK: Possibly not to attach verbal meanings to things when we are painting. Enough meaning will leak through visually.

MP: For me, he worked from his heart with zero pretension out of a necessity of image making.

KK: I agree.

***JG:** If you could be standing in front of any painting in the world right now, which painting would it be, and why?*

KK: Nothing for too long. I'm both obsessed with looking at art and can do without it. I would rather be sitting, adjusting shapes of painted paper.

Maybe *Good and Bad Government* by Ambrogio Lorenzetti. It has everything, city, country, figures, still life. Like nature, enough to look at for a long time. And wonderful to draw from. And I would be in Siena. Surrounded by the Italian countryside. And near great gelato.

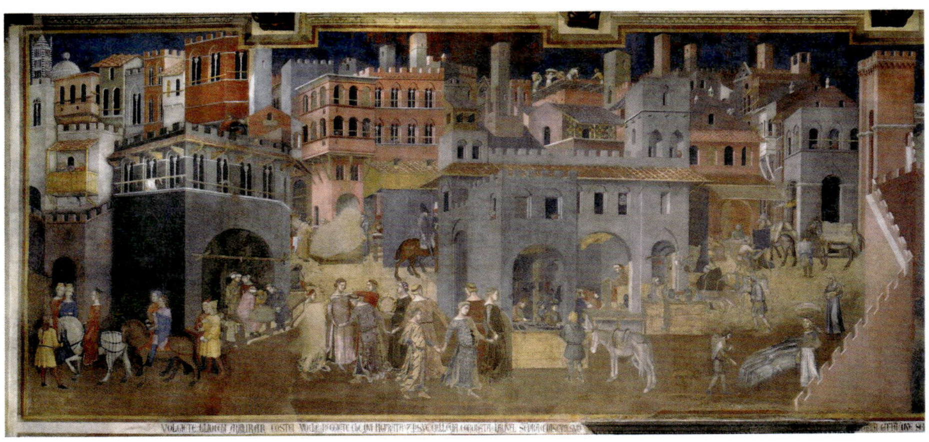

Ambrogio Lorenzetti
Effects of the Good Government on the City Life
1338-40, Fresco, Palazzo Pubblico, Siena

Or, there are these small figure fresco fragments that I saw in the Palazzo Massimo in Rome. I cannot find any reproductions online right now. They are not the major works there. As I remember them, they are partially worn away, but what remains, simple lines and shapes, as much abstractions as representations. Something I want in my work, shapes making representation, while remaining shapes.

MP: If I have to choose just one painting right now, I'd choose Titian's *Bacchus and Ariadne* at the National Gallery in London. The intense blue sky as a backdrop to the dynamic movement of the figures is astounding. I love the palette of the rosy flesh in contrast to the more tawny figures. Talking about moving shapes around, Titian has certainly achieved this with Bacchus leaping through the air in mid-motion.

KK: Yes, true placing of shape. His model could not have posed with his robe flying up the way it does. Titian invented that shape and placed it exactly where he wanted it.

MP: Also, Ken, this painting reminds me of something you discuss in your essay, *Notes on Color*: "Group colors into larger masses that work with and against other masses. A group of similar darks opposed to a group of close value lights. There can be lights within the dark masses and darks within the light masses. These masses must form shapes that play their parts in making up a composition."

Ken, you seem to have found an ease in making art. I find it a challenge, a worthy one, but nevertheless a challenge. Many painter friends with whom I speak find it challenging. How do you account for the ease you have found in image making?

KK: Likely it is a challenge for both of us. We may be just using different terms, or different measurements. I am currently limiting my shapes which makes things a bit easier. Maybe I have always tended to do this. I'm also not trying for any particular thing. I'm placing shapes according to the previous shapes and not attempting to follow any thought or vision. I don't need to get anything correct. I let the image happen step by step.

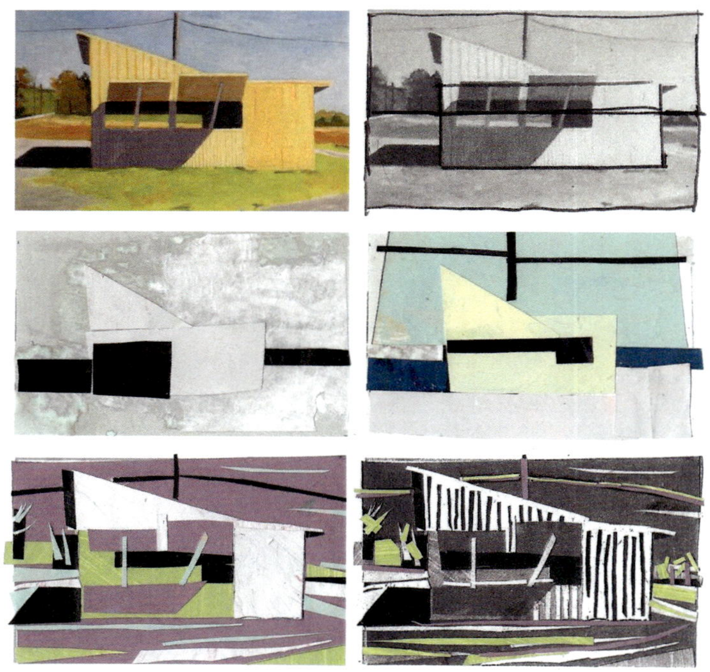

Michele BonDurant
Artist working from their painting Workshop Sequence
2019, Three Pines Studio

When working from life we all take paint and use it to represent something seen. Immediately it's a separation. Separate from nature and thus adjustable. But you don't want too many things to adjust. One must avoid making a mark for each thing seen.

Mary, you do avoid this. Your shapes are limited and strong.

Shapes are easier to move around than marks. If your house is cluttered, in order to remodel, repair, or even clean, requires moving a lot of stuff. That is where the challenge comes in for many. Instead of composing a few shapes, one ends up spending a lot of time just moving paint around, and it does become a difficult task.

MP: Ken, the last time I saw you, you mentioned you are writing a book. Could you tell us a little bit about it?

KK: Currently editing what I hope will be a little book. More than anything else it's about adjusting and composing shapes. It is that simple. That is made hard by unnecessary things one is often told

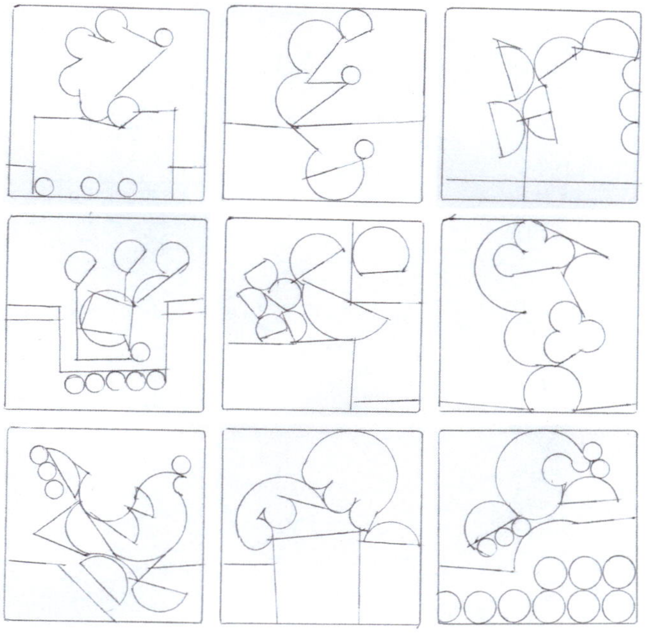

Ken Kewley *Jury Duty Drawings*
November 12, 2019

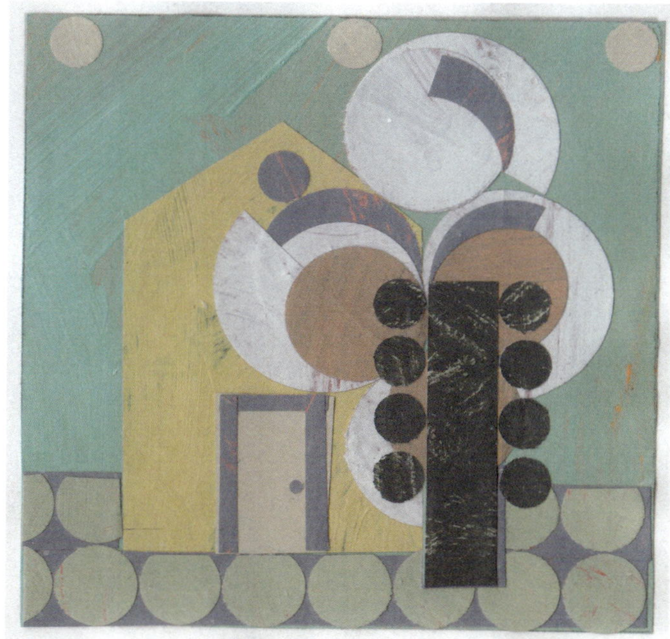

Ken Kewley *New Landscape 4*
2019, painted paper collage, 3 x 3 in.

that one must do. To explain simple is not easy, especially when the opposite of what is true is often also true. Whatever I say to avoid there is a master who does exactly that.

To strengthen one's painting often takes a lot of unlearning. Going back before, as a child, one was praised for making something recognizable, praised for one's rendering skills, and not for one's innate sense of abstraction. It's the latter that one must get back.

MP: When you say, "To explain simple is not easy, especially when the opposite of what is true is often also true," the collages you did of the masters comes to mind. Those were not easy. How do you explain the leap you took between those collages and the work you created afterwards and now?

KK: With those I had set up a rule that I had to use only straight cuts. I had to make curves or circles using straight edges. When you have two straight lines you can immediately see the relationship, how their positions are different. Even though I was copying I was still making a decision about the most exciting placement of each shape. The straight lines made this easier. It also kept me from rendering marks and brushstrokes. I could only render with shapes. Which I do now.

Those complex collages were not easy. But they were not hard. They were time consuming. I was using found color and some colors were very hard to find. On many days I would only place a few shapes. But the master had laid out a good path. I was trying to get as close to the source as I could using my rule.

The stronger the masterwork, and the closer I got, the stronger the collage. This is very different from working from life where getting closer to the subject could be weakening one's work.

***JG:** How has your working process changed over the years?*

KK: In the past I worked more from life. Inventing always eluded me, trying to get an image, in my head, onto the page. I think I was trying to force it whole. Today I find that I can invent. Working with color shapes, moving them around, one at a time, building an image, with no picture in my

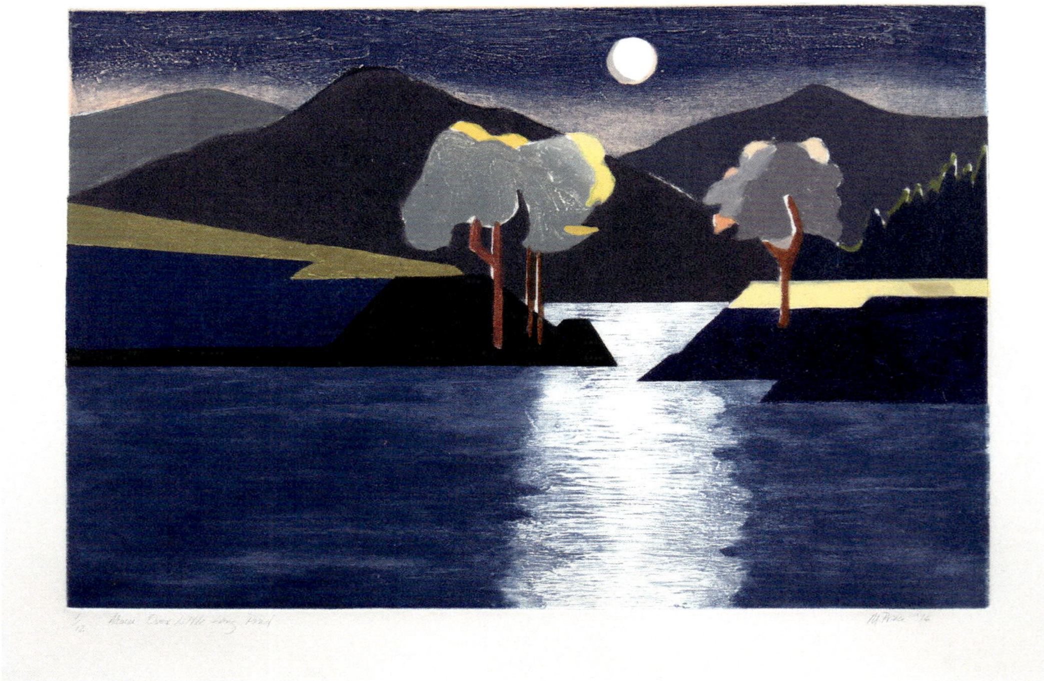

Mary Prince
Moon Over Little Long Pond
Carborundum aquatint, 16 ¾ x 24 ¾ in.

head. Letting the results surprise me. As I did in kindergarten, moving wooden blocks around, geometric shapes, to build a world.

In painting I'm painting up against a straight edge, using stencils, and templates. Nothing freehand. Placing shapes made in this manner. The skill is in placing shapes not mimicking contours and surfaces.

In the past, when working from life, I can see now, that I often did not strengthen my shapes. Today with collage I start with very strong shapes, like circles, and other geometric shapes, with definite edges. If I could go back, paint again those paintings, I would strengthen the shapes. The stronger the shapes, the more definite they are, the easier it is to compare and contrast, and then compose them.

MP: Ken when you say, "If I could go back, paint again those paintings, I would strengthen the shapes," do you mean that if you were painting an orange you would make it more circular? How would you go back and strengthen those shapes?

KK: Not necessarily a circle, just a more definite shape. So that I could compare the straighter edge of one to the more curved edge of another. Too often I was making brush marks, useless nuances at best, without them gathering into adjustable shapes. One cannot transport one's groceries if the bags are tearing and spilling produce.

Since I was not aware enough of the shapes and values of those shapes, I was not making the necessary exaggerations and necessary shifting of those shapes. I was just seeing the color and putting things how and where I saw them.

In adjusting the shapes I mean tweaking more than moving. One does not want to lose what one is looking at. Cézanne might tweak the angle of a road to relate it to the angle of a distant hill. It is still the same road and the same hill that Cézanne saw but the abstraction has been strengthened.

When I work from life again hopefully my sense of abstraction has been strengthened by doing these collages. I'll be more aware that things in nature need to be nudged into abstractions. That one needs to invent in front of life. That in doing so the subject will still be there. One cannot make it up. One must make it up. Both are true.

MP: So you are thinking of abstraction as it incorporates the underlying geometry of specific shapes and how those shapes relate to one another throughout the composition.

KK: Yes, it's the abstract shapes, that make up the things, that make up the composition.

MP: I like to start my process with a thumb nail and then the painting. Often my thumb nails become extended ink drawings. Once I have my basic ideas down in paint while standing in front of nature, I feel free to continue working in the studio. To continue the process into printmaking, I pick a painting and make a larger collage. This creates a more abstract image of the composition. The collage is a pleasure as every color imaginable is available. After the collage is finished, I decide on which relief printing process I prefer, woodblock or linoleum, and the print begins. Colors now have to be limited which becomes a new part of the challenge. By the time I get to the print, the image has moved three steps away from the actual reality of the view, thus creating a more abstract image.

Recently, I've experimented painting with a palette knife and a limited palette. Both are intended to force the abstraction. The limited palette is especially challenging because I have to invent the color through the color relationships. Copying the local color is impossible when I can't mix an approximation of a specific color.

I'm also gearing up my watercolors with the objective of catching a quick impression of the view. Working quickly is challenging, so I am thinking of ways that will force the issue.

KK: Mary, this moving towards abstraction, from painting, to collage, to printmaking, sounds good. Do you feel that going through this process influences you the next time you are painting in front of nature? That you get closer in doing what you do in printmaking while painting from life?

MP: Ken, yes, absolutely! Collage and printmaking are constantly reinforcing my paintings and one another. Through the course of this dialogue with you, I've had a bit of an ah-ha moment. I'm adding small collages to my toolkit to deepen my understanding of the abstraction and the potential color relationships in order to help me solve problems as they arise. It will be similar to the thumbnail, part of my image making process for each painting.

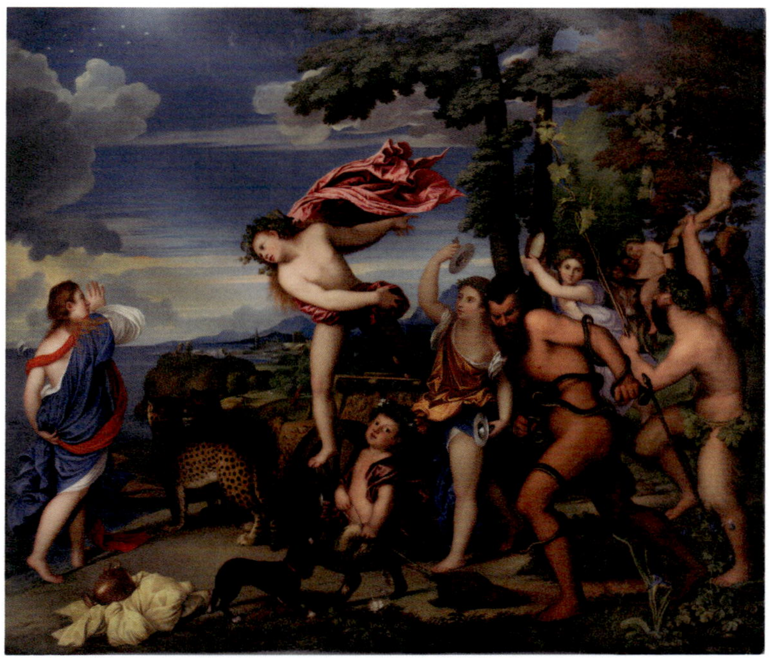

Titian *Bacchus and Ariadne*
1520, oil on canvas, 69 ½ x 75 in., National Gallery, London

KK: That sounds good. In the workshops I've been having people beforehand send me an image of their work. I print them all out onto one page and everyone does collages of these, working from their own image as well as the others. In this way people see how others are seeing their work.

MP: Yes, Ken, your idea for using collage in such a creative way will be very helpful to an artist in numerous ways.

KK: It seems, Mary, that this transition does begin for you in front of nature, with you slightly exaggerating the color instead of matching it, which separates the shape from nature so you can grasp it, thus you are able to adjust it, shift it, compare it with all the shapes you have created. Working from life and at the same time with a world you are creating.

MP: Yes, I do intensify the color. Color allows me to move away from replicating nature. The full array of colors is fascinating.

JG: *Looking back, what events most influenced you as an artist?*

KK: Three things stand out. In 1975. The hundred plus abstract paintings completed for my graduating show at the College of Creative Studies, UCSB. The State Street paintings. Painted in a windowless room downtown Santa Barbara. With nothing but paper, paint, and crayons. I realized that I did not need to have a subject in front of me. That I could do one after another. That it was endless. I knew then that I could do this my whole life.

Then thirty-five years of working from life, painting cakes and pies, working from the model, painting in cities, suburbia, and the countryside.

In 2010. The Aortic Valve Replacement Drawings. I found myself again confined to a small little room. In a hospital bed for a week with a 6 x 4 inch pad of paper and a pen. Finding again that I did not need to draw my surroundings. I made squares and then made abstract compositions within them. Dividing the squares with lines. In the last ten years I have been moving between non-objective and objective. Arranging shapes. Sometimes into a person, place, or thing. Sometimes with those things in front of me. When I am working from life it is my shapes that I'm now most aware of. They must make up the subject without disappearing. I try to be faithful to the observed, but being so cannot make me place shapes in a way I would not do if I was alone in a room.

Today with Clara's calendar I draw a composition into that day's square. If I draw or paint nothing else it still feels like a good day's work. And it only takes two or three seconds. And I produce 365 works a year just with these.

Beyond this I carry a small pad wherever I go and whenever I find myself in a waiting room I make compositions.

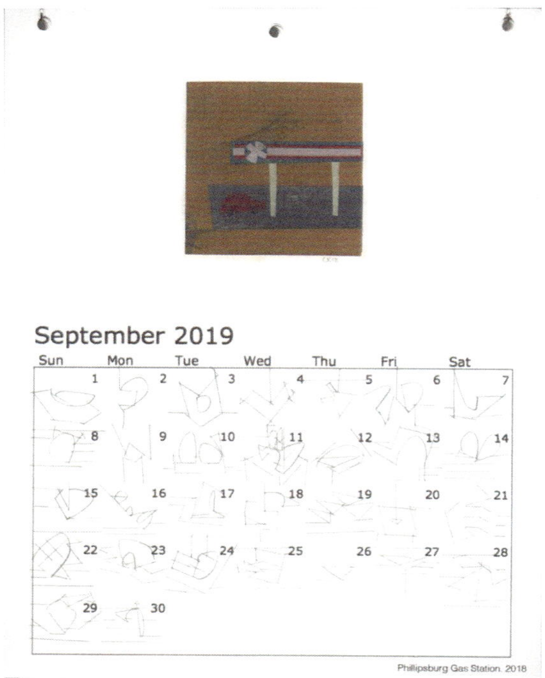

Daily Drawings by Ken Kewley
on Calendar by Clara Kewley

MP: Nature, the material world, has been the one influence that continues to be an inspiration. As a child, I was riding horses with friends when I remember looking up at the horizon where a simple green hill met the blue sky. I wanted to paint that hill and sky. I didn't care about the excitement of horseback riding; I just wanted to paint. That inspiration has stayed with me, whether it is the landscape or a set of objects on a table or an interior scene. Life is an inspiration for art.

As a child it was always the pictures in books that interested me. I would turn the pages over and over again studying each picture. The words were immaterial.

Then there are the numerous good teachers I have discovered: Nieves Billmyer, John Goodrich, and Ken Kewley are among teachers whose knowledge of art I respect and who inspire by their example

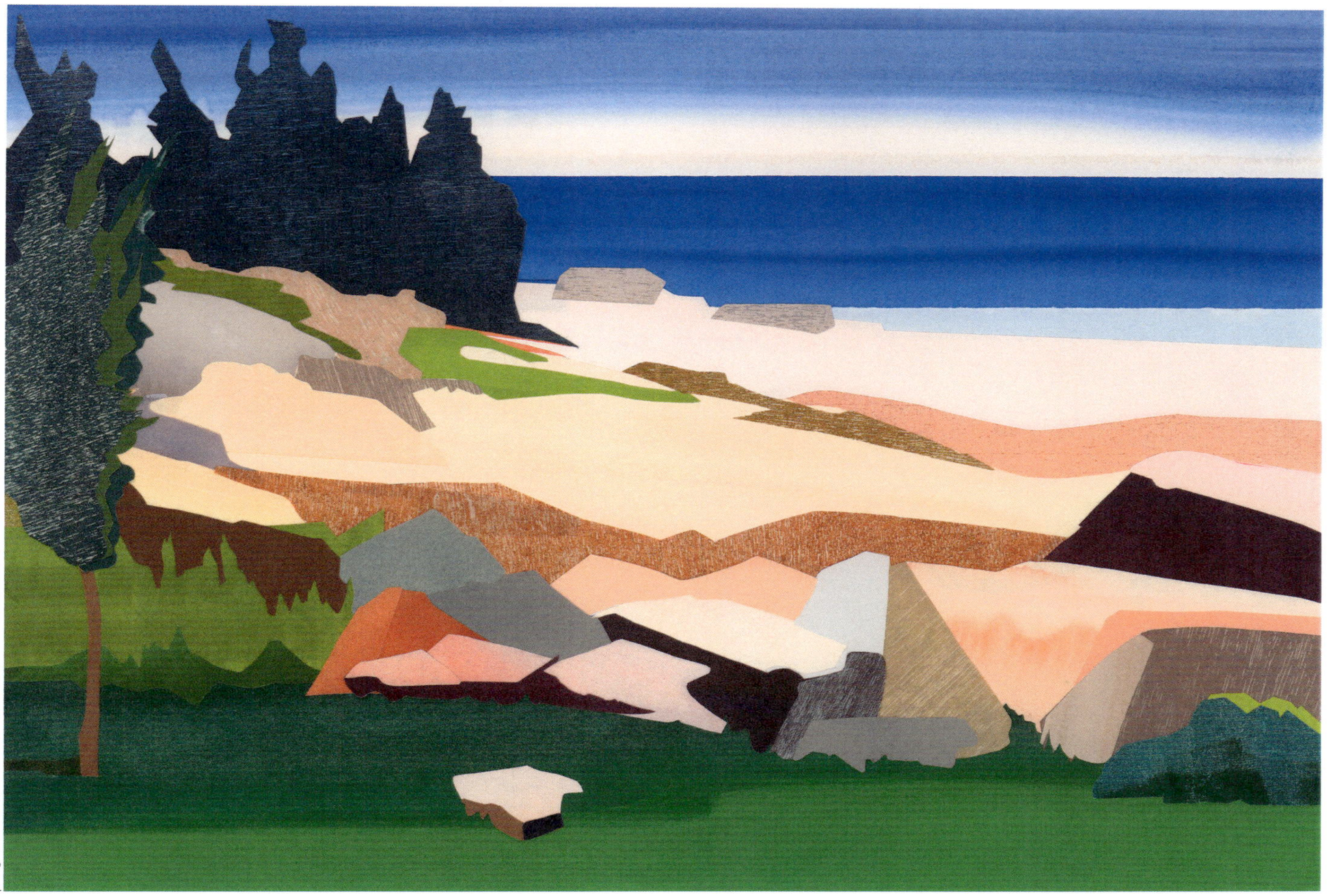

photo@StewartStewart.com

Mary Prince *Schoodic Point*
2019, archival pigment print, 18 x 26 in.

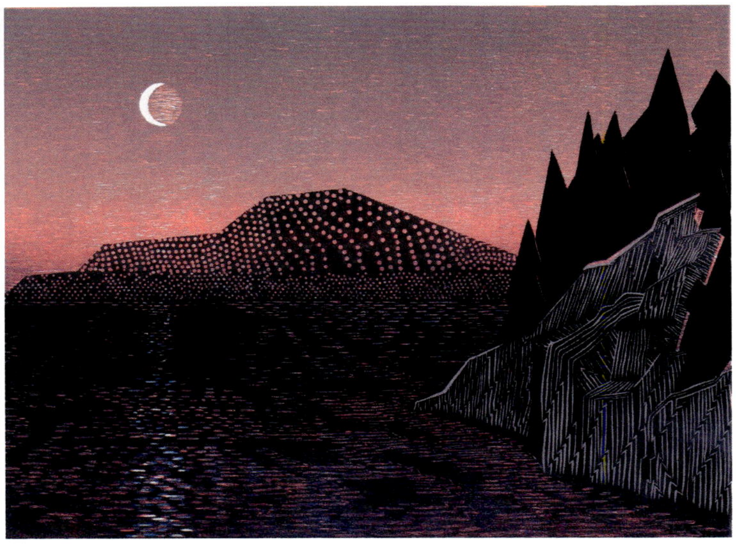

Mary Prince *Hop's View II*
2018, linoleum block, wood block and stencil, 18 x 24 in.

and their insights. Every teacher I have worked with has offered valuable insights.

JG: *I'm flattered! But if you could change one thing about your current work, what might that be?*

KK: I want to push the representation further again. It will most likely happen when I'm back to painting with wet paint again (I think of collage as painting with dry paint).

MP: Pushing the work towards abstraction, considering the dynamic whole of the color relationships, and painting more quickly are directions where I'm headed. I feel that we know what we need to know about image making, so it's a matter of trusting our instincts and intuition to allow our potential to manifest. Working more quickly is a way to encourage my intuitions and instincts.

JG: *What was your most recent artistic epiphany?*

KK: Why shapes are not enough.

JG: *They aren't enough because color adds a new quality to whatever shapes you make? Or because we can't help but read real-world situations into shapes?*

KK: I meant color shapes, or value shapes. Value being more important than color. The color is wonderful only if the value is right. The values are wonderful only if the composition is right. Too often in the past, when working from life, I was trying to get the color right, the drawing right, and forgetting about the need to compose. Instead of getting things right, one needs to nudge things, to exaggerate, to make some values lighter and some darker, to extend or squeeze a shape, to get things wrong.

I'm always working towards controlling the shapes, giving them purpose, having them hold and be held by other shapes, having them take larger and smaller roles, each needed in their own way.

One just needs a few shapes that the eye takes in first, those call attention to another set, and those to others, before the first shapes draw the eye back.

Without this hierarchy the work becomes a wall that we can look at, or turn away from, but it's difficult to enter.

And yes, after the tweaking, shapes will still be read as what we are looking at. One can go towards abstraction without going away from reality.

MP: You make several statements that remind me of the Japanese Koan, in which something is true and not true, like moving "towards abstraction without going away from reality." These contradictions are one of the more interesting and frustrating aspects of honest image making. There are no formulas, skills, or direct paths that lead to a dynamic image. Painting is not a rational endeavor. It's a matter of getting into a place where everything and nothing is present, so it can happen. You mention, and I've heard John mention, getting back to the mindset of a kindergarten child, in which image making becomes play, so one has to drop all preconceived expectations and concepts to succeed. This is why I try new materials or different printing processes: The unfamiliarity leads to discoveries.

Do you have any secrets about getting back to that child-like state?

KK: One must find ways of preventing the use of the skills that one has acquired since childhood. Arranging pre-painted and precut shapes into representations, that prevents one from following contours and surfaces skillfully, is one way I have found.

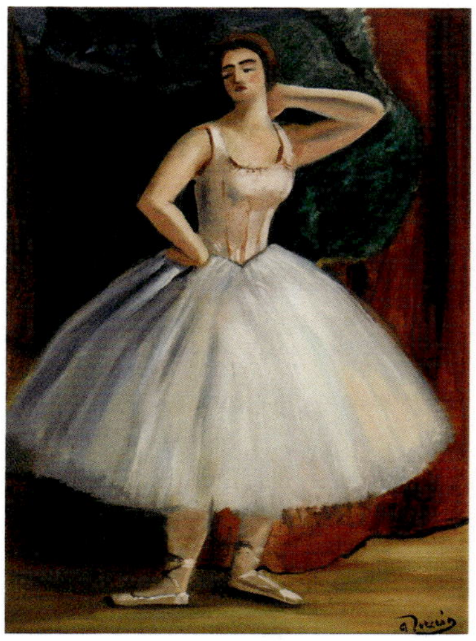

André Derain *Sonia the Dancer*
1927-28, oil on canvas, 18 ½ x 13 ½ in.

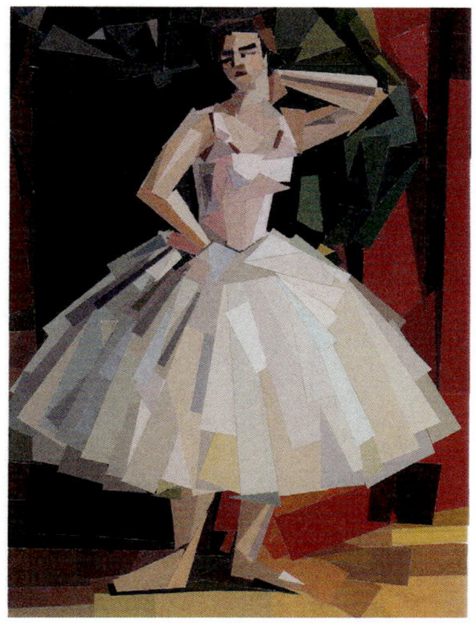

Ken Kewley *Sonia the Dancer (after Derain)*
2008, paper collage, 7 ½ x 5 ½ in.

MP: My most recent epiphany is explore! If I have a comfort zone, it is essential to leave it behind. Explore in every way imaginable: new palettes and new ways to apply the paint. Explore abstractions from finished works, explore starting over and over until I find what excites me. Explore working quickly. Immerse myself joyfully in the pool of artistic exploration. This reminds me, Ken, of some lines in *Notes On Color*: "The life of a painter is a life of exploring." Or another way you put it is "Give up control to let things happen in painting." Exploring and giving up control are actually two sides of the same coin and both lead to the idea of that place where an artist has to go to make honest art.

JG: *Which artists' works do you look at the most?*

MP: Over the past winter, I spent time copying Rembrandt's drawings and etchings of the landscape. I'm also inspired by André Derain's 1907 Fauvist landscapes as well as his later still lifes and landscapes. Recently, I've begun copying Giotto.

KK: I look a lot at the work of Robin Sanford. Her work is always on the verge of losing control, but then shaped by a surprising force. Close to nature, never trying to mimic nature, composed unlike nature, retaining the magnificence and wonder of nature.

I've been posting a work of Georges Braque everyday to Facebook for several years. To focus like this on one artist I think has been good. I look without overthinking or analyzing, just letting it sink in.

I look at my daughter's work with wonder. Simple shapes so carefully placed.

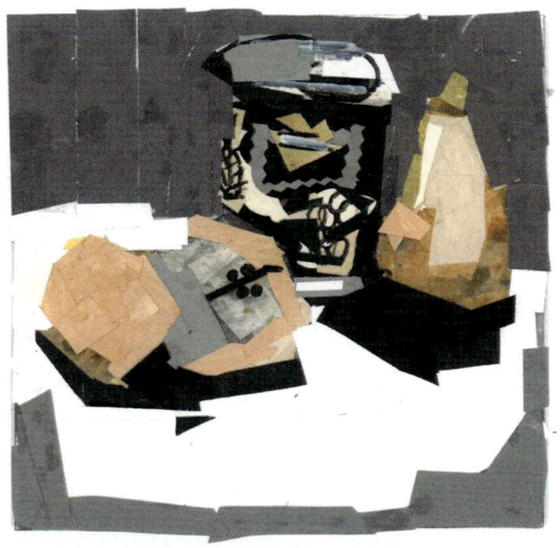

Robin Sanford *Fruit Cocktail*
2017, paper collage, 7 x 7 in.

JG: *What advice would you give to a young artist?*

MP: This quote by Bonnard sums it up: "I am just beginning to understand what it is to paint. A painter should have two lives, one in which to learn, and one in which to practice his art." As time goes by so quickly, it's important to set up a lifestyle that allows an artist to work. It's also important to go to museums, study inspiring painters and find a supportive mentor.

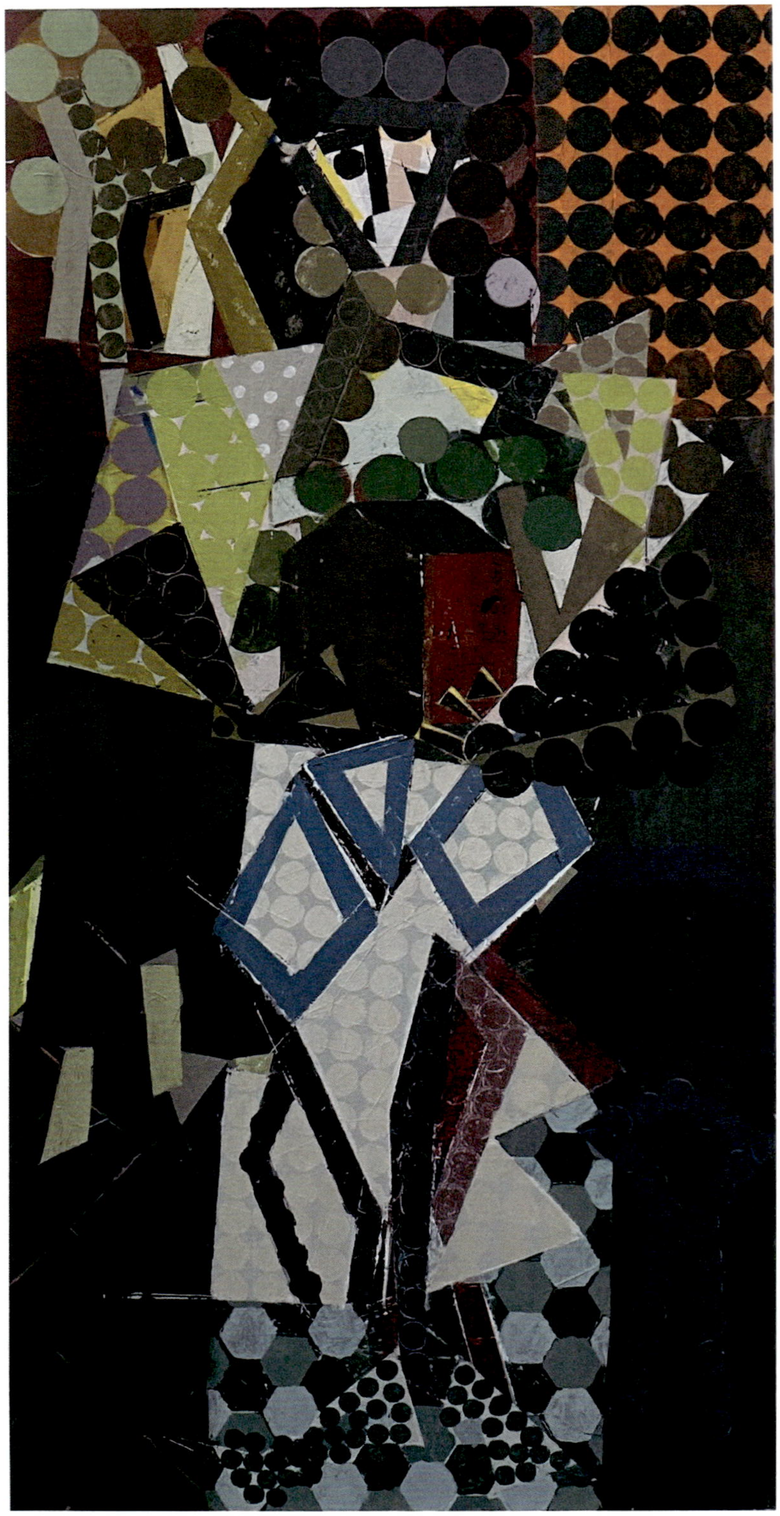

Ken Kewley *Figure 6 (Woman with House)*
2016, acrylic on wood panel, 36 x 18 in.

KK: To start with pure abstraction (most art education has it backwards). Just with shapes and arrange them without thought of representation. Do this until your sense of abstraction takes up a good portion of your brain (like before you started grade school). Then render with abstraction. Avoid any rendering that does not consider the abstraction. Never render in a way that one would not place the shapes in that manner if they were not looking at something. Once something is rendered without consideration of the abstraction it is very hard to insert abstraction into it.

One can build whatever with abstract shapes. Stop thinking that if you get the drawing right, the color right, that it will be right. Those are minor things. It is the adjusting, composing, of the shapes. That is where the excitement is.

Then always go back and forth between non-objective and representation. Always make a shape when making marks. And never try to find your voice.

***JG:** Maybe your voice will find you.*

KK: Yes, if you don't try to find one. And if you can forget any idea you might have about what a painting is supposed to look like.

MP: I agree with Ken.

***JG:** Which of your own artworks are you most satisfied with right now, and why?*

KK: The collages I'm doing at my kitchen table. There is no thought except in the shape I'm placing at the moment. There is not much to think about. Not thinking about the next move, or how many moves there will be, or how it will end. I keep going till it excites

MP: I'm pleased with the paintings and prints I've made over the last couple of years. The parts that I've been working on inform one another without conscious planning. I am constantly curious how they will play out. Still, I'm hoping the best is yet to come.

***JG:** If you could draw the public's attention to any one aspect of art, what would it be?*

KK: Shapes. The arranging of shapes being why one representation is more exciting than another. That it is too easy to get an image without considering the abstraction. Not to be satisfied with a mere likeness. That abstraction has nothing to do with giving up control. That giving up control in order to get what is beautiful in nature does not work well.

MP: If I had billions of dollars, I would give a large sum of money to a major museum with the understanding that the museum design a wing for art that is "perception-based modernism" committed to "updating traditions of composition."

KK: Yes, a museum without any of the contemporary artists who one sees in contemporary museums would be wonderful. There is surely much to pick from and works that are much more affordable than what museums fight over. With a billion dollars each of these artists could be collected in depth.

The only problem is that one person's idea of perception-based modernism may be very different from another's.

MP: Well, yes. That would be up to the curators.

KK: It might be safer if you bought the works yourself then built a museum to hold them.

MP: Well, I have to win the lottery first.

***JG:** How valuable is it to you to work from direct observation?*

KK: I love looking at nature and I love painting. I don't need to do it at the same time. There are things one only gets when working from life. But those things are usually not enough. It's a pleasure to be out in the landscape or to have a model. But I find it best not to look too hard. Measuring one thing against another, matching the color, placing a shape too obediently to where something is seen in nature, can move one away from the needed nudging of shapes, away from making the strongest and most exciting composition.

MP: My process begins with observation, and it never ends. Whether I am starting a drawing or painting or working on a collage or print, I am still drawing inspiration from observation. As the process moves further from the original image, it is still based on the observation of what has preceded. It is never my intention to copy nature, but to find the shapes, values and colors that give form to visual excitement in two dimensional space.

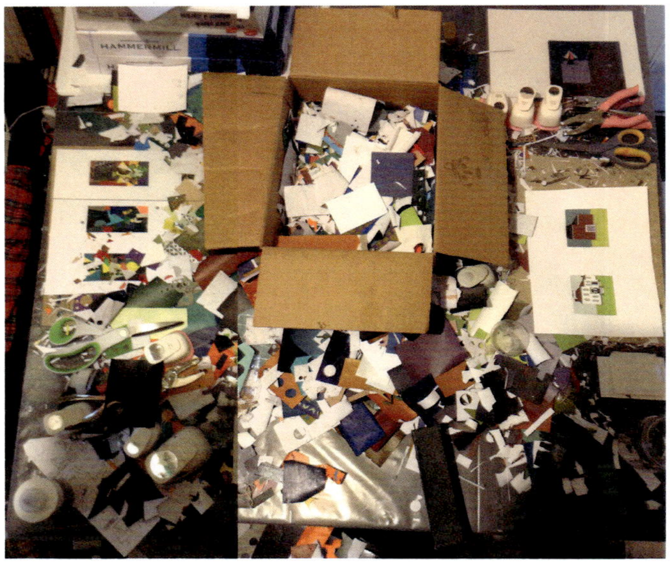

Ken Kewley's kitchen table as shared with Clara Kewley

***JG:** What discussions or writings on art affected you the most?*

KK: The writings of Rhoda Kellogg (*Analyzing Children's Art*. 1969). She basically says everything there is to say about art.

MP: *David Park: A Painter's Life* by Nancy Boas presents a transitional picture of David Park's courage to diverge from the popular art of the 50s, abstraction, and forge his own vision. Park's example gives support to remaining faithful to my own process, whether or not it is in vogue. Boas also mentions that Park claimed he struggled with an image while Diebenkorn could beautifully create an image with ease. As I am an artist who struggles, I find solace in Park's confession.

Ken's *Notes on Color* is a treatise on art that I have been rereading repeatedly. Some of my favorite quotes from *Notes on Color*:

"That art is not something that is learned and then practiced, it is a form of communication and one is always trying to say something clearer. To love and to be honest, maybe one does not exist without the other and a desire to communicate that, this is what it takes to make art. It takes courage to follow one's own vision, whatever that may be."

"In painting you never do what you set out to do. Something else happens."

"Within ourselves we all have great paintings, we all have the colors needed to make these works, and we just need to dig them out."

"Painting is like I am locked out and I am trying every door, looking through windows, trying to find a way in."

"Start by putting down the one color that excites you the most, then the next, relating it to the first. This is the relationship that excites you the most. Then the third color, relating it always to the whole. You are emphasizing what interests you and minimizing other things by putting them in the service of your true passion and leaving out altogether what distracts. Keep it simple." ◼

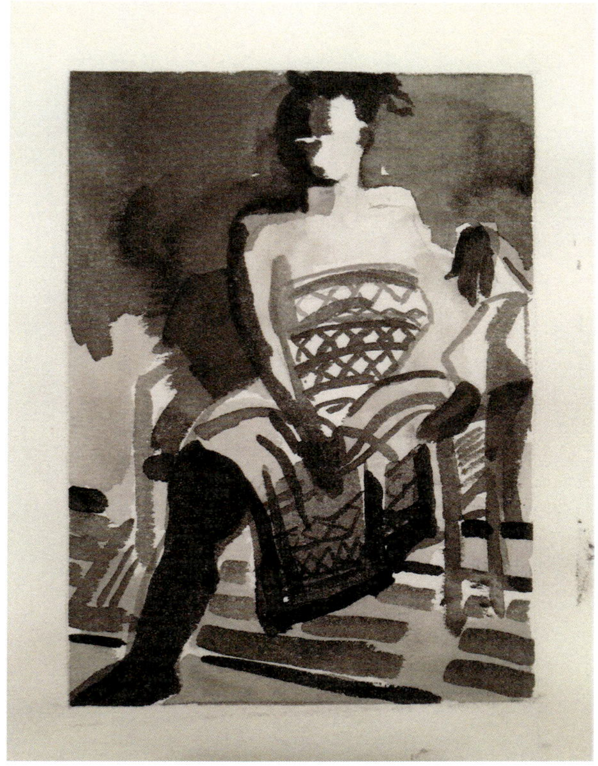

Mary Prince *Woman with a Dress*
2017, ink wash on paper, 7 x 5 in.

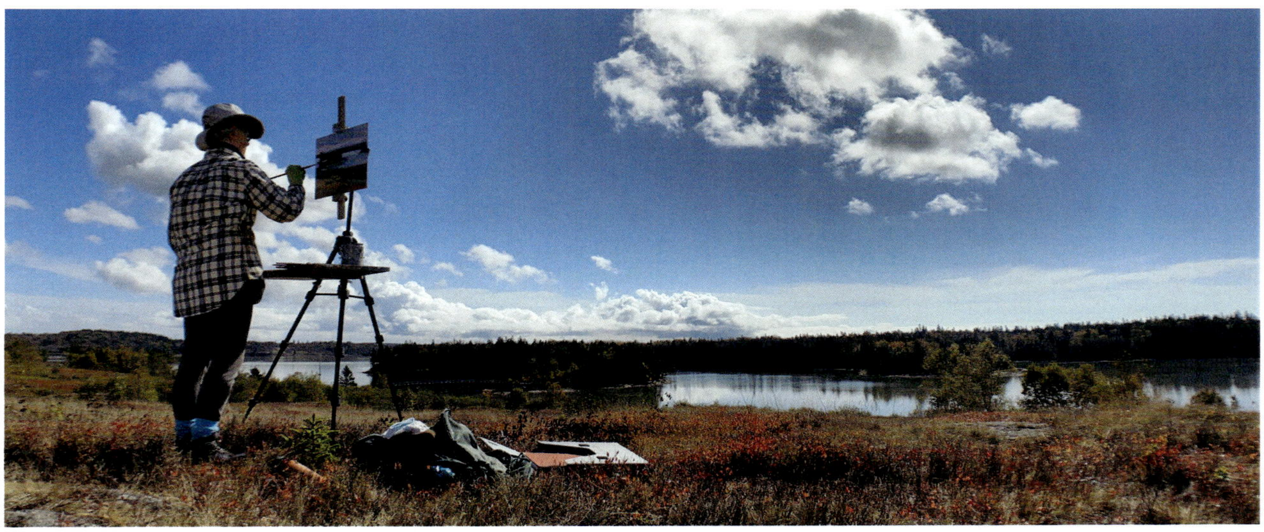

photo credit: Sarah Anderson

Mary Prince painting overlooking West River, Addison, ME

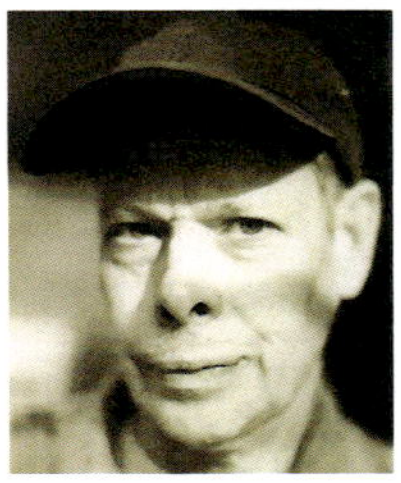

Ken Kewley graduated from the College of Creative Studies at the University of California, Santa Barbara. He was a night watchman at the Metropolitan Museum of Art 1980-1990. In New York his work has been exhibited at Steven Harvey Fine Art Projects, Lori Bookstein Fine Art and Pavel Zoubok. He teaches workshops and lectures at the Pennsylvania Academy of Fine Arts. In addition he has given his workshops in art schools, universities, and museums both in the United States and Europe. His work has been reviewed in *The New York Times, New York Sun, ARTnews,* and *The New York Observer* and included in private and public collections. The artist and his workshops were featured in the December 2017 issue of *Artist's Magazine.*

www.kenkewley.com

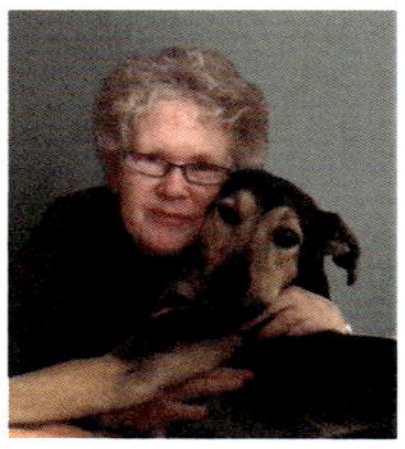

Mary Prince is a landscape and still life painter and print maker who lives in New York City and who paints in Downeast Maine, the Catskill Mountains and New York City. Exploring the dynamics of light, color, and texture of her surrounding world, her paintings and prints vigorously capture the atmospheric changes that animate nature, whether the rugged coastline and pristine islands of the Northeastern coast of Maine, the bucolic landscape of the Catskills, the parks of New York City or the exuberant fabrics and glassy objects of the still life. Her prints are variations of her painting themes. Beginning with an image taken from her painting, she moves to more personal creative variations with relief prints. Mary's artwork is in the Artemis Gallery, Northeast Harbor, ME, Stewart & Stewart, Bloomfields Hills, MI, the Ebo Gallery, Millwood, NY, and the Littlefield Gallery in Winter Harbor, ME, as well as museums and collections throughout the US.

www.zeuxis.us/prince

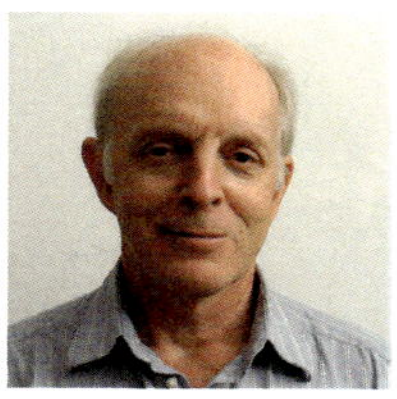

John Goodrich is a New York-based painter, teacher, and writer. His paintings have appeared in solo exhibitions at Bowery Gallery in New York City and the Contemporary Realist Gallery in San Francisco, as well as in group exhibitions at Elizabeth Harris Gallery, Kouros Gallery and Lori Bookstein Fine Art in New York City. He has written about art for such publications as *Review, The New York Sun, CityArts,* hyperallergic.com, artcritical.com and paintingperceptions.com.

www.zeuxis.us/goodrich
www.johngoodrich.net

Unexpected Connections

Lynette Lombard interviews

Deborah Kirklin and Ying Li

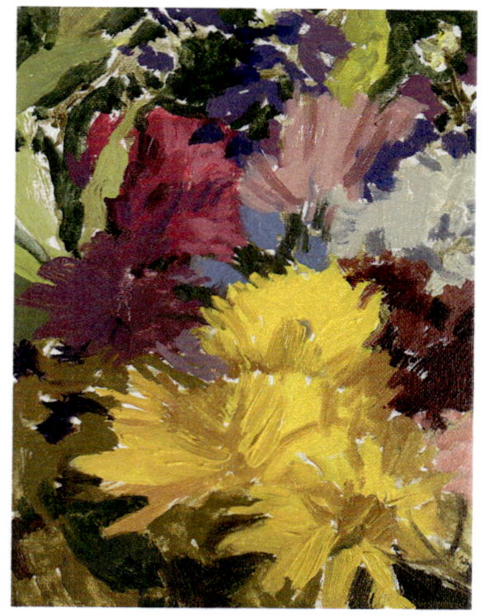

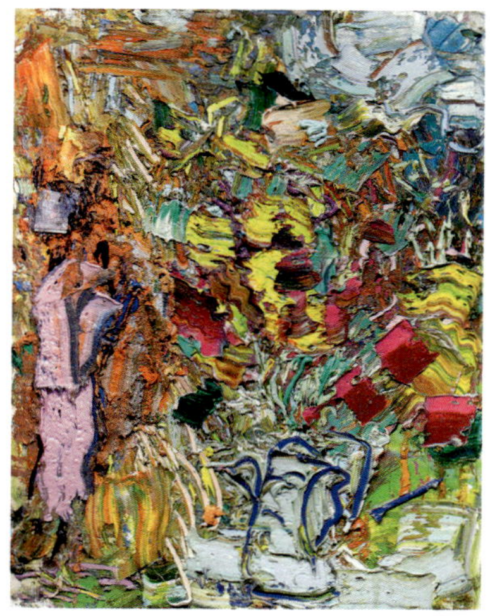

Deborah Kirklin *Two Bouquets, Summer*
2020, oil on linen, 32 x 32 in.

Ying Li *Autumn Blast*
2021, oil/linen, 48 x36 in.

Lynette Lombard: *To begin with looking at both of your work, at first, there seem to be quite a lot of differences, but the more I looked the more I found similarities. Each of you works from observation, there are flower motifs in your respective works, a focus on spatial construction and viscerality—although you have different ways of defining how paint behaves and how you use paint. I'll start out generally and then the conversation will most probably take off!*

LL: *How important is direct observation in your work?*

Deborah Kirklin: Direct observation has been critical to my work since I started painting. I have always felt I could abstract from nature and reality much more successfully and inventively than I could invent abstraction working on my own. I've always been tied to a light, shifting color and atmosphere. Those elements have been my mainstay.

Ying Li: When looking at nature in front of me, there is so much within the process of transforming what I see onto canvas. What's beneficial about working from life is that I don't get trapped in my own logic or my usual way of painting. The Chinese always say you are "such a little dot in this enormous energy." Nature puts me in perspective and gives the painting a sense of scale. Painting what I see onto a surface, working to make structural sense of what I see, takes my own ego away. I really have to concentrate so hard to figure out this thing. It's crazy to work with so much change, how to find structure, how I make sense of things. There's so much surprise. More than my own imagination can offer. It's so huge! So big!

LL: *I like painting something bigger than myself. Nature is huge and it's daunting, chasing the clouds, finding a structure, then, losing it and re-finding it. Working perceptually is so challenging and pushes me to my limits. It demands invention and specificity. There's nothing like working from life. So complex translating what's important and less important, you are always negotiating the relationships.*

YL: Nature sets the bar so high. Complexity, chaos and the structure hidden in nature. Painting for me is about how I make sense of what I see and how I find what holds everything together. You can paint an apple life-size, but you can't paint a tree life-size! You have to make sense of a motif to get at the spirit of what you paint. It's exciting. It's never about copying nature. It's what you take from it from a certain angle—that's what attracts me. Lois Dodd basically paints from observation and she zooms in. She finds a simplicity and a poetry in looking. I was thinking of another landscape painter, Margaret Grimes, whose work is powerful. She painted directly from the landscape, but her choices are very personal—a preference for the linear. We all take something from nature. Nature is amazing because it offers endless diversity and interpretations.

LL: *Yes, talk about complexity, late Vuillard's paintings unfold over time. The accretion of building mark on mark on mark arrives at specific big swelling volumes that have a clarity and a pacing of air, breadth and density.*

YL: It's endless and depends on how I feel. I look for different things from different art historical and cultural periods. Even on different days I search for what interests me at that moment. Lately, I haven't looked at anything. Sometimes you are on your own and that's enough to work with. I look more often when I feel dry. I've been looking at Chinese paintings for quite a while. I studied Chinese painting in China in college and I hated it. This is so boring I thought, stroke after stroke and no color. Looks like a painting with soy sauce. Now I'm turning back around and looking at it. The work is so abstract, but has the essence of what they wanted to say. They put down so little and say so much. They are the opposite of me. I find I look at what's opposite to me. Also, I think about the meaning of landscape painting. What's so special about landscape painting—a good landscape painter says something about life. Bellini at the Frick: Saint Francis. It's the ultimate of landscape painting. I've been looking at paintings by Huang Gongwang, a painter from late Song Dynasty. In Chinese painting he's the ultimate landscape painter because his paintings are about life, the symbolic meaning. There are so many different readings. He doesn't just paint a good tree. And then look at Bellini:heaven and earth, animals, people, tiny rabbits, the creek, huge, fantastic mountains with a great sky. It's all there. Stanley Lewis zooms in as a painter. He says he's just going to paint that fence, but the rawness, the layers, the weight. His paintings have such gravity.

LL: *Stanley arrives at a plastic complexity that's felt out. The rhythm of how we zoom in on neighboring relationships, zoom out to have a distanced view, then zoom in again. It's a back-and-forth focus. I think of Chinese painting as having a stacked space and often I find that feels very real—look up at the sky, you're there; look at the horizon, you're there, look at the ground, you're there. And the rhythm of the strokes.*

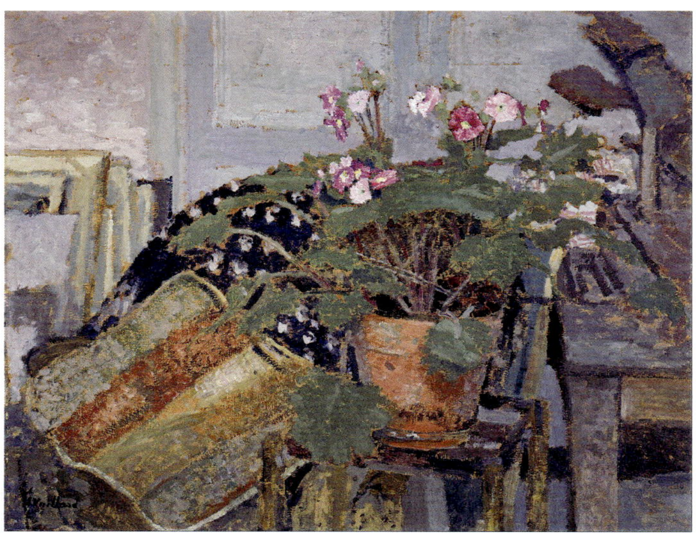

Edouard Vuillard *Le Pot de Fleurs*
c. 1900, oil on millboard, 19 x 24 ½ in.
Scottish National Gallery of Modern Art

YL: The rhythm is created by simple strokes—how the strokes seamlessly weave together through the rhythm. *Dwelling in the Fuchun Mountains* by Huang Gongwang, is 20 feet in length and 11 feet tall; he worked on it through four years and it feels seamless. One breath going through the whole thing! It's a miracle! You listen to Coltrane—one breath: he blows a whole life out. He has a concentration and that makes the energy flow. For Stanley more is more. The opposite is true for Lois Dodd: her distilled images are so paired down—like Haiku. People can take from observation within such an amazing range.

LL: *Process—yes! When does the painting begin? I hate beginnings! When I'm painting and I'm out there, I want to be in the painting, but to start with I paint descriptively, mapping out and finding a structure. When I can see the big relationships coming into a focus, that's when the painting takes on its own life within the rectangle. That's when it begins for me. I see the forces beginning to work in relation to each other. When does a painting begin for you?*

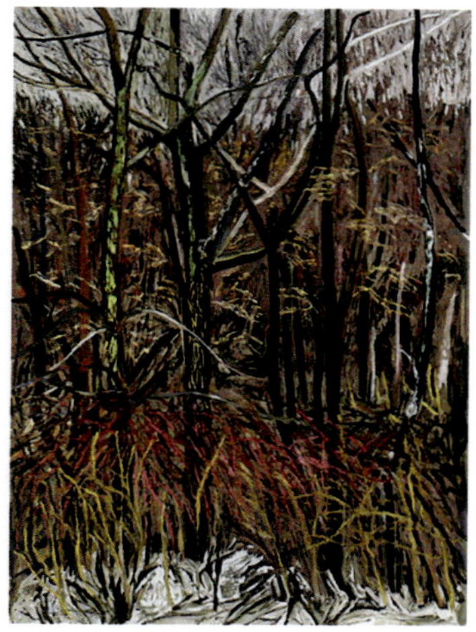

Margret Grimes *March King's Daughter II*
1999, oil on linen, 89 x 64 in.

DK: I have a sense of disquiet and unease when starting something new. Anxiety is part of the beginning. When I'm walking around the motif—my flowers, my props, looking at the light and getting internal feelings inside, the painting starts then. If I don't have an internal feeling, then the painting is not worth starting. In that case, I need to start with a really offhanded small drawing. I'm watching and waiting—the physical enactment is drawing—that's when it begins. I'm looking at the thing not the painting. We're all at the point where we can make a good painting, but what does it feel like? What does it mean? What does it express?

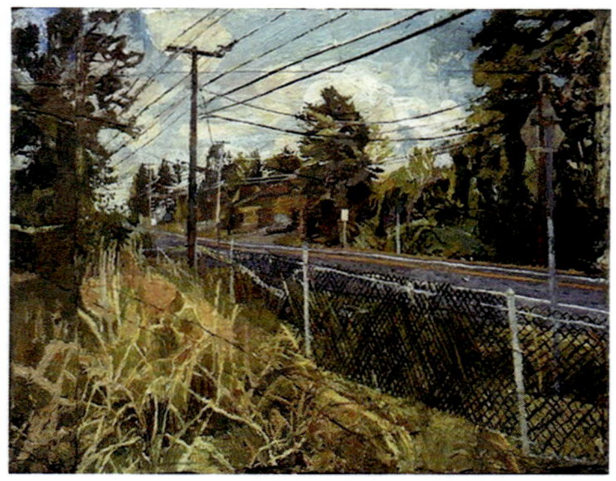

Stanley Lewis *North Gate (Chautauqua Inst.)*
2002, oil on canvas, 33 x 42 in.
Collection of the Center for Figurative Painting New York

YL: Each painting starts differently. Sometimes I just see it—it's right there. Once in a rare while, the painting comes out with no struggle at all. It feels so connected, as if it's feeding out of your hand. Most of the time, it's a process of struggle and frustration. Every touch is a decision and there are so many ways to go. You are constantly battling with yourself. For me what drives a painting is that I feel I painted this. If it's a certain feeling that I've already experienced then, right away, I get rid of it. I get bored and have to do something to break that. Nature offers what I need. When you look harder, the new inventions emerge from seeing what's there. And I say to myself, this is different from what I did in the previous painting. I tell myself "don't be lazy and go back to what I already know."

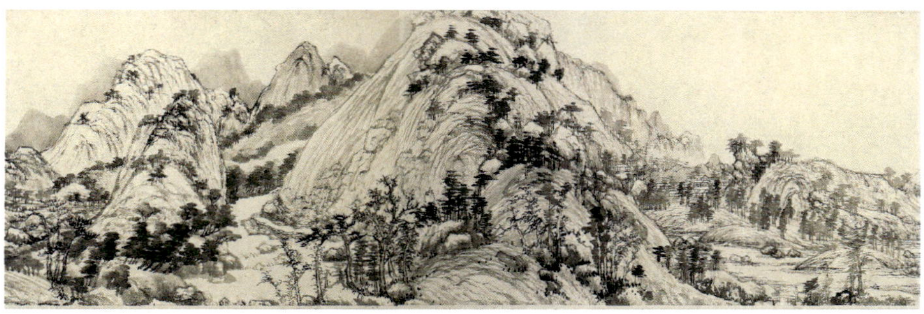

Huang Gongwang *Dwelling in the Fuchun Mountains* (detail), 1350, handscroll, ink on paper, National Palace Museum, Taipei

DK: I have a good feeling when I see a chance for revision and redrawing. When I'm feeling mannered, or the proportion is off, I begin to revise. It's a chance to get back to painting in a true way. I'm always happy when I see I can wipe out a whole corner. I can take it away.

YL: I often feel that I'm in, then I'm out. The painting on the right is a six foot five inch view outside a window in Chelsea, New York City. I've gone back and forth working on it for years. Sometimes you have to step out and have a cup of tea. I put on Art Blakey and he's seamless: how the rhythm and proportion and interval spaces have a subtlety and boldness. It's all there. Something like that can trigger my own feelings about what should be. It's not about details, it's about the whole thing. You can't be passive; you have to be 100 percent there.

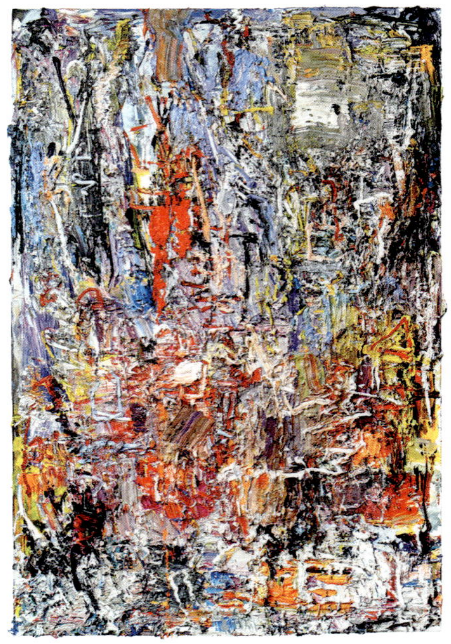

Ying Li *Writing the City #3*
2020, oil on linen, 74 x 58 in.

LL: *For me the process of getting frustrated and pushing beyond what I know involves a leap and I just go for it, no holding back. That is when the whole sensation of what I'm after becomes real and present in the painting.*

YL: Some paintings can be just one session. But a lot of the time I go back to it, work around the area I like, trying to save it, but it never works. I usually end up changing the whole thing. You can never be self-conscious. It's interesting that in my painting classes during the pandemic, students told me over and over that they knocked out a lot of work. Normally, they complain about the hours of work. No one complained this year. They put in the time. "How do you feel" I asked them? They said they felt they're not doing assignments. They need to do this—they need to paint.

LL: *In these two paintings above, I see such similarities of openness, open spaces moving through the whole image. Deborah's painting is very subtle in terms of how the spaces shift—as if there's a table tilted space, then the floor plane sinks down and the distant space of the room pulls back and up. Similarly, in Ying's painting lower left sinks down, flower rises up and the white torques the space, so, it shifts forward and back and builds a volume around the flower. Both paintings share a similar stacked structure.*

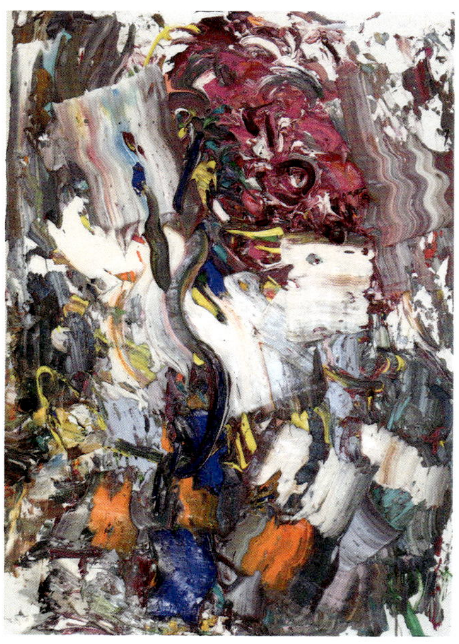

Ying Li *A Happy Orchid*
2020, oil on linen, 74 x 58 in.

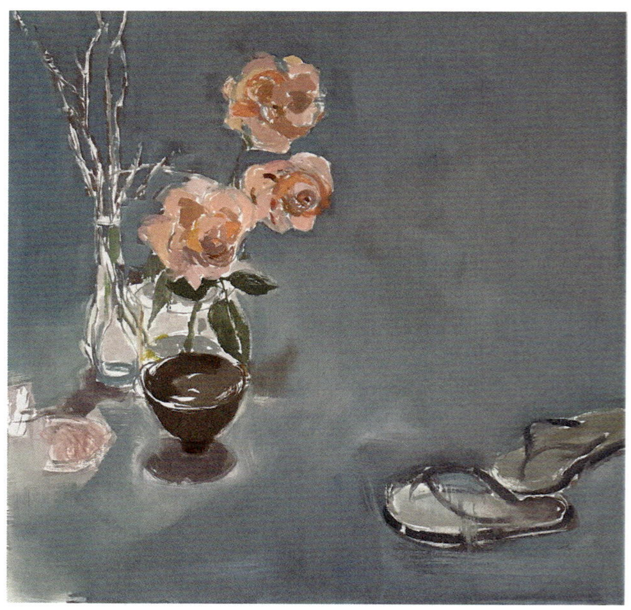

Deborah Kirklin *Still Life with Roses and Flip Flops*
2019, oil on linen, 30 x 30 in.

YL: Deborah, the openness and the air, the vastness of the space: chunk of flowers, the linear lines and the sandals are cool, so it's not just a bouquet painting.

***LL:** Let's talk about the idea of specificity in your work. Both of you are specific in terms of translating what you see. How important is it to keep the specifics of form or how do you define what it means to be specific?*

DK: I'm looking at specific forms and the spaces around them, using the gesture to summarize the form and color. I'm stopping at the moment of form. Specificity is when I create a feeling, a mood, a sensation, which means stopping at the right moment. Like a landscape premier coup approach. When I can't say that the painting is done, then I put it against the wall for a while. Later, I can see clearly what works and what doesn't. Now what I'm doing is quick action painting, trusting in the moment, then, waiting.

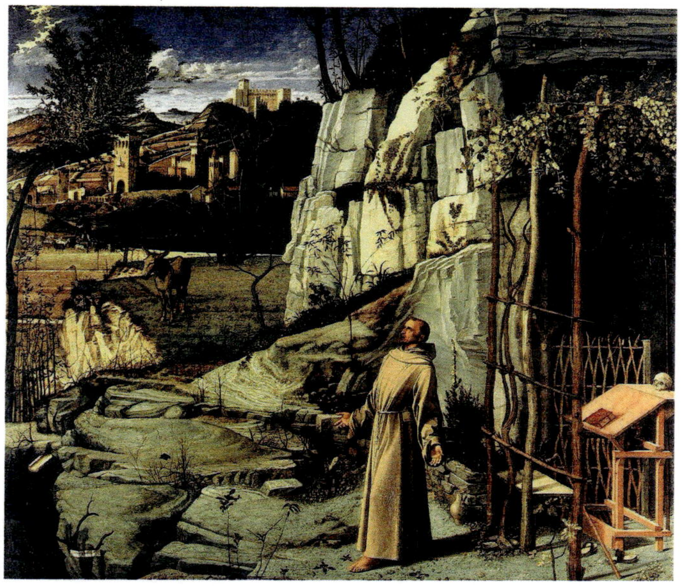

Giovanni Bellini *St. Francis in the Desert*
c. 1480, oil and tempera in panel, 1246 ¼ x 1419 ½ in.,
The Frick Collection

YL: A good painting gives you a very specific spirit. One that can connect with the viewer. There's a different set of criteria for how to make the piece special and unlike the others. Great paintings such as Albert York's—two trees and you can count the strokes—feels very specific. This is related to poetry in that it's not about interpretation, it's directly connected to human feelings. And I find feelings during the process—mapping out at the beginning, then you start to cook.

During that process the painting starts to become something and sometimes I feel I am hitting on a rubber wall, things are floating, but then you zoom in on something. There's a breaking point when I begin to see the other relationships and I make choices. In the end I see that what I thought in the beginning becomes something else.

***LL:** It's about surprise and the painting changes into something deeper.*

YL: You know I was working on a tree for hours and I think "if I can just get that right," but in the end, the tree shouldn't be there! This keeps us going!

***LL:** Color—how much of your color choices are from perception and how much are they poetic decisions from your experience of seeing and feeling the motif?*

YL: When I think about color, I think about Redon: the way he uses color is different from the impressionists. He uses color to serve his subject matter—it's symbolic. The way he uses primary colors and a range of tones is surprising. Color is a personal thing. You cannot force it. We cannot change who we are. I always think drawing is so important then, the color can be used in a crazy way because the scaffolding is there.

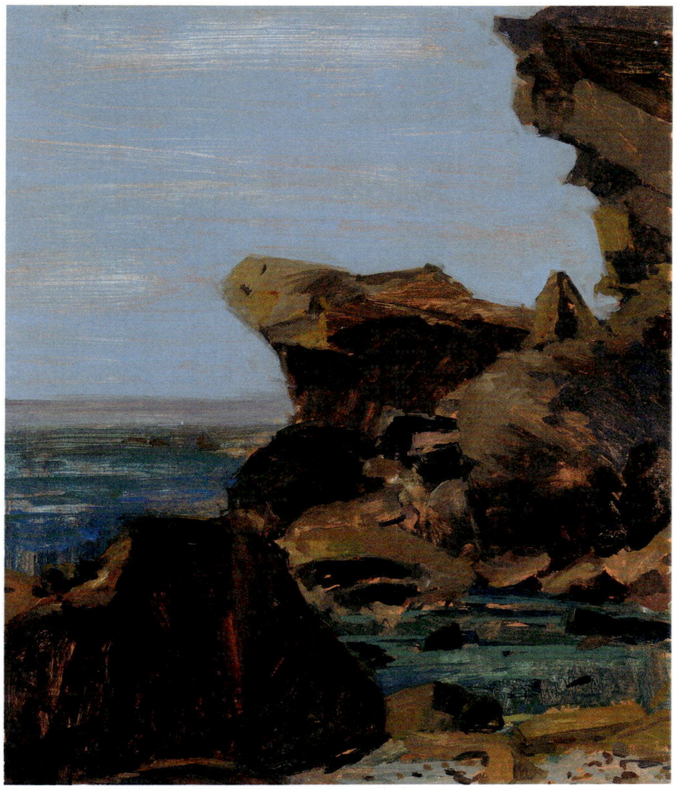

Deborah Kirklin *Rocky Outcroppings at Gualala*
2012, oil on panel, 16 x 12 in.

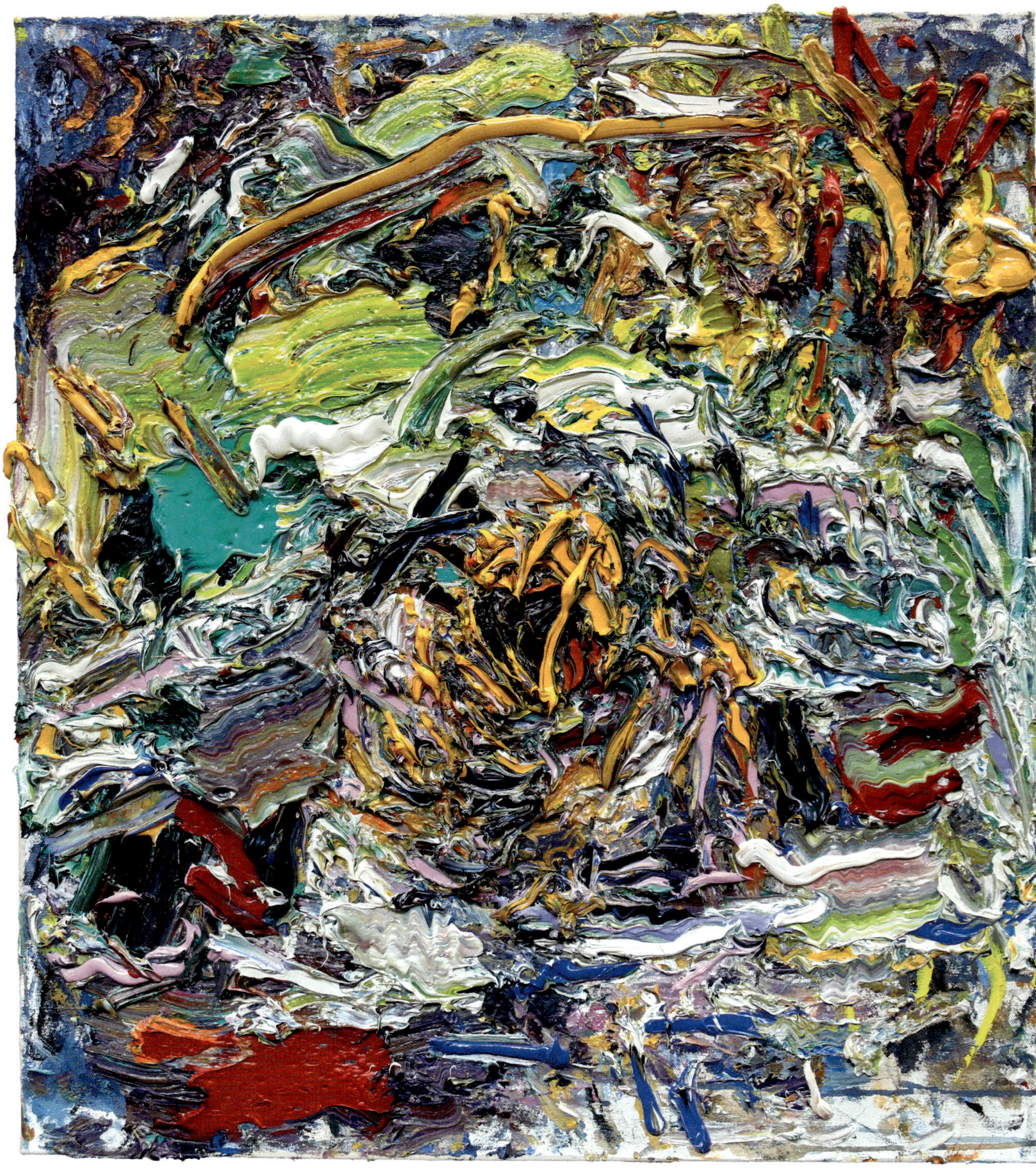

Ying Li *An Empty Nest*
2020, oil on linen, 30 x 26 in.

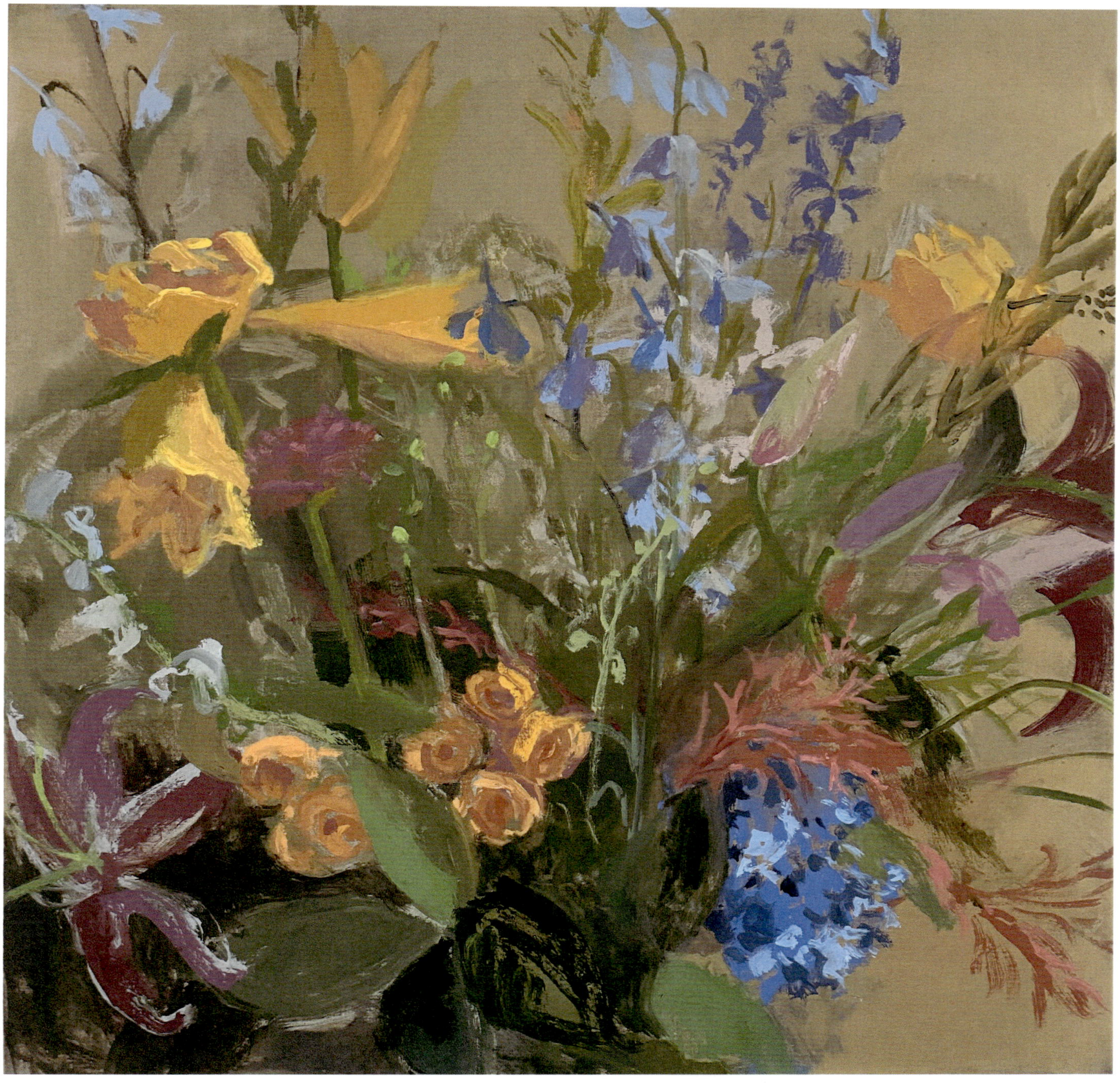

Deborah Kirklin *Stephanie's Bouquet*
2020, oil on linen, 32 x 32 in.

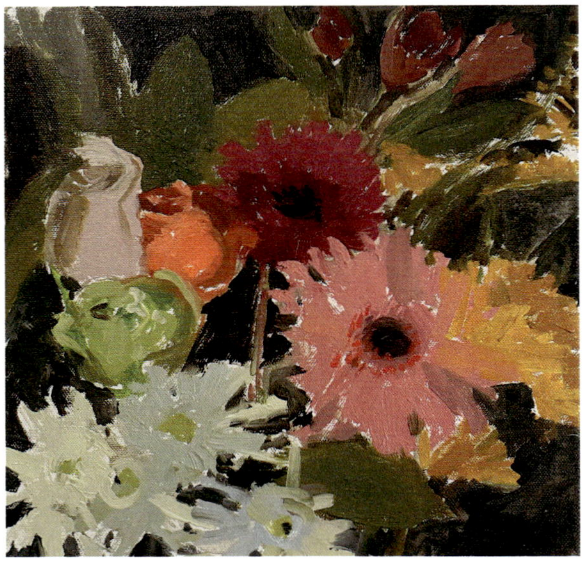

Deborah Kirklin Pink *Gerber Daisy Bouquet*
2020, oil on canvas, 12 x 12 in.

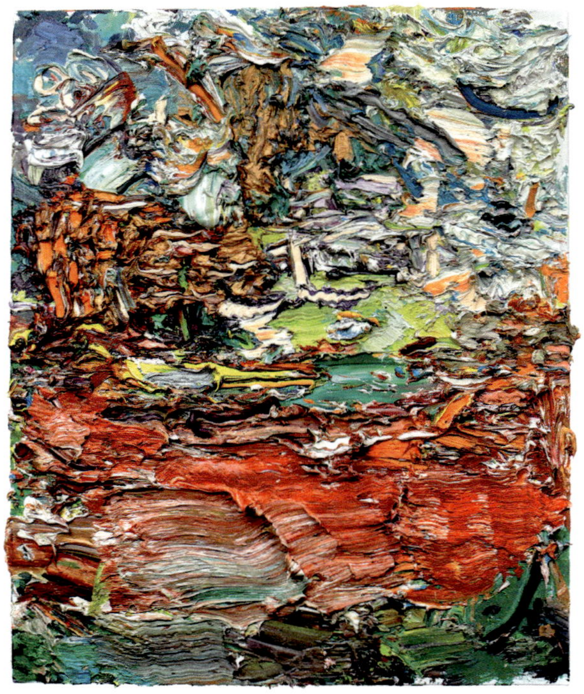

Ying Li *Rosendale Trestle*
2019, oil on linen, 30 x 24 in.

DK: My color is based in perception. I tone the colors. I fall in love and find my specificity with the pigments because of the tones, but my process is instinctive. I previously painted with saturated primaries—they were big interiors with red, blue and yellow influenced by Diebenkorn. I am often influenced by the artists I'm looking at. Seeing color relationships in my mind's eye is an endless source of pleasure and is my main motivator. The colour in my painting here is actually brighter. Really, color is like musical variation. I can work with it forever.

YL: I love this painting of yours (left), Deborah. I guess that's the canvas that comes through the flowers? They are little sparkling areas where the light of the canvas peeks through.

Leland Bell, I learned everything from him. He uses color uncompromisingly to push the light, the rhythm and the space, but it's not through tonal changes. Everything is frontal. His distilled structures are lean and all the spaces and forms have equal importance. He loved to talk about Mondrian and you can really see that connection and Helion's influence. His paintings stand to be looked at for years—they hold.

***LL:** Yes, color is personal, but I recall Nick Carone saying you paint an inner light as well as the light you see perceptually. The inner light can vary—it speaks to something within you, a certain kind of light you are attracted to. Color can be where the internal memories meet the external perceptions and you arrive at a sense of light.*

YL: When a painting gets to the point where it has its own reality, its own world, it's not about the appearances of what we look at. It's same for the light. It doesn't matter whether it's morning or noon or night—I can paint a night painting during the day, if I can feel it and it makes sense. The inner light is when you start to feel it's happening and it's beyond appearance. It's believable.

DK: I am the opposite. I can only paint the time of day I am looking at. I cannot paint the same painting throughout the day. I set the painting aside when the light changes. I'm specific about light and temperature. Yes, we carry different places within us, but I'd feel too self-conscious about defining a specific inner light. I was brought up in Portland, Oregon and I carry the light from there. I moved to the Bay area because I fell in love with the Mediterranean light here. When I was at the University of Iowa, I found it really hard to paint because of the pervasive white light. My better work is tonal. Both of you have such rich color and we come at it from different points of view.

***LL:** How has the Covid pandemic affected your paintings? After teaching in the spring, I felt such an urgency and hunger to paint. I'm introverted and love to paint all the time, so I've found the isolation liberating, but our time is precious. Both of your paintings above are frontal and the space feels intimate, contained, which* *is one of the realities of the pandemic experience. How has Covid impacted both of you?*

DK: The Covid pandemic has made me have a structure for my time, which is essential to my mental health and for those I live with. Every morning I go to the studio to paint. I've been sharing a studio with my husband who paints later in the afternoon. I never thought I could share a space but it worked out. The pandemic and lockdown has brought my family further apart and closer together and painting has been so important. It's an anxious time, especially during the elections, and I lost a dear friend. At times, grief and the anxiety of the election have influenced my work.

LL: I, too, have lost lifelong friends. Covid has brought a profound sense of loss and urgency into our lives and our paintings.

YL: I related to everything you both said. I don't feel that much different in the way that I paint. But I think painting is always a stability within an unstable world and this time intensified that feeling. Painting is what we do. You do it, but there's one new feeling: I feel freer than before. It's as if I can let go. I painted lots of flowers since the Haverford campus is an arboretum and the campus was empty during lockdown, so I could paint all the time. The intensity of the presence of nature has so much energy. No one trimmed the plants and they went wild and I really responded to that. Usually, I'm a messy painter, so I never went to public places to paint, but this time I dragged my stuff right in front of the rose bushes and no one was there. I could paint directly.

Another thing is I like the six foot distance restriction: people walk around you as a landscape painter! And this time really allowed me to paint on larger canvases. I love traveling to residencies, but no one could go anywhere and I have nature around me on campus, so I wanted to take risks and paint larger.

In fact, the painting on the right (top) was done in Rome when I was at the American Academy, which feels so long ago. It's a fence and cypress trees.

DK: There's a lot of Frank Auerbach and Soutine.

YL: Soutine is a genius, totally an individual.

LL: *And Van Gogh is in there in terms of directional marks and the light—a certain afternoon time of day.*

YL: The painting on the right (bottom) is a fake, corny Christmas tree. My boyfriend wanted a Christmas tree, so we decided "let's get a fake one." White is good for painting, so I painted it. I've received all sorts of responses to this painting even in a recent review that said it feels as if you're way up, looking down.

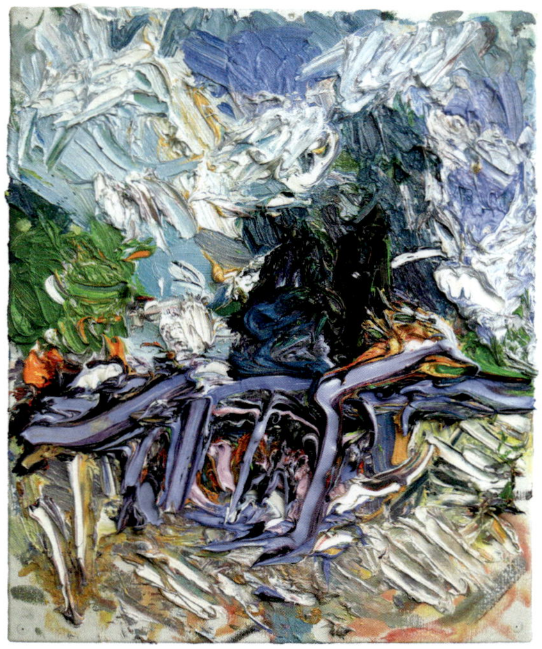

Ying Li *To the Secret Garden*
2018, oil on linen, 20 x 16 in.

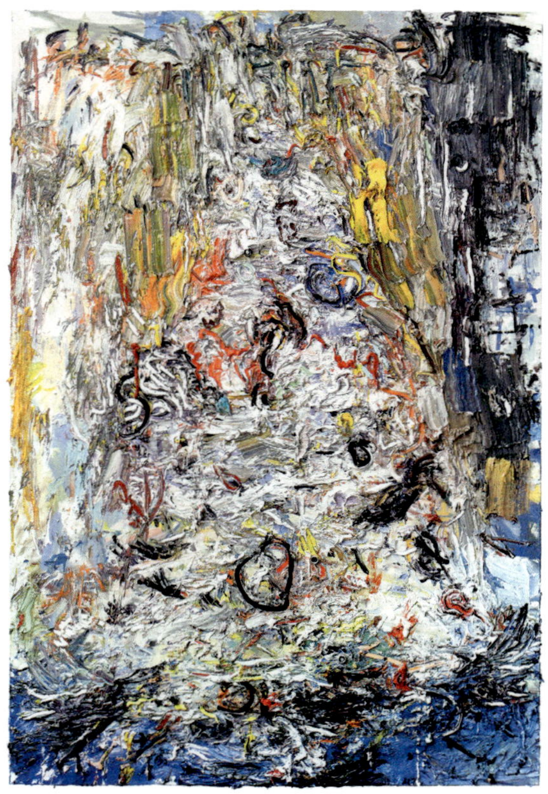

Ying Li *Christmas Everyday*
2020, oil on linen, 74 x 58 in.

LL: *It feels as if the central space cuts back, like a passage through the middle you can walk down.*

In pairing your work, I tried look for images that had something in common. Above, in both paintings, the masses of the flowers move in a more open, but shallow space.

YL: At Haverford, I had a show of three months of work, with this painting. This one I finished in my studio. I started in the daytime then, took it to the studio and finished it at night.

LL: *The piece of paper—on lower left—I do that to test a color and you left it*

DK: Yes.

YL: It's actually a piece of plywood. I use it to paint; it broke and landed right there! I needed that diagonal. Left it there.

LL: *It creates tension in terms of physicality, space, color, everything.*

YL: How big is that painting, Deborah?

DK: 32 x 32 inches.

LL: *So delicate.*

YL: Your marks are so different, beautiful.

LL: *I've seen Ying's painting in the flesh. And it's frustrating not to have seen your actual paintings, Deborah. In these two paintings, you seem to like the square.*

DK: I am experimenting more with my format, especially the square. I go back and forth between the bigger paintings and the smaller ones. Normally, I did several works that were triptychs, 30 x 40 inches in a row. More recently, I've been stretching my own linen because I love painting on linen.

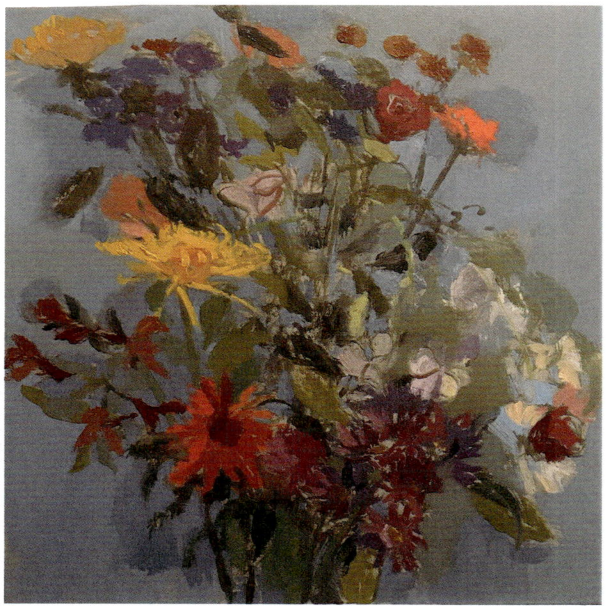

Deborah Kirklin *Bouquet and Shadows*
2020, oil on linen, 32 x 32 in.

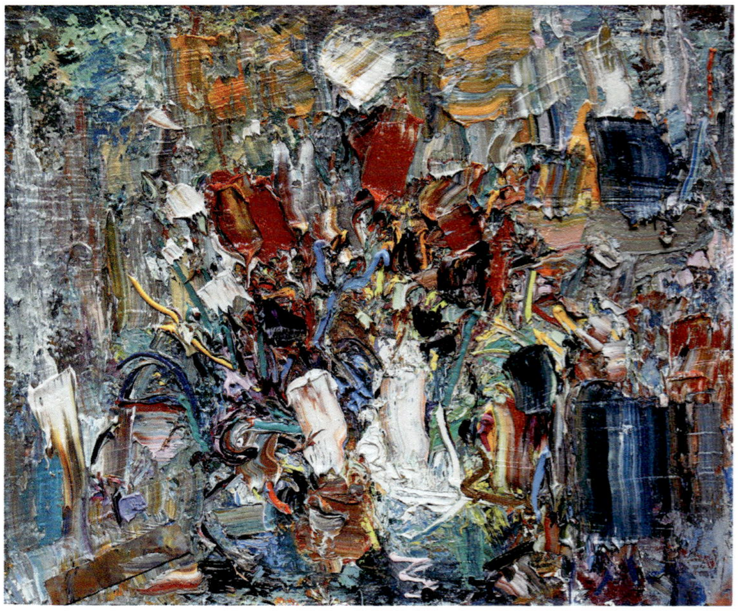

Ying Li *Night Tulips*
2020, oil on canvas, 43 x 50 in.

YL: The pandemic has given us more time, usually we all have so many obligations. So, I've worked every day. I never wash my brushes. It feels like a continuation of this one process.

LL: *Deborah's painting feels very solemn.*

YL: There's life there and energy and the radiance of the flowers.

LL: *You have both mentioned that art is about life. It encapsulates your life and I always think being an artist and the way the three of us paint is about being connected. Other external social connections have been diminished with the pandemic so that has meant we have had a bigger space to be connected to our work, to what we're painting and to what we're painting about.*

YL: That connection is more vivid and stronger and other parts fade away. I remember I was painting a peony and I thought about my friend Charles. I used to go to his garden to paint and I thought, I miss my friend. Associations like this and memories come into the painting. I feel it as I'm painting, I'm having a dialogue with a friend, with paintings and painters from centuries ago and then I think I have to work harder!

DK: I've needed painting more than ever and now I have more time to paint. I do relate to what you've said Lynette about being introverted and having a suit that covers who we are and that we like being on our own and painting, but soon I hope we can emerge!

LL: *Thank you, Ying and Deborah. This has been such an inspiring and lively pleasure to talk with both of you!*

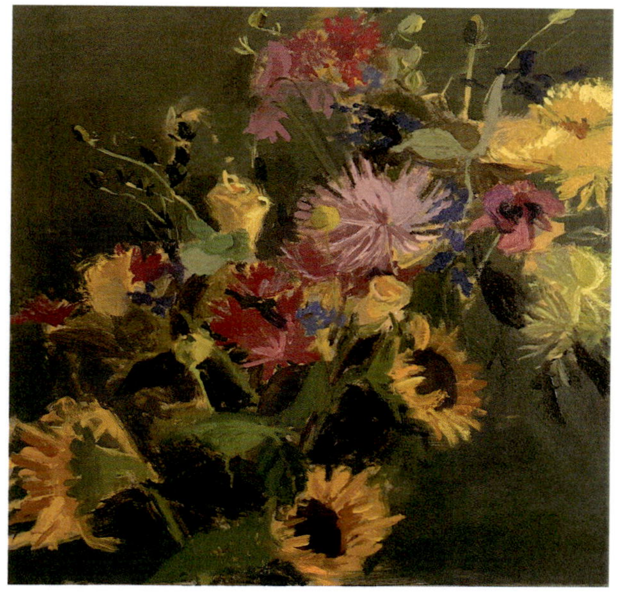

Deborah Kirklin *Sunflowers, Mums, and Greens*
2020, oil on linen, 32 x 32 in.

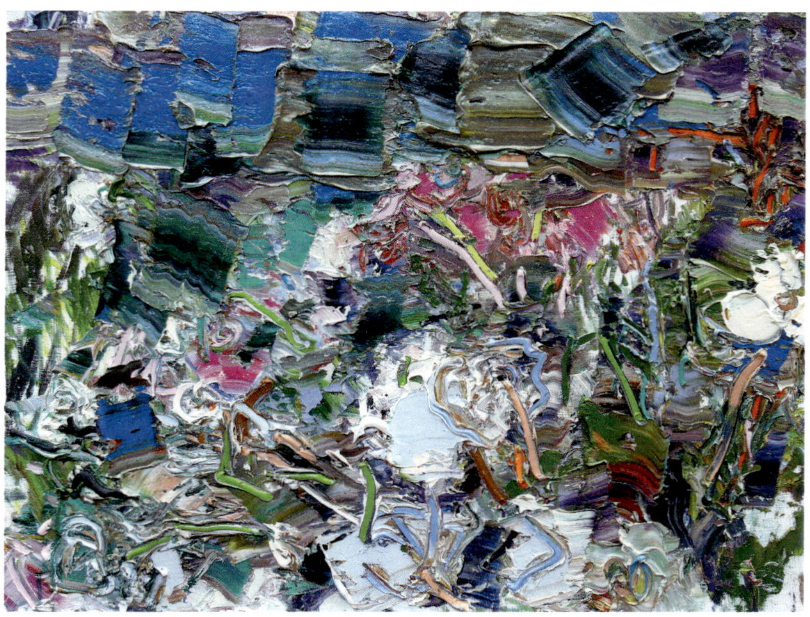

Ying Li *Peonies For Charles*
2020, oil on linen, 36 x 48 in.

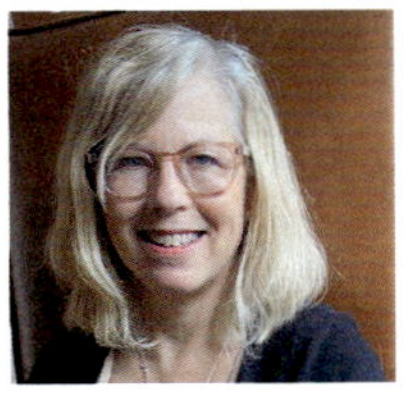

Deborah Kirklin is a San Francisco Bay Area painter who exhibits her work nationally and focuses on still life and landscape. A member of Zeuxis since 1994, Kirklin was also a tenured professor at Santa Rosa Jr. College in Santa Rosa, CA where she taught painting and drawing for many years. She earned her BA in Studio Art from Stanford University and an MFA in Painting from the University of Iowa. Exhibitions include solo shows at Hackett Freedman Gallery in San Francisco, Canada College in San Mateo, CA, Santa Rosa Jr. College in Santa Rosa, CA. She was awarded artist residencies at the Ragdale Foundation (2007) and the Virginia Center for the Creative Arts (2016). Kirklin has been a guest lecturer at Stanford University, CCA in Oakland, CA, the University of California at Davis, Davis, CA, San Jose State University, and University of Notre Dame de Namur in Belmont, CA.

www.zeuxis.us/kirklin
www.deborahkirklinartist.com

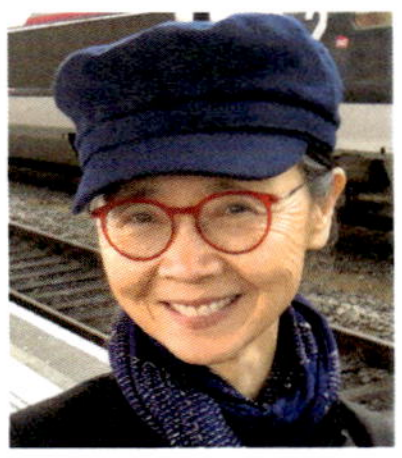

Ying Li, born in Beijing, China, immigrated to the United States in 1983 and received an MFA from Parsons School of Design, NY in 1987. She is the Phlyssa Koshland Professor in Fine Arts at Haverford College. Ying's work has been featured in numerous solo and group exhibitions, including at Centro Incontri Umani Ascona (Swizterland), ISA Gallery (Italy), Enterprise Gallery (Ireland), Museum Rochefort-en-Terre (France), The National Academy Museum, The American Academy of Arts and Letters, Tibor de Nagy Gallery, and many more. She is the recipient of The Edwin Palmer Memorial Prize for Painting and Henry Ward Ranger Fund Purchase Award and was a Visiting Artist at the American Academy in Rome in 2018. Her work has been reviewed in *The New York Times, The New Yorker, Art Forum, Art in America, The New York Sun, The Philadelphia Inquirer, The Washington Post* and most recently by John Yau at Hyperallergic.com.

www.zeuxis.us/li
www.yinglistudio.com

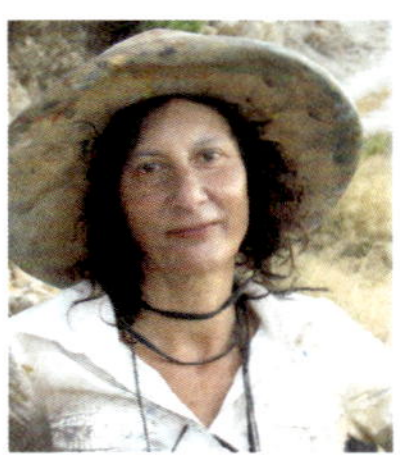

Lynette Lombard, Chancie Ferris Booth Professor of Art at Knox College, received her MFA from Yale University, BAHonours from Goldsmiths' College of Art, University of London and attended the New York Studio School for two years. Lombard received Mellon Grants to Berlin and Spain, the Philip Green Wright-Lombard Award for distinguished teaching and research grants from Knox College. She was represented by the Bowery Gallery, NY, Confluence Collective, Spain, the Midwest Paint Group and Seven on Site. She exhibited at the Centro de Arte, Mojacar, Spain; Newtownbarry House Gallery, Ireland and Chisenhale Works, London, England, the Figge Museum IA, Lohin Geduld Gallery and the Painting Center, NY.

www.lynettelombard.com

Organizing Sensation

Franklin Einspruch interviews

Paula Swaydan-Grebel and Gwen Strahle and John Goodrich

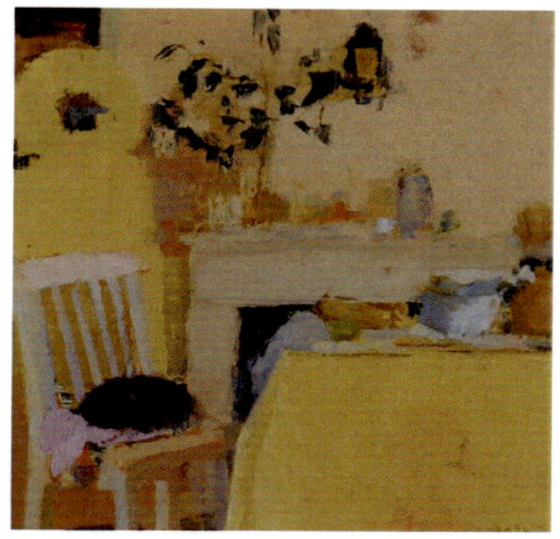

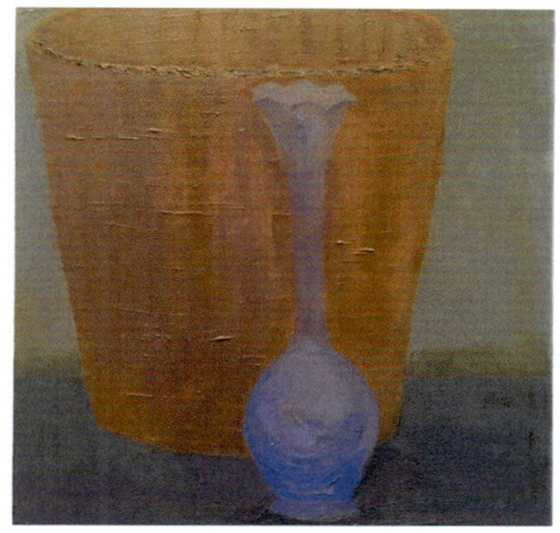

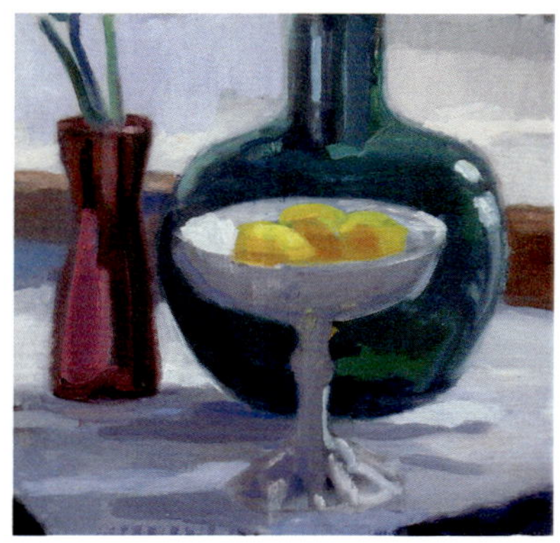

Paula Swaydan-Grebel
Yellow Room and Black Cat
2019, oil on panel, 8 x 8 in.

Gwen Strahle *Untitled*
2020, oil on canvas, 15 x 12 in.

John Goodrich *Purple Vase*
2019-20, oil on canvas on board, 12 x 16 in.

Franklin Einspruch:

Paul Celan (trans. Katharine Washburn and Margret Guillemin):

> *you, never-to-be-counted:*
> *by one null-*
> *token*
> *you are ahead of*
> *them all.*

When I started writing criticism in the 1990s, the question was still hanging in the air of what period of art we were in, pluralism having grown stale as a category. In the years following it became clear that the sheer number of artists and the proliferation of styles was such that an enterprising critic or curator could make a case for just about anything as an ascendant movement. Every so often an excitable critic dubs someone the finest artist of his or her generation, in imitation of the one critic who got away with that in 1945. It never sticks. It won't do to plug some novel phenomenon into the historical position occupied by high modernism. We live in a different time, one that demands a more receptive critical approach, a willingness to look at all anew.

And what times they are. While some critics, the perpetual victims of historicism, are on the lookout for how artists are responding to the pandemic or the political events of the last year, I'm increasingly interested in the opposite, the artists who are able to bear down and work in spite of the mayhem going on in the world. Thus it was my honor and pleasure to interview three intensely committed painters, John Goodrich, Paula Swaydan-Grebel, and Gwen Strahle, all of whom bring their distinct energies to the subject of still life.

FE: *Are you sensitive, personally or aesthetically, to the turning of the year? What sentiments does it generate, either in regards to a new year in general or this one in particular? Does it affect your painting or how you think about it?*

John Goodrich: This year the thought of a vaccine on the horizon is a big boost! But generally seasons don't change my frame of mind, beyond the fact that cold weather means I won't be painting outside. I enjoy painting whatever nature presents at the moment.

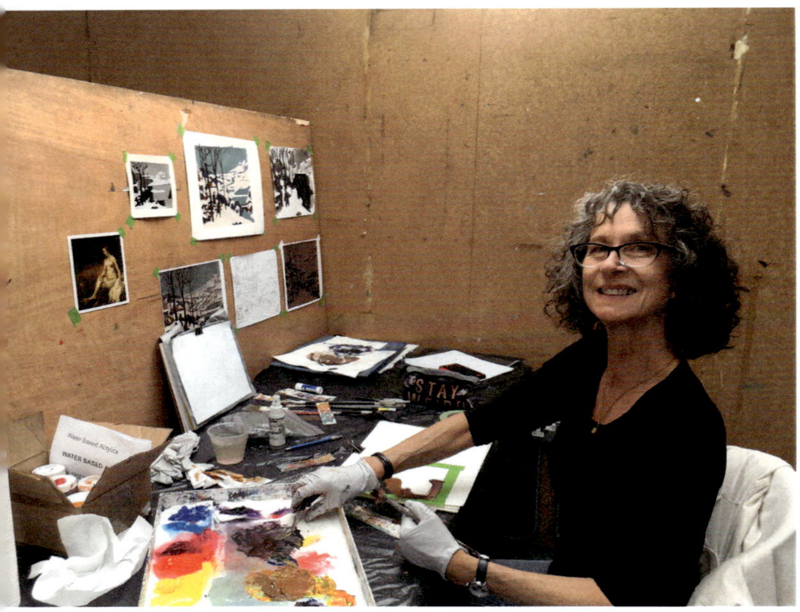
Paula Swaydan-Grebel working in her studio

Paula Swaydan-Grebe: With the turning of the year, I notice that the sky is darker at night, and the sun lowers during the afternoon. There are a lot of greys and browns. I miss the songbirds and all the unusual insects. I am aware of the quiet. Winter is when I travel west to visit with family. This interrupts my studio time, shakes things up, which has some benefits. I take in new views, ideas, and experiences. I will sketch and paint on the road and while visiting family. The key importance is to take the time to draw and paint. Creating art allows me to transcend to a better place. I am uncomfortable when I am not painting.

I paint year-round and never have big plans as the year ends. The quiet winter months are a good time to contemplate the experiences of 2020. It is also time for me to have a conversation with my paintings and set new goals for 2021 to keep me focused. I hope next year it is safer for all to return to some normalcy.

Gwen Strahle: It's going to be hard not to look back on 2020, and be ready for 2021. I can't say that I think too much about the new year in relation to my painting. I am usually entering into teaching a Drawing Marathon in January, at the Rhode Island School of Design. After five weeks, I have spring semester off, so I am geared up to have an uninterrupted time in my studio. I'm more focused on that turn, rather than the turning of the year. I am not teaching it this year as all Winter-session classes will be remote, so as of today I have steady time in the studio through February.

FE: *Conventions, in my opinion, often get a bad rap. I've seen a lot of press releases singing the praises of some artist for defying conventions or nursing an unconventional approach. This seems to reinforce the myth of the artist as a professional flaunter of mores, for which there are examples, but they strike me as beside the point of why one would disdain a convention—it may be limiting, but limits can be productive. You've chosen the conventions of still life and figurative painting in general. What is your relationship with conventions?*

JG: I'd agree that the art world too much resembles the fashion world in that sheer demonstrations of unconventionality seem to get the most attention. You could say that the convention of a painting having rectangular limits is actually what makes it most interesting—a painter can use these limits to give a sense of scale and momentum to whatever happens within the rectangle. At least that's what I get out of great painting, whether abstract or representational.

GS: I consider the still life not a convention but a vehicle. The still life gives me a freedom, in painting. So, it's actually the opposite of limiting.

PSG: I do not think about any relationships with conventions while painting. The decisions I make about the work are intuitive. With that said, to be honest, art history matters in who I am as a painter. From years of study and painting, I am sure that what I have learned has internalized. The elements must feel right, the space, unity, movement, repetition, scale and proportion. Then there are times I'll push these ideas, place the object dead center, then see how I can balance the picture. Cézanne's play with space and scale intrigues me. Right now I am attempting to alter conventional colors to see where it leads me. So, without thinking about it, I both follow and defy conventions.

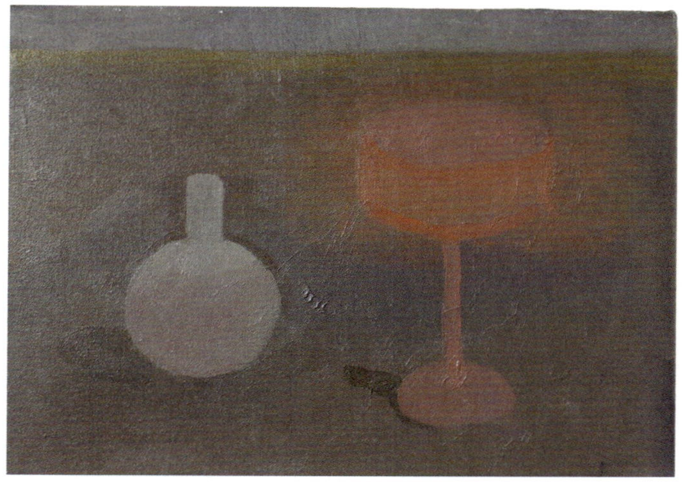

Gwen Strahle *Untitled*
2019, oil on canvas, 11 x 14 in.

***FE:** A common theme I find among the three of you is an interest in taming complexity. You include objects like baskets, scalloped glass, and the like, and then fight your way towards some kind of unifying principle. None of you are painters of detail for its own sake, which is the obvious way to handle complexity. Rather, you're looking for underlying phenomena. Is that a fair assessment? If so, how does it play out in your work? If not, how would you characterize it instead?*

PSG: "Taming complexity"—I like this characterization. Your assessment is fair, I do search for a simplified scheme. It is a constant battle for me because I love to paint all that detail. For my work, I found it takes a lot of drawings, color studies, and rethinking before I find a good design. Afterwards, after all this looking, the details emerge and are placed with a purpose. I also look to historical painters whose work is complex yet solid. One such lesson came from *Hunters in the Snow* by Pieter Bruegel the Elder. I was curious to find the substructure underneath all his details. So yes, the underlying concern of mine is that of a unifying foundation.

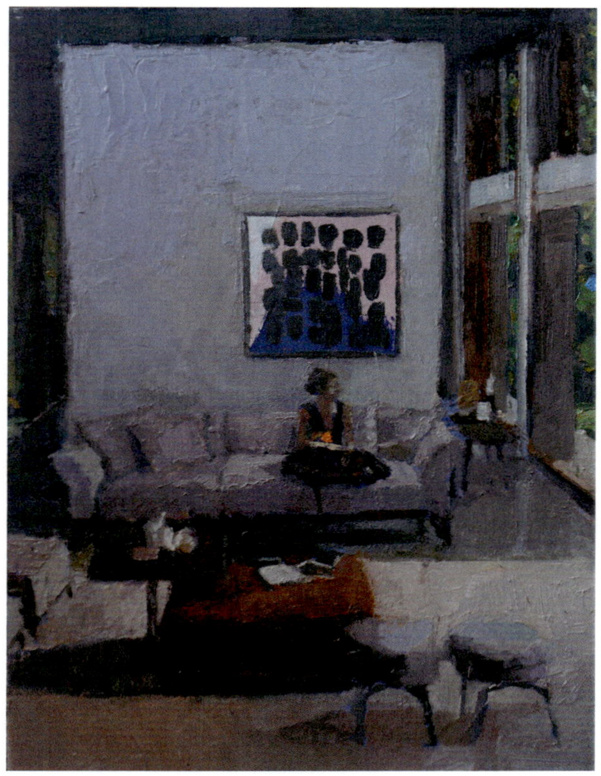

photographed by LivingEtc

Paula Swaydan-Grebel *Room with Artwork*
2020, oil on canvas on board, 12 x 9 in.

GS: That's why I love the still life. It's an arena. The still life is my painting world, and I can put objects in it, take them out, and move them around. One object may have a lead role in one painting, and then in the next painting, a supporting role. The search for "underlying phenomena"—that is absolutely a fair assessment. I see the still life as a zone. A time zone, or a

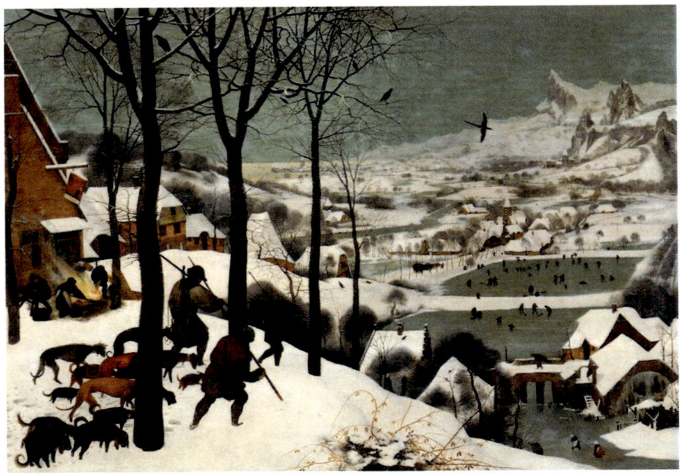

Pieter Bruegel *The Hunters in the Snow*
1565, oil on panel, 46 x 63 ¾ in.

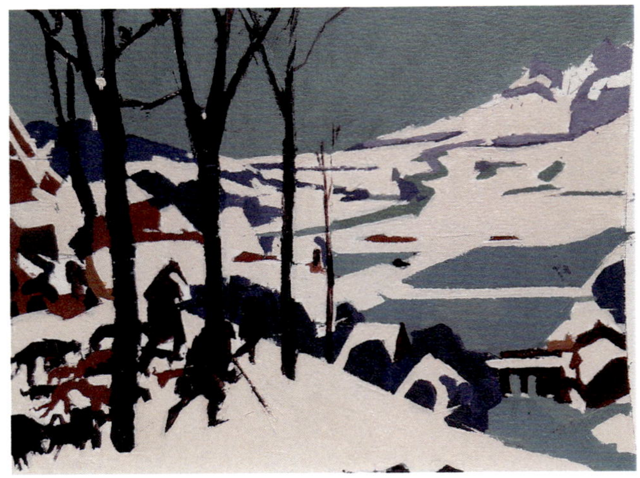

Paula Swaydan-Grebel *Bruegel Study, Hunter in the Snow*
2019, oil on paper, 32 x 32 in.

state of mind. It's a slowing-down. The stillness is always amplified to me because I am painting from something still. Once I have a still life world, an object has to be able to exist in it. The still life world comes first, then the objects. What underlies isn't usually about the literalness of the objects, though I like that I can paint about an object. What underlies is that painting world, which leads the way. I feel like this is a phenomenon.

JG: There's that great quote by Delacroix: "Exactitude is not truth." I tell my students that painting a scene realistically is not a matter of taking inventory, but of figuring out how each element counts uniquely with the painting. So for me the underlying phenomena is the visual energy of a scene, revealed by a particular light. Our perceptions are naturally subjective, and the task is to try to organize them pictorially, in the hope of uncovering the necessary character of each element. Sounds simple, but of course it's anything but!

FE: *What role does the still life play in relation to the rest of your work?*

GS: I've continuously been drawn to the intimacy of the still-life as a quiet, shallow space. But I have also seen the still life as a landscape, a portrait, an abstract opportunity. I like that the still life can be this metaphor for something else, and at the same time refer back to itself. Through painting the still life, I have always felt a freedom. Just thinking about the phrase "still life" slows down time and allows me to contemplate stillness.

I love the objects that I choose to paint. Many I have painted for over forty years. I am interested in a painted world which will allow my objects to exist together in different ways. The particularities of their relationships can enhance and use their idiosyncrasies. Sometimes, I make a painting about a singular object. An object can have a different importance when alone in a painting; and I feel differently when I paint thinking only of one object. If a painting with one object hangs next to another painting with only one object, there might be a connection. Maybe the object wants to be in the other painting. If I am convinced, I may put these two objects together in my next painting.

PSG: The still life offers an excuse to paint indoors in the studio, away from distractions. It is not boring or expected. Each new day I approach the same setup with different emotions, attention, ideas. I may notice something that wasn't obvious to me before. It can be a hidden shape observed by grouping objects within their shadows. Unexpected colors appear when placed side by side with complementing colors. The still life enables opportunities for long moments in looking. This allows discovery, surprises, and exciting occurrences. The still life offers endless perceptual moments and visual experiences that are exciting. It is another reason to make a painting, my favorite thing to do.

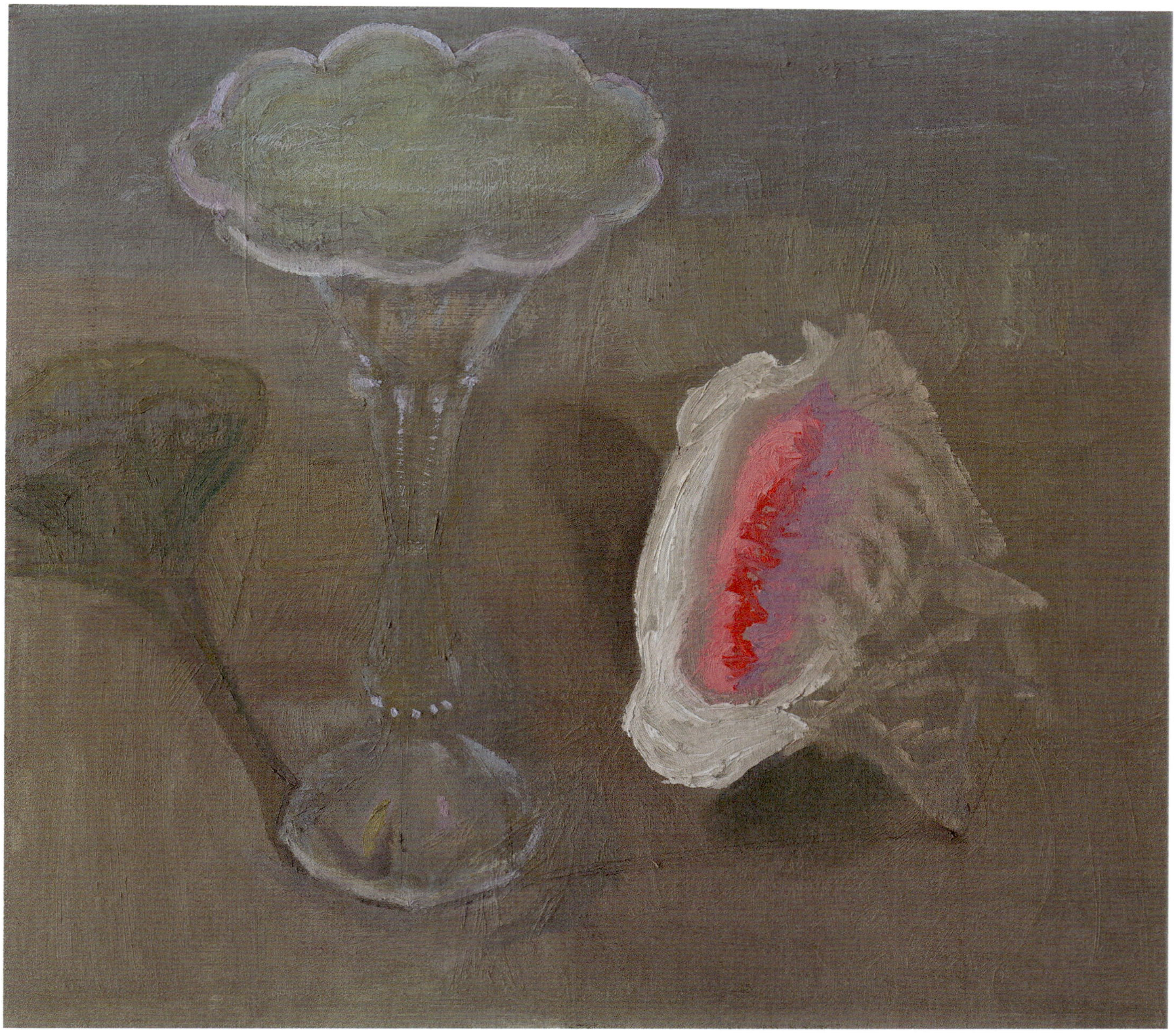

Gwen Strahle *Shell and Vase*
2018, oil on canvas, 17 x 19 in.

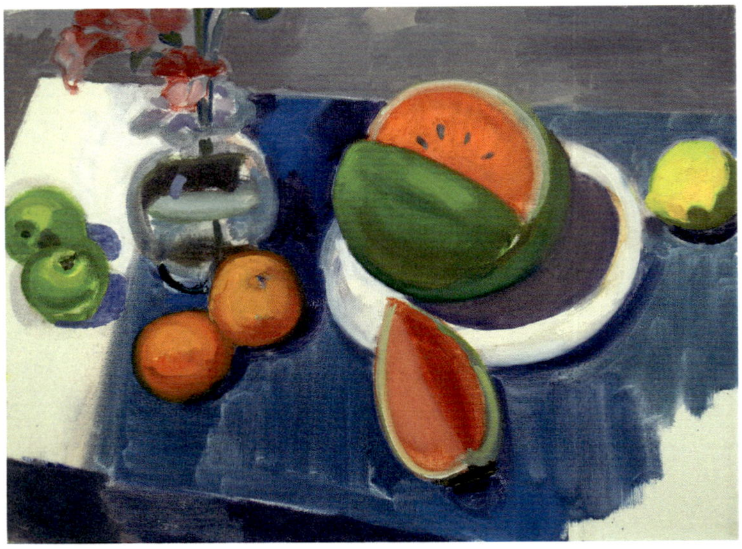

John Goodrich *Watermelon, Oranges and Lemon*
2016, oil on board, 12 x 16 in.

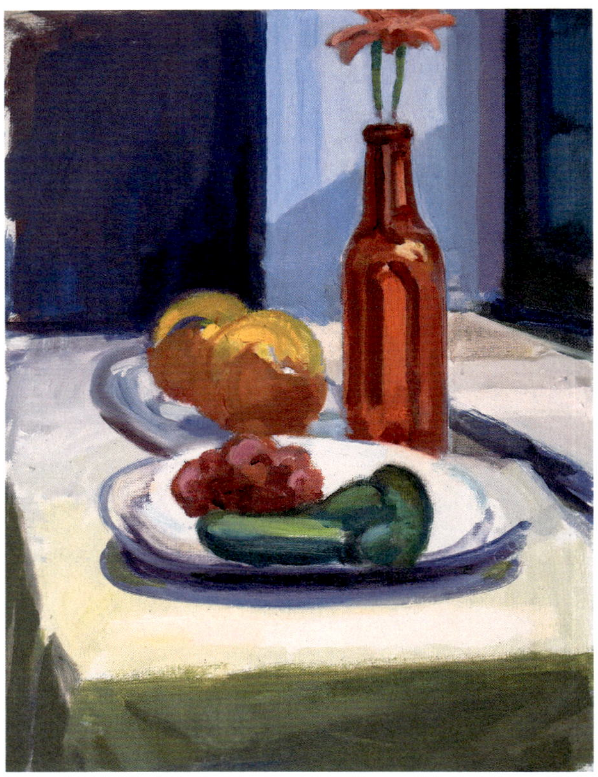

John Goodrich *Red Bottle*
2019, oil on canvas on board, 12 x 16 in.

JG: I like considering a still life as an intimate version of a landscape, the difference being that you oversee the motif instead of occupying it, and you get a chance to re-arrange objects and maybe the light source. The still life is intimate and finite, and the landscape can be overarching and infinite, but for both one has to organize one's sensations.

FE: *John, could you say more about organizing "one's sensations"? What does that entail?*

JG: I'd put it this way: Our visual perceptions are subjective, which means that the way we compose a scene is too. The curve of a road might play a big part in locating other elements on the ground, or be just a faint echo of clouds in the sky. A tree's canopy might be a dense blotting out of sky, or an exuberant eruption from a trunk. Distant houses could be lively interruptions of the long drone of a horizon, or perhaps subtle echoes of foreground fence posts. The challenge is ordering everything at once, and this is so complex and intuitive a task that it may take many false starts and reworkings. Or, for me, countless abandoned efforts.

FE: *Paula and Gwen—do you have your own ways of organizing your sensations? To put it another way, what internal frame do you invoke in order to bring yourself to painting?*

PSG: When I paint the still life, I respond to the depth of colors, shapes, design, and intrigue. The glass holes to look through, the stripes that peak over flat shapes, square versus round. My eyes enter the picture frame, I see the movement of things from here to there. I settle in one area, an area with more detail and brighter colors, harder lines. It is a play of all these that move the eye about. All is an excuse to make a painting, a design within the rectangle. If I am excited and can paint this beauty, then I am happy with the results. Another thing I have done is to make many small studies of the same set-up. I try different values and color combinations. This process has helped me to see what my options are. It helps me to edit, to better understand and express my point of view.

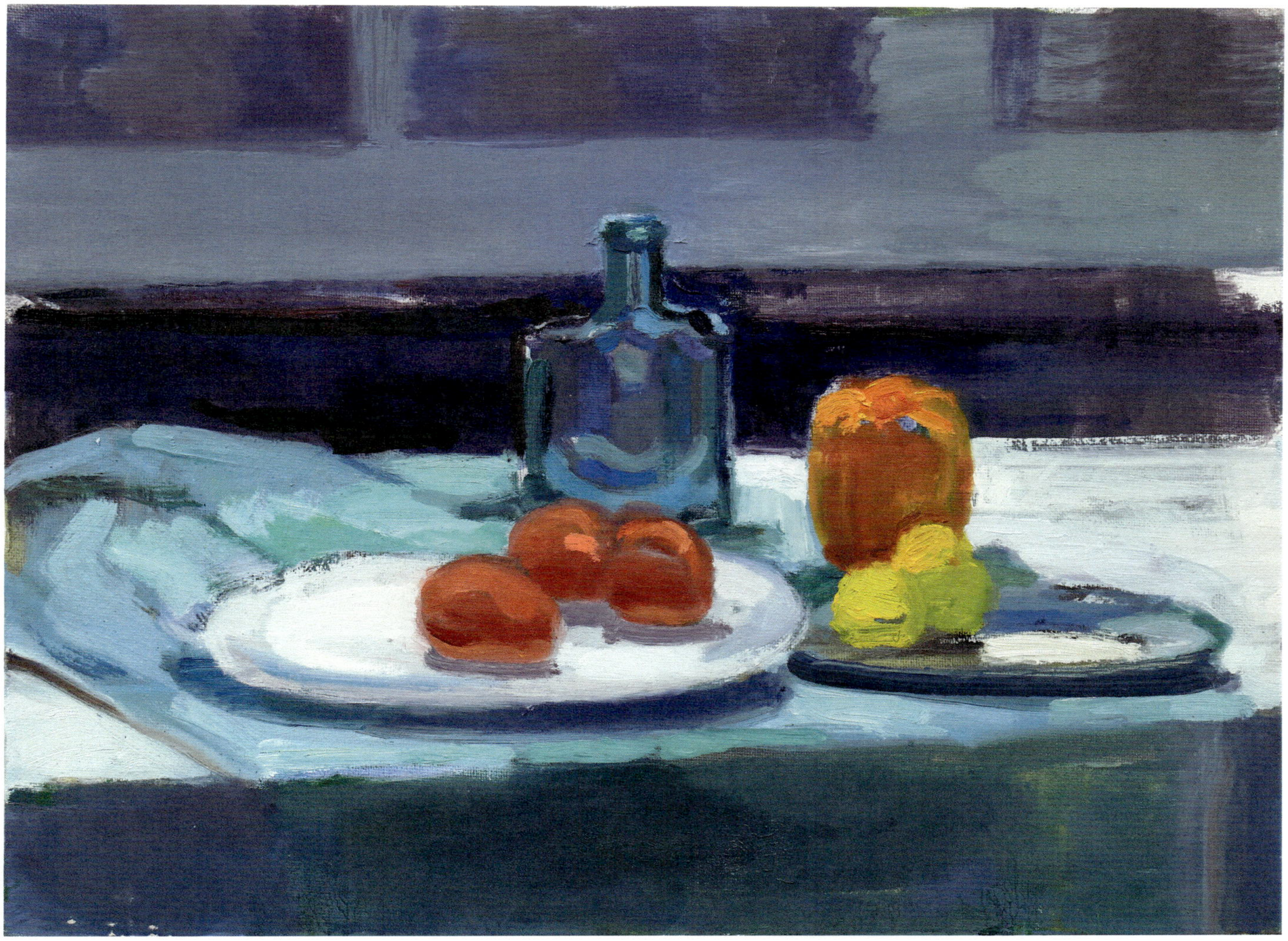

John Goodrich *Square Bottle*
2019, oil on canvas board, 12 x 16 in.

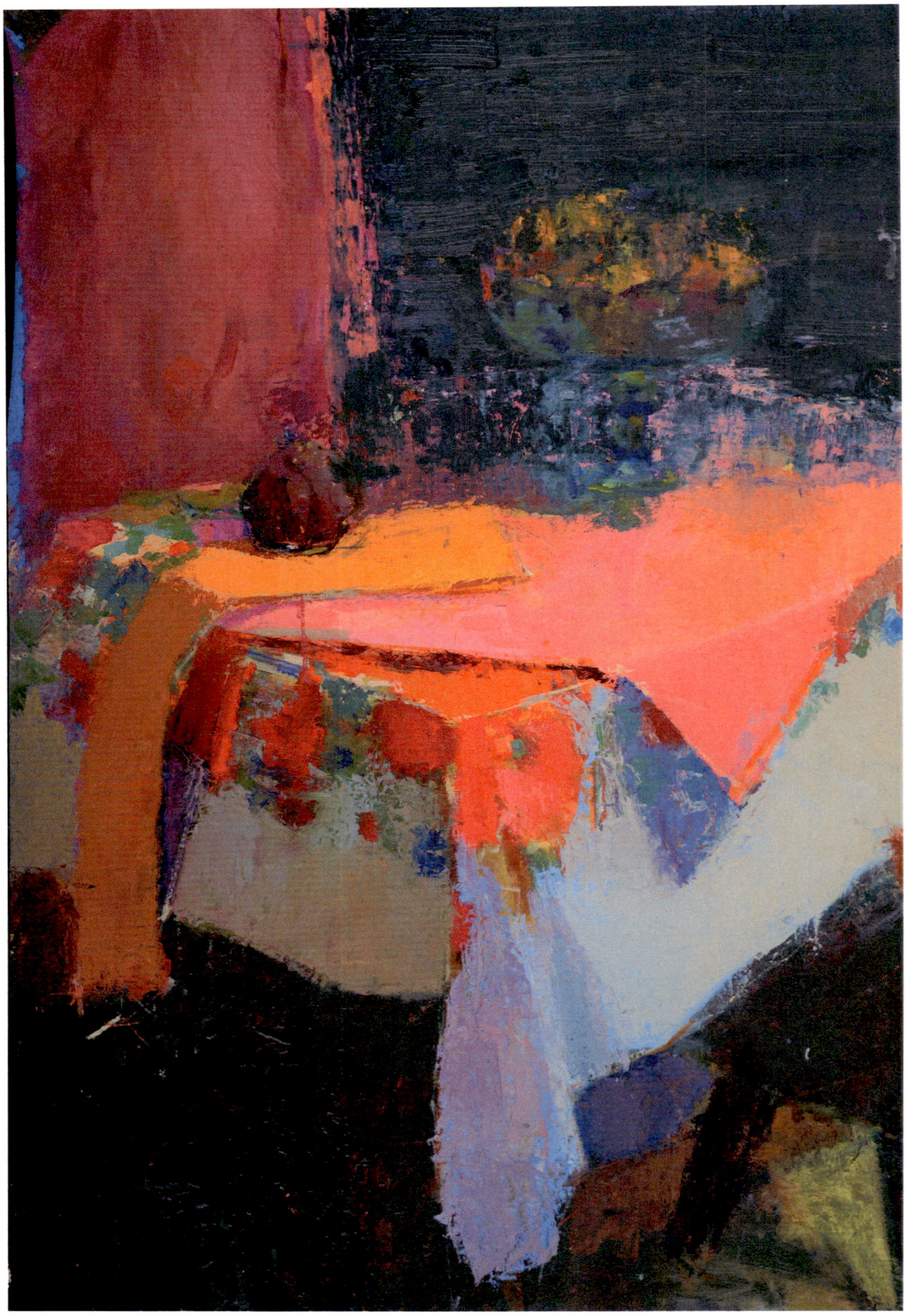

Paula Swaydan-Grebel *Table Setting*
2018-20, oil on panel, 36 x 24 in.

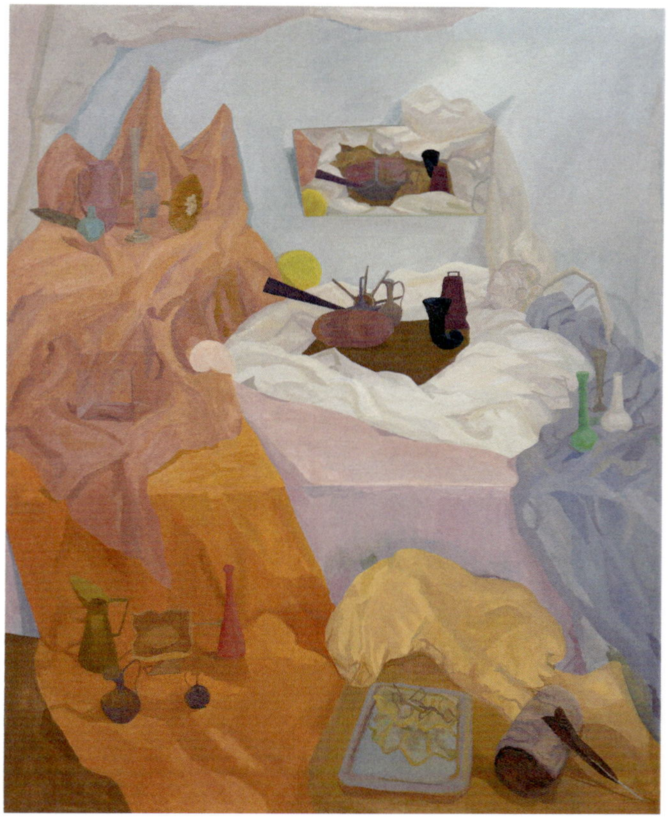

Gwen Strahle *Cities*
2015, oil on canvas, 66 x 52 in.

GS: I have a lot of objects in my studio. I have made paintings where I organize objects into a still life. And, I have found still lifes made by accident. But because I work mostly from memory now, organization is a different, slower process, that seems fitting for the paintings I make. I am adding and subtracting much more than I ever have. I like that only I might know that an object once existed in a painting.

I believe when an artist walks into their studio, who they are as an artist reinforces their paintings and decision making. Of course there are other influences. I walk into my studio, and my paintings are there, with their problems that need to be solved. And that's one way I get started. My own paintings influence me. When I am surrounded by my paintings, I am strengthened by who I am as a painter. That creates a natural organization of responsiveness, and a need to paint. For me, it is an intuitive and most important way of getting started. Also, I love paint. I love my objects. Somehow that combination has always been extremely important to how I end up making these paintings.

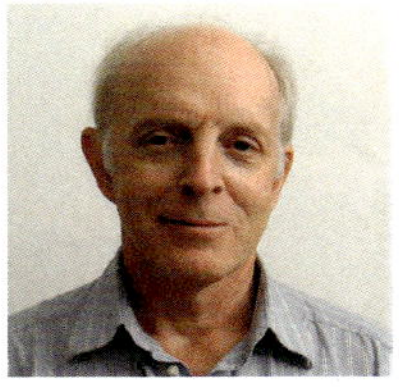

John Goodrich is a New York-based painter, teacher, and writer who exhibits at Bowery Gallery and with Zeuxis in New York City. His paintings have appeared in group shows at Elizabeth Harris Gallery, Kouros Gallery and Lori Bookstein Fine Art in New York City, the Contemporary Realist Gallery in San Francisco and numerous other venues around the country. His work has been mentioned in reviews in *The New York Times, The New York Sun, The New York Observer, The New Haven Register* and other publications.

www.zeuxis.us/goodrich
www.johngoodrich.net

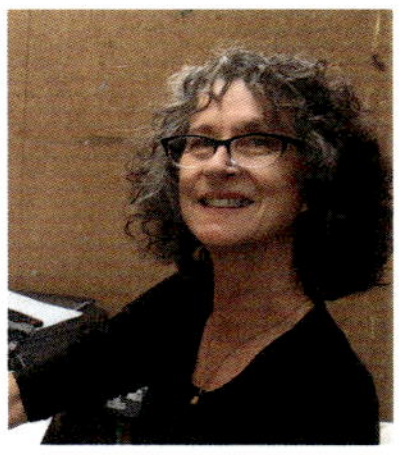

Born in California, **Paula Swaydan-Grebel** received her BFA in Figure Drawing and a Minor in Textiles from the California State University of Long Beach. After moving to Wisconsin in the 1990s she has continued studying there and abroad with key perceptual painters. Paula exhibits and teaches painting and drawing workshops throughout the United States. She is represented by Tory Folliard Gallery.

www.swaydangrebel.com

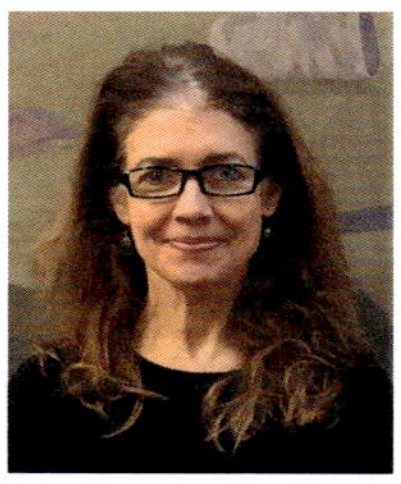

Gwen Strahle lives and works in eastern Connecticut. She has been exhibiting with Zeuxis since 2012. Her work has been exhibited in galleries and museums across the country, and recently at Steven Harvey Fine Arts Projects. She holds a BA from Rhode Island College, and an MFA from Yale School of Art. She has been teaching drawing at Rhode Island School of Design since 1984, and has taught workshops at Art New England and Black Pond Studio.

www.zeuxis.us/strahle
www.gwenstrahle.com

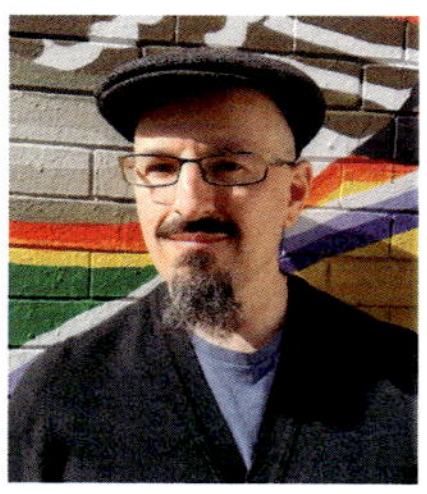

While maintaining a studio practice as an artist in New Hampshire, **Franklin Einspruch** is also active in art criticism, comics, and alternative publishing. His art has appeared in 20 solo exhibitions and 42 group exhibitions. He has been a resident artist at programs in Italy, Greece, Taiwan, and around the United States, and was the Fulbright-Q21/MuseumsQuartier Artist-In-Residence for 2019 in Vienna. He has authored 245 essays and art reviews for many publications including *The New Criterion* and *Art in America.* He has been blogging about art since 2003 at Artblog.net and Dissident Muse Journal. Einspruch has been involved with comics poetry since the form emerged in the mid-2000s, starting with a webcomic, The Moon Fell On Me, and expanding to many other projects and publications.

www.franklin.art

Artisthood and Parenthood

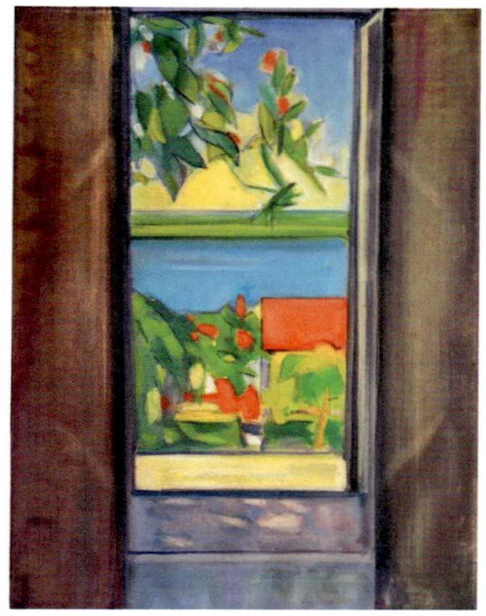

Neil Plotkin interviews

Elizabeth Higgins and Clara Shen

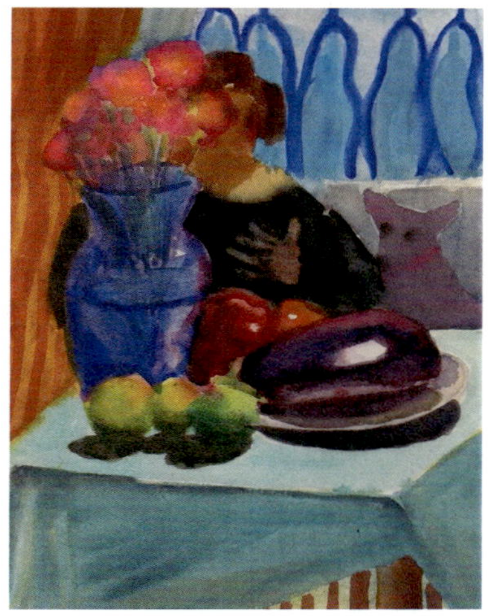

Elizabeth Higgins *Open Window St. Mawes*
2020, oil on canvas, 40 x 30 in.
Clara Shen *Egg Plant*
2017, watercolor on paper, 14 x 12 in.

Neil Plotkin: *The perceived life of an artist is filled with all sorts of draws—a life exploring your mind and the world around you with absolute freedom. The life imagined brims with excitement and stimulation. But what is rarely spoken of is the difficulty of maintaining a family and an art practice. This may be due to the fact that women shoulder the majority of this burden and their work has been undervalued for centuries. Male painters often left the matter of raising children to their wives and female painters had to put their careers on hold while rearing their children. Many of us know artists who have forgone having children in order to avoid many of the sacrifices and trade-offs that artists with children are forced to make.*

My experience as a painter who is also a stay-at-home father fostered my desire to explore the challenges of raising children and continuing my art practice. I had the good fortune to interview two excellent painters who are both artists and parents and tried to understand what their journey has been like. I am very happy that both Elizabeth Higgins and Clara Shen have agreed to spend a lot of time opening up with me about their experiences as artists and parents. All three of us are at different points in our parenting and I would love to think that artists who are early in the parent journey can see that it is possible to be a parent and an artist.

NP: *I want to thank you for doing this interview and I appreciated speaking with you both individually ahead of time in order to understand who you are as people. You both have forged complex journeys to the places you now inhabit as women, artists, and parents. Clara you're a mother of a five-year-old boy and have recently given birth to your second son. Elizabeth you've raised four children—three girls and one son—to adulthood. As we celebrate the entrance into life of Clara's son, I feel that it is important to honor Elizabeth's son, William Jones, a second year Fordham Law Student, who died at home on Christmas Day, 2018, from an accidental drug overdose.*

As a stay-at-home father and painter with two sons, I'd love to hear what your experiences have been and what adaptations you've made by adding this responsibility while maintaining your art practices and how this has affected your work.

Would you mind talking about what painting had been like before you had children and what it was like after having kids? How did this dramatic change adjust your art?

Clara Shen: My memory is refreshed as I am here typing with my son hanging in the baby carrier in front of me. I painted this way exactly 5 years ago, in the same position in my studio with my first born. Right now, I can feel his weight and warmth between me and the canvas. I have to leave the window next to us open a bit even as the chilling wind blows in because I worry about the baby breathing in too much turpentine. I'm sure I don't yet know all the implications how this unique experience will affect my work, but It feels extraordinary to paint this way.

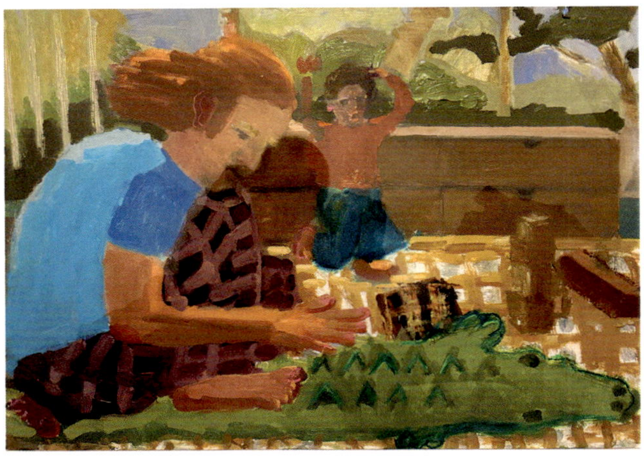

Clara Shen *Father and Son*
2020, oil on paper, 11 x 14 in.

Since my first son came along, he has been a fascinating subject to me, as well as all the domestic images that came with being a family.

But mostly, having a child changed how I paint, because I simply lost the luxury of time to obsess over my paintings. I think it's a change for the better. Now I must work fast and think quickly. For me, spontaneity makes for better art.

In my shortish art career, I have gone and still am going through a few style changes. During my MFA, in the Academy of Art in San Francisco, I was taught the academic style. Since then, mostly after a six-week residence with the JSS in Italy, I tried to "unlearn everything I learned in art school," to quote Israel Hershberg. That was where I met Ken Kewley and Stuart Shils, whose work and ideas influenced me tremendously in the years since. From them I learned how to "see" differently, which really is the key to making different kinds of art. What a struggle it was to break free of all that academic training!

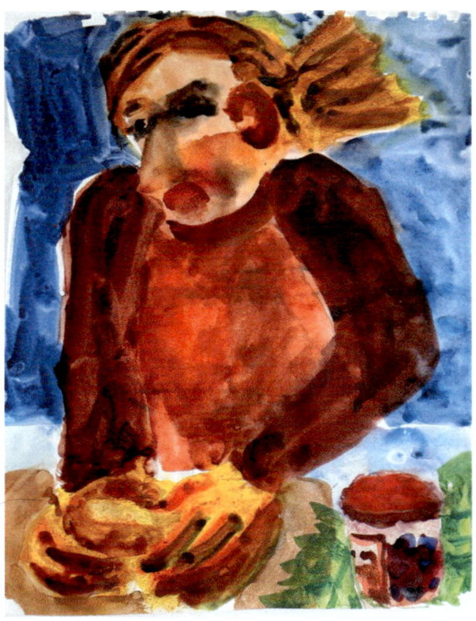

Clara Shen *PeanutbutterJelly*
2020, watercolor on paper, 11 x 14 in.

These two paintings are milestones for me. The still life is more tightly painted, but I took liberty in changing the subject matter for a self-portrait. The other is one of the first paintings I did in a spontaneous style.

I feel grateful to have started learning watercolor in 2012 with John Goodrich who is a most wonderful and illuminating teacher. Watercolor is both liberating and challenging—I so

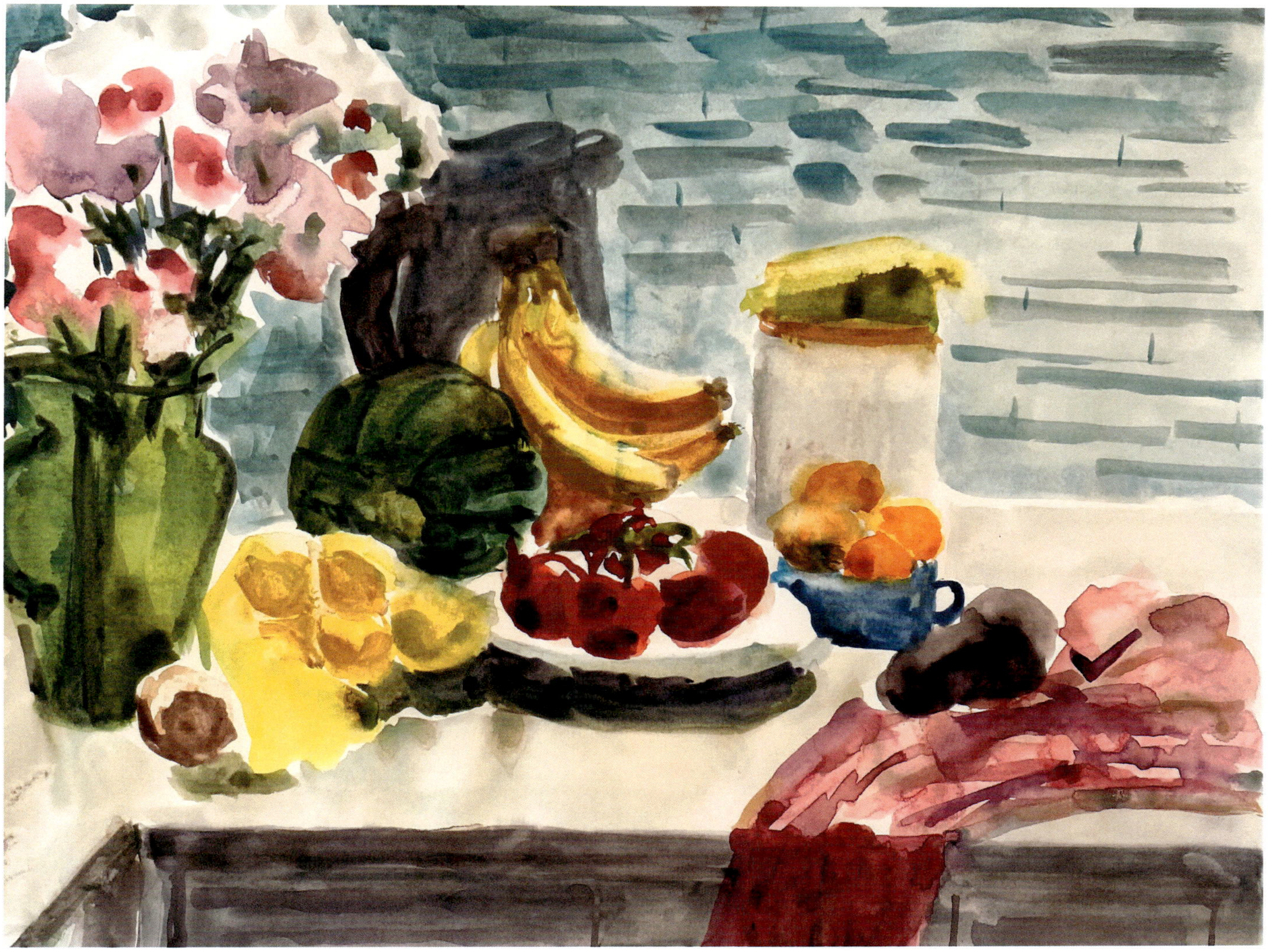

Clara Shen *Still Life with Watermelon*
2020, watercolor on paper, 10 x 13 in.

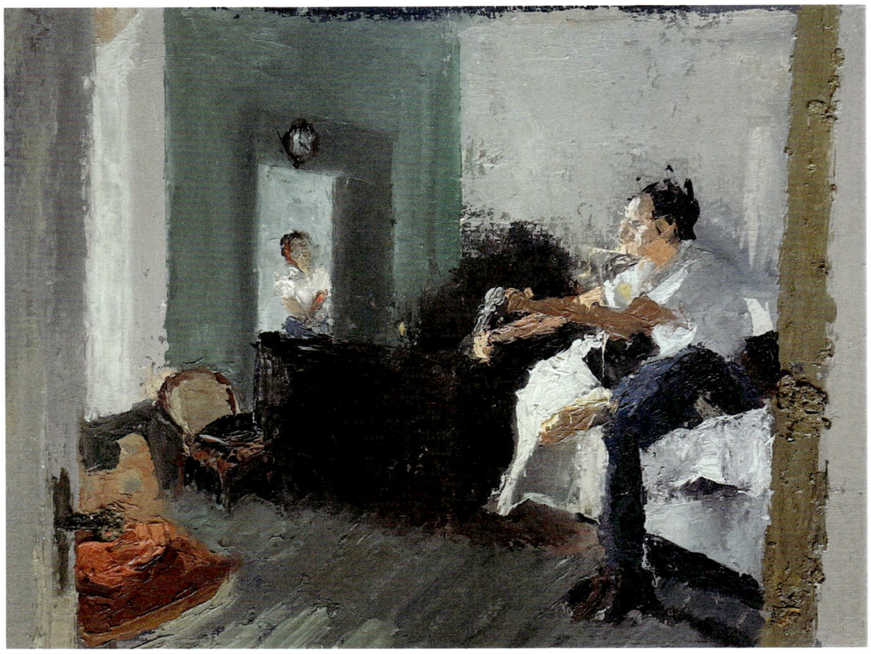

Clara Shen
Somewhere in East Village
2013, oil on board, 11 x 14 in.

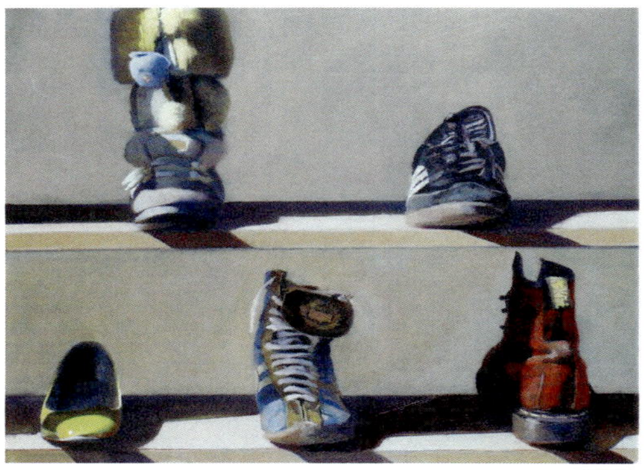

Clara Shen *Self Portrait*
2009, oil on board, 18 x 24 in.

enjoy the fact that water/paint seem to have a mind of their own the second they make contact with paper. That "beyond one's control" property brings immense pleasure to my tightly wound mind. But, as it turns out, it's also the perfect medium when you have a rambunctious boy running around the house making a mess!

Elizabeth Higgins: Clara, being a mother, having given birth to four children, two of whom are twins, born all within 4 ½ years, I certainly understand and share the challenge of focusing on my work, that is my painting, my art.

I've been fortunate to have had studio space attached to my home, so I didn't change my preferred medium which is working in oils.

As far as subject matter is concerned, certainly my art has broadened to include my children in my figurative work. Besides bringing light into my life, my children, I know have found a way into my art.

Certainly, for many years, I didn't have the time to focus on my art while raising four young children, and when they reached high school, my role as a mother became more demanding. I felt that in order to be a good mother something had to give. It was my art. To be committed to my art and to be committed to my young family wasn't possible for me. I now have more time to dedicate to my art as my children have grown up. I wouldn't have done it any other way.

Although my life can be divided into phases: college, graduate school, marriage, motherhood, loss of my son, William, life has been much fuller than that. But I can look at my work during those periods and see that dramatic changes have taken place. Some of these changes might simply be a question of maturity, but I think that it's more than that.

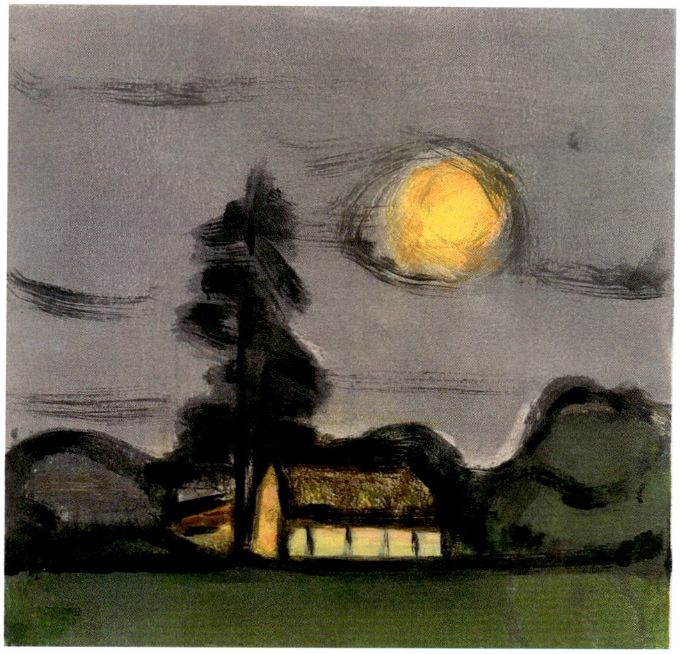

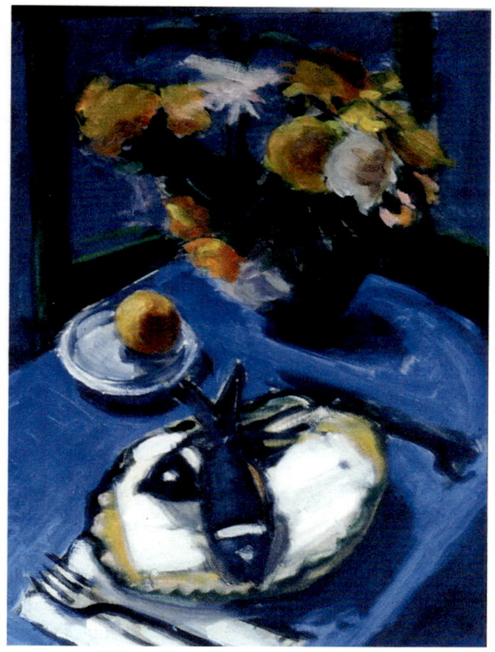

Elizabeth Higgins
William's Light
2020, montype on paper,
8 x 8 in.

Elizabeth Higgins
Still Life with Fish
1985, oil on canvas,
24 x 26 in.

It's the experiences that I've had in each stage of my life and their impact on the way I look at things. But then again, I guess this is what maturity is all about.

When I look at my work from my undergrad school years, I would describe my paintings as being expressionistic in style.

When I look at my work from my MFA years at Parson's, I see that the more formal approach taught there by Leland Bell, John Helliker, and Paul Resika, influenced me and pushed my art in another direction.

In the later stages of my life, marriage, motherhood, and the loss of my son, my work has continued to be affected and changed by a whole new set of experiences and challenges that I could never have imagined as a college or graduate student.

The impact of the cumulative experiences I've had over 37 years of marriage, motherhood and tragedy shapes my art today. Today my art is a mixture of the expressionism of my early work, the formal training of my MFA and the everyday involvement of all aspects of family life.

How this expresses itself now and will tomorrow I think is best described by a respect and fascination with the relationship of shapes, color and rhythms I see in the world around me.

Every detail of my life and every detail in nature, stimulate my artistic expression.

Like many artists, at times I feel so inadequate to do this.

NP: *As you said, Elizabeth, you wouldn't change anything. Despite all the difficulties, I couldn't agree more with that and I imagine Clara you feel the same way. The difficulty is to balance—or not—being an artist with these huge responsibilities.*

The two of you show considerable transformation as artists after having children. Yet both of you appear to go in opposite directions. Clara, you seemed to have gone away from an academic and

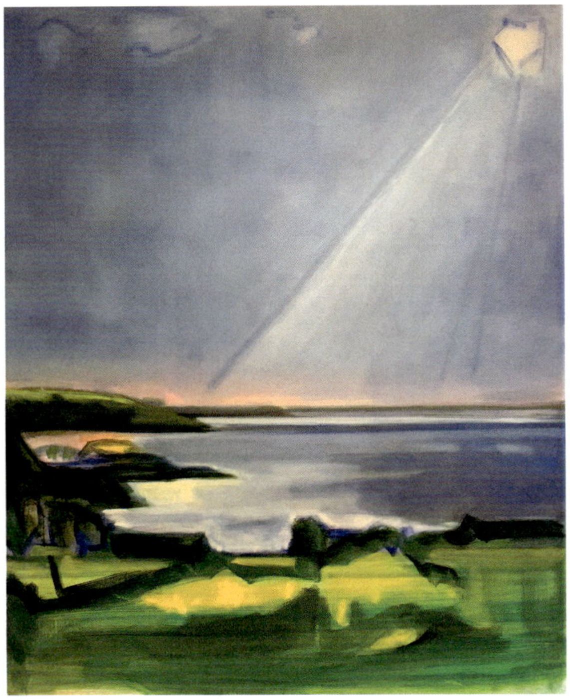

Elizabeth Higgins *Irish Landscape—William's Light*
2020, oil on canvas, 40 x 30 in.

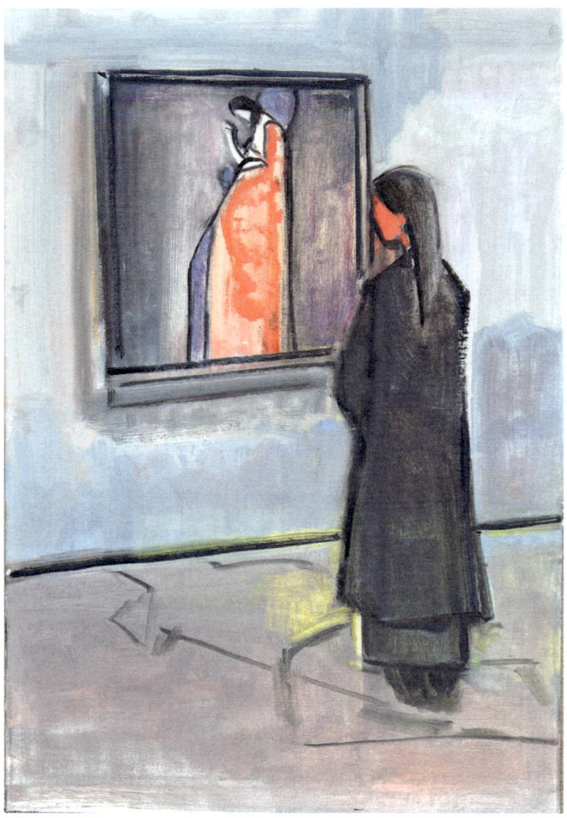

Elizabeth Higgins *Looking for Hope*
1983, oil on canvas, 48 x 72 in.

ordered attitude and towards a more spontaneous approach to your work and Elizabeth, your work looks to have moved towards being more structured and almost meditative. Can you speak to those changes—were they organic or were they part of a particular thought-process/exploration? And what role does the process of making things do for you as a person? For example, I needed calm from the stress of parenting and decided to paint all white objects as a way to soothe myself?

CS: Elizabeth, first of all, my deepest condolences for the loss of your son William. I cannot imagine the pain you and your family must have gone through.

I loved your response. It's an inspiration. So much resonated with me; it offered me a preview of what's to come and a certain degree of consolation in a way—consent to be guilt free if I'm unable to make it a priority before they go to college.

Sometimes, I feel split between the two roles. When I really immerse myself in painting, I feel like I'm ignoring my son; on the other hand, I feel anxious when parenting duties keep me away from my easel.

I think limitations can be frustrating, but they can also serve as points of inspiration. Throughout the years I learned to steal patches of time to make art, which affects my process to a large degree. It forces me to target what I "see" with more precision and requires more vigor and confidence to get what I think I'm after. I realize I really need to hone in on my skills which is why I am going back to copying after old masters.

Neil, to answer your question about what making things do for me as a person: I presume that, like many artists, my desire to make things stems from childhood. I was born and raised in communist China, where making things creatively instead of following the norm meant trouble. I think my progress as an artist, in many ways, has been defined by that experience. I started as a very academic artist, focused on doing things the "right way," and then spent many years in a process of breaking away from that. It has all been about increasingly expressing my creativity, which always gives me deep satisfaction and a sense of belonging, whether I'm working with oil, watercolors or collaging.

It has also definitely informed my parenting! I am always making things for my kids, and my older son has learned from me and we now create together every day. I encourage him to be hands-on and take on projects, and it is one of our favorite ways of spending time together. It is such a central part of my life that it couldn't be any other way.

Regarding maturity and how it affects one's work: I couldn't agree more. Based on my own accumulated life experiences, I believe everything we learn along the way eventually adds up to who we are and how we paint. I feel like my journey has only just begun.

EH: Clara, thank you for acknowledging the loss of my only son. I miss William, terribly, every day.

William told me once that "The making of Art is a noble pursuit." Those words of his have helped me a lot. I hope to honor him by continuing to work hard to create something meaningful and beautiful and provocative. I keep hearing him saying, "What would the world be like without art and artists, Mom? It would be a wasteland."

Please understand, Clara, that the path I chose worked for me—it doesn't mean that my path works for every mother, who is an artist, who is also trying to raise a family. There are so many great female artists, like Louise Bourgeois and Barbara Hepworth for example, who were successful at raising children while balancing their respective art careers.

My mother (I am the middle child of a family of nine) used to tell me "the busier you are the more you get done... " Well I'm a pretty organized person with regard to my family but the birth of my twins threw all of that out the window. While raising William and Julia, I would paint during the evenings. My husband would arrive home and I would retreat into my studio and would often get so "lost" in my work that hours would go by and I'd come into the house after midnight if not later.

I continued to work that way until I was hospitalized, pregnant with my twins, Catherine and Elizabeth, who were born seven weeks premature with a myriad of medical issues. That is when my art really had to take a back seat. I simply had to care for my four small children.

That said (and I know this might sound clichéed), the birth of my four children, was and continues to be, the best work I have ever been a part of.

Neil, you mentioned that my work has become more structured. I don't know if I'd describe it quite that way. I feel that my work now is a culmination of so many influences from my life experiences, from me experimenting and looking at scores of abstract and figurative artists over the years.

Everyone and everything serve as an inspiration for me. As a teenager I copied Vermeer and Goya, Henry Moore sculptures, Jack Bush and the "Group of Seven" at the Art Gallery of Ontario. While a Parsons MFA student, I went to the Met and copied the Old Masters and to MOMA to study the Modernists. Leland Bell and Paul Resika espoused the notion that you had to study and learn from the great artists from the past and the present before you could pursue abstraction. You needed to learn the invaluable lesson of how "to see." This made sense to me, having studied the piano for many years. I was taught that to be an artist, it was necessary for you, as in music, to become proficient in theory and technique so that you would have the ability and the insight to compose your own creation—your own work of art.

NP: *You have both independently mentioned the practice of copying master works. I feel that in doing copies of masters, artists really learn how to "speak" the language of painting, and it's the use of that language in one's own work which connects us to the canon and to each other.*

Elizabeth, you mentioned that you were doing copies before your children were born, and Clara, I assume that you were doing copies before your boys were born as well. To me, working from the masters was a lifeline back to the world of painting and art while I was buried under the responsibilities of raising my boys. It reminded me of why I was an artist.

Why do you, Elizabeth and Clara, work on copies of masters—are you learning composition, techniques, history maybe, or connecting with the artistic tradition or is it the simplicity of opening a book and drawing? You've both mentioned artists that you like to copy from—what is it that draws you into those artists' work?

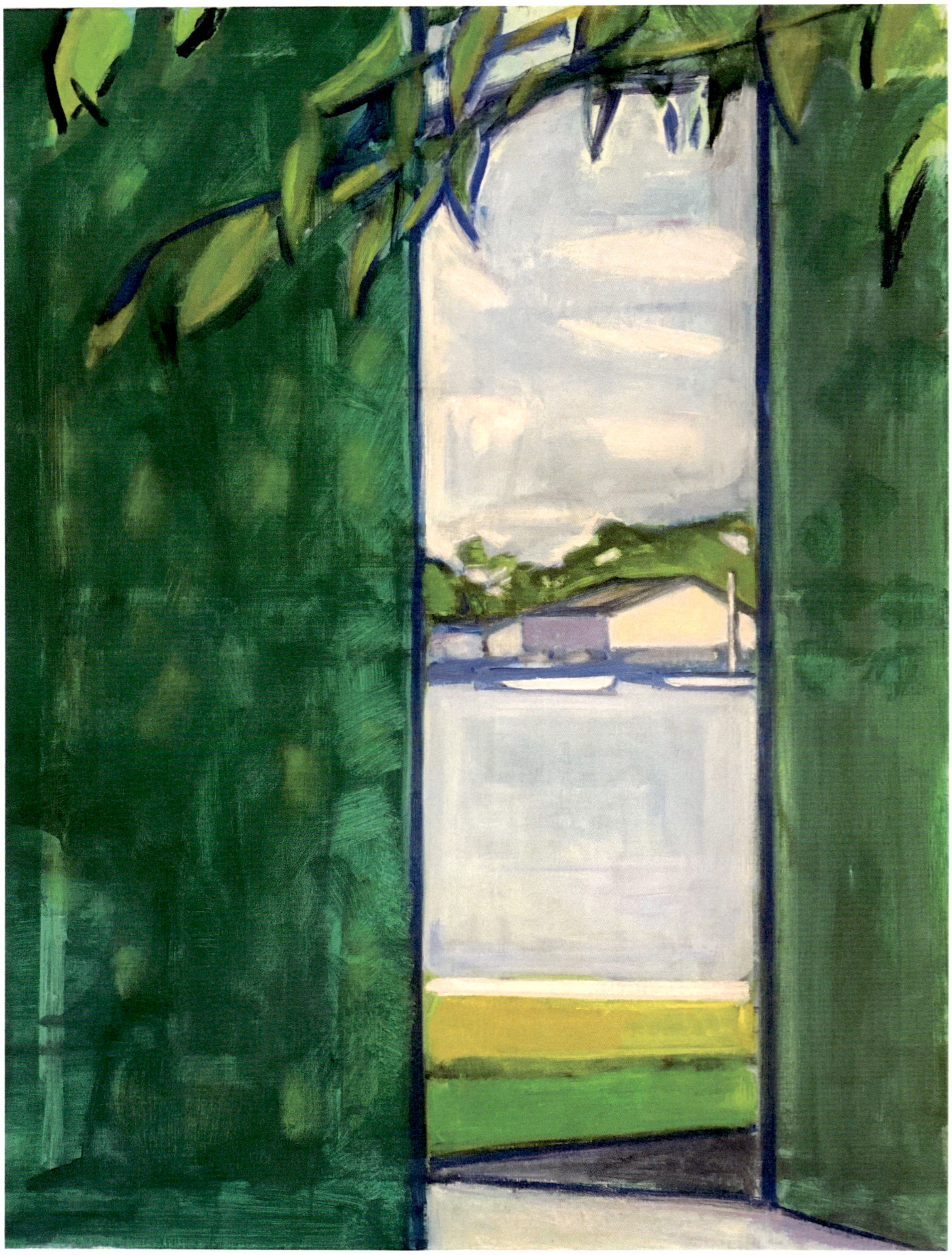

Elizabeth Higgins *Across the River*
2020, oil on canvas, 40 x 30 in.

CS: Neil, you pinned down two of the main reasons I do copies of masters. I mainly copy to learn composition, and the simplicity of opening a book and drawing is definitely a big factor.

I started copying Rembrandt's portraits in grad school. At that time, I was focused on learning technique. In Italy, I learned to do drawings of Giotto and Duccio from the originals, trying to break the works down into shapes and fitting them in a small notebook. Taking all that back to New York, I started to walk around the Met and other museums while creating little thumbnail drawings of whatever catches my eyes. It may be a Titian, Chardin, Matisse or anything else. But of course, the more common thing to do is copy at home. For a while, I copied after David Park using watercolors—I love how he painted the human figure. One of my favorite projects of the last few years was copying oil paintings by Cézanne, Braque and Fragonard as collages.

Playing with the medium naturally makes the copy more interpretive, and copies are fascinating to me exactly because they are interpretations. I love seeing how other artists interpret masters' works! Think about how Picasso completely took over Manet's "Lunch on the Grass" and made it his own, or how Euan Uglow turned Poussin's "The Massacre of the Innocents" into one of his marks-making obsessed creations. It's like one of those rare musical covers or tributes that end up being masterpieces of their own merit, branching from the original work.

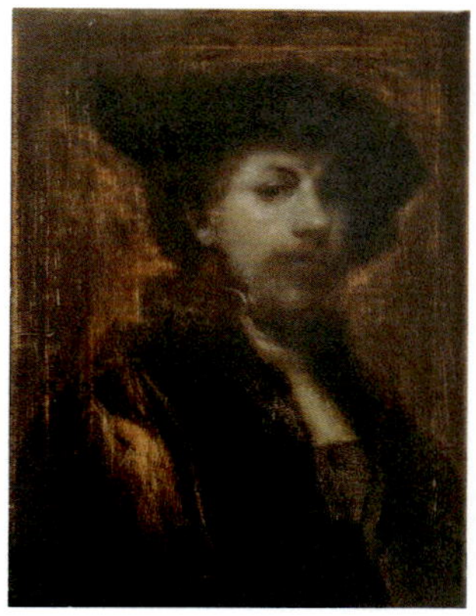

Clara Shen *Study of Rembrandt Self-Portrait*
2009, oil on canvas, 18 x 24 in.

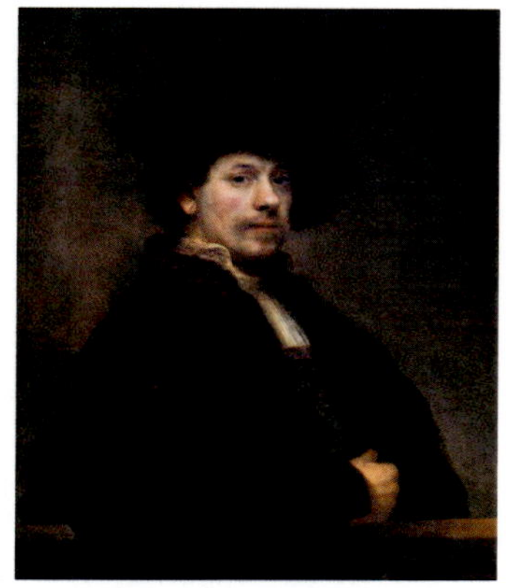

Rembrandt van Rijn *Self-Portrait at the Age of 34*
1640, oil on canvas, 40 x 30 ½ in.

EH: I feel the same way as Clara. By copying or even just looking at great works of art, you learn something new. You have a new insight, a different way of seeing, that you can then incorporate into your own work. My earliest memory of making a copy was when I was 14 years old. As the middle child of nine, I had argued with my mother. I had deeply hurt her by saying something like "Why did you have so many children when you can't love us all equally?" My poor mother responded, "I love each and every one of you with all my heart." I didn't know how to take away the hurtful words that I had spoken. It was then that I copied Feruzzi's "Madonnina" 1897 and slipped it under my mother's bedroom door. A few days later, I found it framed on her bedside table where it would remain until her death. I was aware at that early age of the power art.

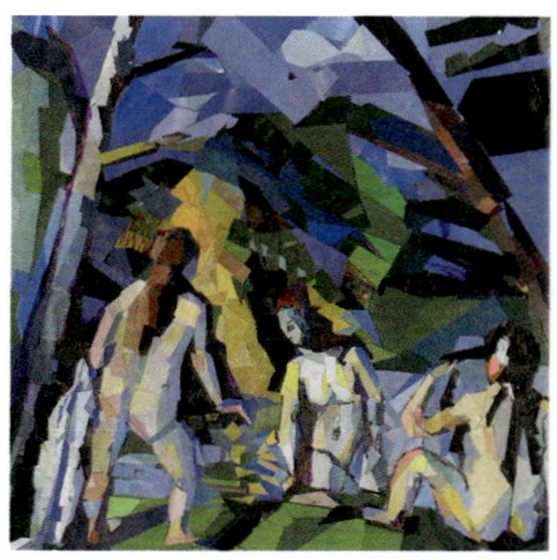

Clara Shen *Cézanne's Bathers*
2013, paper collage, 6 x 6 in.

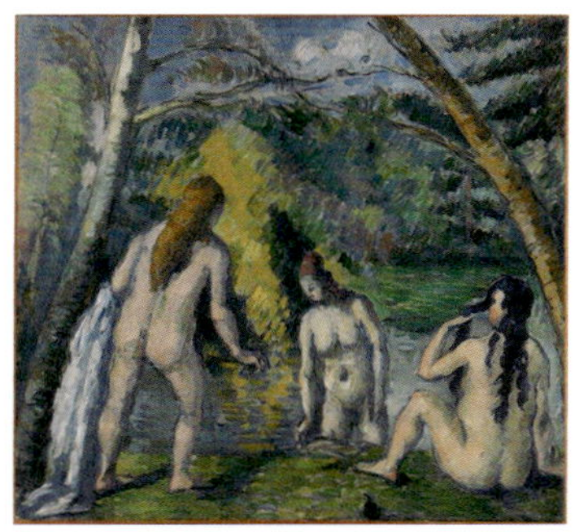

Paul Cézanne *Three Bathers*
1879-1882, oil on canvas, 22 x 20 in.

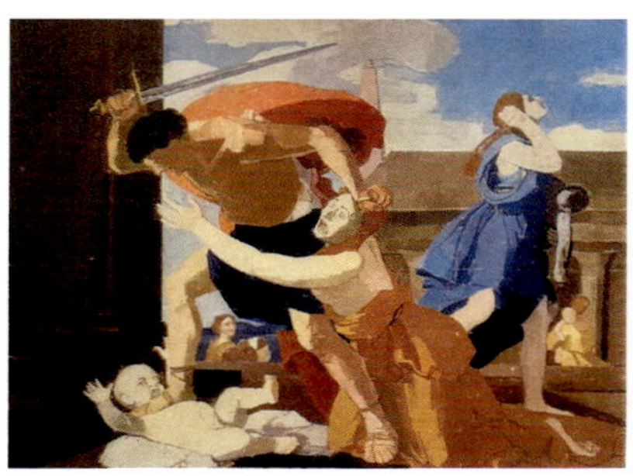

Euan Uglow *The Massacre of the Innocents (after Poussin)*
1979-1981, oil on canvas laid on panel, 16 ¼ x 19 ¼ in.

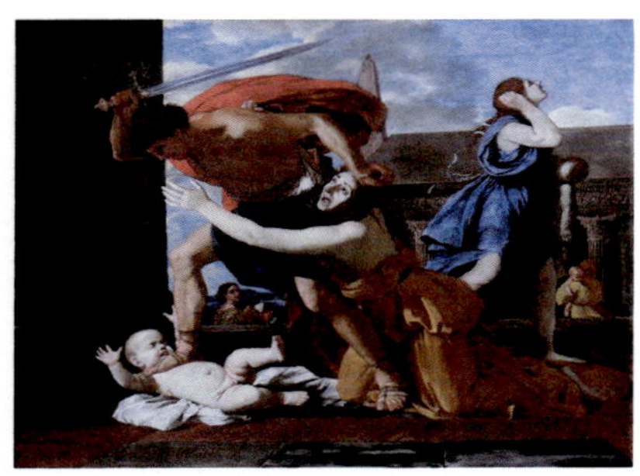

Nicolas Poussin *Massacre of Innocents*
1625-1632, oil on canvas, 58 x 67 in.

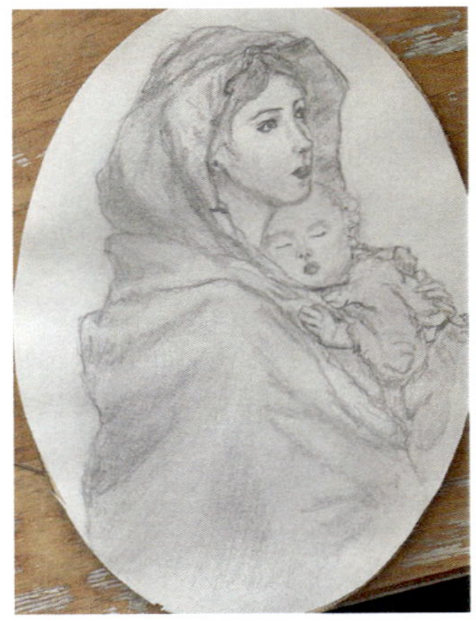

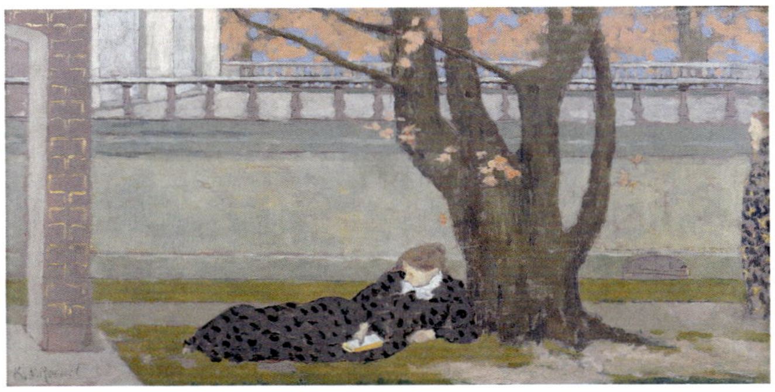

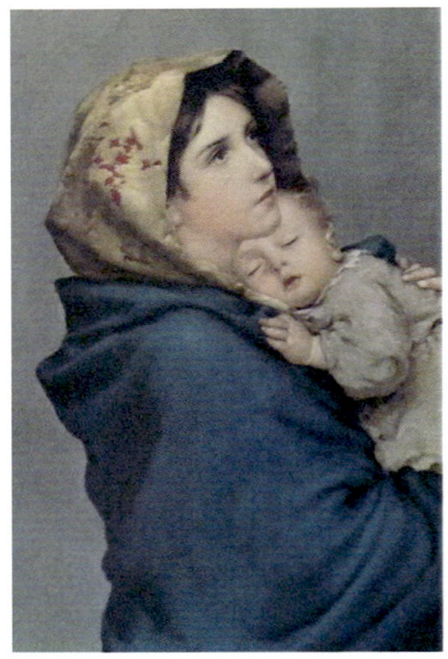

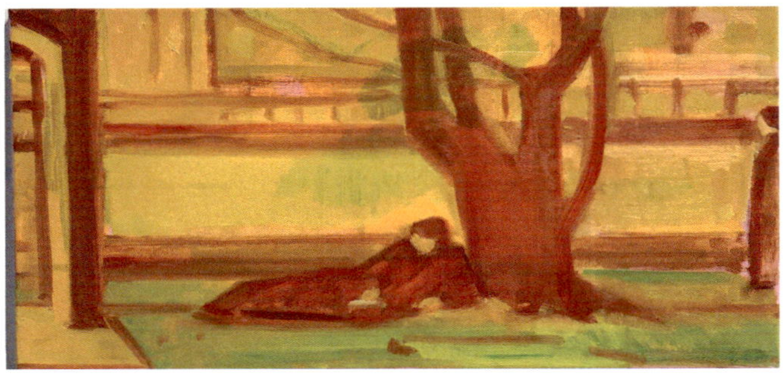

Ker Xavier Roussel *The Terrace at the Tuileries*
c.1892-3, oil on canvas, 14 x 29 ½ in.

Elizabeth Higgins *Sketch after Roussel—La Terrace*
2019, oil on canvas, 10 x 20 in.

Elizabeth Higgins drawing done at the age of 14

Roberto Ferruzzi *La Madonnina*, 1887

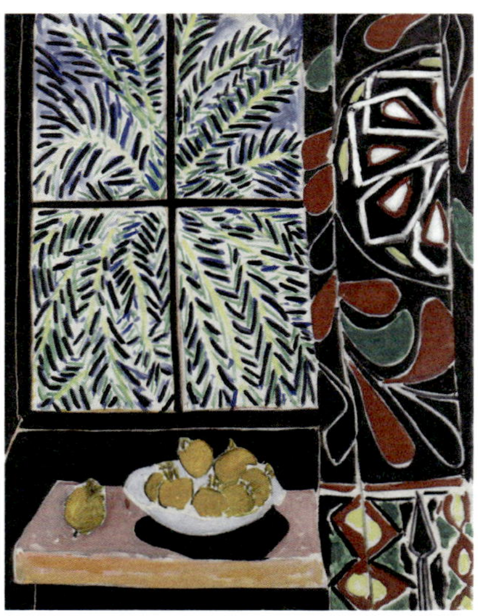

Henri Matisse *Interior with Egyptian Curtain*
1948, oil on canvas, 64 x 35 in.

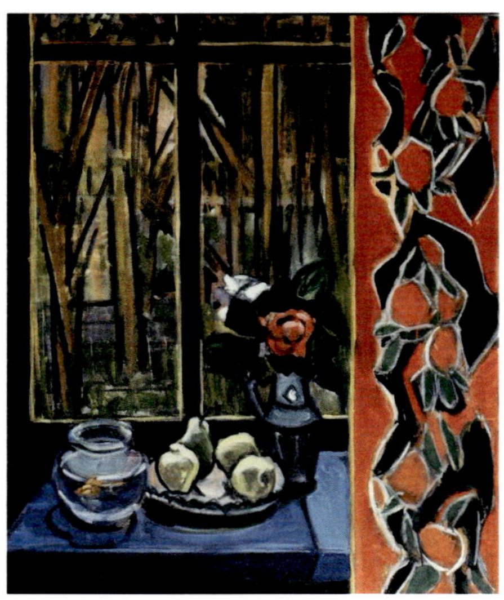

Elizabeth Higgins *Still Life with Apples*
1985, oil on canvas, 48 x 36 in.

But that doesn't explain why I believe copying other artists' work, can play an important role in developing one's own technique. This "process" maybe best described as a discipline from which an artist can either learn or remind oneself of the basic tools of artistic expression.

From this then, the artist's own expression can be shaped by the artist's own imagination and the personal way the artist sees and interprets things. In other words, it is a starting point, certainly not an ending point for artist who is looking to create.

Referring back to our earlier discussion, my training at Parsons centered on acquiring the basic skills of drawing and painting from what was directly in front of us whether it was a still life or live model. This is the role that "copying" has played in the development of my work.

For example, I was so captivated by Roussel's "La Terrace" after seeing it at "Les Nabis" Exhibition at the Musee Luxembourg that when I returned to my studio I did a study of it. I was struck by the color, composition and emotive power of this small painting.

As you can see Roussel influenced me in the small painting "Pilgrimage to St. Anne's" that I completed shortly after having done a study of "La Terrace." It is an example of the powerful role "copying" can play in one own's artistic journey.

NP: *That evolution of the Roussel into your own painting is really incredible. It feels like watching the way Mondrian evolved away from his naturalism. Was this an intentional reference to the Roussel? And if so, can you talk about what your intentions and reasons were for working through that painting to arrive at your own painting. And, is this a part of your regular process of working?*

EH: Thanks for your kind words. The influence of Roussel's work was not intentional at all. In fact, it was only when I was answering your question on the purpose of copying that I saw the direct link and progression between my study after Roussel and my finished painting "Pilgrimage to St. Anne's." I think that is true, from having looked at hundreds and hundreds of pieces of art, when an artist looks at a painting with an "artist's eye" something like osmosis happens. An artist cannot help but take it in like a sponge if they are really looking hard.

And yes, it is part of my process, whether I'm outside looking at a new landscape, or inside looking at a composition of a friend's unintentional still life, or looking at a photograph, I will refer to that as a starting point to begin a painting.

NP: *I want to circle back a little bit to understand both of your origins as people and artists. You both have such interesting backstories and I'd love to hear about them and how they brought you to painting.*

EH: I always drew as a child. Being the middle child in a family of nine I would spend a lot of time alone in my room on the third floor of our home drawing. And although I had studied ballet at the National Ballet School of Canada for a short time, and piano through high school and university, there was little encouragement from my parents for me to study art.

During my high school years at a small Toronto private Catholic girls' school, my parents insisted that I take an extra language and typing in the place of taking an art elective. So that's what I did until the beginning of my senior year. I walked by the art room and the art teacher, welcomed me in and suggested I stay for her class that day. That was the beginning of a lifelong pursuit of my study and making of art.

I loved being in that space, the smell of the paints and inks and all the girls creating while listening to classical music was mesmerizing to me. The teacher suggested that I join the class, but the principal only allowed me to audit the class as I had not received the prerequisite credits. I was undeterred and

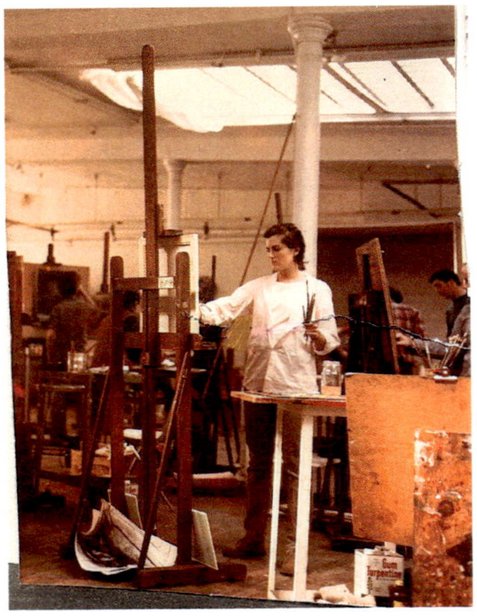

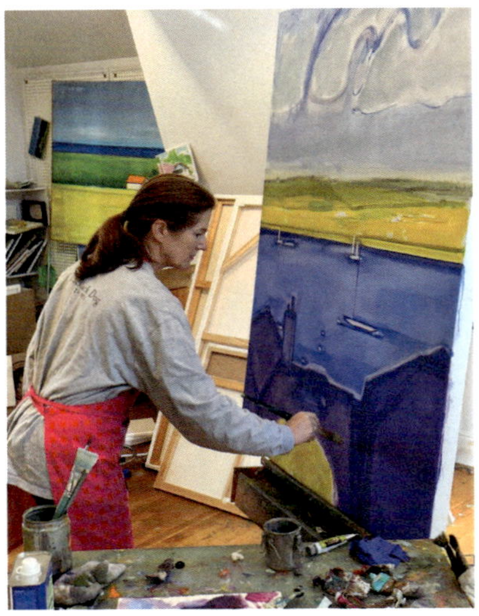

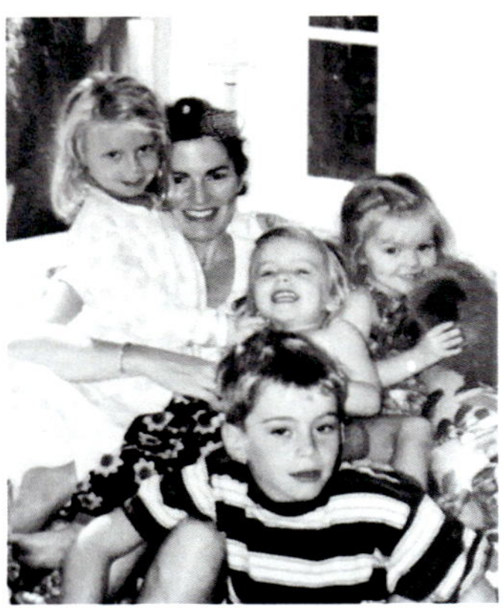

TOP TO BOTTOM:

Elizabeth Higgins at Parsons MFA Painting Studio, 1984

Elizabeth Higgins in her studio

Elizabeth Higgins and family

I knew I wanted to pursue this art thing so I drove across the city to attend a night school class at a public high school so that I would have the required credit needed to apply to Canadian university fine art programs.

My father was a doctor and hoped that I would study to become a doctor. He even went so far as to argue that I could be both a medical illustrator and a doctor. I remember him saying "you see—you can do both, be an artist and a doctor."

I was lucky to have the support of my older brother who was studying to be an architect at the time. Determined to pursue my art, I went ahead and applied to several programs, went for interviews with my portfolio in hand and was accepted into the BFA program at Queen's University, Canada.

I loved it all.

I loved studying, painting with my teachers from the Slade School London and printmaking with JC Heywood. And then to NYC to study with remarkable painters at the Parsons' MFA program.

To answer the second part of your question, I think that the importance of painting in my life is so layered. It's hard to explain really, but when I'm in my studio, in a Zen-like state of concentration, "on a roll," as they say, the whole outside world with all its problems slip away. It's not about resolving the next painting for an exhibition I'm working towards. It doesn't happen all the time...hours go by when I feel pretty worthless as an artist but then when things do come together it is wonderful. That feeling of getting so lost in a painting, so lost in myself that I'm unaware of hours having gone by.

It's similar, I suppose, to when I was a child with a paper and a pencil, alone in my room on the third floor.

CS: My childhood was a lonely one. I was an only child (everyone my age in China was) and my parents were rarely around. As far back as I can remember, pencils and crayons were always there for me. I would color and draw for hours on end, and I think that's when I felt truly content.

My father is an artist at heart, but in order to provide for us he chose to be a businessman. He has always kept art as a serious hobby and during my teenage years he actually started to do oil painting. I found myself intoxicated with the smell of oil paint and turpentine, and I was fascinated with all the painting picture books lying around in his office/studio. That's when I took my first attempt at painting, a copy of a flower bouquet by a Dutch painter whose name escapes me now.

In college, I took all the drawing classes I could as electives while completing my Bachelor's in New Media, a combination of graphic and web design. It was easy to get jobs after graduation, but I never stopped drawing and my heart was always in painting. After a few years, I decided to go back for a Master's degree in Fine Arts and have never looked back. I know that this quest I am on, to explore and refine my artistic expression, will take me a lifetime. That's a good thing, because I feel elated and challenged every step of the way.

NP: *In wanting to highlight the difficulties of balancing a professional art practice with raising children, I wonder if I have underemphasized your lives as professional* *artists. What are the events or markers that made you feel as though you had arrived as professional artists? In what ways did these successes affect the way you work?*

EH: I am a woman who is also an artist, a mother and a wife. I would say that the realization that I was a real, "professional" artist, happened soon after I finished my Parsons MFA when I had my first solo show at the Prince Street Gallery way back in 1987. Barbara Ingber came and saw my work and asked me to be in a group show at her West Broadway Gallery. At the same time a Toronto gallerist from the Nancy Poole Studio Gallery also saw my NYC show and asked me to be a part of her gallery in Toronto... so it was quite exciting for me as a young artist to have had such a positive response. It was at that time that I also received my first commission from VIA Rail Canada and had my work purchased to be included in corporate collections including the University of Toronto. So, I guess when I started exhibiting and people actually bought my work who weren't related to me, that's when I felt like a "professional" artist.

The answer to the second part of your question about how these successes affected my work would be to say that these "successes" were short lived as I was in my head already on to painting the next painting. Seeing my work hung on a gallery wall would initially fill me with a sense of pride and accomplishment but that feeling was fleeting. Seeing my paintings hung outside my studio gave the distance which allowed me to examine my work with a more critical eye. This allowed me to consider how I might make a "better" painting and maybe take a new direction in my work. So, in that way, these "successes" propelled me forward.

CS: My immediate thought is of a location rather than an event: my studio in Greenpoint, Brooklyn. It was in a building full of artists' studios and lofts. I was immersed in a community and in my work and felt so inspired by the creative energy and work routine. It's that sense of belonging, more than anything, that reminds me that I'm a professional in the art world. Since moving to Sleepy Hollow, I have enjoyed my studio at home immensely but had to work harder to find the community. I love being a part of the river towns' art scene. My work has been shown in different venues around here—small galleries, public libraries and restaurants. Each one nudges me to come out of my shell a little more, offers me confidence and helps solidify my identity as a professional artist. My first group show with Zeuxis, "My Studio" at the First Street Gallery, was very meaningful as well. Having my paintings hang alongside those of successful artists in later stages of their careers made something click for me and helped me find confidence to explore directions in my art that I didn't feel free to until then.

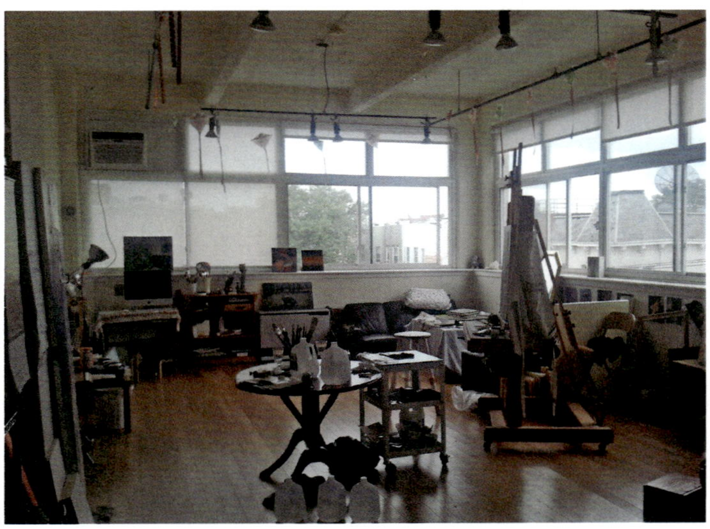

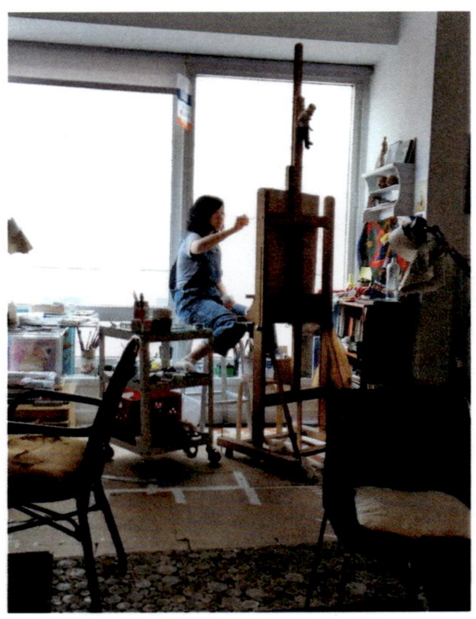

LEFT TO RIGHT:

Clara Shen's Studio in Greenpoint, Brooklyn

Clara Shen painting at home in Manhattan 2014

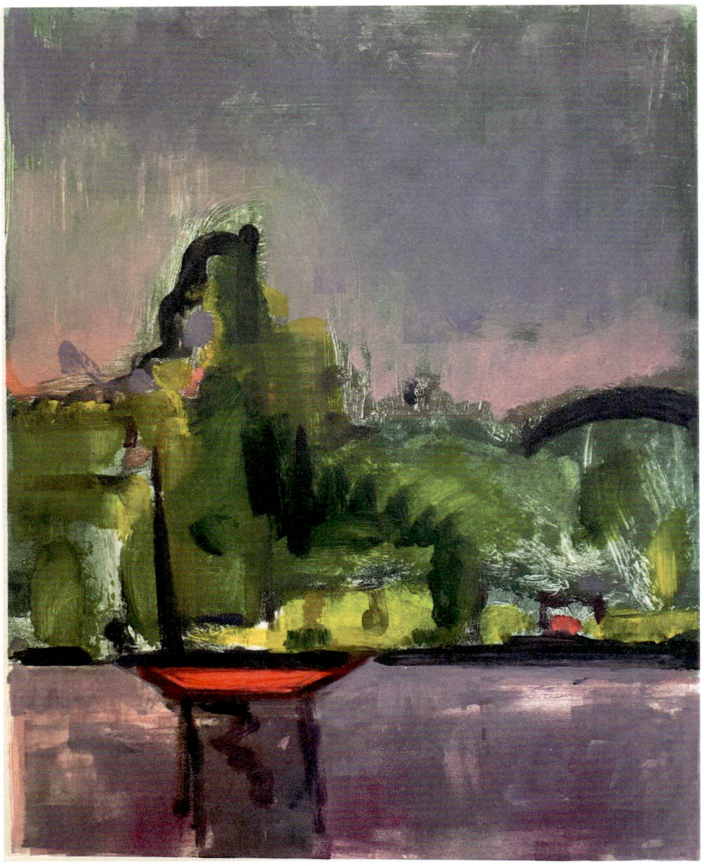

Elizabeth Higgins *Reflected Lake Sebago*
2021, monotype on paper, 18 x 14 in.

NP: *The reason that we are doing this interview at all is because of Covid. It has really changed the world in ways we could never have imagined. In what ways has the pandemic affected your image making and your careers as artists?*

EH: The pandemic has made me look at my work more critically and has made me ask the question, "What do I want to say in my art?" I think Covid has really made me feel a sense of my own mortality and that I better make good use of the time I have going forward.

My show "Light of Day: The Language of the Landscape," curated by Karen Wilkin, which had been scheduled for last May at the Westbeth Gallery, NYC, was sadly canceled due to Covid. I had been so excited to have been included in this amazing group of painters including two of my past teachers, Al Kresch and Stanley Lewis, along with Lois Dodd and other stellar artists. I was looking forward to seeing how my work related to theirs.

CS: The pandemic coincided with my second pregnancy and giving birth to my second son, which really dominated my experience of this otherwise strange year. If circumstances were different, perhaps I could have taken advantage of this isolated period and use the strangeness of the pandemic to create. I haven't had much time to think about my own image making, but I have had fun making art together with my older son. I find it inspirational and enjoyable just to watch him draw and paint. This year, I'm living according to a Chinese concept: accumulate experiences and knowledge with abundance, then release the results into the world slowly and steadily.

NP: *With all of this upheaval, what sorts of things currently excite you to make work? Are you currently looking at anyone who motivates you? What is it about these points of interest that inspires you?*

Elizabeth Higgins *Pilgrimage to St. Anne's*
2019, oil on canvas, 6 x 12 in.

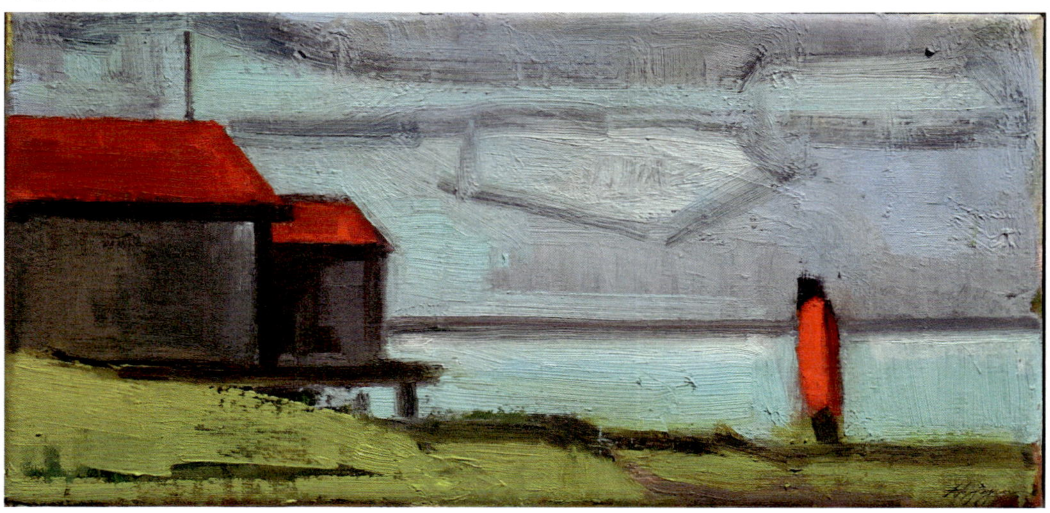

EH: To answer this question, I would again reply by saying that everything around me excites me. I see the beauty of the landscape, of a figure standing by the shore, etc., and that will excite me to begin something, to begin making marks. I continue to be inspired by Peter Doig, the Canadian painter James Morrice, Balthus, Matisse, the San Francisco Bay Area painters... the list goes on and on.

CS: These days I am thinking a lot about friends and family, isolation and togetherness. I am finding a lot of new meanings in these once mundane concepts and experiences as we approach the end of the pandemic. Things we normally took for granted before will be re-examined with a fresh point of view. I am toying with some ideas about the way we connect via Facetime or Zoom, and I wonder if all that mask wearing will make for an interesting visual element in the near future.

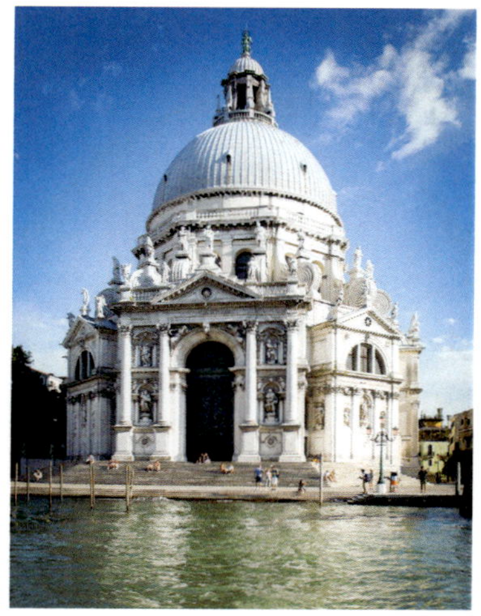

Santa Maria Della Salute

NP: *Can you describe what you imagine the art world/art school/image making might look like in the future post Covid?*

EH: Not sure how to answer this other than to say that all of our isolation will undoubtedly affect every artist's work post Covid. It's inspiring to me that artists are still creating during this stressful time. I believe painters, writers, musicians—all artists—will simply absorb and process this strange time into their work. I'm excited to see what unfolds.

I believe art will be created as an expression of joy and gratitude to celebrate Covid's end. Like the Palladian basilicas, Il Redentore and Santa Maria Della Salute that were built in thanksgiving for deliverance of the plagues of the 16th and 17th centuries, so too, great public large scale works of art, music and architecture will undoubtedly be created.

CS: With so much uncertainty in the world right now, it's still hard to say what life will be like post Covid (assuming there is a post Covid!). Of course, I hope the art world and the world in general will get back to the good old days in terms of culture, with people attending gallery openings and museums. I'm very much looking forward to when we can mingle in real life in front of physical paintings and sculptures again. We have been confined in our personal spaces and doing everything through a screen (including taking art classes and purchasing art online) and part of me fears that people have gotten too used to viewing art this way and will forget how to appreciate art in person or will find it unnecessary. The world is changing fast, and it's hard to say which way the art world will go. **Z**

NP: *It was an honor and pleasure to be invited into the artistic lives of both Elizabeth Higgins and Clara Shen. They are both incredibly strong artists with wonderfully interesting and full lives and this was accomplished while balancing being mothers. I also want to pass on to readers a kindness I received at an opening several years ago. While speaking to artists who were a little older than myself, I explained that I didn't see how it would be possible to work again as my second son had just been born a few days earlier. They countered that yes it would be hard, but I would be able to paint again: they told me I should try to the best of my ability to enjoy my sons' early childhood and that the work would come back again more easily. Many years later, I have found this to be true and am constantly grateful for that advice. I sincerely hope that artists struggling through the challenges of life, surviving Covid, the loss of loved ones or the difficulties of raising children can see that it is possible to balance those struggles and still make meaningful work as both Elizabeth and Clara have been doing.*

If you'd like to read more about Elizabeth Higgins son, William P. Jones III, and the things he accomplished in his too short life, please read:
"A little bit of mercy": A Darien family's loss to addiction
www.stamfordadvocate.com/local/article/A-little-bit-of-mercy-A-Darien-family-s-13847319.php

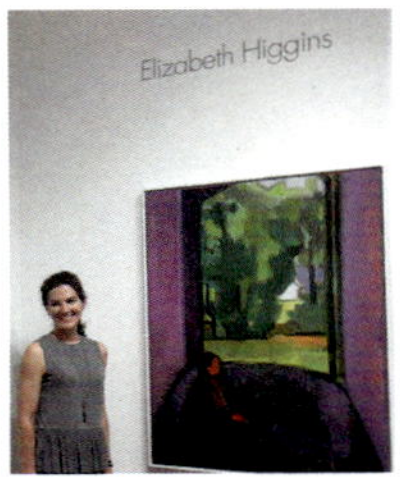

Elizabeth Higgins was born and raised in Toronto, Canada. She received her BFA at Queen's University, Canada. After moving to New York City, she earned her MFA (Painting) from Parsons School of Design, where she was a Helena Rubenstein Scholar. She has exhibited in Canada and the United States and her work is in private and corporate collections. She currently exhibits her work at The Prince Street Gallery, and is part of The Silvermine Guild of Artists as well as Zeuxis. Higgins divides her time between New York City and her home in Connecticut.

www.zeuxis.us/higgins
www.elizabethhigginsartist.com
www.instagram.com/elizabethhigginsartist.com

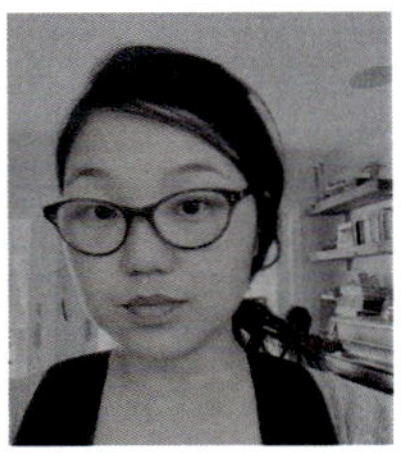

Clara Shi Shen was born and raised in Beijing, China. She received her BFA in New Media and Graphic Design and MFA in Painting at the Academy of Art University in San Francisco. After moving to New York in 2010 she continued studying at the Art Students League and the National Academy of Design, as well as taking residence with the JSS in Italy and traveling to various workshops. Her work, which focuses on still life and figurative paintings in oil, watercolors and collage, has been exhibited in China and in the U.S., at public spaces and private collections. She has been exhibiting with Zeuxis since 2018.

www.zeuxis.us/shen
www.Clarashen.com

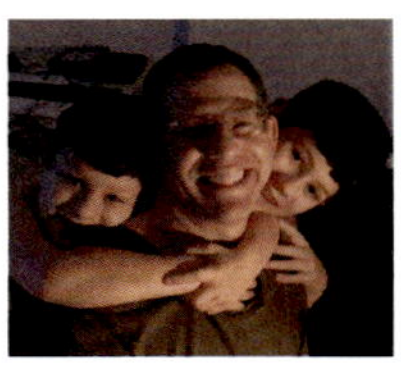

Neil Plotkin was born and raised in Detroit, Michigan. He received his BFA in Drawing and his BA in Art History at the University of Michigan. After living in London, England and Prague, he moved to New York in 1995 and studied at the New York Academy of Art. He has had his work exhibited in Europe and the United States and has work in private and public collections. He has been writing about artists and interviewing artists since the birth of his first son. He currently lives with his family in Brooklyn, NY.

www.zeuxis.us/plotkin
www.Neilplotkin.com
www.instagram.com/neilplotkin/

Form and Feeling

Sheldon Tapley interviews

Philip Jackson and Daniel Dallmann

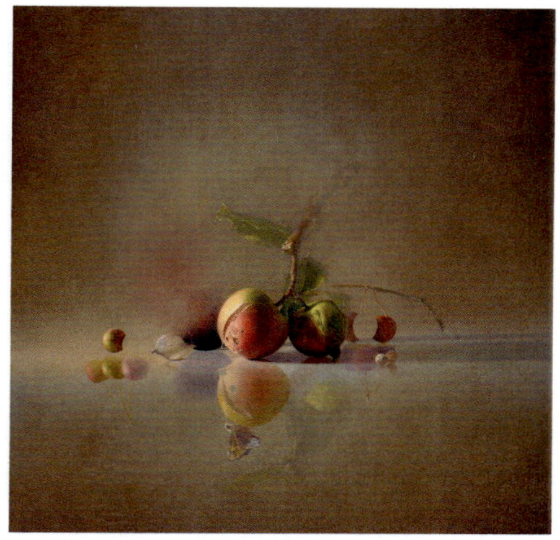

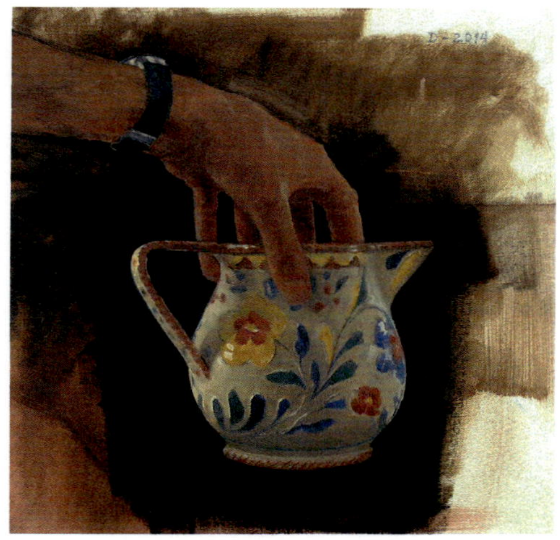

Philip Jackson *Transitory Spaces: Apples, Chrysallis & Moth*
2020, oil on panel, 14 x 14 in.

Daniel Dallmann *Majolica*
2014, oil on linen, 13 x 13 in.

Sheldon Tapley: *When painters get together, we look at pictures. Someone mentions an artist or an image, and soon a book is pulled off the shelf, or a webpage called up, and everyone is offering observations. We educate each other. Thanks to Zeuxis, which has brought together a group of outstanding painters from across the country, I was able to enjoy lively discussions with two masterful and accomplished artists whose work I admire. From our disparate locations in Kentucky, Pennsylvania and Mississippi, we shared pictures, stories and ideas in online conversations.*

For me, this was a welcome opportunity to meet Daniel Dallmann, an artist with an impressive career, who has recently joined Zeuxis. Daniel taught at Tyler School of Art, at Temple University, in Philadelphia, for many years.

Philip Jackson and I first met six years ago, when he spontaneously stopped in Danville as he was driving home to Oxford. Philip invited me to do a workshop for his students at the University of Mississippi, where he heads the painting program. While there, I had the great pleasure of visiting his studio.

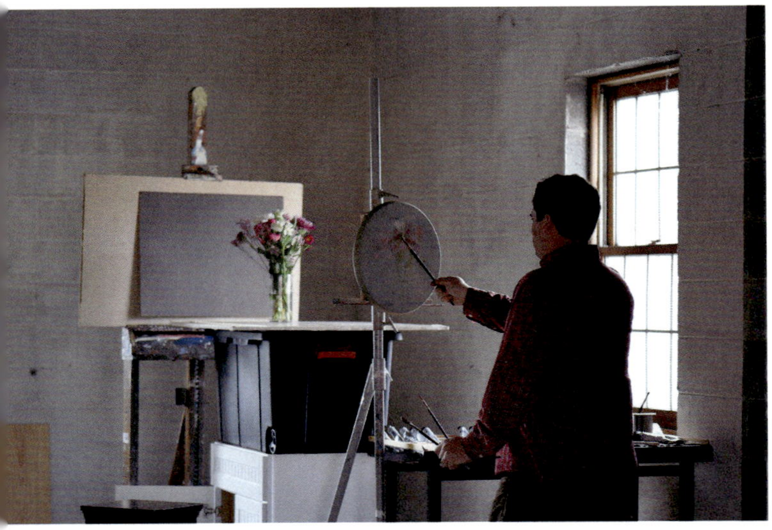

Philip Jackson in his studio

ST: *How do your images germinate? Do you keep a sketchbook, make preliminary studies, use photos, keep a routine, or rely on chance and opportunity?*

Philip Jackson: Typically, my images come from studies from life and reference photography. I am continuously taking photographs of objects all year long. I store them in separate files and as I want to work with the specific subject, I then pull them together to make one complete image. As I choose a particular object, I go back to nature to gather more information from life to further study their anatomy and surfaces. In large part, Photoshop is my sketchbook and means of drawing. I am able to sift through many ways of seeing the subject matter and come up with alternate combination of objects and transparencies.

ST: *Philip, your use of photography is extraordinarily sophisticated. I recall seeing the illuminated box in your studio that you use to stage your subjects. It is fascinating, like a small theater. Please describe your process in greater detail.*

PJ: Yes, I have a stage of sorts that I use to set up objects when documenting them and studying them. The setup is designed to create any light situation possible. I have tracks that are dedicated throughout the box that allow me to achieve not only the right positioning of the light but also control the temperature and contrast of that light.

ST: *Philip, two of your beautiful studies from life are shown below. Please tell us how they fit in with the rest of your work.*

PJ: Although the studies are a development for my longer in-depth paintings, I still see them as final paintings. Individually, they contain a thorough examination of objects but are made with a brief response. These works exist as finished thoughts. I use parts of their observations and color relationships to explore further in my more resolved works.

LEFT TO RIGHT:

Philip Jackson
Study of Yellowberries
2018, oil on museum board, 8 x 10 in.

Philip Jackson
Magnolia Pod, Flower and Berries VIII
2019, oil on museum board, 9 x 12 in.

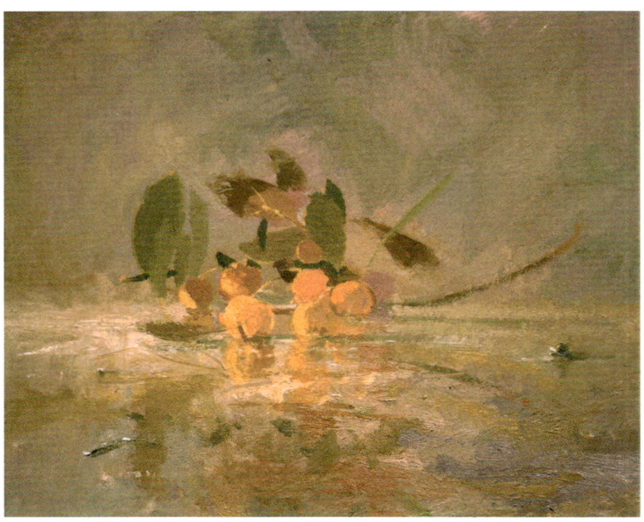

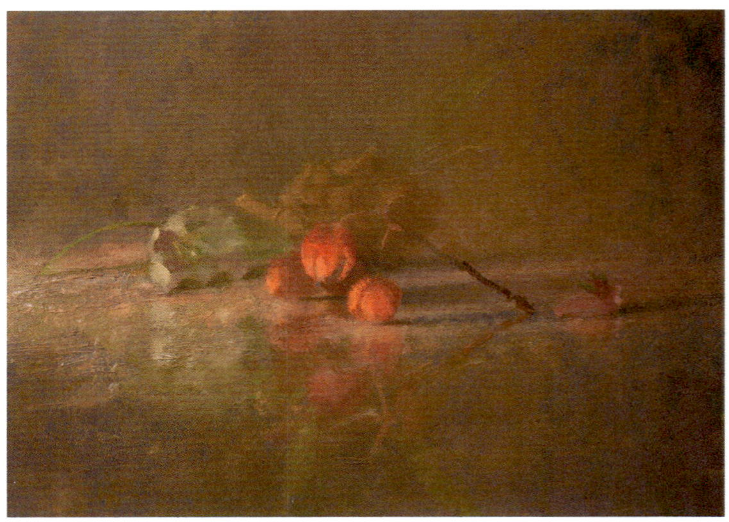

Daniel Dallmann: Years ago, I used sketchbooks profusely, often drawing and re-drawing the same basic image repeatedly as "thumbnail" sketches. When one sketch or another began to come alive for me, I would amplify that composition to a larger size, perhaps 16x20 inches. That would spring the trigger to begin a painting, often quite large, often five feet and more. The sketches and drawings were in anticipation of the scale of the work being planned. I didn't have the confidence to begin a work that might take several months to complete.

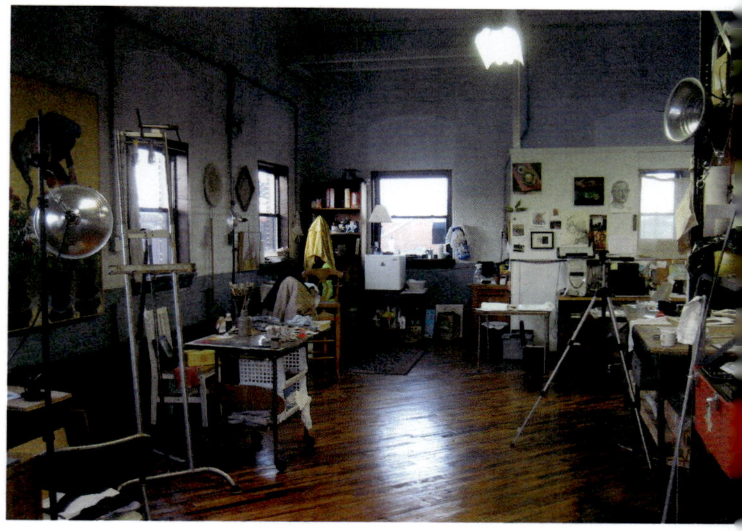

Daniel Dallmann's studio, 2014

I have usually eschewed the use of photos, for all the usual reasons. My figure paintings were mostly done with the models present. In the 1990s and early 2000s I had generous support from the university to pay for models. On rare occasions I would shoot a few photos if the model might be unavailable. The still life paintings, however, are all from life.

One of the most important sources for inspiration for each work is the previous painting. I have tended to work sequentially, pretty much finishing one piece before I begin another. With the year of Covid-19 that has changed considerably. I currently have three or four pieces going at once. It will be interesting to see if I gradually revert back to one at a time or if I continue to work more laterally, left and right, on multiple projects.

ST: *Dan, there's a lot of meaning packed into your phrase "for all the usual reasons" when you mention a reluctance to use photo sources. Artists reading this will be able to make an informed guess at your reasons, but others may find it puzzling. Please explain it a bit more. I wonder if there is something about painting from life that you find particularly rewarding.*

DD: Yes, indeed. I like your choice of words, "particularly rewarding." Working from life presents an infinite number of moments in which decisions must be made. Noticing and responding is the process I find so rewarding. For a plein air painter, choices get made regarding light and shadow; clouds scud across the field of vision, a decision is made and a moment later nature, in her generosity, presents us with another option. In painting with a model there are similar issues, including appointments, exhaustion, and temperament–but also the sense of collaboration when everything is going nicely. Working from a photograph seems as if the decisions have already been made, the ambiance is frozen. During the Covid-19 quarantine I have had to rely on photos more frequently for figure work. But for still life, that has not been a problem.

The photograph provides one with a certain kind of information, of an instant, the product of light. I like the idea that my paintings are an accumulation of moments. (Note here, I am talking about my own, limited, experiences with working from photos. Philip has a completely different use of the technology, including Photoshop. He extends photography in a way that seems to be mixed media. I would not say he is painting "from" a photograph.)

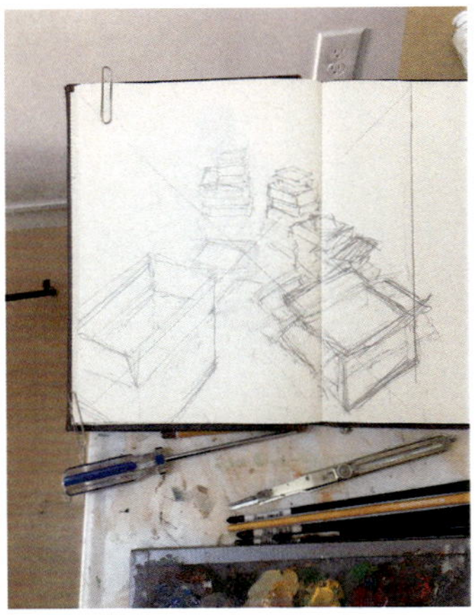

Daniel Dallmann *Sketchbook drawing*

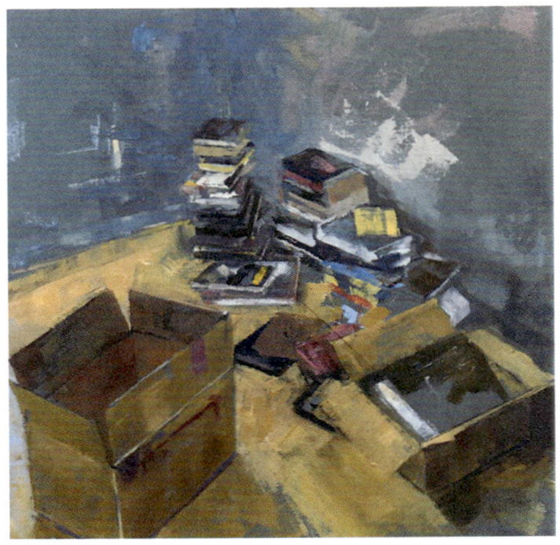

Daniel Dallmann *Early stage of painting*

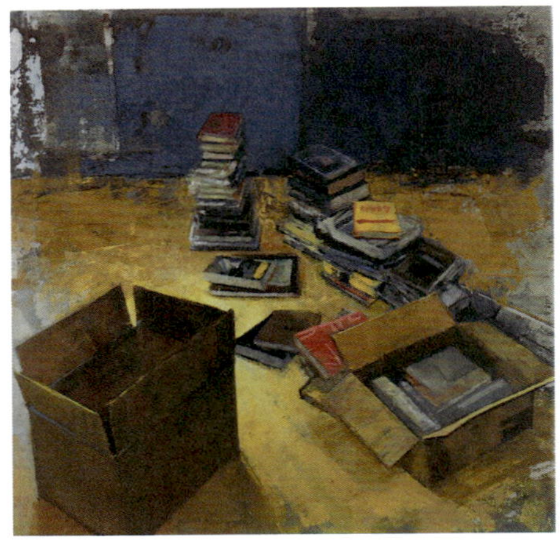

Daniel Dallmann *Sorting Books (Covid)*
2020, oil on wood, 10 x 10 in.

ST: *Dan, it sounds as if you no longer always make preliminary drawings. Does that mean you like to jump in and start painting, resolving the composition as the painting develops? I notice, for instance, that in the painting titled* Sorting Books (Covid) *you changed the walls of the room, in a way that is clearly due to imaginative invention rather than observation. And you did it in the middle of the painting process. It appears that in your sketchbook drawing, you had not yet settled on how the walls might be oriented.*

DD: That is true. In the sketch for *Sorting Books,* I was only mapping the way the objects fit the picture size and format, with attention paid to shape location and rhythm, geometry really, with next to nothing noted regarding value, tone, color, shading or light.

ST: *How would you characterize the precepts that guide your art? Are they rules or simply preferences? How might those have evolved as your art matured? Have you changed your mind dramatically about anything in your creative work?*

PJ: From my earliest interest in making images, I was naturally drawn to representation because I see and describe things in vivid pictures. My work is focused on the micro—the intricacies of things—and I invite the viewer into a greater sense of looking into a painting.

Walter Tandy Murch *Taking Off*
c. 1952, oil on canvas, 16 ⅛ x 16 in.. Toledo Museum of Art

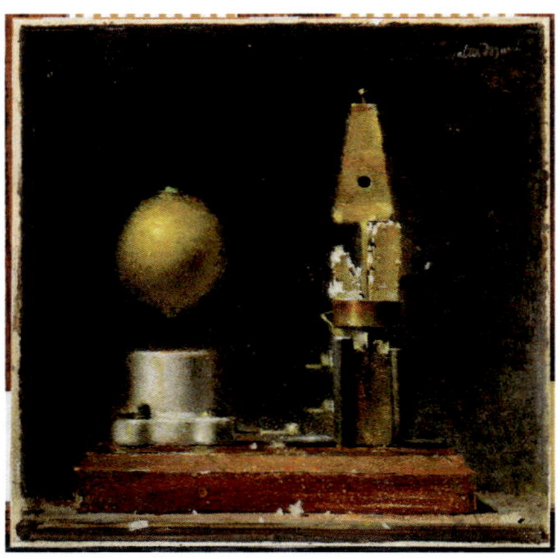

I am equally interested in the illusionistic space the viewer may enter into. After revisiting the paintings of one of my favorite painters, Walter Tandy Murch, I was reminded of something very magical that I have always admired about his diminutive works. Murch said of his analysis of reality, "I must not paint the thing itself, but will paint the air between myself and the thing and beyond." This challenged my observation of the object and my portrayal of it to the viewer.

DD: I don't think about precepts very often. I tend to trust my instincts and allow things to happen, not always successfully, I must admit.

I distrust intentions, whether regarding content or working process; they can get in the way. Intent and content are very often divergent. It's safe to say that my precepts have something to do with how my perceptions get absorbed and translated so they can exist in some art form.

One change that I've noticed over the years: I am less interested in any narrative implications that might be suggested by my images. I think I am more trusting that the form will reveal the content.

The day-by-day work of making art requires countless decisions. Mostly these decisions are abstract, formal choices regarding elements like color, shape, space and energy. Underneath, however, is an unspoken murmur of associations, memories, projections and desires, all triggered by my responses to the subject and formal elements; that murmur is what they call the voice of the muse. Noticing and responding to that soft voice becomes the real challenge of the work, because it is there that I'll find the statement that I didn't know I was going to make.

ST: *Is there a formative experience, person or artwork that may have led you to becoming an artist?*

PJ: I can't remember a time where I was not making objects and thinking through images. But yes, I have had many wonderful people that have contributed to my development as an artist, which I am truly grateful for.

DD: My family was involved in art. My father was a sculptural craftsman who made a living doing commission work for architectural projects, cemeteries, and churches. Our house was filled with books; probably half of them were art books. As a child I loved the books!

PJ: Yes, one in particular has inspired the development of many others. In the painting *Transitory Spaces: Pear, Apples, and Cherries*, naturalistic objects are presented in a seemingly traditional still life arrangement, but I brought them together to form a symbolic family portrait. My wife and each one of my children's lives are reflected in all of my paintings.

In this picture, the pear is a matriarchal presence over the cluster of apples and cherries. Just as a mother hen broods over her young, she is both protective and intimately nurturing to each object as she stands above them. Their lives are reflected through the surface. The mysterious elements in the periphery contain the unknowns that we encounter in our life. I, as the artist, in the place of the viewer, am the voyeur, looking back, watching over them within this small intimate space. This painting is like a brief glimpse into a collection of memories.

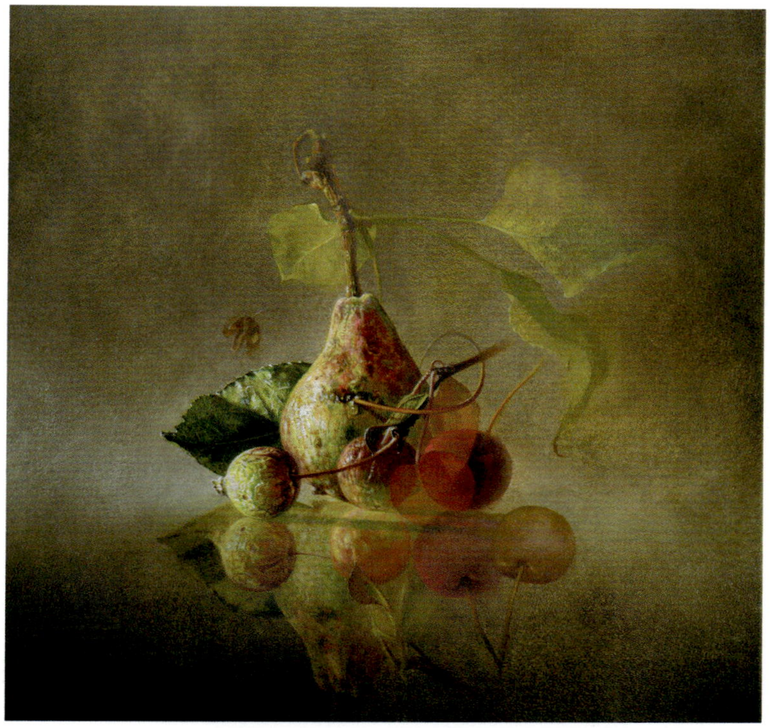

Philip Jackson *Transitory Spaces: Pear, Apple, and Cherries*
2017, oil on panel, 10 x 10 in.

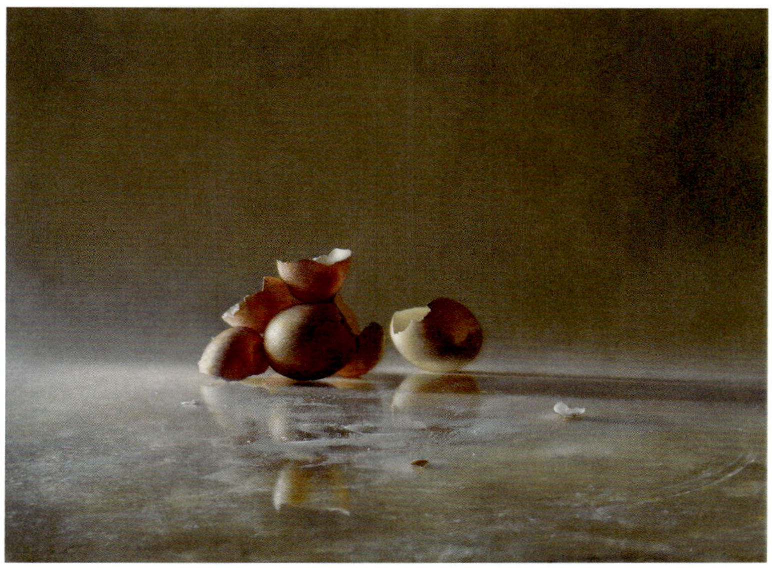

Philip Jackson *Transitory Reflections: Eggshells*
2013, oil on panel, 16 x 18 in.

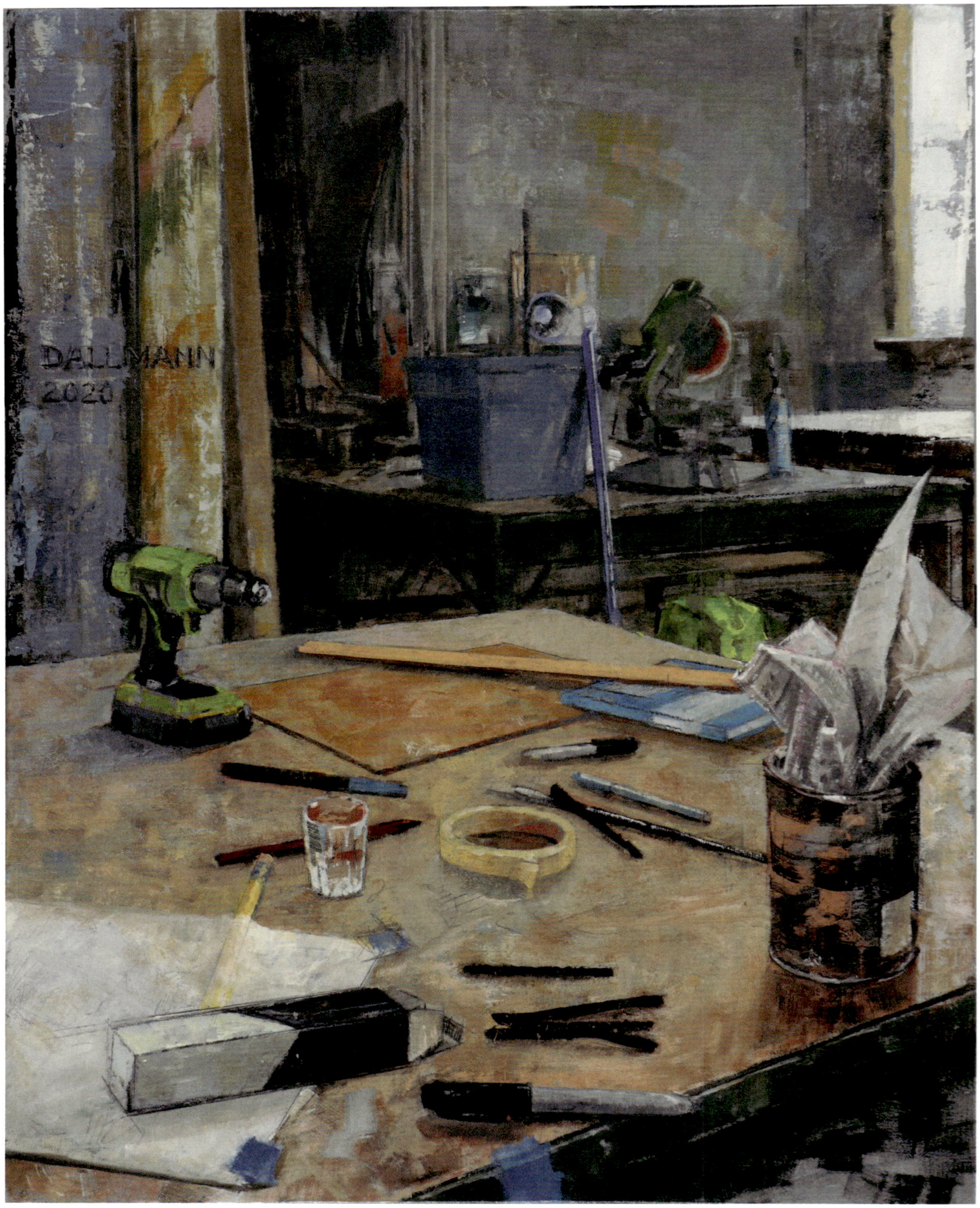

Daniel Dallmann *Studio Space with Still Life*
2020, oil on wood, 15 x 12 in.

ST: *Why do you make still life paintings? And why do we look at them?*

DD: For many years I thought of still life as a boring subject. Bottles of wine, bowls of fruit, and flowers held little interest for me. I began to accept still life as a result of my gradual distrust of narrative and increased trust in form as content. Still life allowed me to forget, or at least neglect, any narrative and allowed me to delight in the power of form (composition, color, gesture, etc.) as a source of content. As example, I might mention *Studio Space with Still Life*, the painting in the current Zeuxis show at First Street Gallery. The objects and spaces have no prescribed meaning; there is no narrative to be "read." But it all adds up to a scattered kind of rhythm, a little like atonal music, or jazz, and is a delight to look at even while contrasted to the more orderly spatial zones.

PJ: My main concern is to present an image that resonates in the mind of the viewer. I choose still life because it contains the simple overlooked things of no inherent value.

The objects I select and the realism of my subjects, however, are only a small part of what is seen within my paintings. It is the conversation between these things that create a life beyond the subject.

Through my paintings, I am attempting to redefine an object's natural purpose and sense of place through the orchestrated exchange between them. The illusions of naturalism are brought into question by the formed relationship of the objects and contradictory reflective surface. The effects of time (aging, the passing of, displacement of, and reorganization of things) are what influence this work. Here objects are presented in opposing stages of life and moved from their original growing place. Somehow, they have been dropped, blown or moved and found their way to a congregated place among the other objects. The intimacy between each object is heightened by the minimal space. Bathed in light, each one reveals its own mysteries. Their surfaces reveal a life lived: dents, bruises, and more. It is as if they were having a conversation long before we approached the picture. These are unusual and banal aspects of space and one might only see the

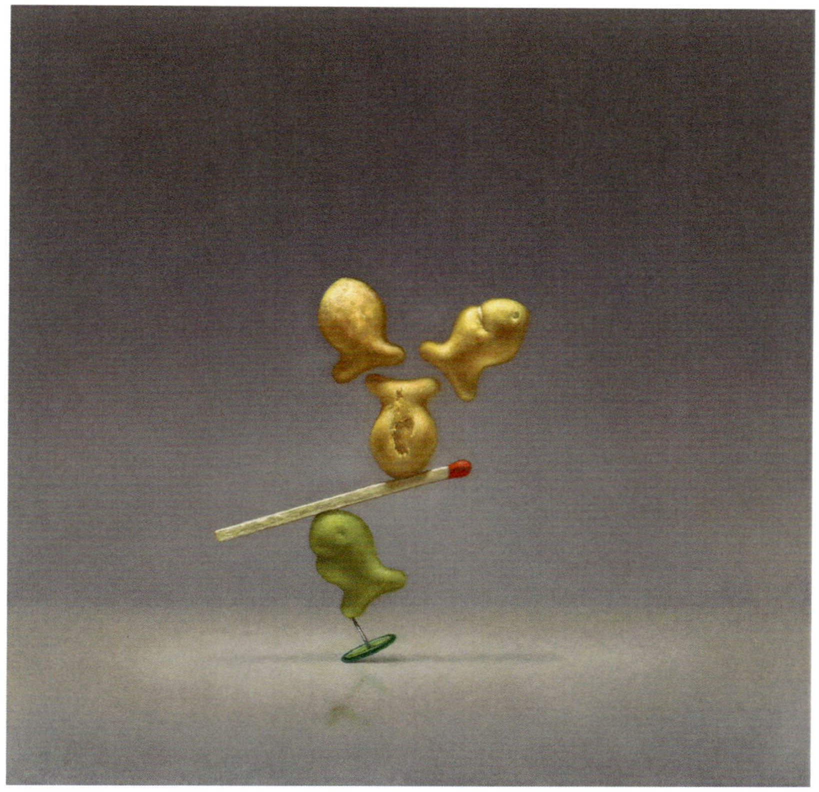

Philip Jackson
Tension Series: Matchstick Balancing Act
2012, oil on panel, 8 x 8 in.

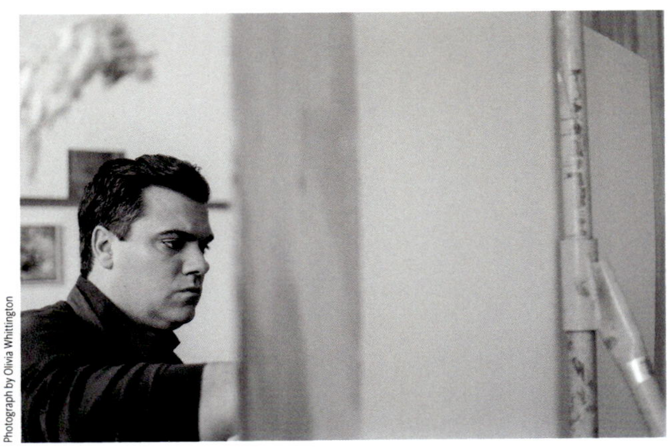

Photograph by Olivia Whittington

Philip Jackson painting

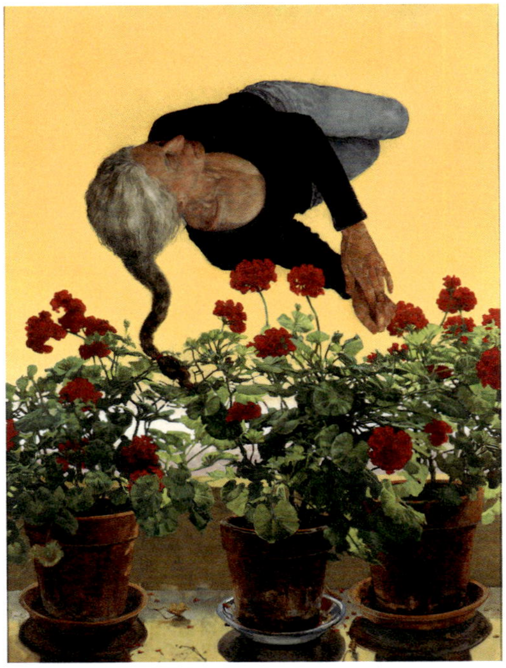
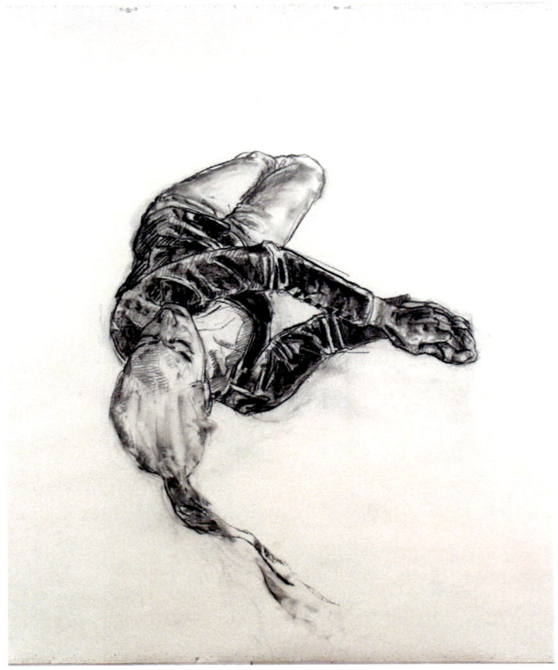
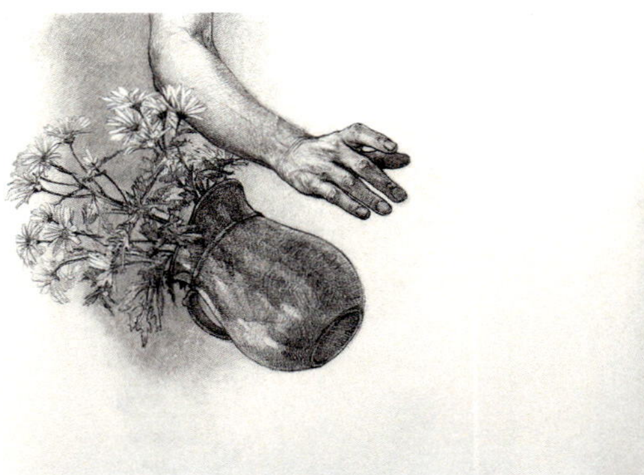
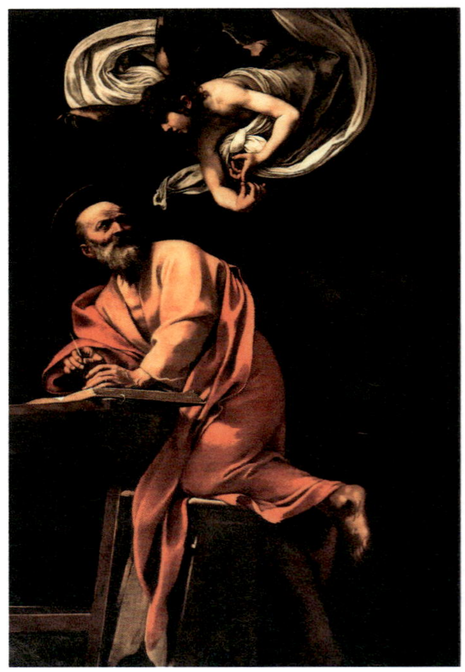

CLOCKWISE:

Daniel Dallmann *Joy of Winter Geraniums*
2005, oil on linen, 66 x 48 in.

Daniel Dallmann *Study of Carol #1*
2005, graphite on paper, 22 x 30 in.

Caravaggio *The Inspiration of Saint Matthew*
1602, oil on canvas, 115 x 73 in., San Luigi dei Francesi, Rome

Daniel Dallmann *Merisi's Gift*
2007, graphite on paper, 22 x 30 in.

relationship if they rummaged the forest floor. There one can see the universe brought together by nature itself.

Why do I make still life paintings? Our world moves at a pace that leaves observation behind. My paintings are an invitation to experience the world again, but through a slower, alternative perspective.

DD: Yes, I would like to echo Philip's statement about the wonderful, enriching, experience of making and viewing the slow art of painting. Fast food is not about nourishment.

ST: *Dan, in our Zoom conversation, you began to tell us some of the process by which you created the painting* Joy of Winter Geraniums *(far left). Please expand on that.*

DD: That was the first of three rather large paintings exploring the instability of life by challenging the phenomenon of gravity. I've heard it said that "gravity never fails," and I wanted to create a picture in which gravity was not a given. I often make pictures without an actual idea, just a hunch that something might be interesting or challenging. When those geraniums in my studio blossomed with such generosity it became a kind of happy ritual, plucking the dying blossoms off and knowing that in a day or two they would be replaced aplenty.

I was not yet certain about the picture and wanted to do a few actual-size charcoal drawings to solve problems of perspective and foreshortening. Practically speaking, the model, Carol, posed on the top of two tables stacked on top of each other, so that she was at my eye level. She lay on the table almost on her back and I rotated the drawing paper to various degrees. I saw her form as illustrative of the geranium joy I wanted to celebrate.

Drawing from the model was related to my love of the baroque paintings that I almost lived with in Italy. I sent you a photo of a Caravaggio painting: the angel inspiring St Mathew. It reminds me of another experience that inspired my series, that touched on the question of gravity. There was a small show in the Vatican complex, called "I Santi ed i Miracoli (The Saints and the Miracles)." The art spanned several centuries, perhaps 12th to 18th century. I noticed, with curiosity, that many of the images contained elements that defied gravity. From a mountain floating away in the sky, shedding rocks and small trees on its way (to heaven perhaps?) to a saint that is swooping in to save children from a burning village, or building, and veritable tons of angels.

I saw that show at least 20 years ago, but the sheer number of images that defied gravity as a way to ensure that the viewers understood that something special was going on, has stayed with me. Here is a drawing of mine that reflected those memories and is something of an homage to Caravaggio's angel.

ST: *Daniel, please tell us more about your experiences living and working in Rome.*

DD: I've lived in Rome on several occasions, a total of about six years. The Tyler School of Art has had a program for many years, housed in the Villa Caproni, near the Piazza del Popolo. I taught printmaking there for two years in the Seventies. Of course, I enjoyed the experience—the museums, the travel—but I was anxious to get back to my studio in Philadelphia and the proximity to New York. In retrospect, I didn't take full advantage of the opportunity.

After having enjoyed and suffered all that twenty-five years of life can throw at you, I had a chance to go back to Rome, 2000-02, to teach painting and drawing. This time I was determined to take full advantage of the experience. I insisted on learning all the Italian language my aging brain could hold. I bought a motorcycle that allowed me to learn the environs, both inside and outside of the city, and made friends with Italian artists and musicians. In the 70s we lived in an apartment only three blocks from the school. I spent most of my time within that small portion of the city. Later, I lived all

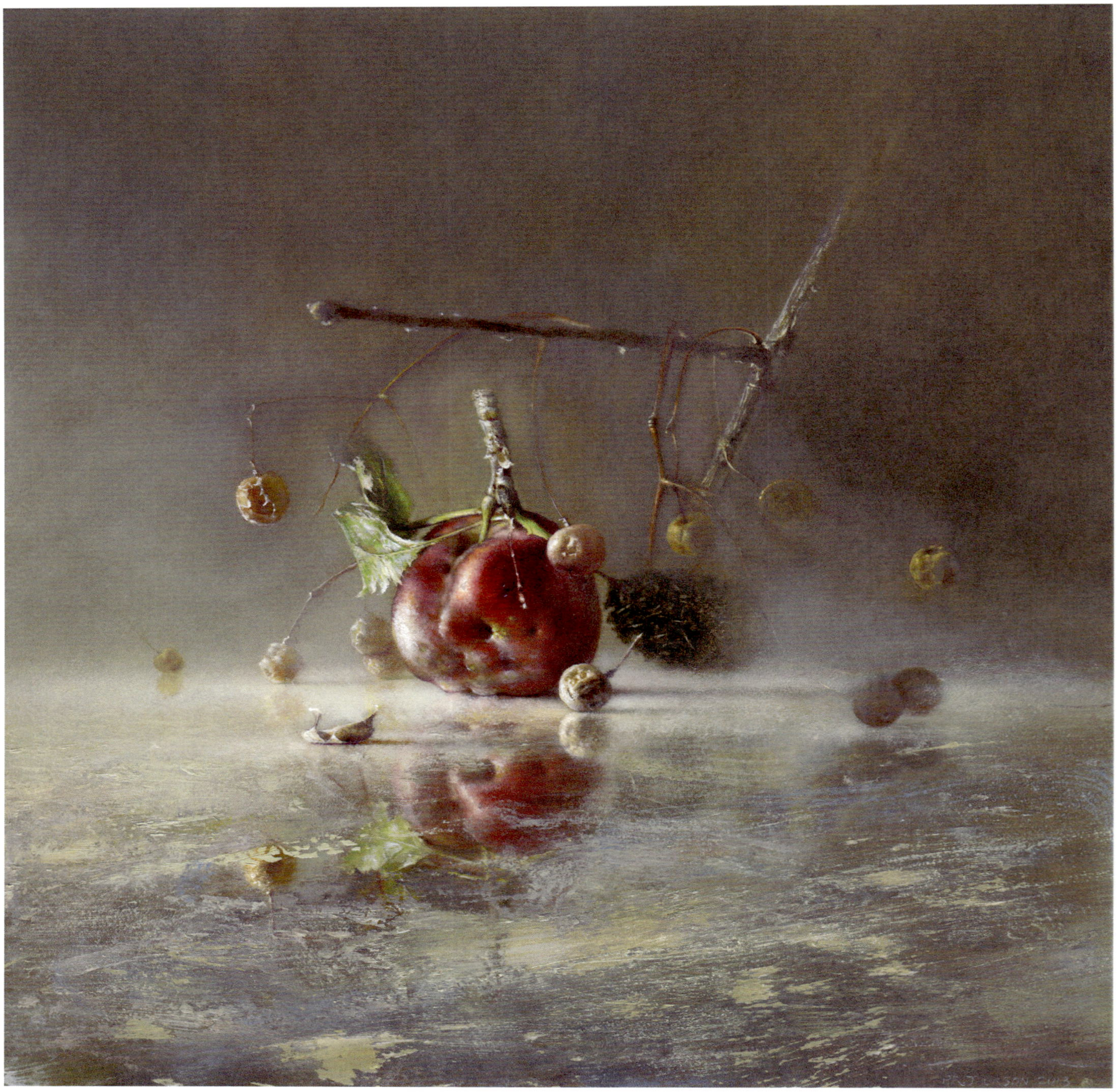

Philip Jackson *Transitory Spaces: Apple, Berries & Fragments*
2014, oil on panel, 8 x 8 in.

over the place: Prati, Esquilino, Trieste and Pigneto. I returned again and again, teaching one-semester contracts, summer school, and visiting artist gigs, arranged by Rhode Island School of Design and by American University—both had Rome programs at the time.

ST: *Thanks, Daniel and Philip, for joining me in this conversation. It is fascinating to hear how each of you have expressed individual experience in your painting. I have so much enjoyed hearing your reflections and I am sure the readers will too.* ■

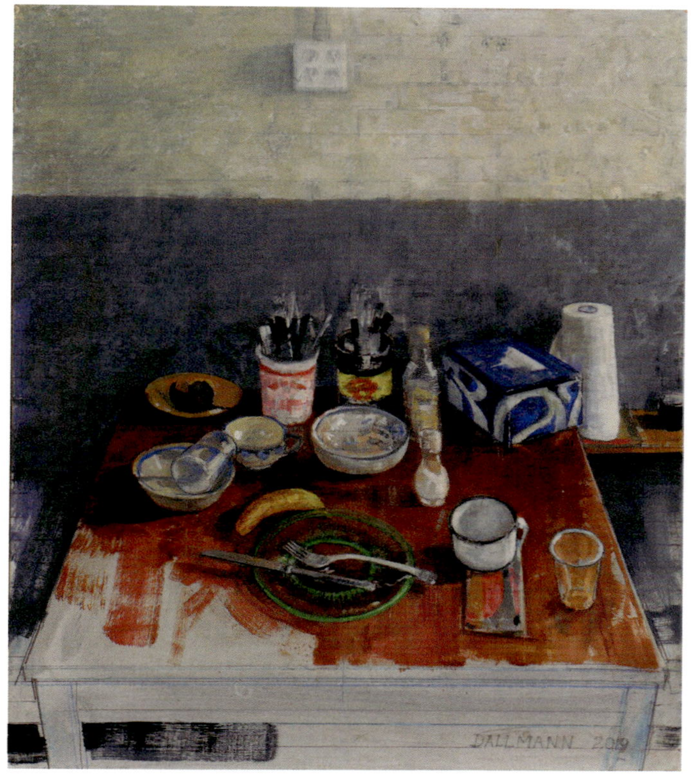

Daniel Dallmann *Hopscotch*
2019, oil on wood, 14 x 12 in.

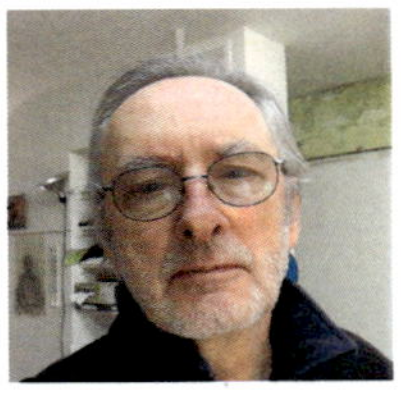

Daniel Dallmann grew up in a family that was accustomed to art; both parents studied at the School of the Minneapolis Institute of Art. After earning an MFA degree in printmaking from the University of Iowa, he moved to Philadelphia to teach at the Tyler School of Art of Temple University for forty-three years. His work in painting and lithography has included themes based on landscape, figure and, more recently, still life. He has been affiliated with Zeuxis for two years. He has presented twenty-five solo exhibitions, participated in dozens of group shows, and can be found in over thirty public, museum and corporate collections.

www.zeuxis.us/dallmann
www.dallmannstudio.com

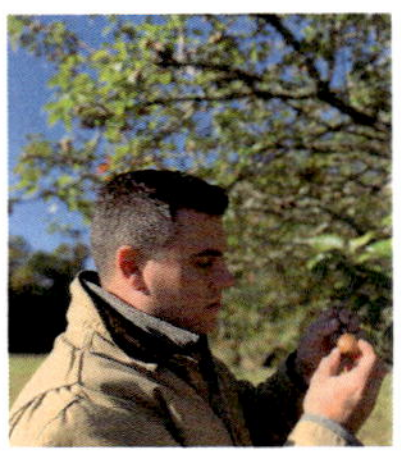

Philip R. Jackson's still life paintings have been and featured in many premiere art magazines and are part of numerous private, corporate and museum art collections nationwide. He has received fellowships from the Elizabeth Greenshields Foundation in Montreal, Canada, the Mississippi Museum of Art, the Mississippi Arts Commission, AIR Serenbe and the Tyrone Guthrie Foundation in Monaghan, Ireland. Jackson received his Bachelor of Fine Arts from the Columbus College of Art & Design in Columbus, Ohio and his Master of Fine Arts from Bowling Green State University in Bowling Green, Ohio. He also studied abroad at Studio Art Centers International in Florence, Italy. He resides in Oxford, Mississippi with his wife and three children where he teaches at the University of Mississippi and heads the painting program.

www.zeuxis.us/jackson
www.p-jackson.com

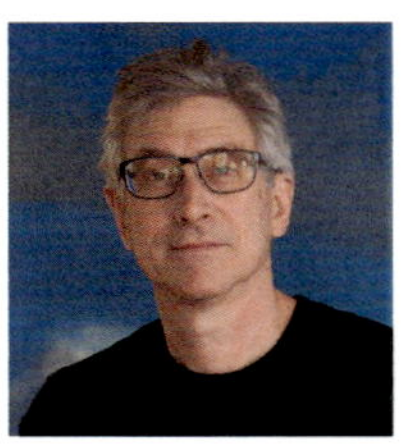

Sheldon Tapley's careful observation and playful invention are the roots of his art. He loves painting directly from life and hopes that it gives his images greater vitality. Still life is an important element of his work and has also become the foundation for images that invoke memory and imagination. Tapley is the Stodghill Professor of Art at Centre College, where he has enjoyed working with his students for many years.

www.zeuxis.us/tapley
www.sheldontapley.com

Paths Painters Take

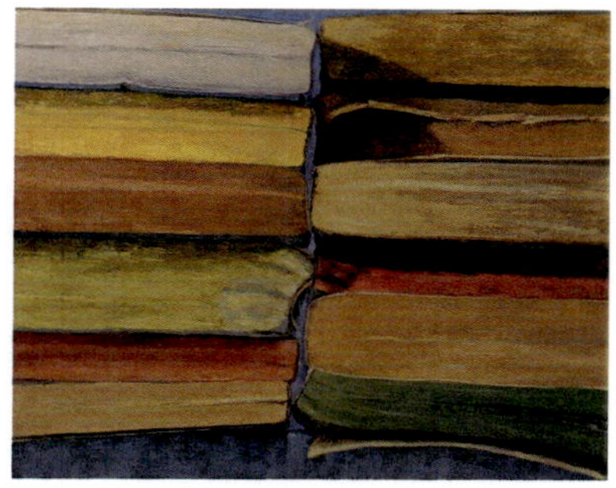

Neil Callander interviews

Neil Plotkin and Emily Zuch and Kimberly Trowbridge

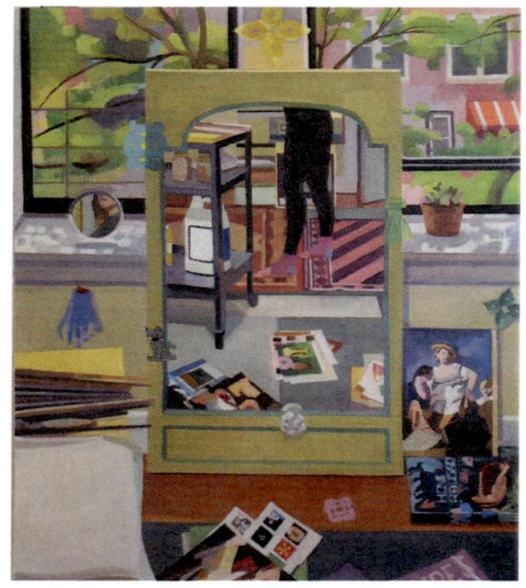

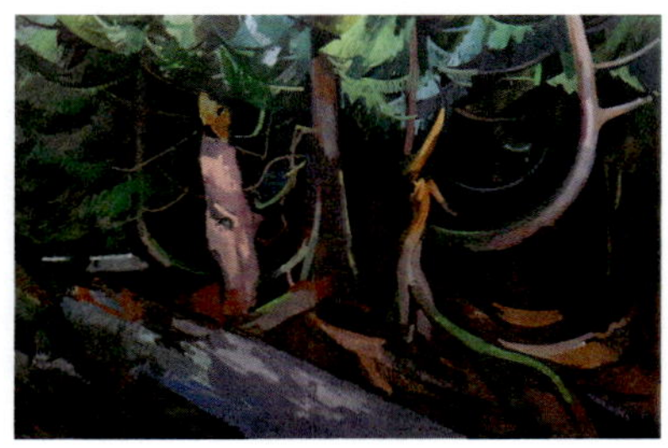

Neil Plotkin *Radke Books*
2019, oil on linen, 24 x 30 in.

Emily Zuch *Legs*
2020, oil on linen, 50 x 40 in.

Kimberly Trowbridge *Theater of Destruction*
2020, Oil on linen on panel, 48 x 72 in.

Neil Callander: *Spread across the country and in the midst of a global pandemic, three painters responded to my weighty questions. Every painter working today reckons with painting's storied canon; over an unhurried email exchange Neil, Kimberly and Emily delivered special insights into how painting's past is active in their practices.*

NC: *One reason I admire each of you is because of your embrace of painting's past—or at least I see overt, embedded and (I suspect) oblique references in your paintings. I'm reminded of that famous John Cage remark to Philip Guston, "When you start working, everybody is in your studio—the past, your friends, enemies, the art world, and above all, your own ideas—all are there. But as you continue painting, they start leaving, one by one, and you are left completely alone. Then, if you are lucky, even you leave."*

In terms of influential painters from the past, who are the last to leave your studio? How would you describe your relationship with these painters?

Kimberly Trowbridge: I love this question, thank you, Neil. The two artists that linger longest for me are Cézanne and Matisse. Cézanne's project, for me, does not diminish in importance, but rather gains more meaning over time. His work attempts the elusive union between an ever-changing perception

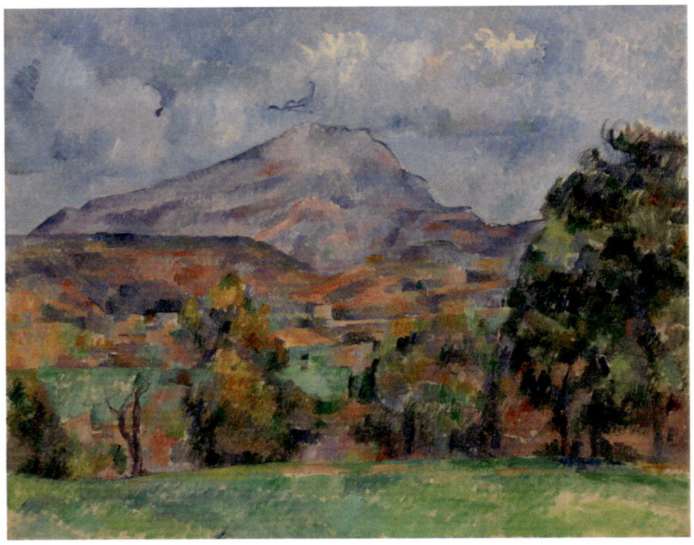

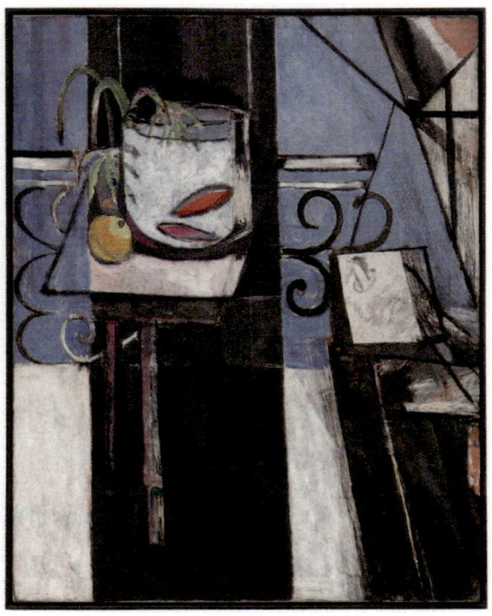

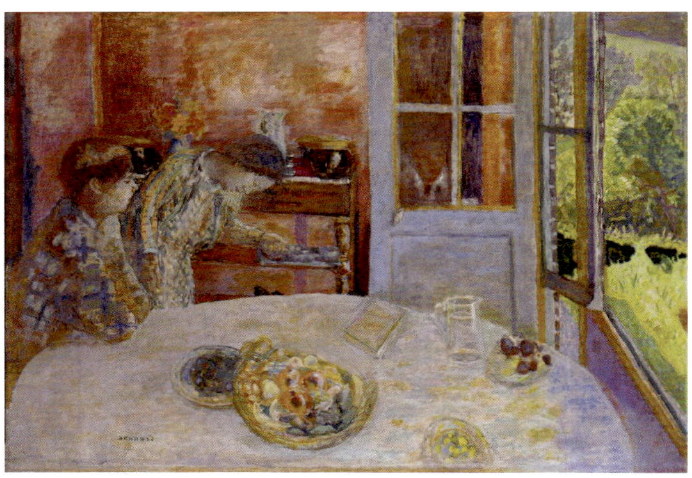

TOP TO BOTTOM:

Paul Cézanne
Montagne Sainte-Victoire
1888-90, Paul G. Allen Family Collection

Henri Matisse
Goldfish and Palette
1915, oil on canvas, 58 x 44 in., MOMA

Pierre Bonnard
The Dining Room, Vernon
c. 1925, oil on canvas, 49 ½ x 72 ½ in.

and a steadfast, bolted structure. I am thinking of him returning over and over to his Mont Sainte-Victoire, building rigorous pathways with colors like bricks, solidifying—but not making static—his experience of looking. I feel intimately close to this project, this desire to "paint Poussin entirely from nature."

Matisse exists in my studio as a kind-of punk rock friend. He helps me get to the big shapes of color and to treat the surface like a layered collage of relationships. I call on him to help when my surface gets stuck or when my forms fall into tedium. In particular, his works completed just before WWI, his closest brush with cubism: *Goldfish and Palette,* 1915; *Bathers by a River,* 1917. The almost brutal physicality of these works, coupled with the tenderness of content, moves me very deeply and I can feel them in my bones.

Emily Zuch: The artist that comes to mind for me is Bonnard. I'm not sure if his influence is visible in my paintings to an outside observer, but there was a time when it was, and I think he sent me down a certain path. The way I approach color is a lot about finding hues in unexpected places and amping them up, letting that color glow. Bonnard embodies that for me, he finds a kind of smoldering color that seems to burn from the insides of things. He also has a certain way of finding a relationship between each object and what surrounds it. He'll have dishes, food and silverware arranged on a table, and each object is an event in and of itself, and the tablecloth serves to isolate each one of them and let it shine in its own way. The spaces between things carry an equal amount of interest; you could spend so much time inching across the distance between two plates in a Bonnard painting. Every mark feels intentional. Nothing feels empty, everything is full.

Neil Plotkin: I don't know if these artists are the last to leave, but they were some of the first to arrive and have remained central to my practice. I first saw the drawings of both Alberto Giacometti and Edwin Dickinson in my first drawing class at university, and their importance has persisted. While living in Europe many years ago, I was given a small article on Antonio Lopez-Garcia which redirected my search for the qualities defining meaningful work. Finally, I have lived off and on in the UK and feel quite connected to the Coldstream and Bomberg schools. And from those schools, Euan Uglow has been the most central to my intentions.

While those four painters came early and stayed late, they remain out of my way. The one artist whom I don't ask to leave is the musician Jason Molina. I find his music thoughtful, filled with integrity and created with a deep sadness all while containing an edge. His music acts as a beacon for me to keep moving towards those traits in my own work.

That's difficult to achieve visually. So, I strive towards the qualities I find unifying in the painters I've mentioned. Their paintings are road maps of a searching process utilizing direct observation. The work is less about the destination of a finished painting and more about an exploration of the world. The pursuit could take years, and during those long periods of time, it shows correction and change. Despite those long efforts, there are often open spaces of the ground showing through. The images often contain large swaths of loose work only to be tightened up with very purposeful marks. The "finished" paintings are often in states of flux and feel neither finished nor unfinished. They are fully formed and still emerging into a finalized state. I hope to make work that has many of those qualities while fitting into the dialogue of American and British painting.

NC: *I bet you all have a long list of diverse artists that influence your practice—thanks for narrowing it down for us. You have me wondering if there is something uniquely American about constructing one's own painting lineage. I'm thinking here mainly about artistic attitude. How deferential, how pioneering, how hybridizing are you in the studio? Do you strive for range, for a narrowing of focus, for originality?*

NP: I love that Kimberly and Emily have different artists with whom they relate and create dialogues. So often it feels like we all look at the same artists, but in reality, we're all on our own paths.

I wouldn't say that I'm directly working with the ideas and modes of these artists but rather that they percolate into my work. As in Lopez-Garcia's, Uglow's and Giacometti's modest subject matter, I generally try to choose simple subjects which allow me to focus on the mark making and physical qualities of the paint. The corrected observations in those artists' work guide me to use transparencies and scraping to reveal changes and past histories. The improvisational quality of Dickinson and Giacometti give me the freedom to change areas of work and not feel obliged to cover the entire surface of the canvas. Like them, I focus my efforts to the areas needing more attention and open space is fine. I seek an accuracy that I find in Dickinson's work and in particular Lopez-Garcia's work. But like Giacometti, I have no intentions to create work in an academic manner. He understood the need for a truthfulness as opposed to accuracy. Because I'm not nearly the artist they are, I constantly need to make corrections, and their work often reveals that they too had to make adjustments. Ultimately, like the artists in my lineage, I want my work to show the journey of the creation of the work rather than to present a finished image.

EZ: In terms of painters that have influenced me, I'm not necessarily conscious of their influence all the time. There will be moments when I will feel very taken by certain approaches by painters I love, and that will lodge in my thoughts while I paint, but it feels more like something on the periphery of my mind than something that is front and center of my thoughts while I'm working. I don't know if I have consciously constructed a painting lineage, but the painters I love greatly affect the

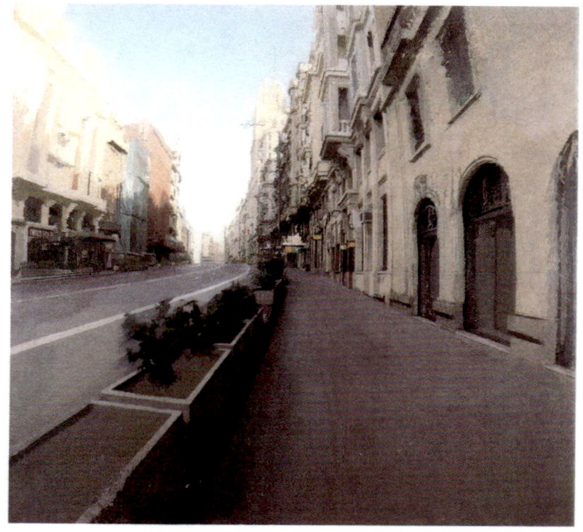

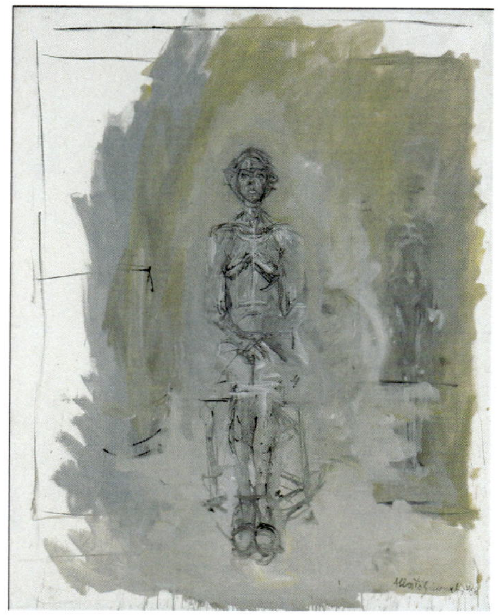

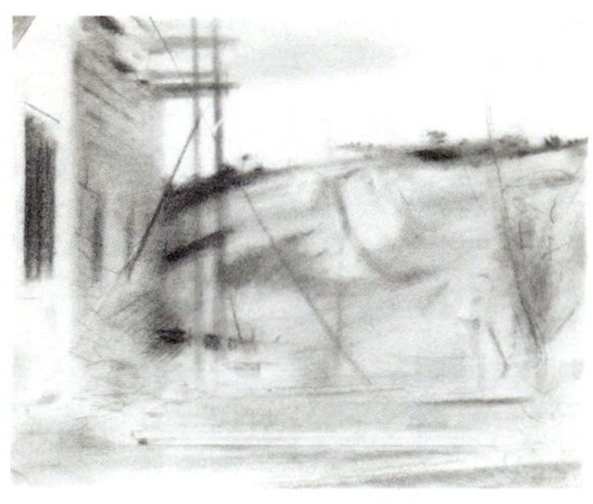

TOP TO BOTTOM:

Antonio Lopez-Garcia *Gran Via, Clavel*
1977-90, oil on canvas on panel, 47 x 48 ½ in.

Alberto Giacometti *Annette Seated*
1958, oil and pencil on canvas, 45 ½ x 35 in.

Edwin Dickinson *Shingling Dickinson House*
1939, charcoal on paper, 10 ¾ x 13 in.

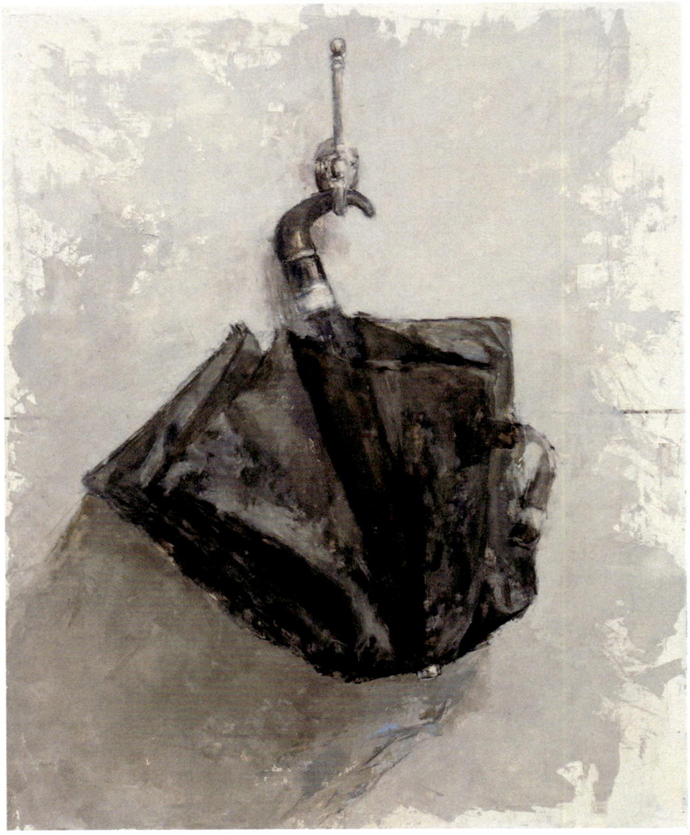

Neil Plotkin *Five Dollar Umbrella*
2018, oil on panel, 18 x 24 in.

way I see the world inside and outside the studio. What I notice, what I choose to paint, and how I frame things are all deeply affected by these painters, although often I don't realize it at the moment.

Originality is always something I hope to achieve in my work, but I think paradoxically the way to get there is often not to think too much about it. I find that delving deeply into what's pulling me in is the most sure fire way to reach something that feels like it's mine, even if what I'm interested in couldn't be more traditional. If I am engaged by a body of work, and have a thread to follow, I feel lucky. I don't think it's necessary to see too far ahead. If I can see my way from the painting I just finished to the next one, that's enough. I think range is possible in so many ways, and it's possible to achieve range within a quite narrow focus (and maybe that's a particularly good way to achieve range that feels coherent). I've learned to resist the pull of lots of new ideas that don't relate to what I'm working on at the time, because I find that often the most exciting thing about them is their newness and that wears off quickly, leaving me disinterested and lost.

KT: I do think there is something deeply American about constructing one's own identity and lineage as a person and as an artist. I also think this necessity and drive to create a meaningful narrative out of disparate histories is now a global, common means for survival. There is something inherently creative in this contemporary construction of self, this collaging-together of experience that is so much a part of our current consciousness. I resonate deeply, Emily, with how you describe Bonnard, his "smoldering color" and the intentionality of each mark spanning the distance between things. This, coupled with your attraction, Neil P., towards artists who exemplify the process of searching, the "exploration of the world," makes me think lovingly of how we as painters look back at the history of painting, both individually and collectively, re-illuminating the philosophical manifestations that help guide us in our own search for presentness and integrity.

Painting is a way of life, a continued effort to translate experience into a meaningful, visual document. Looking to the past gives us wonderful nuggets of wisdom, attitudes for entering, clues on the path through the deep forest of our own consciousness. But ultimately we are called upon to leap into the unknown, into the present relationships building on our surface, right here in front of us in a way that has never existed before. How will we respond? How will we continue to cultivate this unique experience?

NC: *It's fun to be philosophical, important to mull over big ideas, but the painter's craft is visual and there is a moment when you just have to decide what to paint! Will you describe your chosen subject matter and how you arrived at it?*

EZ: Neil P. and Kimberly, I think it's so interesting how you both use metaphors of journeying/searching to describe your processes, the metaphor of a forest rings particularly true for me. So much of the excitement of painting comes from not knowing where it will take you.

I make set-ups in my studio and paint them from life, windows and mirrors are usually a central element. I arrange the space with postcards/reproductions of other artists' work, playing cards, plants,

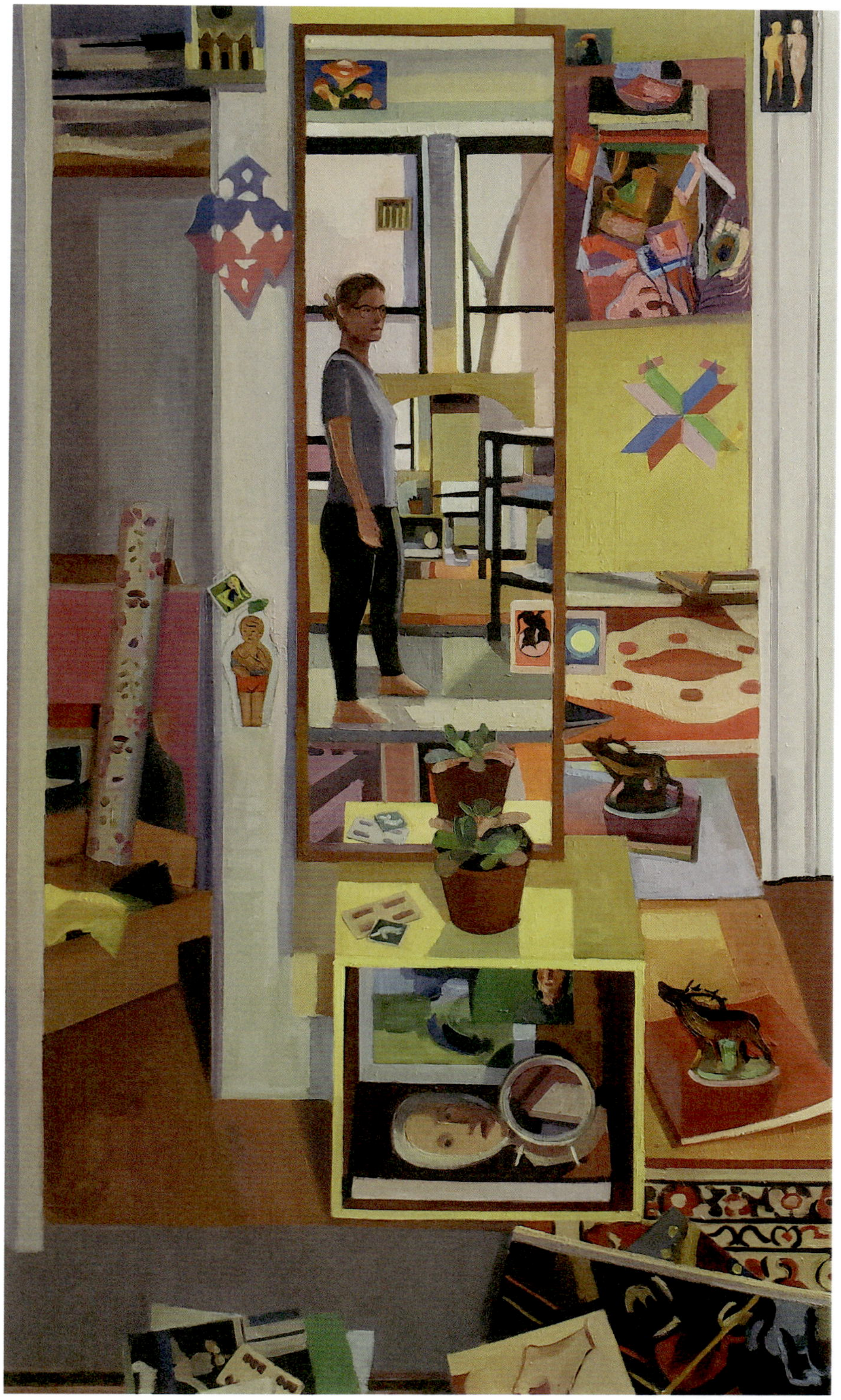

Emily Zuch *Long Mirror*
2020, oil on canvas, 66 x 38 in.

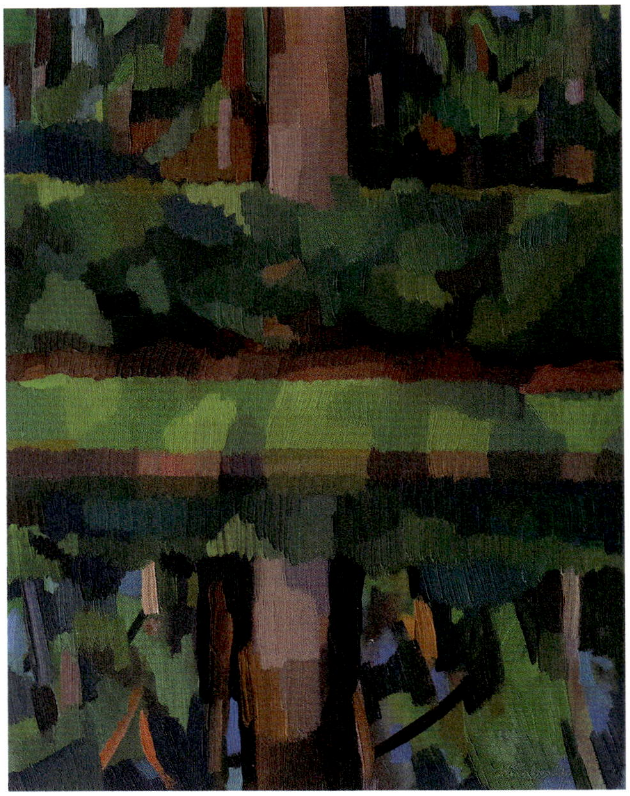

Kimberly Trowbridge
Reflection Pool Double Cedar
2018, oil on paper on panel, 16 x 12 in.

and other tchotchkes. The idea is to create a disorienting, fragmented feeling. It's very fun hearing viewers try to figure out "what is where" when they look at my work.

I came to this subject matter because I wanted to paint fantasy, but I also wanted to paint from life. My solution to this was to create very elaborate installations in my studio to paint, almost like theater sets. These installations would take about a week or so to make, I would use materials like wood, cardboard and paper mache to create these fairytale-like scenes. Eventually I started moving away from this type of imagery and became more interested in the constellations of objects in my studio that would happen without me realizing it, the clutter on a table, for example, or layers of notes and images stuck to the walls. This led me to my current approach. I still control the space by setting up mirrors and objects, but it leaves a lot more space for chaos to enter. I'm always interested in toeing that line.

KT: I love painting nature from observation and the figure as an invented construction.

I began traveling and painting directly from nature about a decade ago, and it has opened-up my painting practice on so many meaningful levels. It has become a whole way of life for me, what I call "plein-air your life," meaning, to directly engage with and witness what surrounds you through the act of painting. I experience incredible joy painting in natural light and responding to the rhythms and forms of plant life. On the field is where I cultivate a deep awareness of color interactions and I consider my plein-air works as my "primary documents" that inform my larger, more conceptual studio paintings.

I think of nature as the stage where human consciousness evolves, and I see my work as a continuation of the Arcadian practice—the Edenic setting where our temporality is revealed. My studio paintings approach nature through the lens of Renaissance painting: the construction of characters interacting on a stage. These characters are both natural forms—trees, vines, ferns—and also figures. I love constructing and inventing figurative forms like hieroglyphics, letters in an

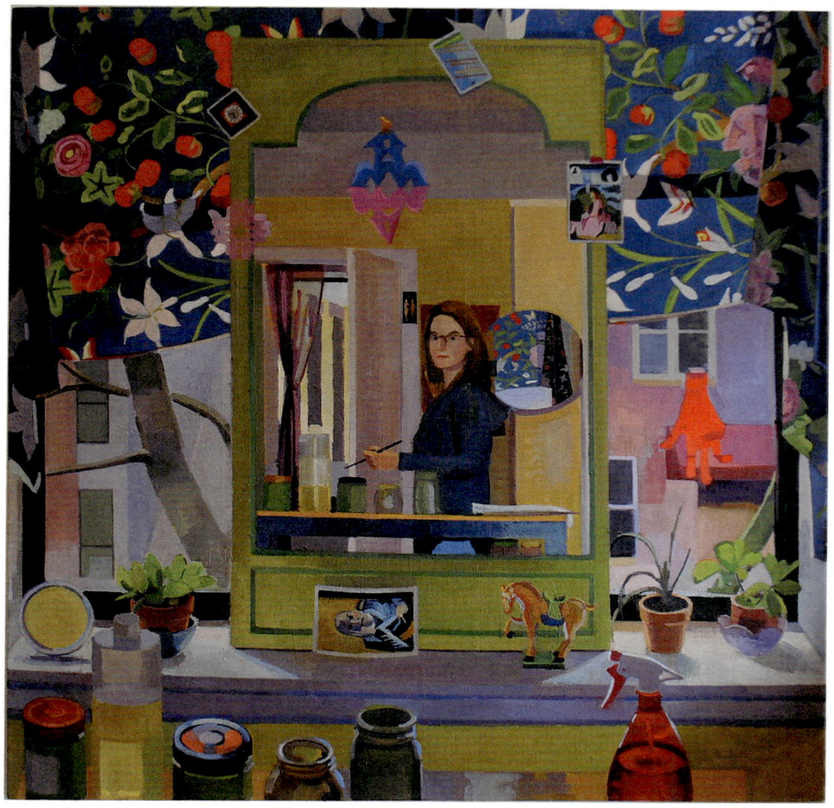

Emily Zuch *Garden*
2021, oil on canvas, 60 x 60 in.

alphabet, gestures that are embedded-in and dictate the overall composition and form of the painting. I love ancient friezes where the figures tell a story like words across a page, like twigs across a forest floor.

NP: I want to be surprised, challenged and ultimately fall in love with my subjects. My work succeeds if I can access an emotional connection to the subject. There is a sense that this painting couldn't exist if I hadn't found these perfect objects in this perfect order. So, the subjects have to work just right.

As a student, I was tasked to draw a view of the classroom studio I was working in. The room was austere, sterile and to my eyes utterly uninspiring and my resulting drawing was uninspiring too. That assignment set my intention as an artist. The challenge for me is not to take something beautiful and recreate it but rather but to find something ordinary, overlooked, and modest and transform that into something to be revered or special.

This translates into much of my current work of paintings of books. When my first son was born, I found it very difficult to balance the duties of being a stay-at-home father while maintaining my painting practice. All I desired during that time was to have some kind of solitude and relief. I envisioned this as a large painting of things only in white. I thought of painting reams and reams of paper and decided to try this first by painting stacks of my art books with only the edges showing. I realized the artbooks offered so much more than the plain paper could have offered. The books are different colors of white in remarkably different shapes. I find it amazing that by limiting myself to just these simple elements, the compositions can be limitless.

NC: *Since you all are working from direct observation in some way, let's dig a little deeper into that. I regularly teach a Painting 1 course with a perceptually based curriculum, and am always struck by how different and distinct the students' paintings are from each other despite assignments with very strict limitations. Why is this? Right-handed vs. left-handed? People operating at different frequencies? Is it*

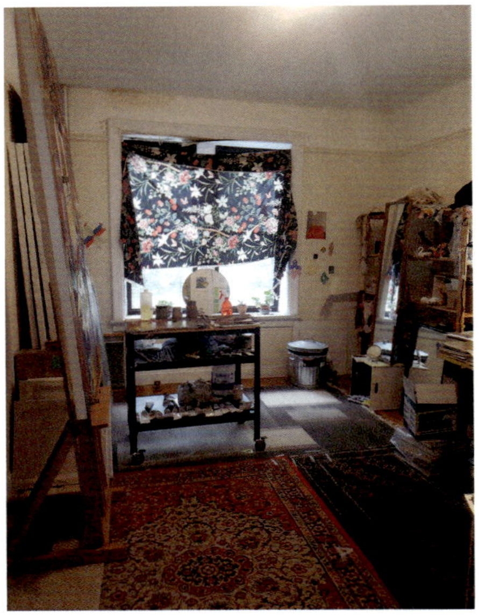

Emily Zuch's studio

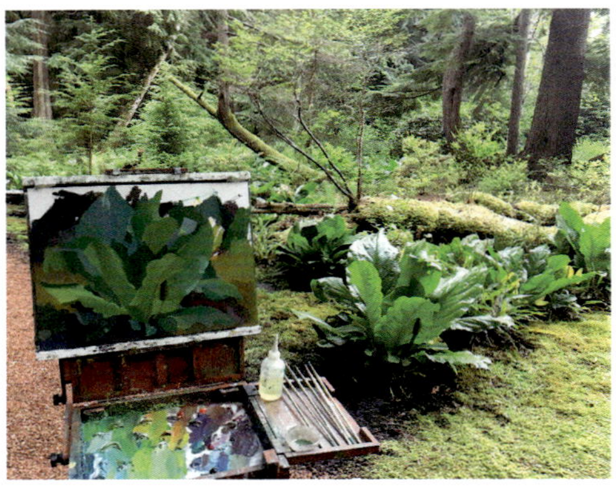

Photograph by David Benharn

Kimberly Trowbridge painting Plein Air in Moss Garden

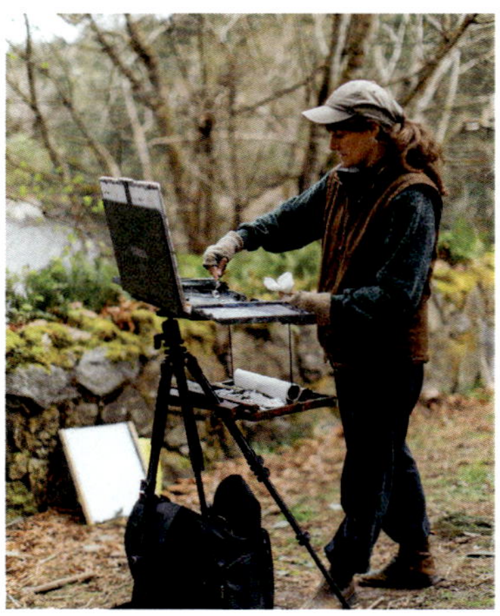

Kimberly Trowbridge painting Plein Air in Moss Garden

more about an unavoidable expression of personality born out of a unique personal history? I mean, even if you tried with all your might you couldn't recreate a Uglow or a Matisse or a Bonnard—not really. I'm thinking about the cumulative effects of the formal elements: mark-making, color and composition. What are the unavoidable qualities that make your paintings unique? Can you share any theories as to why they are unavoidable?

EZ: That's an interesting observation, I have noticed this with my own students as well. I think part of it is that people have different innate ways of mark making, just like people have different singing voices. Another part of it is what people do and don't see. And that is a separate issue from subject matter, what people are drawn to and choose to paint.

It's much harder to notice the elements that make my own paintings unique than those in other people's work. It requires a certain amount of distance. I do think there are certain colors I am drawn to. They don't have much to do with colors I like or dislike, just colors I tend to notice around me. As I've mentioned before, I like finding the color in things and amping it up somewhat, which feels very ingrained to the way I see at this point. Additionally, I know I have a way of making marks that feels largely out of my control. When I look back on old work, I can see how my way of handling paint has changed over time, but this had nothing to do with any conscious decision on my part. When painting, it often feels like there are a lot of thoughts to be had and decisions to be made, but in the end I think a lot of it happens unconsciously. That's where a lot of the magic lies.

NP: To your point Neil, I have spent a great deal of time doing plein air painting and orchestrated still lifes as Emily and Kimberly do, but the work has nothing of what Emily and Kimberly have brought to their paintings. I would love to be able to paint in ways similar to them both, but I just couldn't pull that off. I doubt that one can actually be taught anything in this life—you come as you are. It's like my children—they just showed up. No matter what I do, they revert to being who they came as on their first day home from the hospital. All I can do is to attempt to keep them safe and hope to teach them to be polite.

I think that the most successful artists, and I'm defining success as being able to create work that expresses something unique to themselves, are the ones who understand the need to jettison everything that isn't wholly their own. The *In Line* with Van Gogh show at the Met was a great example of this. His early drawings were quite ordinary, but you could find in them an occasional line that was distinctly his mark. Over time, he discarded the conventional marks and methods while utilizing more and more of his unique marks. In the end, he was only Van Gogh and nothing else. I feel our journey as artists is to eliminate that which is not wholly our own while retaining our own distinctiveness. And that isn't easy.

I have spent so much time and such great effort attempting to be a better painter so that my work could in some way approach the artists I revere. Over and over, I struggled to paint in a manner that contained some of the qualities that drew me to their work. I would inevitably always be disappointed that my work was nothing like theirs. It has taken me thirty years to start to understand that the trail of work that I made is really who I am. It's not what I wanted to be or what I chased after, but the work left

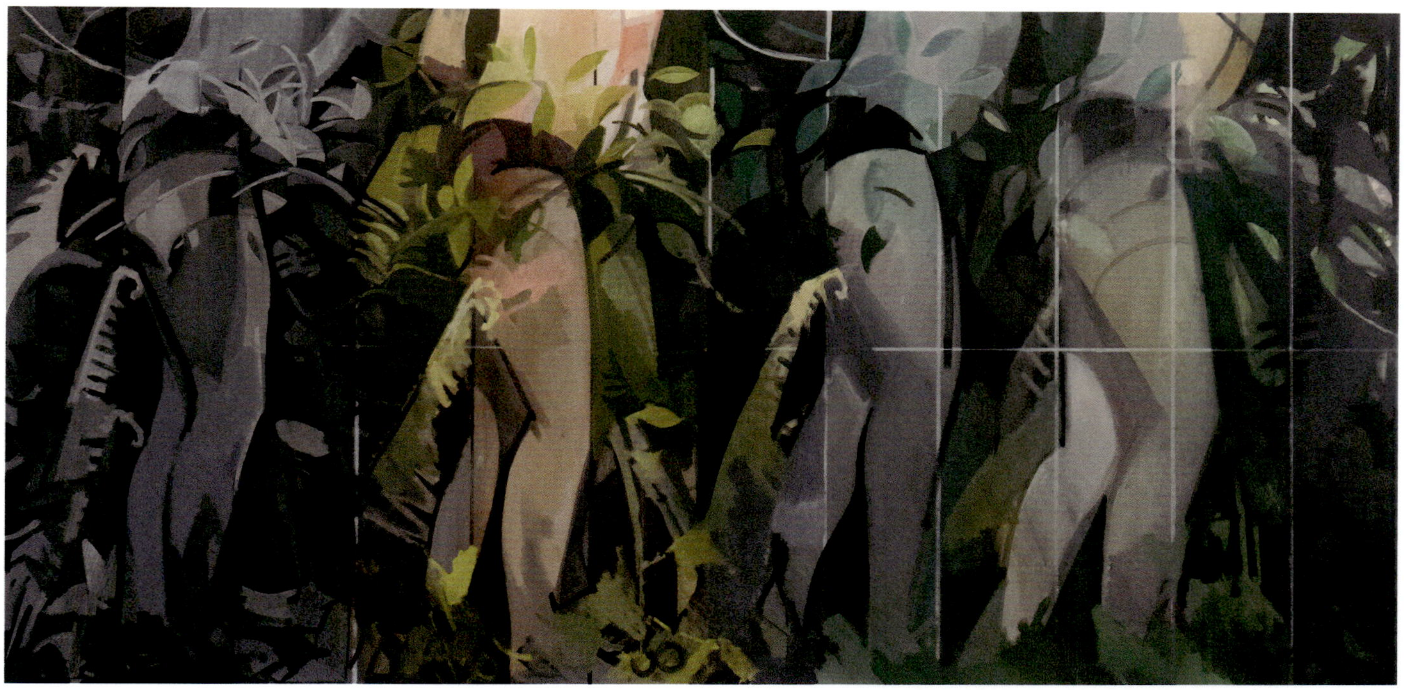

Kimberly Trowbridge *Camellia Walk IV*
2020, oil on paper on panel, 48 x 96 in.

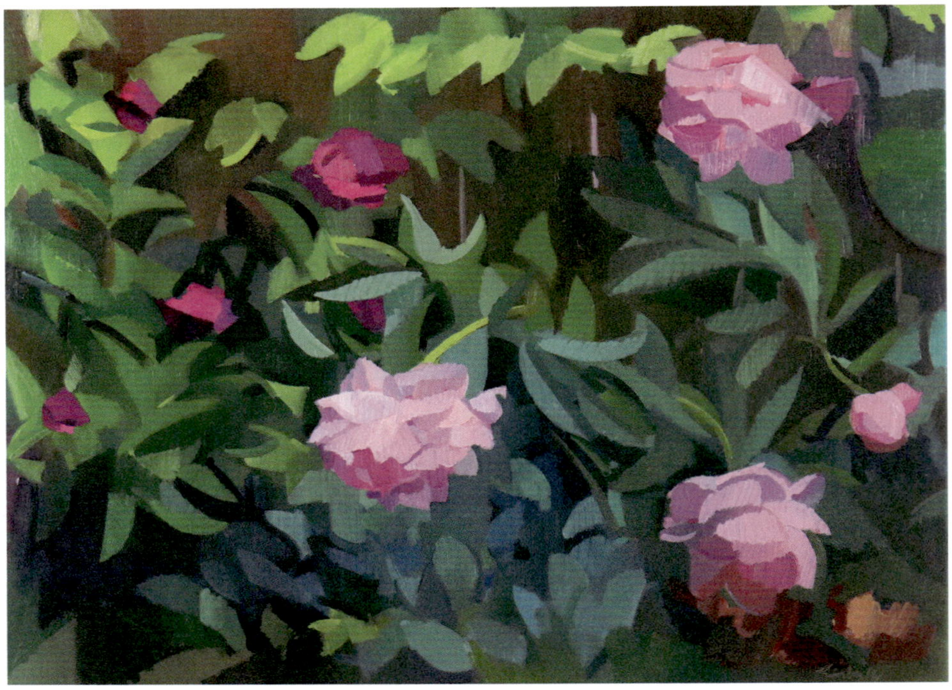

Kimberly Trowbridge *Constellation of Peonies*
2019, oil on paper, 22 x 30 in.

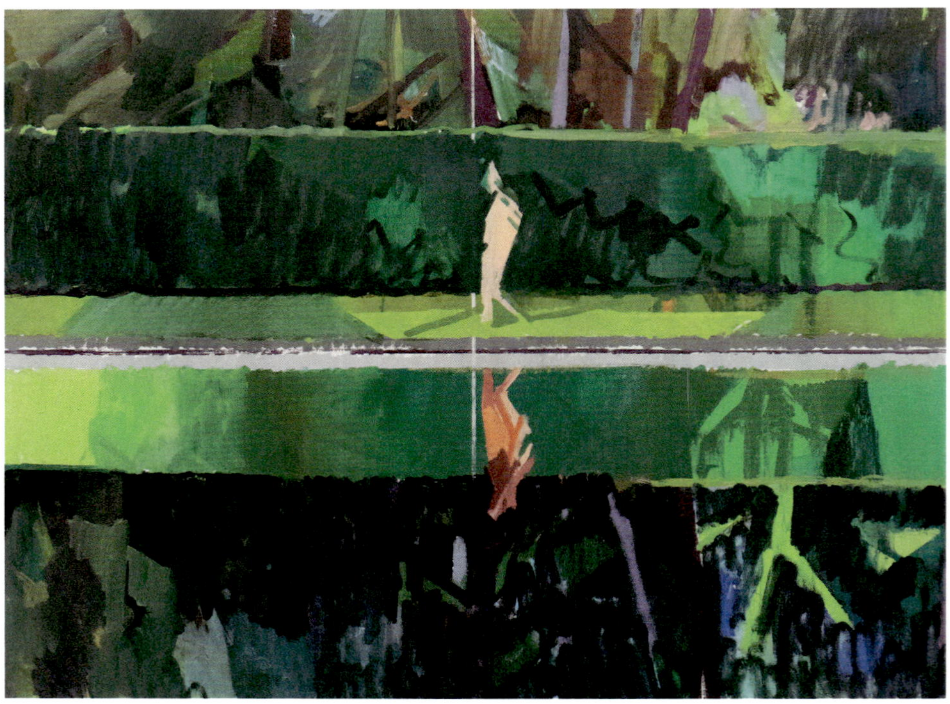

Kimberly Trowbridge *Reflecting Pond Persephone II*
2020, oil on linen on panel, 22 x 30 in.

behind in the wake of searching to become a better artist is the real me. And that was exactly who I was when I started this journey.

KT: Whoa. Big question, Neil. I am also very struck and charmed by the differences in perception and execution among my students. Over time that difference really adds-up into a unique visual pathway— it's the magic. It is also something very difficult to see in one's own work.

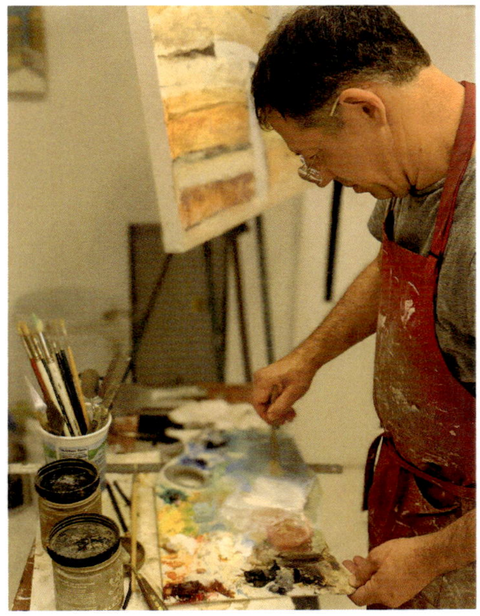

Neil Plotkin in his studio

As we know, the more you paint the more you see. I think of each painting experience as creating a new lens that is added to all of the other transparent lenses, or filters, that we peer through each time we approach a new painting. For instance, I like pairing disparate subject matter with my students: having them do painted studies from epic, multi-figure compositions by Rubens, while setting-up and working from a still-life. The "lens" of Rubens offers new pathways and rhythms for experiencing the seemingly static scene of objects arranged on a table. Or how, a couple of years ago, I was painting a series of blossoming peonies in my backyard, and how clearly I was aided by the Fragonard and Boucher images I was simultaneously working from in the studio. Or how an arrangement of trees in the forest appears to me like characters on a shallow stage as in a Renaissance painting.

But I am describing lenses that are added on. There is still something integral underneath it all that is essentially mine, the attitude and approach towards organizing my perception. This brings me back to Cézanne and how one of his great gifts, so essentially modern, is the earnest tracking of one's perception. In a way his canvases are attempting to answer this question: how do I see?

NC: *For our final question, let's talk about the future. Please tell us about the next steps in your current project, or your next project, or a project you dream of doing. I'd particularly like to know about that last one. Assuming an abundance of studio time and materials, what would you create?*

EZ: One teaching related project I am working on is starting the Chelva Artists' Workshop, a plein-air painting workshop in Chelva, Spain, co-taught with the painter Julie Karpodini. We are planning the first session for June of 2022. This my first time organizing something like this, and I think it will be a lot of fun!

If I had unlimited time and materials, my work might move in both directions in terms of size and duration. With an abundance of space and storage I would maybe work larger, potentially on more than one large painting at a time. If all my time were devoted to painting I might work on more peripheral, small projects alongside the larger oil paintings. I find that drawings, watercolors and collages move in and out of my practice, and I think with more time I could work on pieces more that I don't consider the "main event" so to speak.

Ultimately, I think a lot of the excitement of painting is not knowing what you will paint in the future. Even with a detailed vision paintings tend to turn into something unexpected when they're being made. I hope whatever I paint in the future will be a surprise (in a good way) to my current self.

NP: Clearly, I enjoy painting books. They are imperfect as a subject, and it is those limitations that aid in focusing my efforts. I create rules about how to use the books, what colors the books can be, whether they can be hardback or paperback, and which type of book I can use, etc. But ultimately, the paintings are not about books but rather formal objects.

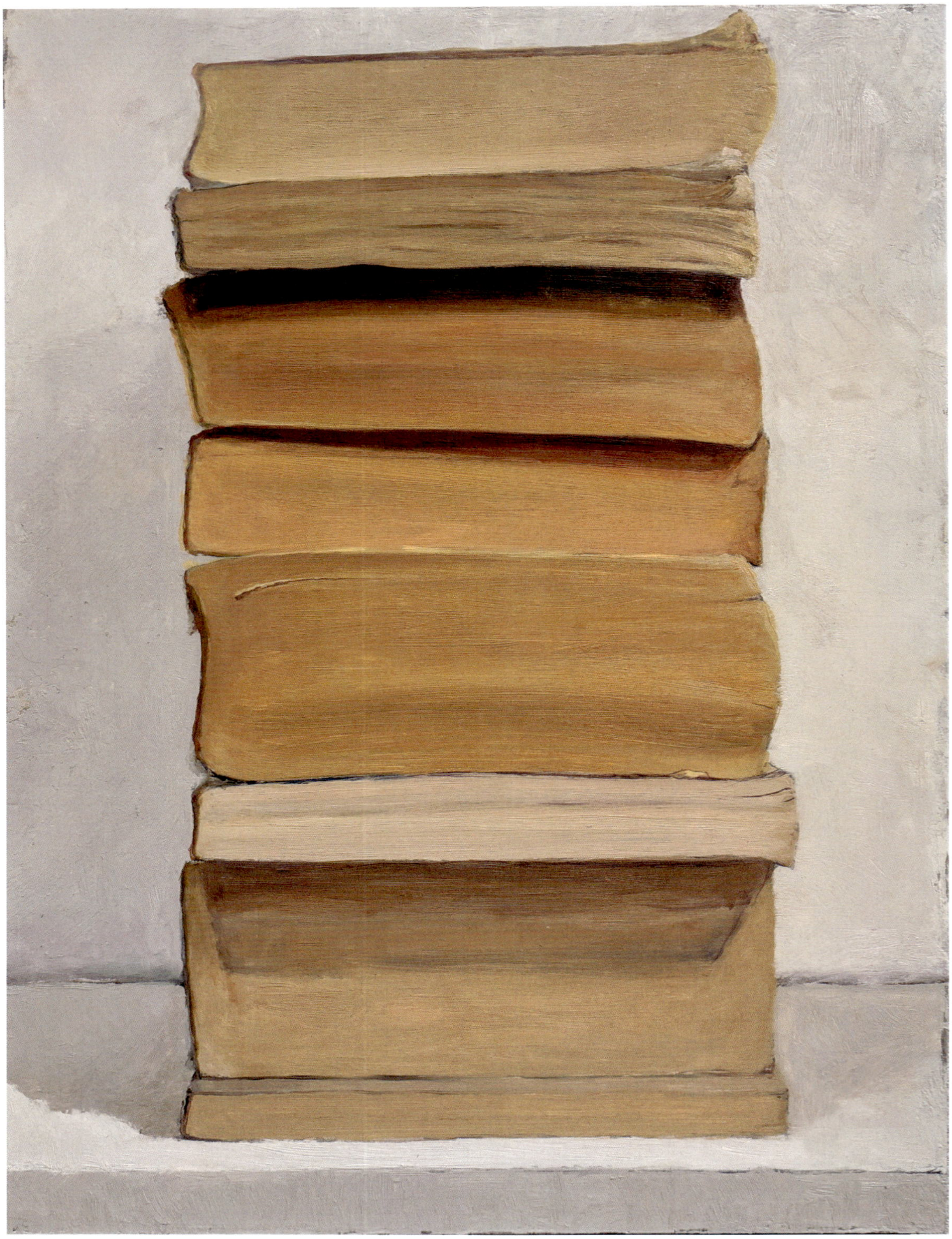

Neil Plotkin *Butter (after Vollon)*
2019, oil on panel, 24 x 18 in.

Currently I am searching for subjects that could help me branch out while continuing this work. While I'm searching for new subjects, my next step with book paintings is to scale up while maintaining a balance with an intimacy. This is challenging and I'm looking at Erin Raedeke and Claudia Carr and others to guide me successfully.

I am also getting more and more interested and excited by sculpture. I'm playing with ideas in my head right now and have just started to make things. I honestly have no idea where this will lead but it excites me a great deal. In the past, I have talked too much about work not yet realized and the work didn't materialize because I thought it to death. I'm hoping to get into the studio and work on these things and see if it holds my attention. I'm aspiring to have some work done by the end of the summer to post on Instagram.

Finally if time permits, I would love to get back to doing more interviews or writing about art. I love to find out about other artists and what motivates them, what their backgrounds were like, who they are looking at, and ultimately to just get to know them. But as you know, Neil, they are very time consuming.

KT: This past year has been one of the most productive years of my life. It saw the culmination of a 3-year project of developing a massive body of paintings based on the gardens at Bloedel Reserve. My current exhibition, "Into the Garden," is on view at the Bainbridge Island Museum of Art. I developed and installed a 30-foot mural as part of the Facebook Open Arts commission; I transitioned my entire painting program online. I've been grateful for the focus and re-prioritizing of time and space that occurred as a result of the pandemic.

So, I am in a much-needed place of decompression and reflection. I am craving more time in my home garden and studio. My peonies are about to bloom. My tomato vines are planted. I am making plans for an azalea garden. I look forward to continuing to develop my long-term project of paintings based on the paradise that is my own yard.

Along with my garden paintings, I am excited to experiment more with mold-making and creating figurines out of plaster, both as objects in themselves, and as still-life subjects to paint in front of the backdrop of my yard.

Thank you very much, Neil C., for your thoughtful questions. It has been such a pleasure to be part of this conversation and to get to know the works and ideas of Emily and Neil P. I am so grateful to be part of this larger community of creative thinkers, pushing into the unknown, exploring and transforming this incredible experience of being alive. Z

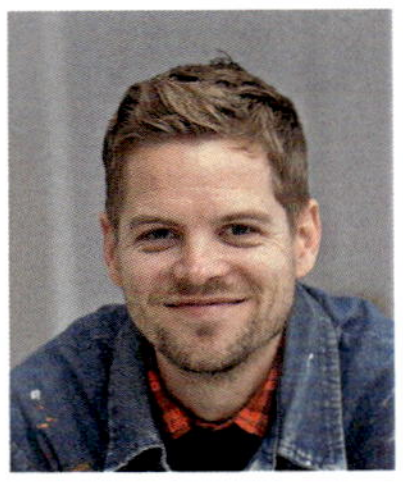

Neil Callander is an artist and educator. Born in Louisville Kentucky, Neil earned his BFA from Indiana University and an MFA from Rutgers University. In 2005 he received a full fellowship to attend the Skowhegan School of Painting and Sculpture. After graduate school he worked as a painter for the artist Jeff Koons in his New York studio. In 2007 Neil and family left New York City to pursue careers as artists and academics. Neil and his wife are currently Assistant Professors of Art at the University of Arkansas. Neil has exhibited widely and often presents publicly on his work and practice.

www.zeuxis.us/callander
www.neilcallander.com

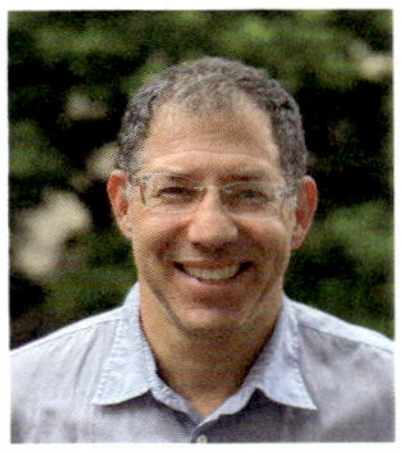

Neil Plotkin was born and raised in Detroit, Michigan. He received his BFA in Drawing and his BA in Art History at the University of Michigan. After living in London and Prague, he moved to New York in 1995 and studied at the New York Academy of Art. He has had his work exhibited in Europe and the United States and has work in private and public collections. He has been writing about artists and interviewing artists since the birth of his first son. He currently lives with his family in Brooklyn, NY.

www.zeuxis.us/plotkin
www.Neilplotkin.com
www.instagram.com/neilplotkin/

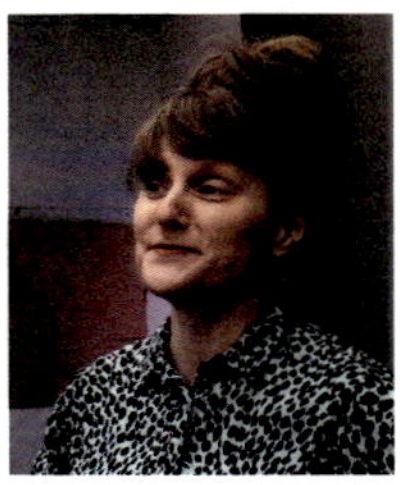

Kimberly Trowbridge was born in Everett, WA. She was Creative Fellow at Bloedel Reserve, on Bainbridge Island (2018-2020) and recently opened her first solo museum exhibition at the Bainbridge Island Museum of Art (2021). She completed a Facebook Open Arts Commission and was Artist in Residence at Oxbow, in Seattle, WA (2021). She is a two-time Neddy Award Finalist (2014, 2016), and an Artist Trust GAP Grant recipient (2014). She received her MFA from the University of Washington in 2006. She is the Director of the Trowbridge Atelier of Painting, at Gage Academy of Art in Seattle. She has led plein-air painting tours in Spain, Portugal, and Twisp, WA. Trowbridge is a plein-air painter, a figure painter, an installation artist, a performer, and a lecturer on color theory.

www.kimberlytrowbridge.com

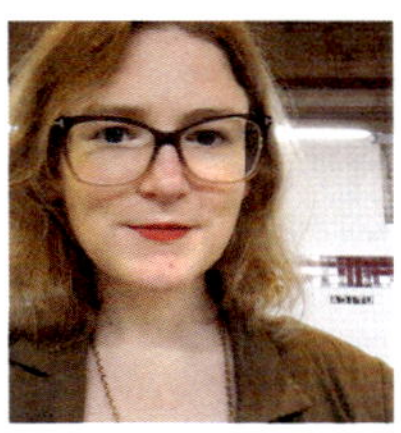

Emily Zuch is an observational painter who works from elaborate set-ups in her studio. She received a BFA from Maryland Institute College of Art in 2008 and an MFA from New York Studio School in 2011. Emily was granted a Fulbright Research and Study award in Painting and Printmaking to Germany in 2014, where she was an artist in residence at the theater Lindfels Westflugel. She has participated in solo and group exhibitions in the United States and abroad, and received grants such as the Hohenberg Travel Award. Emily has attended art residencies including Yaddo, Jentel Foundation, the Woodstock Byrdcliffe Guild, Kimmel Harding Nelson Center for the Arts, the Vermont Studio Center, and Chautauqua. She currently teaches at Pratt Institute and Wagner College, and lives and works in Brooklyn, NY.

www.emilyzuch.com

Expansive Limitations

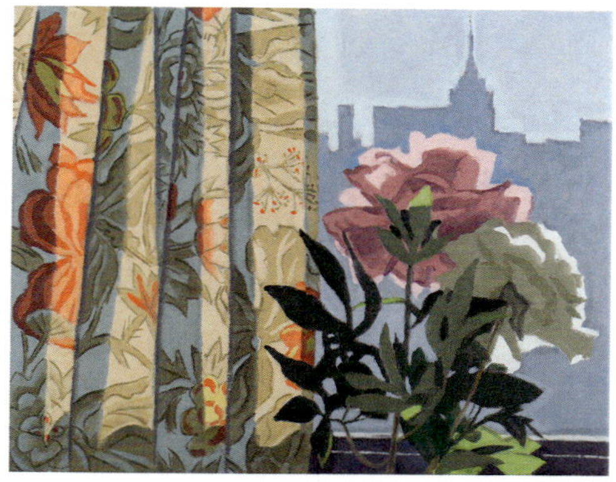

Rachel Youens Interviews

Paula Heisen and Sydney Licht

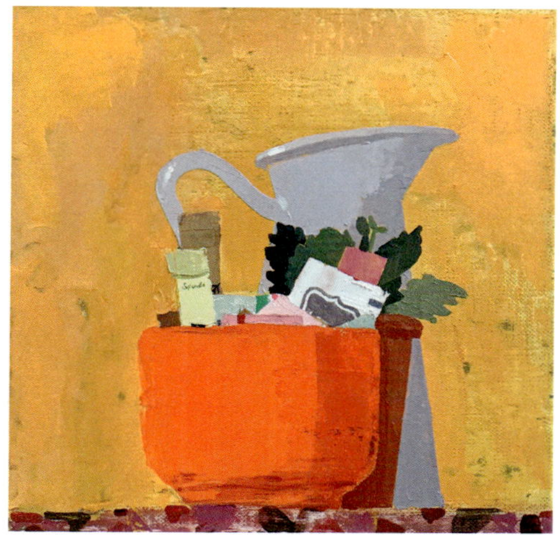

Paula Heisen *Peonies and Curtain*
2021, oil on linen, 16 x 20 in.
Sydney Licht *Still Life with Plant & Pitcher*
2020, oil on linen, 10 x 10 in.

Rachel Youens: *My interview with Paula Heisen and Sydney Licht took place on Zoom, July 1, 2021. Beforehand, I presented Paula and Sydney with a few topics to think about and to guide our conversation.*

RY: *Since we are all still life painters, let's begin with the question of: what was it about still life painting that, when you started to do it, made it the singular place to go, to make paintings?*

Sydney Licht: I've used still life over the past 20-plus years as a means to understand color better. After grad school when I was painting big expressionistic works, I could never resolve them. I realized that I was using color arbitrarily and I needed to give myself some structure. The best way I thought I could do that was to set up a still life with a simple composition that mimicked the composition I had already established in the figurative-abstract painting. I limited my palette and gave myself an assignment. Paint this, just look at it, don't think so much and see where it leads. It is still leading me places and I am still working this way.

RY: *So you set up a structure that was similar to your abstractions?*

SL: Yes, that at least was a semblance of where my interests were and that was a consistency I could carry forward. How about you, Paula?

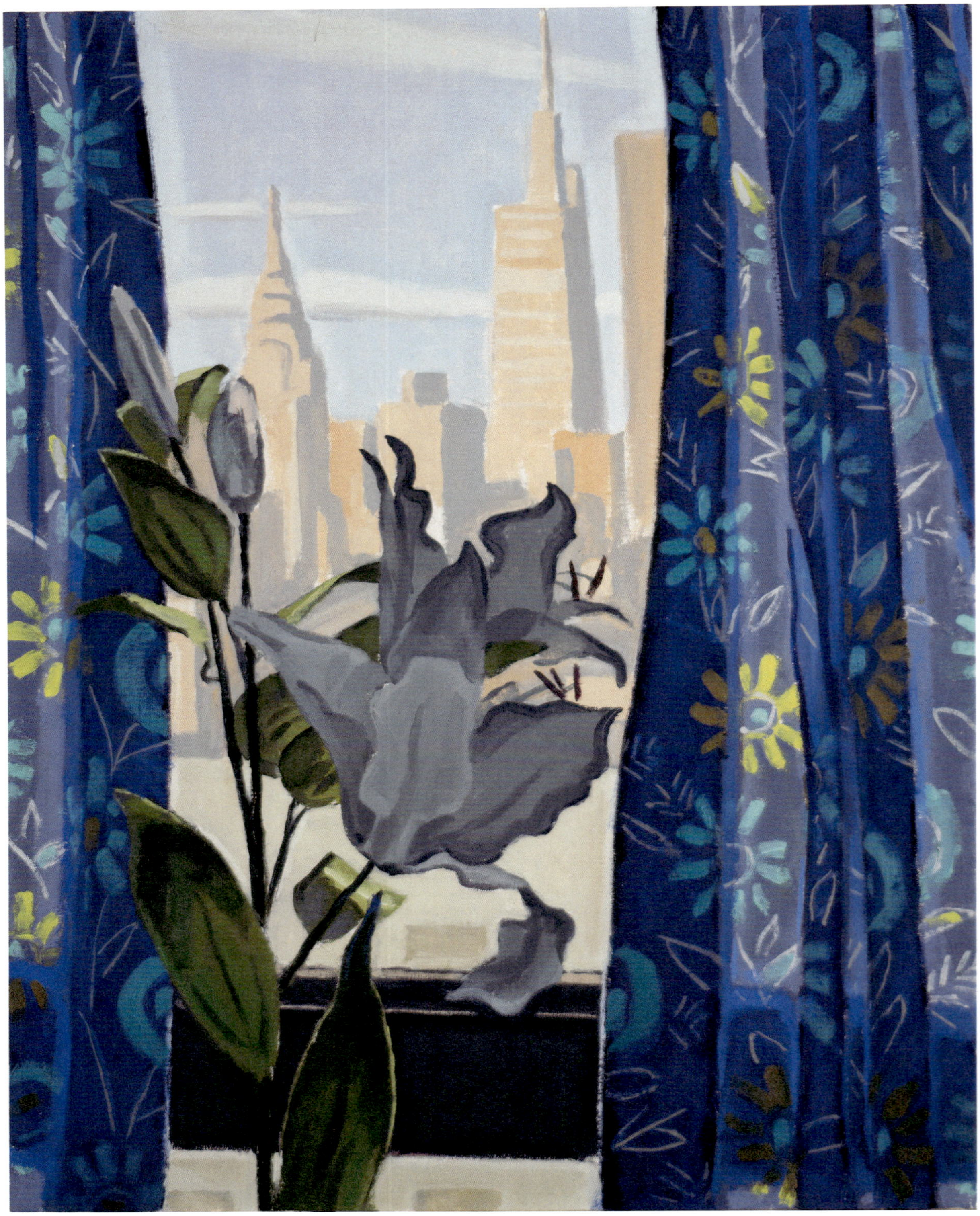

Paula Heisen *Lilies and Skyline*
2021, oil on linen, 18 x 14 in.

Paula Heisen: I moved here from California to go to grad school. I started to paint from the still life because of northeast winters. I had lost interest in the self portraits and narrative figure paintings I'd been doing in school and needed the excitement and challenge of painting from life. It has become a seasonal thing, with summers spent in the Catskills painting landscapes and winters in my Long Island City studio working from still life. I started a garden in the Catskills, intending to paint from it—I was thinking of Giverny, but of course Monet hired people to do the gardening! Eventually I stopped painting from it because I was thinking more about the weeds than the paintings. But it influenced the space in my still life set ups: they became jam-packed with stuff. The collection of objects that I use has grown in response to narrative needs I've had. The motifs and color ideas I have in one discipline tend to influence the other. Since light is one of my main concerns, each studio I've had affected the color key of my work.

RY: *That is interesting about your development. I want to ask both of you about the role of the table. Paula, you are talking about getting rid of the table, and looking out of the window.*

PH: Most still life painters think of the table as a stage of course. You are staging the characters on the tabletop and there are all kinds of relationships between the objects, and the more you know the objects, the more powerful they become in your mind. You are really the stage manager, director—all of those things. I usually had the table parallel to the picture plane—I did think of it as kind of a confrontation. Eventually, the table felt like it got in the way of the image, so I got rid of it. I wanted the paintings to have a sense of floating space.

RY: *Sydney, what do you think about the relationships generated by the painter as director? Your table is like a platform. That places the viewer in a different situation.*

SL: I agree with Paula that the table is a stage and for me it's also a grounding force. I will sometimes make the background color the same or only very slightly different as the presumed table top so the same color that is behind is also below. I try to establish the assumption of a table top without making this distinction by using a different color.

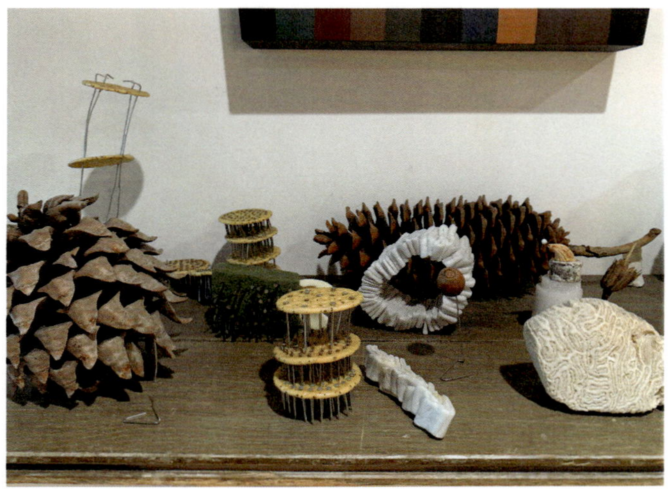

Sydney Licht's collection of objects

RY: *I am fascinated at your different approaches of placing the viewer so differently, both narratively and physically. In some of your paintings, Paula, we are looking out. The viewer is invited to peek behind the curtain and experience and be behind it and look into an exterior world.*

PH: Since flowers have been my focus for the last four to five years, they have become avatars for myself and the viewer. I identity with them as beings. That is the psychic force the paintings are carrying. With these two latest paintings, you are looking at yourself in a way, with light flashing across you at the window. You are watching the flower looking out as you as you look out. Because plants are heliotropic, their bend towards light is a life-affirming act.

RY: *Your identification is with the flower, then, Paula.*

Sydney, I get such a strong sensation of the vertical construction in your paintings. The viewer stands close to the bottom, peering up at constructed space.

SL: Years ago, I had a tiny studio-apartment space without room even for a chair. There was only room for a table and so I was sitting on the floor looking up at objects on a table. I found this

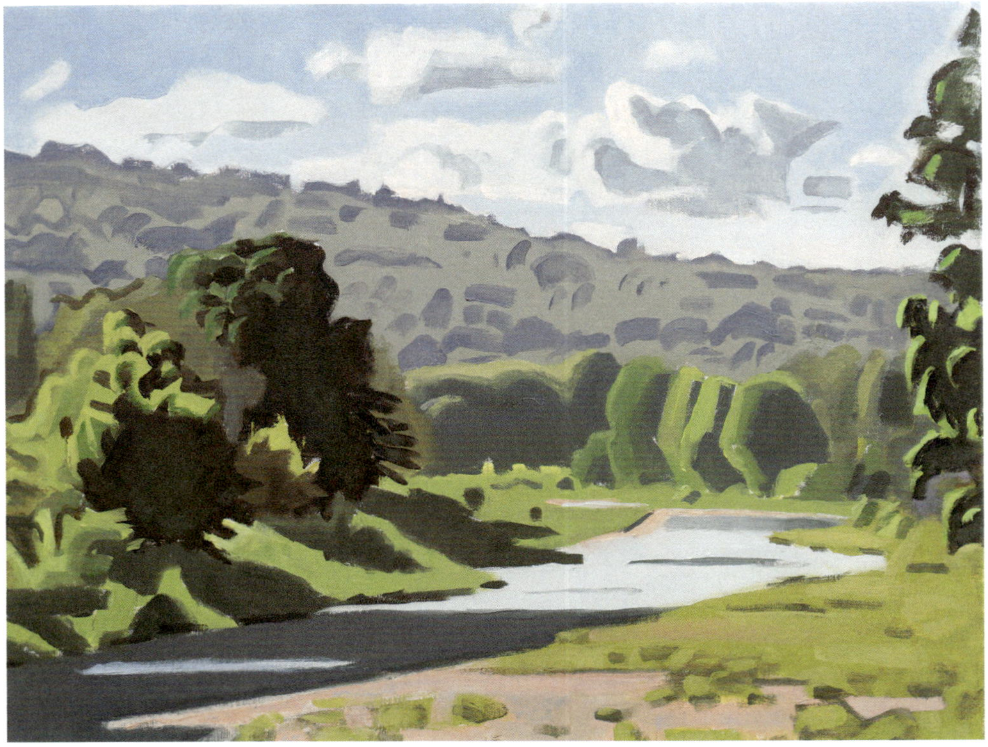

Paula Heisen *From the Bridge*
2020, oil on linen, 14 x 18 in.

arrangement so useful because in looking up, I was exposed to a different point of view than the usual one of looking down at things sitting on a surface. When we look down at ordinary objects we've seen a thousand times before, we immediately put a name to them in our minds, and those names carry assumptions about the object itself. By looking up at the elements, I hoped to take the naming process out of the equation as a way to think about objects more abstractly, just as form and color, without the emotional associations I naturally have about them from my daily life.

RY: *Paula, would you like to talk about the idea of limit, which is so implicit in the still life genre? In your case, the limit of the studio and your relationship to the city.*

PH: What I like about painting still life is that it is so impossible. You can never capture what you see and how excited you are by what you see. That challenge is the thing I am always confronting. The window is such a great metaphor, it operates on so many levels. Because the windows in my Long Island City studio are almost floor to ceiling with western light, the light changes through the day. It is overpowering; it is beautiful and fills the space and it took me a couple of years to figure out how to handle it. Light-filtering shades helped. There are the buildings nearby, the skyline of Manhattan, the studio and all my objects—it was too much! That is the way the world is, it is too much. When I arrived, I did some cityscapes out the window, but felt uninterested. Then I moved to the wall and to a fabric background. Partly, the use of pattern was a way to stop rendering. I love to draw but it gets in the way of painting, so my use of patterns breaks up the space. It helps to keep me aware of the whole and not focus on the details. Limiting the setup to flower-patterned fabric and shadow expanded everything. When you reduce the elements of a task, you paradoxically expand what you can do. In 2016, I taught a color class which helped me get a conceptual grip on the use of color. Now I have a system that allows me to get to what I want to do with a little less anxiety and more understanding.

SL: I can't agree with you more, Paula, that by setting limits for oneself, the possibilities expand. This has been one of the most valuable things I've learned from painting still life over the years. Setting a structure and asking myself questions enables me to expand the possibilities for more questions to come up. When I started, my palette was very limited, then after a while I opened it up a little to a few more colors. There continue to be periods when I reduce the palette once more. These modifications are precipitated by questions that inspire me to start a new painting, like "Can I paint a painting with five colors, or with just the primary colors? What happens when I take white away?" When I set these limits, I really begin to understand how the hues/values of the color spots on my palette relate to one another. All of these revelations come about because of the limits I have set for myself. Narrowing the focus in this way has taught me how I work best. Though I haven't painted many landscapes, I do admire artists who are able to find ways of simplifying the outside world into paint.

PH: I have an easier time with the landscapes than with the still life, that is for sure.

SL: What is your trick?

PH: There isn't a trick. It is my emotional connection to the landscape. I have painted there over thirty years and the trees have real personalities to me. I feel a deep relationship to the place and my abstraction of the landscape comes from that. And I have found inspiration in the paintings of Fairfield Porter, Marsden Hartley and Charles Burchfield—they painted the northeast in its beauty and mystery, creating personal languages in response to the landscape. There are so many still life painters I admire, but I don't feel I have a guide in the same way that I have with my landscapes. The still life works are getting more resolved, but it has been more of a struggle.

RY: *I really enjoy your landscapes Paula, the sense of how you have found these shapes and simplified them in a way that is full, and feels like the Catskills with the character of its trees. You moved backwards in time, from the west coast to the east coast, I am fascinated by that.*

PH: The light of California is still in my paintings. This town, Lexington, NY, is over 200 years old. I grew up in a house that was built two years before I was born. It was all new. I spent my childhood playing in the sun and it still dominates my imagination.

RY: *While we are in the topic of landscape. I want to ask further about other bodies of work you do. Sydney, you make sculpture. What kinds of relationships happen between the two bodies of work? How does it impact your still life painting, or vice versa—or does it?*

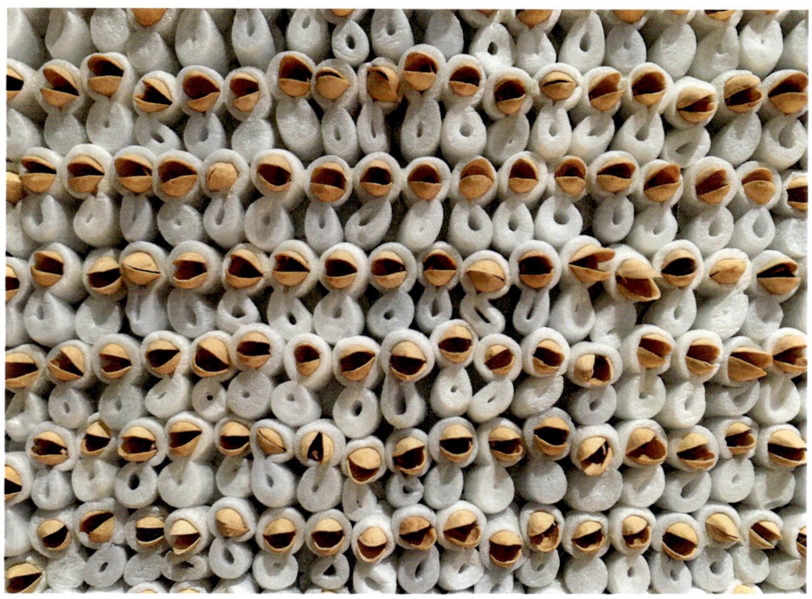

Sydney Licht
Peanuts & Pistachios (detail)
2014, mixed media, 13 x 16 in.

SL: I can answer that because of your last three words, "or does it"? I need the discipline of looking at something in order to focus my mind, so still life painting works for me. But when I am painting a still life set up, everything represents a decision to be made, a split-second response to the initial question I've posed for myself like, what is the relation between "x" and "y," or how light or dark is the object I'm looking at, compared to what's next to it? A million questions need to be answered immediately when you are painting from life. That kind of activity can be wonderful and exhilarating but also exhausting because you are constantly having to pose and answer questions for hours at a time. For my non-objective sculptural works, I decided I don't want to be constantly asking myself questions, so before I start I give myself a rule to follow and I don't deviate. This is rote work. I am making and breathing and wandering rather than focusing my mind. So when I'm having trouble with a painting in the studio and don't know where it needs to go, I do the non-objective works. After a time and my head is cleared, I go back to the painting in the studio and see it in a fresh way. These two distinct

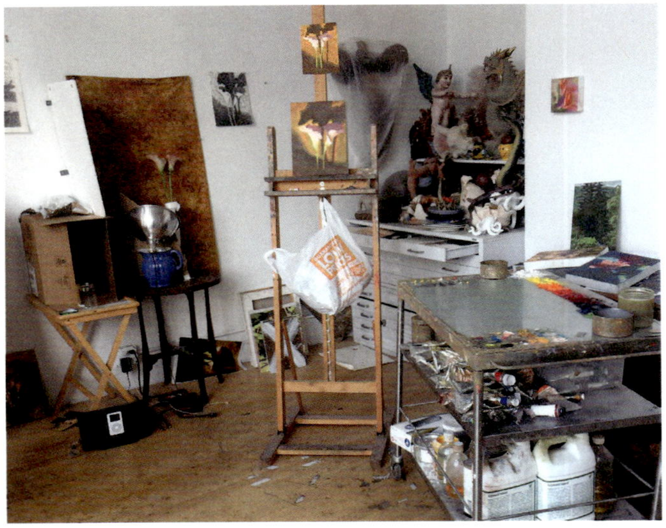

Paula Heisen's Long Island City studio with setup

activities complement each other and are related in that both comment on aspects of our consumer culture, either by what I picture in my paintings or by the materials I use in the non-objective works.

RY: *I can relate with you both, in terms of the exhaustion and stimulation of all the questions we have in the studio, even with the limitations we set up. Paula, in terms of landscape, you mentioned you feel more at home in the landscape you love—you know it; you find it; you discover it. Whereas the artifice of the still life is the set up and all of those questions. But what are the relationships—or are there relationships—between your still life painting and landscape painting?*

PH: Usually my best days in the landscape are sunny days. One of the things I look for in the landscape are cast shadows, the way that light will define something. I do a lot of backlit paintings because the trees take on a clearer personality when they are backlit. The kinds of situations I am excited by in the landscape eventually transfer to my still lifes, like the strongly cast shadows I have been working with. I have created "booths" for my set ups, with light sources directed at the subject. So it is a pretty controlled situation, it doesn't change too much—I need that because I'm a slow painter. What's fun about still life is that I can create any color that I want, not just green. That's the thing about landscape: green. This year I am desaturating almost all of my darks into grays instead of dark green. Enough already with the green! With still life I have bins and bins of fabric. I pull them out, see what mood I'm in. You can create almost any weather you want with the colors of the fabric. After I started to do landscape paintings again in 2010, those motifs of slashing shadows crept into my still life set ups. The shadows became more prominent and darker after Trump was elected, and through the pandemic. This winter—after Biden's election and the beginning of vaccinations—I was moved to look out the windows again and open up the space to the skyline.

RY: *Yes, you go through so much to construct your set ups. Then, there is the whole question of how naturalistic a painting is, and the artifice of naturalism. When I look at your paintings, Paula, and the relationship of the flowers to the curtain, the curtain expands on the lyricism of the flowers and the brushwork has a loose and melodic feeling about it, with different curvatures of flowers, the irises and roses for instance. You feel light coming through the color of your painting.*

But Sydney, your color is compressed and feels like it emanates from the painting. Those are two very different approaches to color, so can you talk

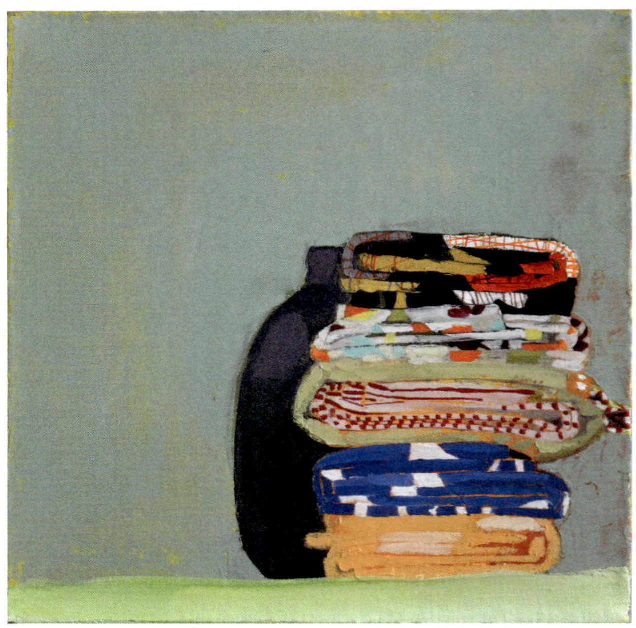

Sydney Licht *Still Life with Fat Quarters & Vase*
2015, oil on linen, 10 x 10 in.

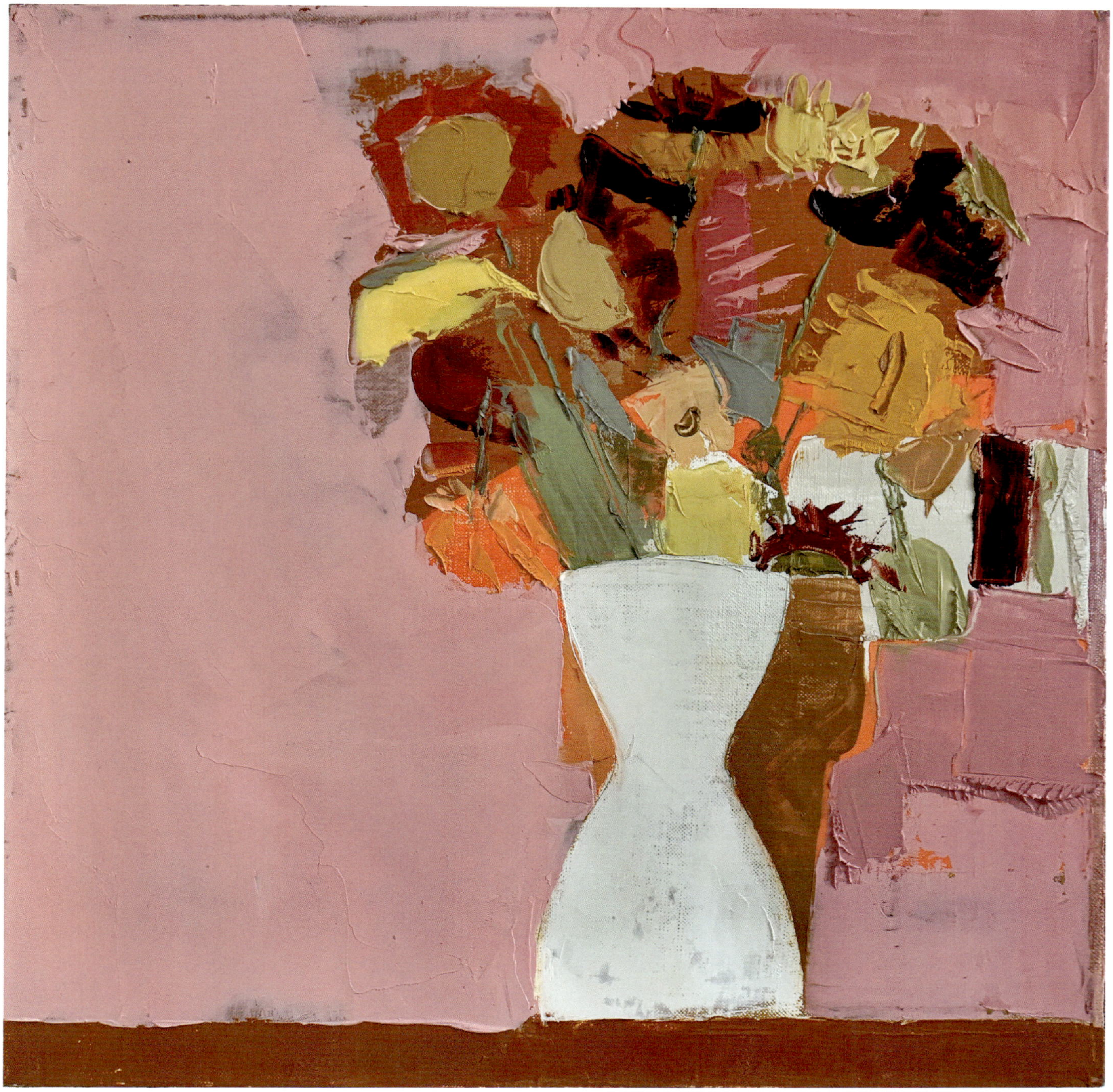

Sydney Licht *Still Life with White Vase and Pot*
2019, oil on linen, 12 x 12 in.

a little more about color and its response to light, to your internal color, or to its relationship to the plane—any approach you like.

SL: I think it's an aspect of another question you had posed beforehand related to shallow vs. deep space, so I'll go into that a little bit to talk about color and space. The space in my paintings is usually very shallow. This is to refer to the two-dimensionality of the picture plane. I don't know if color emanates, but that is an interesting concept. For me, color is a powerful force. The amount of it, how it surrounds the objects, its value and hue...all of these elements together affect how we perceive a particular color's ability to translate into the illusion of space. I am interested in how a painting can be abstract and figurative at the same time. That simultaneity is a balance I don't always achieve, but it has been a looming ambition for quite some time, the space between abstraction and figuration and how color can make something sing or make something scream.

PH: Looking at your work, I am never aware of the tabletop so much, I do feel more that things are floating, that there is an intensity and a happiness in them. There is a freedom in how much you have reduced things to the bare minimum that releases the color. You are responding to color as color, that is how I read your paintings.

SL: Paula, because another thing we have in common is that recently I have been painting flowers as well. I appreciate how you render their form and volume, and as you said, each flower has its own personality and strength, intensity, and tenderness expressed by the way you paint them. It took me a long, long time to allow myself to paint flowers. It has only been in the last four-five years that I have been doing so. It started when I had a friend over to my studio about 5 years ago and she noticed a small study of flowers I had done. This friend sensed my hesitancy about the subject matter and said to me, "It's okay to paint something beautiful." And I thought "... what, really?" It was a revelation. And so I started painting flowers but with a focus more on color relationships as opposed to their particular and nuanced forms.

PH: It does illustrate the difference between our paintings because I am really obsessed with atmosphere and the air around things, that you sense the dimensionality of what I'm painting. While I am interested in abstraction, I do want there to be a feeling that you can travel around the form, that there is air. It is a tricky path to have both those things working at the same time. I've struggled with it. More realistic or less, painting thick or thin, trying different ways to make a painting. Since atmosphere is an obsession, the color key always refers to a particular light situation and I try to unify the painting with that key element.

RY: *Paula, you do feel the air within your flowers and then feel the air within the curvature of the curtains. The rhythm of the flower and rhythm of brushwork in your curtain—continuation and difference—in contrast with Sydney, whose compression and ragged edges are more tectonic. Since we are on the subject of flowers, I'd like to talk more about them. I only occasionally paint flowers.*

PH: Time for a flower painting!

RY: *Re-reading some pages of Norman Bryson's "Looking at the Overlooked" and musing on a few contemporary flower painters has me thinking about what flowers meant to artists. For instance, Kushner and Brainard, and their relation to pattern painting and queerness, the Dutch and their connection to commodity and globalization, flowers, feminism, and women. Are you interested in any of these things, in other things?*

PH: Through gardening I developed a love for flowers. I used to obsess about every inch of my property, every inch. They are all my children, and I worry, a snail got that leaf, are you getting along, don't crowd your neighbor. They are so present and yet gone quickly. So delicate, yet powerful. I respond to them as a fellow sensual creature, not as a feminist or with a political attitude. I have never thought about the clichés. I let my emotional response rule me.

SL: I'd love to see pictures of your garden and see the arrangements you have created. And I know the thrill of seeing something you've nurtured in the ground grow and thrive. It is so satisfying to see what they are doing each day. But I am afraid of them, it is about fear.

PH: You are afraid of growing them?

SL: No, I've been afraid of using them as subject matter because they change so quickly. I'm afraid of losing the moment. I have less control when painting a flower than, say, when I'm painting a rock or a shell or pieces of fabric because, unlike a flower, these are objects that are stable over long periods of time.

PH: But I use silk flowers in my still lifes because there is no way I can do a painting with a real flower! My process takes so long. I do a drawing, a color study, mix the color palette, which can take hours—it can be a three to four day process before I get to the painting, and the flower would be dead by then. On 28th Street I can get beautiful silk flowers; they have to look pretty realistic. I have to control myself when I go there.

SL: I'll have one of everything!

***RY:** For me, flowers are present as characters in a situation, at times as witnesses. I prefer to paint wildflowers rather than store bought flowers. By the way, I plant gardens in tree plots, native species for pollinators. Milkweed that had caterpillars last year are compatible with goldenrod.*

PH: You want goldenrod, I have it!

***RY:** The neighbors might hate to have more. Sydney, talk about the ragged rawness of the way you paint flowers.*

SL: I trowel the paint onto the canvas with a palette knife right from the beginning of the painting. I don't use a brush especially when I start because I can easily get bogged down in detail and lose sight of the big picture. The palette knife protects me from getting focused on one area too quickly so that I can more easily maintain the overall structure of my composition.

***RY:** So your visceral feeling leads to your use of your tool?*

SL: I am attracted to form and try to find strategies to keep myself from focusing on small areas too quickly.

***RY:** On another topic, one has a romance with painters who live in other times, and finds resistances to them. Can each of you touch on that?*

PH: Jan van Eyck is my favorite painter—when I saw his painting *The Virgin and Child with Canon van der Paele* in Bruges, Belgium, I was knocked out by what a wonderful contraption it was! But we are living in a different time and have different needs. I don't have the

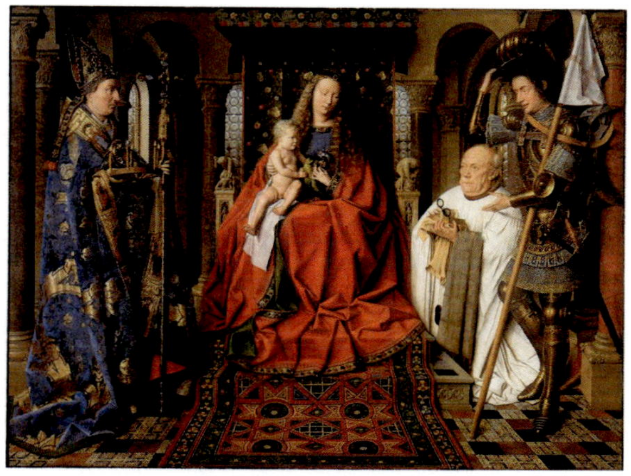

Jan van Eyck *The Virgin and Child with Canon Van der Paele*
1434-36, oil on wood, 48 x 61 ¾ in.

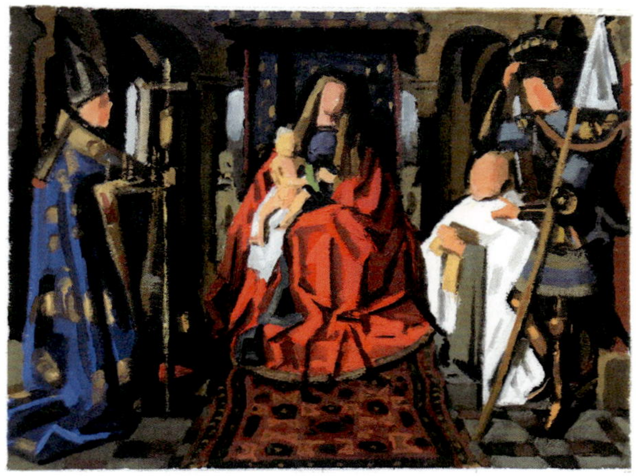

Paula Heisen *Study after Jan van Eyck's "The Virgin and Child with Canon van der Paele"*
2020, oil on linen, 12 ½ x 16 ½ in.

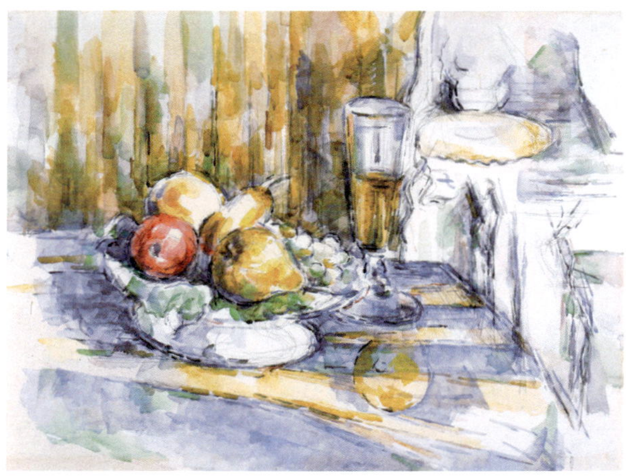

Paul Cézanne *The Dessert*
c. 1900-06, pencil and watercolor, 18 ½ x 24 in.

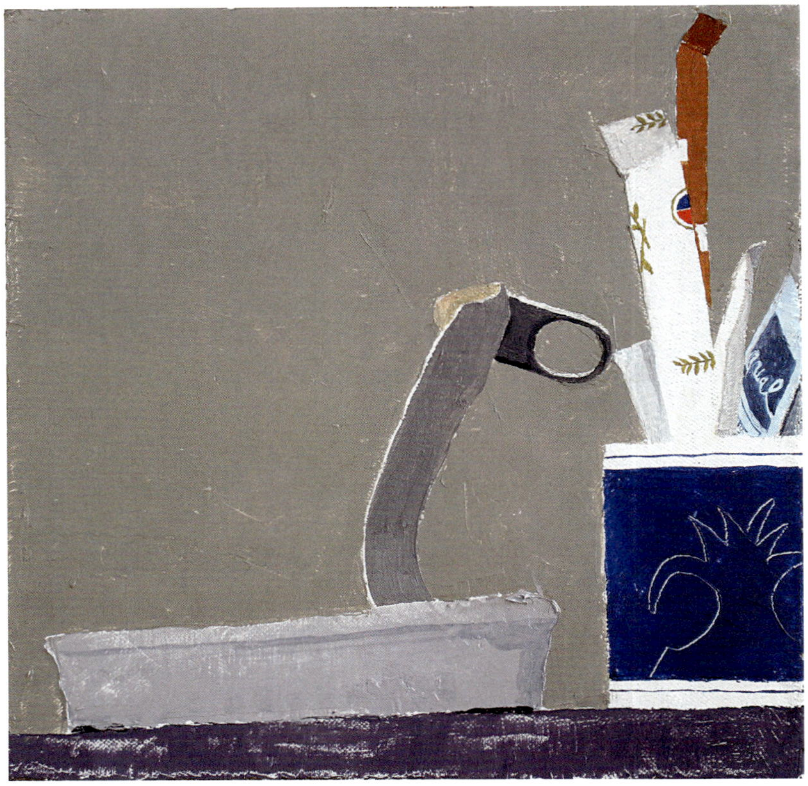

Sydney Licht *Still Life with Sardines*
2015, oil on linen, 8 x 8 in.

techniques he had, I don't grind my pigments like he did, but I am inspired by his work, how he orchestrates those sumptuous details into a powerful whole. Now I tell myself: don't render! The impulse to render underlies my desire to get at what I see, and I have to be careful with it, because it can lead me down a rabbit hole that is no good for the painting.

SL: My first hero was Cézanne but I hadn't focused on him in such a long time. Then I saw the recent Cézanne drawing show at the MoMA and was reminded of his power and intellect. Admiring artists from the past is a bit like having a friend, sometimes you break up with them for a while and then when you resume the relationship, you are reminded of why you became close in the first place. Even now, Cézanne continues to teach me. In the drawings from the exhibition, I noticed again how Cézanne lets the surface breathe by leaving much of the white paper untouched. He doesn't need to cover every inch of the surface with a mark or a color. Sometimes I forget that. Having access to artists from the past and being open to what they continue to teach is such a gift.

RY: *What are the particular things that each artist has to teach?*

PH: I haven't seen the Cézanne show yet, but in a few of the reviews I've read, the critics didn't want to genuflect to the master. Unbelievable that people still have to apologize for their recognition of his greatness. Cézanne is such a towering artist—the biggest thing is his audacity, the simplicity and intelligence in his paintings. My world is more akin to a Matisse or Bonnard, though—because of their sensual interaction with what they were looking at.

RY: *Yes, the distance on Van Eyck and how that is almost irretrievable. About Cézanne, the critics really don't get it.*

I had wanted to ask you about the kinds of objects you collect. For my setups I collect a fairly wide array of natural and man-made things: breads for their sculptural qualities, cultivated and wild fruits, wood and metal fragments, vessels and cloth. I select, strew, push and pull these things to bring together groups of things, which I treat as a tableau. I find that things arrange themselves, and I learn how to paint their forms as they develop—their characters and relationships to each other and the spaces they inhabit. What are your experiences? What do you collect, how do you collect, and what is the life of things in the studio?

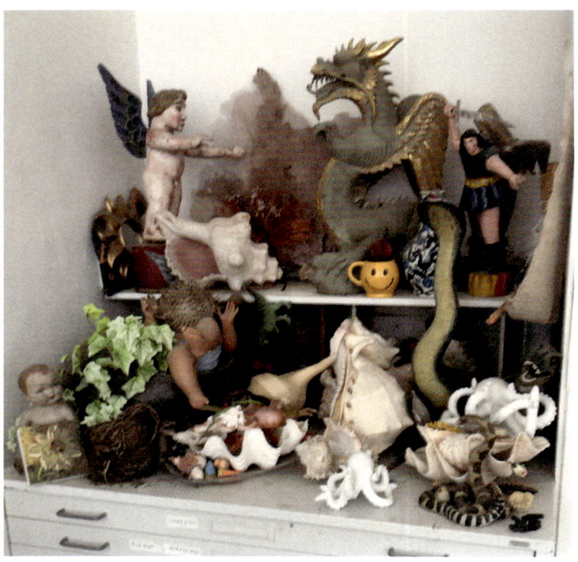

Some objects from Paula Heisen's collection

PH: Early on, I had very simple objects, just fish bowls and maybe a plant, with the feeling of a watery world, and I painted in a watery way, much differently than I paint now. When the figurative-narrative aspects crept into the set ups I bought Mexican figurines, small and large, angels and devils. Then I focused on creatures—ceramic, taxidermied, plastic—a skunk, dinosaurs, fish and birds. Then I went to flowers. I have all the objects in containers or on shelves. When I was working with those objects, I'd pull them out of the bin, see which one wanted me to paint it, which would call to me, and go from there. I allow the flowers to act on me too. My studio is like a cabinet of curiosities. You want to have something around you.

RY: *Sydney, how do objects call on and act on you?*

SL: I am attracted to things that I call "color catchers," objects whose various planes catch the light in distinct ways. Years ago, when I was beginning the still life project, I was interested in natural things, pods and shells, pine cones, etc. Now I am also attracted to man-made items in which the color is more vibrant. Sometimes I look for objects to paint and sometimes the objects find me. For example, when I was a member of Zeuxis, we were asked to paint a particular dishcloth for an exhibition called The Common Object. That experience inspired me to continue painting fabric so I found little bundles of fabrics used for quilting called "fat quarters." Also, being mindful has brought me to things I wouldn't necessarily think of as a subject matter for a still life. For example, several years ago I was having sardines for lunch and as I was throwing the sardine can in the recycle bin, I suddenly noticed the way the light caught the curve of the lid and the tab so beautifully. I was immediately inspired to translate what I saw into a painting. This experience has led me to consider other things I discard as possible objects to paint.

RY: *I too am attracted to these different approaches to collecting: cabinets of curiosities and choosing things as they capture light. I also scavenge for things on the street, being drawn to things that other people think are unwantable. Paula, are you interested in the grand themes, for instance with the dragon, in objects as connected to larger narratives then?*

PH: The paintings I made last year in response to the pandemic were a throwback in a sense because I hadn't used objects for a while. I painted one with the Chinese dragon and one with the Kewpie doll. I had never painted those two objects. When I turned the Kewpie doll upside down—that was how I felt. The dragon of course is a recognizable trope, and its shadow described the feeling at the beginning of the pandemic. It is a beautiful and large object that I loved, but had never felt a real desire to paint it. Last winter was it.

SL: I find the way you are storytelling with the objects you choose, Paula, to be fascinating. In my own work the narrative isn't always so much in the things but in the space between things, the negative spaces and/or in the way things touch or intersect or don't intersect at all.

PH: How would you describe that as narrative? Are the objects or is that space animated by some kind of spirit in your mind?

LEFT TO RIGHT:

Rachel Youens's set up for *Still Life with Pitcher*

Rachel Youens
Still Life with Pitcher
2018, oil on linen, 22 x 42 in.

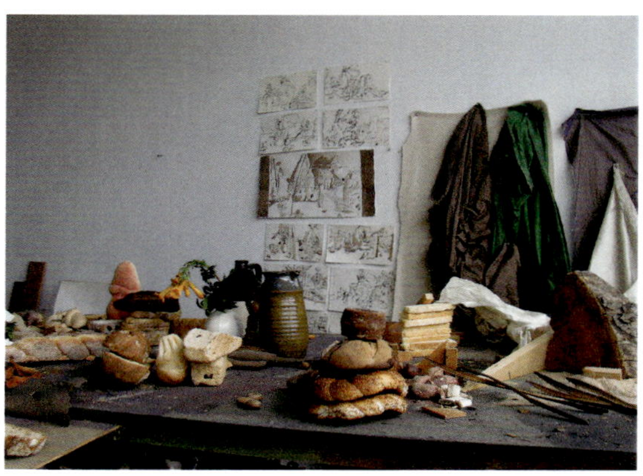

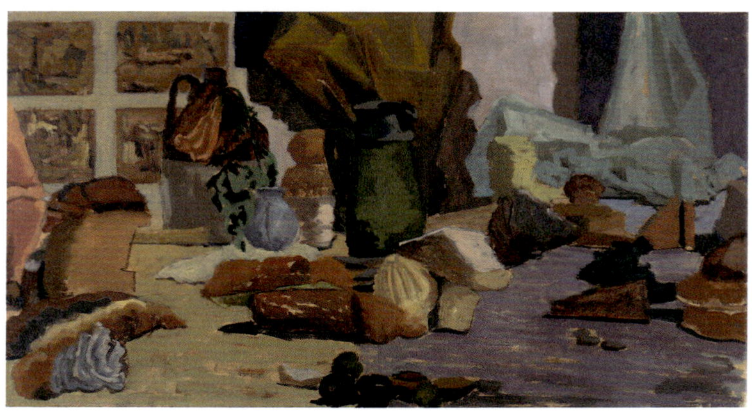

SL: It is more about the way objects do or don't relate to one another by focusing on the space in between them. Perhaps the tab of the sardine can is touching or barely touching some other form in one of my paintings to create a negative shape between the two objects. Could that negative shape be described as lyrical, just as a flower can be described as lyrical? I think so. These relationships can be very evocative. The "way" things relate or don't relate can be the narrative, as opposed to the narrative being expressed by the thing itself.

RY: *I relate totally to the physicality of things that are there and the spaces between them, akin to social and emotional relationships. Now we are getting back to your comment, Paula, about being a stage director and the choreography of a painting.*

PH: Could we talk about creating the set up for a painting—because you want to have something that looks like it is just naturally placed, like something that was thrown up on the shore of a beach. I feel like I have to go into a trance rather than thinking that I want something to do this or that, to let myself be aware of something interesting. You have to surprise yourself when you are setting up.

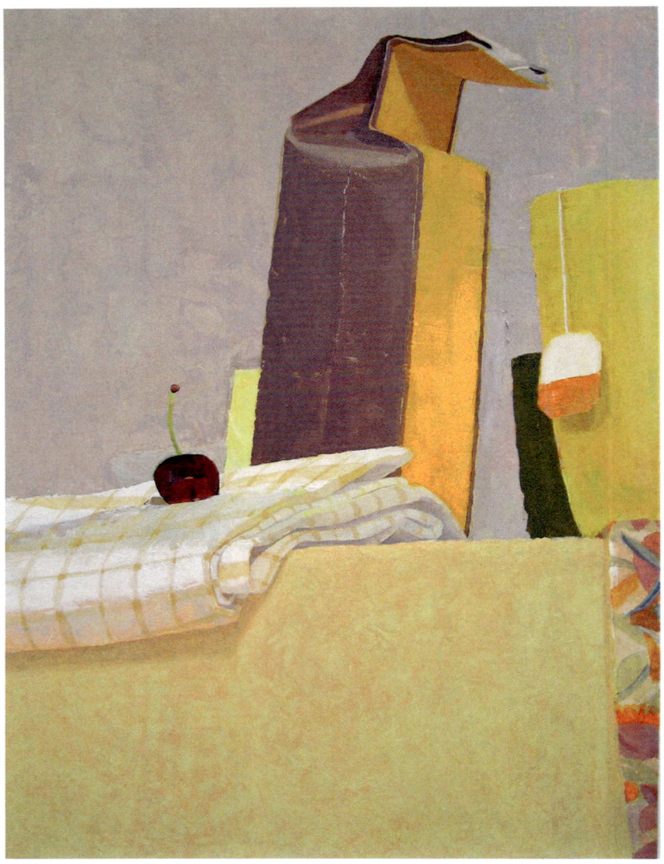

Courtesy Kathryn Markel Fine Arts

Sydney Licht *Still Life with Coffee and Tea*
2009, oil on paper mounted on board, 16 x 12 in.

SL: How do you do it Rachel, because you have so many things that you paint in a vista?

RY: *When I set up a still life I am interested in the particularity of landscape, related to what you are talking about Paula, as a place of surprise. I have a large table that is fairly high. I allow randomness to enter with too many things and too many kinds of things that push my surprise buttons. Things arrange themselves and I walk around the table to find what these relationships are.*

PH: Very interesting, that's not like the frontal space of a stage.

RY: *I do drawings, sometimes two, sometimes ten, to find those changing spaces and points of view. Some objects become quite frontal in relating to those that turn in space. I am drawn to that kind of visual tension.*

SL: The thing that unites all of us is the importance of surprise or the aspect of learning something new as we construct these arrangements. When starting a new painting, I can spend weeks arranging and re-arranging, trying out different relationships. I just went through a whole week where I was looking and looking and nothing was happening, and then yesterday I suddenly saw a new color relationship and thought "That is something I haven't seen or done before." This excitement led me to want to make a painting. I don't do many drawings ahead of time but if I do make a drawing, it's a very minimal sketch to work out a compositional idea before I start laying down the paint. If I do too many drawings ahead of time, my question gets answered so there's no point in making the painting.

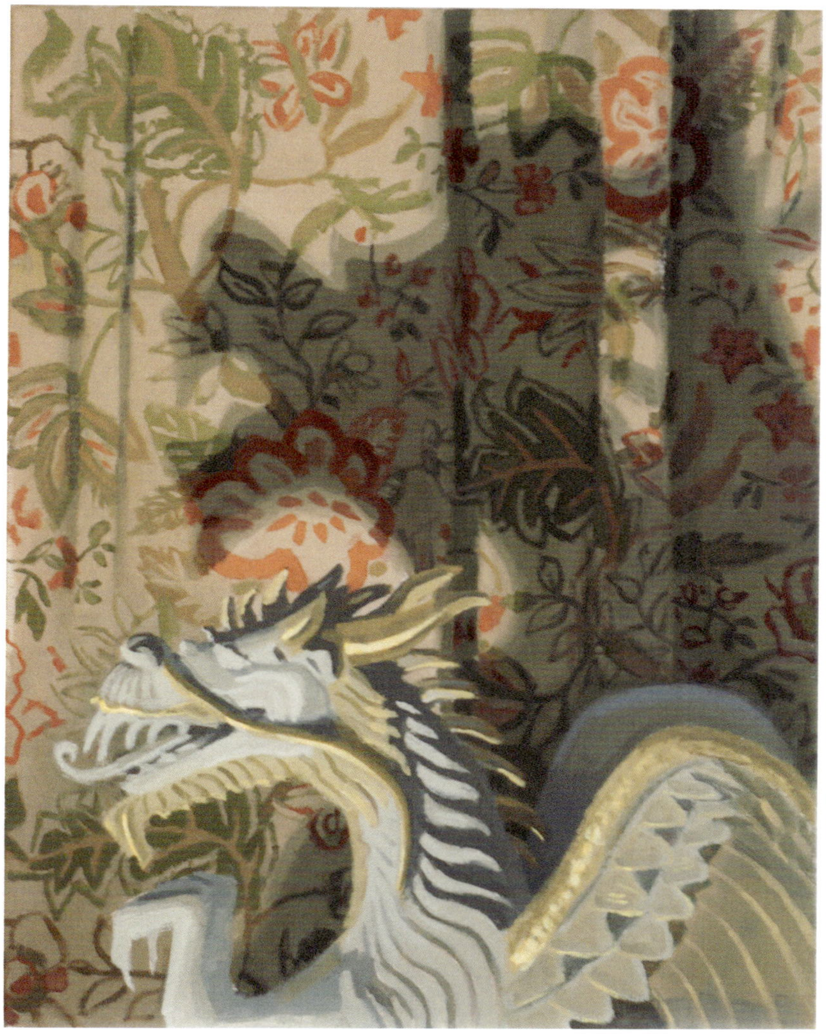

Paula Heisen *The Dragon's Shadow*
2020, oil on linen, 32 x 20 in.

RY: *Yes, my drawings are exploratory and then the painting must open them up to something else. That is a rule I work by.*

SL: Paula, it must be like when you are growing something in your garden, and you think something is going to work but you aren't sure, and then it is like magic.

PH: What happened in that still life, Sydney, did you move something or take something away?

SL: I took something away. In that instance taking something away was necessary in order to move forward. Often when a painting isn't working, I have to determine and eliminate what is standing in the way.

RY: *Yes, the burden and the weight, and yet the promise and the possibility of that history.*

SL: That is why a conversation like this is so valuable, to share the thoughts we all have.

PH: And painting is so damn fun.

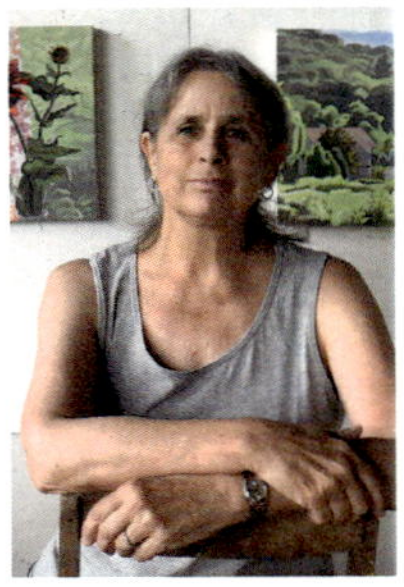

Born in Los Angeles, **Paula Heisen** moved east for the MFA program at the Yale School of Art. Presently, she splits her time between studios in Long Island City and the Catskills. She has exhibited her work throughout the United States, with solo exhibitions in New York, Pennsylvania and Texas. Among the grants and awards Heisen has received are an Elizabeth Foundation Grant, a New York Foundation for the Arts grant, a Joan Mitchell Emergency Grant and an Ingram Merrill Foundation Grant, as well as scholarships to Yale, the Skowhegan School, the New York Studio School and UC Santa Barbara. She has taught at FIT (Fashion Institute of Technology, NYC), Lehman College (Bronx, NY), Oxbow Summer Program (Michigan), Yale University's Summer Program (New Haven, CT) and at the University of California at Santa Barbara. Heisen was a member of Zeuxis from 1999-2000.

www.paulaheisen.com
www.instagram.com/paulaheisen

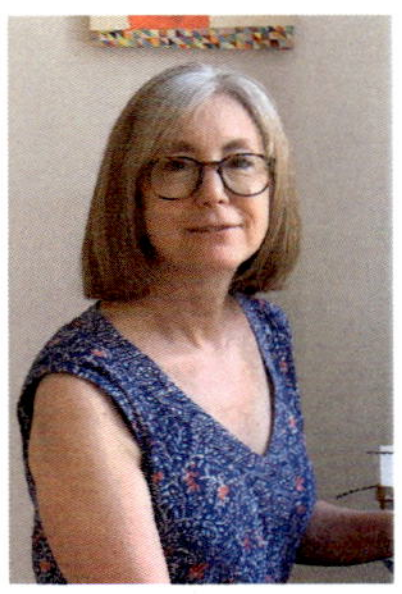

Sydney Licht is a painter based in New York City. She graduated from Smith College and earned her MFA from the School of the Art Institute of Chicago. Her work has been in solo and group shows throughout the country. Licht's most recent solo show was in 2020 at Kathryn Markel Fine Arts in NYC. She received a scholarship to study at the Skowhegan School as well as an Ohio Arts Council grant. She has been a Visiting Artist at The American Academy in Rome and was awarded a residency at Yaddo. Licht has held teaching positions at the University of Rochester, Hobart & William Smith Colleges, Alfred University, the School of the Art Institute of Chicago and at Ohio State University, where she was Assistant Professor and head of the Foundation Program in the Dept. of Art. Licht is represented by Kathryn Markel Fine Arts in NYC and by Thomas Deans Fine Art in Atlanta. Her work has been reviewed in *The New Yorker, New York Magazine, Elle Decor, The Chicago Sun-Times* and other publications. Licht was a member of Zeuxis from 2006-2018.

www.sydneylichtstudio.com
www.instagram.com/sydneylichtstudio

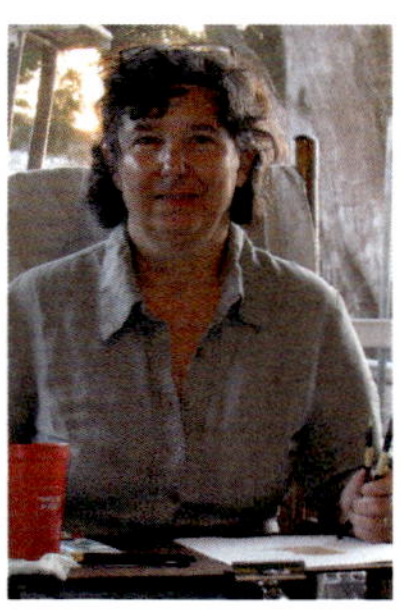

Rachel Youens is a painter, writer, and adjunct professor of fine art in New York City. A graduate of the School of the Art Institute of Chicago and Brooklyn College (MFA 1992), her work has been featured in numerous artist-curated galleries, including Sideshow Gallery, Valentine Gallery, Open Source, 490 Atlantic Gallery, and Talking Pictures. A Guggenheim Fellow (2008–2009), her work has also been recognized with a Pollock-Krasner Foundation Grant and several PSC Professional Development Grants from the City University of New York, as well as residencies at the Fundación Valparaiso (Spain), the Ragdale Foundation, and in Wrangell, Alaska. Youens has written art criticism for *Cover Magazine, The Brooklyn Rail, NY Arts Magazine,* artcritical.com, and *Two Coats of Paint.* She currently teaches at the Parsons School of Design and at LaGuardia Community College, CUNY.

www.ryouens.com
www.twocoatsofpaint.com/tag/rachel-youens

Still Life and Abstraction

Kathleen Craig interviews

Jessie Coles and David Summers

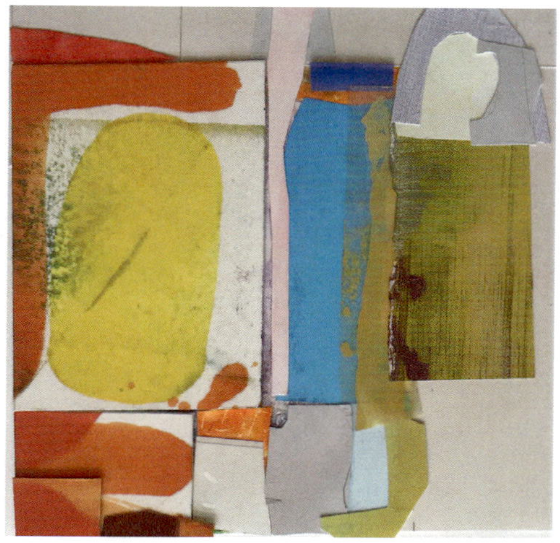

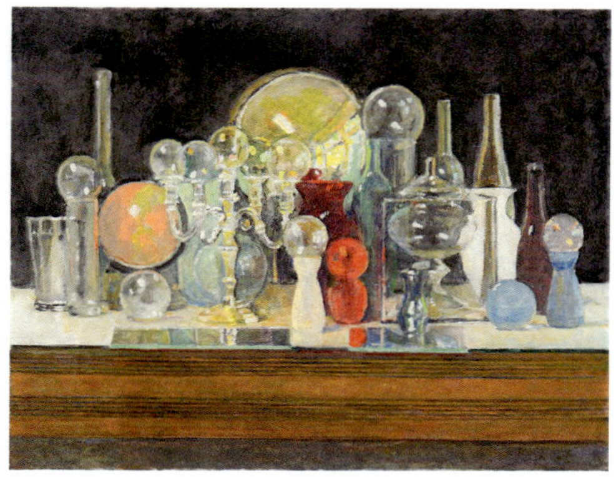

Jessie Coles *Disembroil*
2021, mixed media and collage, 7 x 7 in.

David Summers *No Candles, Apothecary Jar*
2021, oil on panel, 16 x 20 in.

Kathleen Craig: *Jessie Coles, David Summers and I live in or near Charlottesville, Virginia, home of the University of Virginia. A few years ago the town was unwilling host to a well-armed mob of white supremacists, Nazis, and other fine people who put us in the national headlines.*

Although Jessie studied, David taught, and my husband teaches there, we didn't meet at the University. Connections exist—Jessie and I met at Piedmont Community College some twenty years ago, and about the same time David's wife Nancy was my child's third grade teacher.

However, even in a relatively small college town, artists are often quite good at keeping themselves to themselves, and it has been a delight for me to get to know David and Jessie through this digital conversation about what connects us more strongly than mere geography, still life painting.

As Joyce Carol Oates asked, "Where are you going, where have you been?"

KC: *I borrowed my first question from a story by Joyce Carol Oates: "Where Are You Going, Where Have You Been?" How did you come to be a painter? If you can think of your painting life as a story, where are you in that story, and what do you envision for subsequent chapters? And, where have you been—what has the trip been like for you?*

I often feel as if my life as a regular human being is constantly getting in the way of my work. How do you think your life as a whole relates to your work as a painter?

David Summers: How did I come to be a painter? I have been drawing as long as I can remember. I copied things out of magazines and drew the house across the street and the sycamore tree and anything else that might come into view. I always drew things. Since I was the one in the class who "could draw," I did what I was asked to do for school activities but I didn't start to paint until I went to college. From early on, however, I had assumed I would be a painter. There were no paintings (or painters) in Idaho in those days; I had a very 19th-century notion of art, and a fictional and even mythical image of myself in my intended career. Very important to me were the conversations I had with my younger sister, Marilynne Robinson, who has realized similar aspirations as a writer. It was through a series of chance occurrences (including "geographical distribution," an early effort by Ivy League schools to expand admissions nationally) that I wound up "back East" at Brown. I was told I was the first person at Brown from Idaho since 1932. To my Eastern Seaboard friends the state seemed exotic, which it still is, its hospitals now filled with anti-vaxxers.

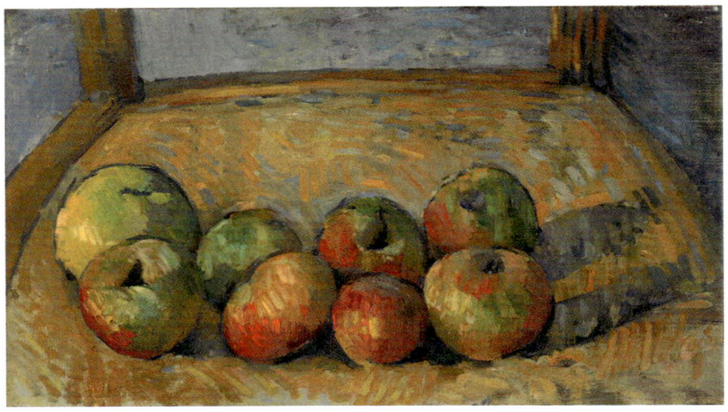

Paul Cézanne *Still Life with Apples*
1878, oil on canvas, 9 x 15 ½ in.

While at Brown I began to see great art, by which I was deeply and indelibly moved. I remember seeing Pollock's *Autumn Rhythm*, but most of all I saw Cézanne, especially a small still life, five or six apples on the wicker seat of a chair, in the museum of the Rhode Island School of Design. If this painter, I thought to myself, made this painting, then I have lot of thinking to do, and a lot of painting to do.

I saw Cézanne as a realist, a descendant of Courbet, who transformed the new color language and facture of Impressionism into a kind of painting that had never been seen before. For me, however, he was never the prophet of formal abstraction. In these same years Abstract Expressionism was waning, Clement Greenberg was in critical control, and I had no desire to make the kind of painting that seemed to be current. I took figure drawing at RISD, and I loved it, as I still do, but no one took it seriously; paper airplanes floated in the air of the studio, and the teacher only came two or three times a term. I took painting courses at Brown, and tried to do all kinds of things with paint. My inclination to observation, and to paint the figure, was emphatically discouraged. I did not know when I went to college that there was such a thing as art history, but I loved it when I found out about it. When I was told again and again that painting was about flatness these days, that seemed to me to be little more than making objects. I felt that it was of great historical interest that painting had come to such a state, but I didn't want to participate in the project. I was also keenly interested in philosophy, and so in the theory of style. To me, art history was cultural and intellectual history, although for most people my age it was social history, and so it has remained.

I applied to graduate school in art history. As it turned out—chance again—the modernist at Yale was on leave, so I wound up getting hooked on the Italian Renaissance. After a couple of years I finished my MA, a translation of Vincenzo Danti's Treatise on Perfect Proportion, which was supposedly based on ideas of Michelangelo. I painted when I could, but I also began a dissertation on Danti's sculpture, which meant a year in Florence and Perugia. I began to teach art history, first at Bryn Mawr, in 1968, then at the University of Pittsburgh, in 1968. I married my wife Nancy in 1970, and in our first summer in Pittsburgh we went to Florence. Nancy bought me pigments, canvases, brushes, and an easel for my birthday, and I began to paint in earnest. I also began my first book project, Michelangelo and the Language of Art, published in 1981. After that, I would paint and then write, never stopping one entirely when I concentrated on the other. Now that I am retired from teaching, I paint more or less full time. My wife, thoughtful and engaged in her own ways, could not be more cooperative. Our two sons were musicians, so I heard a lot of the hard parts of great music.

(Ben gave up the piano, Tim plays the violin in the Mahler Chamber Orchestra in Berlin.) In 1976, our daughter Mary was born. I went to the hospital to draw her in her little incubator and made the best drawing I had ever made. I began to exhibit, still in Pittsburgh. In 1981 we came to the University of Virginia in Charlottesville. I didn't think I wanted to teach here, but on my second visit, I happened to see a branch in evening thin gold-silver light that reminded me of once seeing evening light on the Ponte Sta. Trinita in Florence, which reminded me of Masaccio's light as it has survived best. I can still see that branch, and its place in my mind's eye seems to be permanent. Virginia is very beautiful, although, as might have been anticipated, professionally it has been an inopportune place to devote a life to art. The biggest struggle I have had is the nagging feeling that I would have been a better painter had I just painted, or a better historian had I just done art history, but I could never make the choice. I will paint until I am no longer able.

Jessie Coles: Some years back, I had an extraordinary phone call from a former professor and subsequent mentor, Chica Tenney. "I think your kids may be old enough for you to get back to painting. Don't wait too long." It was completely out of the blue and eerily clairvoyant. They were and I had. Over the years Chica helped me fill in the gaps in my education as an artist and became a real mentor. And yes, "life as a regular human being" had gotten in the way. My kids were 2 and 6. I hadn't painted for a long, long time. I'm not sure what "too long" would have been. But I have always kept a studio and painted since then. Other things have certainly gotten in the way from time to time, but that was a turning point.

At that time, I rigged the world's smallest studio. It was a 3 by 3 foot space that overlooked a stairwell in the eves of our very small house. To my left was a wall just big enough for a piece of 3 by 3 foot gessoed paper. A plywood board straddled the corner of a banister and a ledge on the far side of the stairs. This held my still life setup. The best part was an angled skylight just above my head casting a mellow northern light, both on my setup and the wall that held my work in progress. It was a very private space, at a time in my life when privacy was at a premium. I could abandon all of it when nap

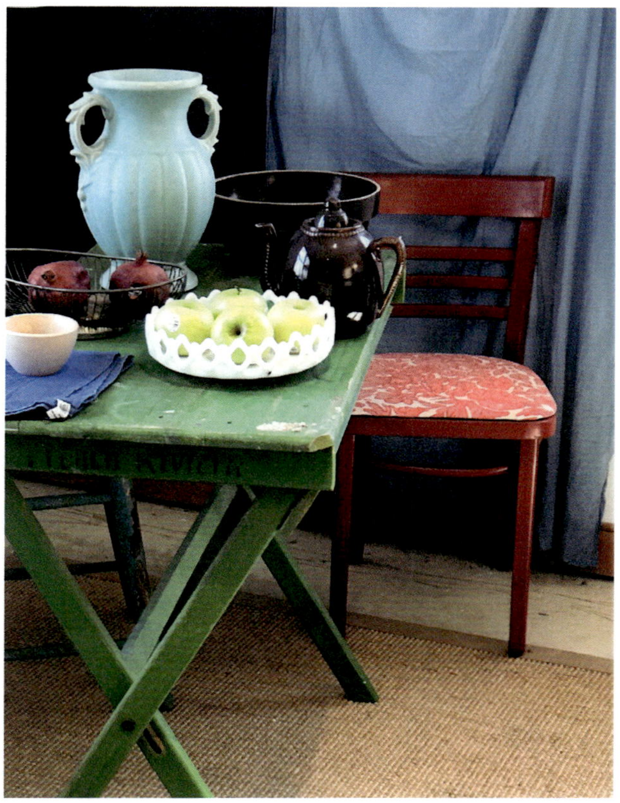

Set up for *Red Chair and Pomegranates*

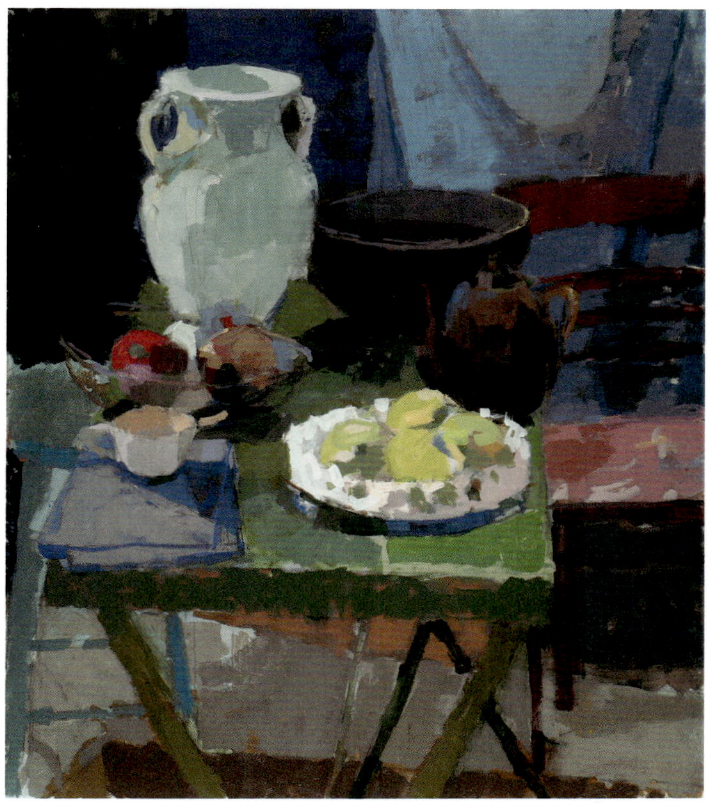

Jessie Coles *Red Chair and Pomegranates*
2017, acrylic on canvas, 42 x 36 in.

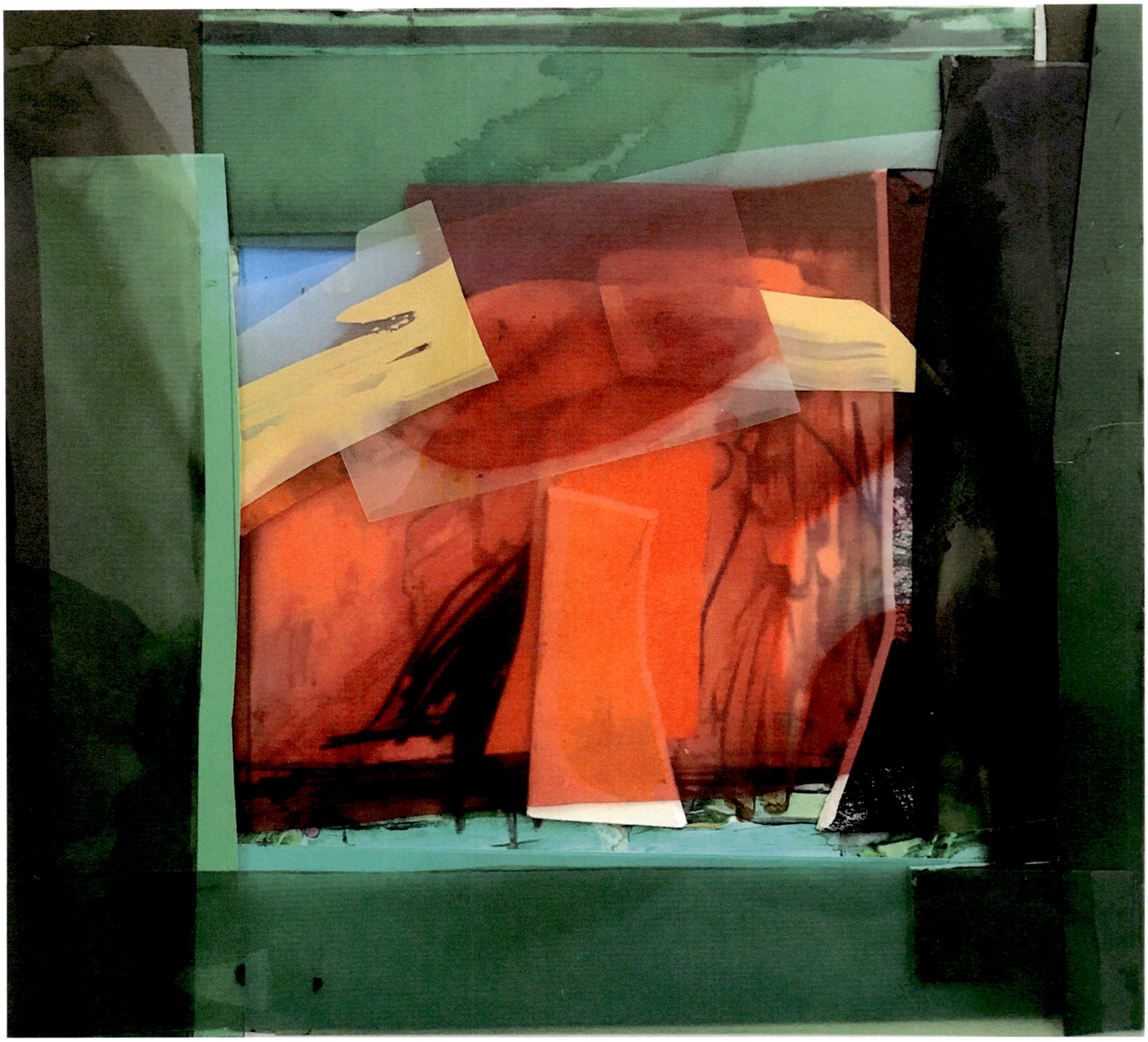

Jessie Coles *Swoosh from Green to Green*
2020, mixed media and collage, 7 x 7 in.

time was over and come back later and nothing would have changed. Still life was efficient. And the intensity of looking, responding, experimenting was a much needed mental escape.

I'm not sure how I came to be a painter. Visual literacy cannot be underrated in the trajectory of an artist and my childhood was rich with it. With my father in the foreign service, our family traveled a lot. We got to spend time in museums, churches, monasteries, temples as well as suks, open air markets, jungles, deserts and coral reefs. Lots to look at. Then, at the University of Virginia, I had a part time job operating the slide projector for art history classes. I have to admit to having tuned out the lectures to a large extent. Youth is indeed wasted on the young. But, pre-internet, soaking up those images was absolutely invaluable.

Later in college, when I finally had the prerequisites needed to learn how to paint, I was lucky enough to study with Phil Geiger. Much of the class was taken up with examining slides of his favorite paintings and gleaning what we could. I feel very lucky to have been provided with such an articulate and inspiring instructor. As a supreme observational painter himself, still life was a natural avenue for his instruction. We were taught to appreciate the dichotomy of creating the illusion of space with paint as well as being sensitive to the picture plane in abstract terms and enjoy the sensuousness of paint as paint. So clear were his instructions, that I can remember digging into my first still lifes and feeling like I was suddenly able to speak in tongues. It was an exhilarating time.

Ever since my 3-foot studio days, still life painting has been a mode that suited the way I thought about making art. The nuances and complexities in front of my eyes gave me limitless options for what to include or edit from a painting, as well as the opportunity for unconscious, responsive mark making. These paintings took weeks and months to complete as elements were painted over, moved around, scraped down and re-imagined. Over time, the abstract elements became more interesting to me than accurate representation. Still, I couldn't imagine what would drive my work if not for looking at something in front of me.

Something did eventually happen to derail that trajectory. Over exposure to oil paint began to cause a serious systematic allergic reaction in me, not just to solvents but to the paint itself, or as a paint maker at M. Graham suggested, perhaps the rancidity of the oil as it cures. This kind of allergy is not that unusual and I painted successfully in acrylic after that for almost

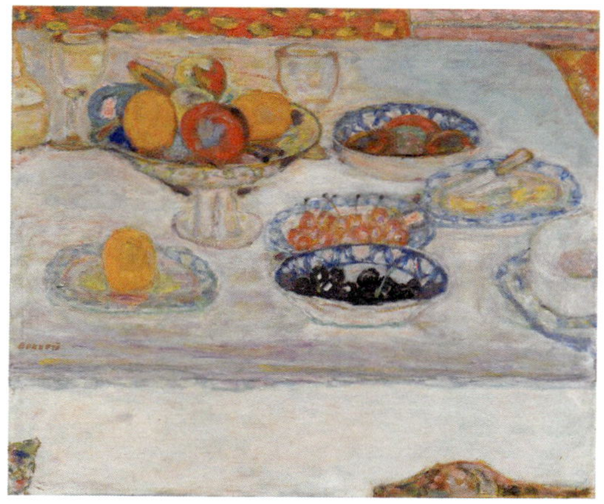

Pierre Bonnard *Compote and Plates of Fruit*
c. 1930, oil on canvas, 23 ½ x 27 ½ in.

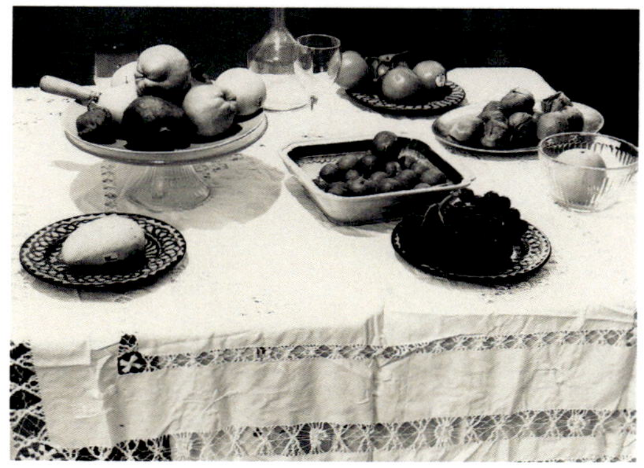

Photograph of set up for Jessie Cole's *Compote and Plates of Fruit, After Bonnard*

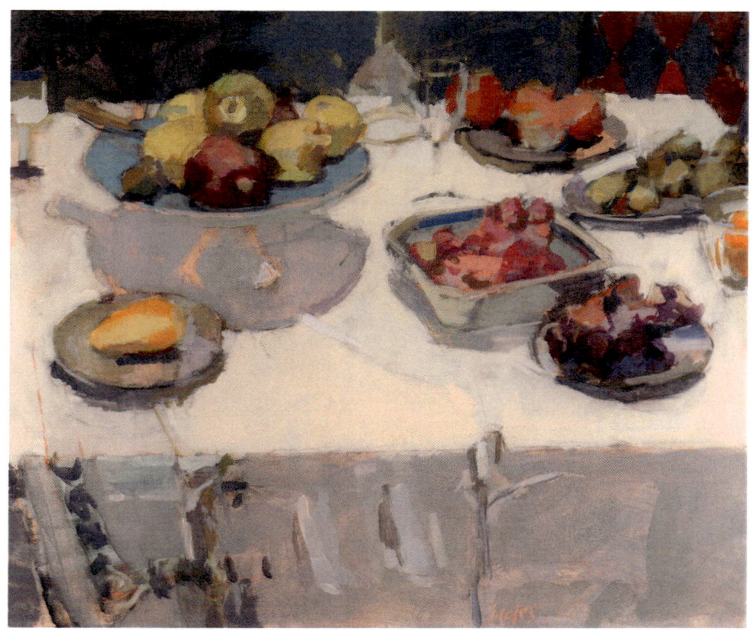

Jessie Coles *Compote and Plates of Fruit, After Bonnard*
2018, acrylic on canvas, 36 x 42 in.

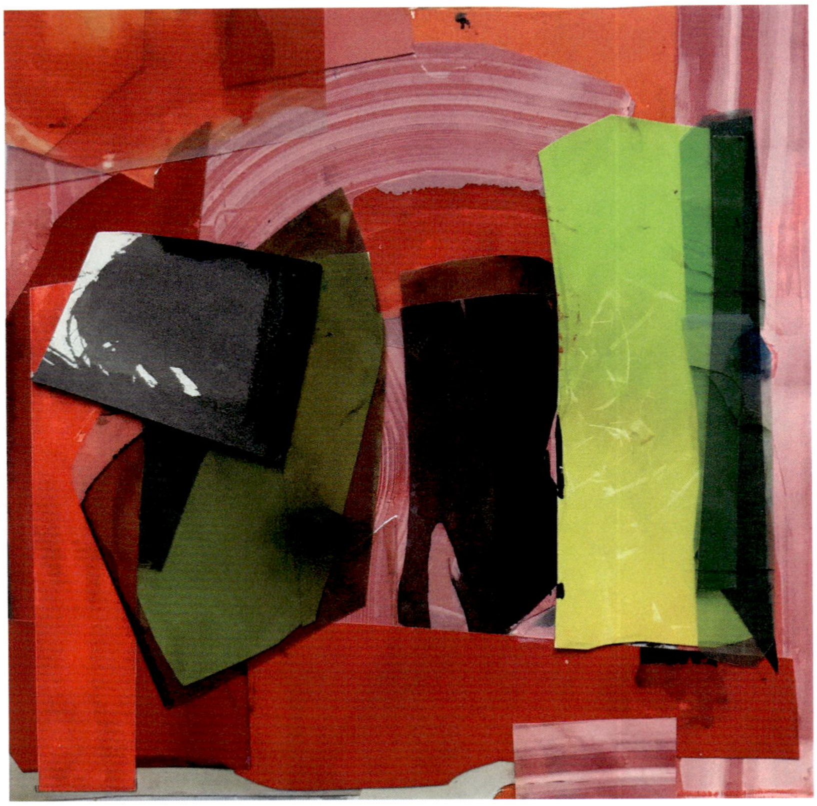

Jessie Coles *Wise Guy*
2020, mixed media and collage,
7 x 7 in.

2 decades, but eventually became allergic to acrylic as well. I believe that an allergy to acrylic paint is a bit more unusual, though not entirely unheard of. I went through an intense time of experimenting with mediums that were new to me: water color, gouache, egg tempera, casein, water color crayons, acrylic markers, alcohol ink, sumi ink, india ink, and finally collage. The search forced me to tease out exactly what experience of painting I was trying to replicate. What satisfies me? What do I wish to express? And what excites me?

I ended up liking collage the best. They allow me to assess color interaction quickly with a lot of experimentation, similar to a Joseph Albers exercise. Somehow, the impact of the color as well as abstract elements in general, have been easier to allow at center stage with collage. I've been leaning more on abstract elements from paintings by Bonnard rather than still life setups as a source for a recent series of collages which has veered into complete abstraction. I've also been finding ways of replicating swooshes of color, glazing and mark making using paper in ways that I have long admired used by abstract painters like Howard Hodgkin. These collages are small. Small things are easiest to affix. But I have a feeling that they should and will get bigger.

To my mind, they also bear a kinship to the still life I used to paint. They are intimate spaces. They contain shapes which have a discourse with one another. Though elements may teeter a little both horizontally or vertically, they are responding to an implied sense of gravity. There is illusionistic space as well as real space created by a concrete layering of materials.

KC: *David, I had just seen a video made for a joint exhibit of Morandi and Albers, in which David Leiber said that their gateway artist to becoming painters was Cézanne. I was tickled then to read in your email that a painting by Cézanne had been a kind of gateway for you as well. If you would like to talk a little about what in Cézanne grabbed you (for me it was composition) I would love to hear it.*

And, of course, the painting you describe was a still life, which helps to introduce our next topic: why still life?

"It is through the still life that one can establish the true essence of what painting is all about. To deny this, is to admit you know nothing at all about painting."

—Ardengo Soffici in La Voce, 1911

*"The viewer is part of the same table top scale.
This makes the objects universal and intimate at the same time."*

*—David Leiber on still life during a discussion video
at gallery exhibition "The Year of the Still Life"*

The quotations above suggest that the choice of still life could, or maybe should, be made with some further purpose than convenience. When you chose, or choose, to paint still lives, is it from a sense that the still life as a form best serves an aesthetic purpose?

Beyond the choice of the still life form, how about the objects involved in your work? Are they items that you value personally or that carry memories or emotional triggers for you? Or are they chosen purely for their rightness in the piece?

More specifically, how do you decide on specific subject matter and how to handle it? I see that the same or similar objects appear again and again—glass balls, fish bowls, piercingly blue bottles. Repetitions and reflections extend as well to the space represented, in the form of reflections on polished surfaces and from gleaming object to gleaming object. Even pomegranates and oranges had been varnished to a high gloss as if you pursue reflection beyond the boundaries of naturalism.

Notwithstanding the former pressure exerted by Clement Greenberg and other fashion mavins of the art world, there are many styles to choose from, even within realism. I often find myself feeling overwhelmed by this freedom to the point of panic. You appear to have an admirable confidence in how you attack your subjects. Has this always been the case?

DS: Cézanne seems to inspire people in a lot of ways that don't look much alike, whereas some people can't see anything there at all. For me, the accidental quality, the just-having-been-put-there of five or six apples was something I had never seen, or never really noticed. For some reason I am often most moved by things that just happen to have been set aside together, forgotten for the time being, perhaps meant for some other time, or simply put out of the way, shelved. They and their juxtapositions are intimate records of life, some with memories attached, some not, always still life. Cézanne said that at a certain point the objects in his paintings begin their conversations. I know what he meant.

I remember Cézanne's little still life (and his oil painting in general, not his watercolors) as modeled all over, virtual space and virtual forms as if everything were of some other density, forms and space alike. Perhaps there really is such density. This is what happened to Impressionism's rainbows. The apples had withdrawn into a stubborn, inviolable presence in their own space, which is how things are. I read somewhere that Cézanne said to a friend, "You are going painting? Where is your Naples yellow?" I don't know if he really said that, but I have always used lots of Naples yellow. It is very bright but also makes beautiful grays in endless mixtures, and makes painting like laying bricks of light. I try to make paintings that are continuous surfaces of light, and light is their real theme. Anything can be in the light, which leads to the matter of subjects, things in that light. Perspective, no matter how sophisticated, is a crude geometry of light that would force forms into my point of view. I don't want to do that. My paintings have lots of highlights. The angle of incidence equals the angle of reflection, which means that there is a source of light reflected to my eye and to the viewer's. That is a real connection, but it means that everything painted is in its own space of light. That's why, as you say, they all gleam. You are right about the naturalism beyond naturalism. My colleague-in-law tells me that there was a great span of time after the Big Bang when the whole universe was nothing but photons. It still sort of looks that way to me.

Kathleen Craig
Still Life with Ape
2020, collage, 12 x 16 in.

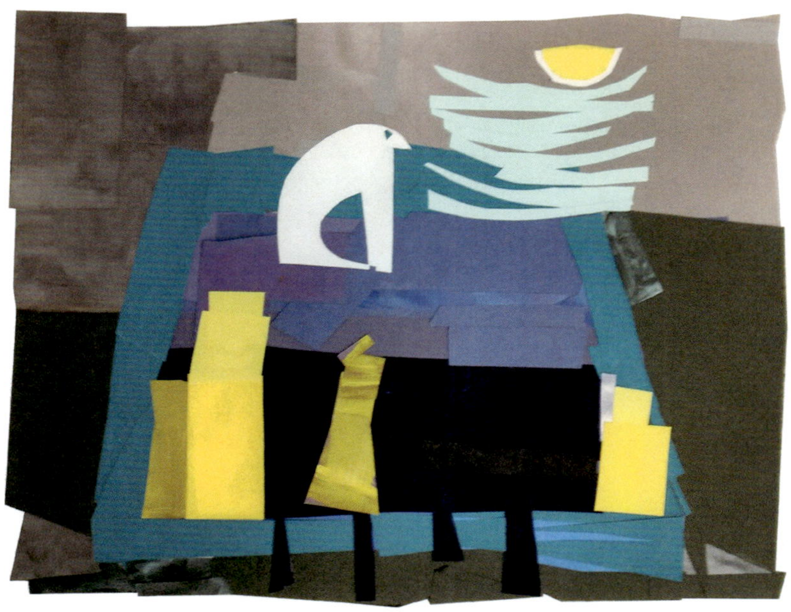

I am very struck by the long historical connection of still life with vanitas. The word means emptiness; when things "vanish" they disappear, are no longer seen. Vanitas is the transiency of things, their fragile and delicate coming to be and passing away. I saw a medieval tapestry in which a fool was blowing bubbles with a pipe, with the legend "Homo bulla est," "Man is a bubble" (woman too). I suppose the skulls in paintings of Mary Magdalene and St. Jerome could be seen as bubbles in this theological sense, but I prefer to think of circles as what happens when a drop falls in still water, and of spheres as what happens when molten glass is blown, or for that matter, when bubble gum is blown. Bubbles burst, but before they do they reflect everything around them, and thus assure us that the great world exists, that it is there to be reflected. Chardin's children still blow bubbles, just as they build houses of cards. I think these fragile constructions have a lot to do with the kind of order he gives his forms in their spaces.

I don't think very much about composition before the fact, although I am always pleased when formal rhymes and resolutions begin to appear. Sometimes I think there should be another bubble here or there.

It is hard not to see a painted bubble as a bubble, and so it is hard to see either the surface on which it is painted or the paint with which it was painted. Bubbles may be the basic illusion.

Gifts have a lot to do with my paintings. Sometimes I give them away (to a good home), and gifts are often "elements" in a still life. I was pleased to find out that the ancient term for still life was xenia, referring to plates of food and fruit given to strangers, that is, to guests, part of the rituals of hospitality (and also part of the tragic stage set, Zeuxis' grapes that fooled the birds, for example.)

As I have said before, the way painting has fit into my life has also made it a fairly solitary and eccentric pursuit. But I have a lot to say about it.

As for how I address painting confidently, I owe it all to drawing. I draw and scumble, draw and scumble. I also scrape a lot. Scraping keeps the drawing and creates all kinds of incident. The final paintings are dozens or hundreds of doings and re-doings, and I like them to show the sequence of realizations. I also like to paint the same things over and over. I am always amazed at how they differ from one to the next. I also read once that Pissarro said of Cézanne that he had the advantage over the rest of us that he was always working on the same painting. I know what that meant too.

KC: *Jessie, I was going to ask you about your choice of still life and what you thought about the quotations below. Unprompted you have offered such a good answer to that not uncommon question, "why still life?" and "what's so great about still life?" that I need to find a new way to approach it.*

In a way, Soffici's remark from earlier sounds a bit silly, as there was plenty of great painting done before "still life" even got rolling! But I can understand the urge to defend it. It seems to me that he might have been referring to abstraction—the effort to separate out the abstract elements of the beauty you see in order to share your perception in a way that works for others.

JC: I get what you're saying. Sure, Soffici seems to recognize a value in painting that goes beyond what is being represented or maybe even the illusion of representation itself. Anyway, I love that he puts still life on its deserving pedestal. Agreed.

KC: *You were interested in abstraction before you began to create your "officially" abstract work. I believe we will be posting, with your permission, samples of your recent collages. (I'm attaching screenshots of a couple of the pieces I was thinking of.) I wonder if you would care to speak a little about one of them, how the abstraction perhaps helps the viewer to appreciate the "essence" of painting even more in some ways than the easily verbalized collection of objects.*

JC: Our response to, or "reading" of, a painting is complicated. If it's representational and objects are depicted, that's probably what the viewer will untangle first. What is being represented here? How is that illusion achieved and how successfully? How do the things I see painted connect to my own experiences of them? These are kind of left brain questions that demand attention before

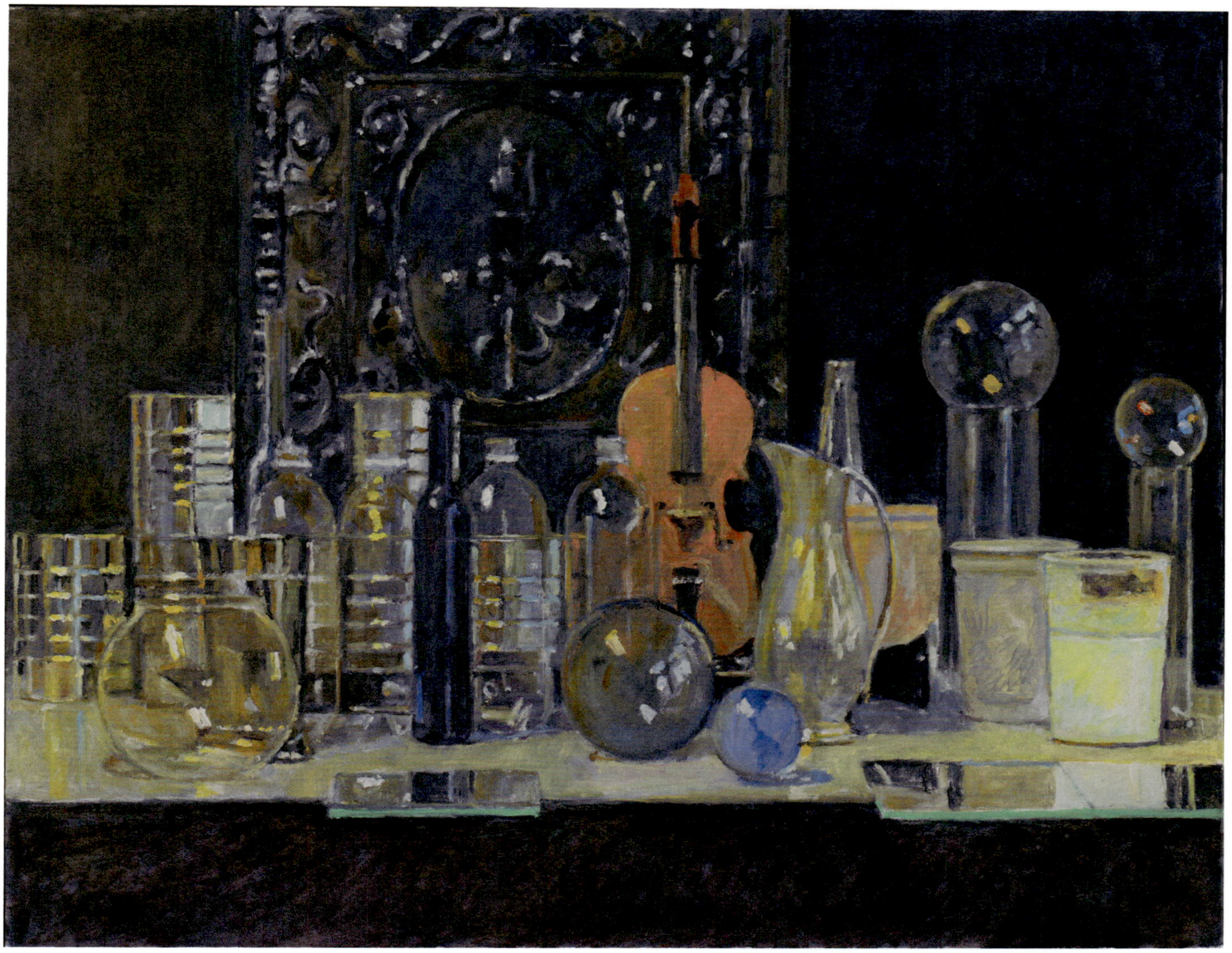

David Summers *Clarinet with Cold Torch*
2021, oil on panel, 16 x 20 in.

experiencing the sensuousness of the paint, the emotion, how it affects you in your gut. I'm not sure if that's what you mean by the "essence" of beauty, but for me, those feelings are at the core of connecting with art.

KC: *Abstraction aside, people are often interested in the choices of subject matter, or objects to paint. I generally choose ugly things, the idea being that beautiful things don't need my help. David chooses mostly things that both contain space and light and reflect them. You spoke of the objects in your still life work that eventually became more interesting to you as abstractions. Do you have any criteria for your choices of things to paint?*

JC: Ha! You're the advocate of ugly things. Do you do it pro bono?

Color is where I usually begin. Maybe a color chord with some interruptions. Setting up is always more physical and emotional than expected. After a little heel tapping, I launch into full throttle pasodoble, swaggering this way and that between table and cabinet, arms outstretched with a flourish of colorful possibilities, cups, bottles, teapots, textiles. I scrutinize the arrangement from one angle, then another, whipping objects away and twirling new ones into place, squinting, furrowing. Love it! Hate it! Ecstasy! Agony!

I also look for forms having clear geometric shapes, cylinders, cubes, cones in an interesting range of scale, as well as a range from dark to light. Anything with handles or a characterful spout adds a splash of gesture. Multiple bowls and plates are great for conveying space as their ellipses tighten the further away they are. Their edges can also act as quick moving directional lines, swinging or spinning your eye around the composition. Organic shapes of plants and produce add mystery. They comprise so many unknowable humps and bumps.

KC: *During another panel I watched David Leiber speak about how both Morandi and Josef Albers considered Cézanne to be their "gateway" artist. I would love to be channeling both of them, to hear in what way that gate got opened... David (Summers) spoke of a small Cézanne still life that seemed to define for him what he needed to do to become a painter.*

Paul Cézanne
The Basket of Apples
c. 1893, oil on canvas,
25 ½ x 31 ½ in.

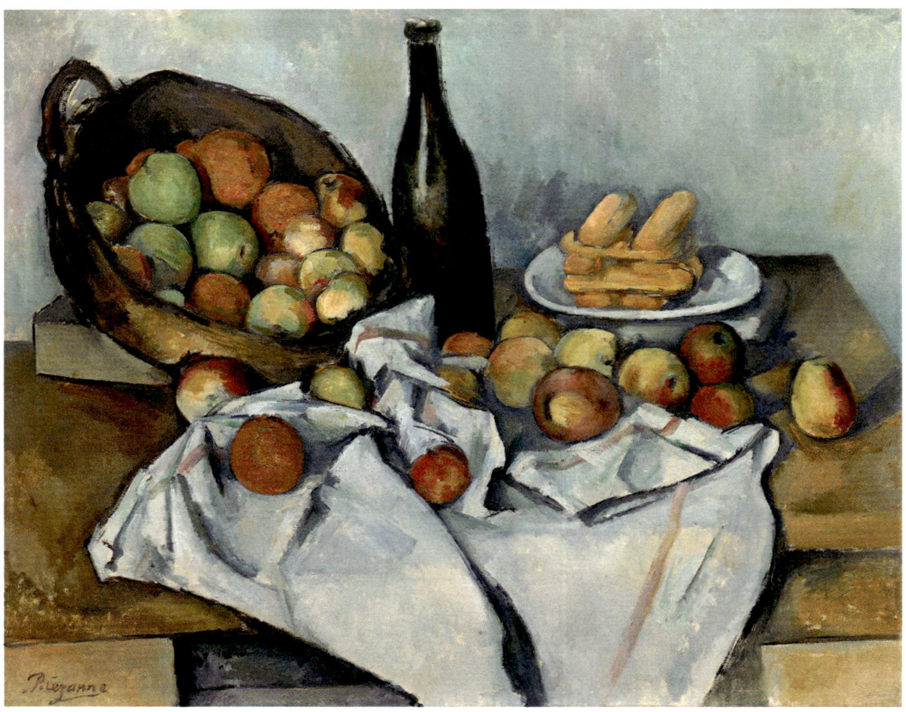

Is there such a figure in your pantheon?

JS: Oh, like a "gateway" drug? That's really funny. Can you send me the link to Leiber's talk? All three of those artists could get you into some serious shit. I should probably be in jail by now. But yeah, I agree, it all goes back to Cézanne. His table top still lifes are the epitome of painstaking specificity while insisting that you pay attention to the abstract elements. I love how un-still they are, with everything kind of lurching and teetering. What brings your eye in and around keeps changing. I love that. I don't think I have as clear or defining a figure as David does. Maybe Diebenkorn comes close. Like Cézanne, his paintings walk the line between abstraction and representation brilliantly, but in a more contemporary way. With his abstract expressionist vocabulary, his paintings give me a huge visceral response.

Similarly, I remember seeing the Matisse/Diebenkorn show in Baltimore. I was excited about seeing the Matisses, who I've always loved, but when the paintings were side by side, the Diebenkorns packed so much more of a punch. He's always been a touchstone for me.

KC: *I didn't put as an official "question" one that I decided was stupid and the answer obvious. If I google collage I get a lot more hits on "how to craft a memory book" than on Matisse. Even actual fellow painters have asked, "Do you still paint or just do collage?" Probably I was just venting, but if you think it worthwhile to address, here it is: Do you ever have to defend collage as "art" and as "painting?"*

JC: Actually, I don't think I have had to defend colleges as "art" or "painting" to anyone except myself. I have certainly noticed a disinterest from some viewers and indeed some galleries. I think painting, with a brush on a single surface, gives people a context, parameters with which they are familiar. It's like game that viewers know how to play. And painting, especially oil painting, holds a huge place in the history of art. It has gravitas. While collage may not be particularly new, it is a way of making pictures that not everyone is ready to embrace. It's a different esthetic with different rules. Though I'm sad to lose some of the audience I had in the past when my paintings were more straightforward, I feel that what I gain is a more intimate and original dialogue with the viewers who do respond to my new work. I find that very exciting.

I was delighted by your premise that collage IS painting, Kathy. I hadn't really thought about it that way. In my mind, collage was just a different kind of picture making, technically a "works on paper." Yet for me, it feels very closely linked to the act of painting. With collage, I am able to play by a lot of the same rules. In other words, my own concerns about making a painting that are in my head right now. These things change. We all have things we're chewing on and then we get through that and chew on something different. When I am in the studio working on collage, it feels absolutely as engaging and satisfying as painting. If anything, it feels like a more pure response to the push and pull of color, the illusion of volume and space, a way to emphasize texture, manipulate edges, respond to rhythms, assert control over the composition... it's all there. When you're painting with a brush, there are so many little tricks for getting something to sit on top, paint on top of paint. It can end up feeling very indirect. You often have to wait for a layer of paint to dry before you can get the next layer to behave in the way you want. With collage, a reevaluation and response can be achieved very quickly. It's easier to stay honest with myself which is very appealing. Is it painting? I experience it as such it as such.

KC:

> *"From the time that I was 6 years old I had the mania of drawing the form of objects. As I came to be 50 I had published an infinity of designs; but all that I have produced before the age of 70 is not worth being counted. It is at the age of 73 that I have somewhat begun to understand the structure of true nature, of animals and grasses, and trees and birds, and fishes and insects; consequently at 80 years of age I shall have made still more progress; at 90 I hope to have penetrated into the mystery of things; at 100 years of age I should have reached decidedly a marvelous degree, and when I shall be 110, all that I do, every point and every line, shall be instinct with life—and I ask all those who shall live as long as I do to see if I have not kept my word."*
>
> *—Hokusai*

David, I loved your comment, that people appreciate—or don't appreciate—Cézanne in different ways! What I noticed, as I said, was composition, in paintings like Basket of Apples 1885, that popped out as I leafed casually through a coffee table book of "impressionist" paintings. The other thing about Cézanne that I learned to appreciate (I admit I was never his biggest fan) was the solidity and massiveness of his subjects, even his glass and china. Like Manet, at the same time he maintained their presence as paint on a flat surface.

I am thinking now about your sense of his apples as belonging to—owning—their space. I feel like your own focus is to carry the same idea in the opposite direction, to the fragility of glass or water or gelatin orbs that also own the spaces they contain, as well as push against and reflect the space around them. (I think you already said this better—imagining the universe made up of photons, only I couldn't even imagine what a photon would look like!)

Jessie mentioned a class she took at the University of Virginia that devoted a lot of time to examining slides of the teacher's favorite paintings and, as she put it, "gleaning what we could."

I feel as if I have already gleaned quite a bit from your discussion of Cézanne and of your own work in relation to it. There must be other paintings or painters you admire. Are there any that you have copied or "learned from"? I hope you will be able to post a favorite painting here and tell us why you like it.

I admire complicated and action-packed paintings like the landscapes of Julian Hatton and the party scenes of Bruegel, also complicated and delicate paintings like yours, but so far at least I myself have fallen flat on complexity and action. Delicacy isn't in me and I can't even hope for it. Are there painters or paintings that you admire without wanting or feeling able, to emulate?

What is the thing you feel is your own greatest asset as a painter, that is, what do you like most about your own paintings?

Hokusai said that although he had gotten really good by age 73, he expected to be pretty near perfect by 110. He managed in that comment to express a supreme confidence in his ability to create, to learn, and to live. What do you think is your next challenge?

DS: I had a little trouble extracting your three questions from your remarks, but I believe I have done it. I think (to begin) I must apologize for referring to some of my own writing. In a book published

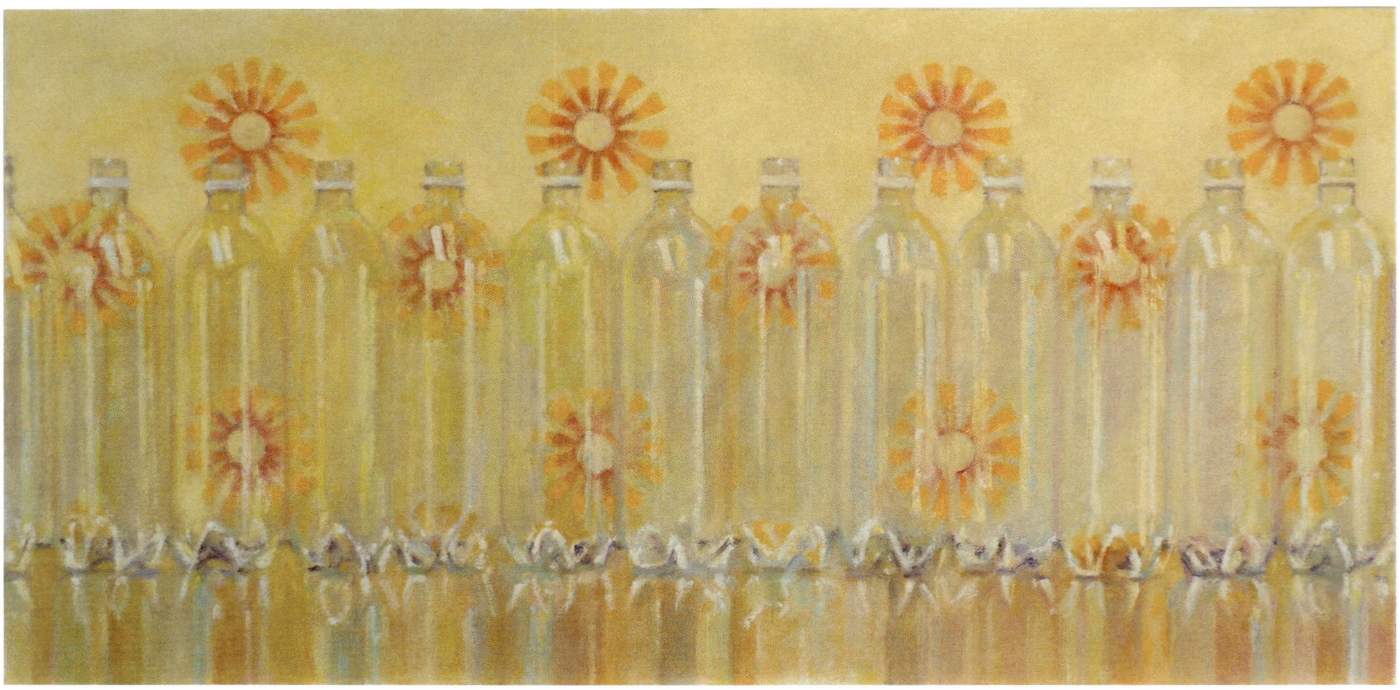

David Summers *Commodity Ghosts Dancing in the Sun*
2019, oil on canvas, 12 x 24 in.

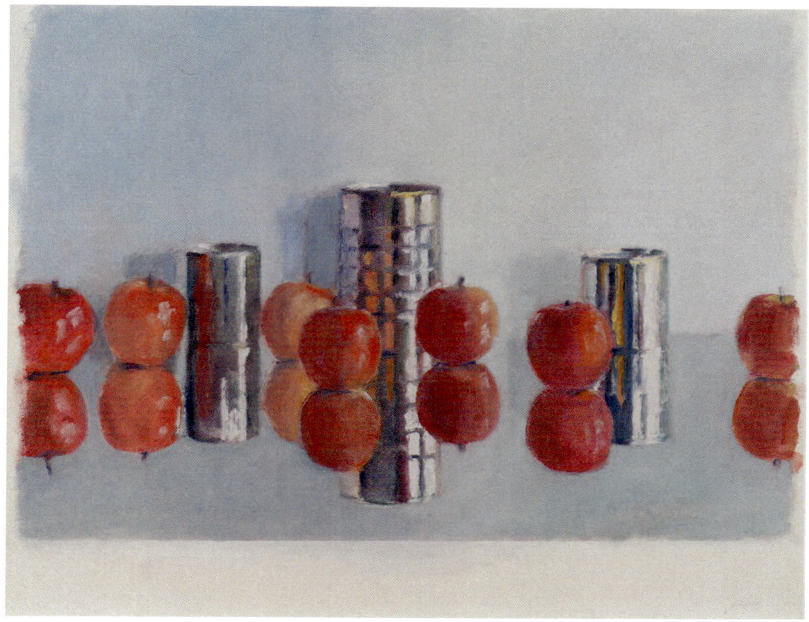

David Summers
Pink Ladies Commodity Ghosts
2008, oil on panel, 14 x 18 in.

in 2003 (*Real Spaces: World Art History and the Rise of Western Modernism*) I argued that painting is not essentially two-dimensional, that instead it is the art of virtual space ("virtuality" being our capacity to see three dimensions in two). When I put a mark on a surface I can see it as on the surface (in which case it might become a sign, a word or number) or I can see it as in a virtual space, which may be further defined in any number of ways. This is the space of imagination. I always saw Abstract Expressionism, insofar as it is drawing, as powerfully spatial. Its transformation into field painting, pure colored surface, was a big mistake, in my view, a view I had held ever since I decided as an undergraduate not to participate in the "flat-object making" projects of the time.

When I begin to paint things, a first mark becomes a shape, or begins to make a shape, and as I paint in response to light, the object—an apple, for example—begins to find its place in the virtual space made possible by the surface. The painting is done when subsequent marks have made the surface the space of the apple. The painting is an apple of observation and imagination, and it is far from its beginnings, vivid in something like the way an apple is vivid, or the world is vivid. Complex paintings must be uniformly vivid.

It is hard for me to think about gleaning from paintings, or of offering my own gleanings to others. I admire everything Matisse ever did, never liked anything Picasso ever did. I greatly admire Giacometti's painting (not his sculpture) because he makes persuasive images out of the spaces marks make. I like Mondrian, but only if I think of his order as three-dimensional. At a certain point in my life I read and taught a lot of formalist criticism, especially Michael Fried, a formalist critic less doctrinaire than most, and unlike most critics, very good at looking at paintings. He made me think a lot about the possibilities of literality. The idea of "all-overness" stuck in my mind, and for some reason I can't forget Olitski's attention to edges, which of course raises serious questions of composition.

As I have said, I have never thought of myself as not painting, but I go about it in a certain way. I often say (I have noticed) that I try to follow my nose, or put one foot in front of the other. I always remember something Albert Pinkham Ryder (?) said. He was like an inchworm at the end of a branch. That's me. I try to make resolved paintings, but the resolution changes. I always have some notion of how a painting should look, and the one in hand may turn out to be like that. But I can't even joke about living to be 110, or even 100, although I might make it to 90. It all takes place slowly, and can't be anticipated. I heard that Africa is drifting northward into the Mediterranean. What will that be like? Z

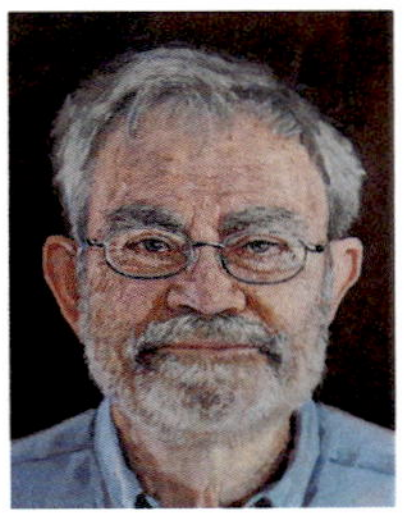

David Summers always loved to draw, then to paint. As a student, he was discouraged from such uncontemporary activities, and went on to study the history of art. He never stopped painting, however, occasionally exhibiting. He always thinks of Chardin and Cézanne. He is represented by Les Yeux du Monde in Charlottesville, VA.

www.zeuxis.us/summers

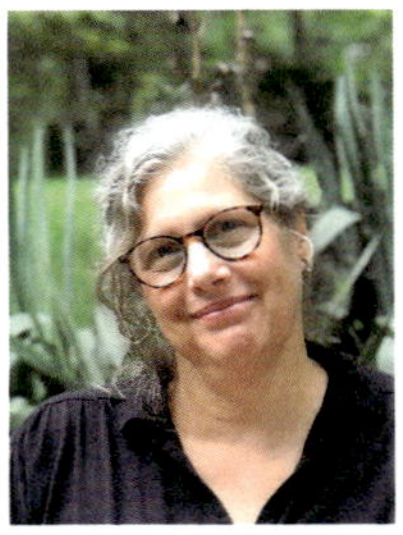

Jessie Coles, born in New York City, spent most of her childhood in Africa and the Middle East. She received a BA in Studio Art from the University of Virginia where she studied painting with Philip Geiger , and continued her studies at the Corcoran School of A rt and Piedmont Virginia Comm unity College. Coles has taught painting and drawing privately as well as at Crozet Arts, Beverly Street Studio, McGuffey Art Center and Nimrod Hall Art Center. Her work is included in numerous private and public collections. She is a two time semi-finalist for the Bethesda Painting Award and is represented by Les Yeux du Monde Gallery in Charlottesville. She lives and works in Charlottesville, VA.

www.jessiecoles.com
www.instagram.com/jessiecolespainting

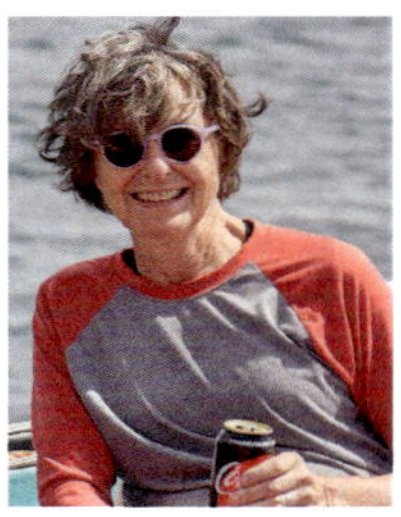

Kathleen Craig paints abstract still lifes, landscapes, and figures, working from observation and memory, with an emphasis on color, composition, and expression. Her work has been influenced by Giorgio Morandi, Nicolas de Stael, and Ken Kewley's essay on color. She currently exhibits with Nancy Margolis Gallery (NYC), Elder Gallery of Contemporary Art (Charlotte), Cerulean Arts (Philadelphia), and Bonfoey Gallery (Cleveland).

www.zeuxis.us/craig
www.kathleencraig.net

Balanced Environments

Matt Klos interviews

Susan Cohen and Daniel Riesmeyer

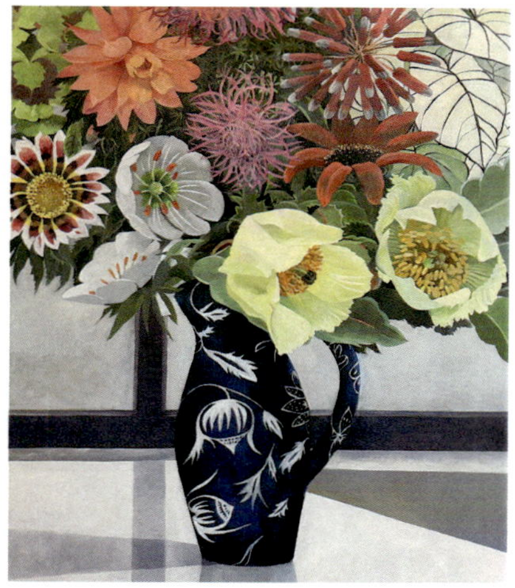

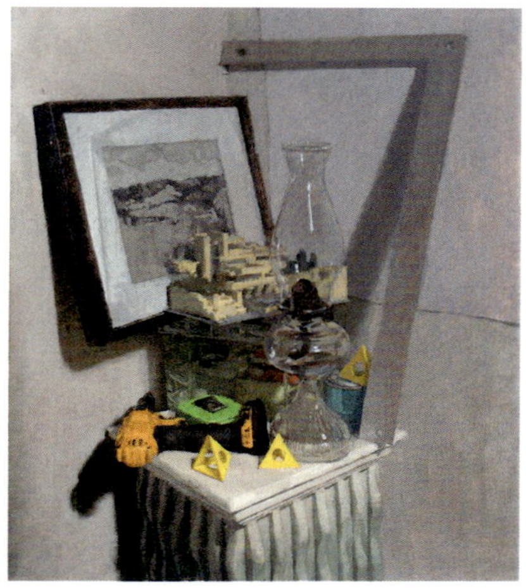

Susan Cohen *Bouquet* (detail)
2022, oil on linen, 36 x 24 in.

Daniel Riesmeyer *The Architect*
2016, oil on muslin on panel, 14 x 12 in.

Matt Klos: *This interview was conducted via email with two artists I admire, Susan Cohen and Daniel Riesmeyer. Susan is an erstwhile member of Zeuxis and Dan is a long-time friend whose work I've seen up close for the last ten years. Through this exchange of questions and answers it has been insightful to learn more about these painters and learn about their experience of observation and decision making, contemporary art, moving from simplicity to complexity, and completeness versus finish.*

MK: *Susan, the city clearly serves as an inspiration for you. Gridded windows hold the background in a number of your still life paintings and collected exhibition postcards feature prominently in some setups.*

Susan Cohen: The city is definitely an inspiration, but I'm not an urban plein air painter. Logistics and the distractions of working on location hold me back. When I'm in the country, I transition pretty naturally into a plein air painter.

Painting still life in my studio allows me to express my complicated feelings about urban beauty by juxtaposing the rigid lines of my windows and view with setups of flowers or curvilinear objects. I'm basically always longing for nature, and I think my city/flower paintings express that longing best. The light of my studio's southern exposure is always changing, and that too, provides subject matter and contrast.

MK: *Ahhh yes, southern light! Light that is constantly shifting is full of surprises and is a strong motivator... or a constant frustration!*

Susan Cohen: Southern light is exciting and dramatic, but what I wouldn't give sometimes for some nice, even, north light...

In my New York City studio, the windows face the back of a huge building with an uninterrupted grid of windows. When I first moved in seven years ago, I was fascinated by the grid's transformation into little colorful icons as night fell and people across the way turned on their lights. The building is far enough away that I can't actually see what goes on inside those spaces, so I painted each window as an abstract arrangement of colored shapes, just as I saw it. The lit-up windows presented an entry to abstraction, although I was only painting what I saw.

MK: *I wonder how you choose, when gazing upon the distant grid of glass, to paint some illuminated windows and not others? To what extent are you consciously making this selection? Gideon Bok did several paintings in a studio with gridded warehouse windows. I remember one painting where he painted each of the several dozen windows independently, treating each as a one-shot, not worrying about how one pane of glass related to the adjacent pane. This was different from the way the windows were treated in the other paintings I remember in that series. In those, the windows seemed to be connected in defining a singular moment. In this painting however, each windowpane marked a particular moment, and when taken with the others one saw an expanse of time stretching across a change of season.*

SC: I think I'm setting out to faithfully paint things just as they are, but inevitably, the painting makes its own demands. Ultimately, what works for the painting is what matters. In the nighttime city paintings, when someone across the way turns on a light revealing something useful for the painting, I'll fit it in. For paintings completed over many sessions, I'm generally consistent about painting at the same time of day, but I'm always open to interesting developments that come up as the light changes.

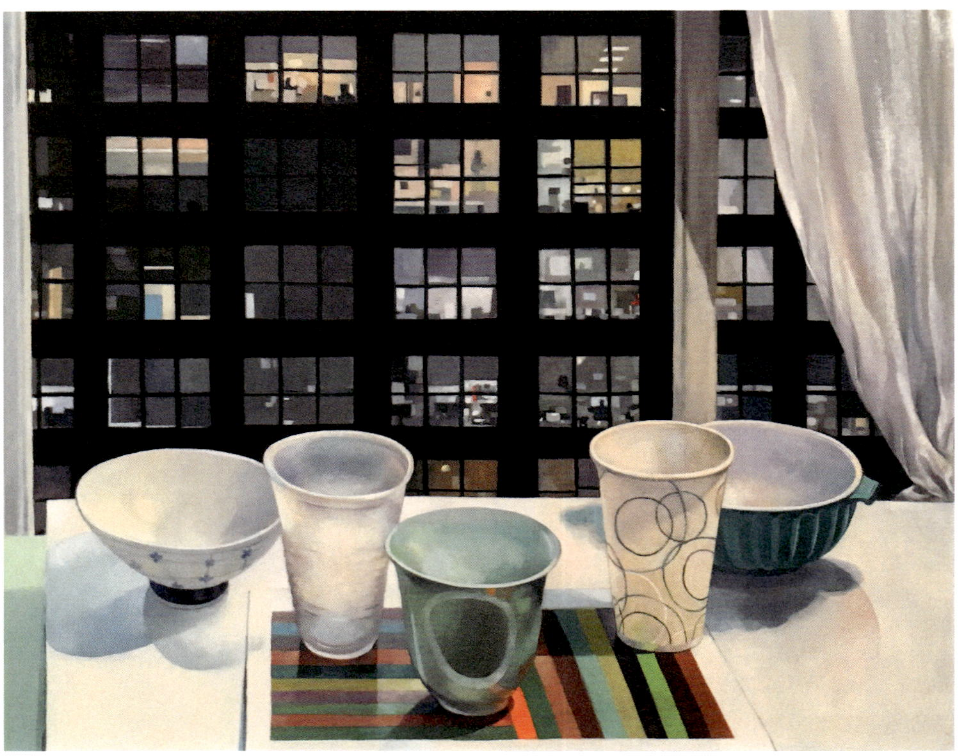

Susan Cohen *Night Still Life*
2019, oil on linen, 20 x 24 in.

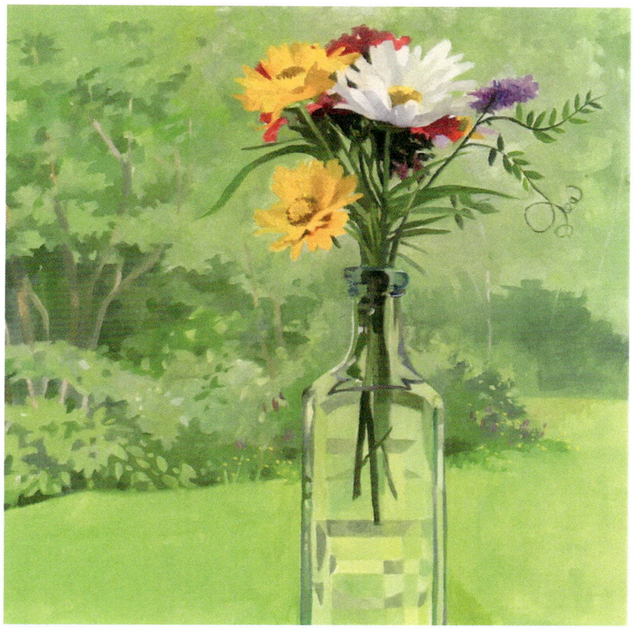

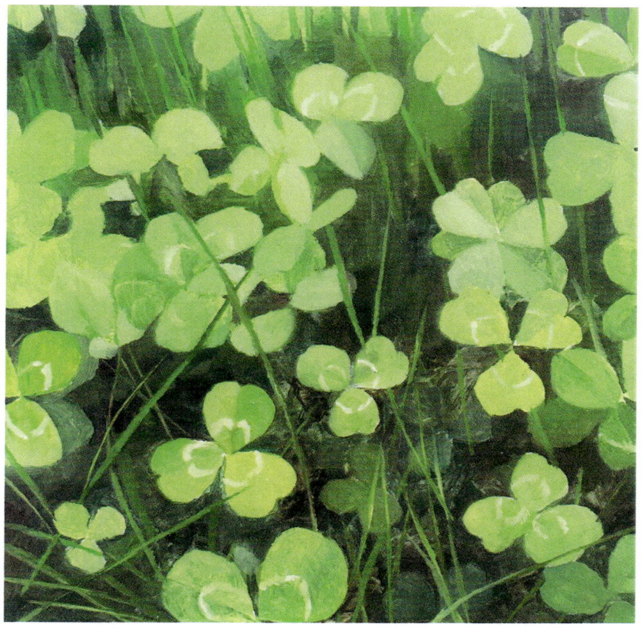

LEFT TO RIGHT:

Susan Cohen
Flowers in a Glass Bottle
2017, oil on panel, 12 x 12 in.

Susan Cohen
Three Leaf Clover
2021, oil on panel, 6 x 6 in.

MK: *Do you feel that the orbit of your work takes on a wobble, or leaning, when you've been particularly struck by an exhibition you've visited? Can you describe a particular instance of this?*

SC: A couple of shows come to mind. The very first museum exhibit I saw after the pandemic shutdown was Agnes Pelton at the Whitney. Her work was new to me and I was moved by her exquisitely painted imagined vessels, flowers, skies and landscapes, as if she were observing and depicting the real, physical world. The specificity of Thomas Nozkowski's precisely composed, mysterious paintings also touch a deep place beyond words. I've always painted from observation, but these shows open the possibility of investigating, and trusting my imagination.

MK: Bowl of Pennies *is perhaps my favorite painting of yours. The spread of fabric around the bowl is extremely chromatic but the color of the pennies is what truly mesmerizes. Indeed, it's not the color of the pennies but the color enacted upon them: the color of the light, the cool white on the inside of the bowl that contains them, and the reds, oranges and blues bouncing about. Your pennies act as water or clouds might act in the landscape. They serve as a conduit to living color in their environment.*

SC: On a small scale, the pennies have a similar quality to the wild disorganization of nature. A field of wildflowers, or a lily pond, or cluttered green foliage looks so random at first, but if you look closely enough, compositional rhythms begin to emerge.

MK: *How are you thinking about color when you work on one of your more sustained still life paintings, like this one?*

SC: A jar of pennies was a fixture in my studio, and although intriguing, it seemed unpaintable. A turning point occurred when I put a handful of the pennies in a bowl and used a clamp light to illuminate it. Not quite consciously, the spark I'm looking for is contrast, and the white interior of the bowl provided such a contrast. Suddenly, they were pennies no more, but an exciting color challenge. In the space around the bowl, I scrambled the plaid, geometric lines by crumpling the fabric. A tube of Old Holland "Naples Yellow Reddish Extra" found among my paints, was invaluable for hitting the pennies' high notes.

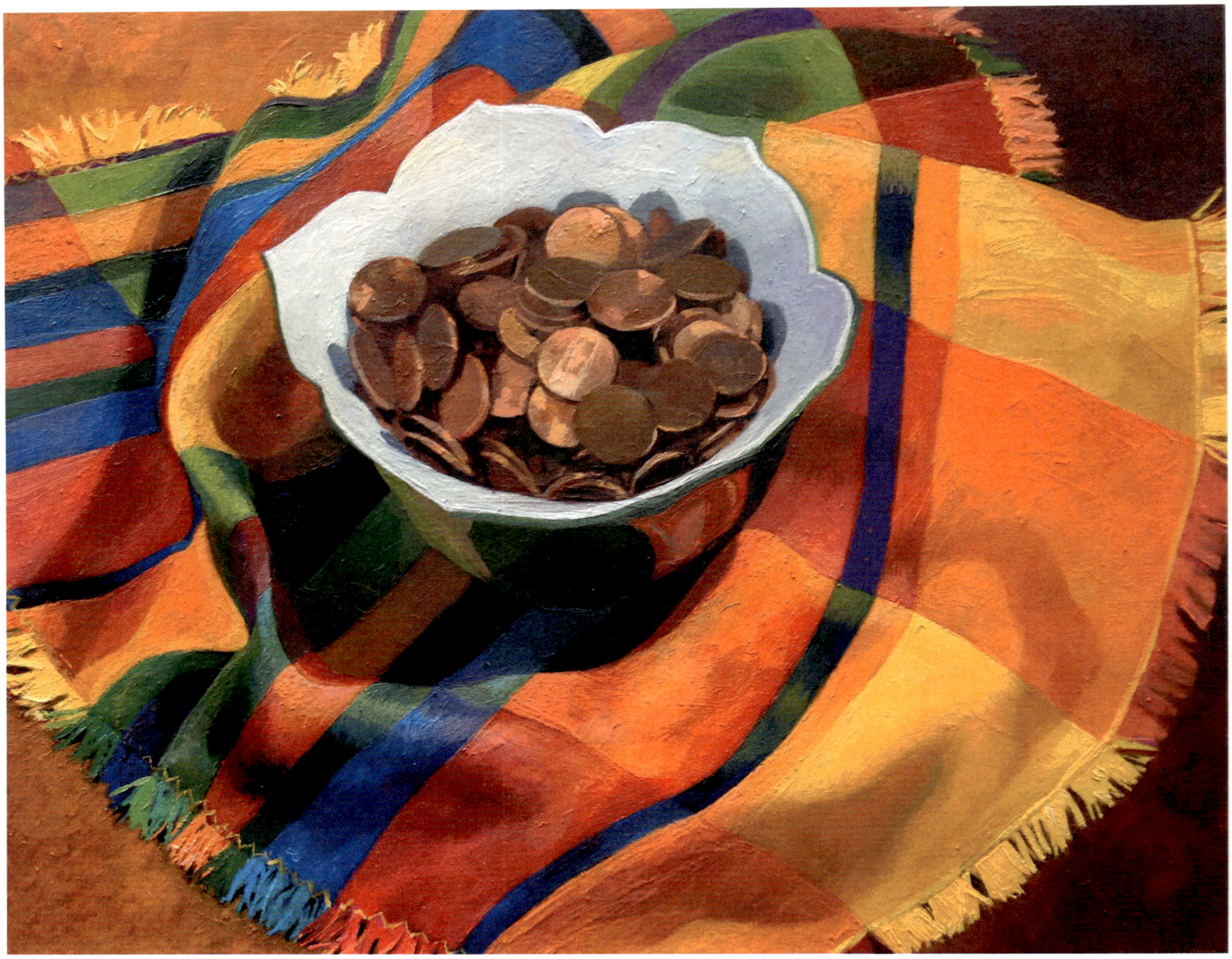

Susan Cohen *Bowl of Pennies*
2014, oil on wood, 8 x 10 in.

MK: *What strategies do you use to get at something quite complex, like the bowl of pennies in this painting?*

SC: The principle strategy when painting the pennies, or painting anything for that matter, is to forget what it is I'm painting, and focus instead on capturing cool and warm colors and shapes. It feels like I'm using the other side of my brain, separate from any sentimental attachment to the things themselves.

With something as beguiling and complicated as those pennies, I didn't want to get there too soon. In general, on sustained paintings, I'll scrape down the day's work with a palette knife, which leaves enough of a trace to re-enter the painting the next day, and keeps me from getting prematurely attached or precious.

Of course, thinking in formal, visual terms doesn't eliminate all thoughts about the objects' identities. Sometimes layers of meaning reveal themselves. While painting *Bowl of Pennies*, I mused on money, and about the person who brought me the fabric as a gift from a recent trip to Mexico.

MK: *You paint some still life paintings of flowers in front of the cityscape and others of flowers in front of the countryside. It strikes me that your flowers serve as the organic element in the former and the geometric agent in the latter.*

SC: I never thought about it that way, but you make a good point. I'm often drawn to complicated, highly structured flowers, and I paint them with the same detachment as if they were inanimate still life objects. Flowers are endlessly surprising, and of course beautiful, but they're still about one shape of color next to another. The challenge is to balance structure with softness and impermanence.

MK: *Can you describe some of the choices you make or some of the phenomena you seek when setting up a still life?*

SC: Setting up a still life or painting in nature are both about isolating what is important. Most still life setups are pretty complicated at first, and it's a matter of adding and adding, and then subtracting objects until all that's left is some kind of formal problem to be solved. It's an ineffable thing I'm looking for, but seems to involve some kind of color, compositional, or for lack of a better word, emotional contrast. When I paint in nature, I am also distilling and paring down, but nature provides the set-up.

MK: *Daniel, some of your still life paintings are quite expansive and complex. More interior than still life actually. I've seen you paint and remember you build up your paintings in an "all over" manner in an alla-prima session. In the very complex paintings I imagine that some areas of the painting may lock in at some point. I imagine that you may spend an entire session painting on the highlight streaming into the interior or the painting within the still life being very careful to hold each mixture and decision to a thin spectrum of color and value. How do you approach your complex paintings when you have crossed into the final stages of making them?*

Daniel Riesmeyer: I think the most important thing for me as I am working on a painting is to strike a balance between an attention to the whole with an attention to the parts—in particular as I get into the latter stages of the painting process. As the painting progresses I may spend more time in particular quadrants but the work is always done relative to the whole—and with an eye only toward what I need to do in those areas to satisfy the needs of the painting.

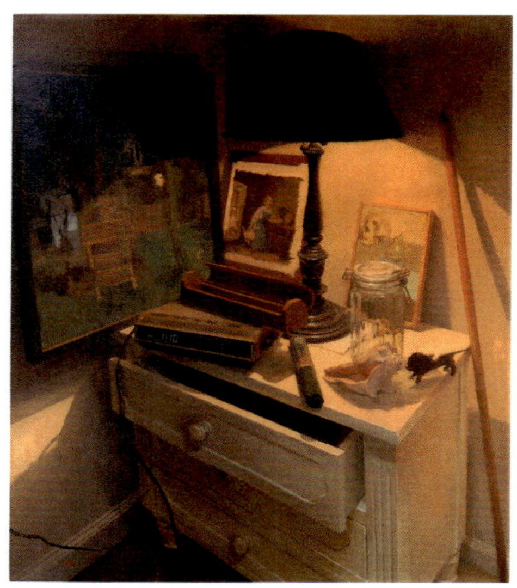

Daniel Riesmeyer *Night Logic*
2016, oil on linen, 24 x 30 in.

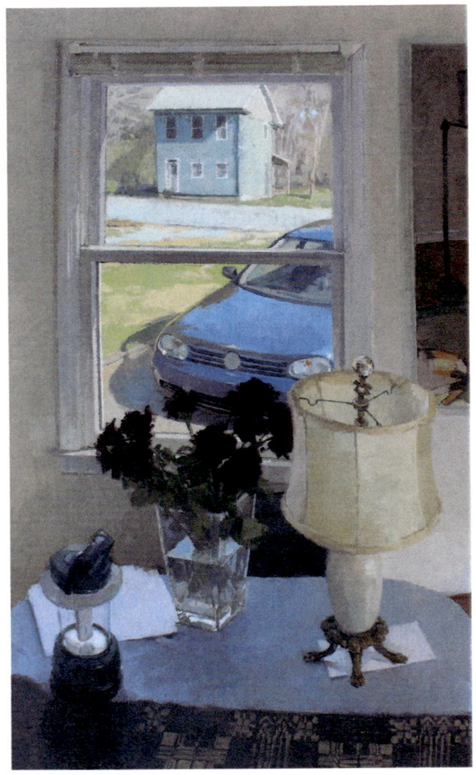

Daniel Riesmeyer
Vase of Flowers in Front of the Window
2018, oil on paper on panel, 26 x 15 in.

The initial stages of the painting don't really have much to do with individual objects, etc., rather, I'm interested in characterizing the light as particularly as possible—where the light (or envelopes of light) is the common denominator. Once a sense of light is established I try to only do what I need to satisfy really basic criteria, relating shapes to each other in terms of proportion, placement, color, and value. I try to avoid getting wrapped up in "detail stuff" if it's not necessary.

In latter stages of a painting I try to focus on adjusting the edges of shapes while I revise color/value decisions—my goal is to have color-shape decisions that carry as much visual information as possible within the context of the painting. Can a particular color-shape of green convey leafy-ness while avoiding actual drawing out individual leaves? What about the texture of a carpet or a brick wall? I tend to link edge quality with contrast of shape—so I am kind of bringing the painting into higher focus as I work, from something totally out of focus and undefined. I don't gauge a painting's success by the level of "finish"—rather by its completeness. I try to do as little as possible but to the greatest visual effect—I gravitate toward other painters' work who do this as well, i.e. think poetically and translate with/through the medium. I want to be as deadpan, understated, or simple in my statements as possible—"nothing fancy here." When I think "all over" painting I am thinking about an artist's equal attention paid to all arts, regardless of the local identity or importance of the stuff. I want a blank wall, etc. to be as considered or important as the "subject" of the painting—because it is. As a painter you are creating a world and there is an obligation to care for all things, nothing is unimportant.

MK: *Haha. That reminds me of some of my beginning students who will leave large areas of a composition unconsidered and completely blank. I'll say, "OK, now what about all this space? What is living in your background?" and they'll say, "Well, that space is empty so I plan to leave it blank." Gets me every time!*

You mention the idea of completeness rather than finish and that you are drawn to other artists that work with a similar ambition. Tintorettos' work immediately comes to mind. What artists do you look to as walking that fine line of completeness while avoiding the entropy that can happen in simply finishing?

DR: I think painters who are most concerned with shape also tend to be more holistic in their thinking, and as such more concerned with completeness as opposed to "finish." A few people who come to mind are John Dubrow, Catherine Kehoe, and Susan Lichtman. Basically, their paintings "work" because of interrelatedness of shape as opposed to rendering across surfaces to form individual volumes. I think most really good painters fall into this category to some extent or another. I think Degas, Bonnard, Corot (his small on-site landscapes), and Morandi also fall into this category.

I will also say that once the light-creating relationships are established I think the hardest part is done (maybe?). I work on-site in environments that change over time—more often than not, the big changes (additions, subtractions, revisions, etc.) come in the latter stages of the painting process. Late-stage openness is baked into the painting process. I try to avoid overcommitting to topical stuff or paying too much attention to smaller areas/identifiable objects because these things end up being a pain to move around or adjust if they are developed too early. Which takes me back to my early thought: what am I accomplishing with what I am doing? Is it necessary or self-satisfying—do I need this level of detail or could I say more with less?

MK: *What are some of your thoughts about the differences and/or similarities between building the one or two shot painting versus the six-month-long studio painting?*

DR: Outside of how size might dictate some aspects of process (brush size, for instance) I don't see much difference between "quick" paintings and something that I work on over an extended period of time outside of the increased risk of overworking.

Bonnie Sklarski said at one point in figure drawing that a good gesture drawing needs to capture all of the essentials that a more "finished" drawing will/would need—developing the drawing beyond the initial five minutes is a process of elaborating on basic truths that need to be present from the beginning.

I think developing a long-term painting is the same way—success is as much about what is included as is not included. With longer-term painting there is a lot more opportunity to lose the essential and get lost. Quick paintings are notational by necessity—part of the trickiness of long-term paintings is that it is easy to lose this quality in overstatement. Ideally, a larger long-term painting should feel like it was constructed with the same motives as a quick one or two session painting.

MK: *Your more traditional still life paintings are arranged in a wonderfully balanced way. They contain items that exist in your household but these things are carefully planted and moved about to make up your motif. These are certainly not still life arrangements that you discover or stumble upon—"Oh, look what Saul (Dan's son) set up!?" Can you tell me how you go about making the decisions for these arrangements? What is the impetus for setting up a still life? How much allegory comes into play?*

DR: I set up arrangements with what I have on hand—some times making the mistake of borrowing stuff that doesn't go unnoticed for very long. With this stuff I try to build something that I think looks interesting in terms of the relationship between light and shadow. I tend to move things around until I find something that looks good to me—I try to arrange or compose intuitively as opposed to having an idea about what will/should work. A lot of times finding/building a "right" feeling arrangement includes moving the light source around as opposed to just moving the objects.

I don't want my setups to feel too "arranged" but arranging is also something I can't avoid—its like trying to explain "finding without seeking."

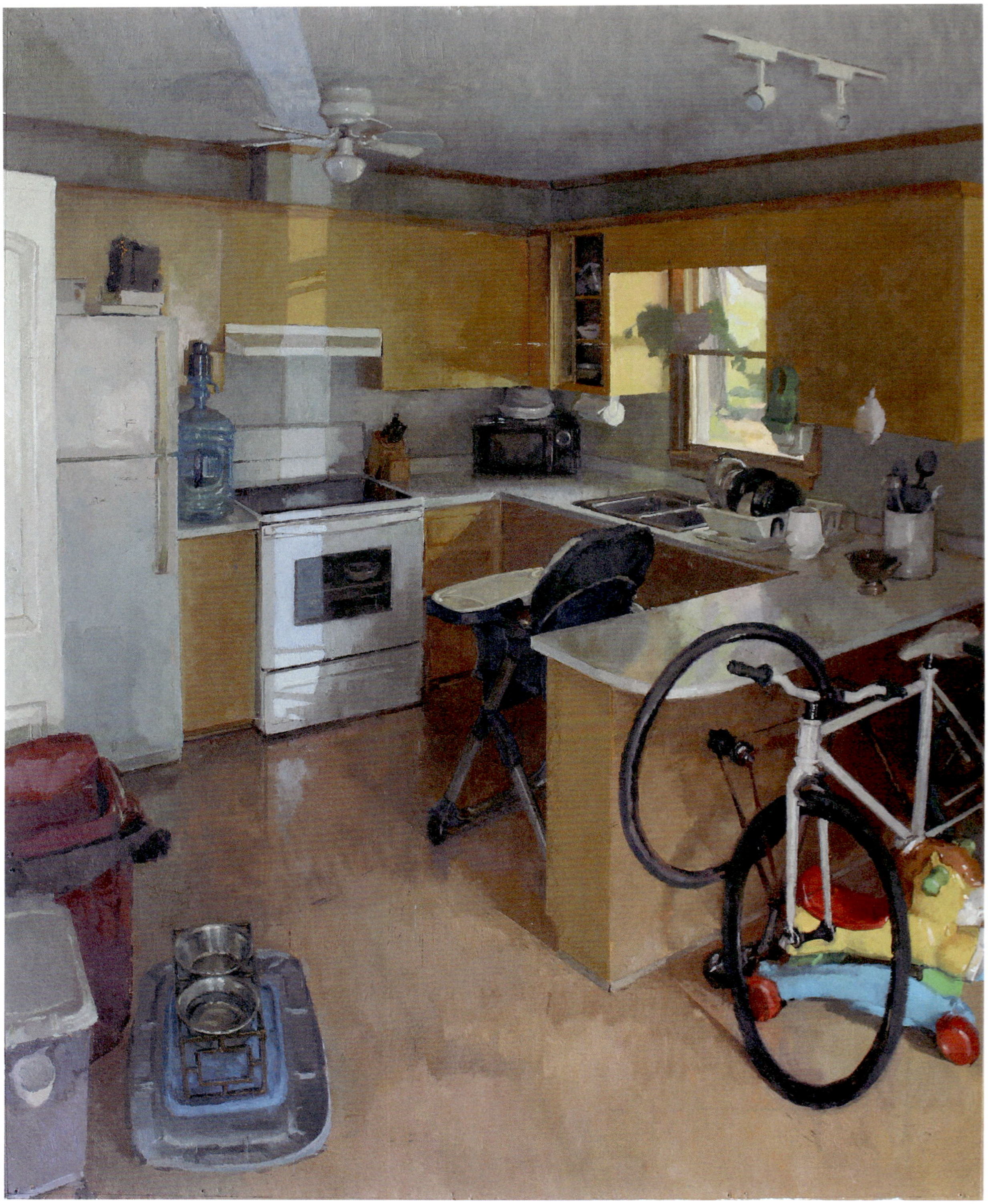

Daniel Riesmeyer *Kitchen at Bozman Neavitt Road*
2016, oil on paper on panel, 29 x 23 in.

I like to think of still life setups as miniature stage sets—like I would play with little toys and blocks as a kid, making environments populated with a variety of characters, etc. Having said this, often I don't start with any particular narrative or allegory in mind—just a collection of stuff with potential. The objects are not arbitrarily selected, just that they are not chosen first and foremost for what they mean to me but rather how they look or could look in a setup.

One nice thing about still life is that I use an incandescent light so painting is not limited to a particular time of day or weather (cloudy vs. sunny). I can set up a still life and the light will be the same, whether it be noon or four in the morning. Typically the harder thing is setting up my painting and palette so that I can see what I am doing clearly but not have the light dramatically affect the still life—that's why there is a very subtle light-temperature shift toward the foreground in a bunch of my paintings. Z

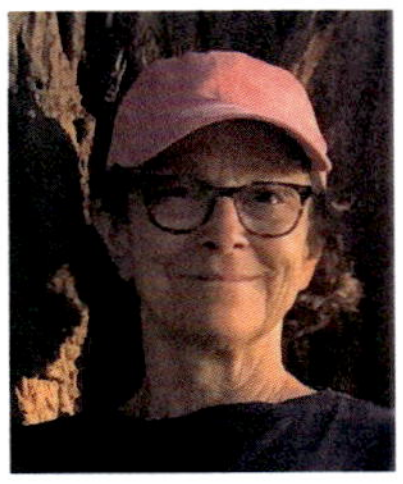

Susan Cohen received her MFA in painting from Brooklyn College, where she studied with Lennart Anderson, Philip Pearlstein and Lois Dodd. While there, she received a graduate fellowship and was the recipient of the Charles G. Shaw Award for painters. She earned her BFA from the Boston Museum School and Tufts University. Susan has exhibited her work at the Painting Center, NYC, and the Cynthia Winings Gallery, Blue Hill, ME, and in juried exhibitions in New York and many other cities. As a member of Zeuxis, her work was shown in venues around the country. Her work is in many private and public collections, among them the US State Department Office of Population, Refugees and Immigration. She was a resident artist at the Vermont Studio Center, the Virginia Center for the Creative Arts, and Cummington Community for the Arts. She lives and teaches art in New York City.

www.susancohenpaintings.com
www.instagram.com/susancohenpaintings/

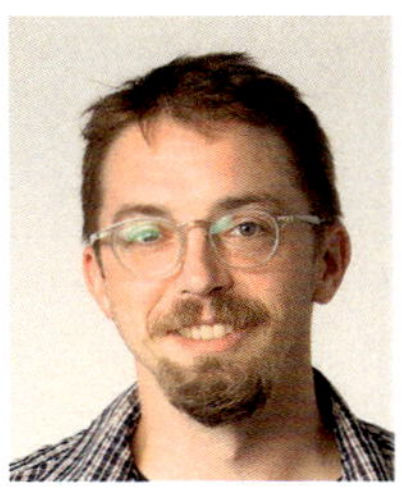

Daniel Riesmeyer was born in Pittsburgh, PA. He received a BFA from The Maryland Institute College of Art and completed his MFA at The Henry Radford Hope School of Fine Arts at Indiana University. He is currently an Associate Professor of Art, teaching Drawing and Painting at Nicholls State University in Thibodaux, LA. Daniel has shown in Washington (DC), Bloomington (IN), Annapolis (MD), Baltimore (MD), Bethesda/Rockville (MD), Oxford (MS), New York (NY), Cincinnati (OH), Hiram (OH), Pittsburgh (PA), and Léhon, France.

www.danielriesmeyer.com

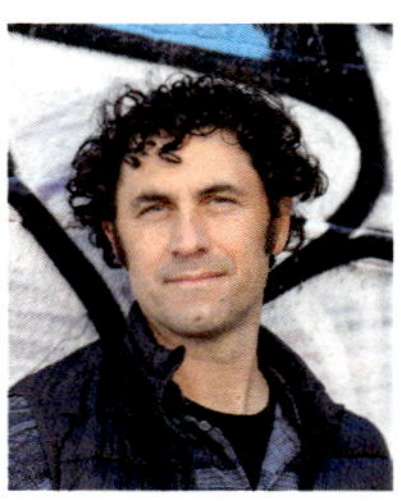

Matt Klos is a recipient of three Individual Artist Awards from the Maryland State Arts Council (2016, 2012 and 2008). His work has been featured in numerous group and solo exhibitions including the Prince Street Gallery in Chelsea, NY. He was awarded first place in the Bethesda Painting Awards in 2007 and received an Elizabeth Greenshields Foundation Grant in 2001. Klos currently teaches drawing and painting full-time at Anne Arundel Community College in Arnold, MD and has served as a guest lecturer/critic at various institutions including the New York Academy of Art, Towson University, and the University of Missouri. He is a member of the collective Perceptual Painters and Zeuxis. He resides in Baltimore Maryland with his wife and children.

www.mattklos.com
www.zeuxis.us/klos

Work Is More Fun Than Fun

Phyllis Floyd interviews

Richard Baker and Barbara Kassel

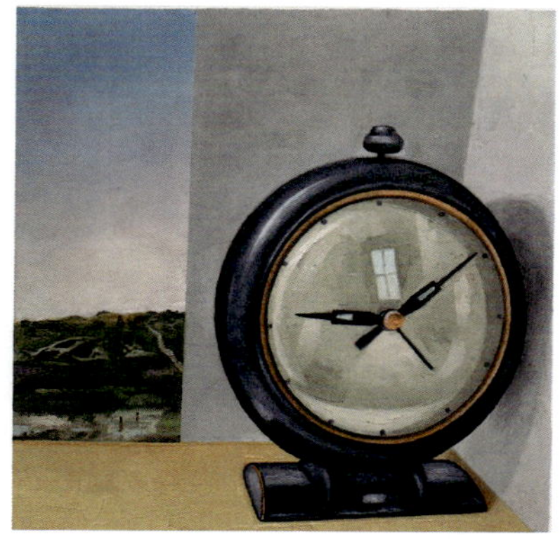

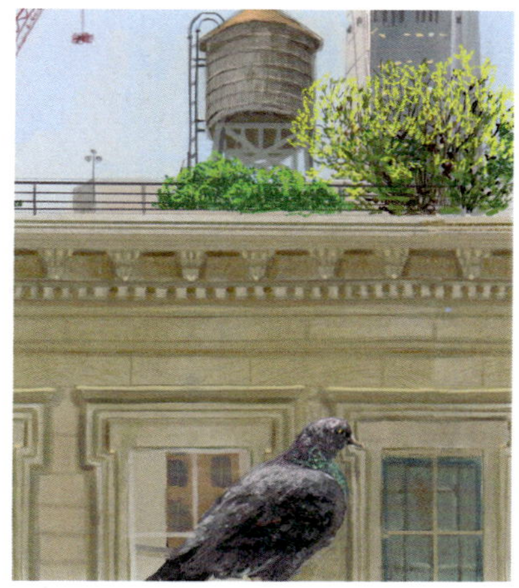

Richard Baker *Untitled,* 2021, oil on linen, 10 x 10 in.
Barbara Kassel *View from Loft,* 2019, iPad using Procreate

Phyllis Floyd: *The interview with Barbara Kassel and Richard Baker is 18th in a series begun 2 years ago when Covid struck and Zeuxis had to cancel an in-person event with Matt Klos and Lynette Lombard. They agreed to discuss their work on line, and their written dialog reached many people who otherwise would not have been able to attend. We decided to continue the project with additional still life painters. Subsequently, some of the Zeuxis artists took on the role of interviewer, and I am now emboldened to try my hand. I had known Kassel's and Baker's work for a couple of decades, but I barely knew them. I've been able to ask away to my heart's desire, and they have responded with the clarity and punch seen in their painting. Though the international news is now worse than ever, painters can lose their worried selves in an activity that is utterly absorbing. It was the playwright Noel Coward who said, "Work is more fun than fun."*

PF: *First, can you tell us something about your early life:—say, up to age 20? Where did you grow up? What was your upbringing like? Can you describe your parents? What kind of a child were you—obedient, rebellious, friendly, introverted? Were there siblings? Did you like school? Was there an event in early years that you remember vividly? Next question is what did you think of the visual arts during this period?*

Barbara Kassel: I was born and raised in Los Angeles, and am a valley girl, having lived in Studio City/ Sherman Oaks until I was 18.

My upbringing was middle class, in a nice ranch house built in the 1940's facing onto the neighbors across the street and foothills behind. It was an area where many people in "The Industry (movie and TV)" lived, but not fancy. It seemed simpler then. Julie London and Jack Webb lived across the street at one time. I remember meeting her with a school friend (her daughter) and she was in bed wearing a silk pink bed jacket with a toy poodle on her lap. It was memorable. I also remember going to a friend's house where there was a large heavily barred cage outside the front door. When I stepped into the house, I was greeted by a full grown lion and a large sofa with the stuffing torn out! My friend had been very nonchalant about it all. Of course, people lived with lions in their houses. His stepmother was Tippy Hedren. The lion was removed some time later after it cornered her secretary.

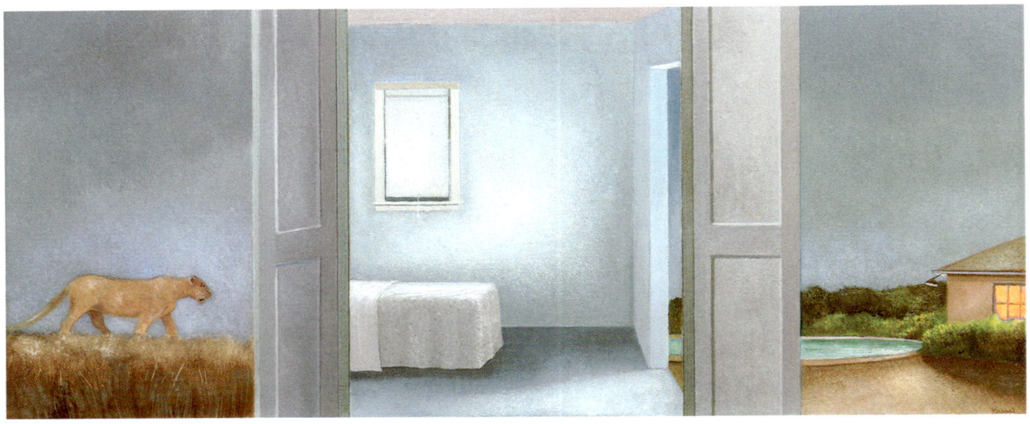

Barbara Kassel
3933 Ethel Ave. (my childhood home)
1997/98, oil on panels, 10 x 24 in.

I had a very loving and supportive family where I was encouraged to be involved in activities that I liked. I had the 1950's panoply of lessons: art, ballet, tap dance, guitar, piano, French (my mother was born in Montreal), swimming. I went to public schools and had a variety of after school and summer jobs. Some lasted longer than others. Telephone Company (lasted one day), Orange Julius (lasted a bit longer), office assistant, and art supply store connected to a lumber yard. I spent a lot of time on the beach and swimming in the ocean. I went to summer camps which I loved. We always had a cat or two. I still do—two. It was a fortunate and happy childhood.

My mother trained as a nurse, but after her marriage to my father at age 20, she gave that up. My father was 28 at the time, a doctor and in the army. He had been born and raised in San Bernardino, CA after his parents fled Germany in the late 1800s. My mother's parents also fled Eastern Europe, my grandfather from Romania and my grandmother, from Russia. Their marriage was arranged by a rabbi. He was a doctor and she was a housewife.

Even though I had what I would call a happy childhood, it was fraught with serious illness in my family. My father had his first major heart attack when he was 42 and died of his third when he was 53 and I was 16. My mother had breast cancer 2 years before and had a radical mastectomy and radiation. My mother became very depressed after my father's death and rather than going to an east coast college as I had planned, I stayed and went to UCLA instead. I learned at an early age how life can turn on a dime.

My time in UCLA was formative. That is where I had RB Kitaj as a drawing teacher, who was terrifying! I had been used to warming up with gesture drawings, etc., but he had us work on a single drawing for the entire class or longer. He told me that to be an artist, I should go to an Art Academy. He asked me to marry him on our second date. This was not in the #MeToo generation. He was 21 years older than I, his estranged wife had committed suicide the year before and he had 2 children. I answered that I'd think about it.

While still at UCLA, Kitaj and I went up to Northern California, to Bolinas where there was a poetry enclave. I remember walking with Bobbie Louise Hawkins, who was married to Robert Creeley,

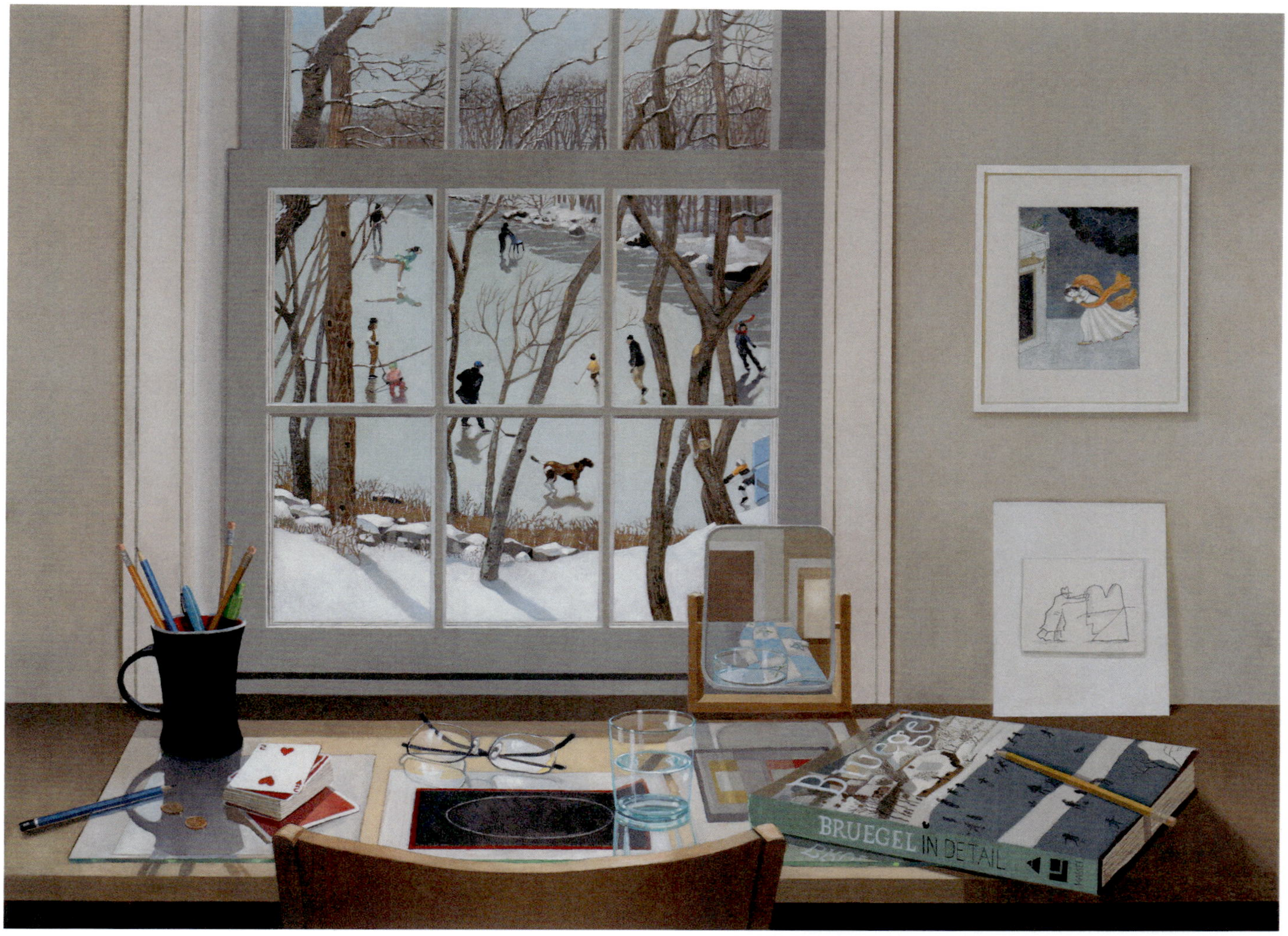

Barbara Kassel *Skaters*
2022, oil on linen on panel, 30x40 in.

and she said to me, “Don’t you want to have your own young life?” It really struck me and stuck with me. In writing this answer, I revisited her and found that she hated when women were just muses for men. Here is a quote from her obit in *The New York Times*: “People are absolutely willing to let a woman be a ’muse,’ and that has to be the worst job description in the world,” she said in an interview in 2011 with the poet and novelist Barbara Henning. “Being a muse means you sit someplace and watch this other person have all the fun.” She has a point!

I went to London with Kitaj that summer and stayed with him at David Hockney’s place for a couple of months while he was renovating a house he had bought. He lived in London and only was a visiting artist at UCLA. Hockney took me to my first opera, Wagner’s *Lohengrin*. I hate to admit, but I would have much rather been at a David Bowie concert. It was an extraordinary time, but I knew that I wanted to have my own life and that I was too young. We remained friends for the rest of his life.

I have an older brother who I remain very close to. I was outgoing, friendly, and obedient. For the most part, that is. In my teens I did stupid things like hitchhiking often late at night with a friend (who I stayed over with and who had a very permissive mother) to the Sunset Strip where we would hang out in parking lots smoking weed. Go to Whiskey A Go Go where girls were dancing in those cages, those sort of things. I would get on the back of motorcycles with guys that I didn’t know, take milk baths with strangers, it was the psychedelic 1960’s. When I think of all the things I did during that period, it makes me think that I was very lucky to have survived.

I liked school and was a good student. I missed being valedictorian by one B+ that I got the year my father died. I loved art classes, and my parents signed me up to learn oil painting at a small place called The Flemish Art Shop when I was 10 or so. My first paintings were of fluffy kittens with dewy eyes, watermelon slices and flowers, also dewy, using copal varnish, Flemish style. From then on, I always had art classes outside of school, including art camps and Chouinard and Otis Art Institutes.

I remember being nine and in the middle of our road on Halloween and suddenly realizing that I was mortal. It was shocking.

I remember having painted a card with a figure with an oval face that I named Calme, and carried her with me. Much later, I realized that it was Calm Me. Art has always allowed me to navigate my life.

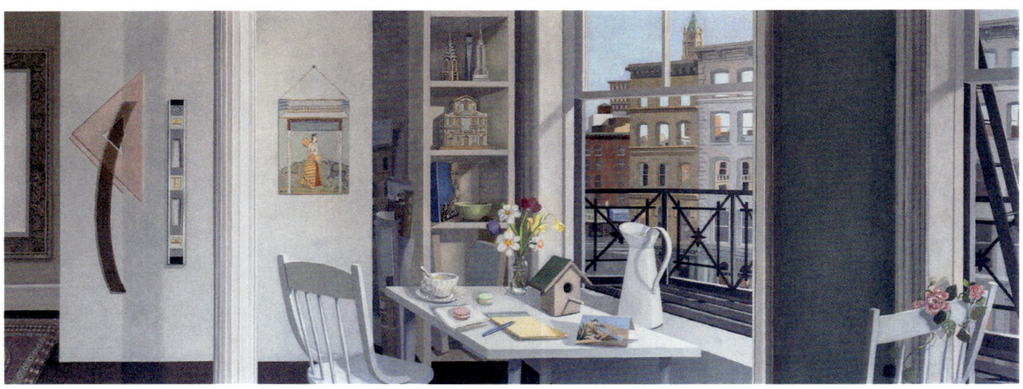

Barbara Kassel
Last Spring in the Loft
2018/19, oil on linen on panel, 48 x 120 in.

My father’s death is seared in my memory as I was there. A few hours earlier he was reading the newspaper in the den on a normal Thursday night and then he was dead in bed where I ran into when I was woken by my mother calling an ambulance in the middle of the night. My life as I knew it was changed irrevocably.

From when I could first remember, I have always loved the visual arts. I loved painting, arts and crafts, pattern, illustration, anything having to do with making something visual. I was not keen on abstract expressionism, and not too keen on pop art, although some of it interested me. I was more interested in art of an earlier time. Ancient up to 20th century and mainly representational. I was interested in and worked from archeology, ancient architecture, mosaic, fresco and sculpture and landscape. I was also drawn to mythology. I hadn't been out of CA until I spent a summer in London when I was 16 with a friend's family. I remember spending time in the museums there, and just being in a city that was so much older and different from LA was amazing for me. During that time, we also spent a week in Rome which I thought was astounding—and still do.

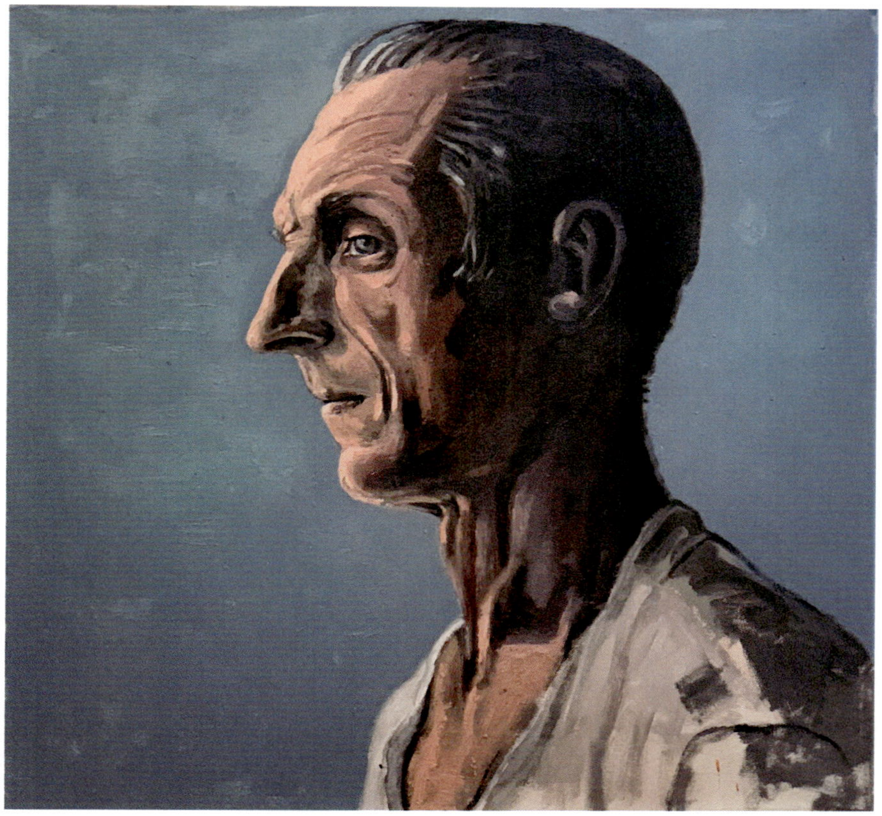

Richard Baker *Uncle*
c. 1984, oil on canvas, 38 x 40 in.

Richard Baker: I grew up in a steel-working household in southeast Baltimore. We lived in a very small, red brick row house in a "white-flight" neighborhood designed by Bethlehem Steel to provide workers with housing so that they could be closer to their jobs. This also allowed many white people to flee urban neighborhoods which were becoming increasingly Black. My parents had been very comfortable living in the inner city with its vibrant neighborhood life, and with their relatives who all grew up there. Did they move to Dundalk because of economic opportunity or racist fear? I'll never know. Streets in my Dundalk neighborhood of West Inverness were named alphabetically A-Z (perhaps not to Z because the end streets ran into steel polluted creeks). The steel company had two plans of row home ownership: you could buy your house and the land it was on, or you could buy your house and rent the land your house sat on. Thank goodness my parents bought our brick row home AND the land it sat on.

Our family consisted of myself, my mother, father, a brother 12 years older than myself, a sister 10 years older than myself, another sister 4 years younger than myself, and two adult uncles—my mother's brothers. The adults chain smoked constantly! These were people from the depression era having only achieved upper elementary school educations. Both of my parents came from families with more than ten siblings on each side. Like most of their generation with similar backgrounds, better education for their children became a priority. Better education simply meant going to school of any kind.

My parents and uncles supported my various interests. For my benefit, depending on my many fluctuating interests, they subscribed to magazines, monthly project/craft kits and bought the entire World Book Encyclopedia including annual editions of science and history supplements. They bought Time/Life science books as well. I pored over images endlessly, reading captions like they were water for the island stranded.

I was interested in the sciences as a young man. Several public school teachers soured my interest. I floundered. The school system I grew up in the nineteen-seventies was rather chaotic and violent. Bullies existed on every corner. My introduction into art may seem cruel now, but I invented a way to deflect the brutal attentions of classroom thugs—magical thinking perhaps, but when I drew caricatures of other kids at the cafeteria table, the potentially dangerous thugs would laugh! I deflected attention away from myself. Without analysis, this was my introduction to being an artist.

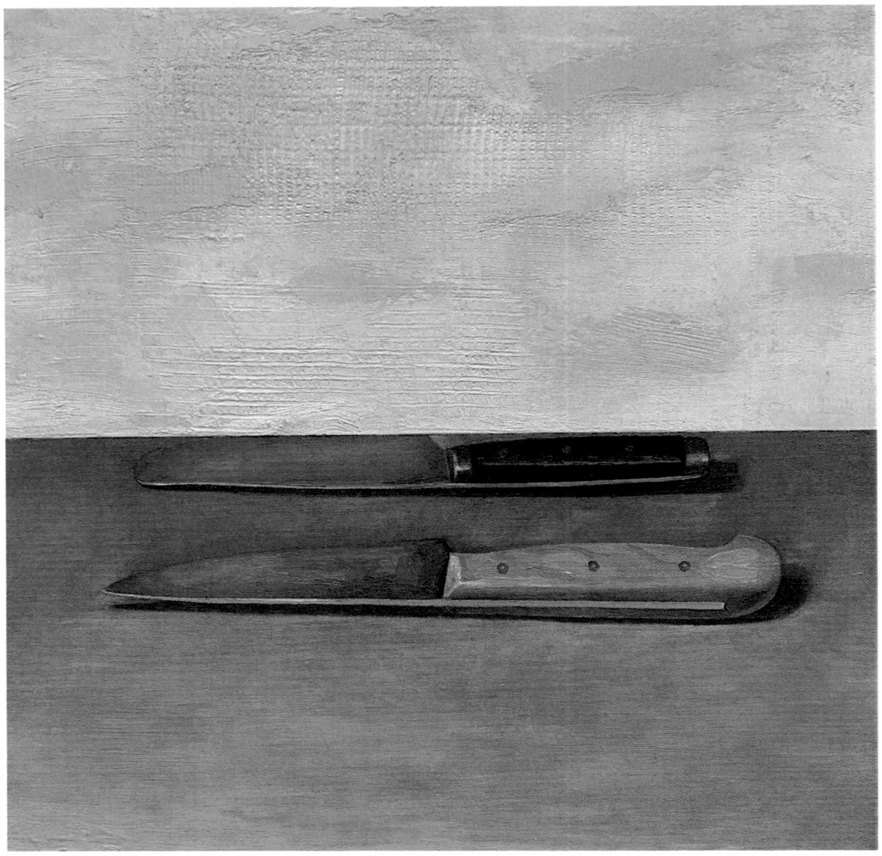

Richard Baker *Knives*
2021, oil on linen on panel, 12 x 12 in.

As a child, I was an opportunistic mixture of being obedient, introverted, strangely outgoing in some environments, and most definitely rebellious. In high school, I conjured inventive, and potentially criminal plans to spice up my neighborhood with various devious adventures. They were always disruptive of the status quo. But that's a story for another time!

Before I entered art school, I knew of a handful of artists: Salvador Dali, M.C. Escher, Picasso... I'm certain that there were a few more but I don't recall who those others were. None of them provided me with a sense of what being an artist was all about. I found my way into art without any clear idea of what it meant to be an artist. I'm certainly not alone in this.

Once I hit art school at MICA, it was an entirely different story! Joe Cardarelli introduced the Beats, NY School poets, and so much other literature; Mark Karnes made me look at things hard, really hard—what was I looking at, how does one translate what one sees onto a two-dimensional surface? James Hennessey showed me how to stretch a canvas when it was the last thing I was interested in doing (drawing was my declared undergraduate major). Despite my reticence, he somehow made painting seem an interesting thing to do.

I moved to Boston, went to the School of the Museum of Fine Arts and the adventure continued.

This is a fragment of the story of my formative years. Still forming...

PF: *I notice that, although your 2 sets of parents came from notably different worlds, they encouraged you to follow your star and to go on to study art. You both went to several art schools, and I'd like to ask both about your formal and informal influences.*

Barbara, is schooling at the Slade quite different from classes in this country?

BK: Going to the Slade from UCLA was like going to the moon, it was so very different! Living in London with its old buildings, the Tube (subway), its very different habits from LA was a shock. At the Slade we started early, broke for "eleveneses," then for lunch, later on for 4:00 pm tea, then off to the pub later. It was housed in an old building and the main drawing room was in a lower level, flooded from above by light. In the past, horses were brought in as models. There were classical plaster casts in the corridors. The "campus" was entirely different from what it would be in the states. At the entrance there was a Beadle, who knew everyone's coming and going. There were no dormitories, so everyone lived off campus. There were no campus activities organized. My class comprised just 12 students who went through the 4 years together. One had a Mentor, mine was an art historian who was very distracted and we hardly ever met. I remember one of our meetings, he was blankly staring out a window and said out of the blue,"... bought my little girl a watch today"...

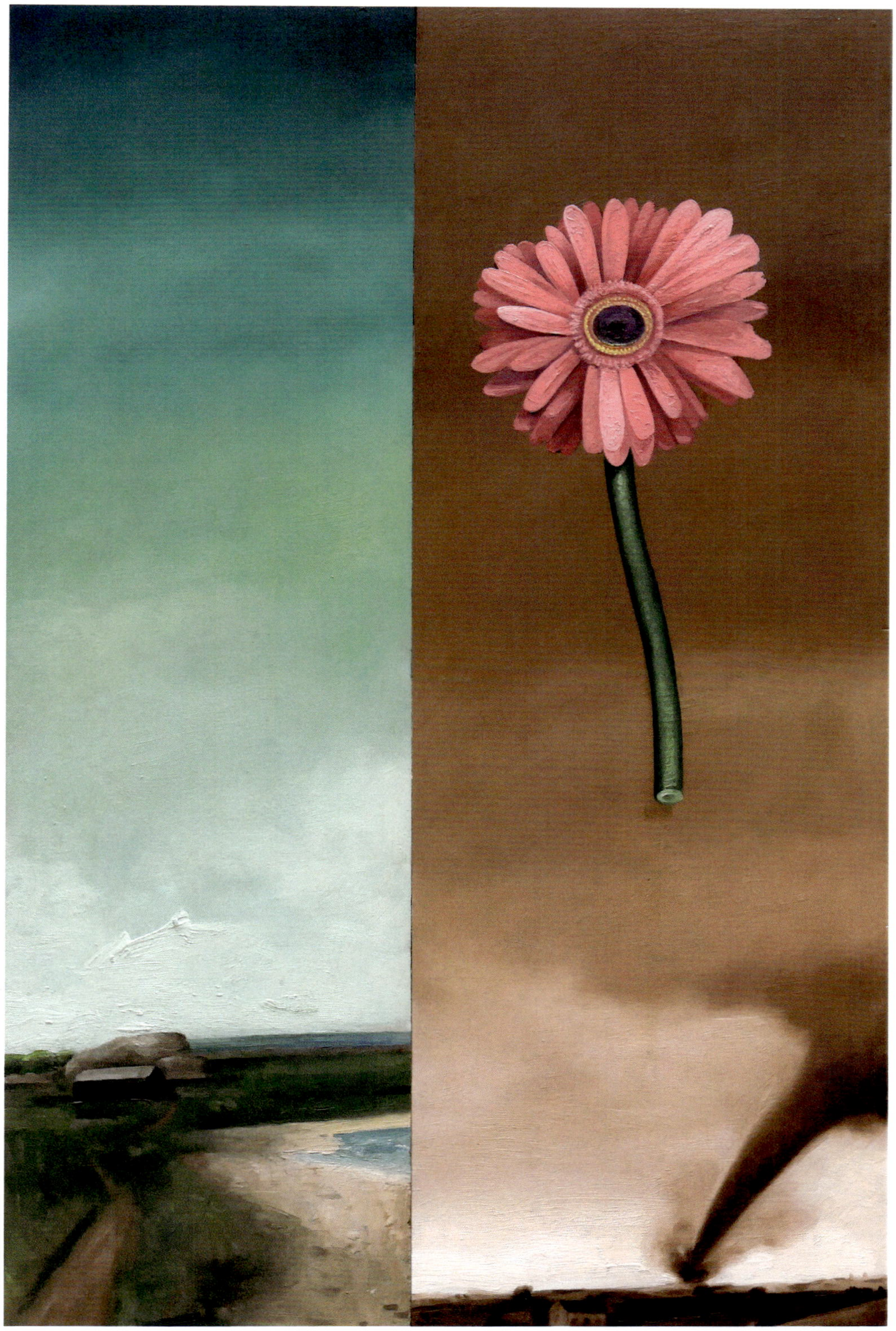

Richard Baker *Untitled*
2016, oil on two joined wood panels, 23 x 15 in.

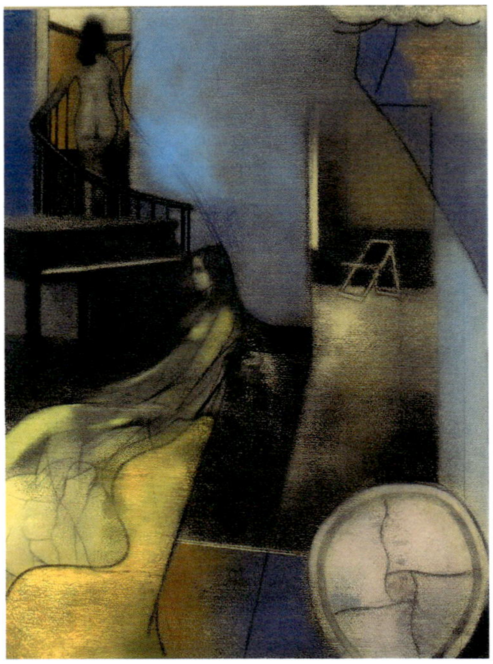

R.B. Kitaj *The Philosopher Queen*
1978, pastel and charcoal on paper, 30 ¼ x 22 in.

and that was it. It was, for me, an eccentric place, although I am sure that they thought the girl from California was pretty eccentric. During our first year, we had 4 very different tutors. Patrick George, Tess Jaray, Stuart Brisley and one other, whose name I can't remember (although I remember that one of his projects was to have us draw a complete interior on a small piece of chocolate using a pin). The classes were full days. My first day at the Slade was with Patrick George. He had us draw straight lines precise lengths without a ruler in the gloomy fall light. I was dismayed and thought "what am I doing here?!" The next session, we drew a pile of potatoes. That was better. We used the Euston Rd School method of measuring everything using one starting measurement. Sometimes we used calipers. These drawings would sometimes last weeks, as in my second year, Euan Uglow had us draw a bed spring for 3 weeks. We also took a class in "Materials and Methods" where we were taught how to properly prepare our canvases with rabbit skin glue and lead white, and how to make pastels and paints which gave me more of an understanding of how pigments bind and work. We took Art History classes at the Courtauld Institute and did studies from paintings there throughout the 4 years. After the first year we were left to mostly work independently with courses being offered by various teachers. The most memorable for me were working with Sir William Coldstream and learning the Euston Rd School method of painting. I remember him telling us that it was like making an omelette. He told us which colors to have on our palette, which brushes, how to set ourselves up so we would not move, position our easels so that we had a clear view, the model's position was taped on the floor, as were ours. We would work all day, for 3 weeks or more on a painting. It was fascinating. Some of the students became acolytes of this method. I dipped in and out of it during my four years. I still use the method, scaled back, when I draw. It teaches one to look closely at the relationships between things. Other teachers who were memorable were Patrick George and Euan Uglow. Frank Auerbach came as a visiting teacher and we worked on a single figure drawing for weeks. Any time it was coming together, he would come by and erase it. All of our paper was worn thin or through.

We also went on a school trip to Russia in 1973 which was wild. It was incredible to be able to see the great museums in Moscow and Leningrad and to meet Russian art students. I remember the Russian minders as always being present. John Stezaker was the instructor who came with us. He was a far left socialist and I remember that he brought many pairs of jeans to sell on the black market there.

When I lived with Kitaj that summer, he encouraged me to apply to the Slade and to the Royal College of Art. I applied to the Slade with a portfolio of drawings and was accepted to start that fall. Instead, I went back to my life in LA and UCLA, deciding not to marry, and asked the Slade if I could postpone my entrance to the following year. Although Kitaj did not teach at the Slade, he remained a major influence in my life. I never would have thought of going to England to an art academy. He was a very intense, driven, literary, Jewish (that was very important to him) person, with a dry sense of humor and I loved his artwork. I remember that he gave me a reading list which started with Madame Bovary. We met often and I modeled for him during my time at the Slade and when he came to the States later. My father had died only 2 years before I met him, and that had a huge impact on the trajectory of my life. I don't think that my father would have been keen on any of that.

PF: *Richard, tell us about MICA and the School at the Museum of Fine Arts.*

RB: This is a Hannah Arendt quote I'm rather fond of, "Education is the point at which we decide whether we love the world enough to assume responsibility for it." That's a good place to begin answering your question. I don't think my education as an artist truly began until after I left art school. As a student, I had the very real demands of earning enough money to pay rent, buy food, art materials, and all else, but it was only when I entered the world at large that I began to assume real responsibility of my life, for my art, and for my fledgling sense of the world.

Art school was incredibly important in supplying me with a foundation of technical know-how, and, as I said earlier, it provided an eye-opening introduction to subjects and ideas broadening my experience and worldview. But nowhere in my "formal" education were certain essential questions raised. For example, the issue of how an artist uses the elements of a lived life as the material of their art was never raised. It wasn't until the studio was empty of assignments and suggestions that the issue of how to think about the relationship between art and life began to truly matter. Of course, Rauschenberg's famous remark, "Painting relates to both art and life. Neither can be made. I try to act in that gap between the two" was well known to me. What it actually meant in practice was lost to me until I had to figure out how to negotiate both life and art as processes.

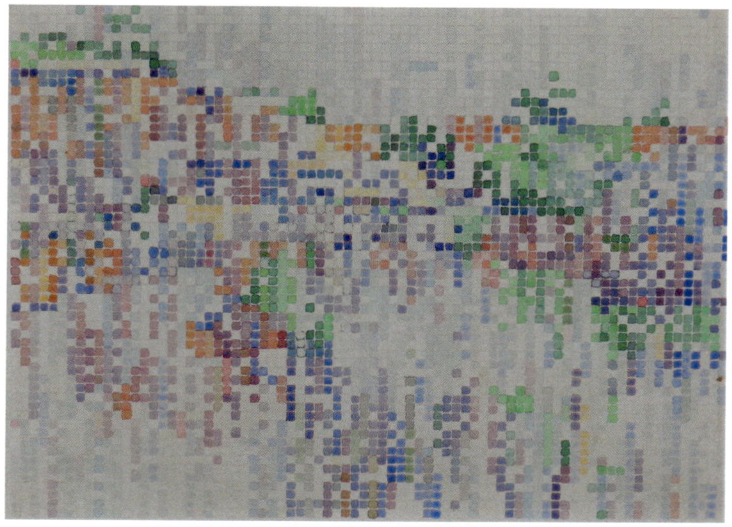

Barbara Kassel
Yale at Norfolk Color Study
1975, watercolor on silkscreened grid printed on arches paper, 12 x 18 in.

BK: Richard, I remember Mark Karnes from MICA when I was teaching there. He is a very nice person and a wonderful painter! I went onto his website after reading your answer and his paintings are terrific. I love their sense of observation and touch.

I applied to the Yale at Norfolk program my third year at the Slade and went that summer. That was also a shock. I remember arriving jet lagged from London to the studio there where everyone was busy stretching up multiple canvases. Our first crit was the afternoon of the first day. A complete change from the methodical, slow work at the Slade! I had a piece of printed graph paper with some squares painted in as a beginning color study. Everyone else seemed to have finished paintings. At the end of the residency, the teachers suggested that I apply to Yale for graduate school, which I did. I would not have done that without that experience.

In graduate school at Yale, William Bailey was a good teacher although he was on leave my first year. He, Bernie Chaet, Lester Johnson and Andrew Forge were the only professors who were not invested in machismo and bullying. Out of the 15 students in my class, one quit, one jumped off Niagara Falls, his body found some months later, and one was taken away literally in a straight jacket. The pressure and the insidiousness of the program were horrible. I was a teaching assistant for Gretna Campbell and she was great. There were no female instructors at the graduate level.

PF: *Are there others, outside of art school, who helped you in painting?*

BK: Phyllis, there are other people, but I have stuck with people who were influential up to my mid 20s. When I was 30, I entered a juried show in Baltimore, where I was living, with Marcia Tucker as the judge. She gave my painting a prize and invited me to meet with her in NYC. I came up with paintings wrapped in cardboard, slung over my shoulder to meet with her in her loft. She bought one. Shortly after, she included me in her Artist Update (I think that was the title) talk. I had no idea she was doing this. I was called by half a dozen NY galleries asking me to come in to meet them. I went up to the city again with my packages of paintings and met with several. I ended up going with Kathryn Markel, who was a wonderfully enthusiastic dealer. The following summer I was on a summer residency at Yaddo, when the phone rang and I was told that I was going to be included in the Venice Biennale, curated by Marcia Tucker. She was a major help for me to get NYC gallery representation and to start a career. And she was such a lovely person.

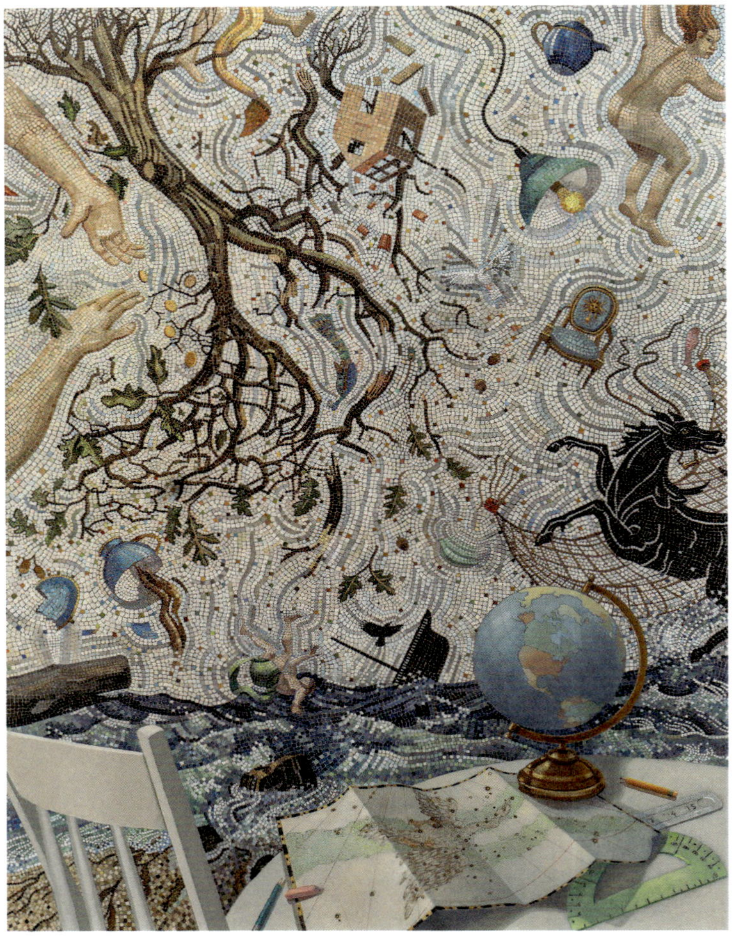

Barbara Kassel *The Plague*
2020, oil on linen on panel, 40 x 30 in.

Fellow artists—for some years I would go in with a couple of other painters and rent a farmhouse in Umbria where we would paint plein air. We were task masters—painting two hours at each site for three or four sites a day. I am still close to those painters.

I was close to Roy Osborne, who was a technician in the print department at the Slade. He studied color theory and introduced me to Seurat and the Science of Painting and other books about color. I began to study color theory and to do almost pointillist work using small graph paper where I would try and record what I was seeing. This continued for some years, and now with my "mosaic" paintings, here I am again, but these are imaginative and not observational per se.

I remember drawing from the model with Sharon Yates while I was living in Baltimore and teaching at MICA. That was great fun and intense.

Traveling extensively drawing and painting in many situations and countries taught me a lot. I loved it. I still do. I always bring my supplies and anywhere I stay becomes a studio. Recently I have started to use my iPad Pro and a program called Procreate to work on. I took it to Paris a few years ago and worked extensively on drawings and paintings from my hotel room or in the parks. In New York last spring and summer, I worked from the city views from the apartment with both my iPad and my oils.

RB: One experience in school has had relevance to many things in creating art and beyond. Barnett Rubenstein was an instructor I had at the Museum School. During one of our more important crits, there was a student who was in great distress over her work. She agitatedly rambled on about numerous disappointments: how the work didn't meet her expectations, how she came nowhere near to fulfilling her intentions, and through her sobs, she stated that she simply felt like a huge failure. Barney asked her to pause for a second, he shook his head from side to side, looked directly at her, a slight smile formed on his face barely detectable beneath his giant white moustache, and said, "Sometimes it's important to simply take the path of least resistance." How true I have often found that nugget of gold! That nugget has been true and useful in many situations.

PF: *Have you yourselves taught, and, if so, did you enjoy it?*

RB: I taught undergraduate painting at the Mason Gross School of the Arts at Rutgers University for eleven years. It was of paramount importance to me that I met each individual student on the bedrock of their own emerging sensibilities. I always sought a give-and-take dialogue seeking a "path of least resistance" which could illuminate the challenging process of growth for each artist, each person. I found the experience immensely rewarding.

BK: I taught at Colby College right out of graduate school. It felt remote and everyone else seemed to be going to the city. Once I settled in though, I liked it very much. I loved teaching the students and stayed two years. I left my tenure track position when I got married and moved to Baltimore where my first husband had an offer from Johns Hopkins. I cobbled together part time teaching at MICA which I also loved, even though it was stressful not knowing what and if I would have a class and the pay was low. I was in the process of going through interviews there for a full time position (which was eventually offered) when I was offered a tenure track position at Goucher College which I took. I taught as a visiting professor in the Art Department at Harvard for a term when I lived in Cambridge.

BK: I had learned a very valuable lesson from my experience at Yale. I am opposed to tearing students apart, belittling them and forcing them to make work that is not authentic. I was told by Al Held that I was a big disappointment as I didn't turn out to be the abstract painter they thought that I was. They couldn't see that my work was about the study of color and although the form was a grid, it all came from observation. After that encounter, I barred my studio and painted what the hell I wanted to. And the subject turned out to be loss and memory. What I see more now in art schools is the teaching on how to navigate the art world rather than focusing on the making. Reading art criticism and studying literary criticism. I have never found any of that of much, if any interest to myself. I've gone to some MFA shows these past years which are all about the resume. Getting in contact with collectors and galleries, explaining what you are doing rather than focusing on the making of the work. It is depressing to me.

PF: *Do you think the study of art history is essential to those aspiring to career as painter?*

BK: I can't say what is essential to others quite honestly. For me, it was and is essential.

RB: There are as many ways of becoming an artist as there are individuals. The study of art history for an artist is a very different beast than it is for an art historian. For an artist, it is by necessity a much more pliable and less restrictive study. The study of art history can offer inspiration and can be a powerful tool and resource—it is one thing to look at the surface of a body of water, and quite another to peer into its depths.

The most useful and fulfilling way to study art history is simply to wander, without aim or purpose, through the halls of great museums—it provides fuel and sustenance. In the end, each path to becoming an artist is a unique story, some stories are more interesting than others, there is nothing more boring than a "professional" artist.

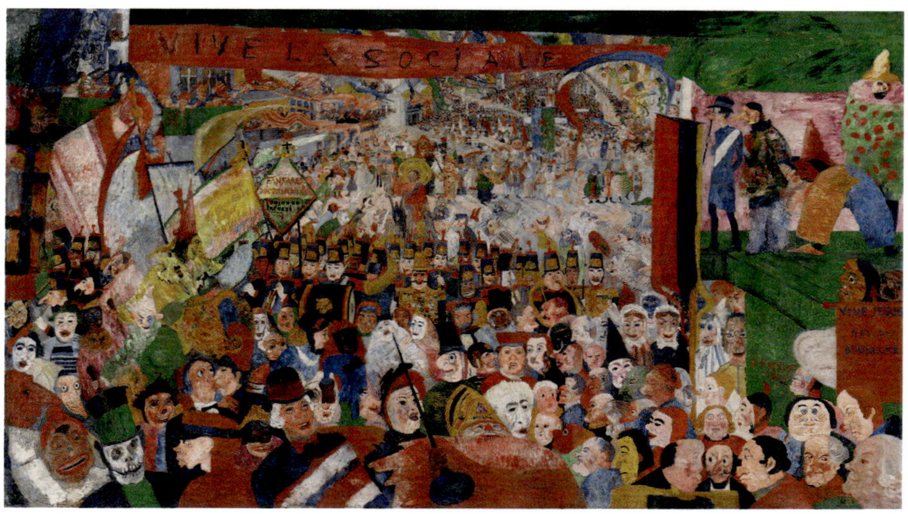

James Ensor
Christ's Entry into Brussels in 1889
1888, oil on canvas, 99 ½ x 169 ¾ in.

PF: *Richard and Barbara: You both have taught art classes and enjoyed doing so. Barbara has had the experience of teaching in quite a few colleges and universities. I am surprised that you both enjoyed it because I found teaching anxiety-producing.*

You both say that bullying in art schools is prevalent, but that you were on guard not to let that practice become part of your classwork. It seems to me that you want to help young people find their own way in their lives as painter. Do you think that any of your students were struggling financially?

Did you ever worry that there would be nothing for them after all that time spent in school? That they wouldn't succeed as you have?

BK: I did get anxious! But after the class got going, that dissipated.

At Colby College many of the supplies were supplied to the students, as well as at Harvard. And there were funds that students could use. I don't remember MICA's policy on that.

I let them know my thoughts about how difficult it could be making a living as an artist. Bu I also thought that many of my students at Colby and Harvard were not necessarily going to be artists. I figured that if you were in an art school, like MICA, it would be more likely that students would want to become artists. I didn't discourage them, only made them open to other possible options along the way. Success is a relative term. And it can come and it can go. Luck plays a large role career wise. I know many wonderful painters who have had a very difficult time career wise. If you can't come to terms with that, if you can live a life without working visually, then a career in the visual arts is not for you.

RB: Before I answer your last set of questions, I need to clarify something. The bullying I mentioned earlier occurred for me in public schools prior to art school. Though the art school environment could indeed be extremely competitive, I was unaware of any outright bullying there.

"Success" in the art world is a rather ambiguous and enormously flexible concept. Because of my successes in finding/fashioning circumstances conducive to having painting be my "job," I came to teaching late in life. Outside of workshops and visiting artist positions, Rutgers was my sole teaching commitment. You ask about whether any of my students struggled financially, yes! Far too many did. The Mason Gross School of the Arts at Rutgers University is a state school and as such, its demographic ranged far and wide. It was frequently painful to work with students who couldn't afford decent basic supplies. Often, the upside was that their resourcefulness and scrappiness had to be inventive regarding material use. In my direct experience, and in anecdotal evidence supplied by friends and colleagues, the elephant in the room in undergraduate classes is considerations of the professional and career aspects of the desire to be an artist. Those issues were confronted only when a student would voice direct questions about how to survive and thrive as an artist in the world at large. Honest answers always brought gasps of surprise and incredulous expressions of horror!

PF: *I'd like to know what you think about moving around as opposed to staying put. Both of you now live in Massachusetts—Richard in Cambridge and Barbara in Martha's Vineyard. Can you describe your surroundings? Are they particularly good for an artist?*

Is your studio in your residence? I believe you have both lived in New York and that your children live here. What do you think of this city as home for artists?

Phyllis Floyd
Flowering Daisies
1998, watercolor on paper, 9 x 12 in.

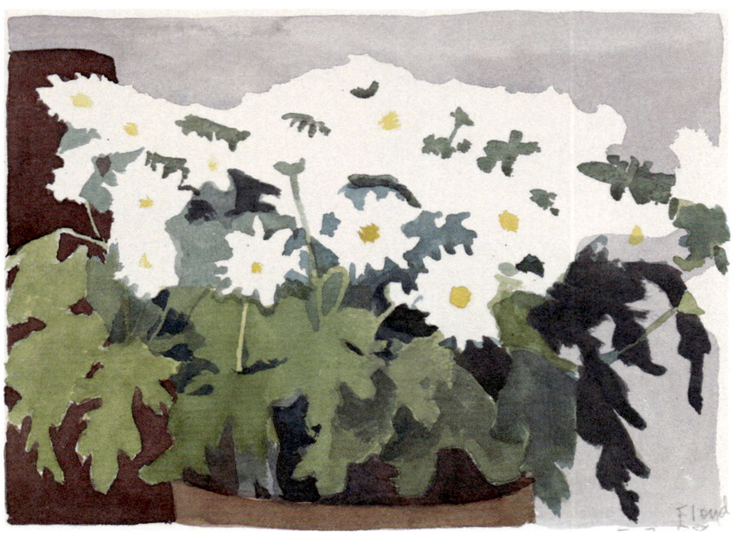

RB: When I attended the Museum School, I worked at Reading International, a bookstore in Harvard Square. A very dear friend and coworker, artist Carolyn May, transferred the lease on her Fort Point Channel loft to me. That was encouragement enough to leave art school. Needless to say, living in a very large, very illegal (commercially zoned) space overlooking the Boston Harbor with views straight out to Logan Airport was a formative experience indeed! It pretty much set the tone for my future endeavors in that it solidified my commitment to art-making as the heart of all my energies.

I lived in New York for twenty-five years. My first years there, I lived in lower Manhattan on Second Street between the Bowery and Second Avenue with my studio a couple of blocks away on Chrystie Street. My studio was on the smallish side but I had

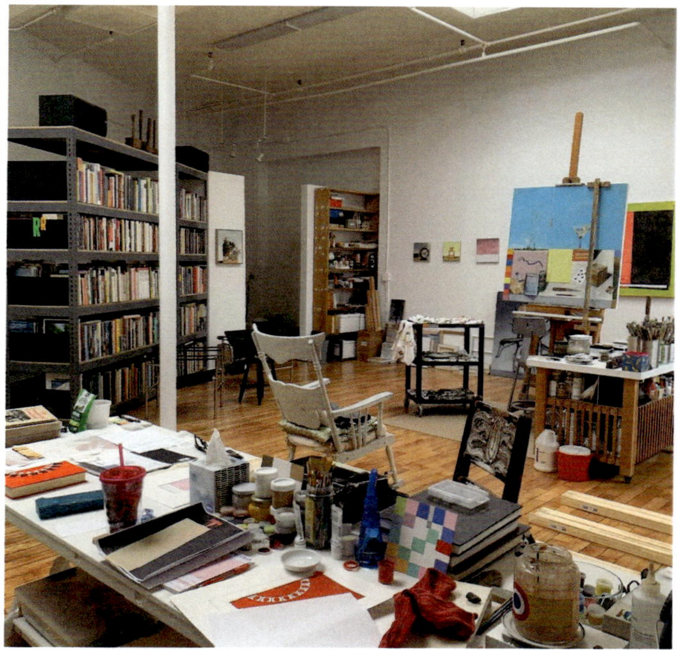

Barbara Kassel's Martha's Vineyard studio

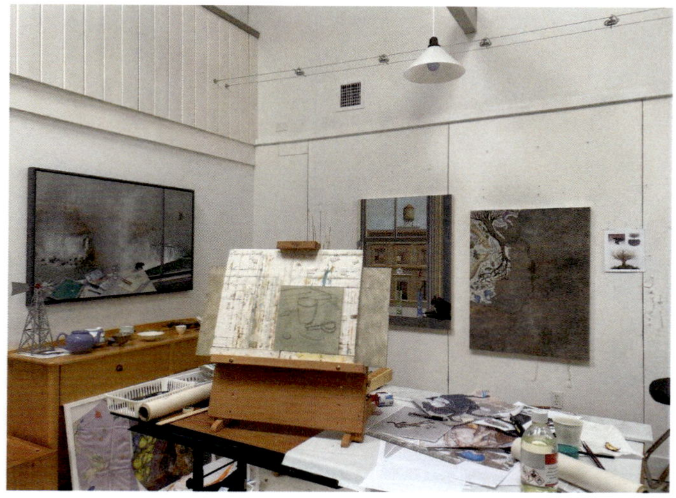

Richard Baker's current studio in Somerville, MA

unobstructed big-sky views straight up to the Empire State building and beyond, and I could walk home for lunch. My remaining years in NY were spent living in Brooklyn Heights with a character-filled studio an easy walk down the hill to DUMBO. That studio had a vaulted red brick ceiling and fragmented views of the East River and over to Manhattan. I rented that studio for nearly twenty years. My current studio in Cambridge is a four-minute walk from home. By some sort of divine magic, most of the studios I've occupied have been absurdly close to my homes.

For an artist, New York is everything said about it, good and bad. By the end of my time there, I found it economically unsustainable, stressful, and counterproductive. In keeping up with the economic and logistical demands I found myself increasingly unable to partake of the many reasons to be in NY in the first place: world-class museums, an enormous and vibrant gallery scene, abundant social events, etc. Exhaustion had set in. What do I think of it as a home for artists? I don't know how young artists can make it work. In recent years, I've witnessed an absurd decrease in the sizes of studios available on the market to rent. There was a point in time when I considered 300 square foot spaces as nearly unworkable. But in recent years I've seen numerous 100 square foot spaces for rent! I've even seen smaller ones listed! Geesh! My move to Cambridge was a much needed change of scene. Honestly, I can't comment on how livable it is for artists here in general—I relocated just before the pandemic hit which clouded my ability to see what Cambridge has to offer under normal circumstances. Despite my having an excellent studio in a great location, one thing I can say for sure, is like in all desirable places to live, decent, affordable studio spaces are in short supply. Beyond that, it would be folly to weigh the benefits or deficits of living anywhere to NY.

In my opinion, I think that moving around a bit geographically is enriching. It doesn't really matter whether one broadens their viewpoint, their worldview, through travel or via occasional relocation. Of course, as I said earlier, there are no fixed rules in how one comes to be an artist. After all, though Titian did visit a few European cities, he was happiest journeying the terrain between his hometown of Pieve di Cadore and his adopted Venice; Giorgio Morandi rarely left Italy; Rene Magritte's epicenter was Belgium; Pablo Picasso held court in Western Europe.

BK: My husband, Jed Devine, who is a photographer, and I lived in a rent stabilized 2500 square ft loft in Tribeca. He lived there from 1974. He fought eviction from almost the moment he moved in with his first wife, a dancer. I moved in 2002 and we fought eviction the entire time with various landlords. There was little heat or hot water during many of those years, and the building was very

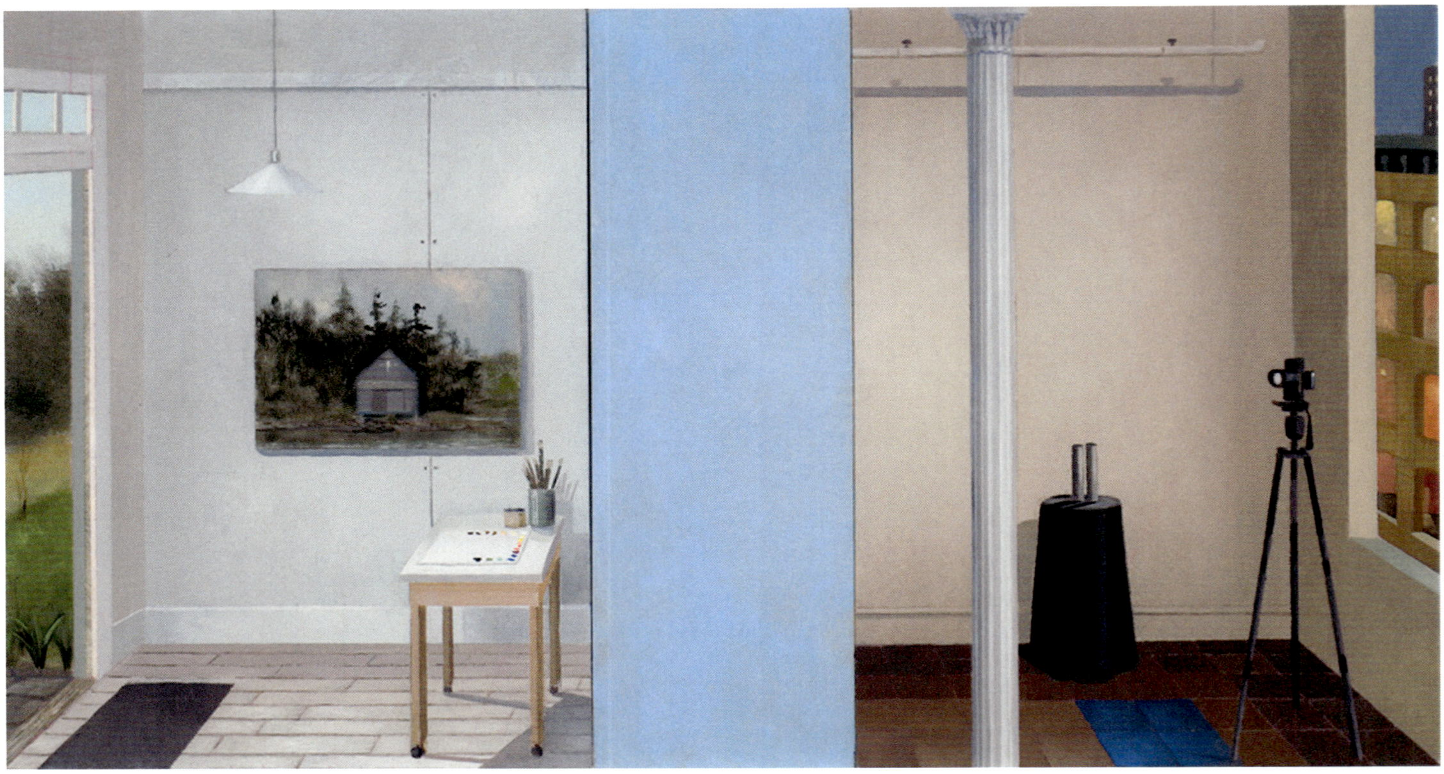

Barbara Kassel *Two Studios*
2002, oil on panels, 12 x 20 in.

run down. But it was a great space! Eventually the building was vacated (death, eviction, buyouts) and only my husband and I and Donna Dennis, a sculptor were left in the building. It was a bit spooky. It was a steep 80 stair walk up for Jed and I and that took a toll. The most recent landlord was serious about buying the last 2 lofts out so we took a buy out and moved two and a half years ago. I have a small house on Martha's Vineyard from the late 1980s with a great light filled studio, so we moved up here full time. I miss the city, but it was the right time for this move for many reasons. We have rented in the city for a few months a year since and hope to do so again, when and if the pandemic lets up.

We live on seven acres surrounded by fields and woods, but we are only 10 minutes from Vineyard Haven or West Tisbury. I love the seasons here and we have beautiful gardens, fields, trees, stone walls and a view of a small pond, which is now frozen and that kids play ice hockey on, which we love. We feel like we are living in a Brueghel! When the ocean is warm enough, I swim a mile or more a day from June into October (that is if I can stand it!).

I would say yes. I enjoy painting outdoors sometimes, or on the screen porch and it is great to be able to walk down to the studio, from the house. There are also a number of professional artists who live here, and an active art community.

I loved living in New York and never thought that I would. I was divorced a year and thought of moving back to LA after 30 years. I even looked at apartments. But then a friend, Sharon Olds, introduced me to Jed and my life took another turn.

Having the loft was amazing, and the rent was incredibly cheap. Without that, who knows what I would have thought. I was able to live in a huge loft, room for both of us to work, the two cats, and be in New York. When I first moved in, I had no idea what I would paint. I was used to working more with far horizon line views, and more dreamlike paintings. The loft faced directly onto the buildings across the street. I found that I "painted my way back into my life." I worked on interiors, views of the buildings across the street, still life. It was always interesting, change of light, time of day, view, objects. One of my shows while living in the city was titled 135 Duane Street. After not thinking that I had a subject, I found that I did, for 17 years. My paintings became more personally narrative.

I think that the city is a great place for artists, except, and this is a big except, the cost of having a place to work and live is so very expensive. It has become even more prohibitive and so very difficult to find. I was extremely lucky in my situation.

The energy of the city seems changed to me, including the art scene. So much of it has moved to art fairs and now digital. Art as commodity. Art as investment, not as experience. It used to be exciting to go to the openings, see the work, see friends. There are still the wonderful museum shows and gallery shows, and I miss being able to go to those so easily. As well as concerts and plays. Maybe my view of this is colored also by the pandemic, where so many in person experiences are just not possible any longer.

Actually, writing this, I miss the city quite a lot! Just walking down the street, stopping for a coffee in a diner or cafe, walking along the Hudson, over the Brooklyn Bridge, Chinatown, the mix of architecture, parks, the people, restaurants, the mix of it all. I really miss my friends who live there and the ease of getting together. It is very quiet where we live now.

PF: *Richard, you cite Rauschenberg's remark "Painting relates to both art and life. Neither can be made. I try to act in the gap between the two." I can't understand the word "made" and, in fact, can you elaborate on that quote?*

RB: For me, the Rauschenberg remark regarding art and life, how "neither can be made," uses the word "made" to express a kind of intentionality. It presumes that one can set out to make art or life and have that happen, just like you might determine that you want to make a cake and then do so. When he speaks of operating in the gap between art and life, he implies movement between the two and in that movement, that dance, either occurs, as if conjured by the movement itself. Life and art happen, they are not "made."

PF: *It is clear that New York residential and studio space is expensive—that is, unless you have a rent stabilized loft or apartment. But remember that in New York you don't need a car, nor do you have to pay someone to shovel snow.*

BK: Ah yes! You are right there! Here you need a car and someone to shovel and plow snow!

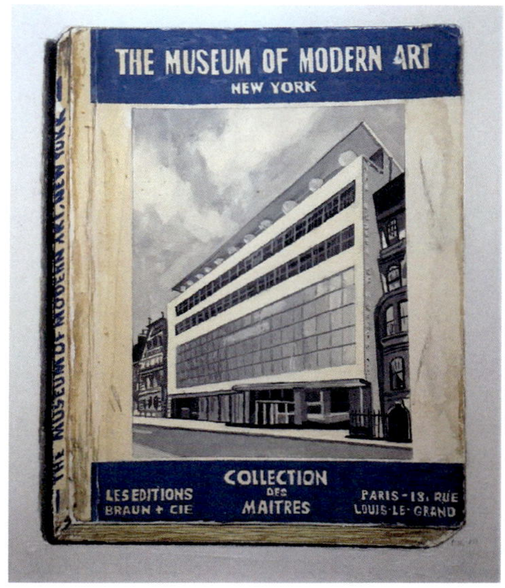

Richard Baker *Collection Des Maitres (MOMA)*
2017, gouache on watercolor paper, 12 x 10 ½ in.

RB: For young artists starting out, real estate affordability is quite an obstacle. I don't know if there are many lucky situations remaining there, certainly, there are few opportunities in the most desirable hubs. Having a car in New York can be an incredible hassle, though it does make difficult-to-get-to neighborhoods a little more accessible. If teaching, most likely as an adjunct these days, commuting can get terribly expensive—when I was teaching at Rutgers, the cost of a monthly MTA pass and a NJT pass ran into big figures. Artists are often rather scrappy and resourceful, so I'm sure that the most clever will find ways to thrive.

PF: *Yes, the word "success" means different things to different people. For purposes here, let's say that you've reached success when your "job" is that of a painter. You both say that luck plays a part in that achievement, and that surroundings, whether city or country, are instrumental for satisfying work. Besides "needing" to paint, what about hard work? Do you have a routine or a certain amount of time allotted to painting?*

BK: I am out of my routine these days. Too much change in the past couple of years, including moving from the loft, adding onto our studio and home here and the pandemic (along with the

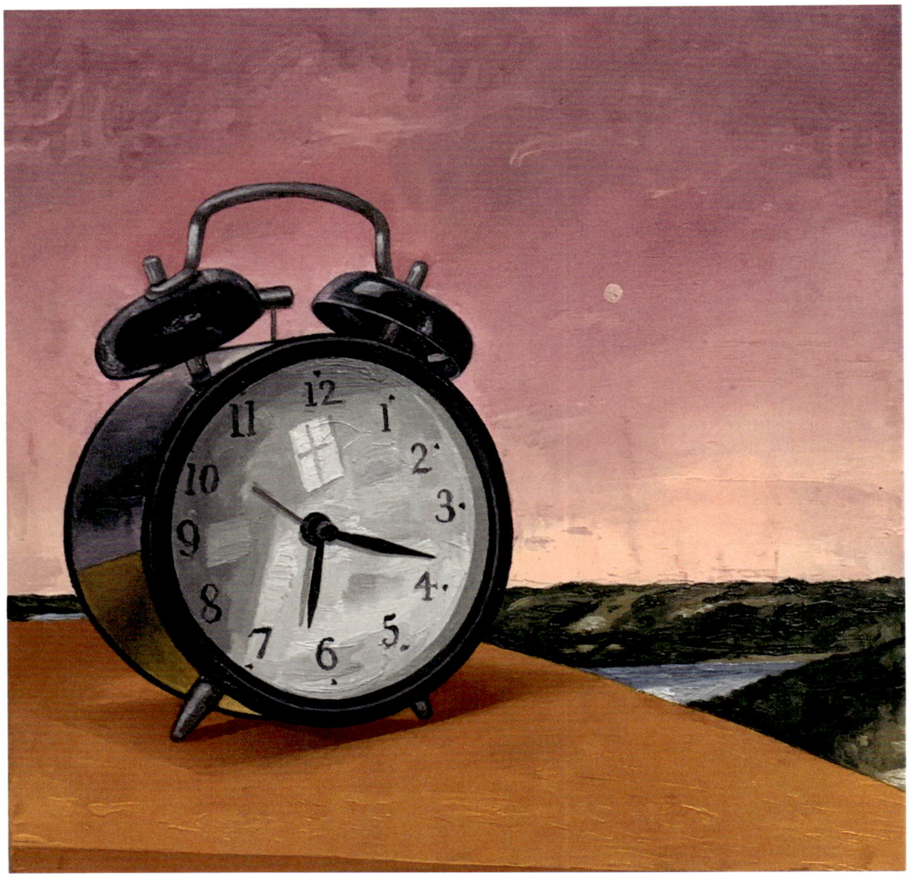

Richard Baker *Untitled*
2021, oil on linen on panel, 12 x 12 in.

imploding of our country). In more usual times, I paint anywhere from 5-7 hours a day. Depends on what I am working on and what else might be happening in my life. I feel out of sorts when I am out of my working rhythm, which is how I feel now. I am working on "mosaic" paintings that are very time consuming, but wonderfully meditative to work on. This means that I have finished far fewer paintings than I am used to.

RB: The artist Carol Bove wrote a wonderful piece about trying to avoid applying the word "work" to what we do as artists. What we do is far more flexible, lively, elemental and experimental than all that. Only my accountant, banker, IRS officials, doctors, or others quantifying matters for themselves, insisted on using the word "job" to describe what we do if we are fortunate enough to make a living from painting. I don't mean to imply that what we do stands outside the norms of regular commerce, but it is a rather strange and unreliable means of making a living. Success is a strange thing: what defines it? Is it making money, having income security, achieving some kind of status or critical acclaim? Who knows, it's a moving target, best determined by each individual artist.

When I was raising young children, I tried to keep "banker's hours." Since I didn't have to punch a time clock, I was always "on call" which definitely had an impact on studio hours. I now visit my studio daily. Not all days are the same. Sometimes I engage in projects at home, sometimes whole days are consumed with matters in the studio. My studio life follows me wherever I happen to be.

PF: *Are you swayed by what others say about your work? Should an artist develop a thick skin?*

RB: Curious question. Creatively, I think the artist's skin should always remain porous, or a semipermeable membrane. But I do think it wise to cultivate an indifference to certain potentially irritating experiences such as witnessing a viewer walk into one of your exhibitions, twist their head around for twenty seconds at best, and then exit quickly on their heels. Of course, best not to take press too much to heart, nor comments like, "I liked your older work better." Despite the necessity of social media, it's also best to have an indifference to the glut of images seen there—everything is seen at the same size, in the same format, and there is very little acknowledgment that the art works exist as objects in the real world, objects with surfaces, a sense of touch, scale, materiality—this "sameness" can be taken far too seriously.

BK: Honestly, I am not very swayed by what others say about my work. Have never been and am even less so as I get older. Do I feel happy if someone responds to my work in a positive way? Yes. I don't seem to have other artists or anyone for that matter, over for studio visits. But when that has happened, I am open to what they might say about the paintings. Part of the reason I enjoyed painting plein air with friends was the ease of us looking at each other's work. I miss that. My husband has a great eye and I have found him to be a great help when I am trying to figure out something. As for having a thick skin? Who knows, depends on one's makeup! I don't happen to have a thin skin. I remember going to an opening for a group show of four artists I was in many years ago. A man came up to me and said "How does it feel to be the only artist not to have sold a painting at the opening?" I smiled and turned away. I paint for myself, which may sound selfish, but I don't know what else to say about why. But I appreciate it when people see my paintings and respond.

***PF:** Why do some smart and savvy people choose to live their lives as painters when it is not practical and the future looks grim?*

BK: Because it is what they want to do in their lives. It is part of what gives their lives meaning. Because you are not yourself without it. This has been my experience at least. None of us has a crystal ball. Who knows what might happen in any given lifetime? No use thinking that a future that hasn't happened yet is grim. We live in the present. Perhaps it was easier years ago. When I graduated with my MFA, I was able to get a teaching position which allowed me to earn income and paint at the same time. That is certainly much more difficult now. But even if I were starting out now, that wouldn't dissuade my pursuing painting.

RB: The future has always been "grim." I don't mean that in a bleak way. Everything has its historical context. The best and the worst among us strive beyond those limitations. Yes, "drive" is an often used word to describe why an artist does what they do in the face of enormous difficulties. But what else motivates us to keep on going? It may sound a bit romantic, but I think it's a kind of core and sustaining optimism about our humanity.

***PF:** You both are submitting work for the next Zeuxis show called "For the Love of Chardin." Do you have any insights about Chardin?*

RB: The absolute poise and frozeness in Chardin's painting *Soap Bubbles* is arresting. Of course, silence is often mentioned when Chardin is discussed and in this painting, it is deafening. The tension, that everything is frozen in anticipation of the

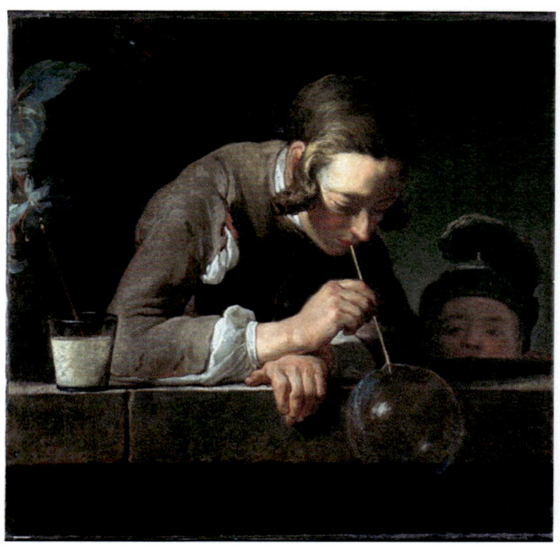

Jean Siméon Chardin *Soap Bubbles*
c. 1933-34, oil on canvas, 24 x 24 ⅞ in.

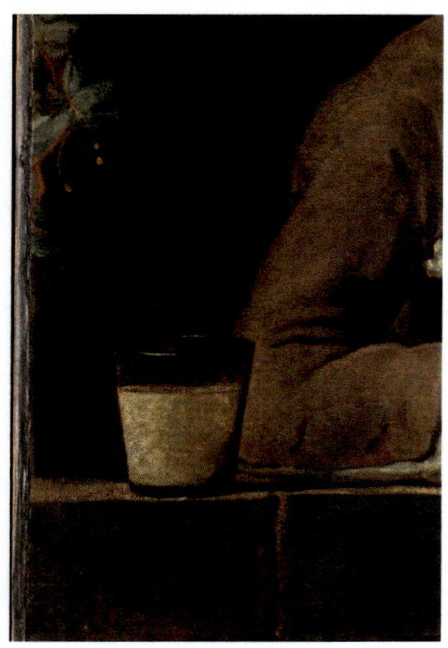

Detail from Chardin's *Soap Bubbles*

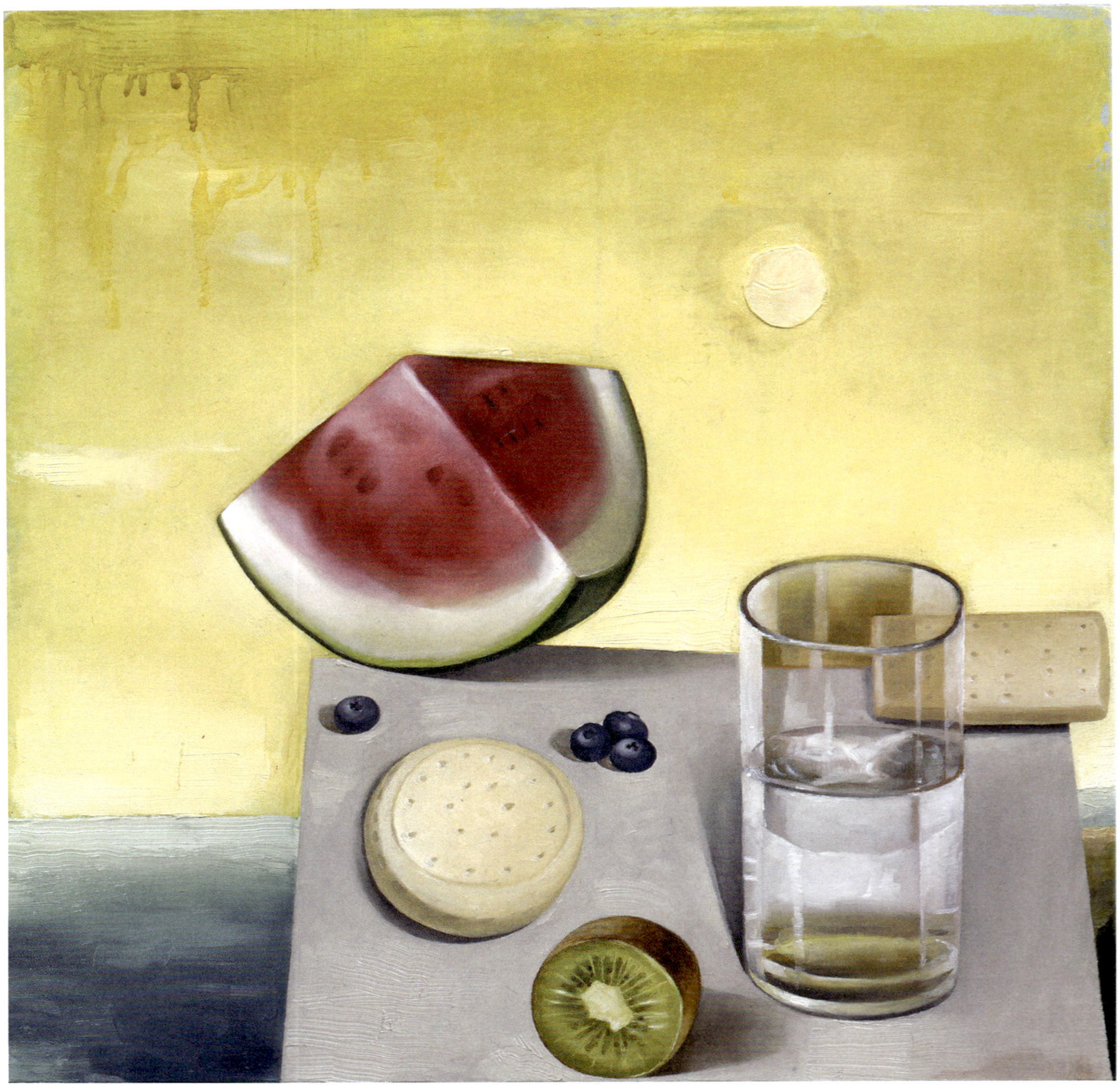

Richard Baker *Wedge*
2004, oil on wood panel, 16 x 16 in.

next moment, and that the image holds prior moments in its memory, reminds me of a loaded gun, or the glimpse of a knife in a Film Noir classic—intimations that the picture of the world we spy upon threatens to radically change. There is also something haunting about how the glass of soap recalls a glass of milk. This is reinforced by the presence of the small child glimpsed beyond the window ledge, curiously beholding the perfect bubble held in suspension. This is a world seen as confident and fragile at once, a secure but vulnerable place, like the illusion of childhood itself, fed on milk and protected by stone walls. For all its solidity, Chardin's depicted world of passing moments and objects, tugs at the edges of insecurity. I find that profoundly beautiful.

BK: I remember looking at Chardin first when I was a student at the Slade. I was first struck by the quality of touch in his work. The beauty, harmony of color and tone, and the buttery quality of his paint. One wants to reach out and touch the painting. I like his choice of subject matter, the everyday, the ordinary and the beauty in that. Nothing of grandiosity or posturing in his work. I like the feel of his direct observation in his paintings. The deep pleasure of that activity and translation into paint on a surface.

He is a virtuoso, but without the bravura or bragging. I love the way that he breaks the picture plane very often in his compositions. Like the ceramic pitchers with their handles turned to the viewer, a

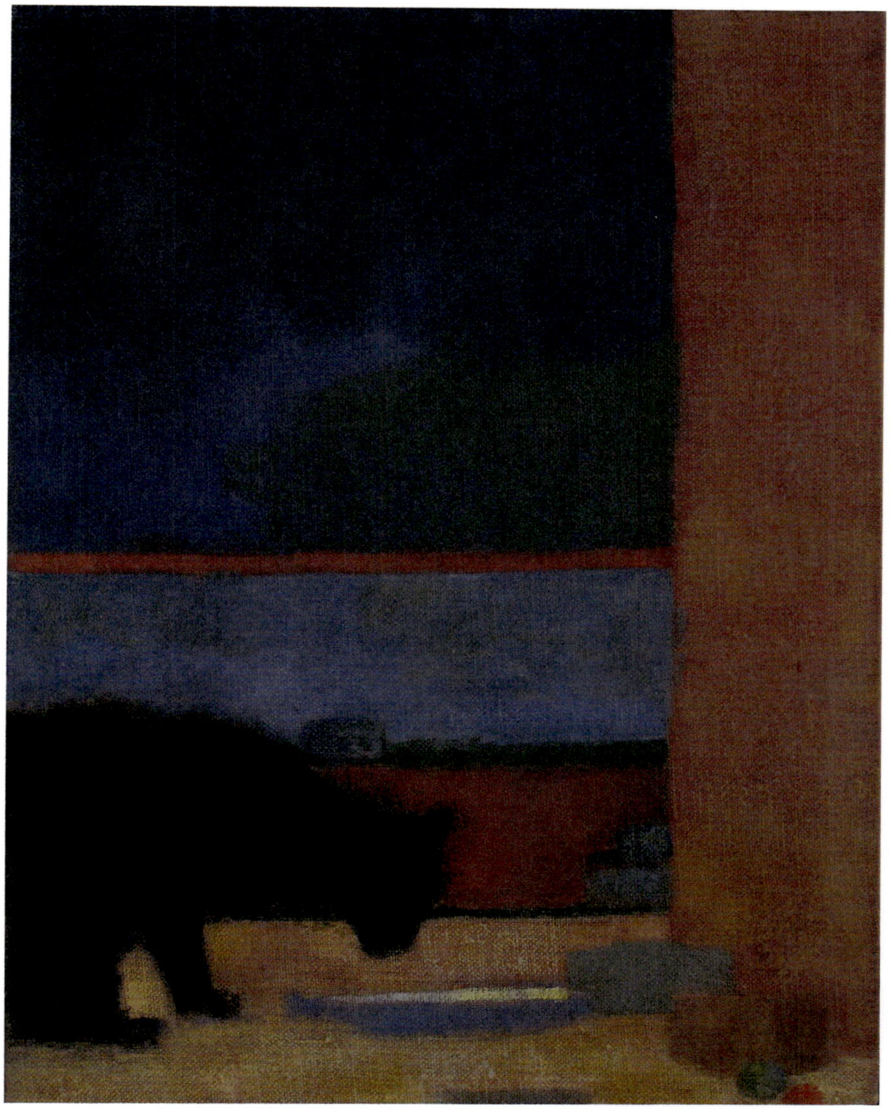

Barbara Kassel
Kipper at Water Bowl
1977, oil on canvas, 21 x 19 in.

rabbit's paw hanging over the edge of a table, a curling lemon or orange peel unfurling over an edge, a sheaf of papers, a pipe, a bubble being blown by a boy with its implicit bursting of that bubble.

I think that there is commentary in his work. The multiple paintings of the young boy constructing a house of cards. Makes me think of the phrase, "The best laid plans…," and how very true that was in his life with the loss of his first wife and 3 of his children. When I look at those very still paintings, the probability of collapse animates them in a prescient way, and from the mischievous cats, coming in to take a piece of fish, a lap of milk etc. Which I have experienced with my cats! Vinny, was particularly interested in rearranging (and breaking things) with my set ups. I found that I painted them in their altered states at some points.

His paintings of figures are beautifully observed, simple and complicated at the same time. One can feel the human connection in them, his eyes intent on the person he is painting, which for me, translate into the viewer's eyes. His moving self portraits are absolutely wonderful and searching. In painting himself, Chardin brings into focus his humanity and humanness and love of the every-day. ◼

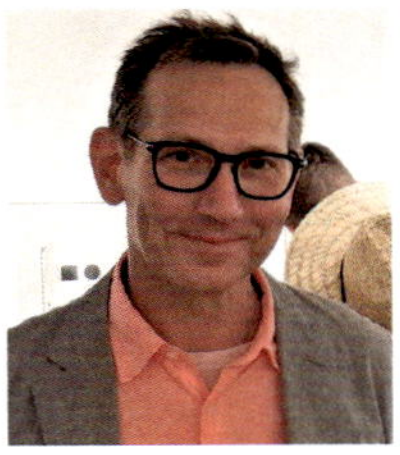

Richard Baker grew up in a steel working family in Baltimore, MD. After high school, he attended the Maryland Institute, College of Art, moving to Boston to complete his studies at the School of the Museum of Fine Arts. After graduating, he worked at a Harvard Square bookstore for several years while painting nights and weekends in a waterfront loft. He then spent a year building poolside sculptures for an artist/gallerist in Palm Beach, FL. After that, for a number of years, he managed a seasonal clothing store, earning enough money each summer to devote himself exclusively to painting through the winter in a shuttered town at the end of Cape Cod. The next 25 years were spent in New York, painting, exhibiting there and elsewhere, raising two children, and teaching in New Jersey at Rutgers University. He now lives in Cambridge, MA dedicated exclusively to daily work in his studio.

www.richardbakerartist.com

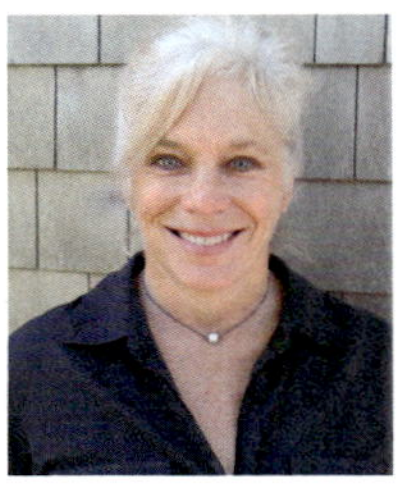

Barbara Kassel was born and raised in Los Angeles. She spent two years at UCLA and then went for four years to the Slade School of Art at University College London for an undergraduate degree in Fine Arts. She studied under Sir William Coldstream, Euan Uglow, Patrick George, Andrew Forge and others. After, she went to Yale University Art School where she did her MFA. She taught at Colby College, The Maryland Institute College of Art, Goucher College and Harvard. She has shown in NYC for 32 years and was represented by the Kathryn Markel Gallery, Maxwell Davidson Gallery and Hirschl and Adler Modern. She is represented presently by the Clark Gallery in Lincoln, MA. She paints still life, interiors and landscape, both plein aire and in the studio, using oils, watercolors and more recently, iPad digital. Her impulses are more metaphorical than realistic and she often mixes motifs. The work comes from her life, and in that way, it is narrative.

www.barbarakassel.com

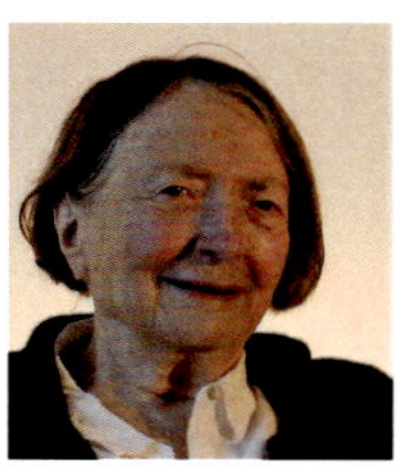

Phyllis Floyd lives and works in a loft in midtown Manhattan, a short walk from the Chelsea art scene. When not attending to Zeuxis matters, she gives her full attention to oil painting and to watercolor, a medium that forces one to "get it right" the first time. Some figures that helped to shape her lifelong search for the essence of pictorial art are her first teacher Donna Norine Schuster, Gabriel Laderman, and several of the painters of Zeuxis..

www.phyllisfloyd.com

Suggestive Interiors

Matthew Lopas interviews

Eric Elliott and Nicole M. Santiago

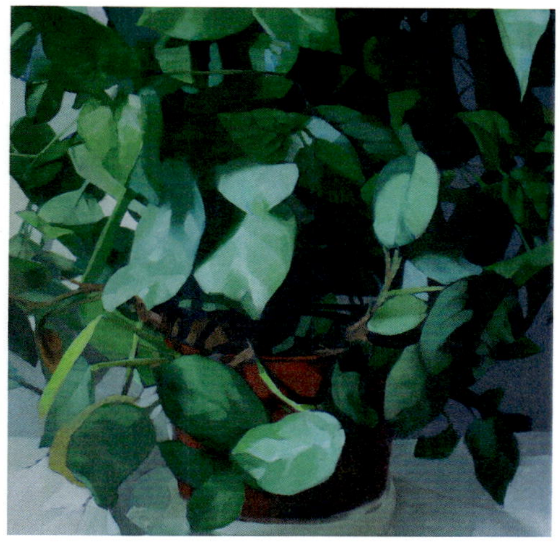

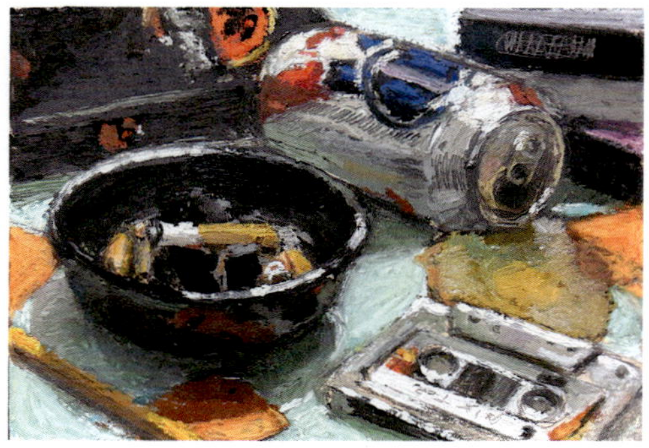

Eric Elliott *Ficus* (detail), oil on canvas, 31 ½ x 21 in.
Nicole M. Santiago *Mix Tape*, 2023, oil & oil pastel on panel, 5 x 7 in.

Matthew Lopas: *When I look at painting, I search for images that dig deeply into the form, show themselves slowly, and delight the eye and heart. The works of both Nicole Santiago and Eric Elliott do this for me. In Santiago's painting,* Transition *(pg. 245), I feel the child immersed in this wonderfully intense imaginative world of nearly abstract forms. She plays in a small private space on the couch, surrounded by a set of moving stripes and dot patterns, She is so intent. In Eric Elliott's piece,* Window Light 1-3 *(pg. 244), my mind swims in richly colored air, searching for substance. Yet I am reassured by the magical sensation of light.*

Who are these two people that speak to me? How did they make such images?

ML: *Please tell us a bit about your early life. Where are you from ? Siblings? Parents? What was your early family life like? What was your first exposure to art and how did that impact you?*

Eric Elliott: I grew up in Anchorage, Alaska, and the biggest influence on my art from my time there was the snow. There is something so magical about how after a fresh snowfall everything is obscured under a huge blanket of white, unifying and abstracting the visual world. I have an older brother and our parents got divorced when I was two, so we lived with our dad, who worked a lot, and when we visited our mom our friends weren't around, so there were a lot of times where we had to entertain ourselves.

I would draw and my brother would play the guitar. I credit becoming an artist to the fact that my dad was an engineer and had a drafting table at work and at home and I loved the big sheets of paper used for blueprints and all the different rulers and pencils. I would draw all the time creating different characters and worlds inspired by comic books. The only art I remember seeing as a kid beyond comics were paintings of snowy landscapes with mountains and arctic animals. My parents were really supportive of my love for drawing and I really wanted to be a cartoonist, but as I got older I realized that I didn't have the desire to draw the same thing over and over again.

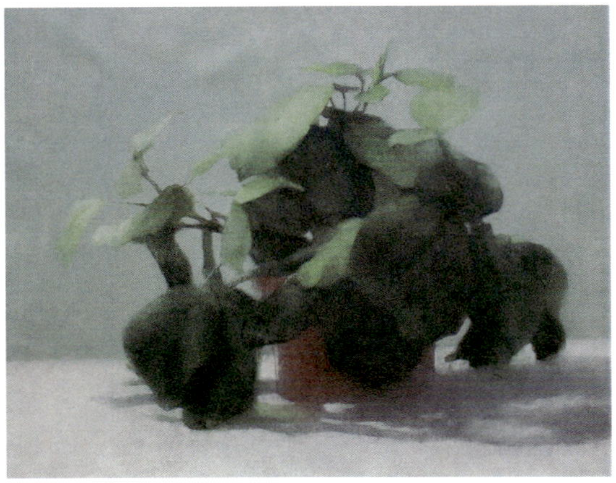

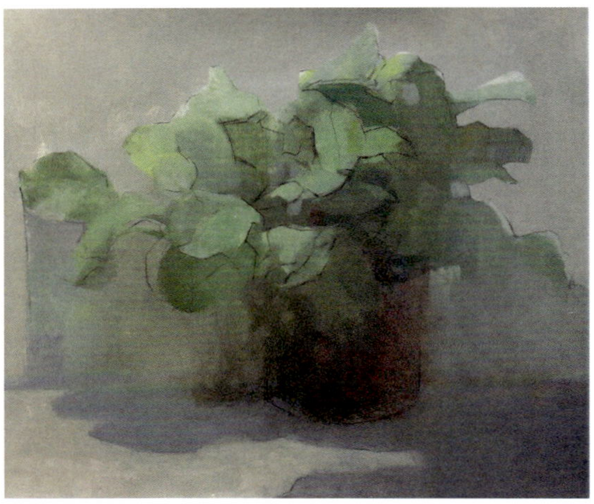

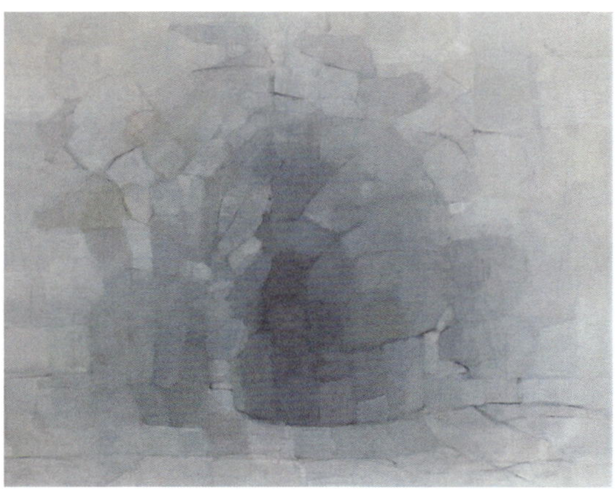

Eric Elliott *Marantas*
2018, acrylic and oil on canvas,
16 x 20 in. each

ML: *What was your education as an artist? Were there any teachers or individuals that had a big impact on you as an artist? What ideas in painting first engaged you? How did you become serious about your painting?*

EE: After high school I went to Arizona to study graphic design, but quickly realized that it wasn't for me, so I started taking painting and drawing classes at the local community college. I was very lucky to have two amazing teachers there, Jim Garrison and Darlene Swaim. They were complete opposites of each other, he was more of a classically trained figurative artist and she was more of a painter's painter who had studied at Yale. They had a wealth of knowledge and both had a following of students that realized how lucky they were to be getting such a good education for such a low price. I spent several years sucking as much as I could from those two and then wasn't sure what to do with myself. During this period were some of my first exposures to paintings that really moved me. The Rembrandt self-portrait in the National Gallery in DC was probably the first painting to stop me in my tracks. The paint handling, color, and expressive quality in that portrait are just amazing. I also took a school trip to Paris around that time and was in awe of all the amazing paintings, but most excited about the room of Rubens paintings at the Louvre. At the time I was doing these terrible angsty twisted figures that were heavily influenced by the baroque, and if I had known about Odd Nerdrum I probably would have gone off that direction, but instead I went to California to finish my undergrad at UC Berkeley.

UC Berkeley was a bit of a culture shock for me; they were more focused on the conceptual side rather than technical skills. There was really no instruction on observational painting, so I felt out of place and really floundered to find my direction, but I had been so focused on the Old Masters previously that it was great to learn more about later art movements and art theory. I had some really great teachers there as well. My primary teachers were Squeak Carnwath, Jane Rosen, John McNamara and Richard Shaw. They were all very different from each other, but all were very generous with their time and knowledge. The second painting that really moved me was by Giacometti. It was one of his portraits made out of swirling black lines and I remember stopping in front of it (never having heard of Giacometti before) and just feeling like I had found what I had been looking for. It spoke to me on so many levels and to this day he has to be one of my heaviest influences. At the end of my undergrad I still had no idea of what I wanted to do except I wanted to deal with the concept of interconnection, something being part of a larger whole, and I wanted to paint figures. In the year after undergrad I was obsessed with Giacometti and Cézanne and was constructing my paintings of figures out of long brush strokes that moved through the figure and beyond.

I started to look around at graduate schools and I decided on the University of Washington in Seattle because of the work of Ann Gale. To this day her paintings mesmerize me with their amazing color and mark making, in my opinion she is one of the best painters alive today. I desperately needed graduate school because I still hadn't really found my voice and still needed a lot of guidance. Graduate school just solidified in my mind just how little I knew. Ann let me know through her questions that I knew nothing about color, and discussions with other professors let me know

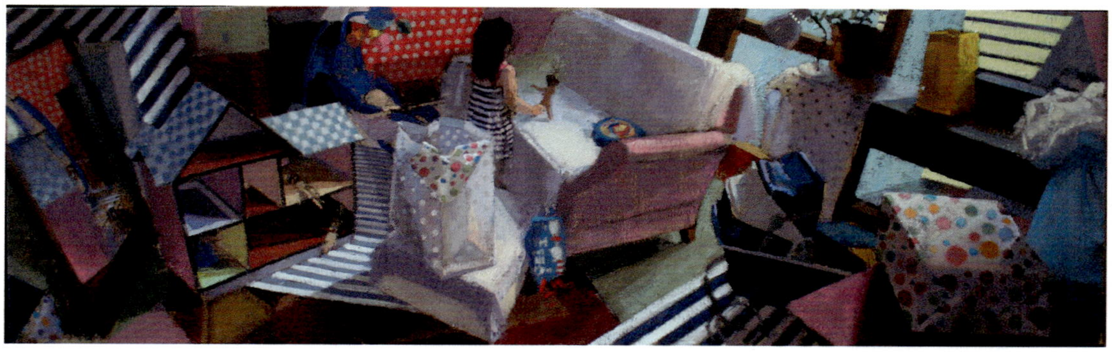

Nicole M. Santiago *Transition*
2017, oil on linen, 16 x 50 in.

how little I knew about art in general. First, I tried to make figures that tried to merge my love for Giacometti paintings and Philip Guston abstractions, but I felt that in critiques everyone focused more on the figures when I was more interested in what the paint was doing. It is hard to explain, but I didn't want to make an abstract painting, when I tried, they just felt too generalized. I found I needed something to respond to, to hang my paint on. I wanted the marks to hold space and volume. I wanted a form/object to be there fully realized while at the same time being one with a larger color field. In order to really consider every aspect of what I was doing and why, I decided to get rid of everything and started over. I got rid of the figures so I didn't have to deal with all the baggage that came with them, I eliminated color, and I got rid of the paint. For a year I did black and white ink drawings of my studio and the objects in it before I figured out a way back into painting.

I started by making thick goopy grey paintings continuing with my studio as my motif. I mixed my greys from the primaries (cad red medium, cad yellow light, and ultramarine blue) and white for a year before attempting to paint observable color, still just using the primaries. Then after another year or so, I expanded my palette to include a warm and cool of each primary. I painted plants, and interiors mostly, dissolving forms on a spectrum from realistic to completely dissolving objects and spaces into color fields. I continued in this vein for a while with decent success, but I got in a rut and no longer liked what I was doing, so I decided to go study at the Jerusalem Studio School for a year to break out of it. I learned a ton there and would have loved to stay longer if I could have. The teaching of Israel Hershberg at JSS is really embedded in the teachings of Lenart Anderson, Edwin Dickinson,

Eric Elliott
Window Light 1-3
2012, oil on canvas,
18 x 24 in. each

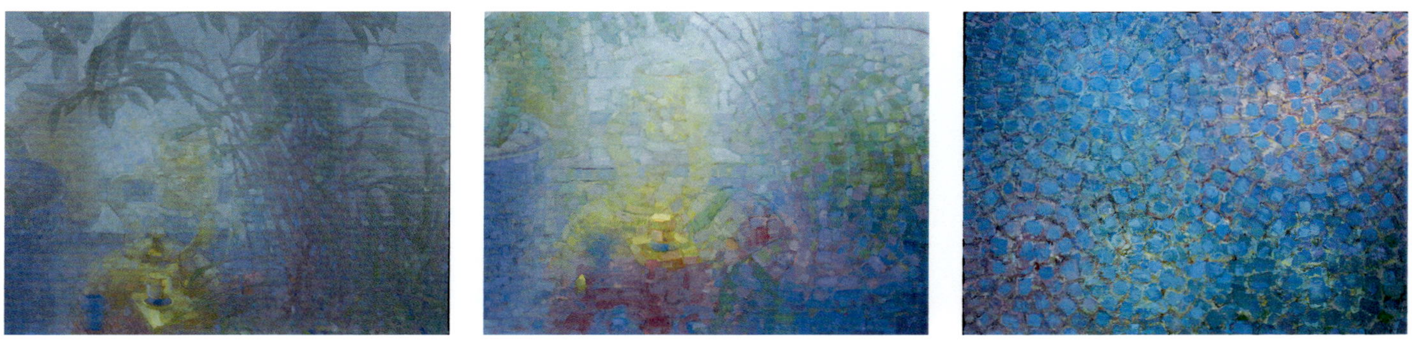

and Charles Hawthorne. Spots of color, premier coup, and seeing the world in terms of abstraction. It was a lot of things I had learned before but taught in a completely new way that really resonated with me and opened my eyes to new possibilities. When I returned from Israel I spent several years just figuring out how to incorporate what I'd learned into my practice, and maybe I still am.

ML: *Please tell us a bit about your early life. Where are you from? Siblings? Parents? What was your early family life like?*

Nicole Santiago: I was born into a working-class family just outside Indianapolis, IN. As an only child, I spent much time alone, submerged in my imagination, pretending to be someone else in imaginary scenarios. Drawing (and just creating in general) was a natural conduit to experience my imagined worlds. I got lost for hours in drawing and other various creative pursuits. I suspect these experiences are relatively common for most children; nonetheless, it is where my love of artmaking began.

While I didn't have much exposure to art with a capital 'A' as a child, my youth was rich in visual stimuli. My grandmother was an amateur painter whose works were the backdrop to my childhood, and of course, mid-century Disney animations also served as a significant influence. But perhaps the most consequential visual impact on my later work was the crowded domestic interiors of my earlier years. Crowded domestic spaces have become a motif in my paintings. Figurative or not, these spaces can speak volumes about the inhabitants' lives.

Another heavy influence, though not directly, was the exceptional creativity of my immediate and extended families. Their lower economic status necessitated a reliance on ingenuity and creativity. This mindset greatly influenced my work ethic, creativity, and general problem-solving abilities in my studio practice and daily life.

ML: *What was your first exposure to art and how did that affect you?*

NS: My first exposure to museum quality work was in the seventh grade during a field trip to the Indianapolis Museum of Art. I was overwhelmed and thrilled by the painted works, from 15th century Flemish, thru the contemporary pieces. A couple of years later, I visited the Museum of the Art Institute of Chicago, which blew my mind! I knew I had to see more museums, so I saved my money for several years, and after high school graduation, I traveled to Europe, visiting many major art collections.

Eric Elliott *Studio #3*
2006, ink on paper,
22 x 30 in.

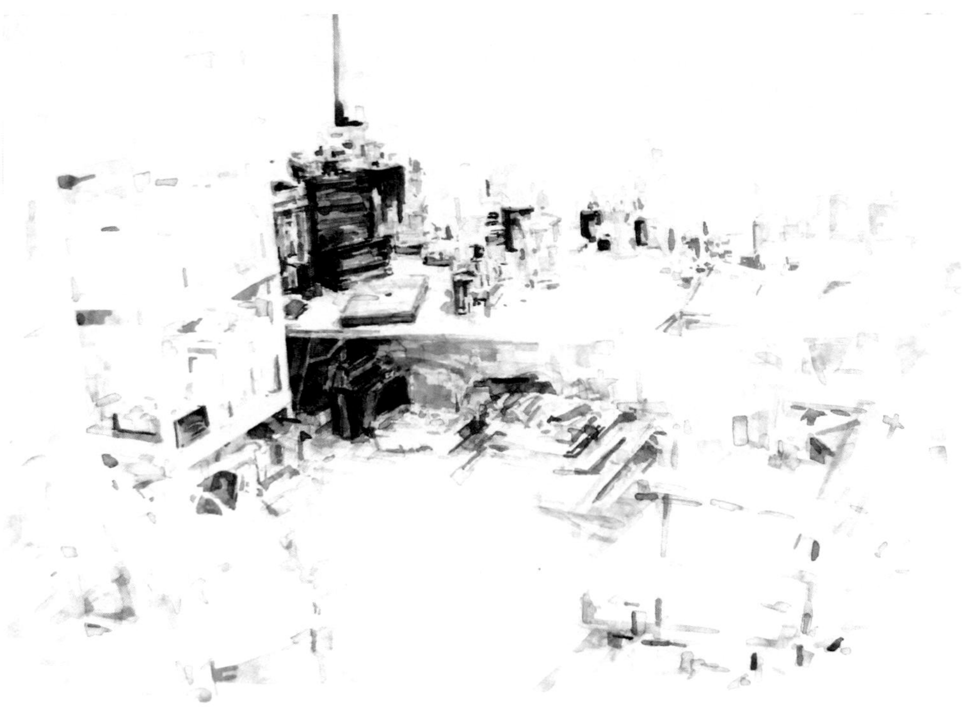

ML: *What was your education as an artist? Were there any teachers or individuals who had a big impact on you as an artist?*

NS: As a teen, I had a fantastic art instructor who was an accomplished local painter and jewelry maker. His critiques were insanely harsh (many students dropped his class), but I enjoyed his honest opinion and rigorous courses. His lessons helped me develop tough skin and, more importantly, a strong work ethic.

During my undergraduate (Indiana University) and graduate studies (University of New Hampshire), I was fortunate to have many accomplished artists as my painting faculty. These revered artists greatly influenced my work and helped me establish my professional career.

ML: *What ideas in painting first engaged you?*

NS: As far back as I can remember, my work has been described as interpersonal, semi-autobiographical narratives. This is what first engaged me and what still captivates my attention. And although I don't think I was consciously aware of it when I was younger, the underlying abstraction was also essential for meaningful engagement. Many of the works I admired as a young painter relied on larger abstract rhythms that carried through the entirety of the compositions.

ML: *How did you become serious about your painting?*

NS: I don't remember a definitive moment when I became serious about making art; naturally, my dedication has only increased with time. But, I suppose if I had to pinpoint a moment, it was likely sometime in my late teens when I started to cut back on other things like musical training, sports, and socializing to dedicate more time to drawing and painting. It was the only thing I was good at. I struggled with academics but did well enough to get by. So I knew I had to push myself as hard as I could. There wasn't a safety net. So far, it's working out alright, but there is always room for improvement!

ML: *Both of you make paintings of interior spaces. The interior has been one of my lifelong loves as an artist. Each of these pieces speaks directly to me. Eric's piece,* Photinia in the Studio, *is a technical tour de force in that it has such a wide range within such a restrained palette. It creates a palpable thickness to the air depicted. I feel my eyes swim though a warm fog. Yet the drawing is so clear that I am comforted.*

The combination of low interior lamplight and a bit of natural daylight in Nicole's Shifting Celebration *sets a self-reflective mood for me that I recognize. The three figures, each in their own world, creates a depth and mystery that resonates with loved experience. It's dynamic compositional movement keeps the eye engaged and in the painting. The way Santiago subtly*

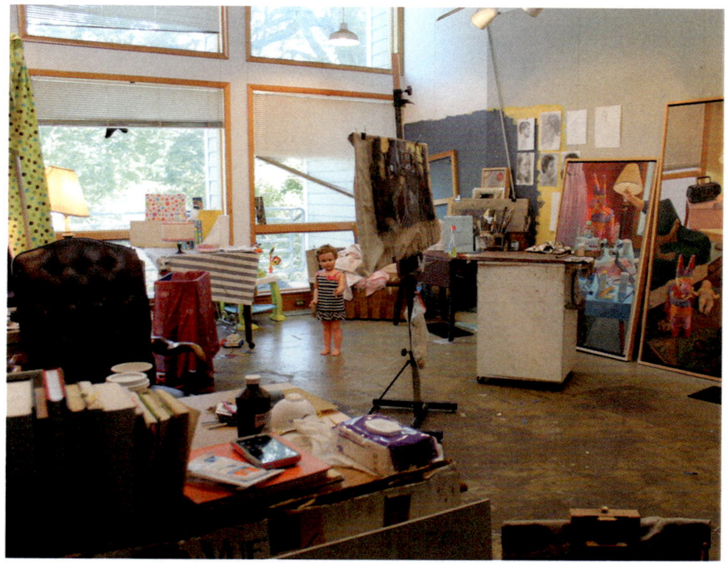

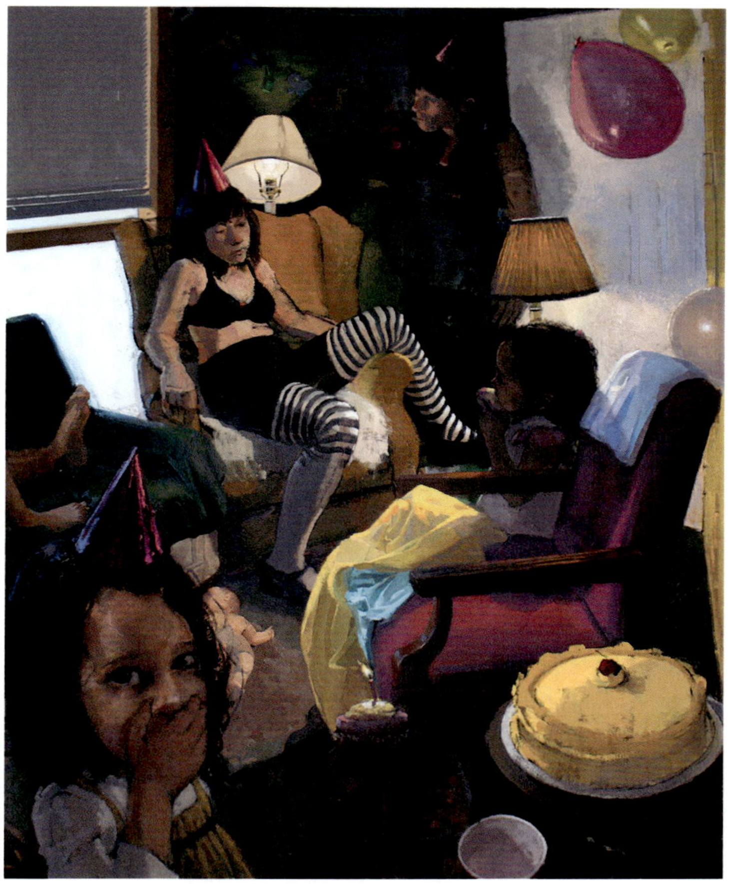

TOP TO BOTTOM:

Nicole M. Santiago's studio

Nicole M. Santiago *Second Time Around*
2017, oil on canvas, 79 x 65 in.

integrates line drawing into her forms and leaves some things incomplete, like the arm of the figure on the lower left, is something that I would like to emulate.

Please tell us about your painting selected here. What led you to paint it? Why this subject? Why this light? Why this palette? Why is it composed the way it is? What methods did you use to make it? What was the hardest part of painting it? What role does narrative play in it? Is there anything more about it you want to say? Please tell us what strikes you about the other's painting.

EE: The path that led to this particular painting, *Photinia in the Studio*, starts with wanting to show that everything is interconnected, everything is equal, all is one, and that there is more to the world than meets the eye. I've always been dealing with the paradox of wanting everything in my painting to become one while at the same time having identifiable form. Maybe my paintings should have been performance pieces where I painted exactly what I saw and then slowly obliterated it, because that is what I was doing then, but instead of leaving it obliterated, I would do this long dance shifting back and forth between dissolution and form trying to find the sweet spot that spoke to me. I think it must be something like what Giacometti struggled with in his paintings. In the paintings of this time period I was wanting to paint the volume of an object and give presence to the air in front of the object as well. A couple of years before *Photinia in the Studio* I did a painting of a bouquet of flowers because I loved the volume of it, the negative shapes, and all the individual parts that made up the whole. The bouquet gave me the idea to paint a plant, so I went to the store and looked for a plant that had the kind of space and volume that I wanted and I found this red tip photinia plant and I fell in love with how I could paint the front, back, and inside of the form. I could dissolve specific leaves or branches while bringing others in focus. I was primarily reducing contrast to create an exaggerated atmospheric perspective. Increased amounts of white pigment diffused the color to give the feeling of atmosphere or fog which felt very relevant to the place I was living at the time (Seattle). In *Photinia in the Studio* I increased the dissolve/contrast not only as you go back in space, but as you go up from the stool to the top of the photinia because I wanted to bend the space, so that the plant is either emerging out of, or dissolving back into, everything else and I wanted this effect to be center stage to emphasize the importance of it.

I created *Photinia in the Studio* by starting with an accurate painting of what I saw. Then I slowly reduced the color contrast to bring everything closer and closer to each other (except the stool that the photinia sits on which stayed the same the whole time). When things would get too dissolved I would bring back more clarity to particular areas and then when I felt like there was too much clarity I would go back to dissolving forms again and this dance would continue until something inside me would tell me to stop. I also wanted the paint itself to have presence, to draw attention to the surface of the canvas and to the individual marks, so I would lay down thick brushstrokes creating a heavy buildup of paint. I was very influenced by Cézanne's constructive brushstrokes, wanting my brush marks to be the building blocks that made up the whole. I was using the minimal palette of cad red medium, cad yellow light, ultramarine blue, and a utrecht white (a zinc titanium blend). The hardest part for me in making paintings is knowing exactly what it is that I want from them, or what they want from me, I want there to be a presence in the painting but you don't really know if you've achieved that until you see it or sit with the painting for a while.

Matt Lopas *Black Swan*
2017, oil on canvas, 45 x 72 in.

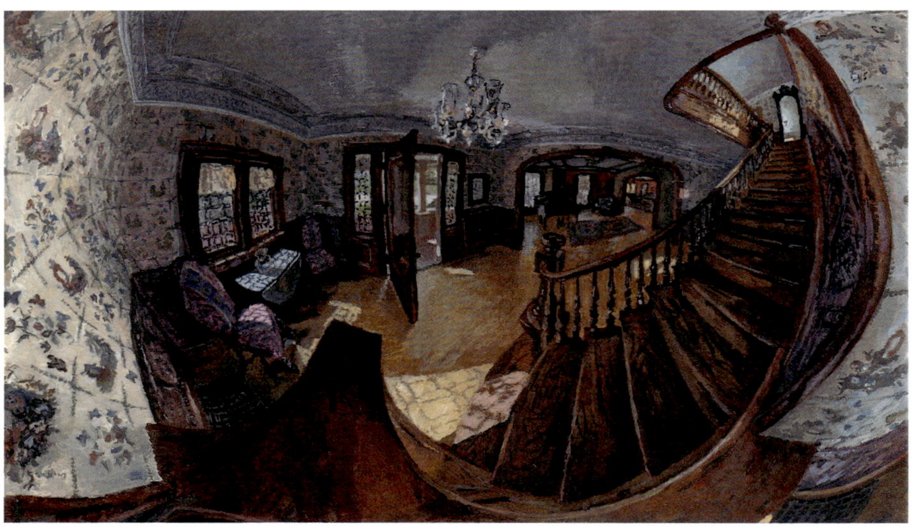

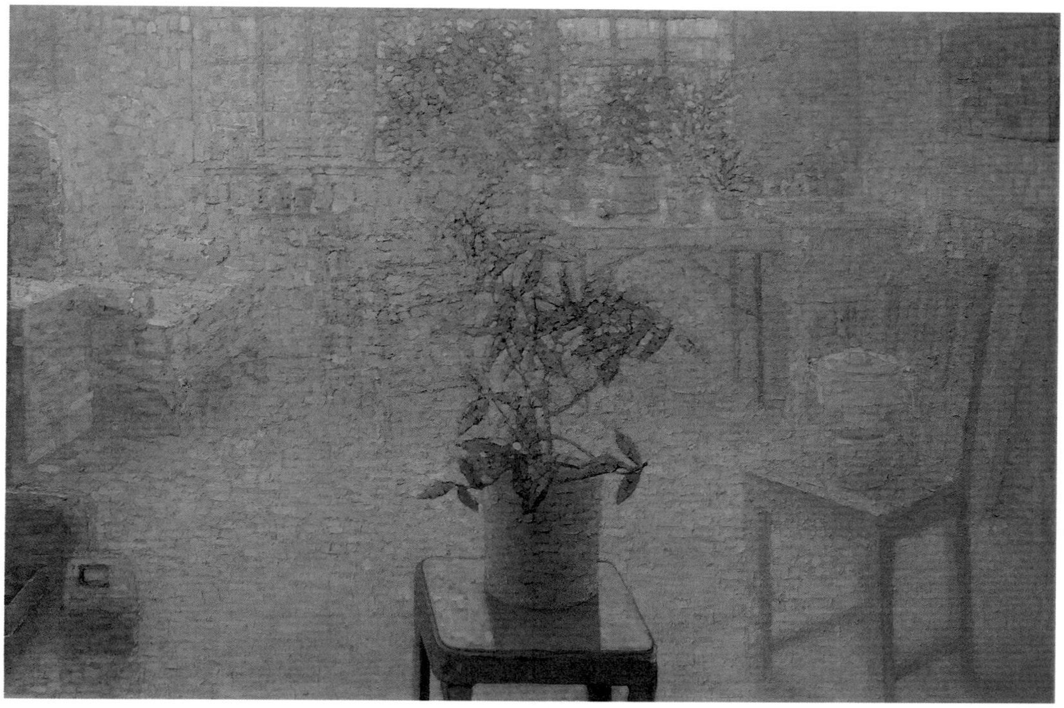

Eric Elliott *Photinia in the Studio*
2010, oil on canvas, 60 x 72 in.

Looking at Nicole's painting, *Shifting Celebrations*, I feel she may have been looking at similar artists as I was when I made my painting, *Photinia in the Studio*. Artists like Vuillard and Susan Lichtman. There is a strong focus on shapes as interlocking puzzle pieces, depth versus flatness, and playing with perception. Although there definitely appears to be more of a narrative in Nicole's painting, I see a lot of similarities in thinking about how to create space. I tend to give little to no thought to the narrative aspect of a painting beyond the idea that any object can be a stand in, or metaphor, for anything else. For example, the photinia sitting on the stool in the center of the room takes on a figurative aspect that can't be ignored.

NS: The painting *Shifting Celebrations* was inspired by a classroom setup for my life drawing course. The longer students worked from the setup, the more I wanted to make my own painted version of the space. I was particularly attracted to the inside/outside color relationships and fractured space. As soon as the semester ended, I reassembled the setup for myself and hired a model. As I worked through the summer, I expanded the setup, taking over a good chunk of the 1200-square-foot classroom. The actual painting grew, too. It ended up being a much larger piece than I had initially planned.

Although I had a general idea of the image's design when I begin the painting, I sort of found my subject and composition through the working process. I spent the first few weeks of this painting merely reacting to the color, form, and space. As the painting developed, forms and colors moved in/out of the picture plane (and in/out of the set up too). During that process, I continually questioned the visual balance, movement, and the geometry of the image. Major compositional decisions were made during the act of painting and eventually, the painting's composition began to congeal. I once read Bonnard painted on large pieces of unstretched canvas to give himself more flexibility with the composition. This makes so much sense to me! So that is how I usually I begin my works, this piece being no different. The unstretched support allows the format of my compositions to expand or compress as needed.

I began without any specific ideas. Instead, I remained open to seeing what the painting revealed during the process. This is often how I approach my figurative work. Conversely, when I work on still lifes, subject matter and content are usually apparent from the beginning. In both my still lifes and figurative works the narratives are nearly always semi-autobiographical. In this piece the content is certainly a thinly veiled reflection of my inner world. At the time I was parenting two small children, caring for aging grandparents, tackling work demands, and attending to my studio practice. I was chronically exhausted and overwhelmed. In a somewhat obtuse way, I feel this painting alludes to the endless struggle to address a mountain of impossible responsibilities both through the mundane domestic debris, actions (or inactions of the figures) and the fractured space that limits the movement of the painted figures..

The studio overlooks a lake with surrounding foliage that floods the space with an intense green light during the spring and summer. I find myself drawn to this light and struggle to capture it. It feels nearly impossible to describe the relationship between outdoor light, dim interior, and incandescent light. It's like a visual riddle that I haven't yet been able to decipher fully. So, I keep returning to it, hoping I can sort it out. I feel like I'm getting close!

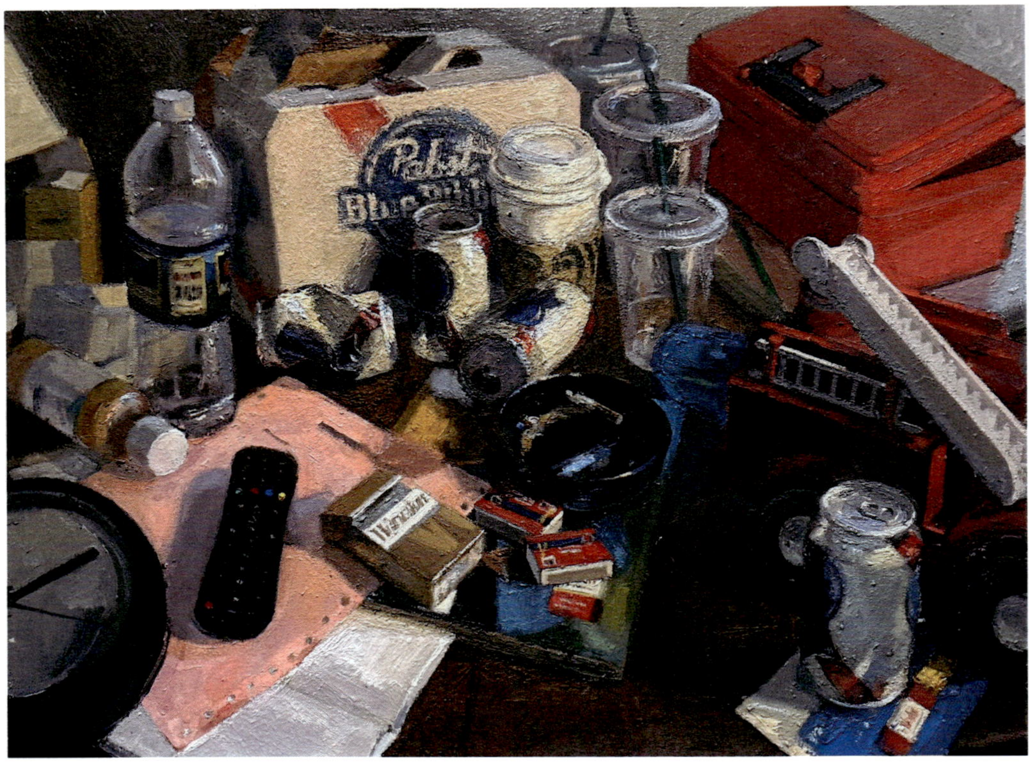

Nicole M. Santiago
A Series of Negotiations
2021, oil on linen, 26 x 26 in.

The methods used in this work are similar to all my works. I usually begin on unstretched, PVA-sized linen. I love working against the color of the linen. As I commented above, the unstretched linen gives me the freedom to expand or crop my images easily during the painting process. I clip the linen to a cheap insulation board for support. Then, lay out a general composition with charcoal and blocks of color. I mostly work from direct observation but also use invention and memory when needed. This painting in particular was in a state of compositional flux for several weeks. I used charcoal and paint interchangeably to shift and adjust the image, continuing to paint and repaint areas until they felt right and the picture was resolved.

Painting my daughter (the young girl in the foreground). She was six years old at the time, and not a willing participant. Her portrait combines direct observation, drawings, photos, invention, and lots of bribes. At one point, I tried to get my two-year-old into the painting, but that proved to be an impossible pursuit. So, I used a mannequin for the child on the chair!

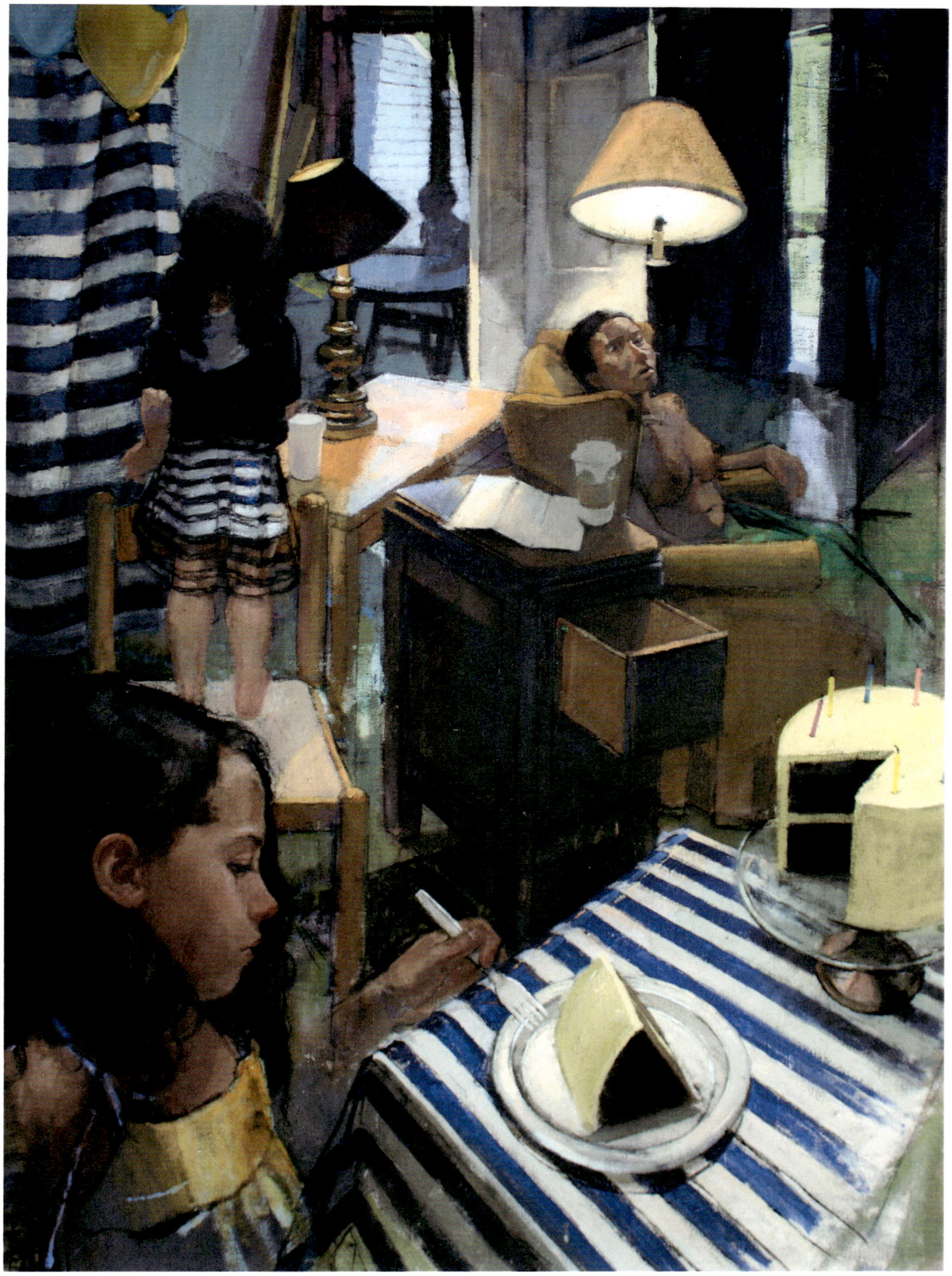

Nicole M. Santiago *Shifting Celebrations*
2018, oil on linen, 62 x 46 in.

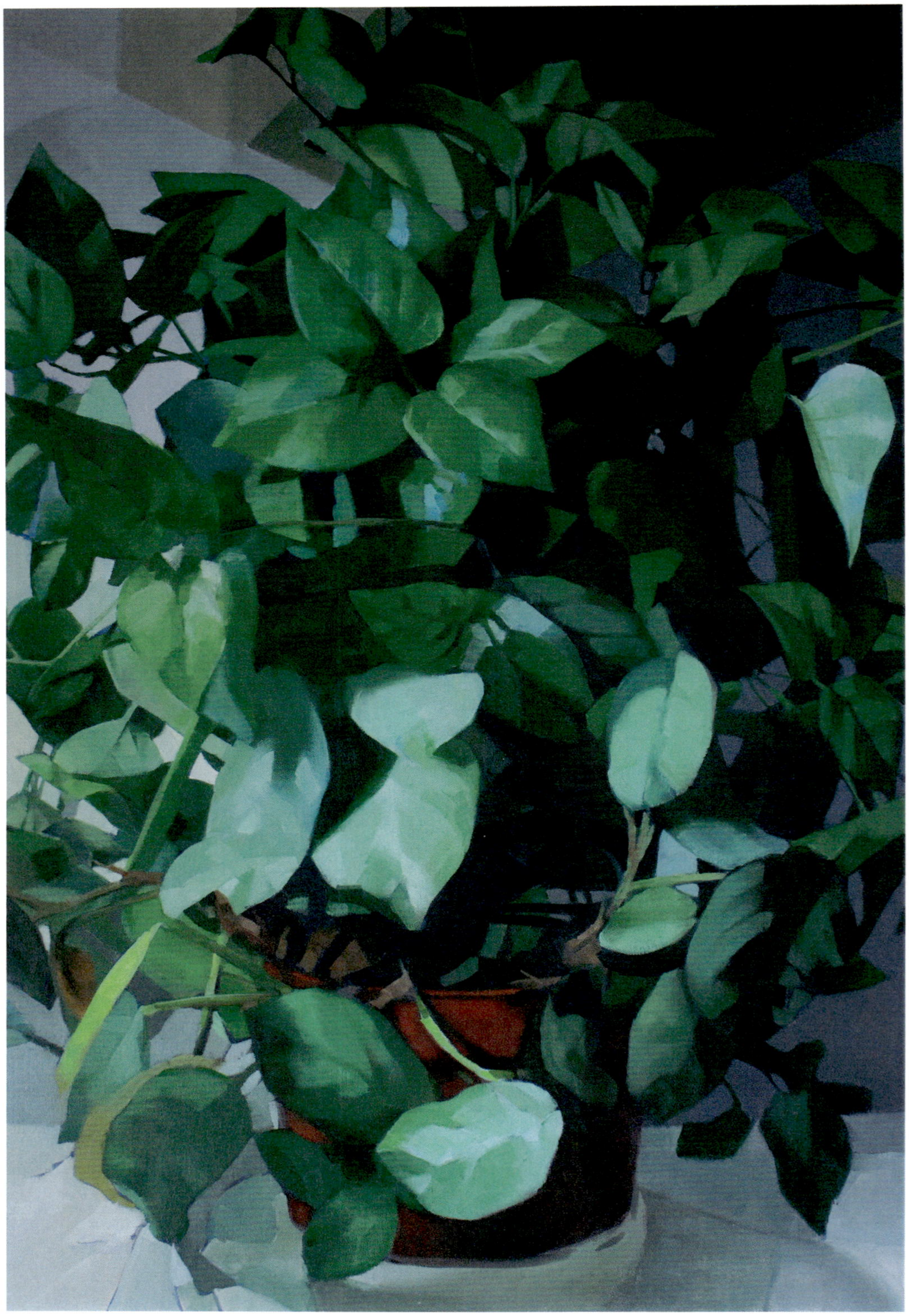

Eric Elliott *Ficus*
2016, oil on canvas, 31 ½ x 21 in.

Eric's painting is exquisite in its refined subtlety; the color relationships are beautifully nuanced, and space, air, and light are expertly described. I'm intrigued by his depiction of space and air. If I were going to talk to my students about how to paint air, this is the painting I would show to them!

I enjoy the slight ambiguity around the overlapping leaves in the foreground and background. The leaves in the foreground advance so clearly but also unify with the plants on the back wall. This area of the work comes alive. There is a simultaneous expansion and collapse in this space here that vibrates. I love the slight ambiguity here, especially when paired with the masterful depiction of atmosphere throughout the painting. It creates a lovely tension and visual play. The geometry within this image is also something I admire. The diagonals (both subtle and overt) activate the picture plane. One of these places is in the way the little green chair that starts a bigger diagonal through to the chair in the upper left. Another is the many diagonal movements that lead us to a point in the larger green plant in the background.

I'm looking forward to seeing this piece in person at some point. I'm sure the work's ethereal quality and nuanced color cannot be wholly captured in reproduction. Z

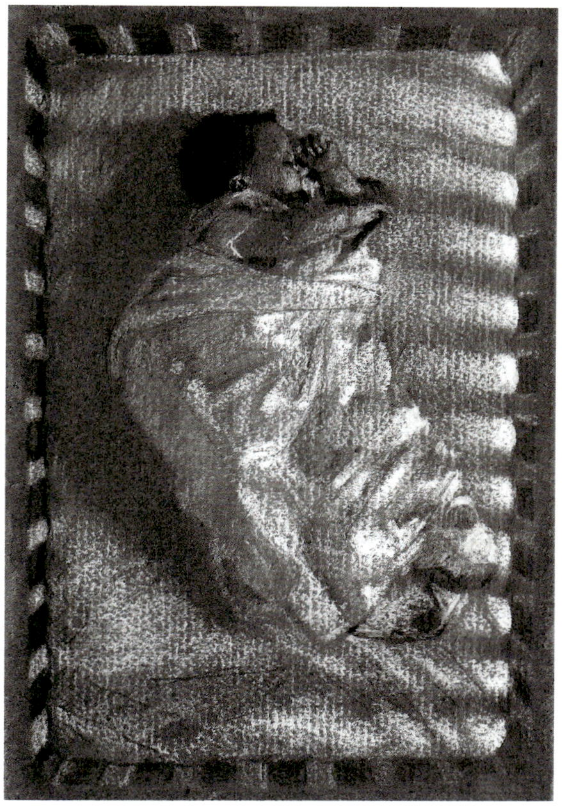

Nicole M. Santiago *Susan Sleeping*
2012, charcoal, graphite, contè, and acrylic on toned paper, 6 x 9 in.

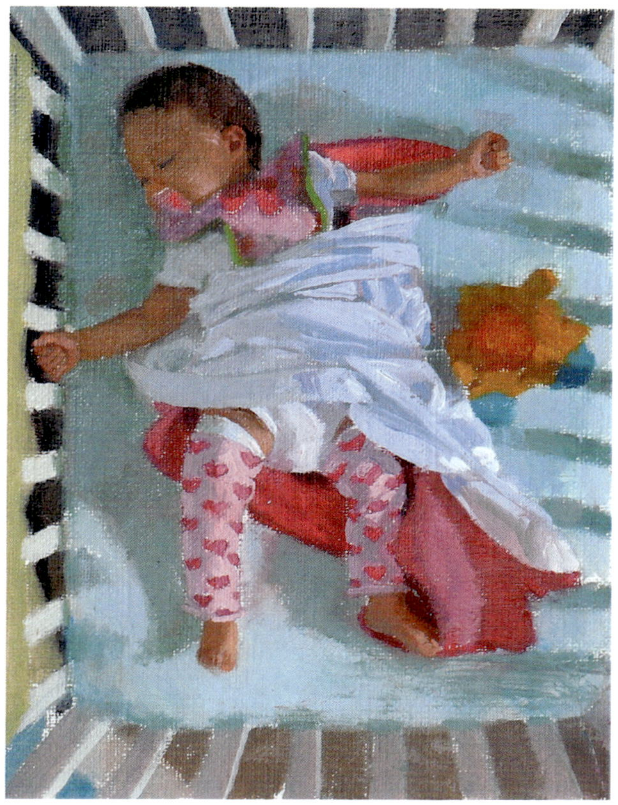

Nicole M. Santiago *Susan Sleeping Crib II*
2012, oil on panel, 8 x 5 in.

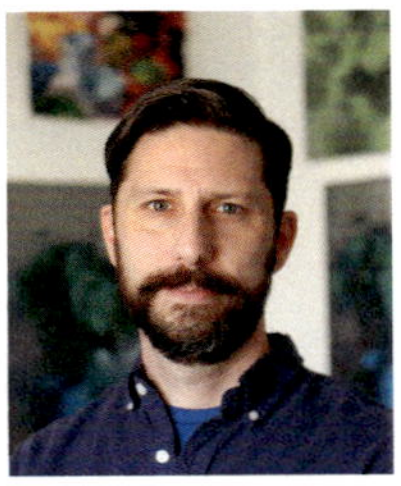

Eric Elliott completed his MFA in Painting and Drawing at the University of Washington in Seattle and his undergraduate work in painting at the University of California, Berkeley. In 2014, he took part in a year-long artist residency at the Jerusalem Studio School in Israel. Elliott was the 2009 recipient of the Behnke Foundation's Neddy Artist Fellowship, was in the 2009 Northwest Biennial at the Tacoma Art Museum, and received the Seattle Art Museum's Kayla Skinner Special Recognition Award. Eric Elliott currently lives in Colorado where he works as an associate professor of painting and drawing, and is the art and design department head at Colorado Mesa University.

www.elliotteric.com

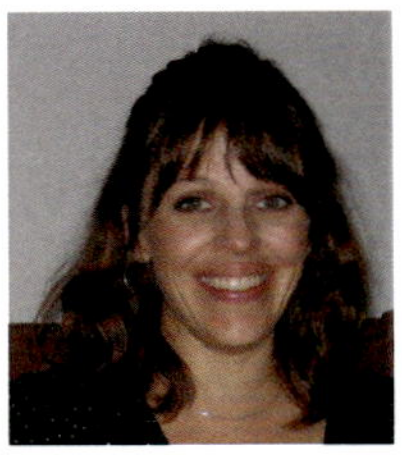

Nicole M. Santiago holds a BFA in studio art from Indiana University and an MFA in painting from the University of New Hampshire. She is a Professor of Art at the College of William and Mary, where she teaches life drawing, drawing, color theory, and 2D design. Santiago's artworks primarily consist of semi-autobiographical paintings, drawings, and prints portraying scenes of everyday life. Within these images, she hints at more universal themes of love, loss, and duty, thinly veiled by the domestic detritus that clutters her picture planes. Santiago exhibits her work often and has shown in over 100 group and solo exhibitions during her career. Her works have been included in many art publications, such as T*he Artist's Magazine, Art New England, INPA (International Painting Annual),* and *Fine Art Connoisseur.*

www.nicolemccormicksantiago.com/

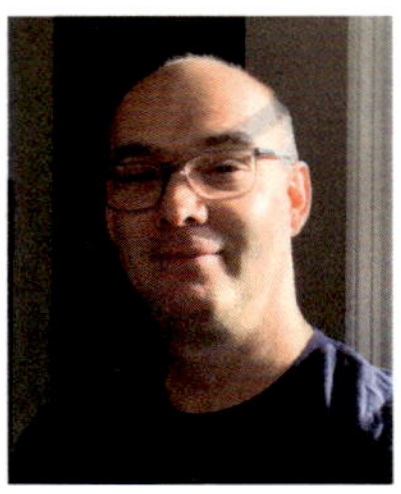

Matthew Lopas was born in 1965 in Chicago. His father, Dr. Harry Lopas, was a hidden child during World War II in Belgium. His mother, Joyce, was a French teacher. Matthew received a BA in Chinese Studies from the University of Michigan in 1988, a BFA in Painting and Drawing from the School of the Art Institute of Chicago in 1991, and a MFA in Painting and Printmaking from Yale School of Art in 1995. He is an artist and a professor of art at Hendrix College. He has lived in Arkansas for 23 years, is married to Susan Clark and has three children.

www.instagram.com/matlopas/

Observation and Memory

Deborah Kirklin interviews

Elizabeth Reagh and Nancy McCarthy

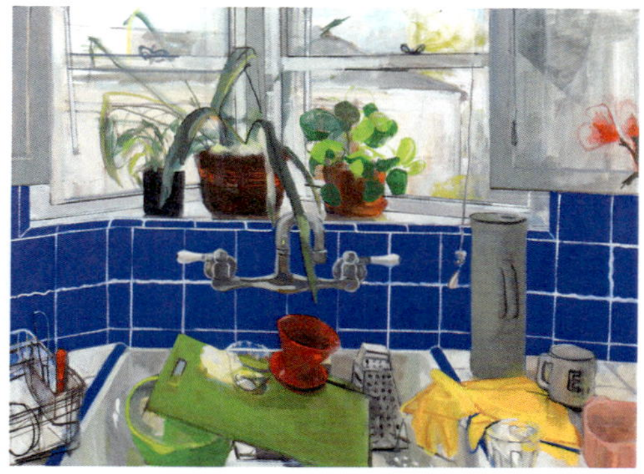

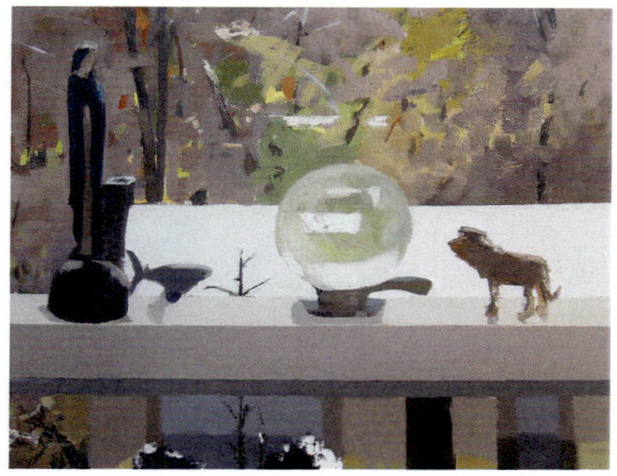

Elizabeth Reagh *Coffee Coffee Coffee*, 2020, oil on canvas, 30 x 40 in.
Nancy McCarthy *Mary, Shark and Lion*, 2019, oil on linen, 12 x 17 in.

Deborah Kirklin: *I want to thank you for meeting today. You two know each other. How did you meet?*

Nancy McCarthy: We met recently for Elizabeth's talk at Black Pond Studios.

DK: *That was such a good lecture. I learned a lot. Let's begin with a little background. What factors in your life contributed to your beginning in art? And how did you gravitate toward painting in particular?*

Elizabeth Reagh: The greatest influence on me in terms of art was my family, because my father was an artist. I grew up surrounded by art and artists. My father was a street photographer, but he started out as a painter, so he always had a painting on an easel in his room, and music playing. I've always had good associations with art for those reasons. He had eclectic taste, and was interested in copying paintings he loved, so he often had some copy in the works in the room he used as a studio. He went through a phase of copying paintings by William Scott, the 60's Scottish abstract still life painter. It made such an impression on me, and I love William Scott to this day.

I was also taken to museums regularly. My brother was given a small printing press when he was a kid and took to it so enthusiastically that he is now a book designer and letterpress printer. We're just a family of people who like making things. Because my father was an art director for a large engineering firm, he brought home a lot of surplus art supplies. I always had supplies. He was in charge of the print shop and had access to great papers and book binding tools. He would make these big blank books for me and bring them home, and I could draw in them.

NM: My story is similar in that it was family that influenced me. My grandfather was a pipe fitter. The story was that he was given tuition to sign up for classes at Wentworth, which is an engineering school in Boston, and instead he went to the Museum of Fine Arts and signed up there. He was promptly pulled out when his father found out. He and his brothers, they're all French Canadians—all painted a little bit and dabbled, and they were always making things. So that influence was there. And then my oldest sister, who was eight years older than I, attended art school. When I was small she was attending classes at the Museum of Fine Arts in Boston, and my father would take me and my other sister there and wait for her class to be over. That was a big influence. My family wasn't particularly sophisticated around art but it was something a person could do and might do.

When I was about twelve at Thanksgiving dinner, a lot of family around, my father said something about me being exactly like my older sister, who was at that time in art college, and at that point I just decided I'm not going to do art. I'm going to differentiate myself. And I started seriously studying music, and was initially a music major. I dropped out of school, and eventually found my way back quite a number of years later to art school, but was constantly making marks and drawing. I think I gravitated to painting because it's a solitary profession, and I need solitude. I need to not be engaged with other people, and I love color.

ER: I would second that. I came to painting relatively late. I was the youngest of three children by many years—eight years and eleven years, and in some ways felt like an only child. I really enjoyed being alone and drawing and making things, and I think that felt very comfortable to me, and led me naturally to art as a career—first drawing and then later, painting.

DK: *So interesting. I'll just briefly say that my family, my parents, were both classically trained pianists. They were amateurs, and they had other occupations, but music was always playing at our house. I studied piano for six years. Then when I started high school I wanted to do something else, and I started drawing and painting.*

NM: Great.

DK: *How important is observation, and how faithful do you tend to be to perception? What role does drawing play in your working process? Do you make studies?*

NM: I think observation is very important for me. It's a starting place typically, not always, but very often. Also, out in the landscape, it's observation and memory, because things are changing so fast. You believe you're working from perception, but actually it's impossible. So, there's a lot of memory. In my still life work I'm also working from observation, and I find that when I'm really honest and get into pure perception, it's more exciting than what I might imagine or fictionalize. But there's also an element of fiction that happens for me, too, and memory.

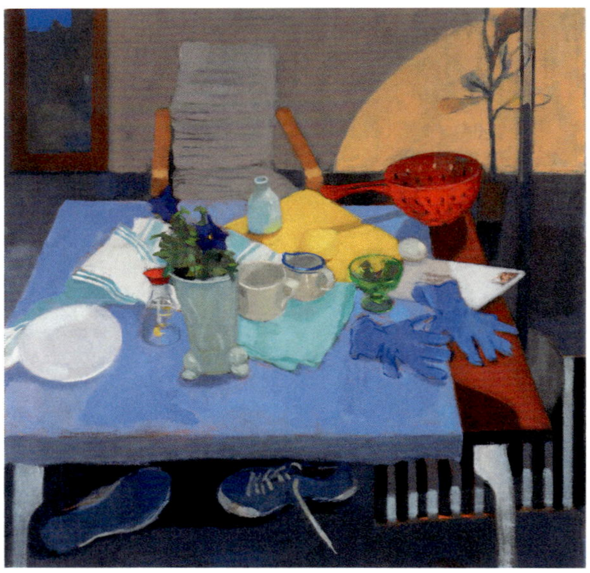

Elizabeth Reagh *Night Studio*
2022, oil on canvas, 36 x 36 in.

ER: Observation is very important to me, depending on what I'm doing. When I'm drawing from life I use close observation to learn about what I'm seeing. When I'm painting it's a combination of observation and imagination. But I agree with Nancy. When I'm painting from observation, what I discover is much richer than anything I could imagine. I see things I wouldn't expect to see, and it's often a surprise when I stand back and look at it—it feels a little like magic!

I never make studies. I'm very impatient to get to the painting. It's similar to assembling something with a manual—I always throw the manual away and just figure it out by trial and error. I think it's really just not having that ability to delay gratification. I just want to skip that step and move to the painting.

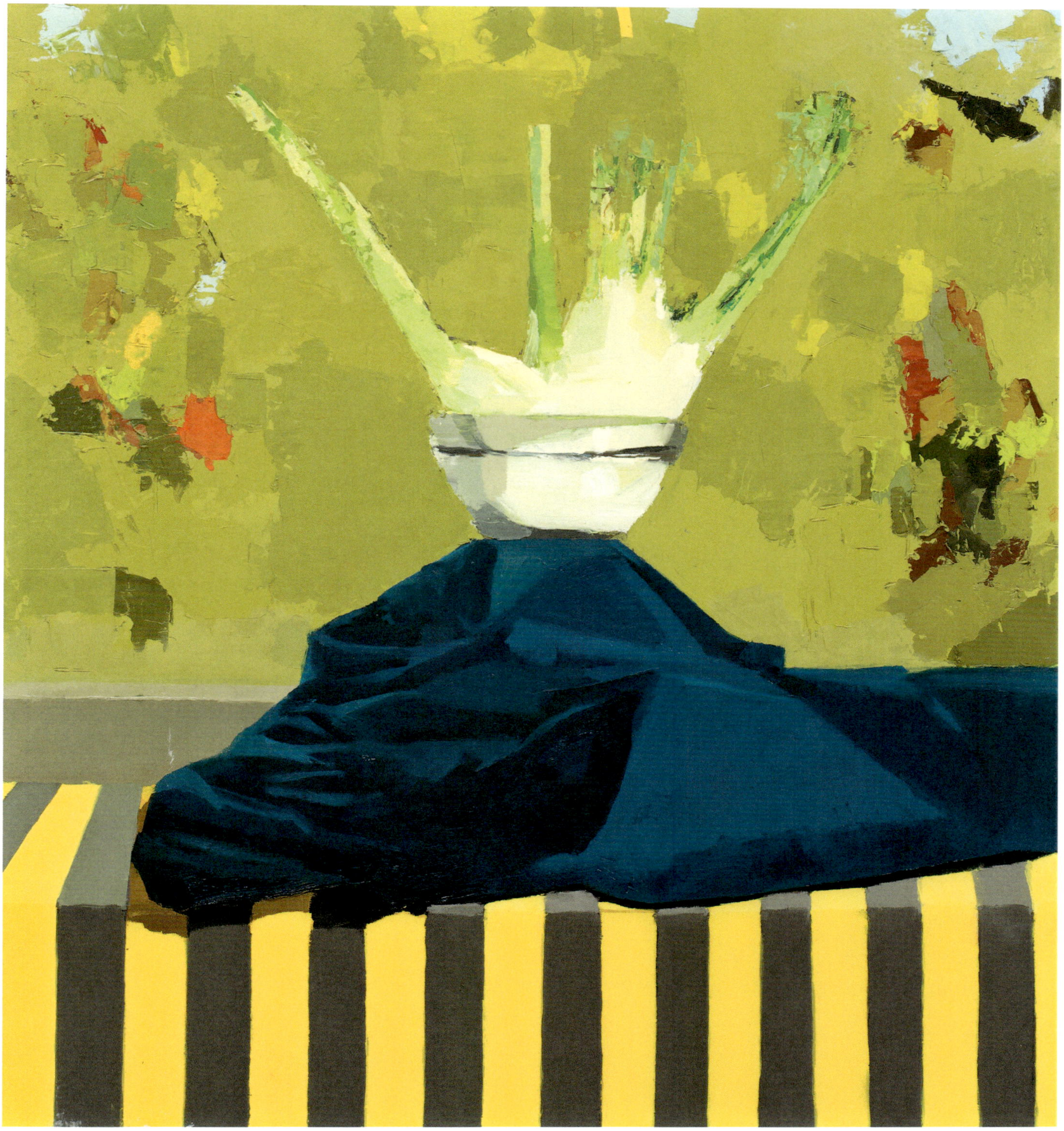

Nancy McCarthy *Fennel*
2016, oil on linen, 20 x 18 in.

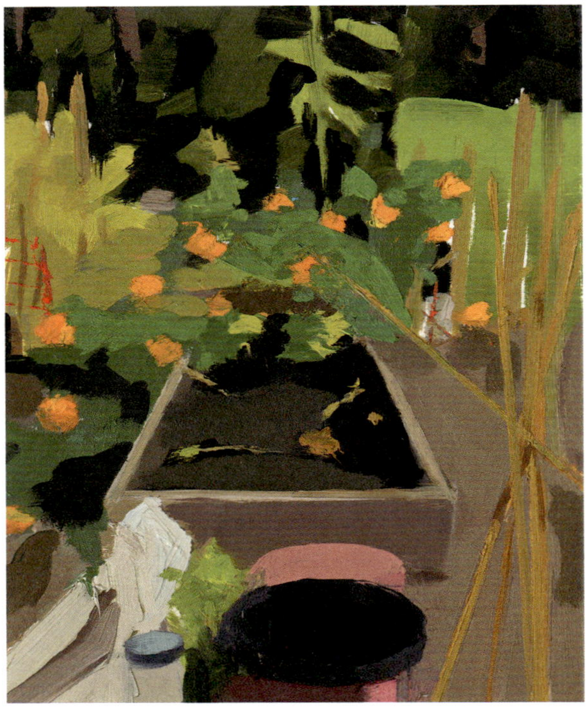

Nancy McCarthy *Marigolds*
2022, oil on board, 11 x 6 in.

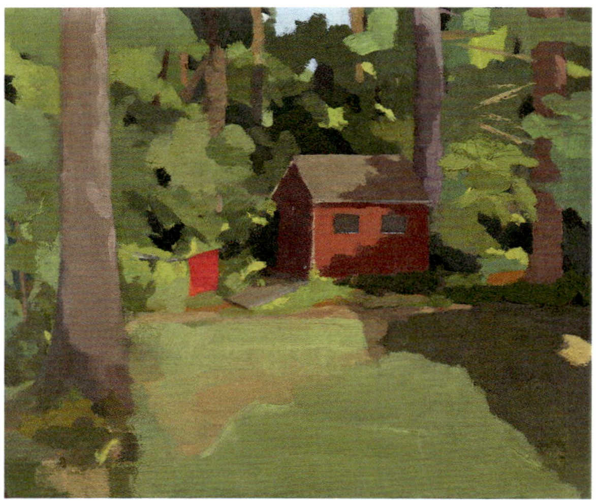

Nancy McCarthy *Shed*
2020, oil on linen, 11 x 14 in.

DK: *This next question is pretty open. What principles or ideas guide you in selecting your motif?*

ER: I think the first principle that guides me is can this work graphically? Do I like the way this thing looks? And can I make this into something visually and compositionally interesting?

In terms of motifs, there are a few motifs I return to again and again. For instance, there are a lot of animals in my work. I definitely resist any kind of sentimentality or romanticism when I'm dealing with animals. I just want to depict them as they are. When I use objects as the motif, I think I'm more interested in how they will look in the whole setup, and whether or not I like the shape and color of them. Do I like the sort of "thing" quality of the objects? I don't want there to be an obvious sentimental attachment to these objects. I'm really thinking about them in formal terms, initially.

As far as drawing, I always draw to figure things out. It's the only way. If I start right into a painting, I'm lost, or I haven't figured it out. I just need to think. It's rare for me to do an extended study.

And then sometimes it'll occur to me afterwards, that I do have a sentimental attachment to these objects. But I don't want to lead the viewer in that direction. I want them to respond in their own way.

NM: Yeah, pretty much the same for me. It's shape and color. And just how they're going to work. But it can take quite a while when I'm setting up a still life, as I'm sure for you two as well. You know it's just in and out with different objects. And putting them against a particular fabric or background, it's how deep the space is, and how far I'm going to zoom in and out. That process is quite involved.

And then in the landscape a lot of times it's determined by the most comfortable place to be. I'll see something, and it'll just be fantastic, but there's no place I can be that I'm not in direct, really hot sun, and I can't do it.

ER: So, Nancy, when you say you spend a lot of time, do you spend a lot of time setting up the setup or do you have a very clear idea when you start painting what the setup is going to be?

NM: Sometimes, yes, I do. I try to figure it out first, but sometimes you get going, you look at it, you say that the red object is not working, so I take it out and find something else.

DK: *So, do you both have collections of objects?*

ER: I have a collection of things because I like things. It's not a specific collection but I cull from what I have. I also might just come into the house looking for something to add to a painting and see a Melitta coffee filter box and grab it, and try it out. A sculptor friend made me a little clay figure when I was trying to get pregnant, her version of a fertility figure. I've put that in so many paintings. It's challenging to paint, but it also allows for so many different approaches.

NM: I have a fairly large collection too. It's also for teaching, but often that's not what I end up using. I scan the house for something that will work.

DK: *You're both exquisite colorists. What experiences or influences have you had that shape your approach to color?*

ER: Well, my childhood again, because where I grew up in LA, there was a mid-century color scheme that was ever present. I really am drawn to it, and I have to try not to default to it all the time. My father had a very similar color sensibility to mine, so I think I was really influenced by his palette. I was married to an Indian man, and we went to India twice. Those visits were such a revelation in terms of color. India is an everyday color explosion. As somebody once said: in India, pink is the new navy. My mother-in-law took me to a sari shop. She thought I needed a sari, but seeing the rows and rows of beautiful fabrics is what I remember most vividly.

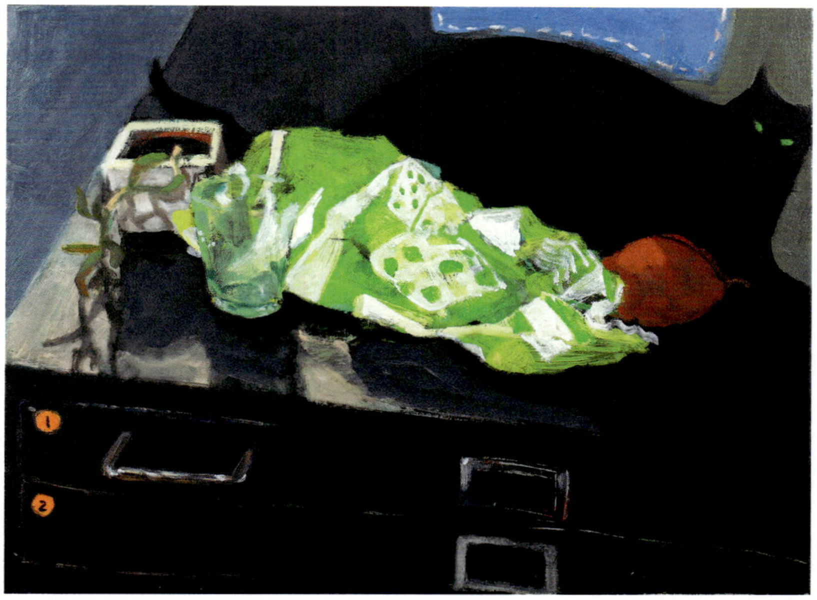

Elizabeth Reagh *Crow on Flatfile*
2020, oil on canvas, 18 x 24 in.

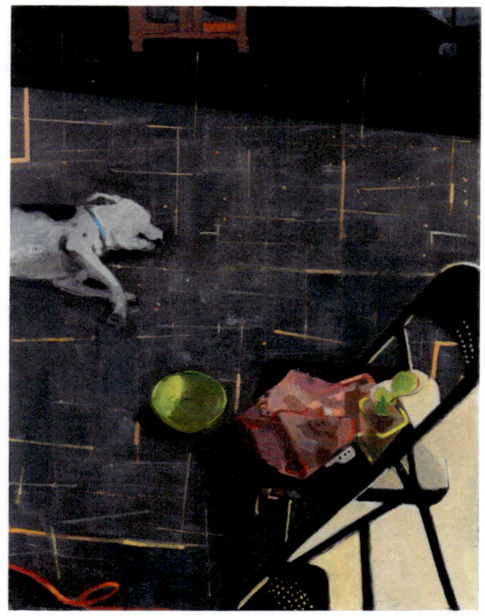

Elizabeth Reagh *Clover on Studio Floor*
2021, oil on canvas, 40 x 30 in.

NM: For me as well—my influences began in childhood. I spent every summer outside, and I was fortunate enough to be in Truro, which is on the lower part of Cape Cod.

I have a distinct memory of being really small, and noticing the difference in color between a shadow that was on sand, and one that was on a concrete block.

DK: *Wow!*

NM: I was thinking about that. Being in sunlight activates those rods and cones in our eyes.

DK: *Are there artists who influenced your approach to color?*

ER: Matisse was a wonderful colorist. Let me think...Vuillard, Milton Avery, the Bay Area artists. Artists such as Max Beckman and Manet inspired me in terms of how they used black. I paint with black a lot and it can be tricky. I think all those years of drawing in black and white got me hooked on the graphic potential of black. I've had to really experiment with adding things to black to make it work better.

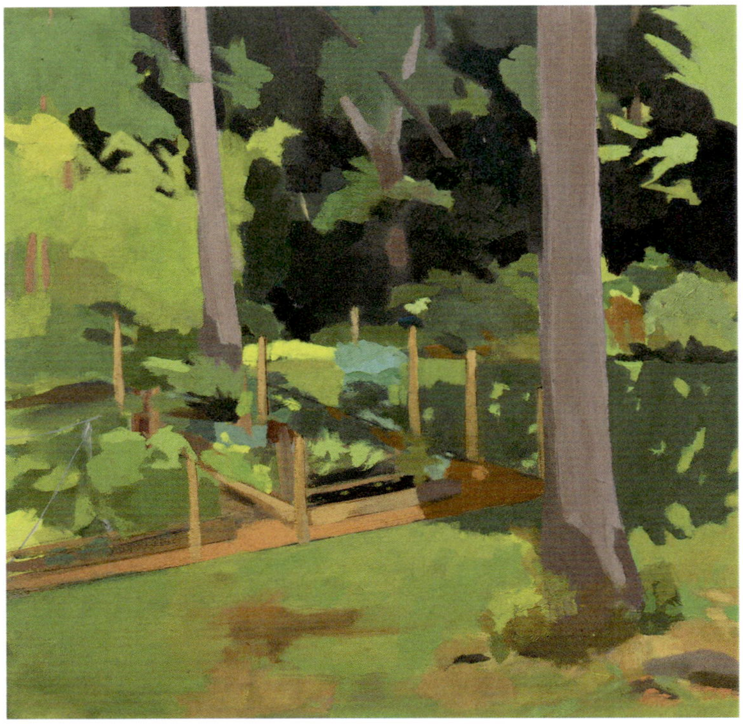

Nancy McCarthy *July Garden*
2021, oil on linen, 24 x 26 in.

DK: *This question is for Nancy. What connections do you make between your landscapes and your still life paintings?*

NM: Well, the process is similar. It's a big puzzle. I'm trying to figure it out and make my way through it. I think there's a difference in my sensibility when I'm outside. I feel a little less constrained, and a little more energized and partly it's because, as I said before, things are changing so quickly that I am ready to dive in. I think I get into the zone quicker when I'm outside. Inside it feels a little more, cerebral isn't the word. When I'm outside I feel like I'm a kid on vacation a little bit, even though I'm struggling every minute. But when I'm inside I feel more like I'm the teacher in the class. As though I'm telling myself what to do until I get in the zone, and all that goes away. I think I'm talking more about the differences than the relationship.

DK: *And do you have a garden? Because I've looked at your paintings on your website, and it looks like you're a gardener.*

NM: Oh, I have a really large garden. So yeah, and I spend way too much time in it, not painting. It's a big draw from my painting. It's a competition actually, because I love it so much.

NM: That's interesting. What kind of black do you use, Elizabeth?

ER: I use Ivory black as a base, and then I add things like pthalo blue or Prussian blue. That seems to give it more luminosity and richness.

DK: *What about you, Nancy? Did that question bring up any other sources for color for you?*

NM: I can't say in particular. Let me think. As a very young person going to the Museum of Fine Arts, looking at the Impressionist collection, which is huge there.

Also, because we were in the Lower Cape, we would go to all the galleries in Provincetown, and when I was young, it was all abstract then. But I remember being excited by it, and thinking it was really cool. So that experience, too.

DK: *Yeah, that's interesting. Bonnard was my gateway color person. I saw his work when I was in Paris when I was twenty, and I'd never heard of him.*

Windows and doorways are present in both of your works. Do you see them as openings to other spaces or realities, as structural, or in any other ways?

NM: A couple of things for me. One is just as a compositional element, you know, either the full rectangle or the rectangle within a rectangle or the implied rectangle

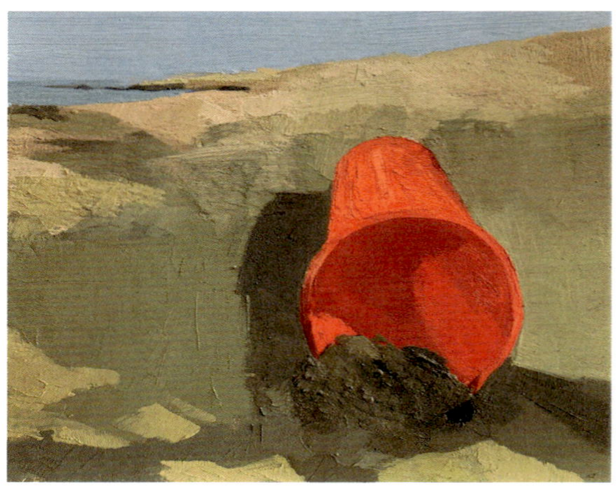

Nancy McCarthy *Red Cup*
2023, oil on board, 6 x 11 in.

if we're seeing a piece of the window. The other thing is the juxtaposition of interior space and outdoor space.

ER: I too see it as compositional. That's the initial attraction. I was painting still lifes in my studio against walls, and I set up one against a window, and it figuratively and literally opened up a whole new world. It added a sense of expansiveness. What I also really like is just how the rectangle of a window creates a painting within the painting.

***DK:** Follow up question. Sometimes, when I look at your recent work, I have the feeling that the still life is a jumping off point for some other kind of meaning, or may be metaphorical. You're also pushing the abstract qualities of still life. Do you want to talk about your recent work?*

NM: You know it's not conscious. And some of my recent work is actually similar to work I was doing a long time ago, twenty years ago. In particular that piece, the *Flamingos with the Moon*. I did a whole series of paintings with a circular table, and that was kind of the basis for that. I can't say that it is metaphorical. Sometimes I think I'm saying one thing, but the painting, as it evolves, says something entirely different, and it's not from my head or from intention, it just kind of comes out. Yeah, and that's kind of the exciting part, I guess, when that happens.

ER: But those and the crystal ball that seems like something very specific. There had to be intention there. I don't know.

NM: I put two flamingos, plastic flamingos, in front of a table, with a crystal ball on it, and initially a gourd as well. I had a big gourd sitting there, and the gourd just didn't work. It was this pale color. I took out the neck, and then I painted it yellow, and made the flamingos a little less plastic. Then I invented the landscape. I often invent landscapes behind things.

***DK:** Elizabeth, your paintings of interiors strike me as domestic landscapes. This is because of their meandering open-ended quality, not in the way that they're painted, but in the way they are composed. Is narrative part of what you're going for in some of that work.?*

ER: Not really. My process is very intuitive, and I often arrive at places where I didn't expect to be. It's hard not to imply a narrative at all in a painting when you've included objects or people, but I like the idea of a do-it-yourself narrative where the viewer can interpret things as they like. I'm not pushing a specific agenda or being overt. I really don't begin with a narrative. I sometimes think I'm really an abstract painter, because I'm so focused on the formal aspects of the paintings.

***DK:** That makes sense. You've both talked about this somewhat. Can you talk any more about your relationship to abstraction?*

NM: I often make, on and off, a series of small abstract paintings. Often in gouache, in between doing a painting that takes me forever. Just as a way to open up my taste buds. I don't think I do enough abstract painting to feel like I have fluency in the language or that I have my own language, but I may move more deeply into it. And basically, I think it's all abstract, whether it's things

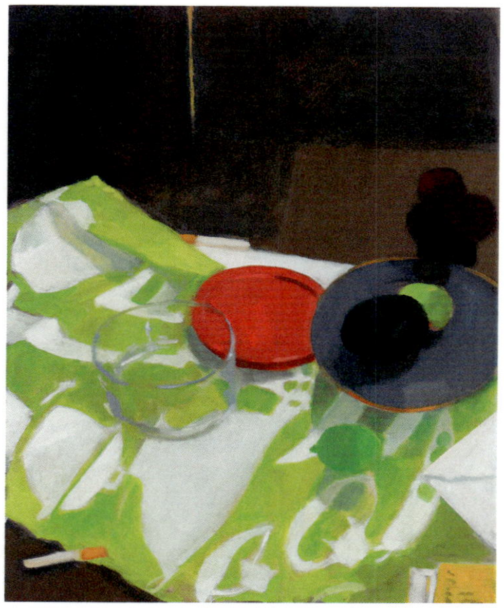

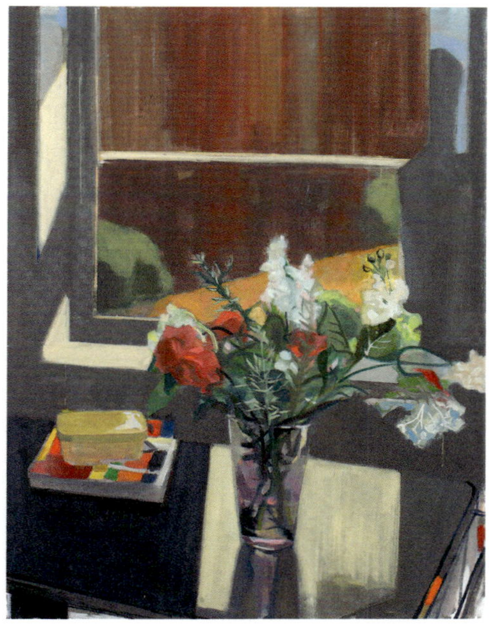

Top to bottom:

Elizabeth Reagh
American Spirit 2
2022, oil on panel, 20 x 16 in.

Elizabeth Reagh *Fall Bouquet*
2020, oil on canvas, 40 x 30 in.

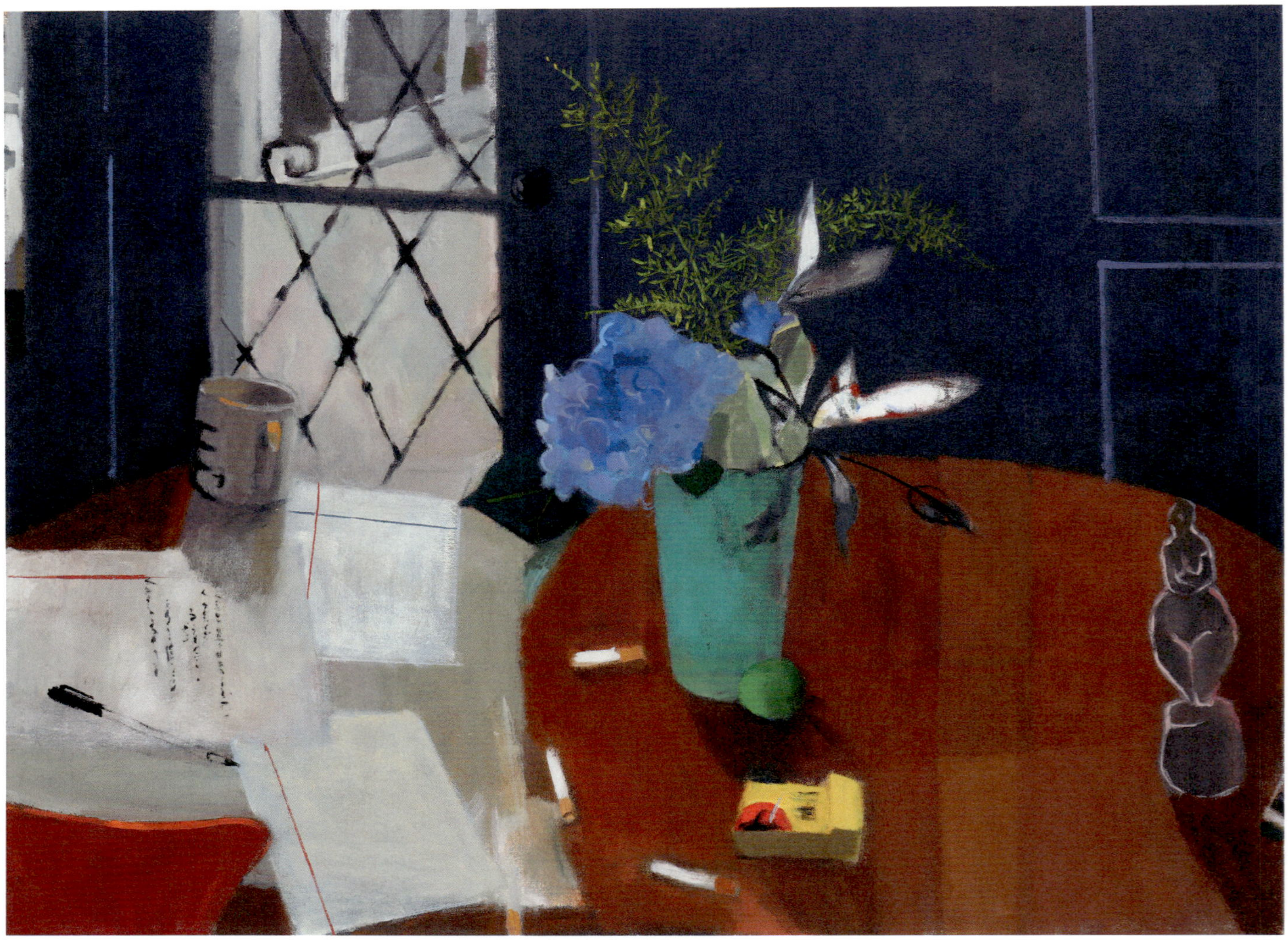

Elizabeth Reagh *American Spirit*
2022, oil on canvas, 30 x 40 in.

we look at and can put words to, or whether it's just shapes of color that don't imply something that we're familiar with. It's all about shapes and color and value.

DK: *You have a pretty developed history with abstraction, too, don't you, Elizabeth?*

ER: I went through an extended period where I worked abstractly. Because I spent so much of my early life as an artist drawing observationally exclusively, and the teaching I received was very traditional, I felt some discomfort with abstract art, as if it just wasn't for me. And then, when I moved to Brooklyn, one of the first people I met was my dear friend Emily Berger—we met through our kids' preschool. Emily is a wonderful abstract painter and through her I met other abstract painters and really began to understand and appreciate abstraction more. Then I just decided to try it, and really enjoyed it. I don't think of myself as an abstract painter, but so much of what I do feeds off abstract concepts. And I like artists like Diebenkorn who went back and forth between abstraction and figuration. I think that's great, because both approaches are so helpful for the other.

DK: *I wondered if there are other pursuits you follow outside of painting. Is there anything that sustains, adds to, or takes away from, your painting life?*

ER: Well, I feel like the older I get, all I want to do is paint, but I realize I have to have a life, and so I really do enjoy the friends and family I have. I also like gardening, but I'm a newcomer to it. I used to really like cooking, but, as I said, all these things take time—time away from painting.

DK: *It's a familiar theme. What about you, Nancy?*

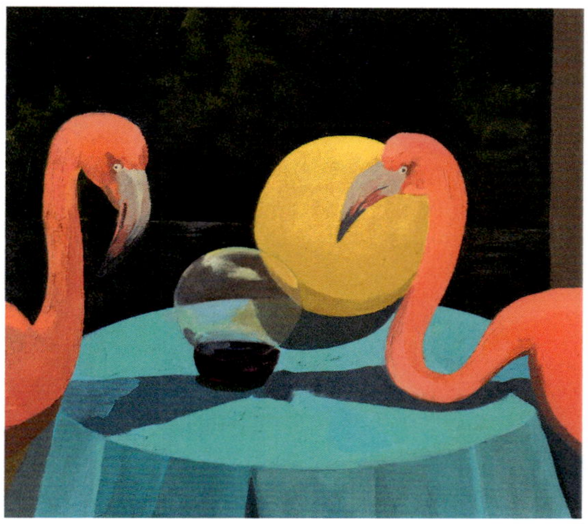

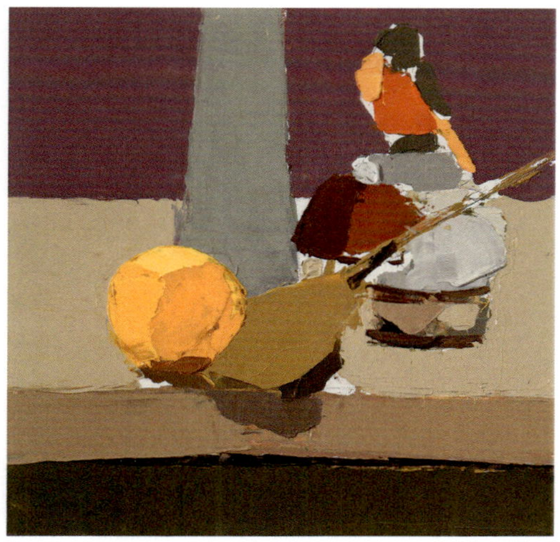

LEFT TO RIGHT:

Nancy McCarthy
Moon Visiting the Fortune Tellers
2022, oil on linen, 24 x 26 in.

Nancy McCarthy
One Robin
2022, oil on board, 10 x 10 in.

NM: Yeah, I do a lot of teaching, both undergraduates and workshops. I get a lot of inspiration and community from teaching, and I enjoy it. But it takes away. It takes time, so it's always like, why did I say I'd do this, you know, and then you get so much out of it. You get fed by it, I think, and energized. A couple of years ago I found a guitar at our local dump, and I've been taking lessons. So that's been great. I love it, but again it's time. But it's my choice.

ER: I know people who have retired, and they look for ways to fill up their time. I just can't imagine that! Yeah, we're really lucky.

DK: *I retired from teaching almost three years ago and it's a different chapter. Opportunities come your way and you can say yes to them. More time for painting and for projects like this one. I want to wrap up by thanking you both for the chance to talk about your work. I'm so glad I got to meet you both; this has been really insightful!*

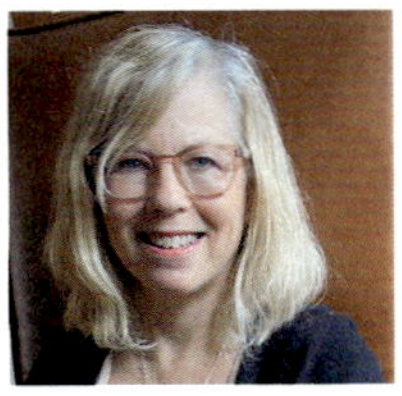

Deborah Kirklin is a San Francisco Bay Area painter who exhibits her work nationally and focuses on still life and landscape. She is represented by Fourth Wall Gallery in Oakland, CA. A member of Zeuxis since 1994, Kirklin was also a professor at Santa Rosa Jr. College in Santa Rosa, CA, where she taught painting and drawing for many years. She earned her BA in Studio Art from Stanford University and an MFA in painting from the University of Iowa. Kirklin was awarded artist residences at the Ragdale Foundation (2007) and the Virginia Center for the Creative Arts (2016, 2022). She has been a guest lecturer at Stanford University, University of California at Santa Cruz, San Jose State University, Notre Dame de Namur University, and CCA in Oakland, CA.

www.deborahkirklinartist.com

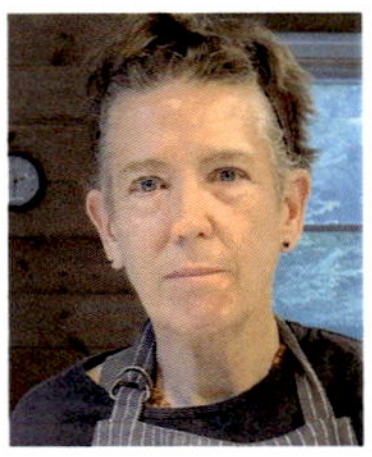

Nancy McCarthy is a Massachusetts based painter. She works from observation, memory and imagination. Recent exhibitions include the Summer Show at the Larkin Gallery, Provincetown, MA., and the Paperscapes show at There Gallery, NYC. Awards include: Visiting Artist, Beijing Royal School; residency at Inside Out Museum, Beijing; a St. Botolph Foundation Award; Vermont Studio Center Artist's Grant and a Ragdale Foundation Fellowship. Her work is represented by the Larkin Gallery, Provincetown, MA. and she shows with Zeuxis in New York. She teaches at Massachusetts College of Art and Design in Boston, MA. and is co-owner of Black Pond Studio in Rehoboth, MA.

www.nancymccarthypainting.com

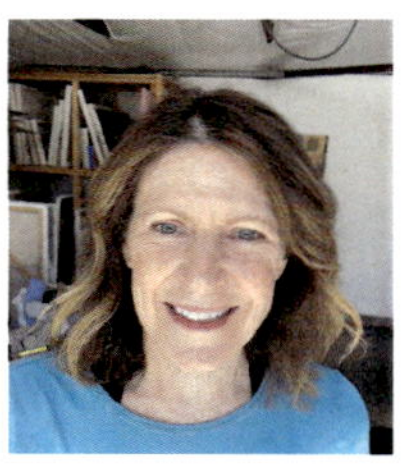

Elizabeth Reagh was born and raised in the Echo Park neighborhood of Los Angeles. She lived and worked in Brooklyn, NY for twenty years, before moving back to California in 2019. She received a BA in art from San Francisco State University, and an MFA from the University of Oregon in Eugene. Reagh's work is influenced by both East and West Coast sensibilities, with a current focus on still life. Observational drawing is an ongoing parallel practice. Reagh has shown in New York and California, and has paintings and drawings in collections across the U.S. and in Europe. In 2021 she had solo shows at B. Sakata Garo Gallery in Sacramento, California and the Project Room at The Painting Center, NY. Reagh will be teaching a 4-week workshop for Black Pond Studio in June, 2022.

www.elizabethreagh.com

Unfolding

Joe Morzuch interviews

Andrew Marcus
and
Christina Renfer Vogel

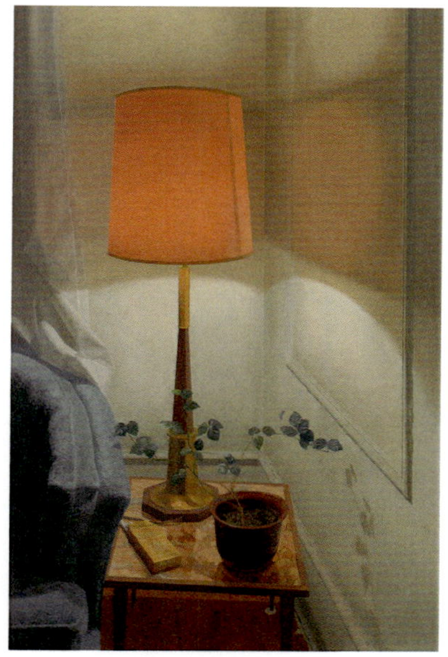

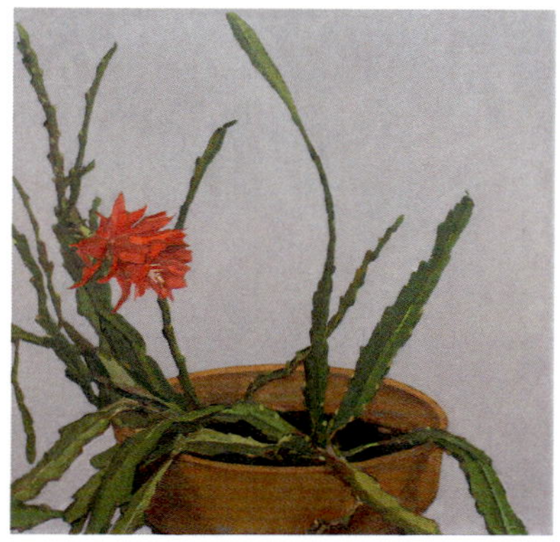

Andrew Marcus *Side Table with Lamp*
2005, oil, 40 x 26 in.
Christina Renfer Vogel *Studio Bloom*
2023, oil on canvas, 20 x 20 in.

Joe Morzuch: *Andrew, Christina, and I had the following correspondence via email exchange over the course of three weeks. I was excited for the chance to get to know both artists through this kind of dialogue, and spent hours studying their work and preparing questions beforehand. After our first exchange, however, I realized that a much more fluid and responsive "conversation" would be far more interesting than anything I could script. Thank you Andrew and Christina for your insightful comments and your wonderful, inspiring work. Enjoy!*

JM: *Thank you both for this exciting opportunity! I am grateful for the chance to discuss your work, interests, and studio practice. My hope is to start with an initial question to get the ball rolling, and follow up from there with a series of exchanges that are organic and conversational. I'd love for each question/response to flow naturally, and will do my best to build on your answers while initiating additional topics and ideas as we move forward.*

I am curious to learn how you came to make the work you are currently engaged with. How did you become an artist? In what ways has your background/upbringing informed your practice, and how did you come to still life as a central theme or subject within the studio?

Christina Renfer Vogel: I am an anomaly in my family. I had no artist models growing up, and going to see art was not something I ever did with my family. But I had strong, encouraging art teachers and a high school history teacher who suggested I look into Temple's art school, Tyler, not far from where I grew up, because he heard it was good—in the end, I landed there. While I have made art since childhood, in many ways it seems quite lucky that I got my start on that path.

In undergrad and grad school, I worked figuratively, making narrative multi-figure paintings, portraits, and self portraits. A body of work that emerged years after grad school was a series of paintings of solitary objects that were stand-ins for figures. I was thinking about archetypes, family roles along gender lines, and societal expectations. The paintings were of significant objects that represented these larger ideas. Looking back, that kind of planted a seed for still life, something I had never explored in my personal work.

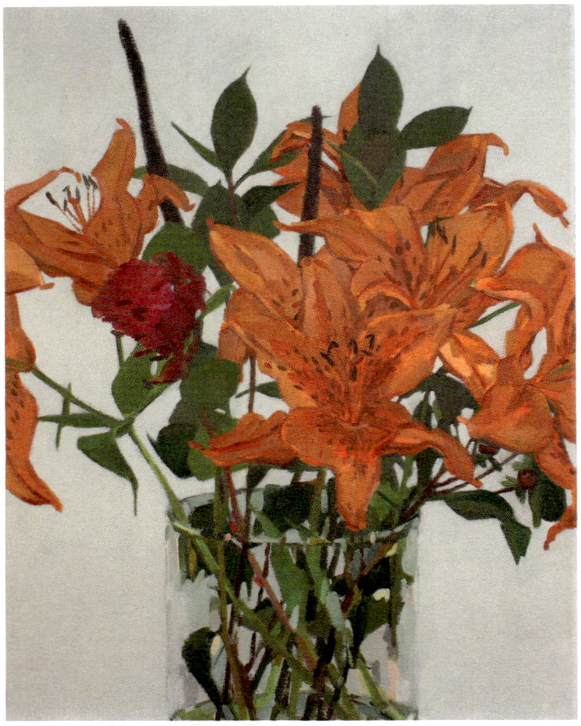

Christina Renfer Vogel
14 Years (Orange Lilies)
2023, oil on canvas,
20 ¼ x 15 ½ in.

The paintings I've been making recently came out of an impulse to bring plants into my studio to serve as subjects. At the time, I was seeking work that felt restorative and nourishing during a difficult period for me personally and professionally. I have always found comfort in plants and have made them a part of living and work spaces throughout my life. Some plants have been companions moving with me through various life stages and locations, and many started as cuttings from artist friends—plants are so generous and generative in that way, and I love that they are imbued with history and in some cases, personal relationships. I started painting flowers for many of the same reasons, but I was also interested in their overt beauty and associations with femininity.

Flowers are fleeting and this encouraged a more urgent, energetic way of working, which felt—and continues to feel—exciting alongside slower work. I sometimes include patterned backdrops to extend and echo the visual relationships found within the plants and flowers to the surrounding space to create a figure ground complexity. While this work is certainly in still life territory, I think the work also feels akin to portraiture. The paintings I am working on now feel most strongly rooted in still life, complex arrangements of multiple objects staged in my studio.

Andrew Marcus: Thank you for your patience. The question, how did I become an artist? I can't say for sure why. I do think my father, who was a writer and used to take me to art museums when I was a kid, was an important influence on why I became an artist. I remember when I was 12 years old, I showed my dad a sketch I made from a Toulouse Lautrec drawing and how excited he was about it and how great that made me feel. I went to art school at a time when new interest in representational art was happening. I always felt a natural bent within me to paint perceptually. How did I come to still life? Again, a question I find difficult to answer. My formative years as an artist came in the 70's when I saw a number of exciting art shows. Artists such as Pearlstein, Laderman, Wiesenfeld, William Bailey, Catherine Murphy, Larry Day and others had shows at the time that were very moving for me and these were all artists that made wonderful still lifes. I'm sure the experience of seeing their work encouraged me in pursuing still life as a direction for my work.

To answer the question, how did I come to do my current work, I'd have to say if twenty years ago I was told what kind of work I am doing today, I wouldn't believe it! From being totally committed to painting as my one and only medium I now, at least for the past several years, do only drawings, in pencil and charcoal. The reason I changed was to speed up my production since as a painter I was extremely slow. The crazy thing is the drawings I do take me even more time than the paintings!

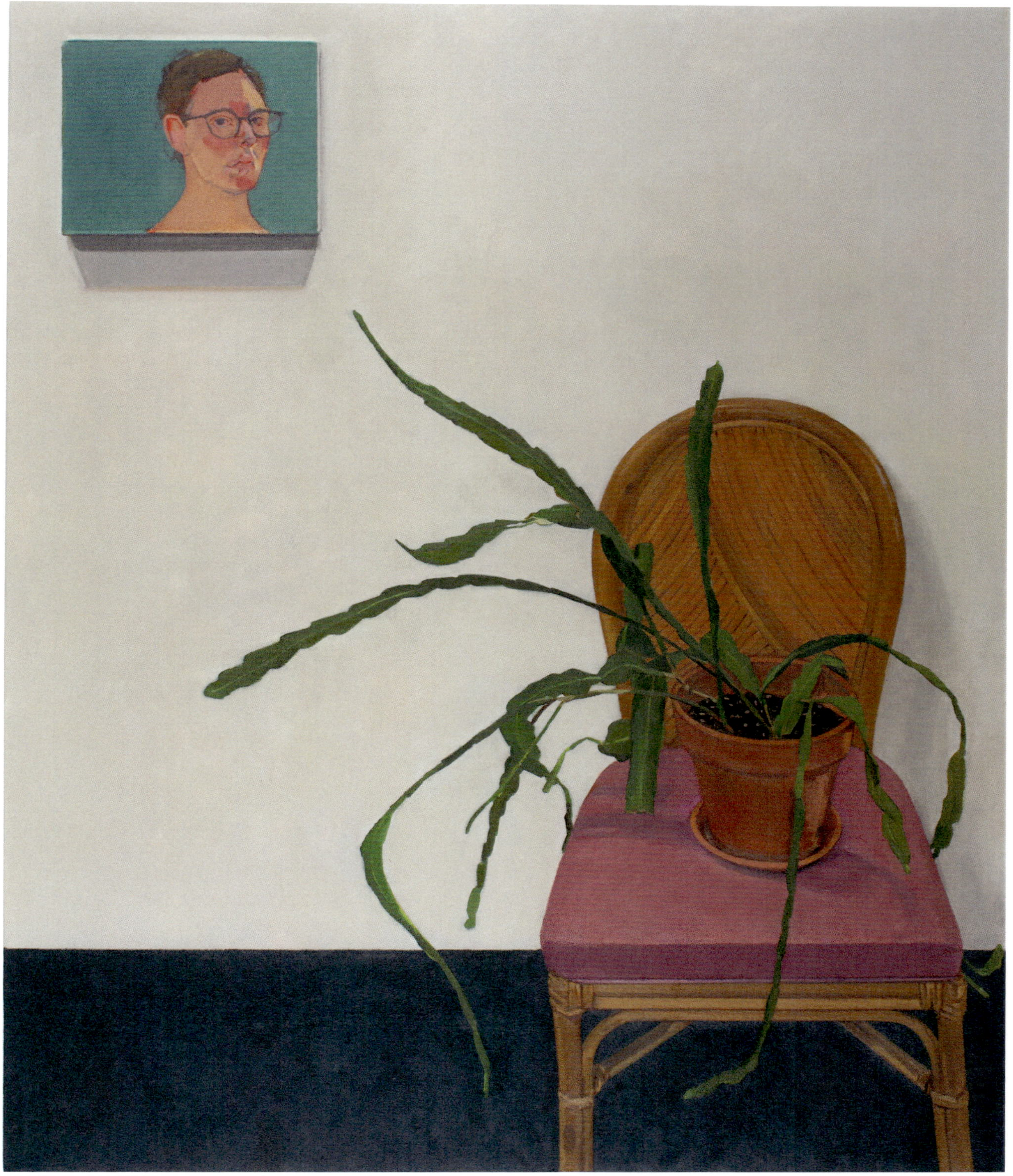

Christina Renfer Vogel *Double Portrait*
2021, oil on canvas, 48 x 40 in.

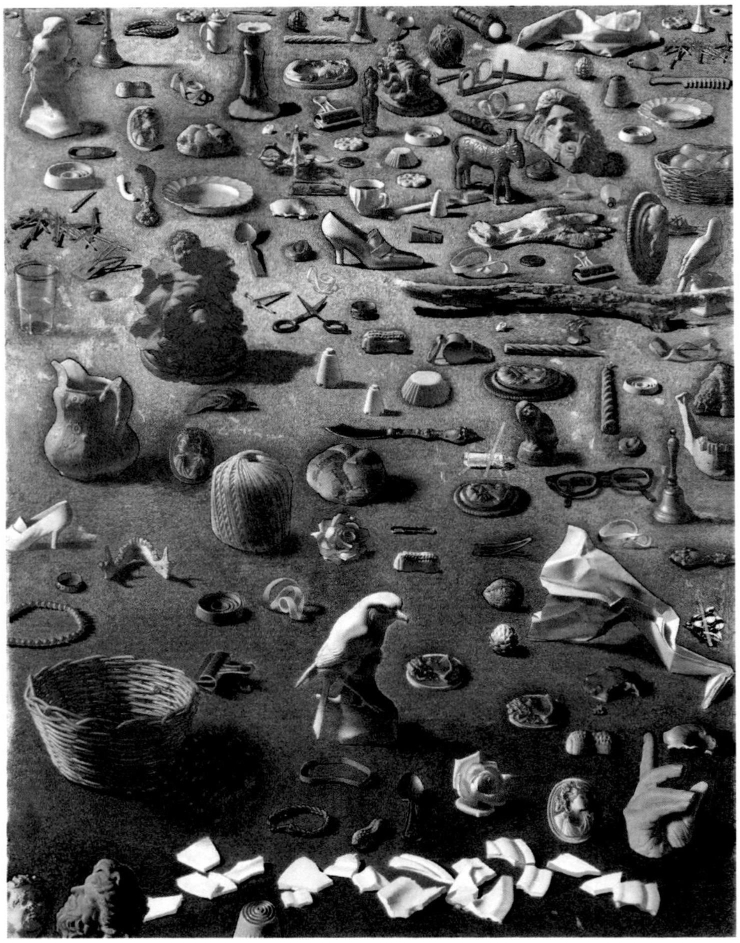

Andrew Marcus *Homage to a Paper Airplane*
2020, graphite on Arches 300 lb. watercolor paper, 32 x 24 in.

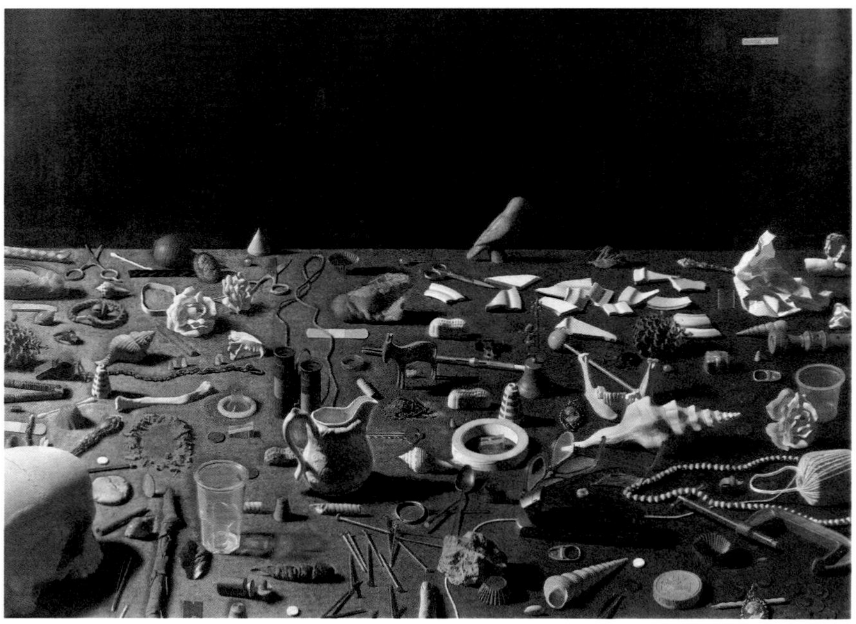

Andrew Marcus *Still life Drawing No. 4*
2010, graphite on Arches 300 lb watercolor paper, 32 x 34 in.

JM: *You both mentioned the importance of other artists to your practice and well-being. Who are the artists, contemporary and historical, that you have carried with you throughout your careers? What about their work do you find interesting or exciting? In what ways have you found support in local, regional, or broader artist communities?*

AM: As a teenager there were two artists that I loved. Salvador Dali and Vincent Van Gogh, two very different artists. I loved Dali for his brilliant technical ability, how he was able to make paintings that had such a powerful illusion of reality, even though that reality was unreal. I loved Van Gogh for his freedom in using color. Another artist I loved as a kid and I still do is Ingres. His little pencil portraits are so beautiful, so precise. Remember, I'm quite an old geezer so I have memories that probably predate Christina. In the early 70's the Whitney Museum put on a show called "Twenty Two Realists". At that show I first discovered the paintings of Paul Wiesenfeld and Gabriel Laderman. Wiesenfeld mainly painted interiors, some with a figure, some without. Unfortunately he died fairly young so now he's unknown. I think of him as an American Vermeer. His ability to control the different elements within an interior was remarkable. I remember seeing a Chardin still life, one of his late works, at the Boston Art Museum, very simple, just a bowl of grapes and a few other things.

Superficially, one would think how conventional, and yet looking at it I had the peculiar feeling that it was ALIVE. A show that William Bailey had in the mid 70's when he stopped painting eggs and started inventing types of crockery was very moving for me. The sense of perfection, of creating an ideal world out of these simple objects gave me a feeling that wonderful things could be done with still life that maybe devoting a big part of one's artistic life to this genre might be worth it. Another still life that stopped me in my tracks was also at the Boston Art Museum, A Harnett of an old violin and some other objects hanging on a door. Why would I find something so commonplace so amazing? This wasn't a painting of the Last Supper, of the Annunciation, of some great narrative from ancient Rome, and yet for me it was just as important, just as meaningful.

CRV: Paul Wiesenfeld and Gabriel Laderman are new to me, Andy, and I am happy to learn about their work. I'm interested in how the work

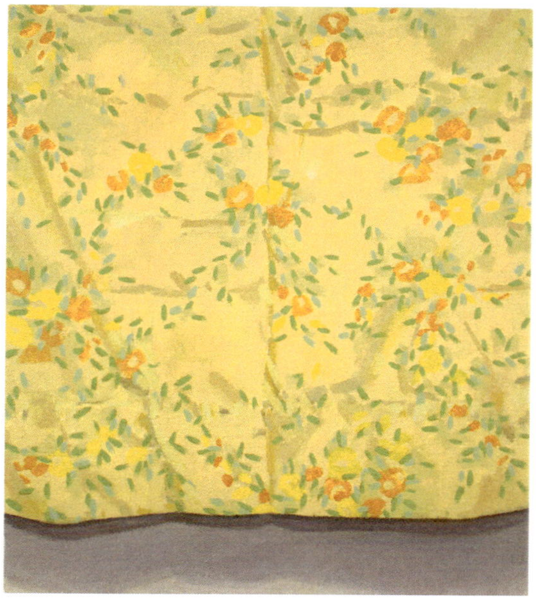

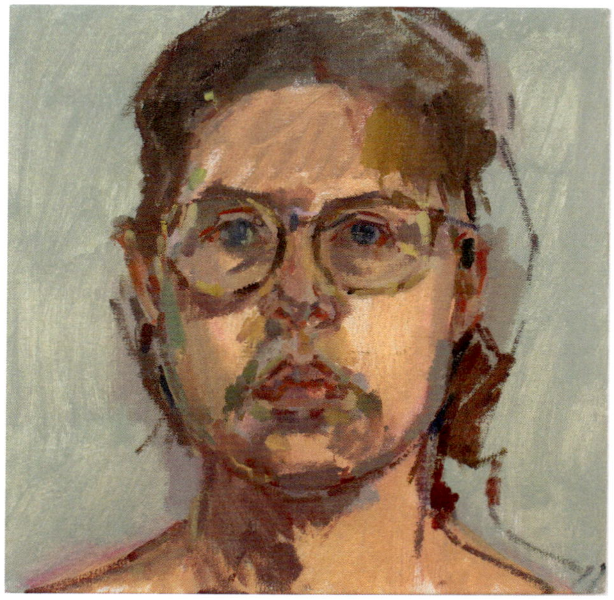

Left to right:

Christina Renfer Vogel
Yellow Roses
2021, oil on linen, 16 x 14 in.

Christina Renfer Vogel
Self Portrait as a Difficult Woman
2022, oil on canvas, 12 x 12 in.

of the artists you mention seem to share a kind of clarity and stillness, and I love how you talk about Wiesenfeld's ability to control the different elements.

Frida Kahlo was an early love for me, and I think her work has certainly introduced an interest in self-portraiture and personal narrative. As I give it more thought now, I also respond to her use of flatness and patterning as well as the direct centrality of her figures; surely these qualities helped to shape my visual language. It was definitely not cool to like Kahlo's work in college, but I think those sorts of prejudices have largely shifted. Much of my beginning awareness of artists was shaped in art school, and I spent a lot of time in the library browsing books and making new discoveries—this was before I was using the internet to research.

I remember checking out and continuously renewing books on Matisse, Seurat (for the drawings), Vuillard, Bonnard, and David Hockney for the color, the touch, and the everyday subject matter. There was an exhibition of Alice Neel's work at the Philadelphia Museum of Art while I was a student, and of course that was so incredible to see in person—Neel's boldness of vision, ability to capture the humanity of her subjects, and her use of drawing, color, and space continue to inspire me. I was also introduced to Susanna Coffey and Euan Uglow due to the work I was making at the time. These are all touchstone artists I continue to revisit.

As a student, I was working figuratively when it wasn't really the thing to do, but I was lucky to have teachers who challenged and supported my developing painting. At Tyler, Susan Moore, who sadly passed away quite recently, was a mentor; as I reflect now, it was incredibly impactful to know her work as well see her model the multifaceted role of working artist, educator, and parent. Susan has truly affected my life and work immeasurably. There are so many artists whose work I have come to know and love, more than I could possibly list here. But among the artists who have been on my mind lately are Lois Dodd, Amy Sillman, Susan Jane Walp, Jennifer Packer, Sangram Majumdar, Josephine Halvorson, Albert York, and Jane Freilicher. Of course their work is quite different, but I think they are all careful observers of the world and simply tremendous painters.

Living in Chattanooga for ten years now, after relocating for my current teaching position, I'm far from an art center but am within a two-hour drive from Nashville, Knoxville, Atlanta, and Birmingham. I feel somewhat isolated in my immediate community, so I try to make it a point to get to those places to see art and connect with other artists. I find artists in the Southeast are excited to meet others who are serious about their work and are making a life in the region. As artists we are part of an ecosystem, and this generous and ambitious community has been so important and nourishing for my practice.

JM: *I know those artists well! It's so fascinating to think of them in connection to both of your work, observation, and the complexities of working perceptually. I'm interested to hear about your connection to observational painting, not just as a process or a means to examine and analyze form, but as maybe something more transcendent..? Vermeer, Van Gogh, Bonnard, Chardin, Neel, Giacometti, Uglow, and Walp, whose paintings are so rooted in the visual, seem so invested in observation as a generative activity. The work is grounded in looking, but also completely opens up and unfolds because of it. I wonder if you two experience something similar when working from life?*

AM: One of the things interesting about painting from observation is that, unlike a photo, the objects represented (still life objects, human figures, mountains, etc) are mere fabrications. That painted (or drawn) bowl, coffee cup, spoon, gun, plant, etc. is only an illusion, just paint or graphite controlled skillfully to make it look real. It's the "not thereness" of realistic painting (whether one is conscious of it or not) that for me is one of the defining things that distinguish it from mechanical forms of visualization. (Although digital representation might be more problematic). For my own work, the "realism" I do is pretty simple minded. I'm interested in a very literal kind of representation, drawing or painting things as close to what my eyes see as I can. Why? Temperament, geography, upbringing, whatever I got from art school, who can say.

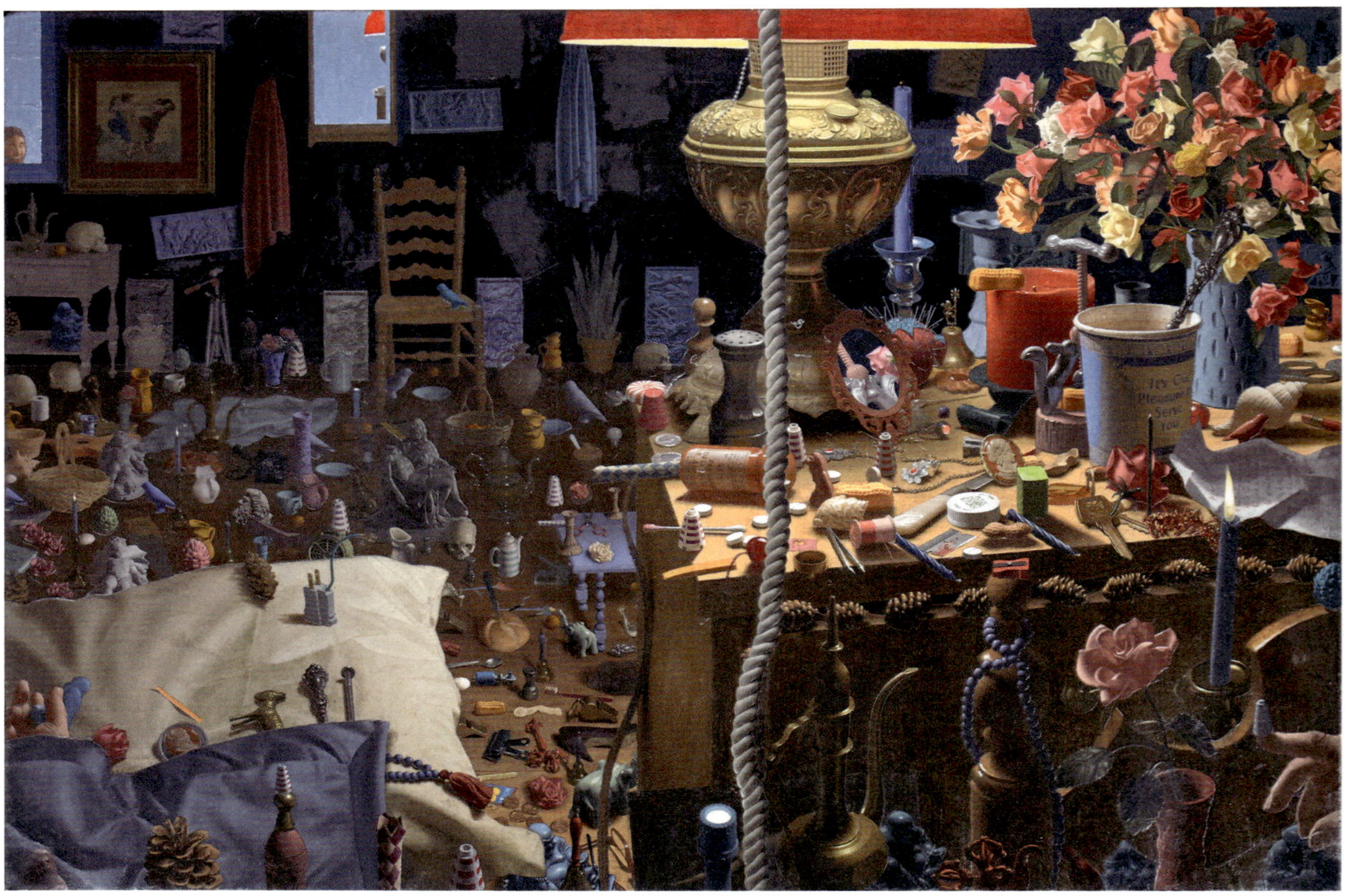

Andrew Marcus *The Still Life Painter has a Nightmare*
2018, oil, 23 x 36 in.

Certainly there is an "unfolding," to use your word, of possibilities as one works perceptually on a painting or drawing. Highly wrought drawing that sometimes takes me months to complete has been my main effort. My still lifes are not based on any set up. There is no arrangement of objects on a tabletop. The drawing paper itself is my tabletop. I use a collage technique throughout the whole process, using individual studies of objects, each cut out separately. This enables me to move them about on the paper, sometimes in dozens of different configurations and finally taping them where they will eventually be drawn on the paper. How the drawing unfolds and develops is never predetermined and has always surprised me when it's completed.

CRV: I do find working from observation to be generative. I know some people consider working in this way to be limiting, but I think that is tied to the notion of copying with exactitude, which is not my goal nor my interest. I do want there to be a sense of accuracy in terms or proportion; that's because I believe it helps me to achieve something akin to the gesture and spirit of the thing painted, but also, as I think on that some more, I do enjoy the struggle of working that part out—sighting and measuring, drawing, finding spatial relationships, working and reworking, etc. Like Andy, your idea of unfolding resonates with me. Rather than feeling bound by my subject matter in a way that some folks might assume would be limiting.

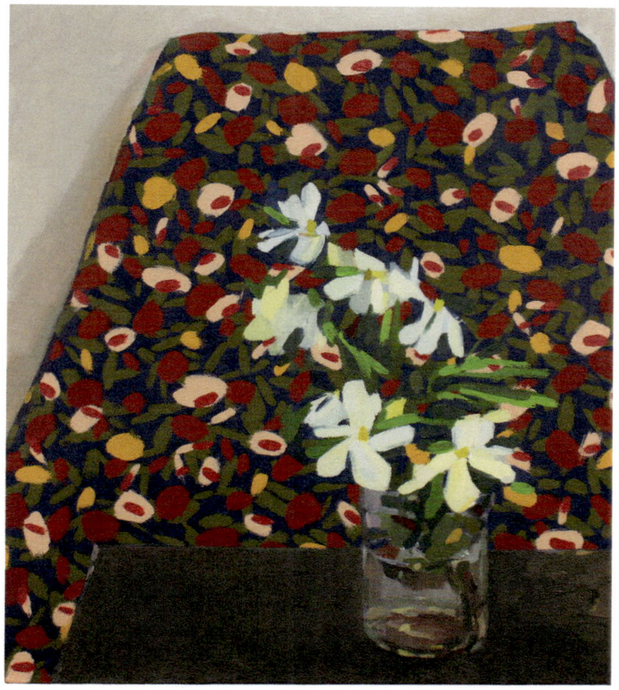

Christina Renfer Vogel
B's Scarf with Delicate Flowers
2020, oil on canvas, 16 x 14 in.

I find working from life to be full of potential. It offers me so much discovery and surprise, and it forces me to get into a zone of focus, deep looking and slowness, that feels somewhat radical these days. This is tied to my teaching practice, too, but I am energized by how artists interpret what they see through painting—and of course this could be applied to more than observational painting. There is so much space for one's own visual language to emerge, even if a whole group of students, for example, are looking at the same setup. As I attempt to achieve a kind of fidelity to my subjects, I think there is room for fiction, abstraction, and invention. I hope there are elements of that in my work even while I aim for a kind of directness or straightforwardness at the same time.

And ultimately, I am making paintings after all, so I try to honor the materiality and make decisions that allow paint to be paint rather than attempt to showcase virtuosity or trick anyone into thinking it's anything other than a painting. Working perceptually is an experiential way of making that motivates and sustains me in the studio.

JM: *These are all such wonderful and interesting points! I am reminded of the idea of narrowing one's practice for the purpose of free and focused exploration. To that end, what limitations, self-imposed or otherwise, have you incorporated into your work? Andy, I'm thinking specifically of the graphite drawings, your choice of composition and framing, and the directness of the drawing process. Christina, you have an interesting relationship with time and how it relates to description, resolution, and finish. How does time play into your work, and how do you see the figurative works relative to the still life paintings? Do they come out of feeling pinned-in with still life, or are they an extension of those works?*

AM: How have limitations affected my work? One very practical one is my work space, that I call, rather pretentiously, "my studio." My wife and I were lucky many years ago to move into an apartment that, by New York standards, is quite large. So two of the extra rooms in our apartment I use as my studio space. The main room is about 15 by 12 feet which I use for my work. The smaller

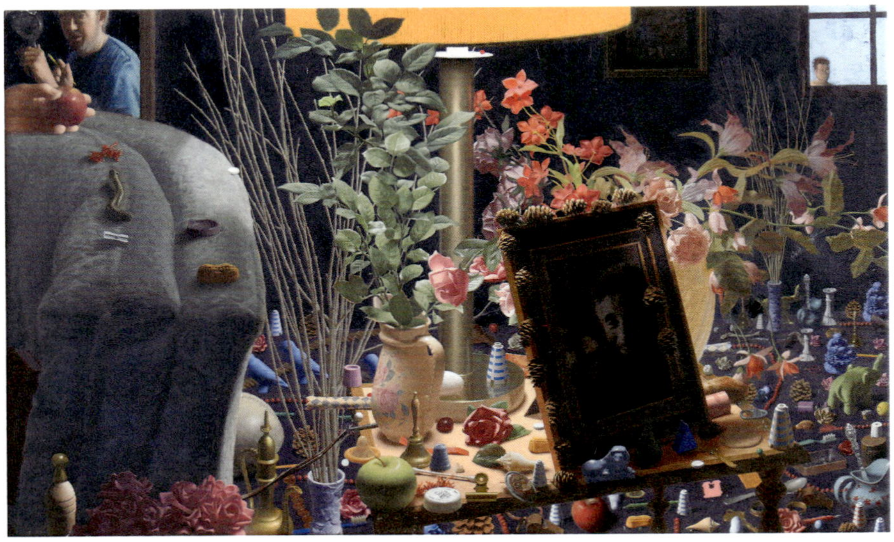

Andrew Marcus
Interior with Family Photo
2016, oil. 23 x 36 in.

room I use to store my work and art materials. This means if I had any grand ideas for doing "Big" painting, it would be impossible. Also my work space has no windows, there is no natural light. Hence all my work is done with artificial lighting. So the limitations of space and light have a direct influence (not only on the dimensions of the work but aesthetically as well) on my practice, ie. modest sized drawings or paintings using only artificial lighting.

Another rule (and a rule always involves a limitation) that I try to follow brings me face to face with a dilemma. I try to limit myself to painting or drawing only what I see, without any mechanical intervention. Why dilemma? I've been blessed or cursed with a desire to represent things, (objects, etc.) as meticulously and objectively as possible. The way I see objects and the way a camera captures objects is nearly identical. This does not apply to how I manipulate space, which I may treat more elastically and freely than a camera. The final limitation I will mention that I have struggled with for most of my career (a word I use with partly tongue in cheek) is Time. I have always been a glacially slow worker. Many years ago I complained about this to a fellow artist and he suggested I switch to a dry medium for awhile. At least, he said, you wouldn't have to wait for the oil paint to dry. So I started doing pencil drawings. The subject matter was the same and my hope was that my production would, if not become prolific, at least speed up. The terrible irony is that the pencil drawings that have become my single commitment as an artist take me even longer to do than my paintings!

CRV: I attended an artist talk by Cynthia Daignault last year, and she talked about painting as a time-based medium; I've been thinking of that ever since. I think of my paintings as marking time, often informed by a life event or relationship. I consider the time spent with my subjects, and then there is the time spent making the work, which varies quite widely. As I touched upon earlier, I like working on faster, smaller work alongside other paintings that build up more slowly (sometimes years, in fits and starts). In response to your observation about resolution and finish, I think it's these different modes of making that result in various levels of description; sometimes I try to work more fluidly and economically and other times I want there to be more of a deliberate and methodical accumulation. As a parent now, and full time professor, focused studio time is difficult to come by, and I try to cherish every moment. Lately I've been thinking about how to work with these limitations, like stopping a painting because I simply don't have more time, even if I might like to push it more.

While still life has become the main thrust of my recent work, I don't think of myself as a still life painter or a figure painter, because those labels feel a bit too limiting. I identify as a perceptual or representational painter certainly, and my work since I've been painting seriously has cycled through portraiture, landscape and interiors, and still life. As I consider the breadth of my work to this point, I don't often see clear divisions between the figurative and still life paintings; I'm working from the same places and continue to revisit core ideas but in different forms.

***JM:** I agree, I feel that time and painting go hand-in-hand. I've really begun to pay attention to time and the effect it has on my work; it feels like one of the main and most interesting variables an artist can work with. In wrapping up, I'd love for you both to discuss what is currently happening in your studio. What are you working on? How is it going? Is there anything you are struggling with, or really excited about? And, if we can project a bit, what do you think might be next?*

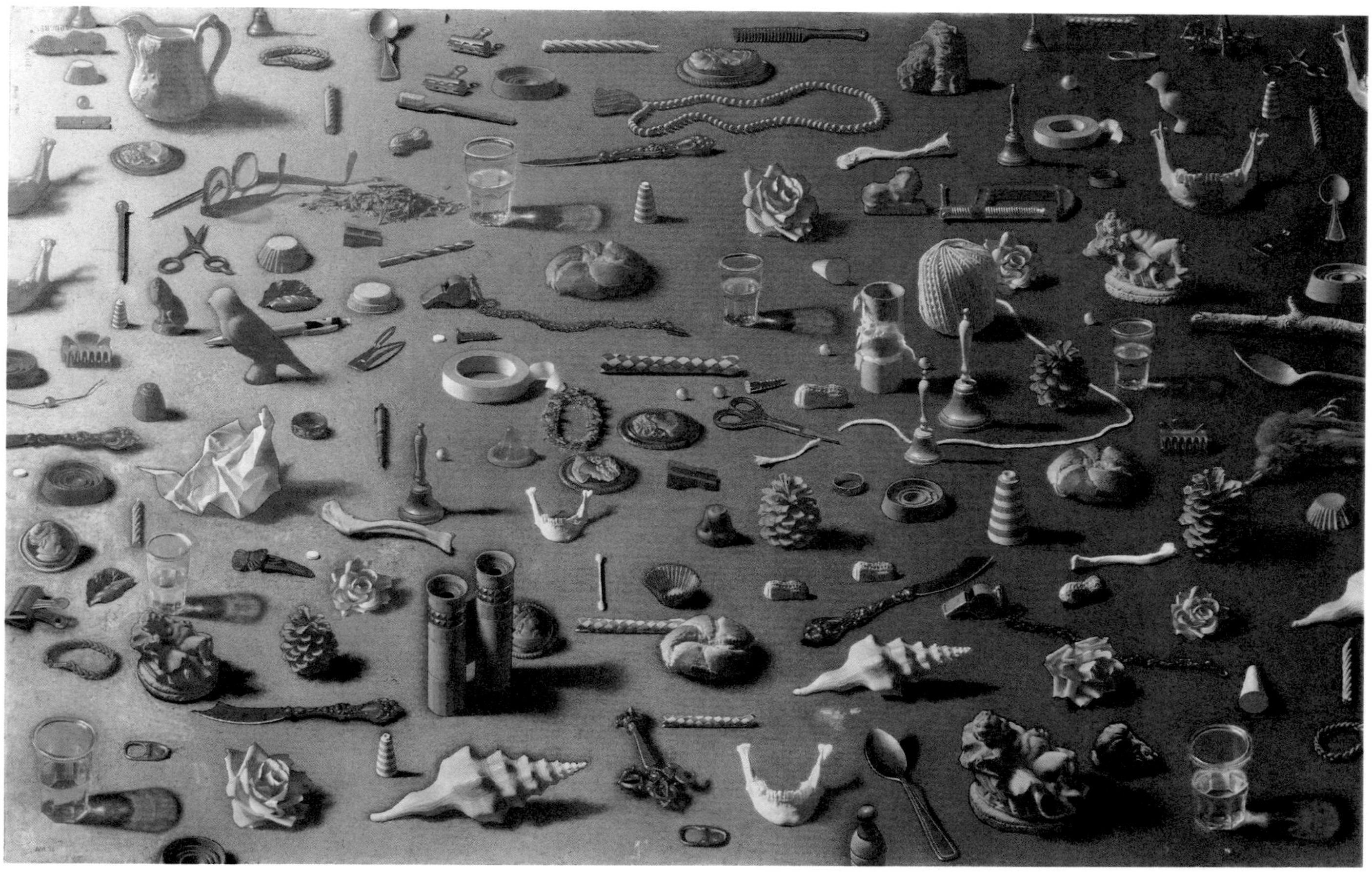

Andrew Marcus *Still Life Homage to Tanguy*
2017, graphite on Arches 300 lb watercolor paper, 24 x 32 in.

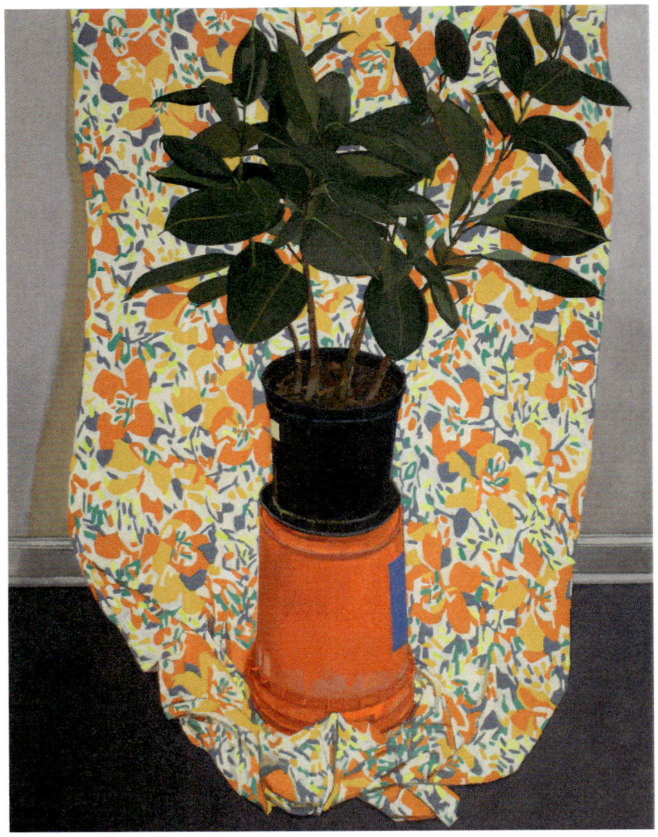

Christina Renfer Vogel *Houseguest*
2020, oil on canvas, 48 x 40 in.

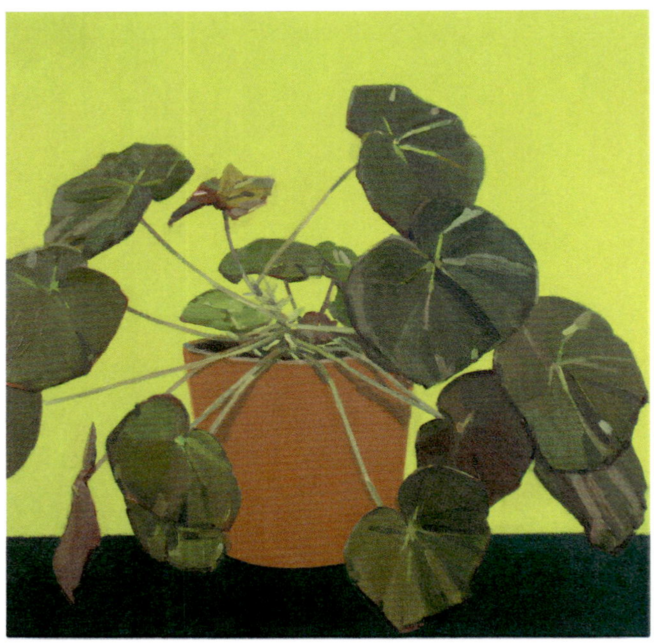

Christina Renfer Vogel *Julia's Begonia*
2023, oil on canvas, 20 x 20 in.

CRV: Lately I've been scaling up to work on more complex still lifes, and some figure paintings, staged within the studio. As painting time feels more precious and harder to come by at this stage of my life, I've been thinking of the studio as a privileged site, a space that is my own for focused thought and work. I honor that space by including utilitarian studio objects such as a Home Depot bucket, extension cord, or studio chair. I am currently working on a painting from a model in my studio, the first time I've done that outside of teaching and since my time as a student, and that has been exciting and challenging. In many ways this work feels like painting about painting, referencing not only the act of making but also my relationship to the rich history of the medium as I consider my place within its continuum. I feel energized by this work and expect that this direction will keep me occupied for some time to come.

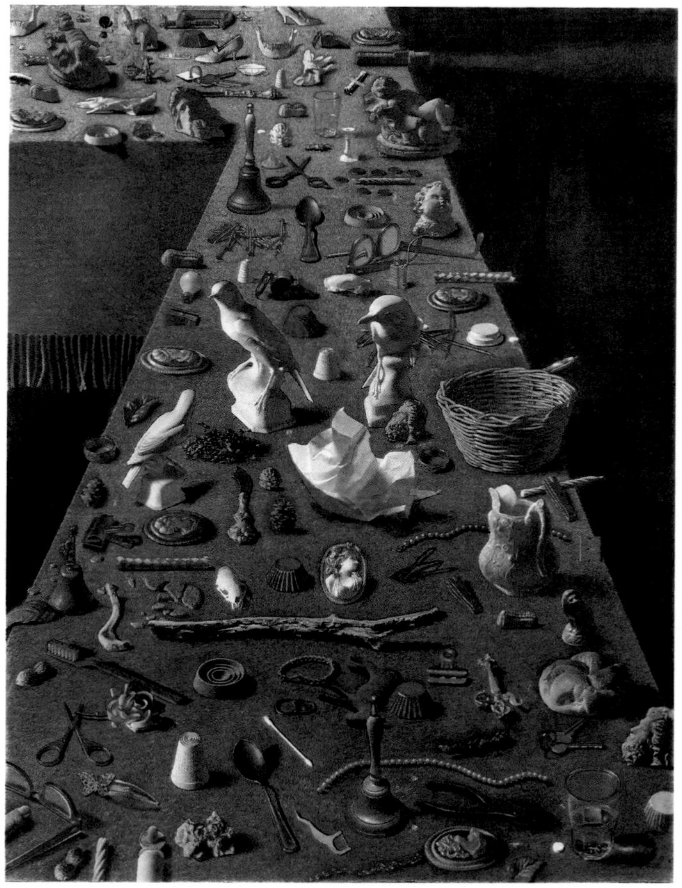

Andrew Marcus *Homage to an Unread Letter*
2022, graphite on Arches 300 lb. watercolor paper, 26 x 40 in.

AM: What I'm working on now is another still-life drawing. When I was in art school I had a teacher who challenged us to work on a drawing for eight hours straight through, suggesting how difficult this would be. Well the drawing I'm doing now was started more than eight weeks ago, maybe even eight months ago! And yes, it is difficult, damn difficult! I don't work from a setup. Another way of putting it, the drawing is the setup. This has advantages and disadvantages. A setup at least suggests a terminus. The setup offers a kind of goal, of course very open ended depending on the sensibility of each artist but at least there's SOMETHING out there to hang your hat on. Without a setup I have freedom to do whatever I want which is great but also daunting. To answer your question "how is it going," some days I think I have a masterpiece, the next day I may feel like ripping it up and either starting all over again or looking for another line of work.

An ongoing question that has nagged at me concerns why my still lifes are so heavily loaded with objects. Is the pressure of the narrative or formal idea that was the original impetus for the drawing such that the resulting abundance of objects represented becomes necessary, or do I have a kind of artistic agoraphobia that causes me to put in many more objects than are necessary to fully express what I'm aesthetically aiming for? Are some of the objects just gratuitous staffage to satisfy what may be horror vacui? Or do all of them have some necessary role to play?

I remember years ago being in Rome and seeing the great Raphael frescoes at the Vatican. Such complexity yet so beautifully composed, a wondrous sense of all in harmony! In my own very modest and imperfect way I try to aim for something like that in my still lifes. But am I enriching the drawing by constantly adding more and more or weakening it by putting too much in? For all the difficulties that come with trying to make something GOOD, of course it can be very fulfilling. As an old person I feel lucky to have something that makes me want to jump out of bed in the morning, go to my studio and "go at it"! As for what's next, I definitely want to simplify. Forget Raphael and think about Morandi. ■

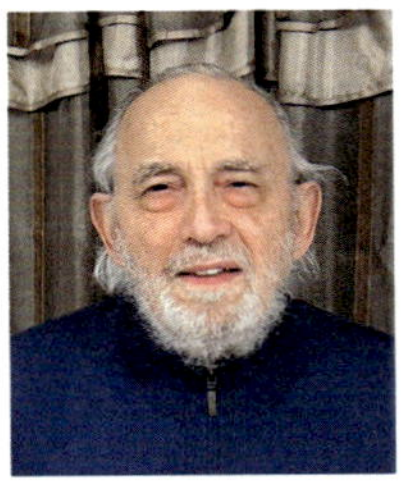

Andy Marcus was born in LA and moved to NYC when he was 16. He early studied at the Brooklyn Museum Art School, then Philadelphia College of Art and the University of Pennsylvania where he recieved an MFA. He has exhibited his work at the Prince Street Gallery, the Artist Choice Museum, and Tatistcheff Gallery. For several years his main interest has been doing black and white still lifes using graphite and charcoal pencil. Some Artists he thinks a lot about, Catherine Murphy, Paul Wisenfeld, Yves Tanguy, early Flemish painting, and old film noir movies.

www.zeuxis.us/marcus

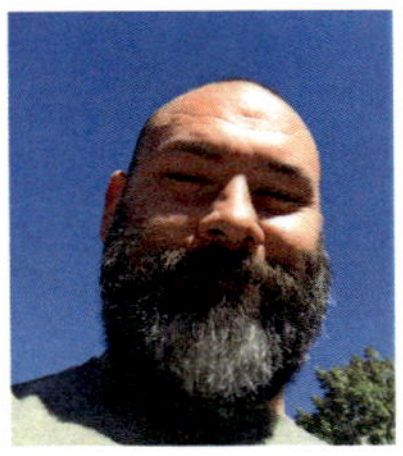

Joe Morzuch is an observational painter currently residing in Starkville, MS. In addition to his studio work, which deals primarily with the still life and self-portrait, he is an Assistant Professor at Mississippi State University. In 2006 he received his MFA from Southern Illinois University Carbondale. He has taught at the college level for nearly 20 years, teaching courses in foundations, drawing, and painting. His work has been exhibited nationwide and abroad.

www.joemorzuchpaintings.com

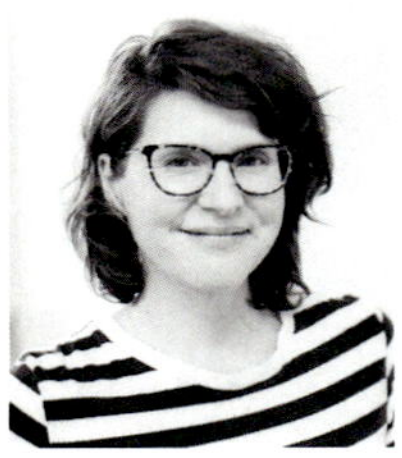

Christina Renfer Vogel holds an MFA from the Massachusetts College of Art and a BFA from Tyler School of Art, Temple University. Her current work represents an intentional turn towards beauty by way of vibrant still life paintings of houseplants and flowers arranged in her studio. Recent exhibitions include a solo exhibition at Spalding Nix Fine Art (Atlanta, GA), inclusion in the 2021 Atlanta Biennial at the Atlanta Contemporary (Atlanta, GA), and a group exhibition at THERE (New York, NY), presented by Zeuxis. Vogel has participated in artist residencies including the JSS in Civita (Civita Castellana, Italy), the Virginia Center for the Creative Arts (Amherst, VA), and the Vermont Studio Center (Johnson, VT). Her work has been featured in New American Paintings, and she is a recipient of an Elizabeth Greenshields Foundation grant and a Lighton International Artists Exchange Program grant, among other awards. Vogel serves as associate professor of painting and drawing at the University of Tennessee at Chattanooga.

www.christinarenfervogel.com

Hanging at the Coffee Shop

Kathleen Craig interviews

Xico Greenwald and Joan Mellon and Cody Heichel

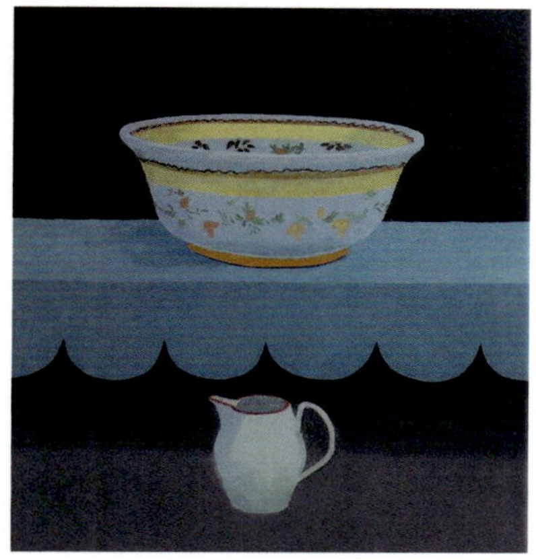

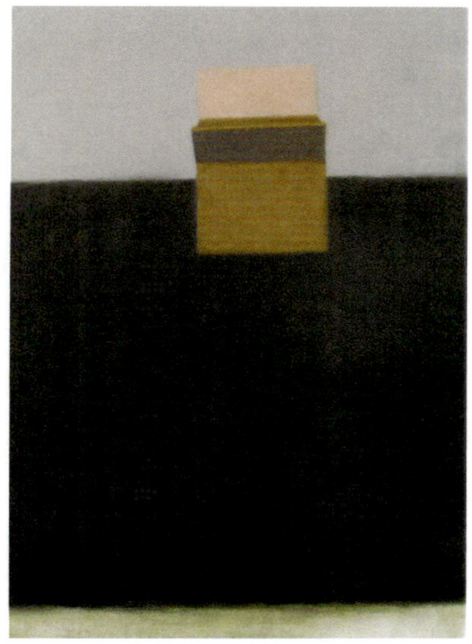

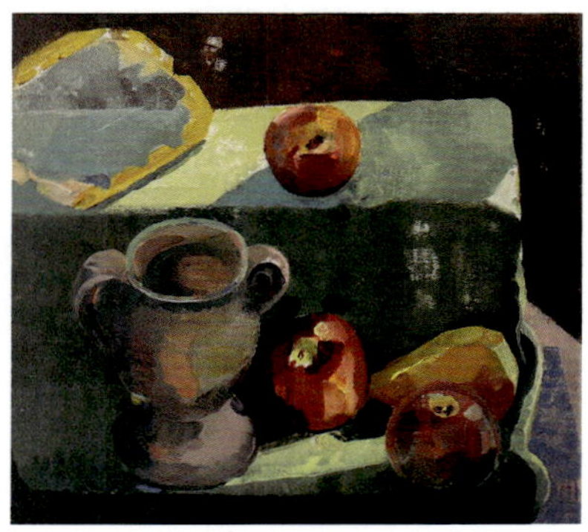

Xico Greenwald *Blue Shelf*
2015, oil on canvas over panel, 55 x 51 in.

Joan Mellon *Box*
2022, oil on canvas over panel, 20 x 16 in.

Cody Heichel *Still Life with Fruit*
2022, oil on muslin mounted on board, 12 ¾ x 14 in.

Kathleen Craig: *Xico Greenwald is a still life painter; Joan Mellon is an abstract painter shifting gears into still life; Cody Heichel is a painter who paints still and other life. Xico and Joan are New Yorkers while Cody and I live in Ohio. In our conversation, I hoped we could make use of the reply-all button to enable a sort of lunch break chat in which the subject could develop more fully or even change direction as the participants spoke with each other rather than to an audience. Cody, Xico, and Joan jumped on this idea; the emails flew back and forth almost faster than I could keep up with them. Their generously shared experience, insights and images have enriched my aesthetic life. I hope they as well as the reader will feel as good as I do about our time together.*

KC: *Some people always knew what they planned to do; some, like me, had to fritter away a lot of time until they made the decision. When, how, and why did you decide to become a painter? Can you describe the moment when painting turned into your job in life?*

I know from your websites that Joan and Xico went to art school and I gather that Cody did not (neither did I). How has that—degree or no degree—worked out for you?

Xico Greenwald: I grew up in Washington DC, around some of America's best museums. My parents appreciated art and we usually made it to major art exhibits. As a youngster I drew regularly. I started painting with oils and drawing from the figure in high school. Looking back, my parents were, on the whole, encouraging.

I went to Bard College where I majored in Studio Art. The faculty there (including Eric Holzman, Elizabeth Murray, William Tucker, Medrie MacPhee, Jake Berthot, Amy Sillman, Joe Santore) were living, breathing examples of working artists and I made the conscious decision to pursue a career as an artist early on my freshman year.

I became a father a couple years after graduating from Bard. When my daughter Imogen was born in 2002, I was working as a part-time art handler at Tibor de Nagy Gallery and Alexandre Gallery, and as a freelance assistant to Jane Freilicher and John Dubrow, among other jobs. I was running around a lot, money was tight and I had a family to attend to. I decided to pursue an MFA at Brooklyn College in 2005, while working part-time, as a way to gain the qualifications I needed to get a college teaching job on a budget. Having an MFA degree is essential to pursuing a career as a college professor and working as a college professor is one of just a few careers that offers the time to conduct "professional research," i.e. time in the studio.

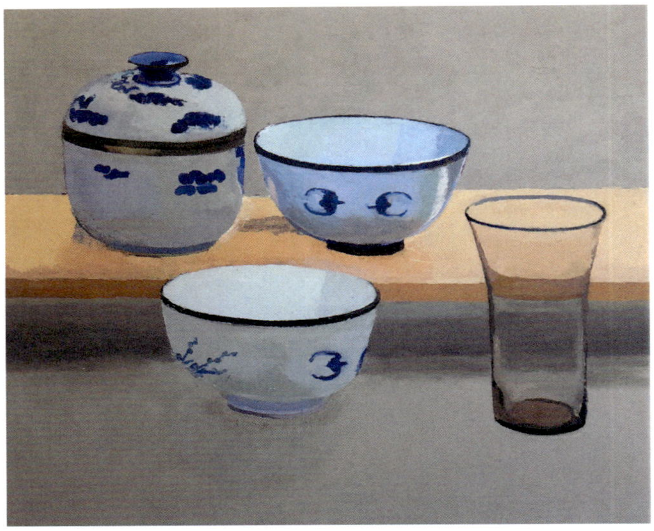

Shortly after grad school, I was hired as an adjunct at Borough of Manhattan Community College (BMCC). I'm still there today, now as a permanent member of the department. It's a marvelous school with wonderful students. I have the best colleagues, including Simon Carr, who demonstrates every day you can teach and make art at the same time.

I'm currently wrapping up a productive yearlong sabbatical. I'll be back on campus in the fall.

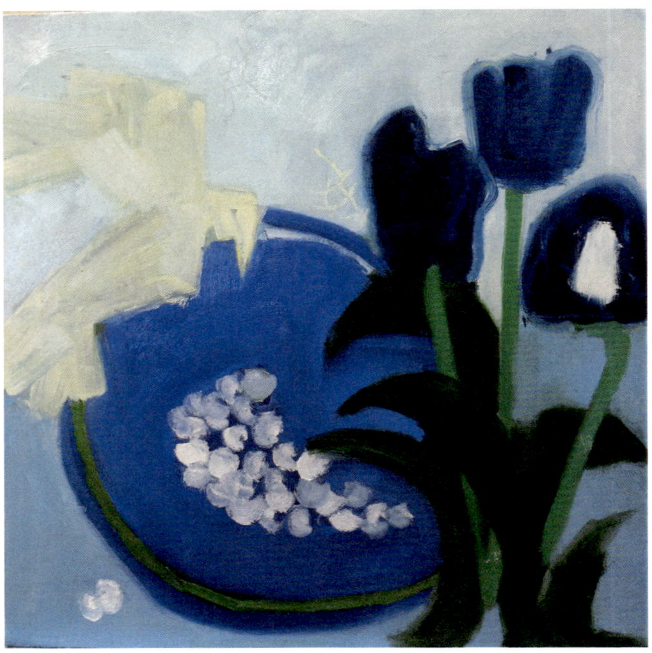

TOP TO BOTTOM:
Xico Greenwald *Chinese Bowls*, 2022, oil on canvas over board, 35 x 41 in.
Kathleen Craig *More Crows, 2018*, oil on canvas, 20 x 20 in.

Cody Heichel: I've always felt a certain comfort in learning on my own time and at my own pace. I was thinking about being a teenager and learning to play the guitar. I had a family friend who offered to give me lessons, and the first thing he had me do was flip my guitar around so that I was playing it as most do: the right-handed configuration. I am left-handed, but I listened and continue to play the instrument today as a right-handed person would. I only took lessons from him for two weeks, but I'm forever curious how I would play or which songs I would have written had I continued to play as a lefty. These choices often come very early on, and can shape so much. I have a lot of similar feelings concerning painting. I wonder what it would have meant for me and for my work had I pursued a degree rather than going alone at it. To be sure though, you never really go alone on anything like this. The teachers just show up in different spaces and times.

In 2010 I became deeply interested in painting. I was 26, and though I no longer see it this way, I felt as if the moment to pursue a degree had passed. In 2011 I found a job in Columbus, OH working for Open Door Art Studio, which is a work space and gallery for adult artists with disabilities. My job was to help artists with varying disabilities to create, exhibit, and sell work. This is when and where I became connected with other artists and the greater arts community. My co-workers were a mixed bag: some held degrees, some didn't, and they all had very complex feelings and advice about the subject. I have ultimately come to view the six years I worked at Open Door Art Studio as my version of college. I learned from my co-workers and from the artists of Open Door. It was my favorite all-time clock in/clock out job; working there really solidified in my mind that I wanted to be a painter. I had been making more money each year from my work, and eventually applied for a fairly significant grant. I decided that if I received the grant then I would use that money and momentum to take the leap and try to make a living at what I loved most. I was fortunate enough to receive the grant, and in 2017 I left Open Door and started painting full time.

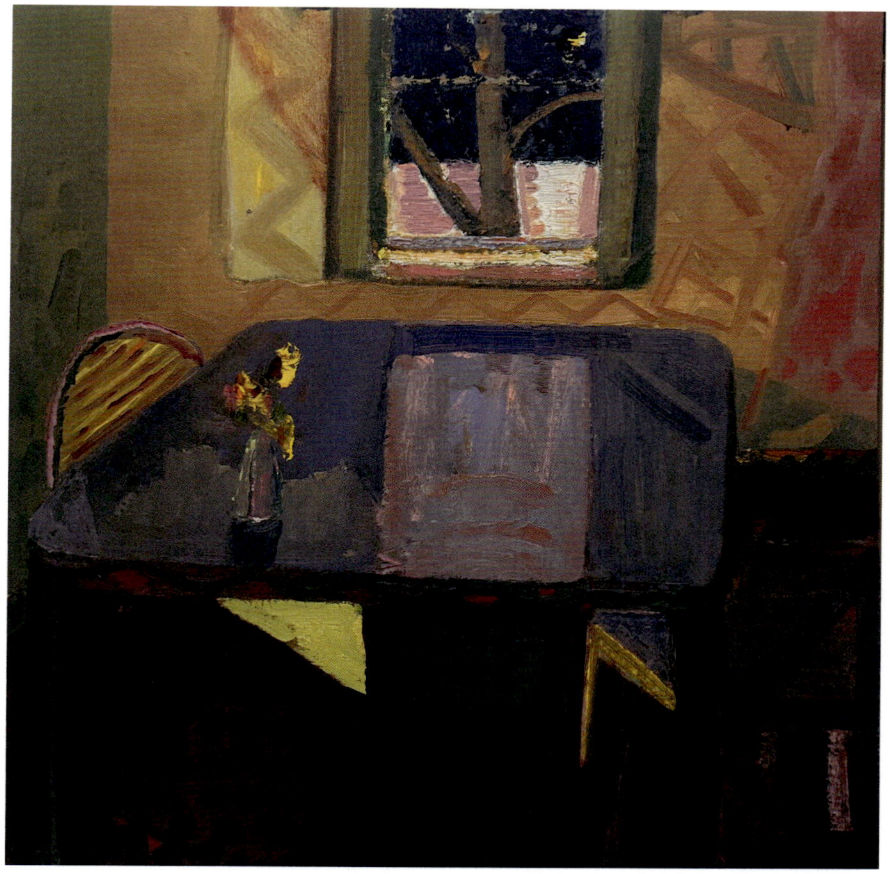

Cody Heichel
Kitchen Table with Flowers
2022, oil on board, 10 x 10 in.

Joan Mellon: I had so many reactions to your seemingly simple question, including laughter and lots of flash backs spanning several decades. I am definitely not one of those people who "always knew what they planned to do" and although I've been making art for a long time, I'm still becoming a painter. I went to School of Visual Arts in NYC in the 60s before the school was granting degrees. I got there "by chance" and applied with the slimmest of portfolios since I had just begun taking drawing classes a couple of months earlier.

Although there were very few academic requirements at SVA (where many went at that time to study illustration), lots of learning took place because we learned by doing and understood through experience, an environment that suited me. The first year was called "Foundation" and included drawing, painting, two-dimensional design, calligraphy, and a techniques class in which we learned a lot about materials including how to make egg tempera paint and rabbit skin glue. I enrolled in the fine arts department for my remaining years. All my teachers (no women) were working artists some of whom served in WWII and studied art using G.I. Bill benefits. Although I took drawing, printmaking, perspective, and anatomy classes, I did very little painting. Let me explain. It was the heyday of Pop Art and I had a teacher who built constructions with various materials and objects, so I started making mixed-media work. Although I loved looking at paintings, it wasn't until years later when I wanted to "just paint" that I began thinking about what I wanted to do as a painter. And that's what I've been doing ever since.

I graduated from School of Visual Arts with a certificate for four years of study and twenty-five years later returned to complete the required academic courses to earn my BFA. Years after that I earned a MA in Liberal Studies from SUNY Empire State College concentrating on art as experience. While being an art student and learning from working artists played a part in my becoming a painter, my degree(s) as such had nothing to do with it—but my love of painting, looking at it in person as much as I could, doing it, and reading and talking about it with other artists, has.

KC: *Thank you! You are giving me a lot to think about. I loved Joan's comment that she is "still becoming a painter." Me, too. I suppose that even in formal art school we all learn by doing, and long* *after the big decision has been taken (I was forty) we have the privilege of continuing to "practice" and learn our job.*

My first impression of Xico's work is one of symmetry, clarity, simplicity and peace, suggested by the beauty of porcelain objects hosting shapes both delicate and brilliant with intense blue and white. But soon, the large scale, the playing about with objects both shadowed and floating, and most of all the relations of the subjects to each other introduce an element of unease and denial.

If they were families, I think they would be the kind that appear smooth and well run on the surface but are at war underneath. Reason appears to prevail but how about that big, out of kilter plate in Still Life with Oval Dish, and its relationship to the small pitcher and dish huddled (fearfully?) together below. And the roles played by the four containers in Chinese Bowls, Glass. Not quite equidistant and, it seems to me, three against one.

I'd like to delve a little more into your painting styles. How do you arrive at your choices of subject, placement, paint application, and color? Can you explain a little what you are trying to achieve? I don't ask for chapter and verse on every brushstroke, but how the big choices in style came about. If my responses to your work seem off the mark, I hope you will enjoy putting me straight.

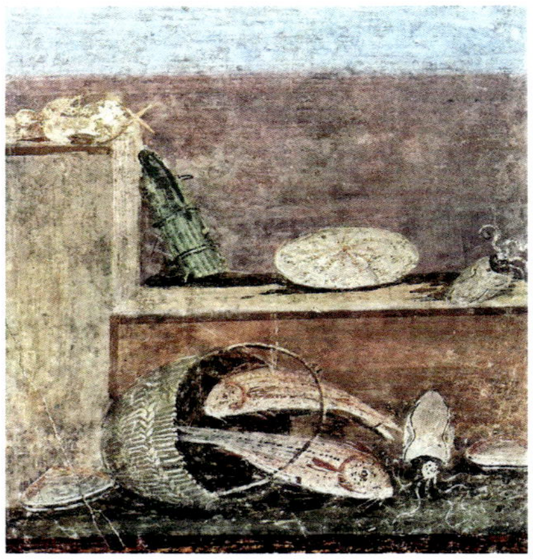

Still Life of Fish and Asparagus
1st century AD, Fresco, Museo Archeologico Nazionale, Naples, Italy

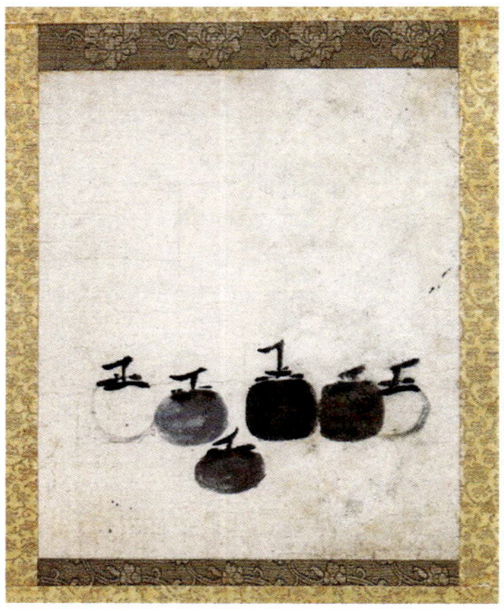

Mu Qi *Six Persimmons*
13th century, ink on paper, 14 ¼ x 15 in.

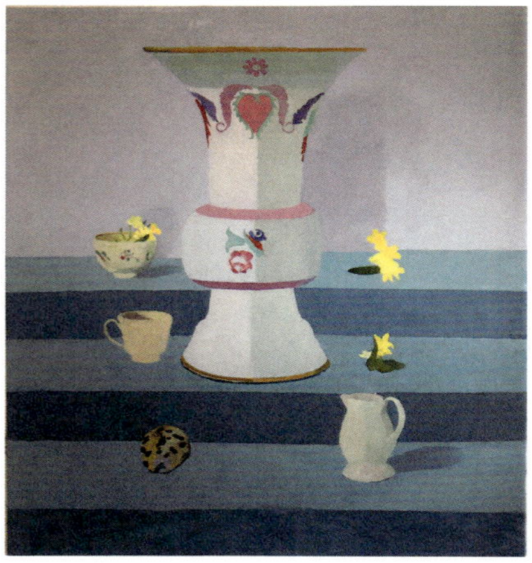

Xico Greenwald *Vase with Items Around, on Steps*
2023, oil on canvas over panel, 54 x 49 ½ cm.

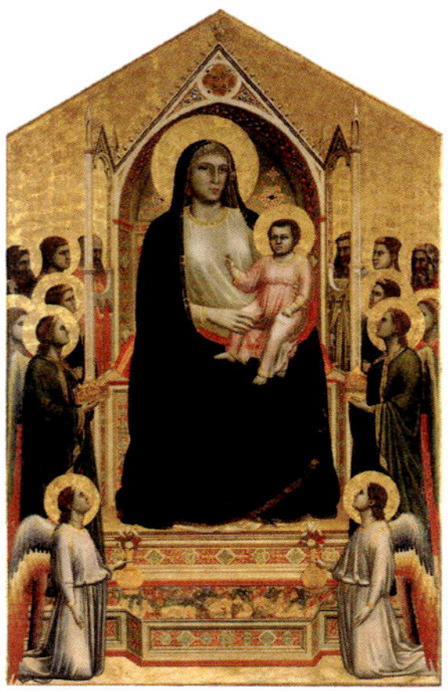

Giotto *The Ognissanti Madonna*
Tempera on panel, 2040 x 3250 cm.

XG: Thanks for sharing your reactions. In both the paintings you mentioned, I was exploring the compositional possibilities offered by a shelf, an idea I'm still working with today.

A couple years ago someone in my studio building threw away a roughly assembled wood shelf. I saw it by the bins and had a genuine eureka moment: With this device, or something similar, I thought, I can juggle items anywhere into a composition. *Shelf,* was the first painting I made using a riser.

In *Chinese Bowls, Glass,* I was using a plank to create a thinner kind of shelf, leaving space beneath the board. I had a couple references swimming around in my head at the time. *Fishes and Asparagus*, a beautiful Roman fresco housed in the Archaeological Museum in Naples, has a thin plank-like shelf and somewhat ambiguous space. Another inspiring artwork, *Six Persimmons,* a well known Song Dynasty ink painting by monk Mu Qi, has a horizontal rhythm across the composition which was also on my mind.

In the painting of the oval dish, I wanted to have the largest shape dominate the top half of the composition. I was thinking of canvases by Adolph Gottlieb as well as the *Ognissanti Madonna* by Giotto, a fabulous altarpiece I had recently seen for the second time at the Uffizi. Giotto's painting of the oversized Madonna and Child has a hierarchical composition featuring some lovely still life elements. In terms of the

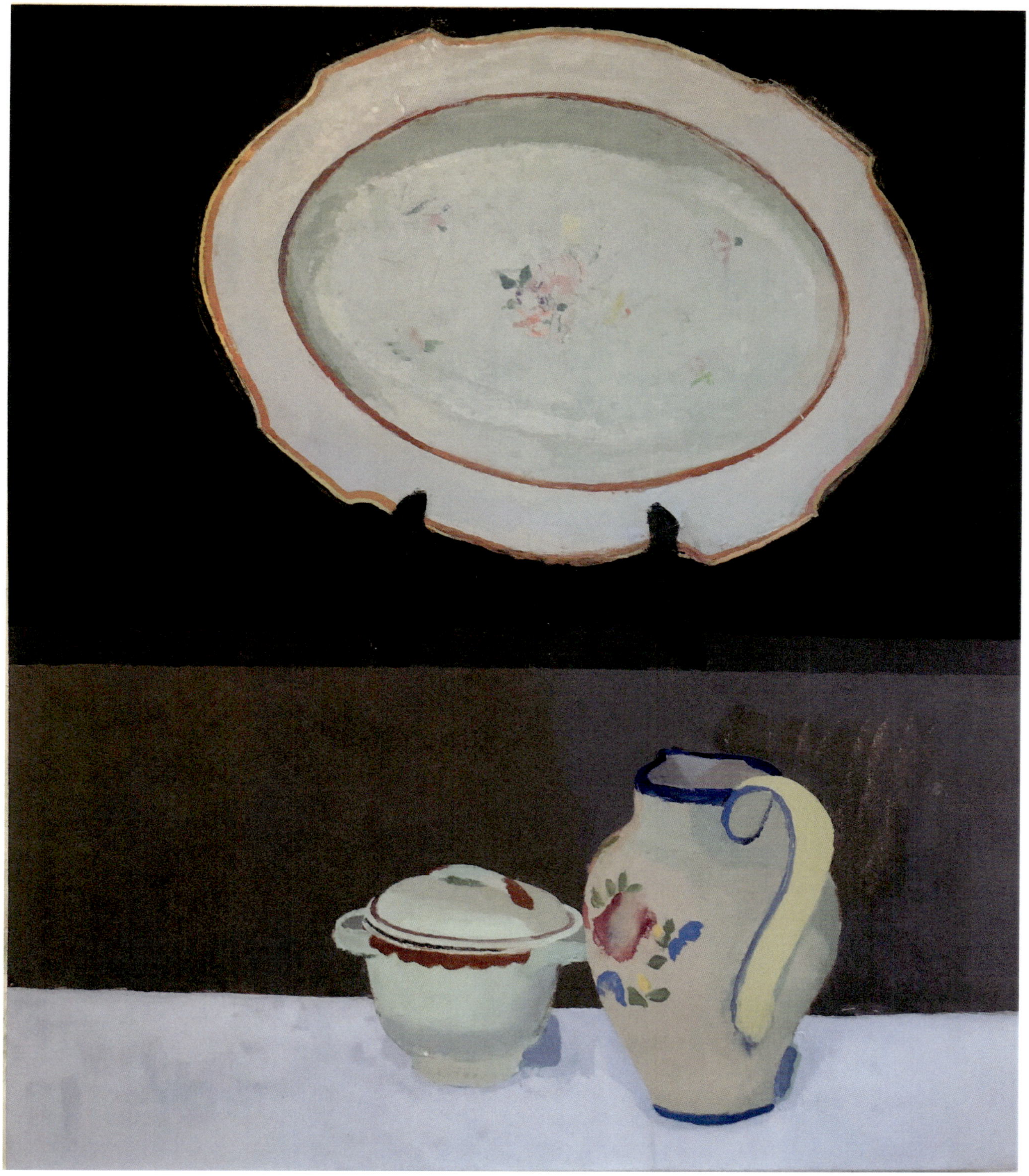

Xico Greenwald *Still Life with Oval Dish*
2022, oil on canvas over board, 54 x 46 in.

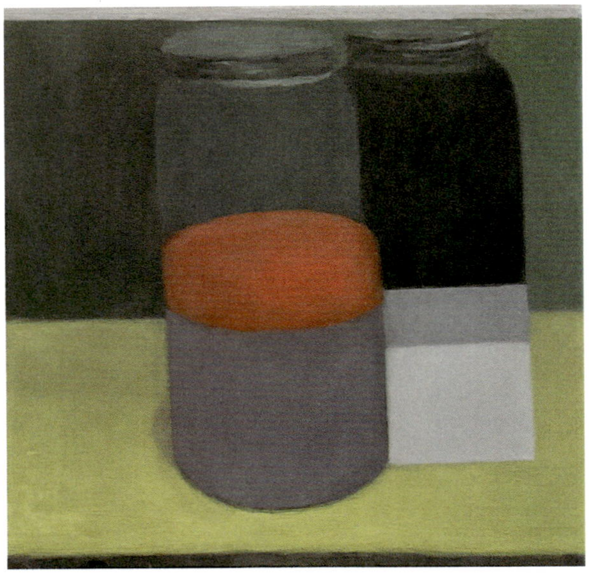

Joan Mellon *Quartet*
2022, oil on canvas, 12 x 12 in.

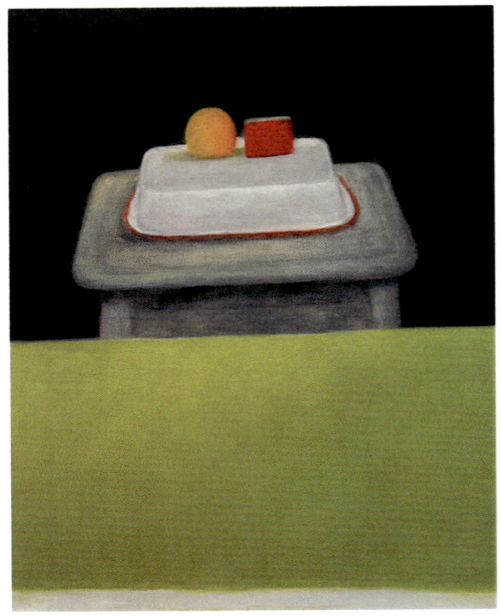

Joan Mellon *Red Rim*
2023, oil on canvas, 20 x 16 in.

black background, I've been researching Spanish and Portuguese "bodegón" painting during my sabbatical and I'm sure that was also on my mind.

Seeing bowls as family members has never been anything I've thought about, but, for the most part, the still life objects I'm painting are handmade, relatively simple items and I do hope my paintings imply a basic, essential shared humanity.

JM: What surprised me, Xico, in the words you wrote about your paintings *Shelf* and *Chinese Bowls, Glass* was your description of how they were explorations of "compositional possibilities offered by a shelf." The following explains why I was surprised. Like Kathy, I first got to know your work through your website. Excited by the first image, *Vase with Items Around, on Steps* and eager to see more, I moved ahead without reading titles, dates, etc. I found myself focused on trying to tease out how you use paint and the feel of the surface of your paintings—they aren't smooth, they aren't rough. How you paint seems to have as much to do with the import of these paintings as what they portray. When I discovered it was a found object—a "roughly assembled wood shelf"—that was the "eureka moment" for your vision of how you could "juggle items anywhere into a composition," it dawned on me that I hadn't seen a single shelf in any of your paintings. Instead, I saw the shelf element exclusively as abstract planes where your recognizable objects were placed exactly where they seemed they should be. Perhaps if I had read the titles I would have seen the paintings differently. I'm glad that I didn't.

KC: *Joan has recently made a shift from abstract or nonrepresentational to representation. From the dates of the images on your website it looks as if the transition was a quick one. I can see also a little the influence of abstraction on your representational work, especially in* Box *and in wonderful* Pods, Cones, Round Things*—witness the stripes masquerading as shelf and wall. You, too, have made considered, contemporary decisions about how to space objects so as to force the viewer to see them as abstract form (*Quartet *for example), monkey with "light" and shadows and juxtapose flat objects with ones that maintain the illusion of three dimensions.*

XG: Joan, can you tell me a bit about your process? Do you work from observation? How do you select your subject matter? What kind of a color palette are you using?

JM: Experiencing your work helped me understand how I perceive things and why Kathy described the horizontal planes of color in *Pods, Cones, Round Things* as masquerading stripes, even though those planes of color are not being anything other than what they are.

At the moment my process is developing one painting at a time. Each painting is teaching me something new and leading me to the next one.

Objects have always been a focus in my work in one way or another. In the early days I included physical objects as part of mixed media pieces I made on structures I built of masonite and wood with oil paint as the source of color. After a number of years making these, I wanted to "just paint" and began by looking at, arranging, and painting actual objects. After a while my interest in the recognizable object became secondary. That's when my focus shifted to abstraction first through the use of gestural brush strokes to convey an emotional content and then using flat color to create depth and a feeling of calm. The physical object resurfaced in 2017 when I made a group of small, three-dimensional objects that lay flat on the wall.

After the onslaught of Covid, a succession of fractured bones, and some loss of mobility, I tried picking up where I left off with abstraction. That wasn't working so I started the next painting with something tangible—four old paint bottles that were huddled together on a shelf in my studio, objects that over the years I imagined I might paint.

I played around creating a space I thought interesting for them to live in and decided how far or close they should be from the viewer (in this instance, me). Then I began thinking about the colors I wanted for each painting making color charts with a dab of the colors and their names/brand names next to them.

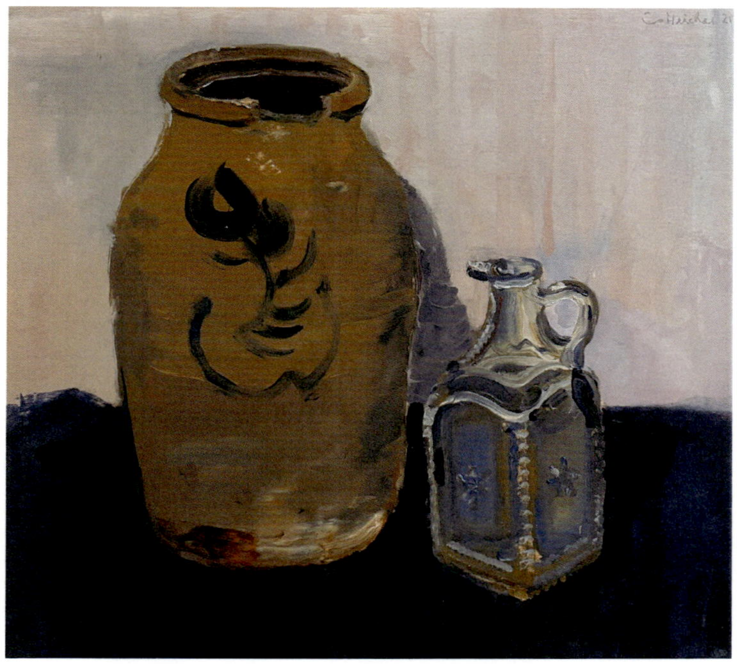

Cody Heichel *Crock and Glass Bottle*
2022, oil on board in handmade frame, 12 x 12 ½ in.

The painting started out okay. The placement of the bottles in the 12 by 12 inch space of the canvas felt right almost from the beginning. And yet every time I went to work on it, something was missing in both the image and how I was painting it. The roughness of the gestural strokes I was accustomed to using were now smooth, the familiar objects now strange. The more I looked at these bottles the less I knew what they were. I began to think I would never be able to translate what I was seeing into paint. Although I was looking at these bottles and they were central to my painting, my interest was not to "observe them accurately" as an observational painter might do. I seemed to be more interested in something about the objects' essence, what they were telling me they were.

Although tempted to abandon the painting, I worked to make it "right." I began by accepting the way I was using the paint. Then I changed the size of one of the bottles, making it look more like a canister and giving it a red top. Another bottle was changed into a small light gray box seen in perspective in the flat space. I fussed with the only small shadow in the painting located behind the left hand object closest to the viewer. As I continued changing the values it seemed as if the painting would never be completed. Then one day it went from being four bottles I thought I knew into a *Quartet* of objects that had not existed until they found their way into the painting. That's when I knew what I was struggling with was resolved. Although I don't know just when or how that happened I was glad it did. "That," I thought, "is the magic of painting." A similar experience repeated itself a year later when I approached looking at another group of objects that had been living in my studio for more than a decade, a group that now exists as *Pods, Cones, Round Things*. This brings me to my most recent

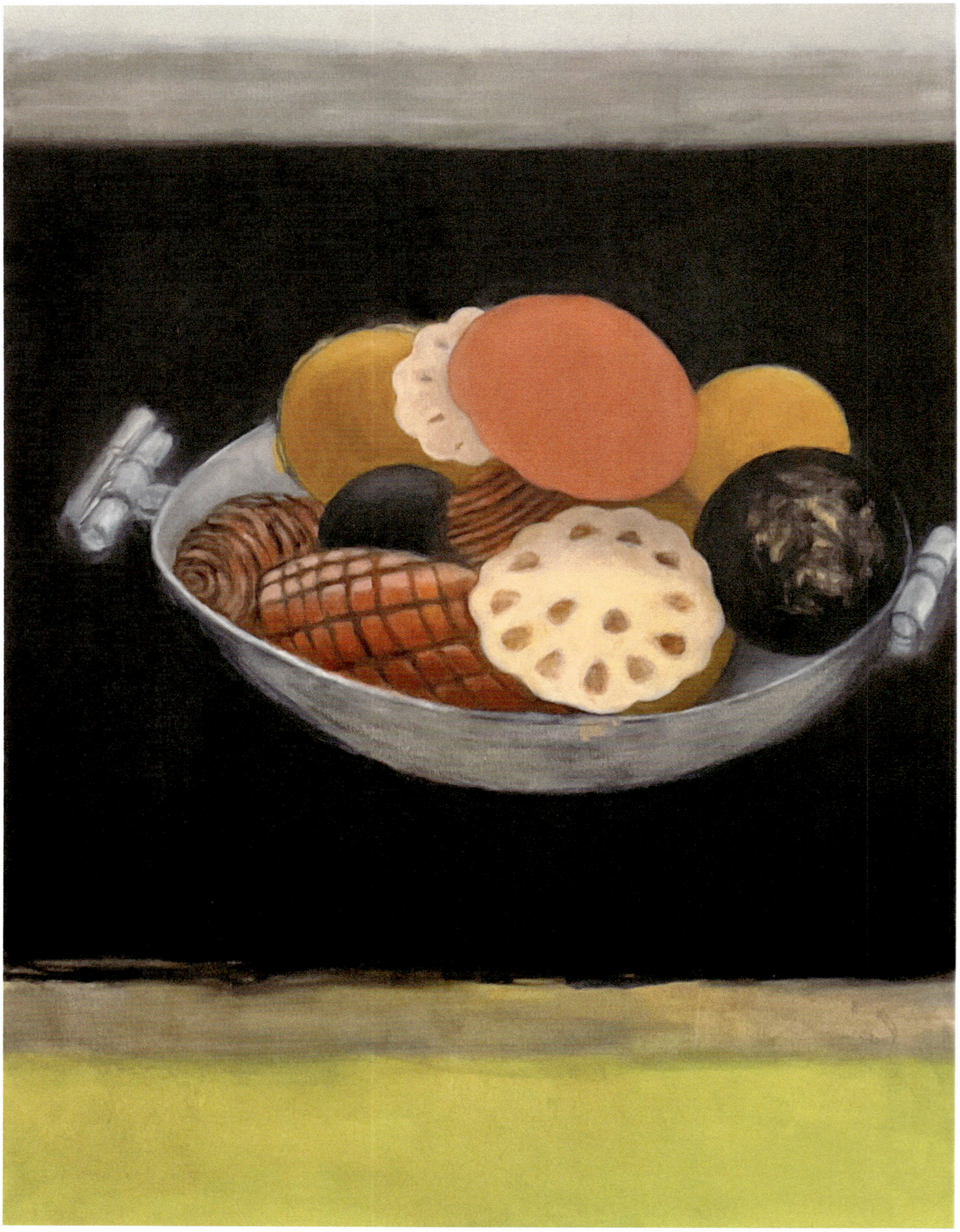

Joan Mellon *Pods, Cones, Round Things*
2023, oil on canvas, 24 x 18 in.

painting (July 2023), *Red Rim*, in which it became clearer to me that what appears recognizable in a painting and the "just paint" of what is seen are continuous.

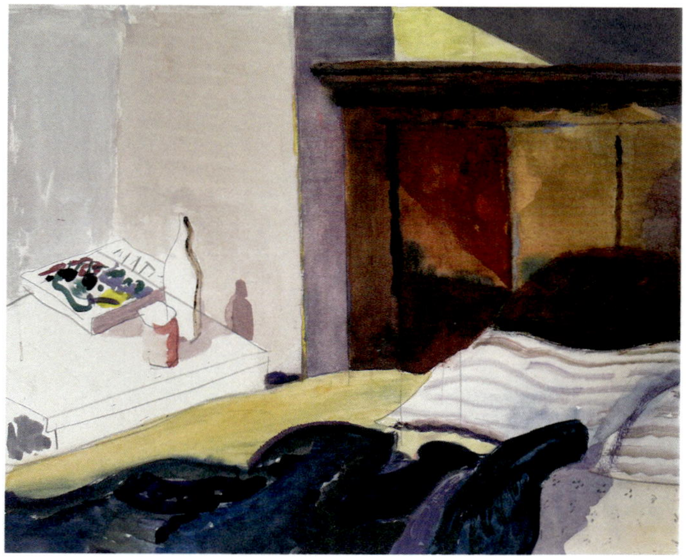

Cody Heichel
Bed and Nightstand
2023, watercolor on paper,
15 x 18 ½ in.

KC: *Cody, I love the way you tackle all the colors of darkness, and indicate humanity by the texture and yielding shapes of your subjects and making sure we know they are made of paint. Your form making brings to mind Ken Kewley's comment: "It is like describing an apple… by enclosing an imaginary object with two hands. You do not try to make your hand look like an apple. Paint takes over the role of the hands and does not hide the fact that it is paint. Painting is talking with the hands made permanent."*

CH: The word that hits me most from your question is "choices," because there are so many of them happening at once while we paint. It's one choice after another, after another. From searching for the subject to finding the off-ramp, I can hardly make sense of it all. The only thing I have to follow is that "yes" feeling, which guides me to whatever it is that day. Sometimes, hastily setting two vessels next to each other and starting. Then, while painting, slowly search for what I like and what I'd like to edit or exaggerate through form, color, composition, etc. On a different day, that feeling might guide me to carefully consider each item and how they are placed, and then paint with a sort of reckless abandon. Choices that feel right one day often don't the next.

There are also the things we consider while we are painting. Cool vs warm, light vs dark, soft or hard edges. Is this bit too strange? Too normal? Is my favorite part of the painting actually hurting it on the whole? Intuition seems to have the biggest voice in the room when it comes to all these choices. To my mind, intuition is our taste combined with our body's stockpile of information and thoughts of previous choices made. Every day we engage with art in any capacity, we feed and hone our artistic intuition, which is our most valuable tool in the studio.

What I'm searching for is an image that surprises me while holding a balance. And I need that "yes" feeling to show up at the end. For me, if the painting is right, I will truly feel a little "ping" in my heart and a sense of relief when I look at it. I will push and push a painting until I find that feeling, or until I push it off a cliff and have to move on to the next one.

JM: Your focus on the word "choices" and how "there are so many of them happening at once while we paint," helps me lessen the gap in my thinking about my earlier nonrepresentational work and recent paintings using tangible objects as a focal point. Your description of how you sometimes "hastily set two vessels next to each other" to get started is not unlike how I have worked abstractly and sounds like an approach I can use just as effectively to paint objects.

Can you give an example of how one of your paintings satisfied your search for "an image that surprises you" and also a painting (could be the same or another) that met your "need [for] the 'yes' feeling" you look for "to show up at the end."

CH: I attached a watercolor painting I recently completed of my bed and nightstand. It's the most recent example of a piece feeling right. Though not a classic still life, I was encouraged by what Kathy said in an earlier email: "sometimes I want to say anything that holds still is a still life." I loved that.

To your question: it held surprise for me, partially because of choices made while painting, but also I think because it ended up being only one quarter of the initial paper/composition I began with. I like adding or subtracting from my initial surface. I find it easier to get going if I know that at any point I can change direction on the size/orientation of the piece. I know this method doesn't speak to everyone, but it's become a pretty important part of my process over the past couple years. I'm curious if anybody else does this?

I suppose every painting which I share in any capacity would have ended with the "yes" feeling. When they don't they just get reworked until they do, or get stuck in painting purgatory–never to be seen!

(Just an extra thought) Something I find difficult is when I arrive at a "yes," but later I find an issue with the piece. I struggle to know which assessment to trust. At its best, following that feeling to "fix it" has helped me push pieces to what I feel are their best versions. But that same feeling has also caused me to ruin many paintings which I wished to get back. Lois Dodd, from my understanding, is a painter who completes her paintings in a few hours and almost never revises what she put down. That idea really resonates with me. But there's also no shortage of painters I admire who rework paintings for years until it feels right and the feeling sticks. I guess I've been trying to find my balance amongst these seemingly opposing ideas.

KC: *Avigdor Arika was another who finished all his paintings in one sitting. When I first learned about him I was in my painting-a-day period and I rushed out to buy a book of his pieces. Many of them were beautiful, but I have to admit I was disappointed in quite a few that I thought he might have put a little more time into. Maybe all-in-a-day is no panacea, but a method that works when it works.*

JM: Cody, you say that part of the surprise of the watercolor painting was that it ended up only a quarter of the initial composition. Was the composition laid out with pale watercolor or pencil and then you painted only part of it? Or did you paint all or some of it and then selected the part that satisfied the "yes" feeling as the final image?

In answer to your inquiry about others working on an ample surface so they could "add and subtract" at will—the following, written in 1998 by Christel Hollevoet, explains that Bonnard liked working on a such a surface: "Instead of following the conventional practice of painting on stretched canvases... on an easel, Bonnard generally chose to paint on unstretched pieces of canvas that were thumb-tacked to the walls of his studios or hotel rooms... Several pieces of roughly cut canvas were juxtaposed on the wall, often abutting, in rows, some very low and others quite high. Bonnard went from one to the other as he applied paint on his various compositions, having several works in progress at any one time. Sometimes he painted various compositions directly on a single large canvas that he cut later on."

CH: Thank you Joan, that quote about Bonnard was really wonderful! This makes me think of how I used to tape my watercolor down to a board from edge to edge, which seemed to lock in the size/orientation, but I now use metal clips to secure the paper to easel and thus am painting edge to edge.

To your question: I started the piece as I often do: with a basic charcoal drawing to lay out my initial compositional idea. As I started painting it though, I began favoring the left side of the paper and not liking how things were looking on the right or as a whole. I eventually removed the sections of the painting which weren't working, and those scrap pieces were fully painted in some spots and unpainted in others. Hope this helps!

JM: Do you use "a basic charcoal drawing" for watercolor too? Doesn't the charcoal mix with the watercolor paint? Do you remove "the sections that weren't working" by physically cutting them out? Do you do this with both watercolor and oil paintings?

CH: Yes, I use a Derwent charcoal pencil to draw for watercolors and oils. Any drawn lines you can see in the watercolor painting I shared are charcoal. The charcoal stays put for the most part, but when it blends into the paint a little I don't mind. How I paint with oils and how I paint with watercolors used to be very different, but now they have essentially met in the middle.

And yes, I just bend and tear the watercolor paper to change the composition. With oil paintings, I will tear away pieces if working on loose canvas, or I will cut the painting with a circular saw if I'm working on board. I often apply a lot of pressure to the surface (scraping away paint) so I almost never paint on stretched canvas.

JM: Xico, could you describe as best you can the surfaces of your paintings? And could you describe what sort of "handmade, relatively simple items" or combination of these items catch your eye and make you want to paint them?

XG: Thanks for the questions, Joan. I know that you painted abstractly for many years. While I have always painted from life, I also love abstract painting and abstraction is often on my mind. Marden, Scully, Rothko, Gottlieb, Kline, de Kooning–these are some of my favorite painters of the last 100 years. By adding risers into my still lifes, I've been able to incorporate new colors and shapes and that was definitely part of the original appeal. But in my artwork I wouldn't say the stripes of color are "masquerading as shelf and wall." I hope for BOTH readings to work together; I want the image to be believable and compelling AND I also hope that the paintings can be enjoyed simply as colors and shapes.

Regarding paint surface–I stretch canvas over wood panels because I, too, frequently scrape the surfaces down to prevent built up texture from previous layers of paint. If I were to paint on a traditional stretcher, I think the canvases would be baggy from all the scraping. This way I avoid that problem. I rarely use much medium because I don't want to have to worry about the chemistry of the paint. I want to be able to paint over any area at any time.

The items in these paintings are from all over. Some are old Portuguese ceramics. (I'm half Portuguese and I love the culture.) Many of the still life objects I've collected over the years are items that looked to me like they belonged in a painting. It can be pretty intuitive. I try to create arrangements that I find intriguing and then work to express in paint the qualities I perceive. That said, my still life painting and the still life set ups themselves often change radically as I work.

***KC:** I loved this exchange. So much of the discussion has been about things that working painters actually are interested in—the "how" of what somebody else does.*

JM: What stands out for me in talking about materials is not so much sharing "shop talk" but how the choice of materials—including the size of the surface one works

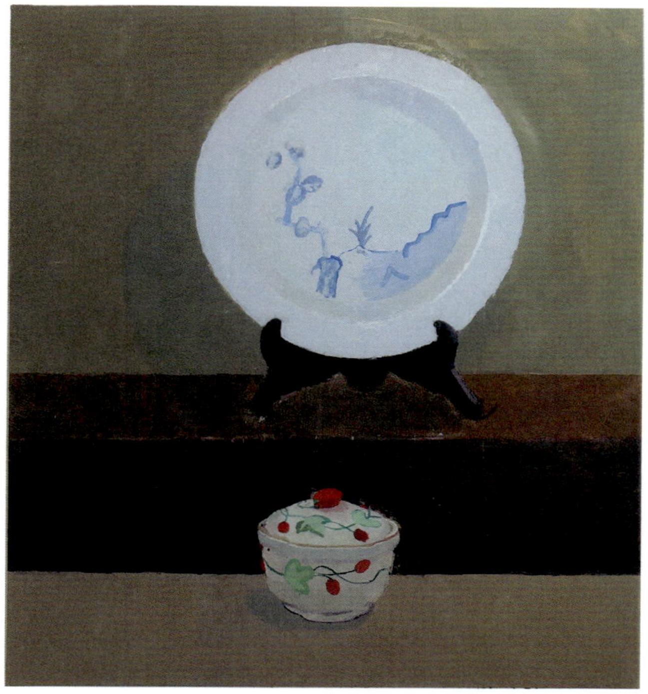

Xico Greenwald *Still Life with Plate*
2021-22, oil on canvas over board, 64 x 58 in.

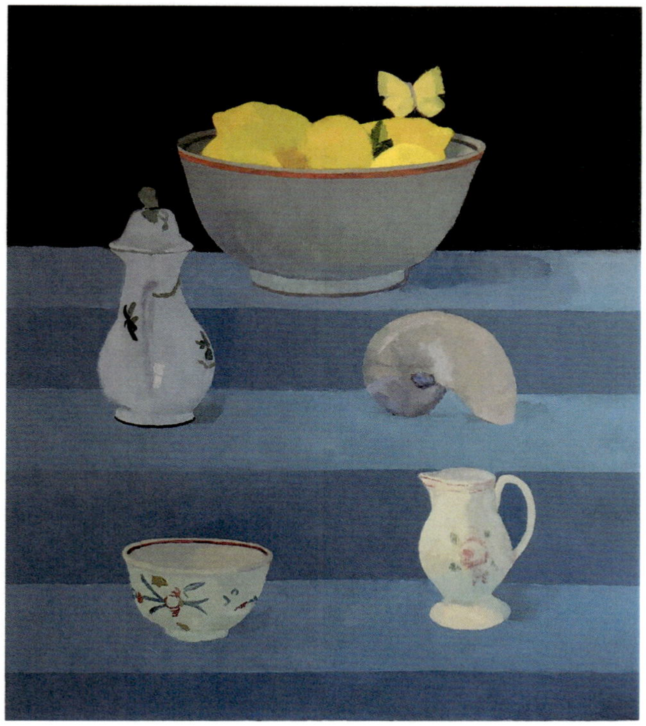

Xico Greenwald *Blue Steps II*
2023, oil on canvas over board, 48 ½ x 42 in.

on and the quality of that surface—reflects the feeling an artist hopes to convey in a painting. For instance, the words "still life painting" usually conjures up images of intimate spaces and familiarity because of the recognizable objects portrayed even when those objects are depicted larger than life as in Xico's paintings or veer off the path of the everyday when, as in my paintings, they can seem to inhabit a world of memory or dreams.

KC: *The first image on Xico's website is an installation shot, which really brings home to me what an effect scale has on my viewing experience. I had seen images of your work in isolation, I knew they were quite large and the subjects larger than life, but I didn't get the bigness feeling until I saw them in (digital) space. By comparison, Cody's and Joan's work is medium to very small both in canvas and subject dimensions. Can you all share your thoughts on scale? Also, my reaction to Xico's installation shot led me to ask myself (now you) what do you think or how do you feel about looking at images of "plastic" art on a flat screen lighted from behind, distorting our experience of color and surface as well as scale. I use my phone camera a lot on work in progress because it isolates the painting from the distracting studio. Do you ever feel (as I confess I do) that you might be judging your own work by how it looks on a screen? Do you use a camera at all, for that or other purposes?*

XG: I agree with Rothko's idea that a painting doesn't need to be small to be intimate.

JM: Yes, he said that he wanted to be "very intimate and human" and by painting "the larger picture, you are in it."

XG: Also, I find that composing in a small painting can feel like a cerebral exercise whereas designing on a larger scale gives me a better sense of how big shapes should be and where they should be.

I begin each painting by taping out the size of the canvas-to-be on the wall, deciding on the proportions of the rectangle for the still life I've set up.

Having a million little paintings hung salon style is a pet peeve of mine. I try to make paintings that won't be lost on the wall.

It's always better to see artwork in person and I don't think we can have those same kinds of profound reactions we have in real life when we are looking at a screen or even a printout.

But these magic phones can definitely be useful. Like Kathy, I also take in-progress photos of paintings. It's been a valuable tool. Sometimes I sketch out possible changes on the phone screen. I like to use the mirror image tool as a way to see the painting with greater distance... a big improvement over using an actual mirror because you can get a straight-on view.

JM: When I was painting abstractly, I always thought of the painting as the object. "It" (the painting) and its size was determined by the space I wanted it to occupy. Its content was determined by the colors I wanted to explore. And its flesh (or something like that) was determined by the gestural brush strokes I was fond of using.

Once I began thinking about tangible objects as the focus of what I was painting, it was those objects that determined the space they would live in. And that space was abstract and nondescript, one perhaps with a name like—"tabletop."

The paintings I make are microscopic compared to the universe and human size compared to my body and the space I work in. No matter what size paintings I make I hope people who see them feel some connection to what I felt making them.

Some years ago, while looking at a few of my hand size abstract paintings in person, an artist I know, who first saw these online, said with great surprise, "I thought these were very large. How did you

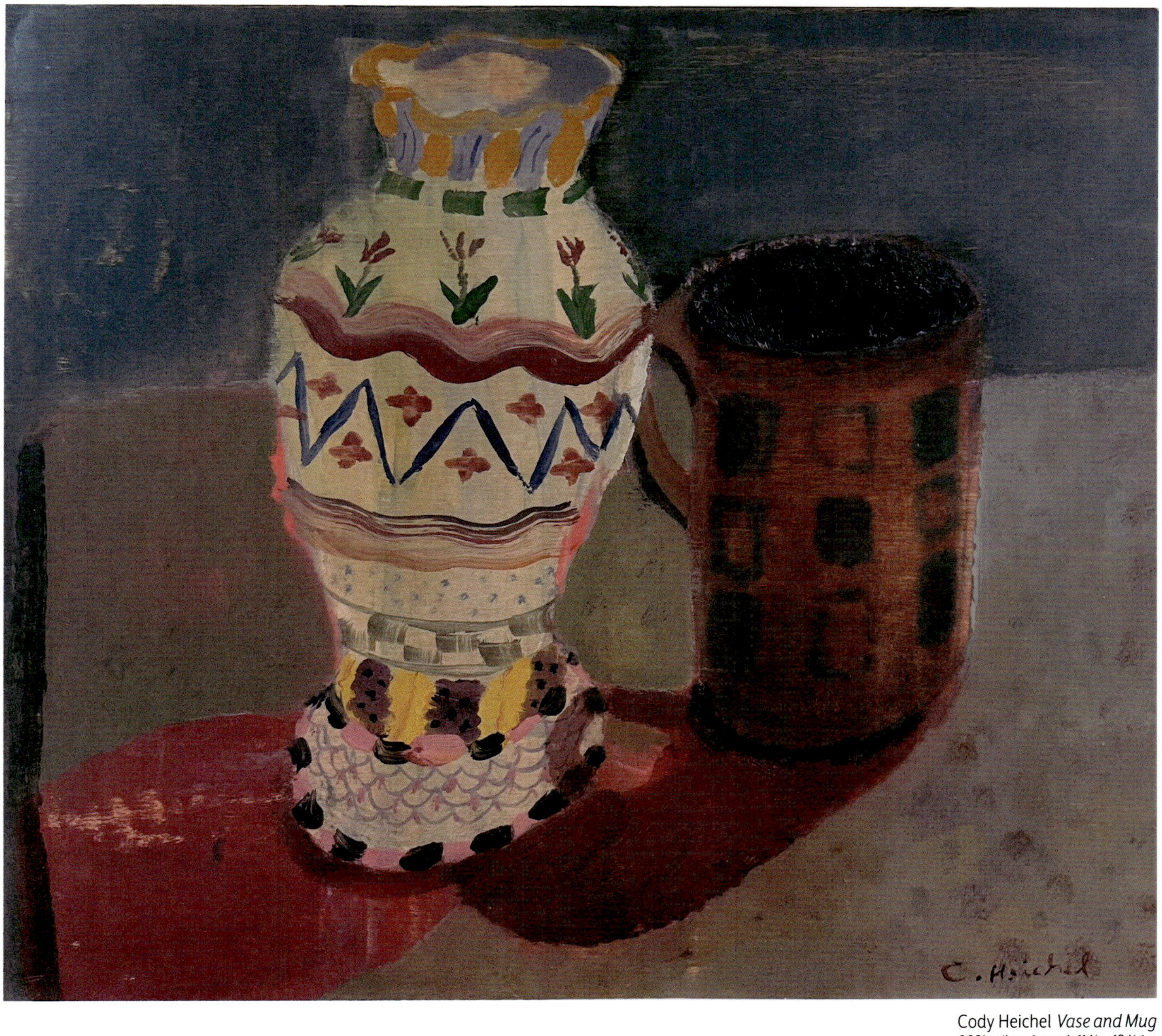

Cody Heichel *Vase and Mug*
2021, oil on board, 11 ½ x 12 ½ in.

make the space in these small paintings look so large?" My answer: "I painted them as if they were large."

Using my iPad camera, I photograph my paintings while in progress and when completed. My computer and website have become the "extra wall" I need to look at these photographs and my work in relation to each another. And even though the tools provided by Adobe Photoshop are electronic and different in feel from the tools I use for painting, I sometimes I use them to try out possible "next steps." Sometimes this is useful, other times, not.

CH: I'll say I've found that the scale of my work is heavily linked to my emotions. I believe my paintings generally reflect how I'm feeling, and that can come through in many ways, scale being one of them. I've had phases where I want to sit comfortably and shrink into myself a bit. Lately I've felt the need to be standing, moving my arms, dancing about, asking for more space. Happily doing so in both scenarios. I hate to bring it up, but Covid (for many reasons) sent me into a phase of working small, and I've only recently begun working large again.

I think scale matters a lot, and it can have such an effect on the impact of any given work. At times, I feel a sense of "this one wants to be small" or "this one wants to be large"... but mostly, I think my emotions dictate how large or small I'm working, and the image follows regardless.

I, too, use my phone to take progress shots and to digitally draw on them. It's very handy being able to try things out risk free. It's also a nice way to engage with work at any point in the day. There are many times I can't be in the studio, but am able to progress a painting along by using my extra 15 minutes here and there to digitally work through issues with any given piece. If I find a solution, I will save it and apply it later to the physical piece. But yes, agreed, if I'm ranking the best ways to view a painting, "through a phone screen" is a distant third place, followed by "printed" in second, and "in person" as the clear winner.

KC: *Zeuxis is contemplating a new traveling show with the theme of Anxiety (just thinking about it makes me anxious). How about you? How would you make a still life painting on such a theme?*

XG: I don't tend to decide on the subject matter in advance in that way. I prefer to allow each painting to inform the next in what I would describe as a somewhat organic studio process.

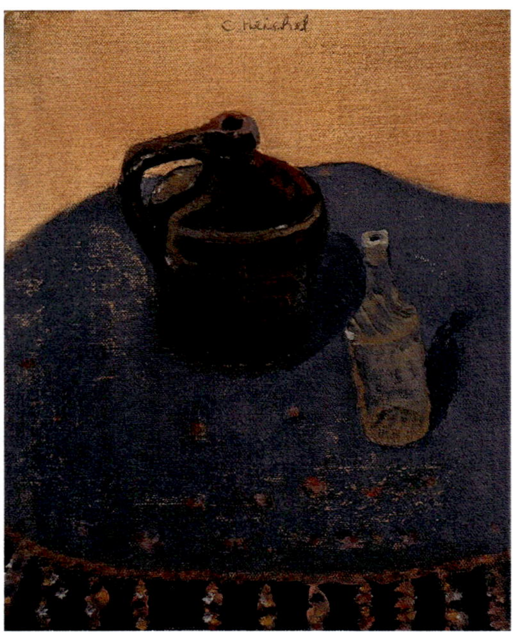

Cody Heichel *Brown Jug and Glass Bottle*
2021, oil on canvas, 9 ¾ x 7 ¾ in.

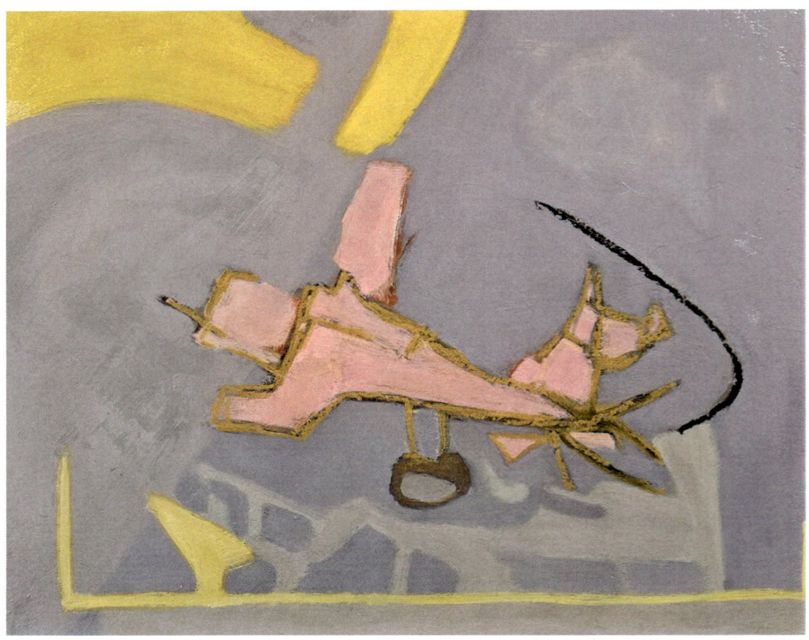

Kathleen Craig *Plane*
2023, oil on canvas, 20 x 24 in.

JM: Like Kathy, just thinking about this makes me anxious. Painting with a theme in mind is not how I work but this is interesting to think about it.

CH: If given the assignment of painting a still life which considers "anxiety," I would probably be focused on a sort of asymmetry, disbalance, or tension in the composition.

KC: *Giorgio Morandi said, "I am comforted by the knowledge that in all my endeavors, even in the moments of greatest uncertainty, my personality has always managed to come through" (pinched from another Zeuxis* Conversation*) Now, Morandi is my favorite modern artist, but this quotation bothers me. Granted the outsized role of personality in all modern painting, I find it nonetheless a little embarrassing; it can come across as a sort of self-congratulation.*

At any rate, it leads me to a question that I think plagues a lot of painters today: Why do we do this thing? What's the point? To whom else does it matter, whom does it benefit? Aren't there already too many lilies in this field? I haven't found an answer yet that flatters me. How about you?*

XG: Thanks for the Morandi quote. What a fantastic painter! I wrote about the influence of fascist ideology on his stylistic development in 2015 when CIMA mounted an illuminating exhibit of his still lifes from the 1930s ("By Giorgio, They've Got It," New York Sun, 2015).

CH: I love your piece on Morandi, Xico! Fascinating, and perfectly titled as well.

JM: I have loved Morandi's paintings since I first saw them by chance in a gallery in my home town, NYC, in the 60s. About the quote—the hardest part for me is to be pleased that, "my personality has always managed to come through"—especially when I hope my "personality" and my paintings reflect the surprise and wonder I feel when looking at paintings I love and admire by a long list of artists past and present.

Xico, because of Morandi's fascist ideology, do we now have to worry about liking Morandi for the wrong reasons?

XG: No, he's great. I think his ideology played a part in his artistic development. His paintings remain incredibly inventive. Though he was deeply involved in this nationalist movement, it served him well artistically. But he usually isn't discussed in these terms.

Kathy's question, "Why do we do this?" is a big one! This is probably something everyone needs to figure out on their own. In my case, I'm sure there are lots of factors. I can tell you that I love art, all kinds of art, from cave painting to contemporary art, and I'm motivated in part by an aspiration to contribute to this.

JM: Although I don't know why continuing to move paint around on a surface matters to me or if what I do matters to anyone else, I keep doing it. Your question "Why do we do this?" is one I also ask and find both more difficult and in some ways easier to answer each decade.

CH: I have to feel it's inevitable that our personalities come through in our work, for better or worse, at every stage of our journey. Yet somehow it is also something that takes work to achieve, that is to have your work truthfully reflect what you'd hoped to share. Which, to me, seems to answer the "why" of it all. Brings to mind the David Hockney quote: "What an artist is trying to do for people is bring them closer to something, because of course art is about sharing. You wouldn't be an artist unless you wanted to share an experience, a thought."

*Matthew 6:28-33 King James Version (KJV) "Consider the lilies of the field, how they grow; they toil not, neither do they spin: and yet I say unto you, That even Solomon in all his glory was not arrayed like one of these." Z

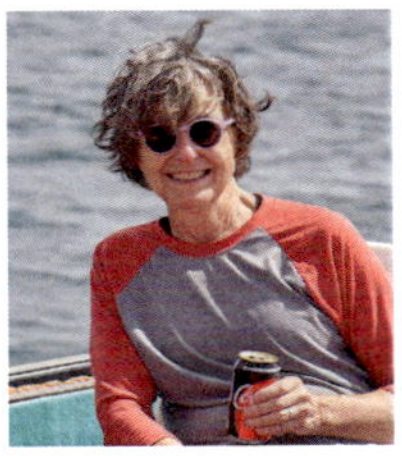

Kathleen Craig paints abstract still lifes, landscapes, and figures, working from observation and memory, with an emphasis on color, composition, and expression. Her work has been influenced by Giorgio Morandi, Nicolas de Stael, and Ken Kewley's essay on color. She currently exhibits with Nancy Margolis Gallery (NYC), Elder Gallery of Contemporary Art (Charlotte, NC), Cerulean Arts (Philadelphia), and Bonfoey Gallery (Cleveland).

www.zeuxis.us/craig
www.kathleencraig.net

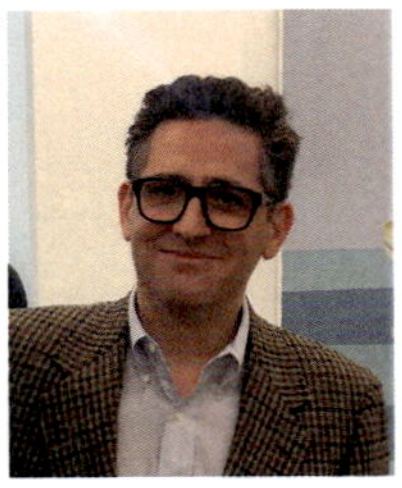

Xico Greenwald is a New York City–based artist. His paintings have been exhibited at numerous galleries, including George Billis Gallery, Nancy Margolis Gallery, Alice Gauvin Gallery, Dibboll Gallery at Loyola University and Andrews Gallery at College of William and Mary. He has taught at Pratt Institute, Rider University, and Mount Gretna School of Art, and currently serves as Associate Professor at Borough of Manhattan Community College-CUNY. His essays, reviews and interviews have been published by various media outlets including *The Wall Street Journal, The Spectator, The New York Sun* and ArtCritical.com.

www.xicogreenwald.com

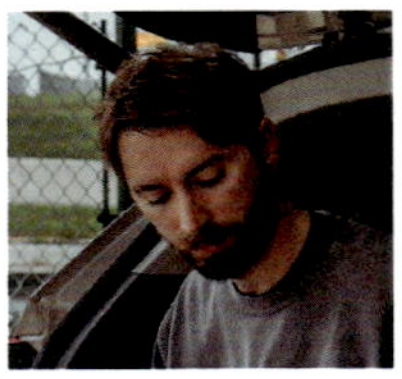

Cody Heichel is an Ohio-based painter working primarily with watercolor and oil. His paintings combine direct observational work with moments of improvisation and play. Informed by his love of Modernist and Expressionist painters such as Charles Burchfield, Georgia O'Keeffe, and Ernst Ludwig Kirchner, Heichel manipulates form and color, leaving his subjects somewhat abstracted yet tethered to an understood reality. In 2017 he was awarded the Greater Columbus Arts Council Visual Art Fellowship, and was selected for the Greater Columbus Arts Council's 2018 Artist Exchange Residency Program in Dresden, Germany. His work is represented by Brandt-Roberts Galleries in Columbus, Ohio, and Visual Index in Winston-Salem, North Carolina.

www.codyheichel.com

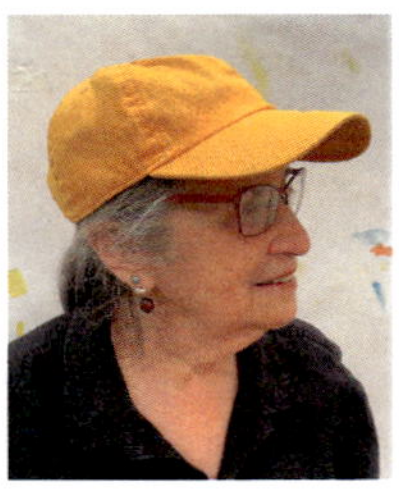

Joan Mellon's exhibition highlights include one person shows in the New York metropolitan area and group shows in the U.S. and abroad. Her work is in the collections of the Franklin Furnace Archives at the Museum of Modern Art, Johnson & Johnson, New York Public Library / Artist Books & Prints, and private collectors. She has a BFA from School of Visual Arts and a MA in Liberal Studies from SUNY Empire State College where she has been an adjunct mentor. After painting abstractly for many years, Joan Mellon has refocused her attention on objects and still life. What has surprised her most looking at familiar objects is how strange they seem and how, in the process of painting, they tell her what they are. With each painting Joan's curiosity has grown about how what's recognizable in a painting and what's "just paint" are continuous—something she is always learning about from the long list of artists, past and present, she admires.

www.joanmellon.com

Contrast and Connection in Conversation

Daniel Dallmann interviews

Nancy U. Granda and Stanley Bielen

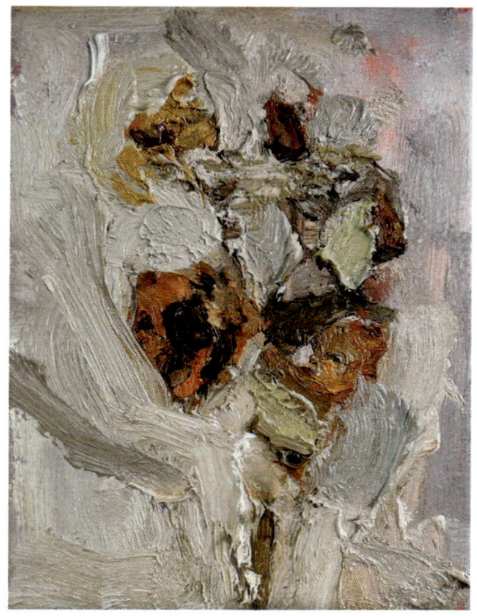

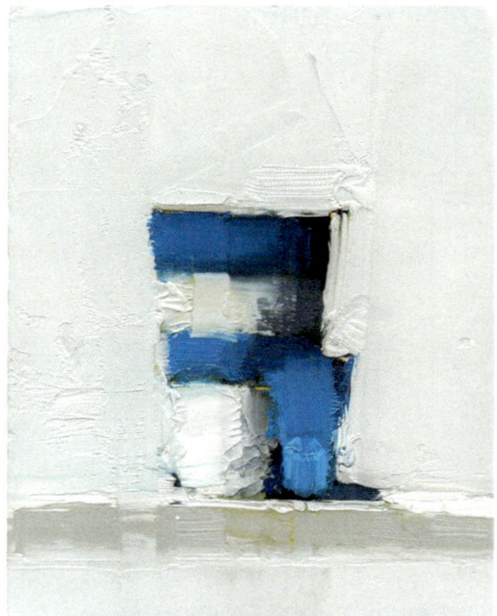

Nancy Granda *Wilted*
2023, oil on panel, 8x6 in

Stanley Bielen *Minor Blue*
2022, oil on paper mounted, 8 x 6 in.

Daniel Dallmann: *When I took on the challenge of facilitating one of the interviews published by Zeuxis, an organization of painters that focuses, to a large degree, on the ancient category of still life painting, I had only a slight idea of what it might entail. Zeuxis has been around for quite a while, and they've been publishing these interviews for several years. I took the opportunity to contact two wonderful Philadelphia painters that I had never met before, although I had known their work for some time.*

Nancy U. Granda and Stanley Bielen: I want to thank them both for their generous agreement to engage with this project and for their gracious permission to visit their studios to begin the interview process.

DD: *At our initial introductions during our studio visits, while being knocked over by the wonderful works I saw, I gained a cursory understanding of your backgrounds. First and foremost is the fact that you each have had a very different path to arrive at where you are now. Nancy is relatively new to the profession of artist/painter and Stan has been in this milieu for decades. That in itself, is of some significance in the topics we'll be discussing, especially in regard to backgrounds.*

Nancy, I learned from your short bio on the Zeuxis website that you studied English literature in college. Can you give us an idea of how you got from there to the time you began showing your works?

Nancy U. Granda: I grew up north of Wilmington, Delaware in a comfortable suburban neighborhood on the edge of Brandywine Creek State Park. I was an introverted, dreamy kid, who loved reading, writing, drawing, looking at pictures, and being outside in my backyard or the nearby woods. The house I grew up in was full of books— both parents read a lot— and they encouraged my interest in the arts by providing music lessons and trips to museums. At the same time, though, their ideas about careers were extremely practical, and the idea of going to art school would've been utterly unfathomable.

I studied English at the University of Pennsylvania and spent some time pursuing a PhD in Early Modern English Literature (Shakespeare, Milton, etc) as well. I then married my husband, Carlos, settled in Philadelphia, and chose to stay home caring for our two children. When they reached school age, I found myself looking for a creative outlet and began taking oil painting classes at Woodmere Art Museum, near my home. And I was instantly captivated. I found that time stood still when I focused on a drawing. I found that the tactile pleasure of oil paint was something I hadn't realized was missing from my life. After that first class, I found a tremendous community of teaching artists and students in the Philadelphia area.

I sometimes regret that I did not go to art school full-time. But I think there's been a great benefit to me starting later in life. As a young person, I was just so self-conscious. I put tremendous pressure on myself to succeed, without appearing to work hard. I kind of felt the same way about being a parent—really, I'm an extremely anxious person. When I started painting, on the other hand, I had no expectations at all. I remember thinking, "I can make a really terrible painting, and it just won't matter." Oddly enough this idea was incredibly freeing.

DD: *Stanley? What brought you to the Pennsylvania Academy of Art in 1976?*

Stanley Bielen: In 1957 I was born in the People's Republic of Poland, a country that no longer exists. My family comes from 2 villages in the foothills of the Carpathian Mountains near the border with Ukraine. In 1964 we emigrated to Connecticut where my father's parents were living. My father had not seen his father since 1939. My parents were war children. They grew up under occupation, education was not possible, and restarting life here was difficult.

I have always loved to draw and paint. It was not until high school, however, that I was able to receive any instruction in art. It was at the end of my freshman year that I discovered the art department at Stamford High School. For the next three years it was an oasis for me. The discovery of painting, drawing, and art history created a homeland for me. It has remained that way to this day and in many ways it is the place where I am most at home.

The students from my high school who pursued art usually went to design schools like Pratt or Parsons. The head of the art department gave me a catalogue for the Pennsylvania Academy of Art and I applied there. I attended the Academy from 1976 to 1980. While there I studied primarily with Arthur DeCosta. He has had the deepest impact on my development as an artist.

DD: *You each have widely different backgrounds and widely different epochs in which you began to exercise your interest in visual art. You both had to make choices in the kind of art you were about to make, and this in a time period when there were many art moments, if not art movements.*

SB: Thinking back, Dan, I had a sense fairly early on about the general direction that I wanted to go. After receiving some basic instruction in drawing in high school, I started to draw things that were around me; my family, myself, landscapes, and still life. In the art teacher's lounge in high school

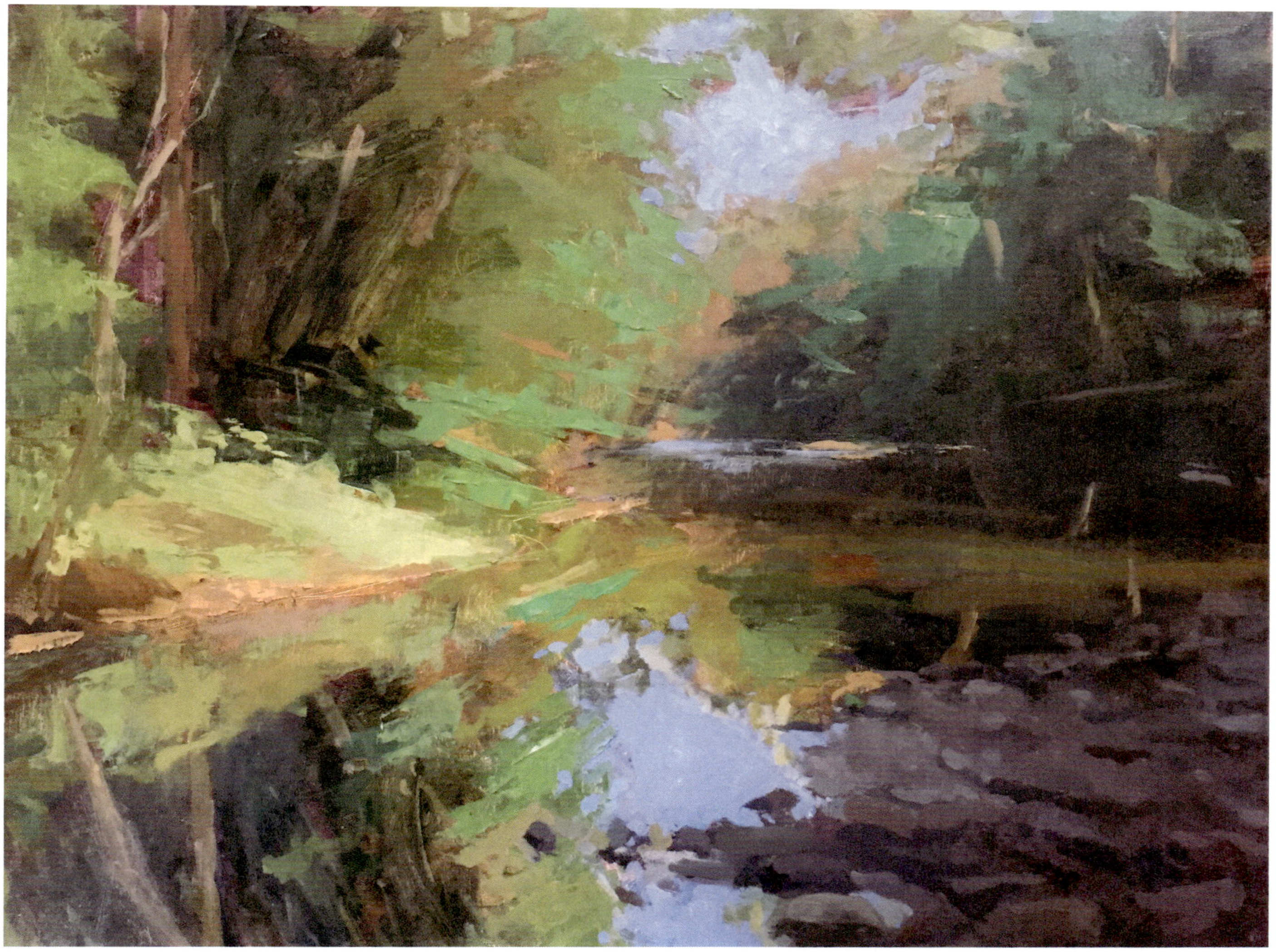

Nancy U. Granda *Wissahickon*
2017, oil on panel, 24 x 30 in.

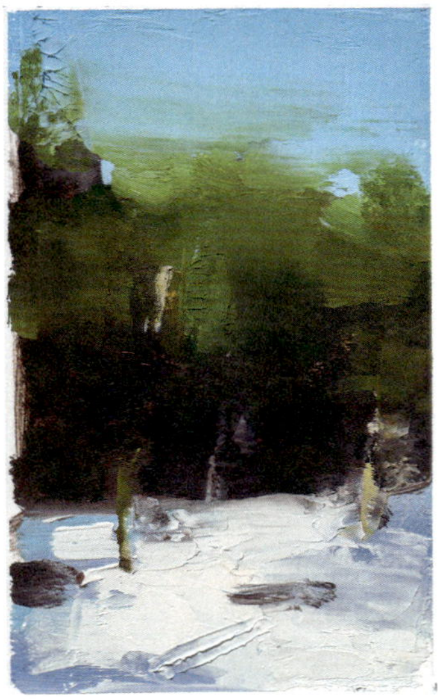

LEFT TO RIGHT:

Stanley Bielen
Mantua Then
2018, oil on paper, 6 x 5 in.

Stanley Bielen
March Pines
2013, oil on paper, 12 x 4 in.

there was a very good art library and I spent a lot of time there. It was heavy on late 19th century early 20th century art. Going through the volumes, I found that in looking at someone like Matisse, I would be very drawn to the early tonal work; also very early Picasso, Manet, and Kathe Kollwitz. In terms of non-representational work at that time, Hans Hoffman's abstract work was very attractive. A painter who I was aware of in those early years, whose work I liked very much was Raphael Soyer. A contemporary painter working in a personal realist style, painting the people and things around him, and with an Eastern European background, on top of it. That was a direction that I wanted to follow.

A topic that is easy to overlook is, how do you train a painter? If you want to become a musician you have to become familiar with an instrument. When I got to the academy in 1976, I had almost no experience in oil painting. My time there and really years after were spent in trying to understand a medium that is not super friendly to beginners. There was a realist reemergence at that time. I was aware of that and there were plenty of art magazines in the library that we students went through, however, those years were mostly about going to the studio and trying to "fail better."

DD: *Stan, lots of interesting stuff in your last statement. In particular, I latched on to the statement regarding the early tonal works of Matisse, etc, "... I would be very drawn to the early tonal work; also very early Picasso... and Kathe Kolowitz." Nancy mentioned being attracted to tonal works, early on, as well.*

It might be said, and for purposes of our discussion I will say it, that the early tonal works of Matisse and Picasso were leaning toward depiction of the subject matter while their later works leaned toward the concepts around modern painting that would change the face of painting forever. Realism was never enough to make a great painting. Maybe Cézanne set the table, but both Matisse and Picasso respectfully upset the apple cart of Cézanne's still life paintings, in their own way.

NG: As a very young person I was drawn to many different kinds of art. When I was quite young, I developed a real love for medieval and Egyptian art and artifacts. I don't know that I would have been able to express why at the time, but in hindsight I think I was really attracted to the powerful presence of these objects that had survived many centuries and still had the ability to affect me emotionally. I liked that they were not "realistic" but seemed to belong to their own universe outside time. I spent a considerable amount of time in Penn's museum of anthropology, where I was struck with the enduring human need to make beautiful, powerful objects.

In my undergraduate days I took some art history classes but hadn't yet cultivated any really specific appetites. When I was a little older still and the kids were in the stroller era we spent a lot of time in museums and various Philadelphia galleries. I became interested in what contemporary painters were doing in Philadelphia. However, I was still thinking about painting fairly passively, strictly as a visual consumer; at this time I still had no thoughts of becoming a painter myself.

DD: *I love your use of the word "appetites" in the paragraph above. I lived in Rome for a couple of years back in the mid 1970's. I visited hundreds of museums and churches, viewing lots of over varnished paintings of angels and saints. When it became clear that we'd be returning to the states I felt a real "hunger" for the directness of American painting, especially the bold, rocky, oceanfront paintings of Winslow Homer.*

NG: When I did finally start painting, I immediately began looking at art in a much more critical way. Why did I like the things I did, what kinds of paintings specifically appealed to me? I realized fairly quickly that I tended to prefer more tonal work, or work with fairly close color harmonies. In those early days of painting I was looking at work that was "painterly" but quite naturalistic. Learning to create a realistic illusion of the things I saw was pretty compelling for a while. Once I began to feel that I had acquired some good fundamental painting skills, though, I began to think about the other things that a painting could do. I started looking in earnest at work that was less defined by realism—Vuillard. Bonnard. Giacometti's drawings. Morandi. Auerbach. This was work grounded in close looking but wasn't purely observational. It was not bound by a need to depict. It was work that seemed to be about the interplay of perception and the artist's need for expression.

Quite serendipitously, about this time the Barnes Foundation had a wonderful Soutine/de Kooning show. I had known a little bit about Soutine from paintings in the Barnes foundation's permanent collection, I had never seen his landscapes or even much of his still lives. That show was a revelation to me.

DD: *Representational art has two distinct aspects, that of the subject that exists apart from the painting and that of the painting itself. (That's an oversimplified statement, but I hope clear enough, for this purpose.) I heard an art history professor once say that Matisse was challenged by a viewer regarding his* Woman in Blue*—"Why did you put that big ugly hand on the lady?" His reply: "Sir, that is not a lady, that is a painting."*

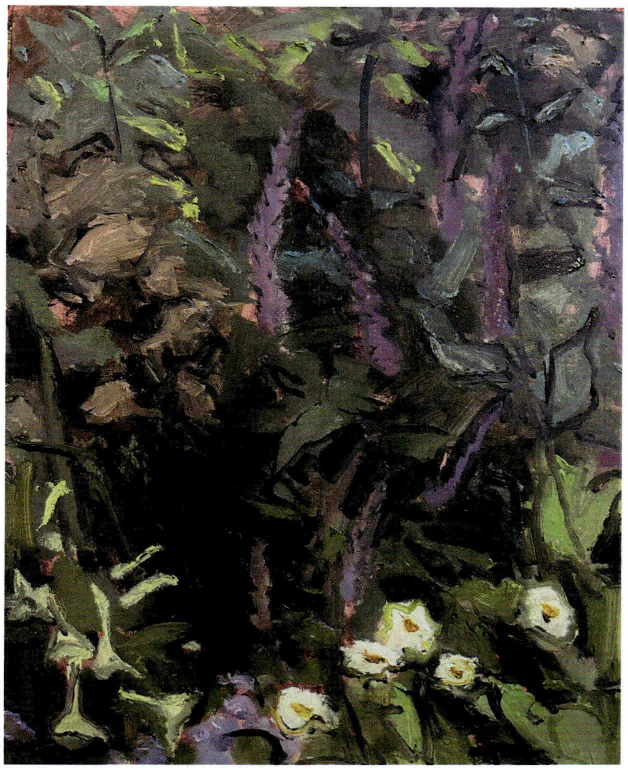

Nancy U. Granda *Midsummer Garden*
2023, oil on panel, 20 x 16 in.

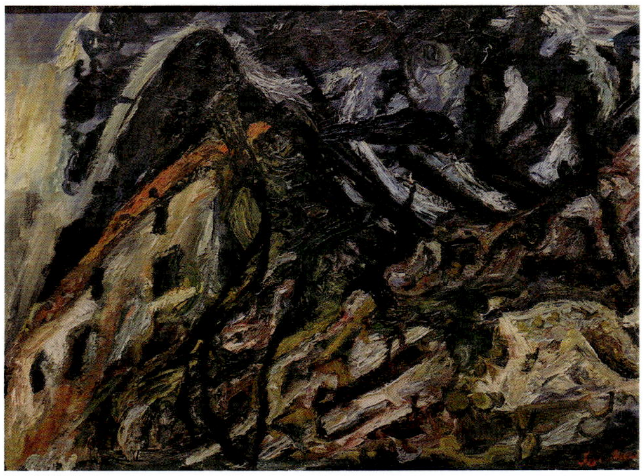

Chaïm Soutine *Landscape at Cêret*
c. 1920-1, oil in canvas, 22 x 33 in.

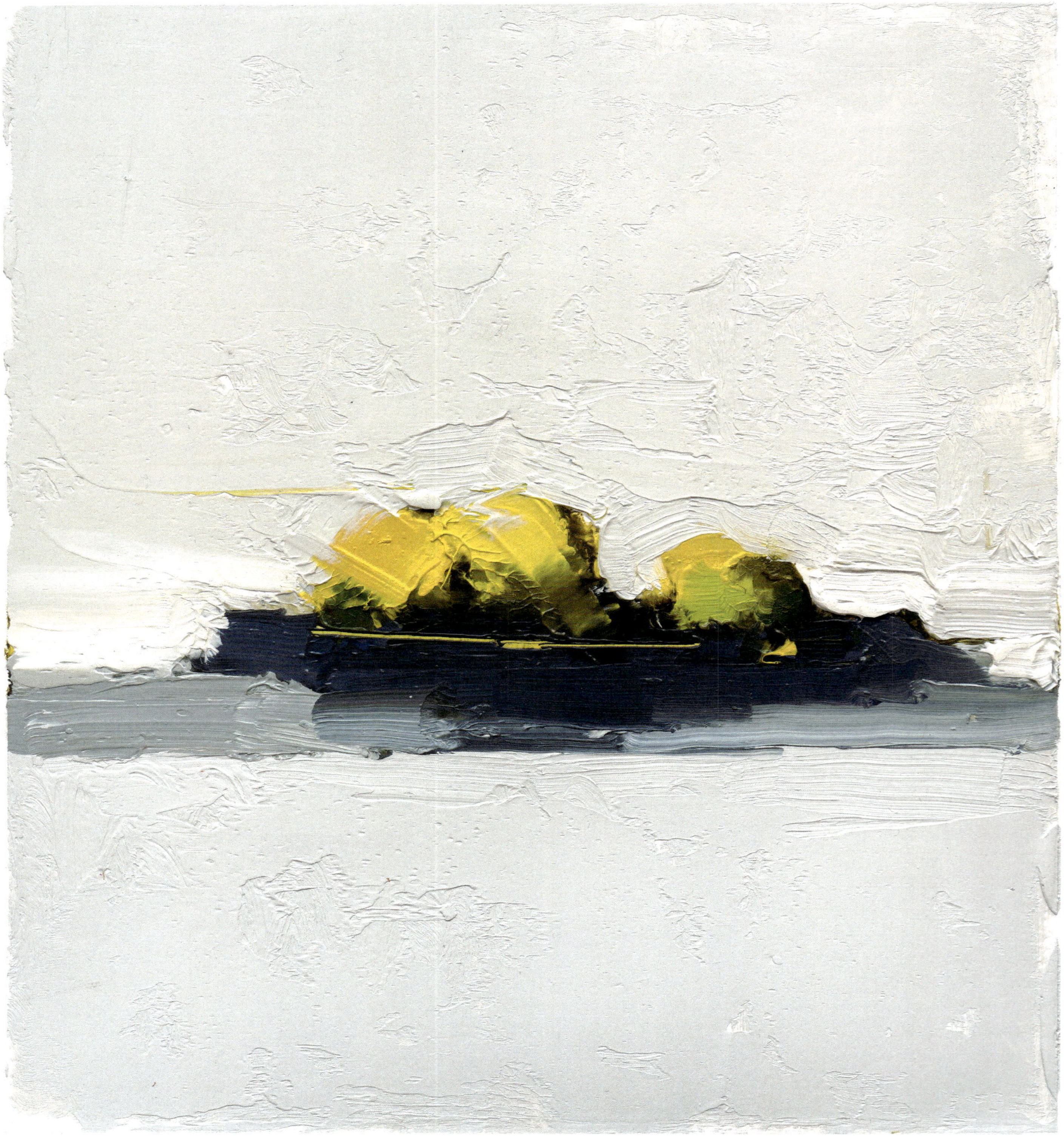

Stanley Bielen *Essen*
2022, oil on paper mounted, 8 x 7 in.

There is a way to balance those two aspects, even to shift the primacy of one or the other, to add tension or create harmony, and infinite shades between. I certainly see that balance in works by each of you. Stan, in your single subject works, some of which have these wonderful slurries of paint, applied with a knife, that attract attention to the material itself, which asserts the presence of the painting as an object in and of itself, apart from the identity of the subject matter, perhaps a plate of ripe fruit. Nancy, I see something similar happening in your works as well? Maybe with the dark color range as well as the turgid, almost liquid quality of the surface?

NG: I guess I sort of was approaching this question by the end of the last answer— but yes, I do absolutely feel that the best of my paintings are as much objects made of paint as they are images or representations. And I always hope that they will function as their own little worlds, independent of both the subject and of me. I think it is important for me to see the beauty in the struggle, rather than in a polished final product. I'm thinking of Giacometti's searching lines, and Stanley Lewis's beautifully dense surfaces.

SB: In response to your last question I would like to share with you the opening paragraph of an article about painting mediums written by Arthur DeCosta. Occasionally I teach a workshop and I like to read this paragraph to students.

"One of the most difficult problems of technique in painting is finding a medium that will permit the brush to move with the same facility as a drawing point. An example of this problem, perfectly resolved, can be seen in the red silk cape on Pope Innocent X, in the portrait by Velasquez. Here, the integration of drawing and painting calligraphy is complete. One's awareness of gorgeously spread paint is simultaneously experienced as an incomparable illusion of shimmering silk. This subtle balance between evidence of means (the paint and the brush) and the illusion of appearance (the reality of the subject) is the classic painterly ideal."

DD: *I like his subtle description of those two aspects of representational art; the "illusion of appearance" and the "evidence of means." Notice that the parenthetical additions in the above paragraph are mine.*

For either or both of you: What do you like/love/desire to see in your own paintings? Is there a quality that you feel is necessary for you to be excited about doing the work? To be satisfied enough to call the painting done? To mourn the loss when you screw it up and find that quality has vanished? That quality, those qualities, might be ephemeral or concrete, or both?!) How do you know it when you see it, or feel it?

NG: I mentioned earlier that I love many different kinds of painting. I think the paintings I've made that I would consider the most exciting, the most meaningful, come from exploring the tension between various opposing qualities— structure/chaos, mystery/clarity, poetic brevity/teeming copia, observation/invention, object/image.

For a long time I felt my most successful paintings were very fast, small sketches. They had a lot of freshness and energy, but I started to feel that they were missing something ineffable that only arrives with time. Lately I've been trying to build up some of these small

Nancy U. Granda *Dead Flowers in a Mirror*
2022, oil on panel, 10 x 8 in.

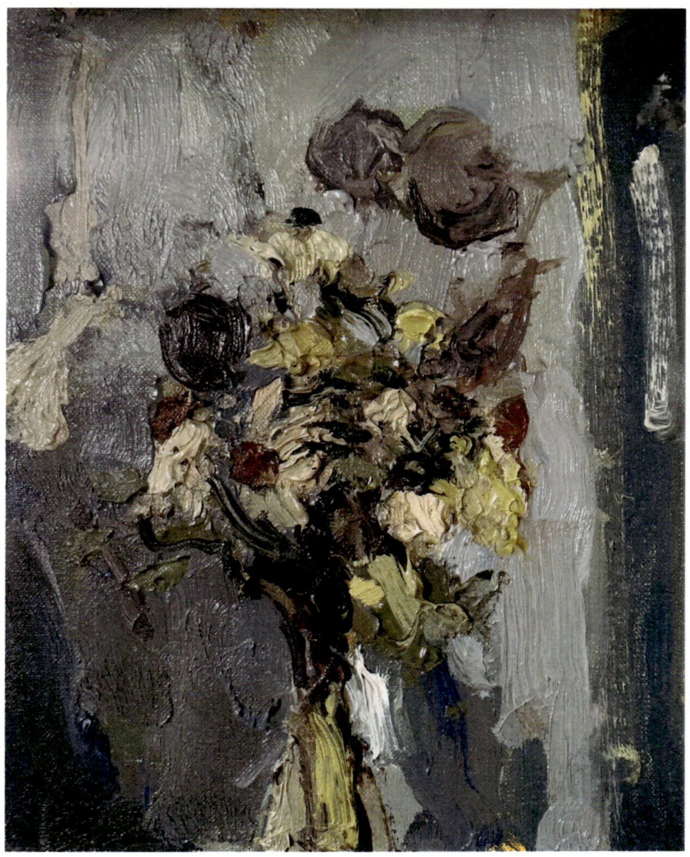

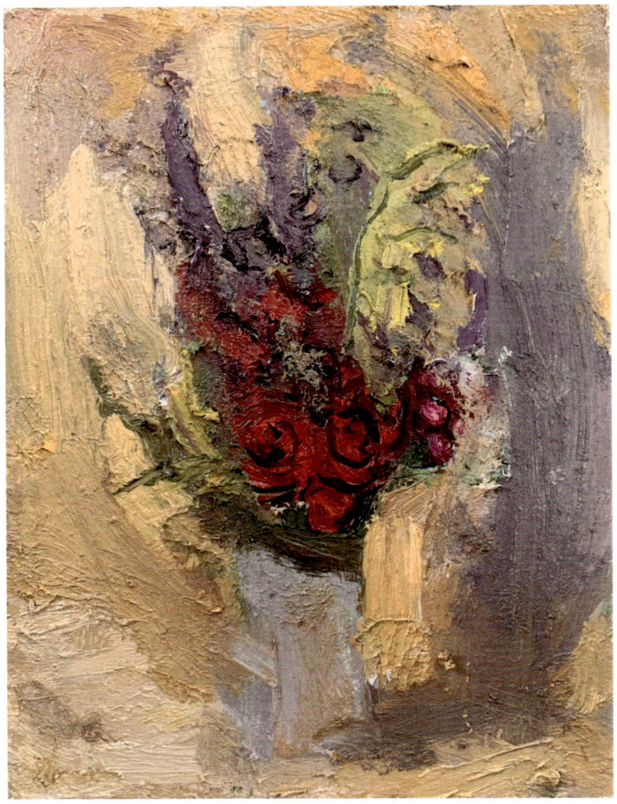

Nancy U. Granda *Blaze*
2022, oil on panel, 12 x 9 in.

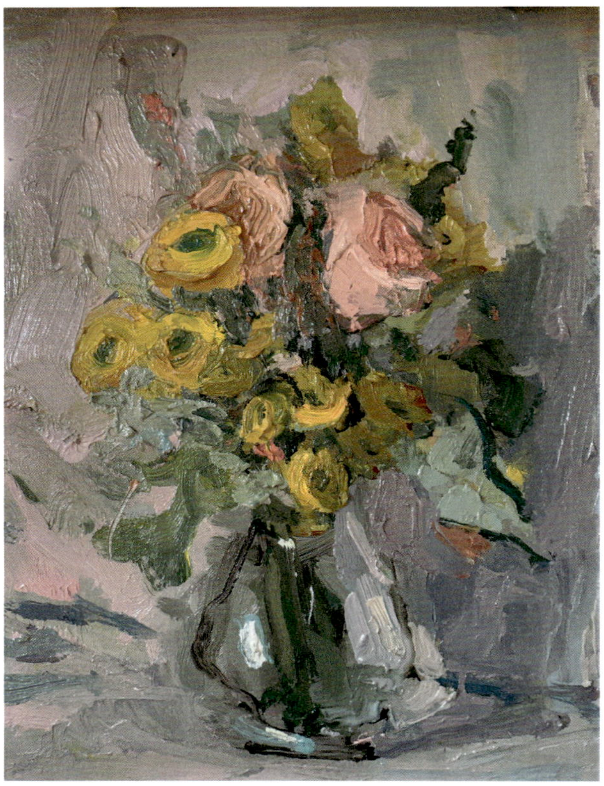

Nancy U. Granda *Golden Suns*
2022, oil on panel, 12 x 9 in.

paintings in many layers; I can repaint the entire painting many times in a single session, and continue to add layers over weeks or months. While the paintings begin from observation, I eventually find myself responding more to the paint on the canvas than to the subject itself. Ideally at some stage it feels as though the painting has broken free of me and my expectations, and has taken on its own life, its own gravity.

I like to feel immersed, even kind of overwhelmed when I'm painting. This is the opposite of how I am in the rest of my life. I struggle with perfectionism and the paralysis which often accompanies it. In painting I find great joy in embracing imperfection and courting disaster. I can take big risks without fear of consequences. There are so many good paintings in the world—it's okay if I destroy a few in the attempt to make something beyond good, something that surprises me.

SB: In my case, it was in the 90's that still life started to become my main focus. A friend, and fellow painter, put it this way once; "painting, it's like being a miner, you go down into the mine, you find a vein and you mine that vein." Still life has been that vein for me.

DD: *And finally, what is your particular attraction to still life? Why not landscapes or some other category of representational painting; or non-objective abstract painting for that matter. I found it interesting that in the response to the last question and the related question, "why still life?," you both chose to talk about studio practice... and paint, light and gardens.*

SB: This past year my wife and I became grandparents and our granddaughter recently turned one. I have been thinking about what it might be like for her to be seeing the world for the first time. When we take her outside and she sees the light, trees, leaves, you can see the wonder on her face. I think that is why we become painters. In painting a still life, it is these eternal elements that are explored: light striking a form, space, atmosphere. And, all of this is local, it is a particular light, it is a particular atmosphere, in my case the mid-Atlantic, that my still life paintings are a product of.

And as far as everyday studio practice goes, I prefer an informal what's-in-season approach. I have been involved with gardening most of my life. My parents farmed in their early years. My wife, Elizabeth, along with neighbors started an urban community garden. Often I start my day by going to the community garden to look around and see what I can bring back to the studio to paint. Once in the studio, I spend some time arranging elements to see how I

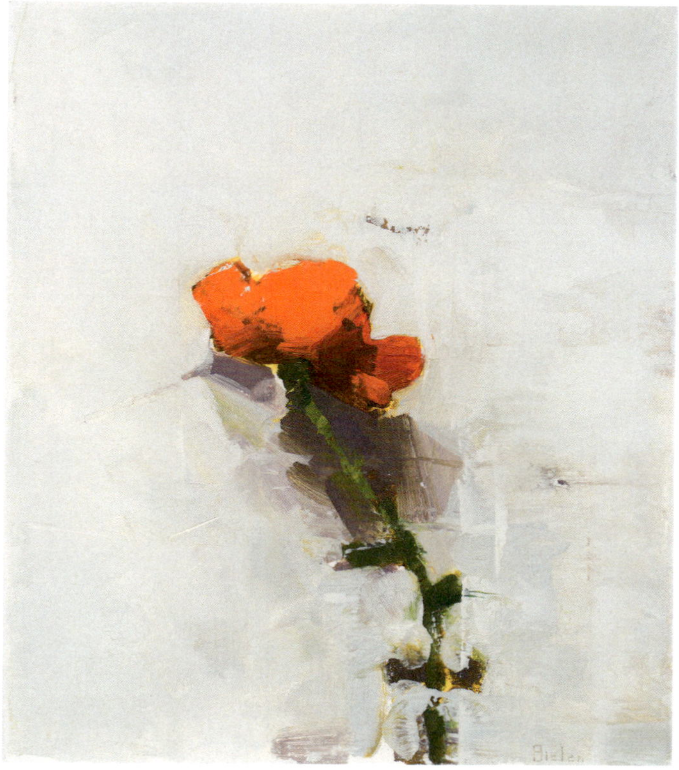

Stanley Bielen *Saudade*
2018, oil on paper mounted, 14 x 12 in.

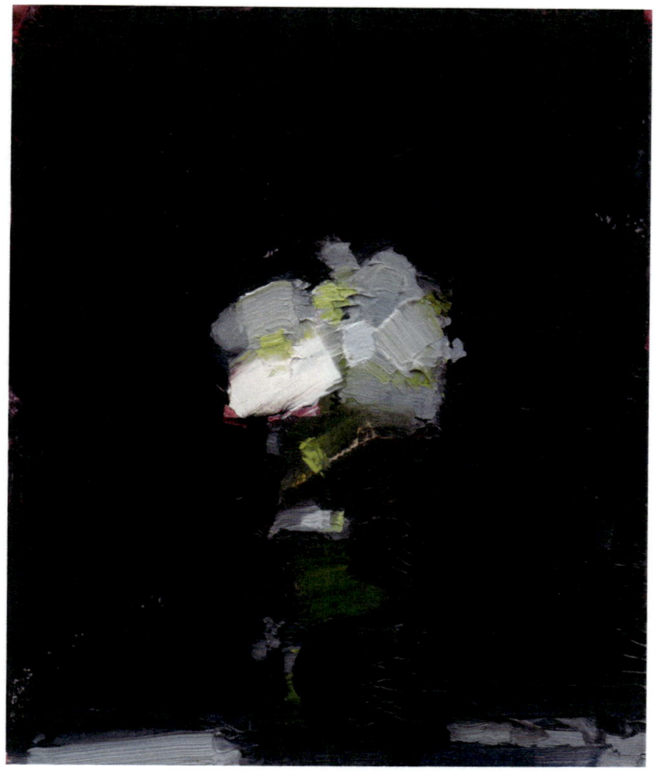

Stanley Bielen *Waning Crescent*
2020, oil on paper mounted, 7 x 6 in.

might paint them. I work directly from the subject. Most of the paintings are done alla prima, hence the generally small (although life size) scale.

NG: Early on, I painted a lot of still lifes in part for the convenience—they were something I could easily set up in my studio. But after a while, I started to find the set-ups stiff and awkward. I had come to prefer the feeling of finding a composition in the landscape to that of orchestrating a composition.

When I started painting the small flower sketches, it felt like the best of both worlds. The flowers are almost always little bunches I pick from my garden, and I don't really arrange them in any particular way. I like that they have a little bit of the chaos of the garden about them. I also like that they move and change and wilt. I usually set them up in the same place, on a shallow shelf; I only use natural light so the outdoor weather has a way of working its way into the paintings.

DD: *It has been a delight as well as a challenge, to organize this conversation for Zeuxis. My thanks to Nancy and Stan for putting up with my often clumsy questions and slow replies! I have loved learning about your lives and your devotion to painting.*

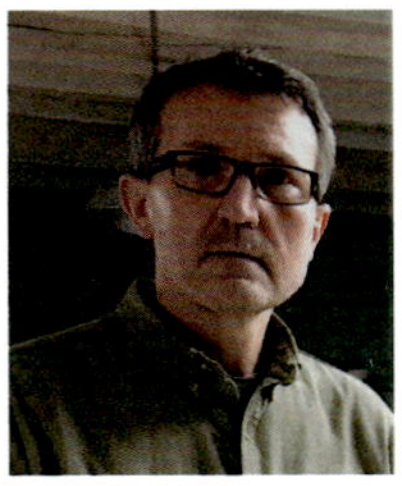

Stanley Bielen was born in the Podkarpackie region of Poland. He studied at the Pennsylvania Academy of Fine Art and is influenced by the long regional realist tradition called the Philadelphia School. He exhibits nationally and is represented in public and private collections including the Hirschhorn Museum and Sculpture Garden and the Pennsylvania Academy of Fine Art. Stanley lives and works in Philadelphia, PA and Bridgton, ME.

www.stanleybielen.com

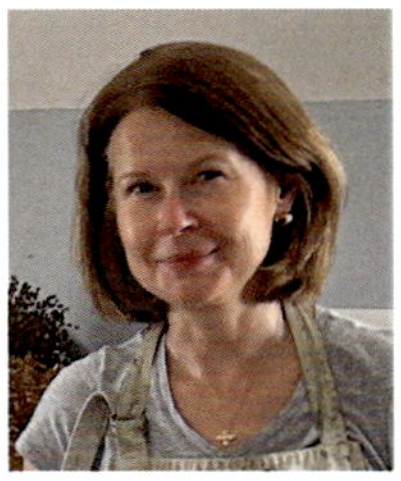

Nancy U. Granda is a painter from Philadelphia, Pennsylvania. She graduated from the University of Pennsylvania in 1994 with a degree in English literature, and she has studied at the Pennsylvania Academy of Fine Arts. In her work she strives for a spontaneous and deeply engaged response to her subject, whether working solely from observation or from a combination of sketches, photographic reference, and imagination. Her recent paintings explore questions regarding atmospheric color and the physical properties of paint.

www.nancygrandapaintings.com

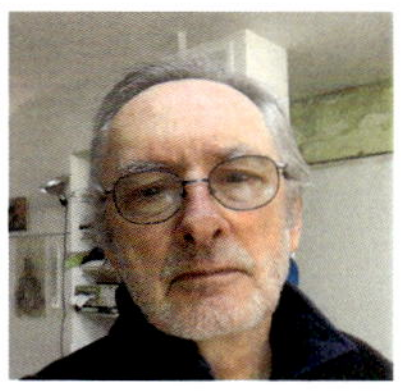

Daniel Dallmann has spent about 50 years making paintings, prints and drawings. while living and maintaining a studio in Philadelphia, PA. For the first 40 of those years, he also taught these subjects at the Tyler School of Art. Dallmann's focus on still life is relatively recent. Figurative subjects played the primary role in earlier work, with objects and environment of secondary importance. He has exhibited with Robert Schoelkopf and Peter Tatistcheff in New York City and Charles Moore and Richard Rosenfeld in Philadelphia when these were active galleries. He is presently represented by InLiquid in Philadelphia.

www.dallmannstudio.com

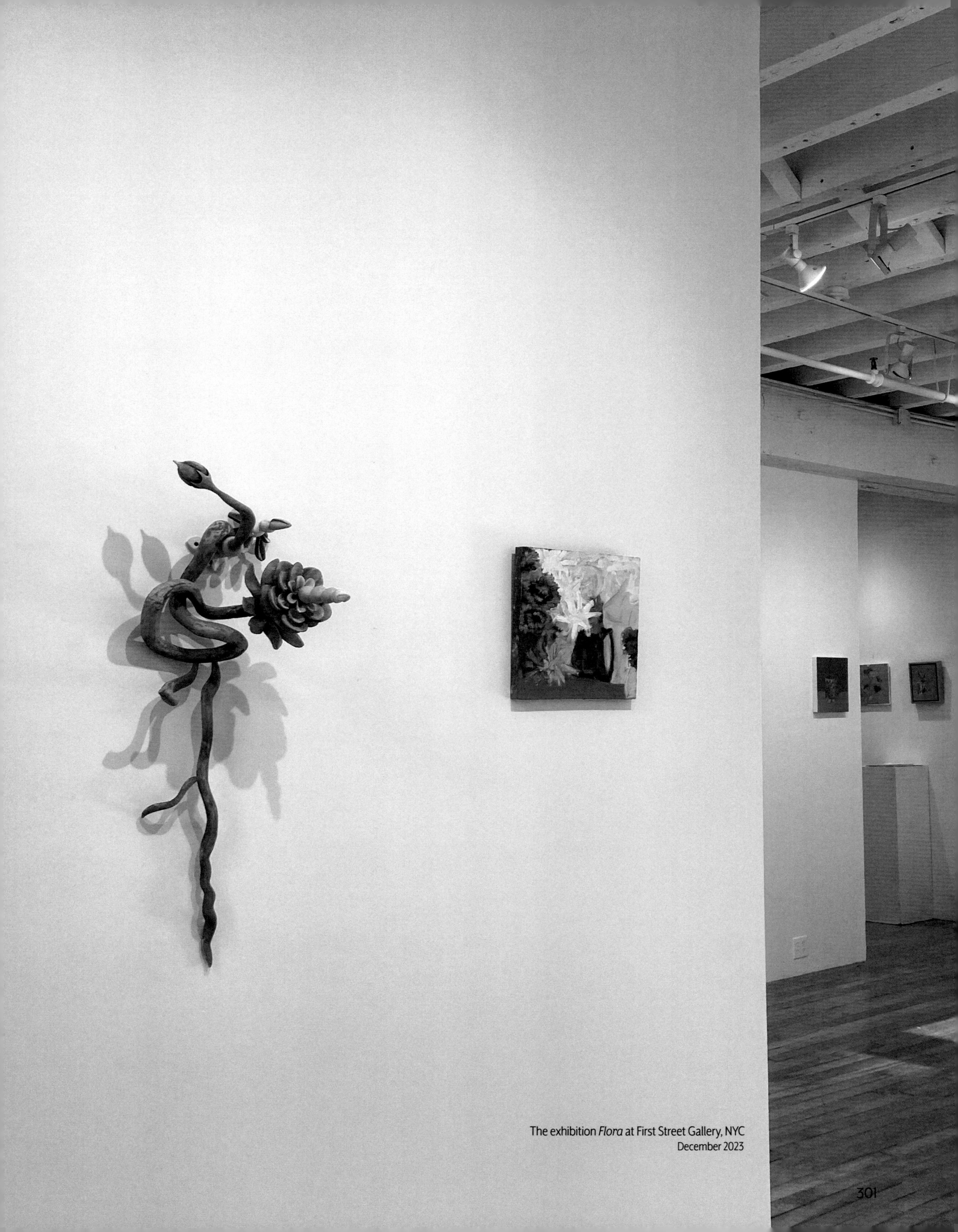

The exhibition *Flora* at First Street Gallery, NYC
December 2023

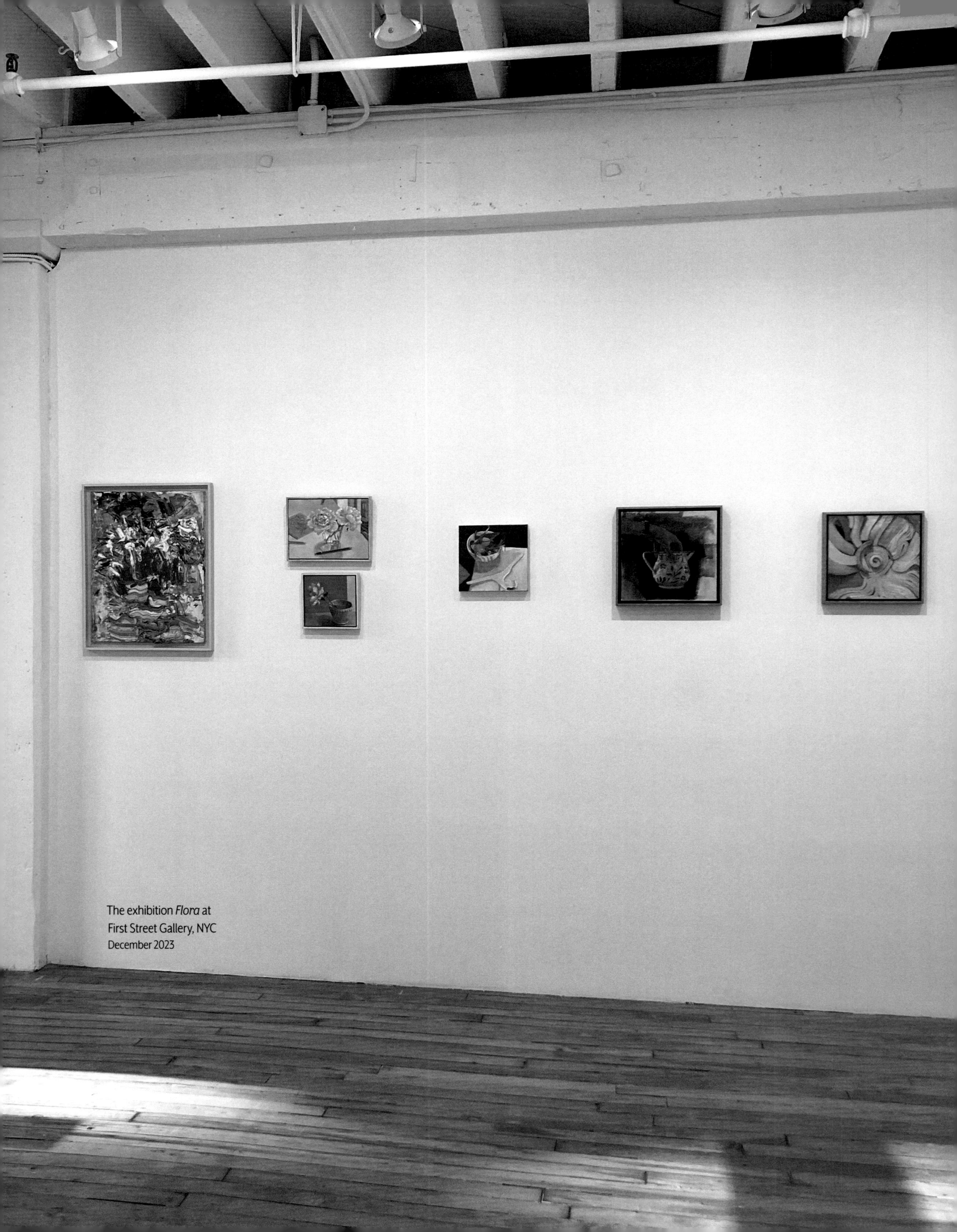

The exhibition *Flora* at
First Street Gallery, NYC
December 2023

Afterword:

The Life of Zeuxis

Phyllis Floyd

July 2023

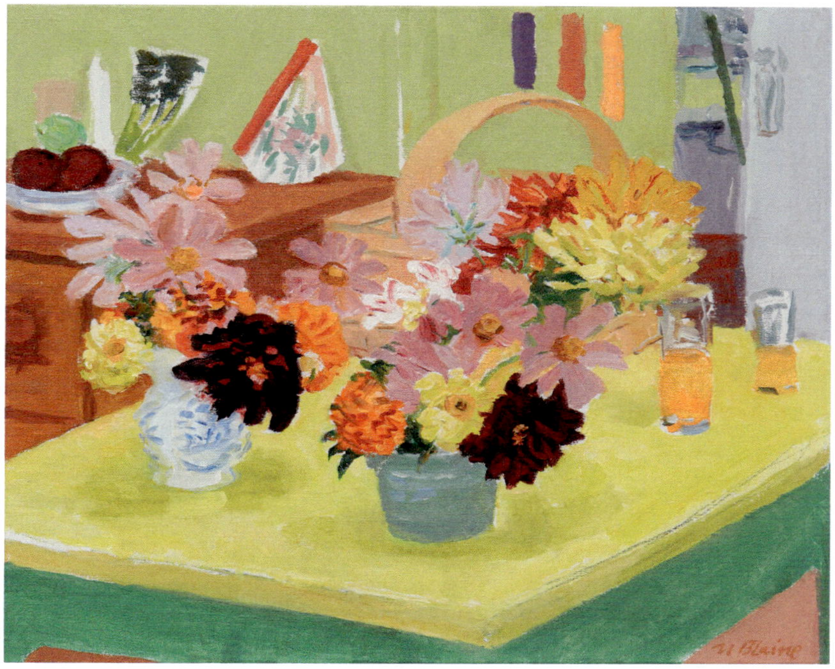

Nell Blaine

Sometime in the mid 1990s, it occurred to me that I might put together a group show. An entity, called the Organization of Independent Artists, offered a small amount of money for publicity to an "independent" painter—that meant a painter who was not part of a for-profit gallery—who could gather together some artists, introduce a theme, and find space for an exhibition. I had been wrestling with still life for years, and I proposed a still life show. I had a strong feeling that the directors of O.I.A. never in this world wanted anything other than "cutting edge" art and that my proposal caught them off guard. (I used to say to myself that I wanted to *épater l'avant garde*.) I reasoned that in a big city like New York there must be some like-minded painters. I hunted them down east side and west side and then by word of mouth. The nucleus consisted of Paul Carrellas, Lucy Barber, Suzanne Biggins, Tim Kennedy, Rita Baragona, Catherine Drabkin, Catherine Kehoe, Bill Barnes, Joe Byrne, and maybe others. Brian Jermusyk joined and then left us. We used slides in those days to present our work and communicated by telephone!

The nucleus became an association committed to exhibiting our still life paintings in likely venues. Finding a space to exhibit our paintings was then, as it is now, the biggest hurdle. Rita offered a show at her school in Blairstown. We also showed at a large gallery in the Steinway Building under the auspices of Kohn, Pederson, Fox architects. A Nell Blaine watercolor was on view and I believe a piece by Ruth Miller, who later joined Zeuxis. We showed at the Erector Square Gallery in CT, and I associate Carmela Kolman with that show because she went to a lot of trouble to procure the space for us.

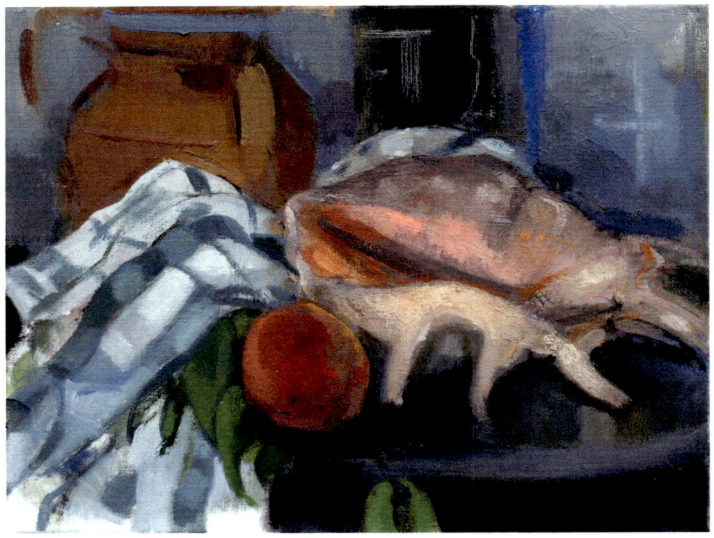

Ruth Miller

In 1998 John Goodrich (recommended by Bill Barnes) joined, and John, Joe Byrne and I became a Steering Committee with Carmela Kolman as treasurer. We used my loft as meeting place and proceeded to teach ourselves how to communicate with our group of painters. We found out early that the possibility for misunderstanding is infinite, but at least we didn't have to endure the squabbles that arise when many people try to make decisions. Some of our decisions were seen as unfair, dues for example, and artists left us. I had to be prodded into buying a computer, and I still find it a mixed blessing. War broke out when we asked artists to ship their work in Masterpak cartons, and two or three refused.

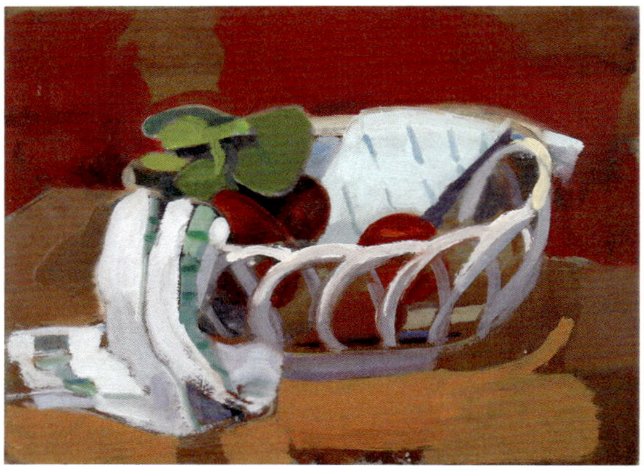

John Goodrich

One day John and I took a walk down Madison Avenue and, within one or two hours, made a connection with Lori Bookstein Fine Art and another with Kouros Gallery. During the next five years, Zeuxis organized several theme shows at each gallery. The husband and wife who owned Kouros eventually retired to their residence in Connecticut where they had a sculpture garden. Lori Bookstein moved from the Upper East Side to a larger space on West 57th Street, then to an even larger space in Soho and following that to East 66th Street. At present, she shows work on 39 East 78th Street.

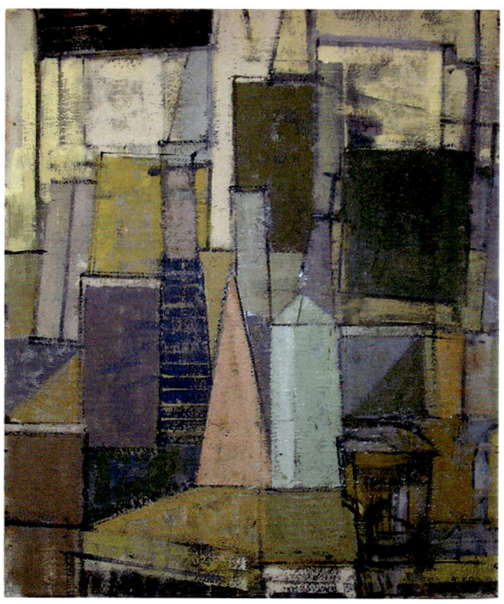

Joe Byrne

Zeuxis exhibitions were on display in New York whenever possible, but also around the country. We planned themes to enhance the exhibitions' coherence and increase interest. (Some of the Zeuxis artists didn't like the restriction of themes, but others have said that they enjoyed the challenge.) We relied on our artists to give us leads. Many of them were in the academic world, and so our shows traveled to college galleries and museums such as Colby College, Haverford College, Santa Rosa Junior College, Hollins University, Coe College, University of New Hampshire, Tulsa University, University of Arkansas, University of Alabama. All of the traveling shows were accompanied by handsome catalogs with full color reproductions. There is evidence that the catalogs have a life of their own because every once in a while one is spotted far from home.

We produced a big catalog for the show called "The Common Object." It had an especially long run at Maryland Institute College of Art beginning in 2011, and the gallery director arranged a series of talks featuring Zeuxis artists and guests. Elizabeth Geiger stood before her large painting and spoke so movingly that everyone was quiet for fear of missing a word. Temma Bell did a dance as she talked about her piece, evidence that she and the painting were one. In the evening, another talk featured John Goodrich and Bevin Engman. Bevin surprised me by describing her experience teaching painting to students. She has focused on light and color in her classes at Colby College, and has a reputation as an inspiring teacher. The same has been said of Mark Karnes who had a small piece in the exhibition. I believe he still gives classes at MICA where many know him as devoted in both classroom and studio.

After about seven years on the Steering Committee, Joe and John said that they had served long enough. They were replaced by Lynn Kotula, Susan Cohen, and Sydney Licht. We met for about a year, and I was dismayed when they announced that they were no longer able to serve. I had thought that I couldn't manage on my own, but my years of investment in Zeuxis had instilled in me

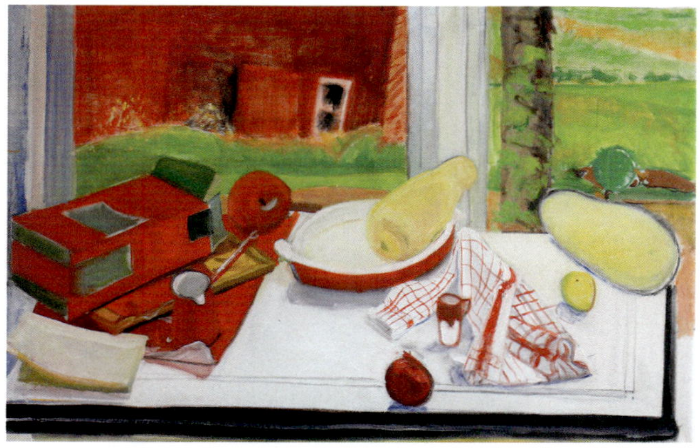

Temma Bell

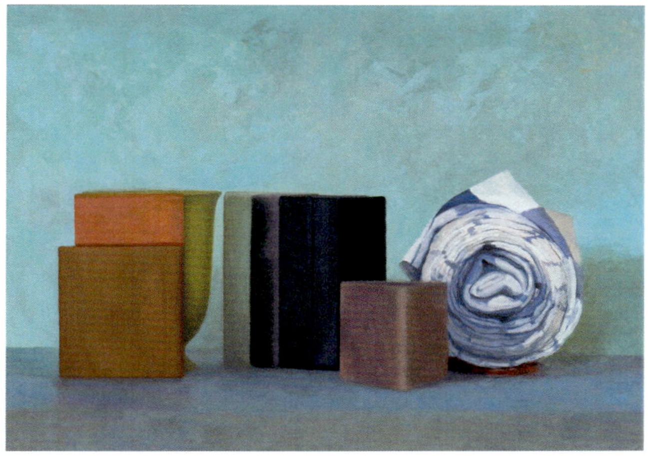

Bevin Engman

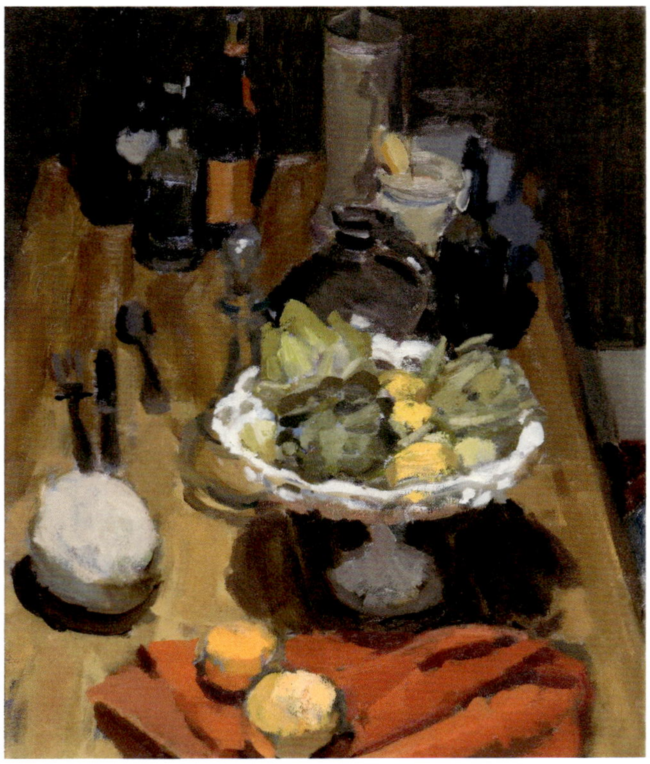

Elizabeth Geiger

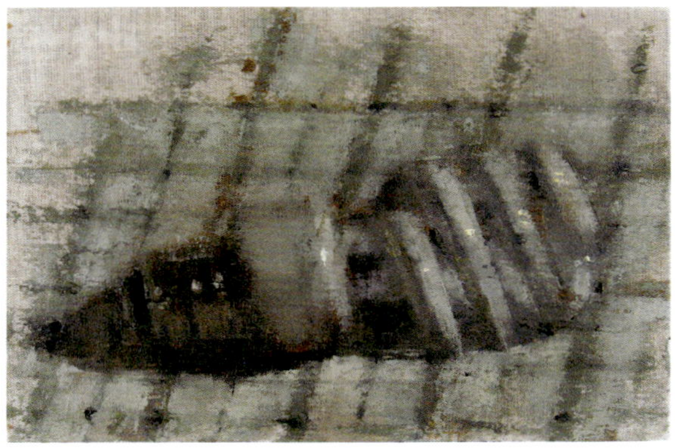

Mark Karnes

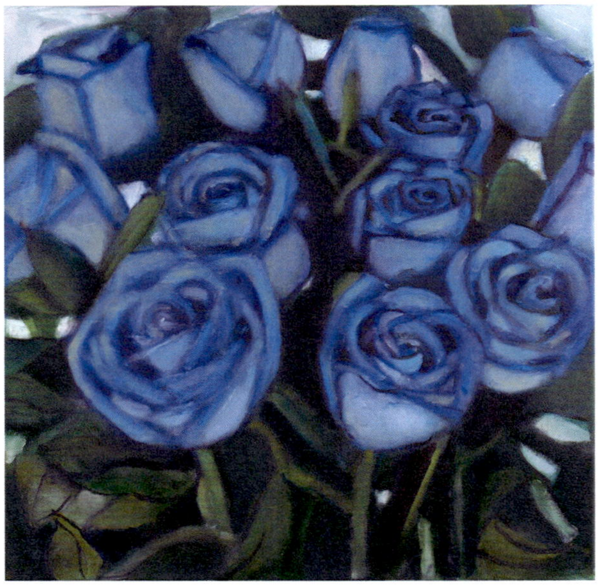

Carmela Kolman

a habit from which I couldn't break free. After several sleepless nights, I decided to manage on my own. Ruth was kind in listening to me complain about the rough spots as I tried to deal with my new role as crisis manager. Zeuxis hired Stacy Mohammed, later Shazzi Thomas, then Seth Schoenberg to work part time, and each year we planned publicity that required ever more complicated uses for the computer. During 2022, Kayla Edmonston worked with Seth to learn the ropes because Seth found a full-time job as archivist. Kayla recently graduated from FIT, and is involved with her own painting. John has continued to help when we need him most, hanging the shows that more and more people have come to enjoy.

We lost five artists when they lost their lives. Suzanne Biggins was one of the first to join. In 1995 I saw a couple of her still lifes in NY, and in that same year she moved to Waldron Island and then to Seattle. Victor Pesce came to my attention when his work was praised in the *The New York Times*. His wife Elizabeth Harris promoted his work. Carmela Kolman's work is illustrated in several of the Zeuxis catalogs. She died at a young age of Marfin's syndrome. Lynn Kotula joined Bowery Gallery where her husband Tony Stewart has done a remarkable job of dealing with her legacy. Sandra Stone loved painting but hated careerism. Her daughter, Alix Bailey, has organized shows for Sandra to take place in fall 2023 at the Painting Center and at THERE. All were fine painters and much-loved personalities. They must not be forgotten.

It became apparent that, while we couldn't accomplish everything we'd have liked, we had some unique options. One of them was to invite illustrious guests. Zeuxis catalogs are full of paintings by Lois Dodd, Louisa Mattiasdottir, Leland Bell, Gabriel Laderman, William Bailey, Richard Baker, Trevor Winkfield (see complete list on following pages). Tibor de Nagy Gallery has lent us work by several of its artists, and we appreciate their good will.

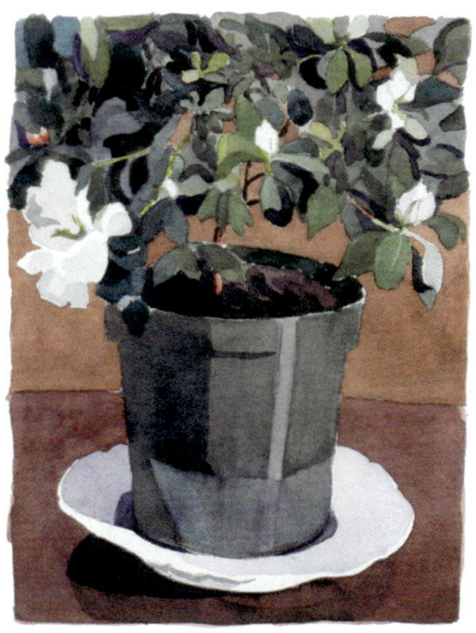

Phyllis Floyd

I ask myself how I have changed over the past 28 years and what I have learned from my association with Zeuxis. It's been a pleasure to meet so many accomplished people. We are a competitive bunch, but the most experienced painters are willing to support others and even to give time to Zeuxis. We all try, not always successfully, to appreciate contributions made by others. Human nature, for better or worse, is exaggerated in artists.

Exhibiting one's work has its hazards. In the long run, it matters most what one likes and dislikes in one's own work, even when over time such opinions might change.

At present, Zeuxis is organizing two shows—one called "Flora" and the other "The Anxious Still Life"— both to be seen in New York this year and next. Zeuxis has a life. Z

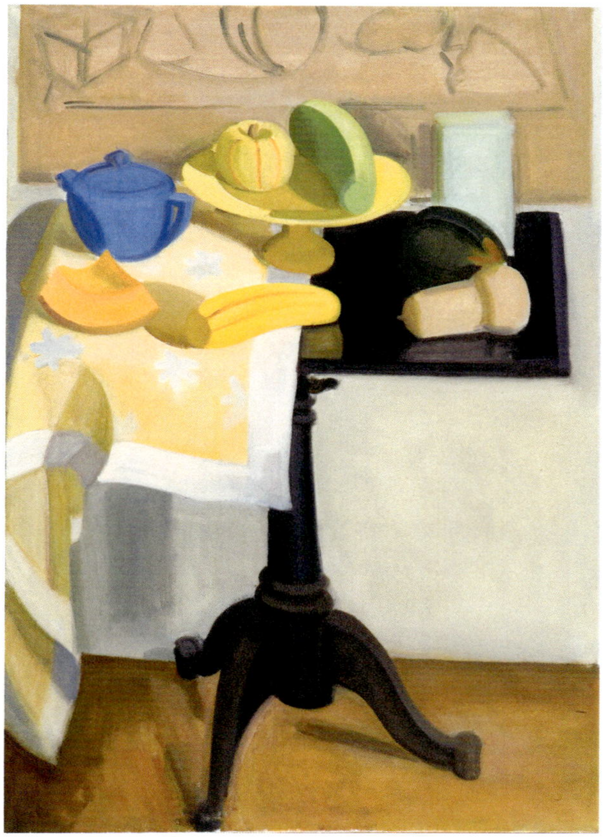

Lynn Kotula

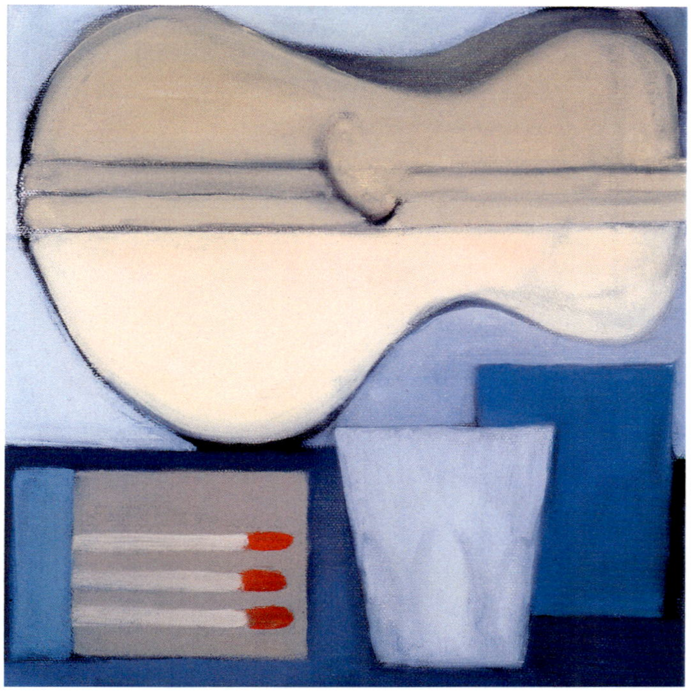

Suzanne Biggins

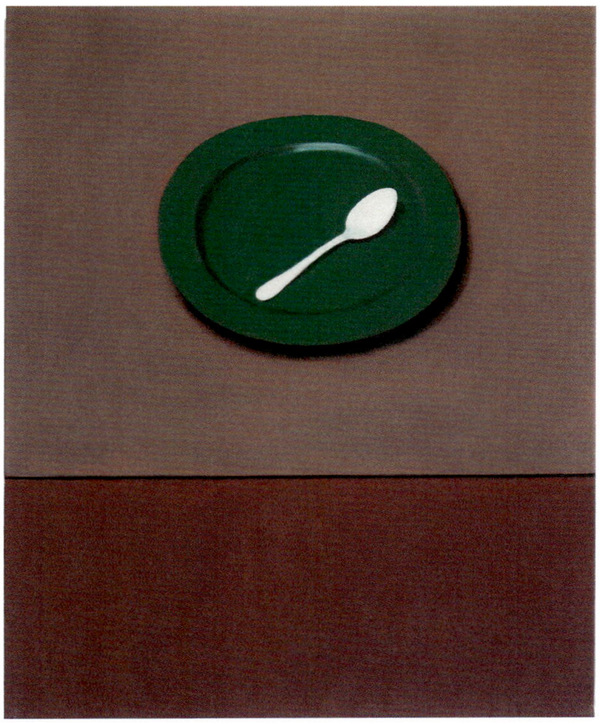

Victor Pesce

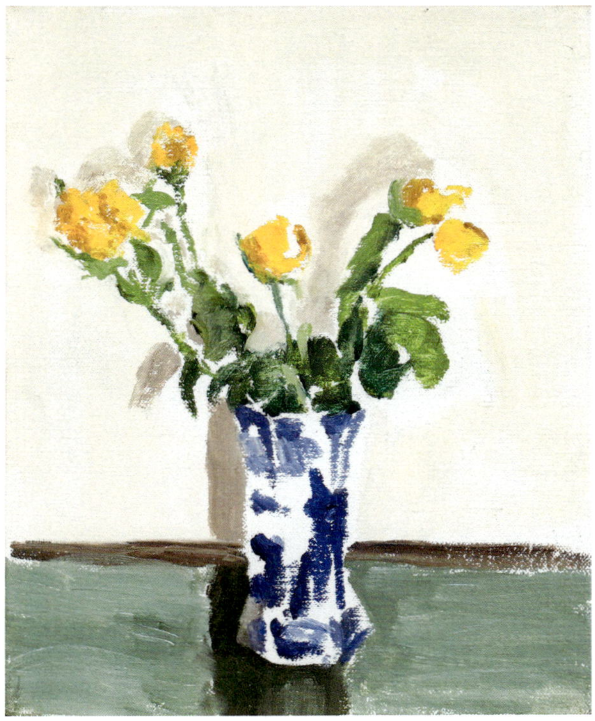

Sandra Stone

Zeuxis Guest Artists

1995-2023

Lennart Anderson
Martha Armstrong
Alix Bailey
William Terranouva Bailey
Richard Baker
Nancy Balliett
William D. Barnes
Victoria Barnes
Violet Baxter
Leland Bell
Sallie Benton
Biala
Stanley Bielen
Suzanne Biggins
Nell Blaine
John Bradford
Rick Brazill
Tom Burckhardt
Joseph Byrne
Caren Canier
Richard Castellana
Donna Cehrs
Bernard Chaet
Richard Chiriani
Anna Contes
Colleen Cox
Robert De Niro
Lois Dodd
Catherin Drabkin
John Dubrow
Franklin Einspruch
Kate Emlen
Bevin Engman
Nancy Flanagan
Jane Freilicher
Stanley Friedman
Elizabeth Geiger
Owen Gray
Elliott Green
Nancy Grimes
Nancy Hagin
Carolyn Harris
William Harsh
Christine Hartman
Paula Heisen
Elena Lehman Hilfer
Delphine Hogarth
Diana Horowitz
William Hudders
Su-li Hung
Dee Jenkins
Robert Jessel
Mark Karnes
Catherine Kehoe

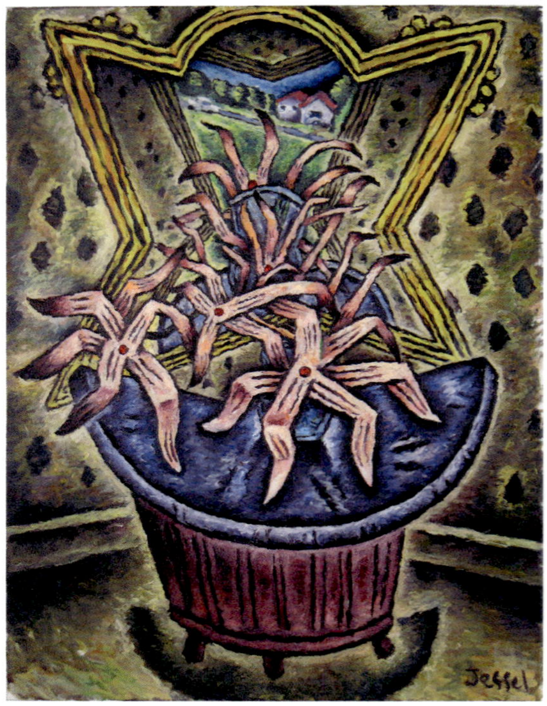

Robert Jessel

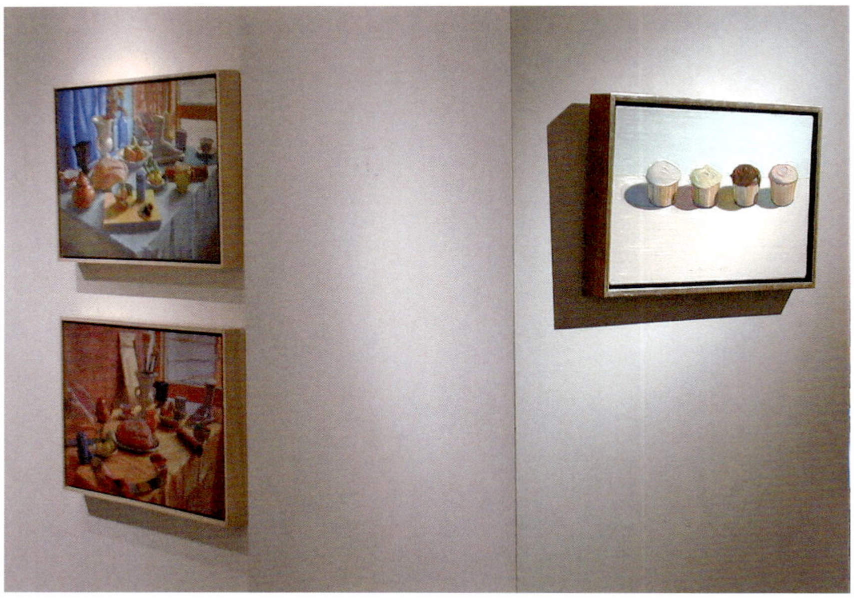

Wayne Thiebeau (on right) at Serial Thinking

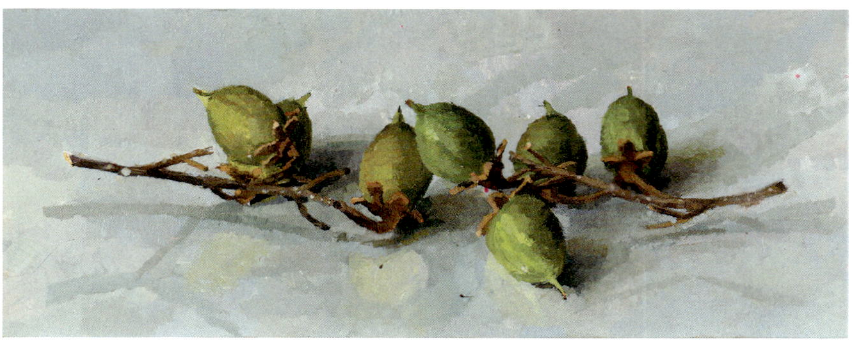

Susanna Coffey

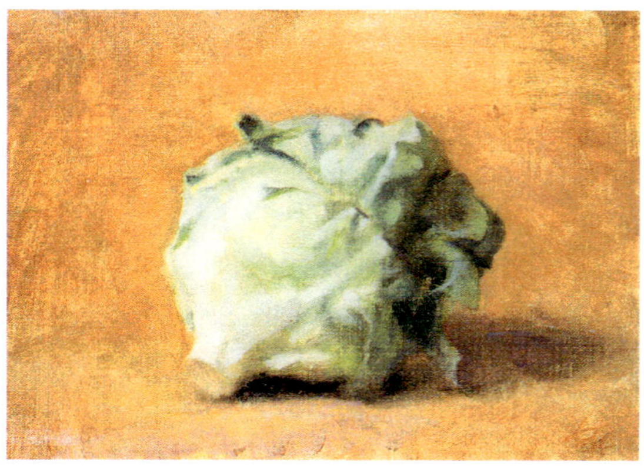

Lennart Anderson

Niki Ketchman
Ken Kewley
Arthur Kleinfelder
Matt Klos
Ernest Koerlin
Carmela Kolman
Lynn Kotula
Al Kresch
Penny Kronengold
Robert Kulicke
Gabriel Laderman
John Lee
Marion Lerner-Levine
Ginger Levant
Stanley Lewis
Mark Lewis
Bruce Lieberman
Susan Lichtman
Matthew Lopas
Catherine Maize
Jennifer Maloney
Eves Mansdorf
Janet Manyan
Max Mason
Louisa Matthíasdóttir
Cynthia Maurice
Stacy Mohammed
Gael Mooney
Kathy A. Moore
Ben Frank Moss
Patrick Neal
George Nick
Wilbur Niewald
Scott Noel
Janice Nowinski
Elizabeth O'Reilly
Margaret Olney-Mc-Bride
Victor Pesce
Susannah Phillips
Linda Phillips
Langdon Quin
Stephanie Rauschen-busch
Emil Robinson
Stephanie Sanchez
Laura Shechter
Don Southard
Clintel Steed
William Stewart
Carol M. Stewart
Walter Strach
Anne Tabachnik
Wayne Thiebaud
Ian Tornay
Mary Jo Vath
Susan Walp
Amy Weiskopf
Bill White
Trevor Winkfield
Sharon Yates
Rachel Youens

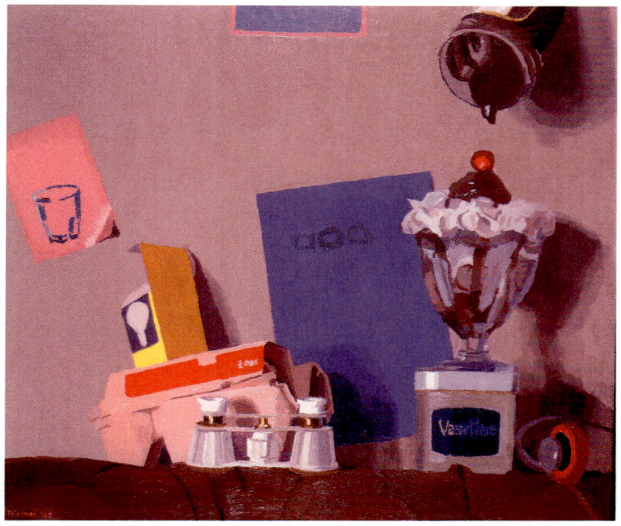

Stanley Friedman

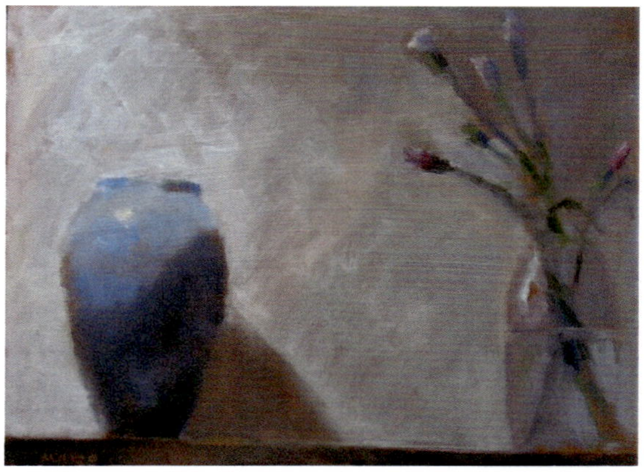

Catherine Maize

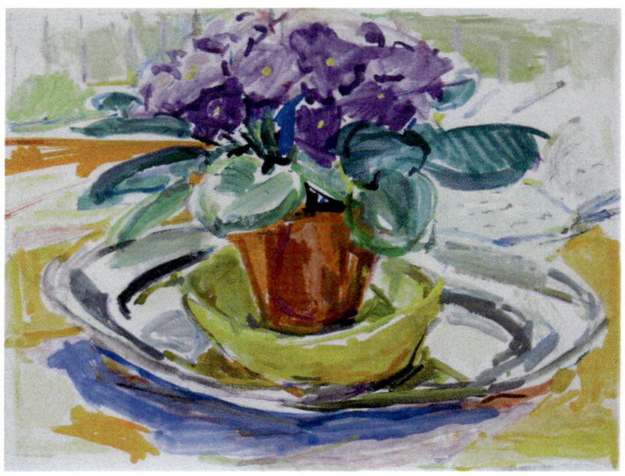

Rita Baragona

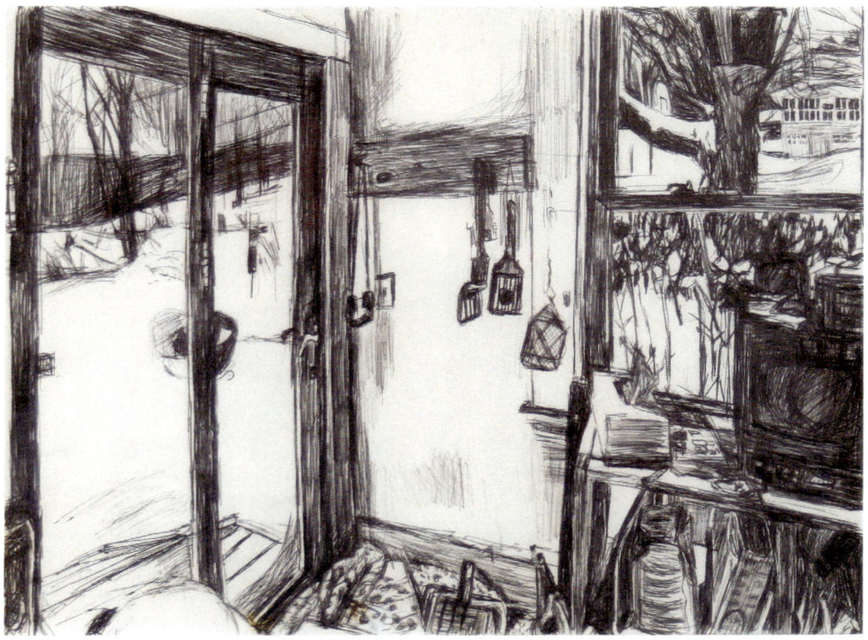

Stanley Lewis

Zeuxis Exhibitions
1999-2023

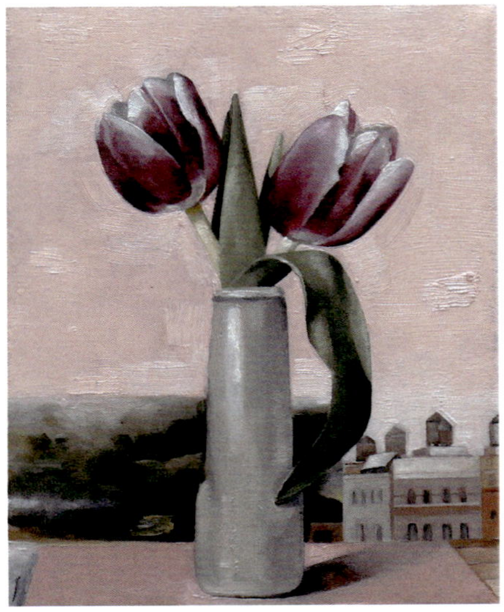

Richard Baker

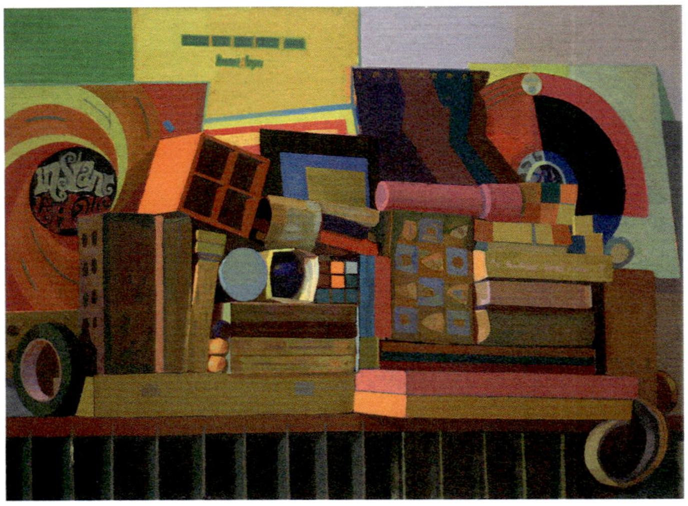

John Lee

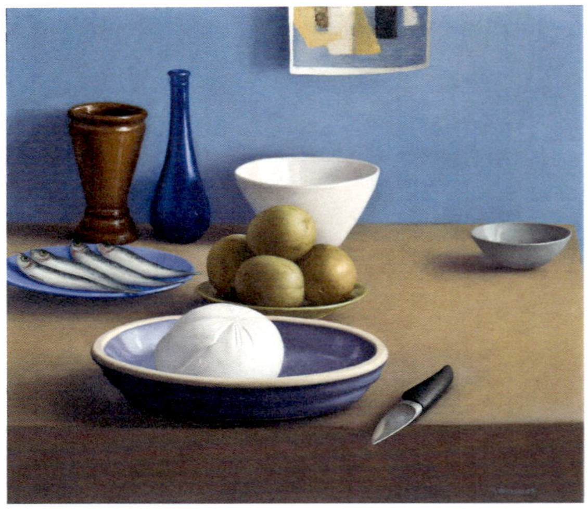

Amy Weiskopf

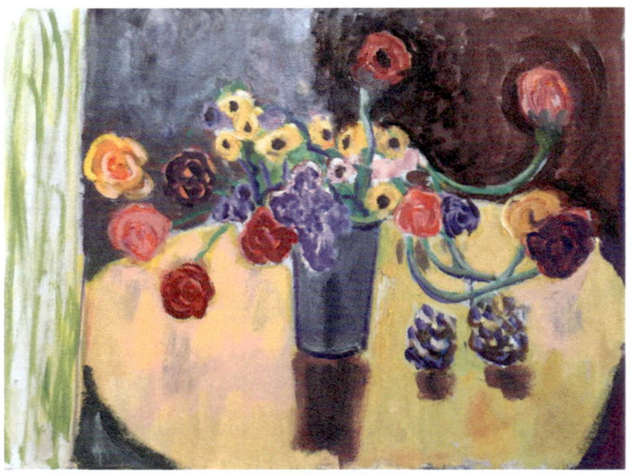

Richard Castellana

Zeuxis at Marywood – 1999
Contemporary Gallery, Marywood University, *Scranton, PA*

Zeuxis An Association of Still Life Painters – 1999
Butler Gallery, Marymount College, *Tarrytown, NY*

Distilled Life – 1999
Prince Street Gallery, *New York, NY*

Still Life: The Human Presence – 1999-2000
University Art Gallery, University of Wisconsin at La Crosse, *La Crosse, WI*
Peninsula Fine Arts Center, *Newport News, VA*
Courtyard Gallery, The Washington Studio School, *Washington DC*
Erechtor Square Gallery, *New Haven, CT*
The Painting Center, *New York, NY*

Serial Thinking – 2002
Wright State University Art Galleries, *Dayton, OH*
Kouros Gallery, *New York, NY*
Augustana College Art Gallery, *Rock Island, IL*
Purdue University Galleries, *West Lafayette, IN*

Zeuxis An Association of Still Life Painters – 2002
New England College Art Gallery, *Henniker, NH*

Uncommon Perspectives – 2002-03
Denise Bibro Fine Art, *New York, NY*
Hermitage Foundation Museum, *Norfolk, VA*
Attleboro Art Center, *Attleboro, MA*
Washington Art Association, *Washington Depot, CT*

Works on Paper – 2003
Pennsylvania Academy of Fine Arts, *Philadelphia, PA*

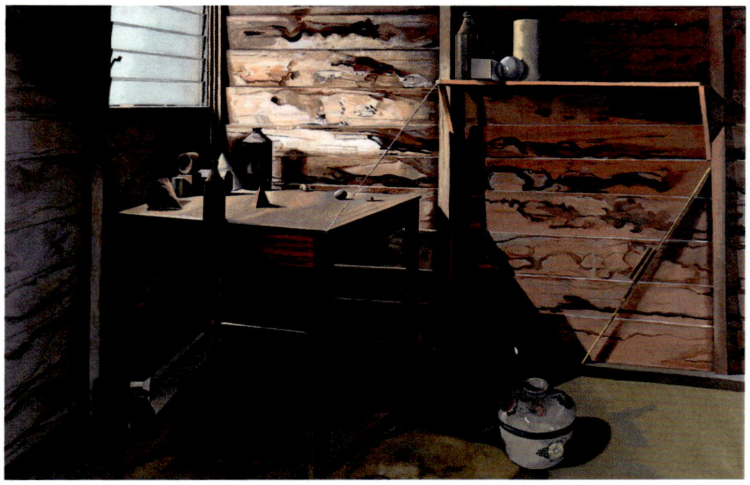

Gabriel Laderman

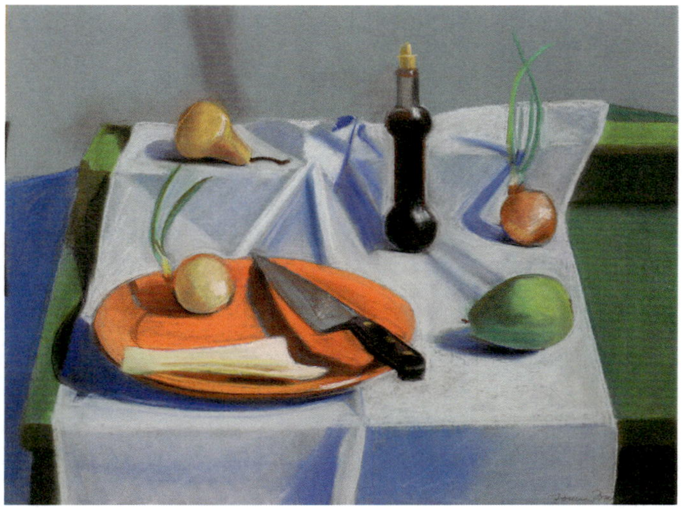

Louisa Matthiasdottir

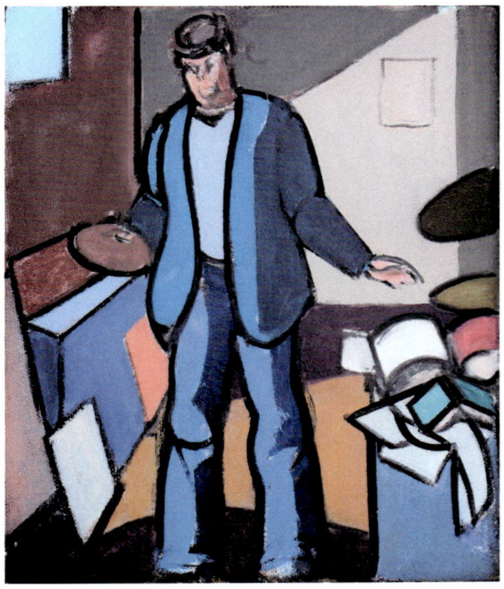

Leland Bell

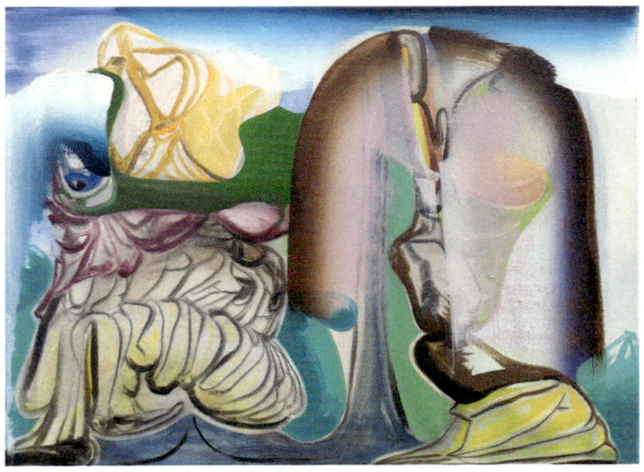

Elliott Green

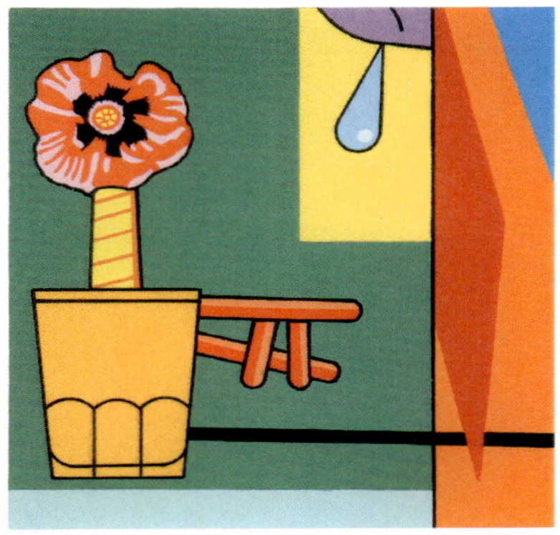

Trevor Winkfield

Zeuxis at LIU – 2003
Salena Gallery, Long Island University, *Brooklyn, NY*

A Moveable Feast – 2003
Westbeth Gallery, *New York, NY*

Table Top Arenas – 2004
Colby College Museum of Art, *Waterville, ME*
Lori Bookstein Fine Art, *New York, NY*

Poetic Dimensions of the Modern Still Life – 2004-05
Hofstra Museum, *Hempstead, NY*
Kouros Gallery, *New York, NY*
DuPont Gallery, Washington and Lee University, *Lexington, VA*

Facets of Perception – 2006-07
Snug Harbor Cultural Center, *Staten Island, NY*
Schweinfurth Memorial Art Center, *Auburn, NY*
University of Tulsa, *Tulsa, OK*
Eleanor D. Wilson Museum, *Roanoke, VA*
Wiegand Gallery, *Belmont, CA*

On Board – 2007
Lori Bookstein Fine Art, *New York, NY*

Small Takes – 2008
First Street Gallery, *New York, NY*

Outside the Box – 2008
Delaware College of Art and Design, *Wilmington, DE*

In/Out – 2008-09
Hobart College, *Geneva, NY*
Broome Street Gallery, *New York, NY*

Contemporary Perceptions—Zeuxis Still Life Painting – 2011
Blair Academy's Romano Gallery, *Blairstown, NJ*

The Common Object – 2010-12
Lancaster Museum of Art, *Lancaster, PA*
Peninsula Fine Arts Center, *Newport News, VA*
Prince Street Gallery, *New York, NY*
MICA, *Baltimore, MD*

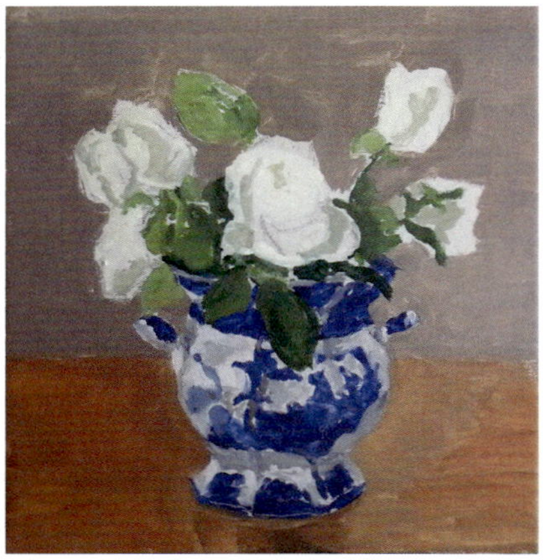
Sandra Stone

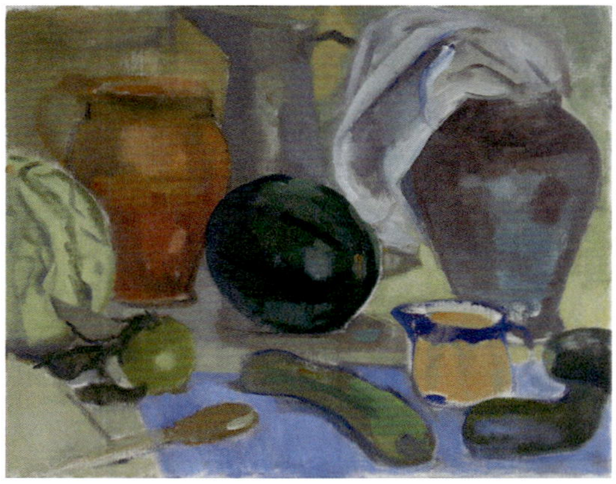
Ruth Miller

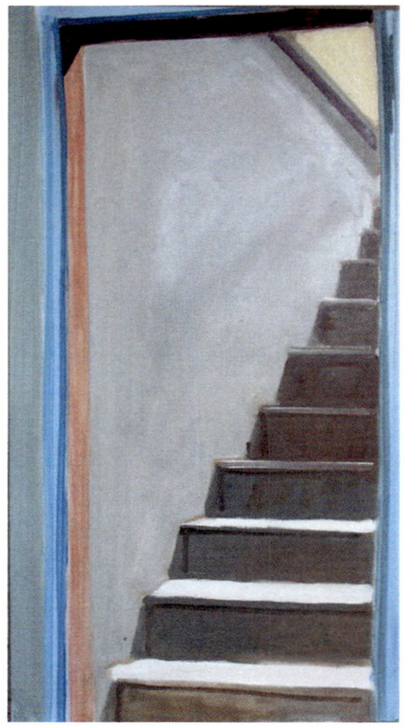
Lois Dodd

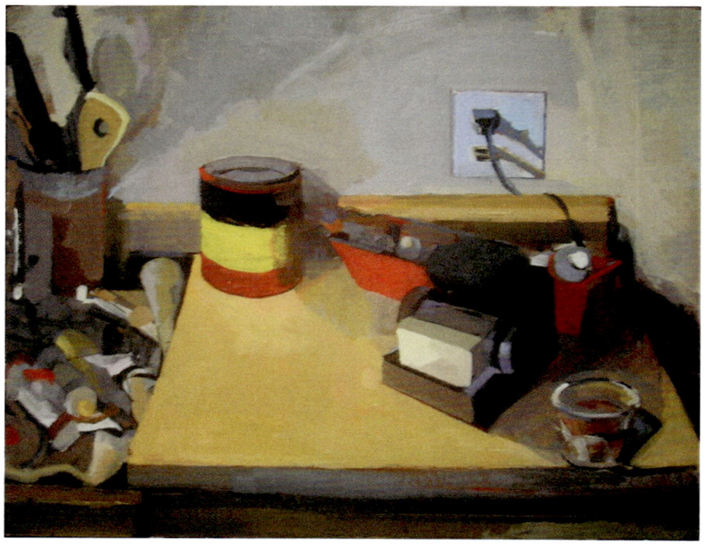
Nancy Flanagan

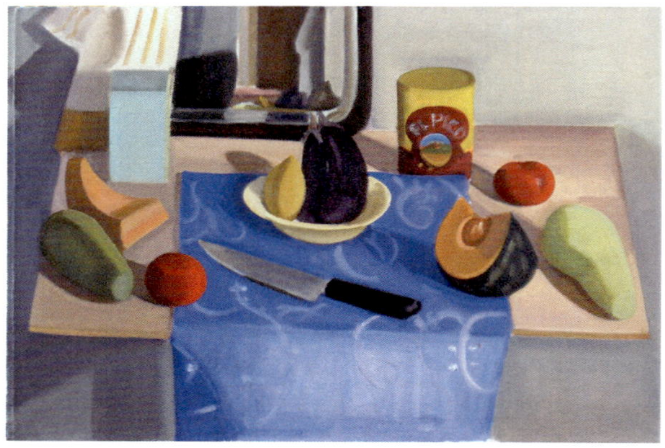
Lynn Kotula

Reflections – 2012-13
Boyle Family Gallery, Lindenwood University, *Saint Charles, MO*
Rosemary Berkel and Harry L. Crisp II Museum, Southeast Missouri State University, *Cape Girardeau, MO*
The Painting Center, *New York, NY*
Pennsylvania College of Art & Design, *Lancaster, PA*

Still, Blue – 2013-14
Schmidt Art Center, Southwestern Illinois College, *Belleville, IL*
Wilson Galleries, Anderson University, *Anderson, IN*
First Street Gallery, *New York, NY*
Maryland Hall for the Creative Arts, *Annapolis, MD*

Beyond the Window – 2015-16
Gallery of Art and Design University of Southern Mississippi, *Hattiesburg, MS*
Norton Center for the Arts, Centre College, *Danville, KY*
Bowery Gallery, *New York, NY*
Alexandre Hogue Gallery, University of Tulsa, *Tulsa, OK*
Mark W. Potter Gallery, Taft School, *Watertown, CT*

Flowers As Metaphor – 2016-17
Hendrix College, *Conway, AR*
Santa Rosa Junior College, *Santa Rosa, CA*
Wiegand Gallery, Notre Dame de Numar University, *Belmont, CA*

The Unstilllife – 2017-18
Toni and Stuart B. Young Gallery, Delaware College of Art and Design, *Wilmington, DE*
The Painting Center, *New York, NY*
Windgate Art and Design, University of Arkansas Fort Smith, *Fort Smith, AR*
University of Mississippi Museum and Historic Houses, *Oxford, MS*

Drawing the Curtain – 2018
First Street Gallery, *New York, NY*

My Studio – 2019-20
First Street Gallery, *New York, NY*
Alabama Center For The Arts, *Decatur, AL*
Robert and Elaine Stein Galleries, Wright State University, *Dayton, OH*

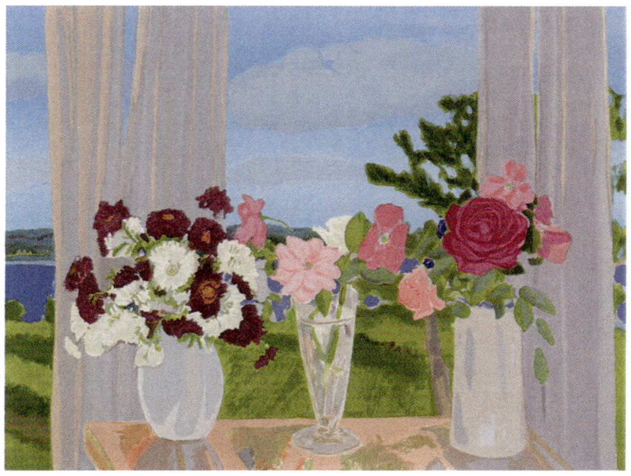

Jane Freilicher

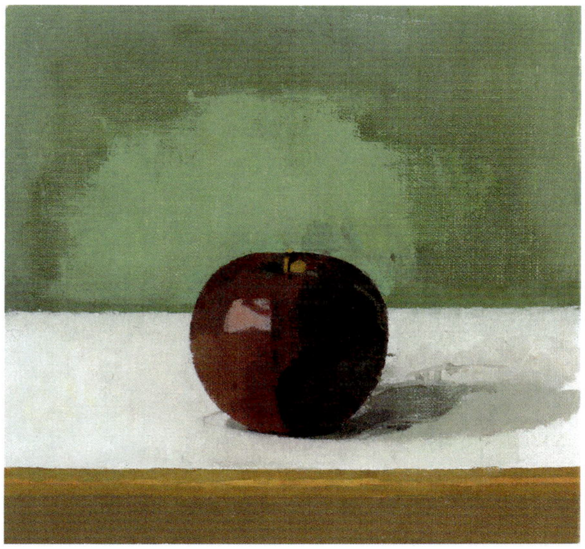

Susan Walp

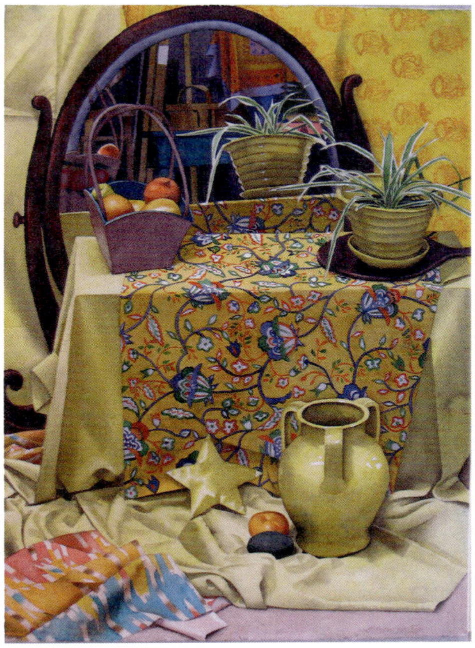

Nancy Hagin

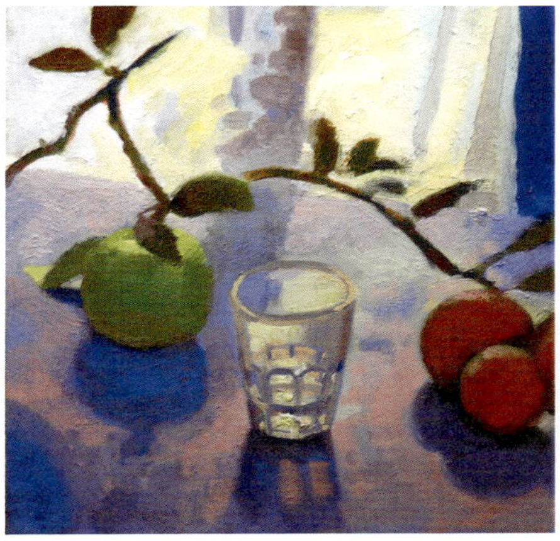

Bill White

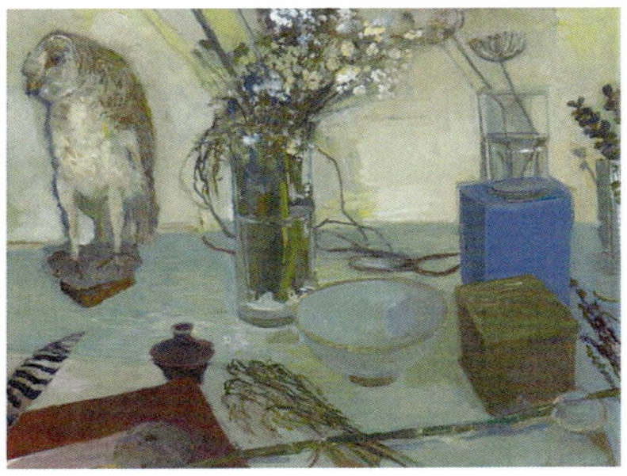

Stephanie Sanchez

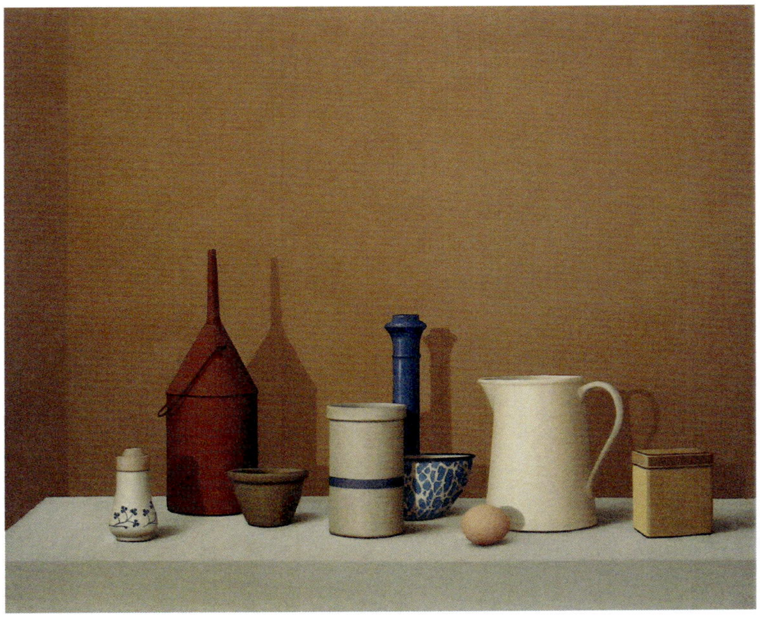

William Bailey

Composing in the Key of S – 2021
First Street Gallery, *New York, NY*

For The Love of Chardin – 2022
Miller Art Museum, *Sturgeon Bay, WI*
First Street Gallery, *New York, NY*

Flora – 2023
First Street Gallery, *New York, NY*

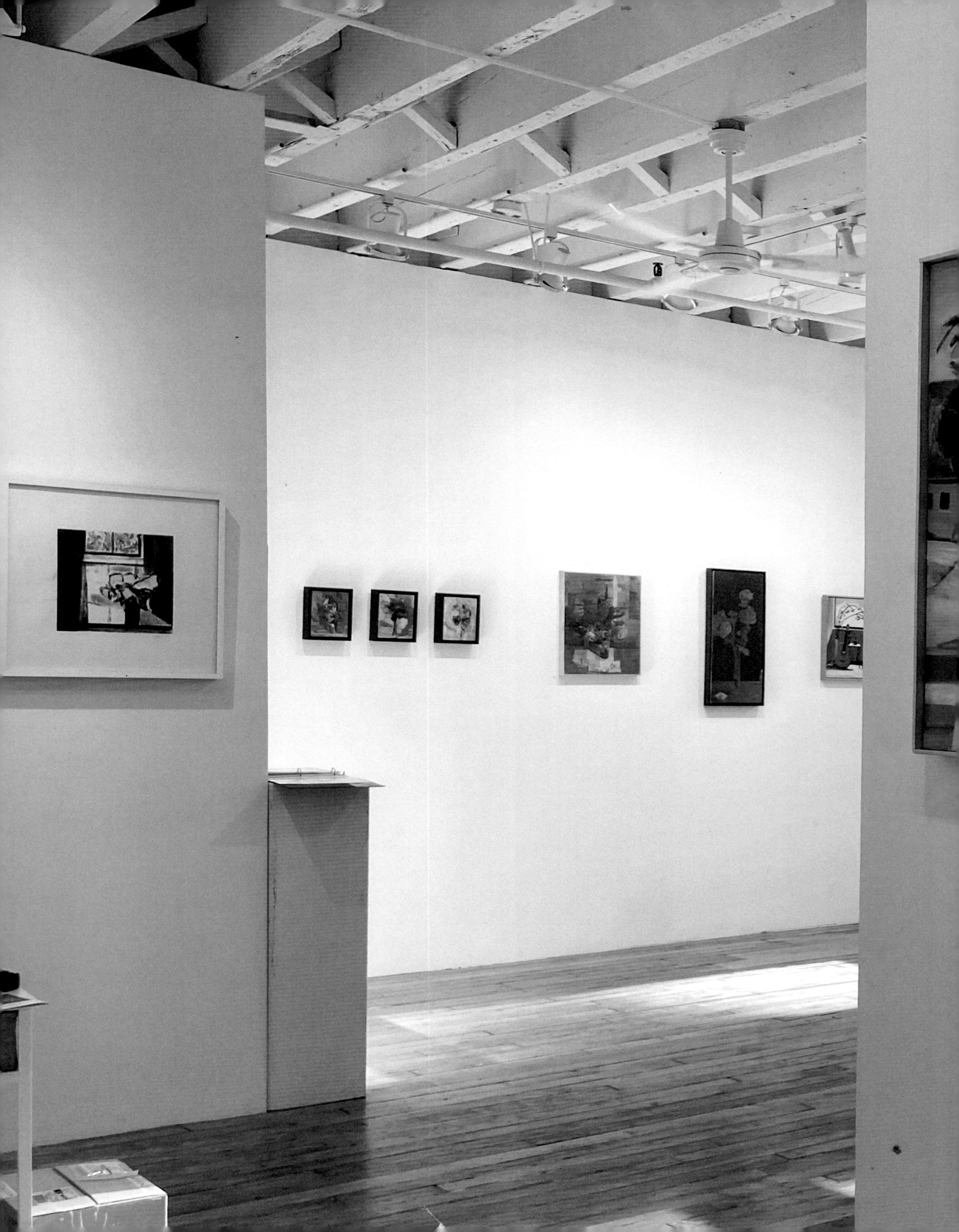

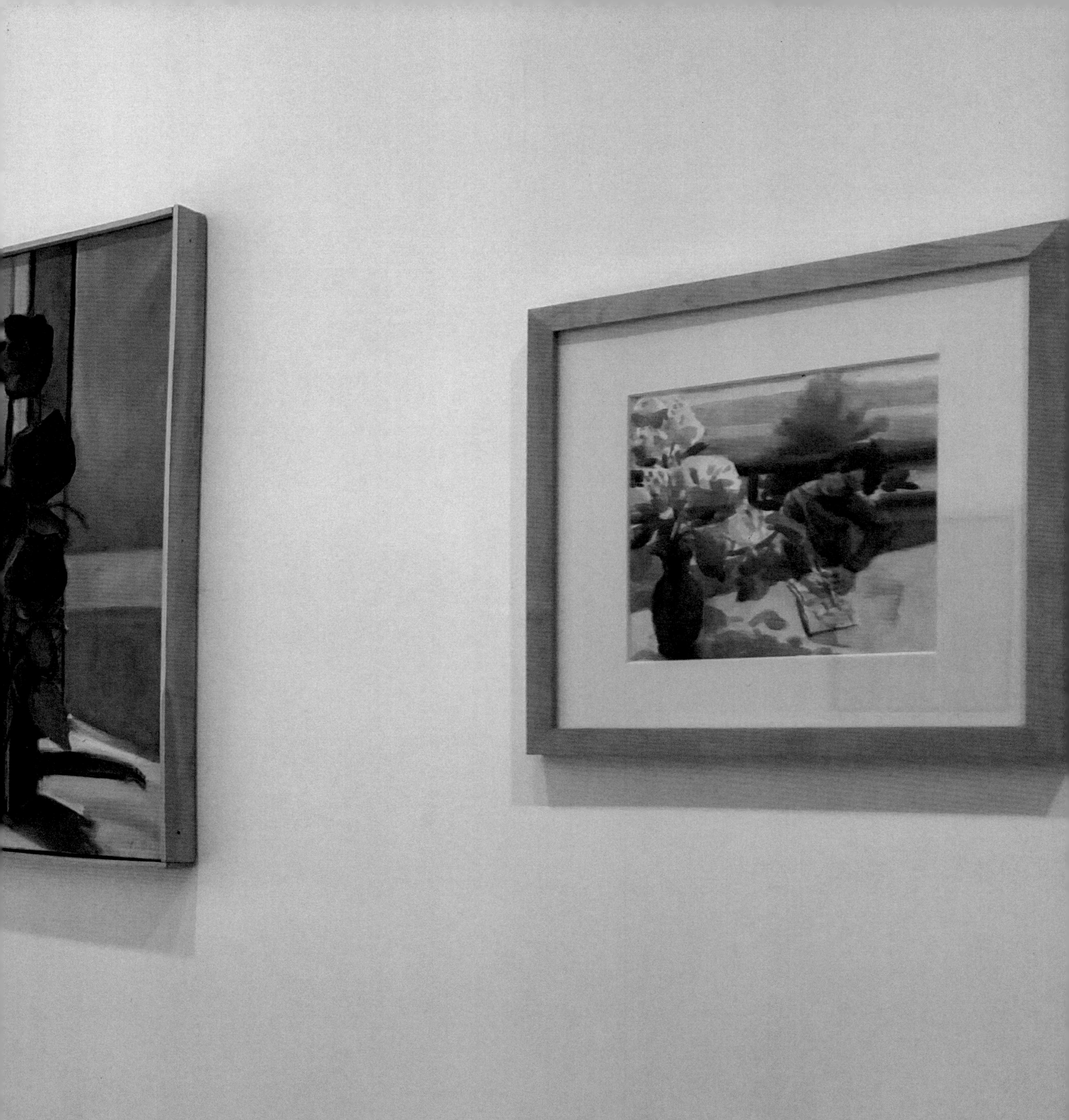

The exhibition *Flora* at First Street Gallery, NYC
December 2023

Acknowledgments

Having wordlessly produced untold numbers of paintings in the quiet of their studios, these still life artists here speak out on their lives and what their practice has taught them. We are grateful for the interviewers' thoughtful questions and for the artists' candor.

Seth Schonberg, who in 2020 was administrator for Zeuxis, had the foresight to publish these interviews on our web site. During the ensuing three years we thought of compiling them in the form of a book.

John Goodrich enthusiastically took up the work of book design. Because of his long association with Zeuxis, he was the ideal person for the job. He planned the structure and the style of the book in a way that made sense to us, and, along with Ying Li, shot the black and white photographs. Ultimately, the job was passed on to Cheryl Conrad, graphic designer. She worked at length on each page and communicated with artists and with Suzanne Salinetti of the Studley Press.

Kathleen Craig, and later Nancy Granda, volunteered to proofread 300 pages plus four times that many captions. We appreciate their diligence.

Thank you also to Zeuxis artist, Elizabeth Higgins, for her financial contribution toward the cost of production.

Little did we know a year ago what a huge job we'd undertaken. It has drawn on all our resources.